AMERICAN IMMIGRATION & ETHNICITY

A 20-Volume Series of Distinguished Essays

EDITED BY
George E. Pozzetta

A Garland Series

TITLES IN THE SERIES

VOLUME 6

THE WORK EXPERIENCE

Labor, Class, and Immigrant Enterprise

EDITED BY
George E. Pozzetta

GARLAND PUBLISHING, INC.
New York & London
1991

Library of Congress Cataloging-in-Publication Data

The Work experience: labor, class, and immigrant enterprise/ edited by George E. Pozzetta
p. cm.—(American immigration and ethnicity; v. 6)
ISBN 0-8240-7406-8 (alk. paper)
1. Alien labor—United States—History. 2. Immigrants—United
States—History. 3. United States—Emigration and immigration—
History. I. Pozzetta, George E. II. Series.
HD8081.A5W67   1990
306.3'6'08693—dc20   90-48320

Printed on acid-free, 250-year-life paper
Manufactured in the United States of America

INTRODUCTION

*Once I thought to write a history of the
immigrants in America. Then I discovered
that the immigrants were American history.*

Oscar Handlin,
The Uprooted (1951)

When it first appeared forty years ago, Oscar Handlin's startling observation occasioned disbelieving reactions; today, changes in historical scholarship have moved immigrants much closer to the central position posited by Handlin than perhaps even he ever considered possible. Once relegated to the fringes of historical investigation, immigrants now speak to the main themes of American history with an eloquence that belies the lack of attention they received earlier. In large part this is true because of what has happened to the field of immigration studies. Drawing from the momentum of the new social history, with its perspective "from the bottom up" and its insistence on exploring the experiences of ordinary people, the scholarly inquiry into immigration and ethnicity has produced an astounding outpouring of books and articles over the past several decades.

This rich and complex historical literature has drawn heavily from the methodologies and insights of the other social sciences and humanities, and the wider investigation into immigration has criss-crossed disciplinary boundaries at a rapid pace. The major journals of History, Political Science, Anthropology, Sociology, and Geography, for example, regularly carry essays dealing with the immigrant experience, and hundreds of articles appear in the more specialized local, regional, and topical publications of each discipline. Simply finding the relevant essays on any given topic within the general field has become a substantial challenge to researchers. This collection, therefore, represents an effort to bring together a selected cross section of the most significant articles on immigration and ethnicity. It is not definitive, no compilation treating with such broad-ranging and dynamic topics can ever be, but it is indicative of the scholarship that has shaped—and continues to shape—these important subjects. The major themes and issues of the field are discussed below, and each volume contains an individualized listing of supplemental readings for additional guidance. Taken together the collected essays contained within these volumes explore the manifold ways in which "immigrants were American history."

The liberation of immigration studies from its previously marginalized position has flowed from a number of critical interpretive and conceptual advances. One of the most important of these has been the effort to place immigration to America in the context of broader patterns of movement. Alerted by Frank Thistlethwaite's pioneering work, which showed how European migration to America was only part of a much larger transatlantic population and technological exchange, researchers now realize that an American-centered perspective is too restrictive to comprehend the full dimensions of migration. Immigrants from all quarters of the globe often envisioned America as only one destination among many, and then not necessarily a permanent one. Outmoded conceptions of "America fever" and exclusive one-way movement have given way to more complex understandings of the various manners by which America attracted and retained immigrants. The best works have taken into account the ability of multinational labor markets, economic cycles, transportation networks, as well as individual familial strategies, to propel immigrants outward in multi-step journeys.

At the same time as Thistlethwaite called for attention to large scale movements, he also urged that scholars be sensitive to the highly particularized nature of small scale migrations. Instead of studying "an undifferentiated mass movement" of individuals from loosely defined nation states, he insisted that immigrants be seen as emanating from "innumerable particular cells, districts, villages, towns, each with an individual reaction or lack of it to the pull of migration." This perspective necessarily involved linking the homeland with the new land in very precise ways, accounting for the specific influences of such factors as chain migration, kinship networks, travel agents, steamship companies, and repatriation flows, as well as the highly individualized economies of local regions.

Rudolph J. Vecoli's seminal work on Italian peasants in Chicago has pushed the study of premigration backgrounds in new directions. By pointing out that old world cultures survived the ocean crossing and significantly influenced adaptations in America, Vecoli stimulated a broad-based inquiry into the various ways in which immigrant traditions articulated with new world realities. The resulting scholarship has shifted the emphasis of investigation away from attention to the forces of assimilation and cultural break-down to those of cultural persistence and ethnic continuity. Immigrants did not succumb passively to pressures for conformity, but rather followed patterns of resistance and accommodation to the new land by which they turned themselves into something new—ethnic Americans. The ethnic culture that they created has proved to be a dynamic quality that has had influence into the third and fourth generation and beyond.

Such a viewpoint has led to different conceptions of assimilation and acculturation. Less often have scholars viewed these processes as easy, straight-line movements from "foreign" to "American." Nor have they continued to be captivated by images of a vast "Melting Pot" at work that has thoroughly erased differences. Rather, newer studies have posited a syncretic outcome in which both immigrants and the mainstream society have been changed, and the overall process of immigrant integration has emerged as more contingent and unpredictable than previously imagined. Attempts to preserve immigrant languages, value structures, and tradition, for example, could not, and did not, result in the exact replication of old-world ways. In a process of "invention" and "negotiation," immigrants adapted their ethnic cultures to meet changing historical circumstances and to resolve the problems of duality inherent in their straddling of Old and New Worlds. At the same time, the host society was changing, or "reinventing," its own cultural traditions, in part because of the need to accommodate the presence of diverse clusters of immigrants.

Much of the most stimulating new research carried out along these lines has adopted the urban immigrant community as its setting. Community studies have not only examined the institutional structures of settlements, but have also typically attempted to penetrate into the "interior worlds" of newcomers to discover the mentalities, values, and life strategies that shaped immigrant destinies. Such inquiries have probed deeply into the families, kin groups, and neighborhoods that formed the core of immigrant districts. Their conclusions have revised older conceptions of immigrant neighborhoods that emphasized the social pathology of family breakdown, crime, and deviant behavior. Immigrant communities emerge as remarkably vibrant and complex entities that provided effective cushions between the often strange and harsh dominant society and newly arrived residents. They also were far from the homogenous bodies so often envisioned by outsiders, but rather were replete with various "subethnic" divisions based upon distinctions of class, religion, ideology, and local culture. The process of immigrant adaptation to America, therefore, was as often marked by tension and conflict *within* ethnic concentrations as it was by friction between the group and the receiving society.

Internal divisions were also features of immigrant communities in rural and small town locations. However, the distinctive physical and cultural contexts encountered in such settings meant that immigrants usually experienced different adjustment patterns from those of their urban-dwelling cousins. More isolated from mainstream contact and better able to establish a local hegemony, immigrant settlements in these settings often maintained traditional languages and folkways for longer periods of time and with less change than was possible in city neighborhoods. The ethnic culture that rural immigrants crafted correspondingly reflected these particular conditions.

Eschewing a reliance on sources generated by the host society and utilizing a broad range of foreign language materials, researchers have demonstrated the existence of a remarkable range of civic, labor, religious, recreational, cultural, and fraternal organizations created by immigrants. Each of these played important roles in mediating the difficult adjustment to new-world conditions, and the presence of these institutions points to the need of recognizing immigrants as active agents in determining their own futures. To be sure, they were often circumscribed in their actions by poverty, nativism, discrimination, and limited skills, but they typically responded with imaginative adaptations within the limits imposed upon them. Many formal immigration institutions such as labor unions and mutual aid societies, for example, employed collective strategies to overcome the constraints restricting immigrant lives. Informal familial and kin networks often assisted these initiatives with adjustments of their own to ease the process of insertion into America.

The most fundamental institution of all, the immigrant family, reveals these patterns clearly. Families did not disintegrate under the pressures of immigration, urbanization, and industrialization, but rather proved to be remarkably flexible and resilent. Family structures and values responded to the multiple challenges imposed by migration—both in urban centers and rural spaces—by expanding their roles to accommodate a variety of new demands. Immigrant women, in their capacities as mothers and daughters, played critical functions in these transformations. Recent work, however, has attempted to move the study of immigrant women beyond the family context and to view women as historical actors who were able to influence the larger society in many different ways. The broader challenge has been to reveal how women confronted the multiple dilemmas posed by migration, and, more generally, to insert the issue of gender into the wider interpretations of the immigrant experience.

Since most immigrants entered America in quest of work, and after the 1860s usually industrial work, their relationship to the labor performed assumed a special importance. The vast majority arrived with preindustrial cultural values and confronted a complex urban-industrial economy. This encounter was a crucial factor not only in understanding the patterns of immigrant assimilation and social mobility, but also in comprehending the nature of American industrialization and the processes by which an American working class came into being. Through their collective labor as workers, their actions as union members, and their varied responses to exploitation and insecurity, immigrants were critical elements in the shaping of a modern American economy and labor force. Researchers are continuing to explore the exact nature of this dialectical relationship as they attempt to link immigrant values and expectations with the demands of the workplace.

Just as scholars have pursued the immigrant into the factory, home, and mutual aid society, so too have they entered the doors of immigrant churches in their investigations. The denominational pluralism that has characterized American society is a direct outgrowth of the nation's ethnic pluralism. Older works concentrated on examining the institutional histories of different immigrant religions and on the conflict engendered by such issues as parochial education and the formation of national parishes. More recently scholars have moved the study of America's religious tapestry out of church buildings and diocesan boardrooms and into the streets and neighborhoods. By examining the "popular piety" of immigrants, researchers hope to understand more clearly the ways in which new arrivals integrated the actual practice of religion into their everyday lives.

Investigators have already learned much about the relationships between ethnicity and political behavior. Indeed, one of the most surprising findings of the "new political history" was the discovery that ethnocultural considerations—often in the form of religious indentifications—were critical influences in shaping American voting patterns. Election outcomes in many parts of the nation often hinged on such factors. Indeed, perhaps no aspect of the American political arena has been immune to the force of ethnicity. Currently, researchers have been interested in determining how immigrants shaped a political culture of their own as they adapted to the American environment. Arriving from dissimilar backgrounds and frequently containing within their ranks followers of many different political ideologies, immigrants cannot be neatly classified into simple categories. Whether as supporters of urban machines, leftist critics of American capitalism, or as second and third generation politicians pushing group demands, immigrants and their progeny have been essential ingredients in the American political equation.

The American educational system similarly underwent profound transformation due to the immigrant presence. Many newcomers approached this powerful institution with ambivalent feelings since education in America offered both an opportunity for future progress and a danger to valued traditions. For their part, schools and school officials were forced to cope with unprecedented problems of space, curriculum, rules of discipline, attendance, and staffing. Immigrants ultimately found it necessary to judge the worth of education defined in new-world terms, both in relation to themselves and their children. They reacted in various ways, ranging from the formation of separate educational initiatives that sought to maintain cherished values to the avoidance of formal educational institutions altogether. One thing was certain: both sides of the equation were changed by the contact.

America responded to the immigrant presence in varied ways. During periods of crisis, the host society often reacted by promoting rigid programs of Americanization that sought to strip away foreign customs and values. Research has shown that even programs of assistance and outreach, such as those offered by settlement houses and philanthropic agencies, often contained strong doses of social control. Immigrants were not unaware of these elements and frequently reacted to these and such programs as bilingual education and affirmative action have engendered sharp public division. The present collection of essays, therefore, should be seen as providing the first installment of an important research agenda that needs to be open-ended in scope, responsive to new methodologies and interpretations, and cognizant of its relevance to contemporary American society.

The editor wishes to thank Leonard Dinnerstein, Victor Greene, Robert Singerman, Jeffrey Adler, Robert Zieger, and especially Rudolph Vecoli and Donna Gabaccia, for their helpful advice on this project.

GEORGE E. POZZETTA

SUPPLEMENTAL READING

Tomas Almaguer, "Racial Discrimination and Class Conflict in Capitalist Agriculture: The Oxnard Sugar Beet Worker's Strike of 1903," *Labor History*, 25 (Summer 1984), 325–350.

Mie Liang Bickner, "The Forgotten Minority: Asian American Women," *Amerasia Journal*, 11 (Spring 1974), 1–17.

Melvin Dubofsky, "Organized Labor and the Immigrant in New York City, 1900–1918," *Labor History*, 2 (1961), 182–201.

Melvin Dubofsky, "Success and Failure of Socialism in New York City, 1900–1918," *Labor History*, 9 (Fall 1968), 361–375.

Charlotte Erickson, "Emigration from the British Isles to the U.S.A. in 1831," *Population Studies*, 35 (1981), 175–197.

Frances H. Early, "The French Canadian Family Economy and Standard-of-Living in Lowell, Massachusetts, 1870," *Journal of Family History*, 7 (Summer 1982), 180–199.

Howard M. Gitelman, "No Irish Need Apply: Patterns of and Response to Ethnic Discrimination in the Labor Market," *Labor History*, 14 (1973), 56–68.

Philip Gleason, "Confusion Compounded: The Melting Pot in the 1960s and 1970s," *Ethnicity*, 6 (1979), 10–20.

Philip Gleason, "The Melting Pot: Symbol of Fusion or Confusion?" *American Quarterly* SVI (Spring 1974), 20–46.

Bruce C. Levine, "Immigrant Workers, 'Equal Rights,' and Antislavery: The Germans of Newark, New Jersey," *Labor History*, 25 (Winter 1984), 26–52.

Hubert Perrier, "The Socialists and the Working Class in New York, 1890–1896," *Labor History*, 22, No. 4 (Fall 1981), 485–511.

Thaddeus Radzialowski, "Immigrant Nationalism and Feminism: Glos Polek and the Polish Women's Alliance in America, 1898–1980," *Review Journal of Philosophy and Social Science*, 2 (1972), 183–203.

Robert Swierenga, "Dutch Immigrant Demography, 1820–1880," *Journal of Family History*, 5 (Winter 1980), 390–405.

Peter Temin, "Labor Scarcity in America," *Journal of Interdisciplinary History*, 1 (Winter 1971), 251–264.

CONTENTS

UNITY AND FRAGMENTATION:
CLASS, RACE, AND ETHNICITY ON CHICAGO'S SOUTH SIDE,
1900-1922

The concept of working class fragmentation — the failure of workers to identify with one another across ethnic, racial, sexual, and skill lines and to act collectively on the basis of class interests — is often assumed in the historiography of early twentieth century America. American workers probably were more heterogeneous during this era than at any other time in the nation's history. Employers in many basic industries reorganized production methods and in the process restructured labor markets, drawing their workers from a much wider social and geographic spectrum than they had in the nineteenth century. While an earlier generation of "old immigrant" and native-born men remained dominant in most skilled occupations, the "new immigrants" — largely unskilled farmers and farm laborers from southern and southeastern Europe — were rapidly displacing them from the ranks of common laborers and machine tenders. The number of women entering the manufacturing labor force actually leveled off after the turn of the century, but their overall proportion in the wage earning population continued to increase. Finally, Blacks secured positions in many manufacturing industries for the first time during World War One as a result of war production and the shortage of immigrant labor. Racial diversity grew, considerably complicating the process of class formation.[1] While the uniqueness of the American working-class experience has often been exaggerated, it is difficult to imagine a more complex population than the one which experienced the birth of the new corporate political economy at the beginning of the century.

Nowhere was such diversity greater than in Chicago's Union Stock Yards and the surrounding slaughtering and meat packing plants. When Immigration Commission investigators studied the industry in 1908-1909, they found more than forty nationalities represented. The workforce was demographically diverse not only in terms of ethnicity but also in terms of race, age, and work experience. Mixed in with older, skilled Irish and German butchers were thousands of young eastern European peasants and laborers only recently arrived from the forests and farms of the Austro-Hungarian and Russian Empires. While men did most of the industry's heavy work, they were joined by a growing stream of young, single women and later, during World War One, by housewives and mothers. Thousands of Black migrants from the Deep South arrived during the war, making the industry one of the most important employers of Black labor in U.S. manufacturing. Packed into the crowded neighborhoods of Chicago's vast industrial South Side, these workers seem to exemplify the divisions within the American working class during this era.

Yet a study of these butcher workmen demonstrates that the existence of diversity did not lead inevitably to fragmentation. How did workers from such diverse backgrounds interact with one another, as they undoubtedly did in many circumstances? Is it possible to distinguish factors which contributed to class cohesion from those which led to fragmentation? This case study reminds us just how complicated social relations among American workers were and are. It considers several approaches to the problem of class fragmentation in light of what

1

happened in the Chicago Stock Yards during the early years of this century and concludes with some observations about what the case study can tell us concerning the interplay of class, race, and ethnicity.

I

Several labor historians have analyzed the problem of fragmentation similarly. Herbert Gutman has argued that the continual influx of "preindustrial" migrants into American society meant that various groups — native-born artisans, earlier immigrants, and the new immigrants of the early twentieth century —experienced the wrenching process of adjustment to life and work in industrial society at different times and paces. There was no one generation which saw "the making of the American working class." Indeed, Gutman seems to suggest that continual migration contributed to a process of disintegration, an *unmaking,* throughout the late nineteenth and early twentieth century.[2]

David Montgomery and others have discussed the same problem in generational terms. Montgomery suggests that there were two generations of industrial workers in America by the turn of the century, the first consisting of the native-born and members of older immigrant groups (particularly Germans, Irish, and British) and the second composed largely of eastern and southeastern European immigrants augmented later by Black migrants from the South. By the late nineteenth century, many of the more "mature" workers from the earlier generation had lived in industrial towns and cities most of their lives. They had, to use Hobsbawm's phrase, learned "the rules of the game," creating subcultures built on strong social, economic, and cultural institutions which supported them daily and in times of stress. They governed themselves at work and often in the community as well through a moral code emphasizing solidarity, mutualism, and craft if not class pride. Often these subcultures were supported by ethnic and religious organizations which took on class characteristics because of the occupational makeup of the communities and their problems.[3] The dominant milieu in many parts of Chicago's South Side, for example, was a traditional Irish-American Catholicism fused with militant craft unionism.

By the turn of the century, however, such subcultures were increasingly undermined by the introduction of mass production work and the massive influx of new immigrant groups. While new production methods rendered craft organization much less effective, the creation of new ethnic communities, populated by workers who shared neither the industrial nor the social and cultural experiences of the earlier generations, threatened the prospects for solidarity among American workers.[4]

In the steel industry, the primary division between the first generation of skilled Irish and British steelworkers and the second of Slavic common laborers was fundamentally psychological. While the earlier group was firmly-rooted in the mills and the towns which grew up around them, many of the new immigrants viewed their stay in the industry as a brief sojourn. They bore their troubles patiently, for they hoped to return home and resume their old way of life on the land. Separated by a generation of work and trade union experience as well as by profound cultural differences, the two groups held little in common and found it difficult to identify with one another on the basis of class interests.[5]

Labor economists have explained class fragmentation by focusing on the divisive effects of segmented and hierarchical labor market structures. They argue that employers accentuated or arbitrarily created status distinctions among workers by providing a wide range of wage rates and benefits and by making

2

employment for some workers more secure than for others. The consequent stratification of the working class on the basis of differences in status, wages, and benefits inhibited class organization and action. Where these objective differences in work situations overlapped with significant racial, ethnic, and sexual divisions — as was so often the case in American industry — their divisive effects were enhanced.[6]

Like the Marxist theory of a labor aristocracy,[7] labor market segmentation theory attempts to explain the role of the more privileged strata of the working class. These workers, the theory maintains, were incorporated into the developing structure of monopoly capitalism through higher wages, greater employment security, and various welfare schemes. In this respect, radical labor market theory is the economic counterpart to the argument that the labor movement was ideologically integrated into corporate society during the early twentieth century under the auspices of a pervasive "corporate liberalism." Enlightened corporate leaders insured a relatively high standard of living and labor reform legislation for the AFL's constituency in exchange for stable industrial relations and conservative labor politics.[8]

Gabriel Kolko's formulation of the fragmentation theme comes closest to putting labor historians out of business entirely. Drawing on evidence of strong ethnic subcultures, figures on reemigration and wage differentials, and other data, Kolko pictures the working-class community as a "splintered society," unable to unite around common grievances and goals. This failure and the frustration and despair which it bred have been reflected, he argues, in unusually high rates of crime, insanity and emotional problems, alcoholism, and other forms of social deviance. Their failure to develop class consciousness and a social democratic labor movement has rendered twentieth century American workers "lumpen people in a lumpen society."[9] While not always drawing such dire conclusions regarding the social worth of contemporary American workers, many historians and other scholars share Kolko's view of early twentieth century American workers as a highly-fragmented social group.[10]

Both the New Left historians of corporate liberalism and the radical labor economists relate their analyses of class fragmentation to specific characteristics of monopoly capitalism. On the one hand, the strong market position of the largest firms in each industry allowed them to buy off many of the skilled, organized male workers, most of whom came from native-born or older immigrant backgrounds. On the other, the expansion of labor markets through immigration and internal migration not only kept the lid on labor costs, it also discouraged the growth of class consciousness by increasing the diversity of the working class population.

II

The packing house workers make an excellent case study of the unmaking or perhaps the remaking of the American working class during the early twentieth century. Both the strong market position of the "Big Five" packers and the sophistication of their huge corporate bureaucracies made them prime candidates for corporate liberalism. The situation of the butcher workmen themselves and their behavior over time demonstrate both the obvious potential for fragmentation among such a group of workers and considerable success under certain conditions in uniting on the basis of class interests.

The packers were pioneers in work organization and technology. Extensive division of labor and a primitive sort of assembly line had emerged in hog slaughtering by the mid-nineteenth century, but the complete conversion of the

3

industry to mass production methods awaited the perfection of the refrigerated railroad car and the emergence of a national market for dressed meat in the late 1870s. As late as 1880 the job of slaughtering and cutting up a steer was still often done by one man, the "all-round butcher." During the next two decades, the big packers reorganized this process, gradually introducing more and more division of labor, as they consolidated their hold over the national market and expanded overseas. By the turn of the century, the same was executed in assembly-line fashion by a gang of 230 men, each person doing the same minute manipulation a thousand times during a full workday. The same extreme division of labor was applied to canning, sausagemaking, and byproduct departments throughout the plants. This dramatic reorganization of work seriously undermined the power and control of the skilled butcher, facilitating great increases in production speed.[11]

The new production methods also allowed the packers to reorganize the labor market. By the early twentieth century the industry relied on what labor economists term a dual labor market. About one third of the workforce was spread out over a hierarchical job structure ranging from the common labor ranks to the few highly-skilled jobs left in the industry. The other two-thirds of the butcher workmen were considered common labor. In practice, this meant that they were paid a standard wage rate which fluctuated with economic conditions and unemployment in the industry. It also meant that many of them were essentially casual laborers hired for a week, a day, or even a few hours at a time. Chicago, was, in fact, the home of a very large casual labor market in which immigrant packing house workers were but one component. The existence of this large, heterogeneous, floating population might be expected to inhibit the development of class solidarity among common laborers and between them and the more skilled butcher workmen to whom they posed a threat.[12]

TABLE I
NATIONALITY OF EMPLOYEES IN THE SLAUGHTERING AND
MEAT PACKING INDUSTRY OF CHICAGO, 1909

	1909 (N = 15,489) Proportion
Native-born:	
White	18.9
Black	3.0
Foreign-born:	
Bohemian and Slovak*	10.0
German	10.4
Irish	7.5
Lithuanian	12.0
Polish	27.7
Russian	2.9
Other	7.6
Total	100.0

*Includes "Austrian."

Source: Calculated from U.S. Immigration Commission, *Reports, Immigrants in Industry, Slaughtering and Meat Packing,* XIII. Washington, D.C.: GPO, 1911, 204.

The creation of a large market for common labor resulted in a constant social recomposition of the industry's labor force from the 1880s through the early 1920s. Bohemians, Poles, Lithuanians, and other eastern Europeans increasingly displaced the original generation of skilled Irish and German butchers, so that by 1909 Slavic groups represented more than fifty percent of the labor force in Chicago (See Table I). Like Brody's Slavic steelworkers, most of these butcher workmen had come into the country since the turn of the century. Blacks entered the industry as strikebreakers during an 1894 strike, and there were about 500 of them in the stockyards ten years later. By the First World War, when thousands of Black migrants poured into the plants, many of the Slavic immigrants had still been in the country less than ten years. In the early 1920s, when Mexican migrants began arriving, Blacks already made up about a third of the labor force in the city's two largest plants. Generally, skill levels reinforced racial and ethnic differences. Recent immigrants and Blacks settled into the common labor ranks, while the shrinking group of older immigrants clung to the more skilled jobs. Finally, throughout the early twentieth century women comprised an increasingly large proportion of the industry's work force. By 1920 thirteen percent of the butcher workmen were, in fact, women. Their wage rates and employment security were even worse than those for male common laborers.[13]

Employers tried to turn such diversity to their advantage. John R. Commons, the noted labor economist, found during his study of the industry in 1904 that the large firms intentionally mixed nationalities in the various departments of their plants, hoping that language and cultural differences would keep the workers divided. An employment agent at Swift explained how the strategy worked.

> Last week we employed Slovaks. We change about among various nationalities and languages. It prevents them from getting together. We have the thing systematized. We have a luncheon each week of the employment managers at the large firms of the Chicago district. There we discuss our problems and exchange information.[14]

Newer ethnic groups entering the yards often came first as strikebreakers. This and the fact that some foremen and strawbosses practiced favoritism toward those of their own nationality only heightened the danger of inter-ethnic and inter-racial conflict.[15]

Meat packing, then, was a model of the dual labor market which radical economists have described as characteristic of early monopoly capitalism. It is difficult to fully appreciate the problem of class formation and fragmentation, however, by focusing exclusively on the workplace and labor market as labor economists and historians of mass production work have done.[16] Here the emphasis of labor historians, notably Gutman, Brody, and Montgomery, on the cultural diversity of the laboring population and the generational quality of class formation becomes crucial. In the case of Chicago's packing house workers and among American workers more generally, some of the most significant factors affecting class formation were cultural and community-based.

The diversity of the labor market was not only reflected in but also reinforced by separate racial and ethnic communities, each of them with its own social structure and cultural institutions. Most of the remaining Irish and German butchers lived either in Bridgeport and Canaryville, just east of Union Stock Yards, or in one of the outlying neighborhoods of the South Side. The more recent Slavic immigrants clustered in ethnic enclaves in Packingtown, the area immediately south and west of the Yards. Black workers were isolated in the Black Belt, a deteriorating ghetto more than a mile east of the Yards. These three communities were separated from one another by various man-made barriers — elevated lines, railroad tracks, factories, and the Union Stock Yards themselves. (See Map.)[17]

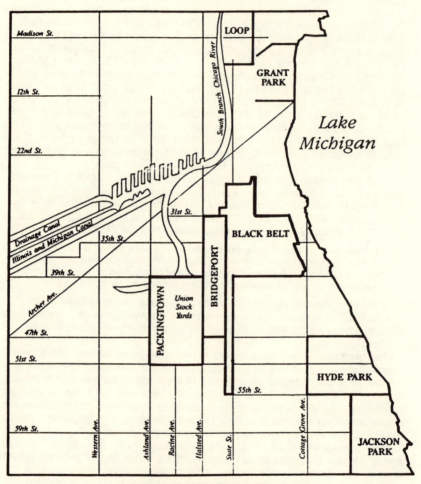

THREE WORKING CLASS COMMUNITIES
ON CHICAGO'S SOUTH SIDE, 1920.

Behind these physical barriers lay more important social and cultural ones. Each community spawned its own leaders as well as religious, fraternal, and political groups all organized along ethnic or racial lines. Polish workers attended Polish parishes, socialized with one another in the Polish Falcons or other fraternal groups, drank together in Polish neighborhood bars, married within their own ethnic group, and sent their children to Polish Catholic schools. Lithuanians, Bohemians, and other immigrant communities all had comparable networks. Blacks went about a similar process of institution building over in the Black Belt where the Urban League, the YMCA, and local churches were particularly active in helping migrants settle into jobs and housing during the era of the great World War One migration.

The creation of such subcultures was, of course, a natural and healthy response of migrant people seeking to adjust to the rigors of life in a large industrial city and at the same time nurture traditions and values which were distinctively their own. But it is also true that the ethnic and racial identification reflected in the creation of such communities could be and sometimes was used not only by employers but also by ethnic leaders within the communities to divide workers and maintain their own power.

Community-based barriers to class formation were most dramatically demonstrated in the July 1919 race riot which rocked the city's South Side, claiming the lives of 23 Blacks and 15 whites, including several packing house workers. While white butcher workmen had little to do with the attacks on Blacks, the riot ended any prospect of creating an interracial labor movement in the Yards for more than a generation.[18] In both workplace and community, it seems, Chicago's packing house workers were divided from one another.

Having documented these very real divisions, however, we are faced with a paradox: Between 1900 and 1904, in the midst of a very heavy influx of recent Slavic immigrants and young women, and once again in the First World War, during the great migration of Blacks from the Deep South, packing house workers achieved considerable unity.

In the early twentieth century, unionization spread quickly from the older generation of butcher workmen, particularly the Irish who had a long tradition of union organization and solidarity, to the Slavic immigrants. The new immigrants not only flooded into the union but also built the kind of strong shop-floor organizations that labor historians have generally associated with more "mature" industrial workers. They restricted output and engaged in wildcat strikes, adapting these and other tactics to mass production work and challenging management's prerogatives in the workplace. Young women workers — often viewed as a particularly docile group — organized, struck, and fought for their rights within the union as well as in the plants.[19]

During the war years the new immigrants provided the main source of union strength and worked to integrate Black migrants into the movement. Shop-floor organization emerged once again, this time with a small but solid core of Black activists sharing rank-and-file leadership with Slavic immigrants and German and Irish veterans. An organizing drive swept through the neighborhoods of the city's South Side, galvanizing workers from a wide range of backgrounds into an effective movement which significantly improved conditions in the plants.[20] In the industry's two major strikes (1904 and 1921-1922) immigrant communities remained solidly behind the workers' movement.

In both of these periods the butcher workmen overcame labor market segmentation and significant social and cultural barriers. Yet both of these movements eventually disintegrated. How can we explain their impressive unity in the face of such striking diversity and still account for their ultimate fragmentation by the early 1920s?

III

Several factors help to explain the apparent paradox: (1) the degree of social contact in the plants and community among various groups of workers; (2) the structure and strategies of the packing house unions themselves; (3) the attitude of community leaders and institutions toward working-class organization; and (4) the general political and economic context and the balance of class forces within which the organization took place.

The broad shape of work and community life suggests that the butcher workmen were deeply divided, but when we go beyond the aggregate statistics to analyze the sort of microscopic units which are most significant in socialization — work group, tenement house, saloon, union local — we find more interaction among diverse groups than the broader patterns would suggest.

The apparent ethnic and skill stratification in the plants, for example, is somewhat deceptive. As a result of the packers' hiring policies, work groups in packing were quite mixed ethnically, racially, and in terms of skill. The following ethnic breakdown for a 225 man cattle killing gang at the turn of the century certainly understates the importance of Slavic immigrants who poured into the industry in the following two decades, but it suggests the diversity in the labor force.

TABLE II
ETHNIC DIVERSITY IN A CHICAGO CATTLE KILLING GANG, 1900
(N = 225)

Germans	98	English	6	Welsh	2
Americans	50	French	3	Swedes	1
Irish	29	Dutch	2	Norwegians	1
Polish	13	Canadians	2	Swiss	1
Bohemians	13	Russians	2	Finlanders	1
				Italians	1

Source: Charles J. Bushnell, "Some Social Aspects of the Chicago Stock Yards," I, *American Journal of Sociology,* 7 (1901), 168.

By 1917 the same gang was apt to include many Polish, Lithuanian, and other "new immigrant" common laborers, as well as Black migrants, and a residue of skilled butchers from the ranks of the native-born and the older immigrant groups. The most highly-skilled Irish splitter worked with Polish and Black laborers at his side. While the pace was often grueling, killing gangs and other work groups spent part of the day standing around talking, waiting for the next batch of animals to arrive. Even among the newest ethnic groups there were significant numbers of English-speaking people who provided links between the generations of butcher workmen. This allowed for an informal process of acculturation which facilitated unionization in both periods.[21]

This ethnic pluralism in many of the packing house work gangs contrasts sharply with the situation in the steel industry where ethnic and racial segregation by department minimized inter-ethnic social contact on the job. Significantly, relations in steel between "new" and "old" immigrants and between skilled and unskilled were notoriously bad. In contrast to packing, labor organization in the steel industry remained weak up until the 1919 strike, and even during this strike steelworkers remained divided with the new immigrants providing the bulk of the strikers.[22]

In packing, the same work process and labor market which seemed to divide workers from one another also created serious shared grievances which offered a basis for unity. Irregular working hours, frequent lay-offs, intense speed, and arbitrary foremen were all problems which the most skilled knife man shared with the common laborer. Because of widespread division of labor in the industry, it was relatively easy for common laborers to fill in on more skilled jobs. Thus, the army of laborers that gathered outside the stockyards gate each morning looking for work represented a very real threat to the wages and conditions of the skilled men.

Saloons in the vicinity of the Stock Yards were another point of social contact among the myriad groups comprising the labor force. While neighborhood saloons were ethnically-segregated, those bordering the Yards and the packing plants were quite mixed, tending to draw workers from particular departments in a plant regardless of skill or ethnicity. Many of the men who owned and tended bar in these saloons were Irish butchers who had retired or been blacklisted for labor activity during the late nineteenth century. It is doubtful that these establishments were racially integrated, but they clearly provided a common ground for the "mature" generation of butcher workmen and the Slavic common laborers. Here, in fact, much of the early organizing went on, while the settlement house served a similar function for the ethnically-diverse group of young women workers in the industry.[23]

Turning from workplace to community, we find more common ground. Urban and ethnic historians have noted recently that the popular conception of the "immigrant ghetto" is misleading since most immigrant neighborhoods were, quite heterogeneous, providing frequent contact among a number of ethnic groups.[24] The apparent ethnic residential segregation in Packingtown is a case in point. While ethnic groups certainly clustered, most blocks were mixed, frequently containing two or three and sometimes as many as four or five different ethnic groups. More importantly, individual tenement buildings were also ethnically-mixed. Over half of the multi-family Packingtown dwellings in 1905 housed at least two different ethnic groups. Poor ventilation and overcrowding meant that families sat together on front porches and children played in streets and alleys. The social ecology of the community, then, also suggests considerable opportunity for inter-ethnic contact.[25]

Historians have generally viewed the acculturation of immigrant workers as a top-down process and an instrument of social control employed by personnel managers, evening school teachers, and settlement house workers.[26] Such efforts represented an element in the immigrant worker's process of adjustment, but their influence has probably been exaggerated. Formal "Americanization" — through citizenship classes and government naturalization procedures, for example — proceeded very slowly in these communities. The University of Chicago Settlement's Citizenship School reported a total enrollment for 1908-1909 of 112, a tiny fraction of the community's foreign born. The packers, like most employers, took little interest in Americanization until the war years when they did sponsor classes and patriotic pageants. In these cases there were large numbers of workers involved, if only because they were captive audiences at the affairs which were generally held during work hours. But even the packers' own study of literacy and naturalization conducted during the war found that less than two-thirds of foreign-born women in the plants could speak English. Three-fourths of male immigrant employees were not citizens, and 43 percent of them had not even filed their first papers in the naturalization process, despite the fact that they had been living in the country an average of fifteen years.[27]

Yet such figures do not necessarily mean that immigrant workers failed to come to terms with their new lives. There were alternative conceptions of Americanism to those of management, but historians have largely ignored acculturation as it took place among workers from diverse backgrounds and through the efforts of working class institutions.[28] In packing, there was an informal but conscious push by union militants to assimilate new groups into the broader working class community and the labor movement, an effort which might be termed "Americanization from the bottom up."

In a world organized largely along nationality lines, the union was a rare institution because it brought the immigrant into contact with those from other ethnic backgrounds on the basis of shared class interest. Commissioner of Labor Ethelbert Stewart, who studied the problem among Chicago packing house workers in 1904, argued that the union represented "the first, and for a time the only, point at which he (the immigrant) touches any influences outside of his clan." Settlement house reformer Mary McDowell agreed.

> The labor union has been the only institution that has brought the immigrant in touch with English-speaking men for a common purpose and in preparation for self-government.[29]

If foremen emphasized punctuality, diligence at work, and respect for private property in their Americanization programs and company papers, the union had its own message which stressed standing up with fellow workers for one's rights and expressing one's opinions freely. An immigrant's introduction to the workings of the American political and economic system frequently came through conversations with fellow workers, discussion and debate at union meetings, and labor movement publications.[30]

In the 1900-1904 period the Irish were the "Americanizers," and they made their bridges to the new immigrant communities in a number of ways. The use of interpreters at local union meetings encouraged participation by even the most recent immigrants. Hog Butchers' Local 116 provided spontaneous translations into five different languages; the more ethnically-diverse sheep butchers required seven. Local 116 located an organizing gold mine in their vice president Frank Klawikowski who spoke several eastern European languages as well as English. Multi-lingual union leaflets and newspapers were printed in both periods of organization. The *Butcher Workman* carried columns in Lithuanian and Spanish during the World War One years, as well as in Polish, Bohemian, German, and English. The Stockyards Labor Council which directed the wartime organizing campaign appointed Polish, Lithuanian, and Black organizers and collaborated with the Women's Trade Union League on special educational programs for immigrants. In both periods newcomers were quickly integrated into the leadership at both the official local union level as officers and business agents and at the unofficial shopfloor level as committeemen and shop stewards.[31]

Antanas Kaztauskis, a Lithuanian laborer on the cattle killing floor, described his experience with the union in 1904:

It has given me more time to read and speak and enjoy life like an American. . . . It is combining all the nationalities. The night I joined the Cattle Butchers' Union I was led into the room by a negro member. With me were Bohemians, Germans and Poles, and Mike Donnelly, the President is an Irishman. . . . We swore to be loyal to our union above everything else except the country, the city and the State . . . to do our best to understand the history of the labor movement, and to do all we could to help it on. . . . I help the movement by being an interpreter for the other Lithuanians who come in. That is why I have learned to speak and write good English. The others do not need .ne long . . . they are quickly becoming Americans.[32]

The structure of the union itself could facilitate or obstruct this process of acculturation. In the 1900 to 1904 era, organizers steadfastly refused appeals from some ethnic leaders to organize on a nationality basis, opting instead for departmental locals. All the workers in the city's cattle killing gangs, for example, were members of the same Amalgamated Meat Cutters and Butcher Workmen's local, regardless of skill or nationality.[33] This arrangement maximized contact and solidarity across ethnic lines and provided the institutional context for the Americanization process. Each local union became an instrument of education, reflecting the values of the labor movement and the broader working class community and imparting these to the immigrants.

In contrast, the complicated organizational structure introduced during World War One actually reinforced existing divisions by creating separate locals based on skill, nationality, and race. The full explanation for this tragic decision remains obscure, but some of the pressure for racially-segregated locals came from leaders within the Black community who feared that the voice of the Black minority would be muted in an inter-racial mass local. These organizational divisions were aggravated by factional conflicts among the movement's leaders which drew immigrant laborers, Blacks, and native-born whites into opposing camps. The residential, social, and organizational segregation of Black workers in particular deprived them of the informal social contacts and conscious program of assimilation which had drawn Polish and other new immigrant groups into the movement. Black and white union militants made valiant efforts to bridge this gap, while the packers manipulated it to their advantage.[34]

The existence of separate racial and ethnic communities could lead to either unity or fragmentation, depending upon the role played by important community leaders and institutions. In the case of Packingtown, strong ethnic identity and organization facilitated class mobilization. In both of the industry's major strikes community leaders and ethnic religious, fraternal, and business organizations supported the workers morally and financially, while large crowds comprising all segments of the population turned out to attack scabs. In the 1904 strike, the overwhelming majority of strikebreakers had to be recruited from other neighborhoods and even other cities because of the pressure for community solidarity in Packingtown. Scabs could neither drink nor cash their checks in neighborhood saloons. Polish and Lithuanian newlyweds turned over wedding gifts to the union's strike fund, while priests in all but one of the community's ethnic parishes urged their flocks to remain loyal to the union.[35]

The community's response during the 1921 strike was comparable. The White Eagle Dairy distributed free milk, while a Lithuanian bakery provided hundreds of loaves of bread. Newspapers reflecting a broad range of opinion covered strike activities sympathetically, while both clerical and freethought fraternal groups offered support. Catholic parishes, fraternal groups, and small businessmen were particularly supportive in the Polish community which provided the real backbone of resistance in both strikes. In Packingtown the welfare of the communty was seen as linked to that of the union.[36]

The role of community in the Black Belt was very different. Like the recent Slavic immigrants, most Black packing house workers were relative newcomers to urban industrial society and they faced a difficult process of adjustment. In the case of the white immigrants, unions played an important role in this process and greatly influenced the immigrants' views. In the case of the Black migrants, however, this formative experience was shaped by individuals and institutions whose interests were tied to those of the packers. While some race leaders clearly identified with the union, the Chicago Urban League, the Wabash Avenue YMCA, several Black churches, and other community institutions depended directly on the packers for financial support and urged Black butcher workmen to be loyal to their employers. Certainly the packers took an instrumental view of this relationship. Their contributions to the Urban League, for example, rose sharply during union organizing drives and strikes but fell away after the packers had destroyed labor organization in the industry. More generally, packing house employment provided the community's most important source of income. By 1920 the packers employed over half of the Black manufacturing workers in the city. At a time when white employers and craft unions excluded Blacks from many occupations, the packers offered well-paying jobs and critical financial support for Black community institutions.[37]

The packers developed personnel programs tailored to the needs of the Black migrants. "Efficiency Clubs" sponsored choral groups, picnics, and a very successful sports program. As a result, the clubs were popular among the migrants, many of whom were searching for social contacts.[38]

The packers supplemented this community strategy with one aimed at creating racial friction within the plants. They victimized Black and white union activists and favored non-union Blacks in hiring and advancement. Considerable evidence suggests that the packers also employed small groups of anti-union Blacks who were responsible for attacks on union workers in the weeks preceding the 1919 race riot.

Austin "Heavy" Williams, for example, quickly became a strawboss on the cattle killing floor at Wilson's and also served as a recruiter for the Wilson Efficiency Club which met at the Wabash Avenue YMCA. In both capacities Williams counseled new Black workers against becoming involved in the union. While Williams himself was never accused of violence against union men, several Black workers under his influence were. Some carried knives and guns to work, and one of them badly wounded a Black union activist with a heavy, pointed pritching stick normally used to move cattle carcasses. Many of the wildcat strikes and other disturbances which broke out in the plants during the weeks before the 1919 race riot involved this small group of anti-unon Blacks and similar groups at other packing houses.[39]

Racial conflict, then, was not simply the inevitable, if tragic, outcome of labor market competition. The packers exploited racial divisions through their paternalistic policies. Their efforts paid off in the 1921-1922 strike when most black workers stayed at their jobs and helped to defeat the union.

Finally, the general political and economic climate and the balance of class forces in Chicago directly influenced the limited success and the ultimate failure of the butcher workmen to overcome their divisions. Union strength was greatest during the economic boom just after the turn of the century and during the severe labor shortage of the war years. It was weakest in the high unemployment of the 1904 recession and the post-war depression. The butcher workmen's organization was particularly vulnerable in such downturns because of the large proportion of unskilled in the industry.

More importantly, union strength in both periods grew within the context of strong social movements. Chicago's working class was one of the most highly organized and militant in the world during the early years of this century. Nearly every union in Chicago was a constituent of the powerful Chicago Federation of Labor and by 1903 these unions had organized over half of the city's entire labor force, including many unskilled immigrants and more than 35,000 women. Once again during the First World War, the city's labor movement was "more closely organized, more self-conscious, more advanced in its views" than any other in the country. The progressive wing of the city's labor federation created, staffed, and partly financed the early wartime organizing in the Yards. In 1919 the Federation launched an independent labor party in which packing house workers played a prominent role. But labor strength was more than a matter of organizers and money. During the 1904 strike, the packing house teamsters went out in sympathy with the butcher workmen, and workers from other neighborhoods helped with picketing. A woman or man working in the Yards during the early twentieth century was surrounded by a *labor-ethos* which bolstered her or his own efforts.[40]

Likewise, the fragmentation of the Stock Yards movement was part of a general collapse of the labor movement in Chicago and indeed throughout the country. Most of the strikes which engulfed the nation in 1904 and 1921-1922, like those of the butcher workmen in these years, were defensive actions in which workers fought to save their unions. Conditions in Chicago were particularly grim in the years following the First World War. The cumulative effects of economic depression, political factionalism in the labor movement, and the emergence of nativism and racism among the more "Americanized" skilled workers caused the virtual disintegration of a movement which had been quite strong during the war.[41]

Often in American history when class solidarity did emerge it was crushed through government intervention. Certainly state power hobbled efforts to sustain an inter-ethnic, inter-racial class movement in the Chicago stockyards. During the early stages of the 1904 strike police showed restraint and even fraternized with strikers. But as the struggle dragged on, the packers brought their influence to bear on city authorities. Once it became clear that the police, and not the union or crowd, controlled the streets around the Yards, strikebreakers poured in, and the strike was lost.[42]

In keeping with the national pattern during the war and the early 1920s, government action during the 1921-1922 strike was resolute and decisive at both the federal and local levels. Government arbitration offered the packers a degree of flexibility in the tight wartime labor market and saddled union officials with the responsibility of disciplining their members. The packers took this opportunity to develop an alternative to independent labor organization by erecting an elaborate welfare system and an employee representation plan. But the packers' version of the American Plan included a stick as well as a carrot. Federal arbitration ended precisely when the union was weakest, and the packers declared war with a large wage cut. When workers resisted, local government power was thrown decisively on the side of management. A sweeping injunction outlawed virtually all picketing, and hundreds of mounted policemen invaded the immigrant neighborhoods surrounding the plants. The strike was crushed, ending labor organization in the industry until the late 1930s.[43]

13

IV

The story of Chicago's packing house workers suggests that the problem of working class fragmentation in the early twentieth century remains a matter for investigation rather than assumption. On one level, the situation provides substance for economic and cultural theories of fragmentation. The labor force was divided through hierarchical job structures which reinforced racial and ethnic divisions. On Chicago's South Side, the varied work experiences of skilled Irish butchers, recent Slavic immigrants, and Black migrants were also reinforced by the physical and social distance separating these groups. Not surprisingly, many of the packers' personnel policies were designed to accentuate these barriers.

But this study also suggests that such divisions can easily be overdrawn. The butcher workmen were clearly divided between primary and secondary labor markets, but in opposition to this tendency toward fragmentation there were countervailing pressures inherent in the changing character of manufacturing during these years. Much larger plants with finely-integrated production systems could link the fates of very large, socially-diverse groups of workers who might otherwise have had little in common with one another.[44] In packing, a significant intensification of work and the downward pressure on wages caused by casual hiring methods and the army of unemployed at the Yards gate provided a rationale for more skilled, Americanized butcher workmen to reach out to the unskilled Black and Slavic newcomers. In a peculiar way, the hiring practices of the packers and the structure of work in the industry actually facilitated this effort. Rather than Balkanizing the various social groups which composed the labor force, mixed work gangs brought them together, presented them with shared grievances, and offered the opportunity to begin an informal process of socialization.

The effects of social and cultural division are also complex and require further study. In the community, as in the workplace, there were numerous points of contact among white immigrant workers and between them and native-born whites. The existence of strong racial and ethnic subcultures, for example, was not necessarily an impediment to class formation. As Greene has shown for Slavic coalminers and Brody for immigrant steelworkers, the cohesion of such communities often facilitated organization and mobilization in strikes.[45] This was clearly the case with the new immigrants in packing during both union periods.

In addition to analyzing the position of important community leaders and institutions on the question of inter-ethnic and inter-racial working class solidarity, we must also consider the influence of both employers and the broader working class movement in the process of integrating newcomers into the industrial workplace and community. The packers and the unions contended for the loyalty of the new immigrants and the Black migrants. Considering the diversity of the labor force, the unions were remarkably successful at integrating the immigrants in both periods of organization. Although the Black community was divided over the issue of unionization, the labor movement was generally less successful among the migrants. Here paternalistic personnel practices, continuing discrimination in the labor market, racially-segregated neighborhoods, and a lingering suspicion of the "white man's union" combined to keep most Black butcher workmen in the packers' camp. Because of the diversity of the working class population in the United States, a careful analysis of the conditions under which various minorities "settled in" is essential to understanding the problem of class formation and fragmentation.

Here the Chicago case study draws our attention to the social, economic, and political context — the situation within which class formation took place. In both periods of union strength, cohesion and organization along class lines developed as part of a general upsurge supported by a militant, well-organized labor movement and by mobilized ethnic working class communities. Fragmentation and decline came within the context of economic depression, unemployment, and government and employer attacks on the metropolitan and national labor movements. Under such pressures, the racial, ethnic, and skill "fault lines" in the broader working class community contributed to the disintegration of the class movement. But such diversity is not sufficient in and of itself to explain the relative weakness of class identity.

The Chicago case study demonstrates that there are important questions which must be probed before conventional assumptions concerning class formation and fragmentation in the highly-diverse American population are accepted. How common were relations across skill, ethnic, and racial lines, and what form did they take? How did these relations affect class organization and conflict? What is the most realistic way to conceptualize the connection between class and ethnic consciousness in light of the fact that some groups exhibited both simultaneously? Such questions can lead us to a better understanding of the remaking of the American working class in the early years of the corporate political economy.

North Carolina State University   James R. Barrett
Department of History
Raleigh, NC 27650

FOOTNOTES

For comments on earlier versions of this essay, the author wishes to acknowledge the efforts of David Brody, John Bodnar, Steven Vincent, Anthony LaVopa, and James Crisp.

1. Philip Taylor, *The Distant Magnet: European Emigration* (New York, 1972), 48-65; David Montgomery, *Workers' Control in America: Studies in Work, Technology, and Labor Struggles* (New York and London, 1979), 34-7; Daniel Nelson, *Managers and Workers: Origins of the New Factory System in the United States, 1880-1920* (Madison, 1975), 81-5, 145-7; David Brody, *Workers in Industrial America: Essays in the Twentieth Century Struggle* (New York, 1980), 14-21.

2. Herbert Gutman, *Work, Culture, and Society in Industrializing America: Essays in Working Class and Social History* (New York, 1976), Chapter One.

3. David Montgomery, "Gutman's Nineteenth Century America," *Labor History* 19 (1978), 416-429; "Labor in the Industrial Era," in Richard B. Morris, ed., *U.S. Department of Labor Bicentennial History of the American Worker* (Washington, D.C., 1976); *Workers' Control in America*, 1979), 9-31; E.J. Hobsbawm, "Custom, Wages, and Workload in the Nineteenth Century" in *Labouring Men* (London, 1964); Richard J. Oestreicher, "Solidarity and Fragmentation": Working People and Class Consciousness in Detroit, 1877-1895" (Ph.D. dissertation, Michigan State University, 1979), 122-32, Chapter Five.

4. Oestreicher, "Solidarity and Fragmentation," Chapter Eight; John Bodnar, *Immigration and Industrialization: Ethnicity in an American Mill Town* (Pittsburgh, 1977), Chapters One and Two; David Brody, *Steelworkers in America, the Non-Union Era* (New York, 1969) *passim.*

5. Brody, *Steelworkers in America*. On reemigration of the new immigrants of the early twentieth century as a group, see J.D. Gould, "European Inter-Continental Emigration, The Road Home: Return Migration from the U.S.A.," *Journal of European Economic History* 9 (Spring, 1980), 41-112; Frank Thistelthwaite, "European Migration Overseas in the Nineteenth and Twentieth Centuries," in Herbert Moller, ed., *Population Movements in Modern European History* (New York, 1964), 73-91. See also, "A Century of Immigration," *Monthly Labor Review* 18 (1924), 1-19.

6. Richard Edwards, *Contested Terrain: The Transformation of the Workplace in the Twentieth Century* (New York, 1977), especially Chapters Nine and Ten; David M. Gordon, Richard C. Edwards, Michael Reich, *Segmented Work, Divided Workers* (London and New York, 1982); *Labor Market Segmentation* (Lexington, Mass., 1975); Andrew Friedman, *Industry and Labour: Class Struggle at Work and Monopoly Capitalism* (London, 1978); Jill Rubery, "Structured Labour Markets, Worker Organization, and Low Pay," *Cambridge Journal of Economics* 2 (1978), 17-36.

7. On the concept of a labor aristocracy, see Frederick Engels, "Preface to the English Edition," *The Condition of the Working Class in England* (London, 1969), 29-35; E.J. Hobsbawm, "The Labor Aristocracy in Nineteenth Century Britain," in *Labouring Men*. For critical evaluations of the theory, see John Field, "British Historians and the Concept of a Labor Aristocracy," *Radical History Review* 19 (Winter, 1979), 61-85 and the conference papers abstracted in *Bulletin of the Society for the Study of Labour History* 40 (1980), 6-11.

8. James Weinstein, "The IWW and American Socialism," *Socialist Revolution* 1 (1970), 3-42; *The Corporate Ideal in the Liberal State* (Boston, 1968); Ronald Radosh, "The Corporate Ideology of American Labor Leaders from Gompers to Hillman," *Studies on the Left* 6 (1966), 66-8; "Labor and the American Economy: The 1922 Railroad Shop Crafts Strike and the 'B&O Plan'" in Jerry Israel, ed., *Building the Organizational Society: Essays on Associational Activities* (New York, 1972); Gabriel Kolko, *Main Currents in Modern American History* (New York, 1977), 80-3, 176-7.

9. Kolko, *Main-Currents in Modern American History*, Chapter Three. (The quote is on page 99.)

10. For a sociologist's view of the problem, see Gerald Rosenblum, *Immigrant Workers and American Labor Radicalism* (New York, 1968).

11. John R. Commons, "Labor Conditions in Slaughtering and Meat Packing" in John R. Commons, ed. *Labor and Trade Union Problems* (Boston, 1905) 223-6; Ethelbert Stewart, "Productivity in Meat Packing," *Monthly Labor Review*, 18 (1924), 14-21; U.S. Bureau of Corporations, *Report on the Beef Industry* (Washington, D.C., 1905), 17. On the growth of a national market for dressed meat and the structure of the big packing corporations, see Alfred Chandler, "The Origins of Big Business in American Industry," *Business History Review*, 33 (1959), 1-31 and Mary Yeager, *Competition and Regulation: The Development of Oligopoly in the Meat Packing Industry* (Westport, Connecticut, 1981), and on the early technology in the industry, Siegfried Giedion, *Mechanization Takes Command: A Contribution to Anonymous History* (New York, 1948), 93-6, 213-40, and the illustrations on 89, 97, and 217. For a full analysis of the transformation of work referred to here, see James R. Barrett, "Immigrant Workers in Early Mass Production Industry: Work Rationalization and Job Control Conflicts in Chicago's Packing Houses, 1900-1904" in Hartmut Keil and John Jentz, eds. *German Workers in Industrial Chicago, 1850-1910: A Comparative Perspective* (DeKalb, Illinois, 1983).

12. Commons, "Labor Conditions in Slaughtering and Meat Packing," 243, 245-6; U.S. Bureau of Corporations, *Report on the Beef Industry*, 17-18. See also U.S. Department of Labor, *Bulletin* No. 252 (Washington, D.C., 1919). For discussions of the casual labor problem in Chicago, see Carlton Parker, *The Casual Laborer* (New York, 1920), Chapter

Two, Grace Abbott, "The Chicago Employment Agency and the Immigrant Worker," *American Journal of Sociology* 14 (1908), 289-305, and Alice Solenberg, *One Thousand Homeless Men, A Study of Original Records* (New York, 1919), 7-8.

13. U.S. Bureau of Labor Statistics, *Report No. 56* (Washington, D.C., 1905), 3; U.S. Immigration Commission, *Reports, XIII, Part 11, Immigrants in Industry, Slaughtering and Meat Packing* (Washington, D.C. 1911), 199-201; Alma Herbst, *The Negro in the Slaughtering and Meat Packing Industry in Chicago* (Boston, 1933), xxii; Paul S. Taylor, *Mexican Labor in the United States: Chicago and the Calumet Region* (Berkeley, 1930), 37-40, 50-1, 74, 153; Sophinisba Breckinridge and Edith Abbott, "Women in Industry: The Chicago Stockyards," *Journal of Political Economy*, 19 (1911), 632-54; *Fourteenth U.S. Census, 1920, Manufactures* (Washington, D.C., 1923), 364.

14. John R. Commons, "Introduction" in Elizabeth Brandeis and Don D. Lescohier, *History of Labor in the United States, 1896-1932*, III (New York, 1935; reprinted, New York, 1966), xxv.

15. Herbst, *The Negro in the Slaughtering and Meat Packing Industry*, 16-17; Ethelbert Stewart, "The Influence of Trade Unions on Immigrants," U.S. Bureau of Labor Statistics, *Bulletin No. 56* (Washington, D.C., 1905), reprinted in Robt. M. LaFollette, ed. *The Making of America, Labor* (Chicago, 1906; reprinted, New York, 1969), 228; Sterling Spero and Abram L. Harris, *The Black Worker* (New York, 1931; reprinted, New York, 1968), 264.

16. Harry Braverman, *Labor and Monopoly Capital: The Degradation of Work in the Twentieth Century* (New York, 1974); Daniel Nelson, *Managers and Workers;* Edwards, *Contested Terrain;* Gordon, Edwards, Reich, *Segmented Work, Divided Workers.* Each of these works has influenced my own approach considerably.

17. On Packingtown, Bridgeport, and Canaryville, see Barrett, "Work and Community in 'The Jungle,': Chicago's Packing House Workers, 1894-1922," Ph.D. dissertation, University of Pittsburgh, 1981, Chapter Three and pp. 326-8, 346-52. The best social and economic profile of the Black Belt in this era is Allen Spear, *Black Chicago: The Making of a Negro Ghetto* (Chicago, 1967), 129-200.

18. For a thorough, scholarly analysis of the riot and the social problems from which it sprang, see William Tuttle, *Race Riot: Chicago in the Red Summer of 1919* (New York, 1970). Tuttle, however, argues for a causal link between the growth of class consciousness and organization on the one hand and the growth of white racism on the other, a view with which I disagree. See Barrett, "Work and Community in 'The Jungle'," pp. 318-58.

19. David Brody, *The Butcher Workmen, A Study in Unionization* (Cambridge. Mass., 1963), Chapter Two; John R. Commons, "Labor Conditions in Slaughtering and Meat Packing" 243-5; Barrett, "Immigrant Workers in Early Mass Production Industry"; Alice Henry, *The Trade Union Woman* (New York, 1905), 52-8. Leslie Woodcock-Tentler, *Wage Earning Women: Industrial Work and Family in the United States* (New York, 1979) argues for the docility of women workers in this era.

20. Brody, *The Butcher Workmen*, Chapter Four; Barrett, "Work and Community in 'The Jungle'," pp. 306-8, 316-8, 320-5.

21. For the ethnic and skill composition of work gangs, see the Commons article cited above and Carl Thompson, "Labor in the Packing Industry," *Journal of Political Economy*, 15 (1906). For figures on English speakers among the new immigrants, see U.S. Immigration Commission, *Reports, XIII, Part 11, Immigrants in Industry*, 260, and for unionization as a process of acculturation. Barrett, "Work and Community in 'The Jungle'," Chapter Four.

22. Bodnar, *Immigrants and Industrialization*, 35-50; Brody, *Steelworkers in America*, 120-21, 246-47, 260-61.

17

23. Dominic Pacyga, "Villages of Packinghouses and Steel Mills: The Polish Worker on Chicago's South Side, 1880-1921," Ph.D. dissertation, University of Illinois, Chicago, 1981, 189-91; Thompson, "Labor in the Packing Industry," 107-8; "Prohibition Survey of the Stockyards Community," 1926, Folder No. 7, McDowell Papers, Chicago Historical Society; Perry Duis, "The Saloon and the Public City: Chicago and Boston, 1880-1920," Ph.D. dissertation, U. of Chicago, 1975, 639, 645-6; Charles J. Bushnell, "Some Social Aspects of the Chicago Stock Yards," Part II, *American Journal of Sociology* 3 (1901), spot map number five. See also, John M. Kingsdale, "The Poor Man's Club: Social Functions of the Urban Working Class Saloon," in Elizabeth and Joseph Pleck, eds., *The American Man* (Englewood Cliffs, N.J., 1980).

24. Thomas Philpott, *The Slum and the Ghetto* (New York, 1978), 67, 72, 141; Kathleen N. Conzen, "Immigrants; Immigrant Neighborhoods, and Ethnic Identity: Historical Issues," *Journal of American History* 66 (1979), 603-15.

25. These observations are based on Edith Abbott and Sophinisba Breckinridge, "Housing Conditions in Chicago, III: Back of the Yards," *American Journal of Sociology* 16 (1911), 435-68 and on a computer-assisted analysis of a unique 1905 manuscript census of the community. For a fuller description of this data base, see Barrett, "Work and Community in 'The Jungle'," Appendix B.

26. Edward G. Hartman, *The Movement to Americanize the Immigrant* (New York, 1948). For the efforts of managers and middle class reformers to use Americanization programs as a means of social control, see Gerd Korman, "Americanization at the Factory Gate," *Industrial and Labor Relations Review,* 18 (1965), 396-419; Nelson, *Managers and Workers,* 144-5; Brody, *Steelworkers in America,* 189-97; Stephen Meyer, "Adapting the Immigrant to the Line: Americanization in the Ford Factory, 1914-1921," *Journal of Social History* 14 (1980), 67-82. The most subtle treatment of this theme remains Herbert Gutman's "Work, Culture, and Society in Industrializing America, 1815-1919," in his collection of essays under the same title.

27. *Chicago Record Herald,* Oct. 10, 1909; "Citizenship School in 1908-1909 School Year," Folder 11, "Community Study, 1918," Folder 20, Mary McDowell Papers. On the packers' Americanization programs, see *National Provisioner,* 63 (Sept. 25, 1920), 18-19, 25-6, 42-3; *Swift Arrow,* 1 (May 12, 1922), 5; Records of the Mediation and Conciliation Service Record Group 280, Case 33/864, Box 44, 632-82, National Archives and Record Service, Suitland, Maryland.

28. For brief, perceptive comments on informal socialization of immigrants at work, see Montgomery, *Workers' Control in America,* 42-3 and for a treatment which considers the efforts of both management and unions to "Americanize" Slavic immigrants, Neil Betten, "Polish-American Steelworkers: Americanization through Industry and Labor," *Polish American Studies* 33 (1976), 31-42.

29. Stewart, "The Influence of Trade Unions on Immigrants," 226. McDowell is quoted in Howard Wilson, *Mary McDowell, Neighbor* (Chicago, 1928), 99.

30. Stewart, "The Influence of Trade Unions on Immigrants," 231-3.

31. *Ibid.,* 229-31; *Amalgamated Meat Cutters and Butcher Workmen Official Journal,* 2 (July 1901), 2 (May 1902), 2 (Nov. 1902), 2 (Mar. 1903); Olive Anderson, "Chicago League Organizing Stockyards Women Workers," *Life and Labor,* 7 (Apr. 1918), 84; Wm. Z. Foster, "How Life Has Been Brought into the Stockyards," *Life and Labor,* 7 (April, 1918), 64-5. I derived the following breakdown for 25 floor committeemen for whom I was able to determine race and ethnicity: Polish - 9; Black - 5; Bohemian - 3; German - 3; Irish - 3; Lithuanian - 2.

32. Antanas Kaztauskis, "From Lithuania to the Chicago Stockyards — An Autobiography," *Independent* 57 (Aug. 4, 1904), 248.

33. Theodore Glocker, *The Government of American Trade Unions* (Baltimore, 1913) 19-20, 28; Commons, "Labor Conditions in Slaughtering and Meat Packing," 233.

34. For evidence of Black support for segregated locals, see the testimony of William Z. Foster, Secretary of the Stockyards Labor Council before the Chicago Commission on Race Relations in the Commission's *The Negro in Chicago* (Chicago, 1922), 428-29; William Z. Foster, *American Trade Unionism* (New York, 1947), 22-3; and Alma Herbst, *The Negro in the Slaughtering and Meat Packing Industry*, 30-1. On the factionalism of the World War One movement, see Barrett, "Work and Community in 'The Jungle'," 318-67.

35. Chicago *Tribune*, July 20, 24, 26, 29, 30, August 5, 8, 1904.

36. *Dziennik Ziednoczenia*, Feb. 4, 15, 1922; *Dziennik Chicagoski*, January 1, 3, 5, 7, 9, 10, 11, 12, 23, Feb. 4, 10, 1922. See also, Dominic Pacyga, "Crisis and Community: Back of the Yards, 1921," *Chicago History*, 6 (1977), 167-77. (Translated articles and editorials from the Polish newspapers are available in the Chicago Foreign Language Press Survey which is on microfilm at the Chicago Historical Society.)

37. Spear, *Black Chicago*, 169-74; Tuttle, *Race Riot*, 99-100, 140, 147-148, 151; Arvarh Strickland, *History of the Chicago Urban League* (Urbana, Illinois, 1966), 38, 44-5, 48-9, 74; Walter A. Fogel, *The Negro in the Meat Industry* (Philadelphia, 1970), 29; Chicago Commission on Race Relations, *The Negro in Chicago*, 147.

38. Chicago Commission on Race Relations, *The Negro in Chicago*, 147-8; Tuttle, *Race Riot*, 151.

39. See the testimony of Robert Bedford, William Bremer, Gus Grabe, Frank Custer, Austin "Heavy" Williams, Jack Johnstone, Joseph Hodges, and Louis Mihora before Judge Joseph Alschuler in the Records of the Federal Mediation and Conciliation Service, RG 280, Case 33/864, Boxes 42 and 46, at the National Archives and Record Service, Suitland, Maryland.

40. Steve Sapolsky, "Class Conscious Belligerents: The Teamsters and the Class Struggle in Chicago, 1901-1905," seminar paper, University of Pittsburgh, 1974; Glocker, *The Government of American Trade Unions*, 24; Montgomery, *Workers' Control in America*, 57-8; Foster, *American Trade Unionism*, 19-22. The quote, from Ray Stannard Baker, is in Tuttle, *Race Riot*, 141.

41. Montgomery, *Workers' Control in America*, 20, 97. For a full analysis of the relationship between the general decline of the labor movement in these years and the disintegration of the movement in the Yards, see Barrett, "Work and Community in 'The Jungle'," 318-67.

42. Howard B. Meyer, "The Policing of Labor Disputes in Chicago: A Study," Ph.D. dissertation, University of Chicago, 1929, Chapter Nine; Chicago *Tribune*, Aug. 14, 1904.

43. Pacyga, "Crisis and Community," 166-77; Benjamin Stolberg, "The Stockyards Strike," *The Nation*, 141 (Jan. 25, 1922), 90-2; *Dziennik Chicagoski*, Dec. 8, 9, 1921.

44. Gordon, Edwards, and Reich, *Segmented Work, Divided Workers*, Chapter Four.

45. Victor Greene, *The Slavic Community on Strike* (South Bend, Indiana, 1968); Brody, *Steelworkers in America*; David Brody, *Labor in Crisis, the Steel Strike of 1919* (Philadelphia, 1965).

19

Natives and Immigrants, Free Men and Slaves:
Urban Workingmen in the Antebellum American South

IRA BERLIN
and
HERBERT G. GUTMAN

OF NECESSITY, HISTORICAL RESEARCH IS PIECEMEAL. But the growth of historical understanding is not simply an additive process. Instead, new discoveries transform older conceptions and necessitate reconsiderations at the highest interpretive level. A re-evaluation of the place of immigrant workers in antebellum Southern cities suggests how the process works, for it forces a reformulation of ideas about the entire structure of the urban work force and raises questions about the nature of Southern society, urban and rural, and the beliefs of Southerners, native and immigrant, free and slave.

FEW OF THE BULWARKS OF SOUTHERN DISTINCTIVENESS have withstood the battering ram of historiographic iconoclasm better than the overwhelmingly native origins of the Southern people. While scholars of all persuasions have challenged the unique character of the South's economy, its social structure, its politics, and its institutions, the weight of historical evidence has left this mark of Southern difference undisturbed.[1] Even a passing acquaintance with transatlantic migratory patterns

An early version of this paper was prepared in 1975–76 while its authors were fellows at the Shelby Cullom Davis Center for Historical Study at Princeton University. They remain indebted to the center's director, Lawrence Stone, for encouragement and support. Rebecca Scott ably assisted with the initial research and analysis. Judith Rowe and Nita Roberts of the Princeton University Computer Center and Bertha Butler of the Computer Science Center at the University of Maryland guided the statistical aspects of this study. Another version of this paper was thoughtfully criticized at the 1981 Annual Meeting of the Organization of American Historians by Harold Woodman. Research grants from the Ford Foundation and the Rockefeller Foundation facilitated additional research, and we thank Robert Schrank and Joel Colton, respectively, for making this work possible. We also want to acknowledge the thoughtful criticisms offered by W. Elliot Brownlee, George Callcott, Eric Foner, Ronald Hoffman, Michael P. Johnson, Bruce C. Levine, Sidney Mintz, Joseph P. Reidy, and Leslie S. Rowland.

[1] For a recent attempt to deny the distinctive nature of Southern society, see Edward Pessen, "How Different from Each Other Were the Antebellum North and South," *AHR*, 85 (1980): 1119–49; also see the comments that follow in "*AHR Forum*—Antebellum North and South in Comparative Perspective: A Discussion," by Thomas Alexander, Stanley L. Engerman, Forrest McDonald and Grady McWhiney, and Edward Pessen, *ibid.*, 1150–66.

affirms that few of the thousands of Europeans who journeyed to the United States in the years before the Civil War settled in the slave states. At mid-century, when fully one Northerner in seven had been born outside the United States, only 5 percent of the Southern free population was foreign born, and a disproportionate number of these resided in the border states. Ten years later, the margin had widened as European migrants surged into the North, while they continued to dribble into the South. On the eve of the Civil War, when fewer than one free Southerner in fifteen had been born outside the United States, immigrants composed nearly a fifth of the population of the free states.[2]

Historians have found this massive imbalance reason enough to ignore immigrants in antebellum Southern society and to argue that slavery repelled foreign settlers. While lavishing attention on the role of foreign-born people in the transformation of pre–Civil War Northern society, scholars have neglected their place in the development of the antebellum South. This is particularly true in accounts of the immigrants' part in the making of the urban working class. Although the portrait of antebellum class formation in the cities of the North has been constructed as a rich ethnic mosaic, in the urban South the process has been etched in black and white.

The conventional treatment of Southern urban workers leaves little room for immigrants—indeed, for white labor generally. Drawing on the antislavery argument, particularly that of political abolitionists, historians have emphasized that the presence of slave labor degraded free white workers. With William Seward, they have maintained that slavery denied the white workingman employment and expelled him "from the community because it cannot enslave and convert him into merchandise." The rules of the free market economy simply did not apply to labor in a slave society. As Charles Nordhoff, another opponent of slavery, observed, it mattered nothing to the slaveholder "how low others can produce the article; he can produce it lower still, so long as it is the best use he can make of his [slaves'] labor, and as long as that labor is worth keeping. A free white mechanic is at the mercy of his neighbor, the capitalist, in a slave state, because, if the capitalist does not like the price, he can go and buy a carpenter and sell him again when the work is done." Conceding that slaves worked at lower rates than free laborers, historians have concurred in the abolitionist argument that, "when the two are brought into competition, white labor is crowded out."[3]

[2] U.S. Bureau of the Census, *The Seventh Census of the United States, 1850* (Washington, 1853), xxxvi–xxxviii, and *Population of the United States in 1860* (Washington, 1864), 620–23. If slaves are included in the analysis, the proportion of immigrants in the Southern population shrinks (to about 3 percent in 1850, 5 percent in 1860), and the differences between the proportion of immigrants in the North and that in the South grows. For a survey of recent scholarship about immigrants in the Old South, see Randall M. Miller, "Immigrants in the Old South," *Immigration History Newsletter*, 10 (1978): 8–14. Also see the discussions in Clement Eaton, *The Growth of Southern Civilization* (New York, 1971), 150–76, 221–70; Ella Lonn, *Foreigners in the Confederacy* (Chapel Hill, N.C., 1940), 1–32; Herbert J. Weaver, "Foreigners in the Ante-Bellum Towns in the Lower South," *Journal of Southern History*, 13 (1947): 62–73, and "Foreigners in Antebellum Mississippi," *Journal of Mississippi History*, 16 (1954): 151–63; William L. Barney, *The Secessionist Impulse: Alabama and Mississippi in 1860* (Princeton, 1974), 26–43; and Edward L. Ayers, *Vengeance and Justice: Crime and Punishment in the Nineteenth Century* (New York, 1984), chap. 3.

[3] Nordhoff, *America for Free Working Men* (New York, 1865), 1–39; and David Bertelson, *The Lazy South* (New York, 1967), 201. For an important exception to this conventional wisdom, see Carville Earle and Ronald Hoffman, "The Foundation of the Modern Economy: Agriculture and the Costs of Labor in the United States and England, 1800–60," *AHR*, 85 (1980): 1055–94.

TABLE 1

Selected Southern Urban Populations, 1850–1860

City	Total Population in 1860	Percentage of Increase/Decrease from 1850 to 1860	Percentage of Population in 1860		
			White	Free Black	Slave
RICHMOND	38,000	+38	62	7	31
CHARLESTON	41,000	− 6	58	8	34
MOBILE	30,000	+43	71	3	26
NASHVILLE	17,000	+67	77	4	19
LYNCHBURG	7,000	−18	56	5	39
BATON ROUGE	5,000	+27	68	9	23

NOTE: Percentages here and in all subsequent tables do not always add to 100, owing to rounding; total population rounded to thousands.
SOURCES: U.S. Bureau of the Census, *The Seventh Census of the United States, 1850* (Washington, 1853), and *Population of the United States in 1860* (Washington, 1864).

According to the extant historiography, black freemen and bondsmen did most of the labor in the South, including most of the artisanal work. In his classic study, Charles H. Wesley put the proportion at about 80 percent. Others have suggested the same without Wesley's precision. Historians have maintained that native-born white workingmen fled the slave states when they could. Those who remained in the South protested slave competition but had little success against the potent combination of slaves, who monopolized skilled labor, and masters, who reaped a handsome profit from their slaves' work. Such circumstances could hardly encourage foreign immigration, and those few feckless migrants who alighted in the slave states generally found employment at tasks that masters deemed too dangerous for their valuable slaves.[4] Foreign-born workers have thus appeared marginal, rather than central, to an understanding of the working population of the urban South.

The dominance of the urban work force by black laborers has been challenged implicitly by recent work on urban bondage, which emphasizes the sharp decline of slavery in the cities in the late antebellum years. But scholars have posed the question of urban slavery far too narrowly. They have vigorously debated whether the peculiarities of urban bondage pushed or the nature of plantation demand pulled slaves out of the cities, while ignoring the character of the urban work force and the relations between slaves and free workers. Even the most detailed scholarship has left the immigrant the South's invisible man.[5]

Yet the peculiar pattern of European migration and settlement in the slave states gave immigrants importance far beyond their numbers and projected foreign-born workers into a place in the Southern working class that rivaled the role played by

[4] Wesley, *Negro Labor in the United States* (New York, 1927), chaps. 1–3; Herman Schlüter, *Lincoln, Labor, and Slavery* (New York, 1913); Kenneth M. Stampp, "The Fate of the Southern Antislavery Movement," *Journal of Negro History*, 28 (1943): 10–22; Roger Shugg, *Origins of Class Struggle in Louisiana* (University, La., 1939), 20–110 but esp. 86–92; Robert S. Starobin, *Industrial Slavery in the Old South* (New York, 1970), 146–89 but esp. 153–63; and Frederick Law Olmsted, *Journey in the Seaboard Slave States* (New York, 1856), esp. 193.

[5] Richard C. Wade, *Slavery in the Cities: The South, 1820–1860* (New York, 1964); and Claudia D. Goldin, *Urban Slavery in the American South, 1820–1860: A Quantitative History* (Chicago, 1976).

TABLE 2
Occupational Distribution of Employed Free Adult Men, 1860

City	Number	Percentage of Employed Adult Free Men		
		Non-workers	Skilled Workers	Unskilled Workers
RICHMOND	7,954	38	42	20
CHARLESTON	6,985	45	35	20
MOBILE	7,306	38	30	32
NASHVILLE	4,307	41	35	24
LYNCHBURG	1,273	48	34	18
BATON ROUGE	887	40	47	13

SOURCE: Computed from the U.S. manuscript census schedules, 1860, Records of the Bureau of the Census (Record Group 29), National Archives, Washington [hereafter, U.S. Census MSS., RG 29].

immigrants in the North. Although a comparatively small number of Europeans migrated to the South during the nineteenth century, those who did generally settled in cities. South Carolina, Georgia, and Alabama had few immigrants, but Charleston, Savannah, and Mobile had many. At mid-century, the foreign-born population of these states reached 3 percent only in the case of South Carolina. But more than a fifth of Charleston's residents, more than a quarter of Savannah's, and almost a third of Mobile's had been born outside the United States.[6] Moreover, since men formed a disproportionately large share of the foreign settlers in Southern cities, immigrants composed a still larger share of the urban male work force than they did of the urban population as a whole. As a result, like Mobile (where half of the employed free men had been born outside the United States), many urban places in the Lower South could be appropriately described as immigrant cities.[7]

The same processes that drew immigrant men disproportionately to Southern cities concentrated them in specific places in the social structure of the urban South. As a group, immigrants entered Southern society at the bottom of the free social hierarchy and made up a large part of the lower ranks of urban society. On the eve of the Civil War, native-born white men composed better than two-thirds of the male merchants, political officials, and professionals in Mobile, Charleston, and other Southern cities, while foreign-born men equaled a similar proportion of petty proprietors—grocers, restauranteurs, stable keepers, and the like. Immigrants were

[6] J. D. B. DeBow, *Statistical View of the United States* (Washington, 1854), 399. This disjunction between rural and urban patterns of immigrant settlement also existed in those areas of the South that received the largest numbers of foreign settlers. In 1860, immigrants composed 13 percent of Louisiana's population but foreign-born men and women accounted for almost two-fifths of the inhabitants of New Orleans; U.S. Bureau of the Census, *Population of the United States in 1860*, 615.

[7] The data on nativity of employed free men in Mobile, along with similar information of employed men in Baton Rouge, Charleston, Lynchburg, Nashville, and Richmond have been calculated from a tabulation of all men for whom either an occupation or property (real or personal) is listed in the 1850 and 1860 manuscript censuses, the 1850 and 1860 manuscript slave schedules, and the 1850 and 1860 manuscript industrial schedules, National Archives, Washington, Record Group 29.

TABLE 3
Skill Distribution of Free Working Men, 1860

City	Number of Free Working Men	Percentage Skilled	Percentage Unskilled
RICHMOND	4,929	68	32
CHARLESTON	3,846	63	37
MOBILE	4,552	49	51
NASHVILLE	2,533	60	40
LYNCHBURG	661	66	34
BATON ROUGE	529	79	21

SOURCE: Computed from the U.S. Census MSS., RG 29.

also disproportionately represented among urban workingmen, the largest occupational group in every major Southern city. Immigrants commonly dominated the free male working population and formed a large proportion of the entire male working population, free and slave. For that reason, foreign settlers helped shape social relations in the urban South and had a profound influence on class and racial relations throughout Southern society.

The composition of the urban male work force on the eve of the Civil War suggests the significance of immigrant workers in Southern cities.[8] Four Southern cities and several towns have been studied: Richmond, the South's premier industrial city with a population of some 38,000 in 1860, of which more than 60 percent were whites, about 30 percent were slaves, and less than 10 percent—the remainder—were free Negroes; Charleston, an older Atlantic port with a population slightly larger but of similar composition to that of Richmond; Mobile, an expanding cotton port of some 21,000 whites, 7,500 slaves, and fewer than 1,000 free people of color; and Nashville, a rapidly expanding interior marketing and transporting center, three-fourths of whose residents were white. In addition, two smaller cities have been examined: Lynchburg, a regional Virginia tobacco manufacturing center of 7,000, with proportionally few immigrants, and Baton Rouge, a Louisiana river town of 5,000, with proportionally many immigrants. Except for Charleston and Lynchburg, these cities grew rapidly during the antebellum period. In some respects, their populations increased more rapidly than those of Northern cities.[9] (See Table 1) In these selected cities and throughout the urban South, laboring men were sharply divided by legal status, nativity, and race. Native-born white men monopolized occupations in the upper ranks of Southern society. The vast majority of merchants, bankers, factors, doctors, and lawyers in these cities

[8] This essay focuses on the role of men in the Southern urban working population. We are preparing a companion essay that examines the composition of the female sector of the work force of Southern cities. The presence of large numbers of slave women, almost all of whom worked, had a profound impact on the role of free working women and throws into sharp contrast the lives of all women in Northern and Southern cities. In this essay, unless otherwise stated, work force and working population refer to male work force and male working population.

[9] Leonard P. Curry, "Urbanization and Urbanism in the Old South: A Comparative View," Journal of Southern History, 40 (1974): 43–60.

TABLE 4
Employed and Propertied Adult Free Men by Nativity and Race, 1860

City	Number	Percentage by Nativity and Race				
		Southern-Born White	Northern-Born White	Foreign-Born White	Free Black	Unknown Origin
RICHMOND	8,122	51	7	31	8	3
CHARLESTON	7,256	41	6	42	8	3
MOBILE	7,457	31	16	50	2	1
NASHVILLE	4,415	50	13	31	3	3
LYNCHBURG	1,295	70	3	16	7	4
BATON ROUGE	927	44	11	39	5	1

SOURCE: Computed by the U.S. Census MSS., RG 29.

were white men born in the slave states, frequently in the states in which they resided. Generally, the more successful—as measured by wealth and slaveownership—the greater the likelihood that these men had been born in the South. At the bottom of free society, the free laboring population was a good deal more hetereogenenous. Native-born Southern whites, Northern-born whites, foreign-born whites of various nationalities, and free Negroes (almost all of whom had been born in the South but who divided among themselves by their degree of racial admixture) formed the free working class. The remaining portion of the laboring population, the slaves, was also almost entirely native born and, like the free Negroes, divided by color—black and brown. By its legal status, nativity, and race, each group played carefully defined and usually distinctive roles within the urban work force.[10] Free workers constituted a majority of the adult free men in all cities studies. Except in Mobile, skilled workers predominated among these free wage earners. (See Tables 2, 3, and 4.)

On the eve of the Civil War, immigrants composed a large portion of the free urban work force—sometimes stretching to a clear majority. Generally, the further south the city, the greater the proportion of workers of foreign birth. In Mobile, that classic immigrant city, almost two-thirds of the free workingmen were immigrants. Although the proportion of the foreign-born free workers was smaller in Charleston and Baton Rouge, it still equaled about half of the free work force. Immigrants were not nearly as prominent in the cities of the upper South, especially in land-locked interior cities like Lynchburg. Even in Richmond and Nashville, however, foreign settlers totaled 40 percent of the free workingmen. (See Table 5).

[10] For purposes of this essay, workingmen have been divided into two categories: skilled and unskilled. Among those classified as unskilled are day laborers, boathands, draymen, dock workers, sailors, and tobacco factory workers. The skilled workingmen have been further divided into two subcategories: those working in the building trades (including bricklayers, carpenters, painters, plasterers, plumbers, and stonemasons), and other skilled workers (including bakers, barbers, blacksmiths, bookmakers, brewers, butchers, carriage makers, cabinet makers, clock makers, confectioners, engravers, founders, jewelers, pilots, printers, shoemakers, tailors, tanners, wheelwrights, and watchmakers).

TABLE 5
Adult Free Workingmen by Nativity and Race, 1860

City	Number	Percentage by Nativity and Race			
		Southern-Born White	Northern-Born White	Foreign-Born White	Free Black
RICHMOND	4,929	39	8	39	14
CHARLESTON	3,846	28	6	52	14
MOBILE	4,552	19	14	64	3
NASHVILLE	2,533	42	12	41	5
LYNCHBURG	661	62	4	20	14
BATON ROUGE	529	35	11	47	7

SOURCE: Computed from the U.S. Census MSS., RG 29.

Black freemen and Northern-born whites also played an important part in the laboring population of the urban South. Free Negroes or free people of color—the specific nomenclature depended on the region—made up a small and variable portion of the urban working class in every Southern city. In some places, like Charleston and Richmond, they constituted an important minority of the free workingmen—amounting to more than one in seven. Elsewhere, however, they slipped to numerical insignificance. In Mobile, free men of color totaled only 3 percent of the free workingmen. Northern-born white workers also varied widely in number from place to place, although they played a more important role in the newer cities of the west and the Lower South than in the older ones in the Upper South. They, too, equaled about 4 to 14 percent of the free work force. Taken together, free Negroes and Northern-born whites totaled about a fifth of all free workingmen in Southern cities. (See Table 5.)

Although the proportion varied from city to city, immigrants, free Negroes, and Northern-born whites together constituted nearly three-quarters of the free workingmen in Charleston and about 60 percent of those in Richmond and Nashville. In Mobile, immigrants, Northern-born whites, and free people of color totaled a full 80 percent of the that city's free workingmen. Except in the interior marketing and manufacturing center of Lynchburg, white workers native to the South made up only a minority of the urban South's free working class. Within the context of an overwhelmingly native-born regional population and the predominately native origins of the upper ranks of urban society, native-born Southern white workers were a conspicuous minority in most Southern cities. (See Table 5.)

Whatever the dynamics of slavery in the city, enslaved black laborers remained an indispensable part of the urban work force on the eve of the Civil War. Although their share of the total urban labor force shrank during the late antebellum years, nearly all slaves did manual labor of one kind or another, and they remained a large component of the laboring population everywhere except in the border cities. In Charleston, Richmond, Mobile, and Nashville, adult slaves still

TABLE 6
Workingmen by Status, Nativity, and Race, 1860

| City | Number | Slave | Percentage of Workingmen | | | |
			Southern-Born White	Northern-Born White	Foreign-Born White	Free Black
RICHMOND	9,557	48	20	4	20	7
CHARLESTON	7,887	51	14	3	25	7
MOBILE	7,002	35	13	9	41	2
NASHVILLE	3,408	26	31	9	30	4
LYNCHBURG	1,623	60	24	2	8	6
BATON ROUGE	843	37	22	7	29	5

NOTE: For the classification of workingmen, see note 10, above.
SOURCE: Computed from the U.S. Census MSS., RG 29.

constituted between one-half and one-quarter of the workingmen, skilled and unskilled.[11] In Lynchburg, they constituted over 60 percent of the workingmen. The presence of slaves reduced proportionately the weight of various groups of free workingmen in the urban working class and made Southern whites (like everyone else) a still smaller proportion of the whole. Only a minority of Southern urban workers had been born in the South and shared the most prized Southern attributes: whiteness and freedom. Most urban workers were born alien to the dominant characteristics of Southern culture. (See Table 6.)

Slaves, free Negroes, immigrants of various nationalities, Northern-born whites, and Southern-born whites played different roles in the Southern urban work force. By the various combinations of color, status, and nativity, workers toiled at different skill levels, practiced different trades, and labored in different sectors of the economy. ;See Table 7.) For free workingmen, these differences can be discerned by disaggregating the census enumerations. The antebellum census, however, provides no occupational designations for slaves—an omission that has fueled erroneous speculation about the kind of work slaves did in Southern cities.[12] So many free men (immigrants and native born) practiced skilled crafts in Southern cities that it is unlikely urban slaves could have been similarly skilled. Had slaves possessed skills in the same proportion as free workers, the ranks of unskilled labor and domestic service would have gone unfilled and Southern cities would have been like no others in the Western world. An analysis of patterns of slave ownership and employment on the assumption that a slave's work was related to his master's— that an adult slave man owned by a blacksmith was likely to be a blacksmith, while an adult slave man owned by a banker was not—and within the context of the known occupational structure of the free working class confirms this inference. It also provides a rough estimate of the level of urban slave skill and a still rougher guide to the character of urban slave occupations.

[11] All slave men between age fifteen and sixty are presumed to have worked and are included in the work force. For a more extended discussion of slave occupations, see pages 1185–87, below.
[12] A recent example is Robert William Fogel and Stanley L. Engerman, *Time on the Cross: The Economics of American Negro Slavery*, 2 vols. (Boston, 1974).

TABLE 7
Free Workingmen, Skilled and Unskilled, by Nativity, and Race, 1860

City	Number	Percentage of Workingmen			
		Southern-Born White	Northern-Born White	Foreign-Born White	Free Black
A: Skilled Free Workingmen					
RICHMOND	3,341	48	10	36	6
CHARLESTON	2,413	38	6	40	16
MOBILE	2,211	25	17	54	3
NASHVILLE	1,522	46	17	33	4
LYNCHBURG	434	70	5	18	7
BATON ROUGE	416	36	12	44	8
B: Unskilled Free Workingmen					
RICHMOND	1,588	20	4	46	30
CHARLESTON	1,433	11	5	72	11
MOBILE	2,341	14	12	69	4
NASHVILLE	1,011	35	4	51	9
LYNCHBURG	227	46	2	25	27
BATON ROUGE	113	34	5	57	4

NOTE: For the classification of workingmen, see note 10, above.
SOURCE: Computed from the U.S. Census MSS., RG 29.

An examination of slave ownership in Mobile, Charleston, and Nashville reveals that most artisans (here including those who might classify themselves as manufacturers employing skilled workers—founders as well as blacksmiths, contractors as well as carpenters) did not own slaves, and those who did controlled only a small portion of the city's slave population. Workers were the largest occupational group, but slave ownership by workers (almost always artisans) never exceeded 15 percent of the slave men. (See Table 8.) Moreover, women (usually adolescent girls) composed a disproportionate share of artisan-owned slaves, suggesting that, when a skilled worker purchased a slave, the slave was usually a servant for the owner's household rather than a journeyman for his shop.[13]

With slave prices rising rapidly in the 1850s, slave hiring grew more commonplace throughout the urban South. Many free workers may have been among those who rented rather than purchased slaves. Both masters and slaves found slave hiring profitable. It provided slaveowners—particularly widowed women—a steady

[13] For example, in 1860 only 40 percent of the slaves employed by Richmond's white men (including tobacco manufacturers) were women, but women accounted for 60 percent of the slaves employed by white artisans. A similar pattern can be found in Lynchburg, another city where the distribution of slaves was reported by employer rather than by owner. Elsewhere, the disparity between the white male ownership and the white artisan ownership was smaller, and, in Charleston, artisans proportionately owned more men than the white male population as a whole. See note 16, below.

TABLE 8
Ownership or Employment of Adult Slave Men, 1860

City	Total Number of Slaves	Occupation of Owners or Employers							
		Merchants, Planters, Professionals, and Politicians	Manufacturers	Petty Entrepreneurs	Artisans	Unskilled Laborers	White Women	Free Blacks	Unknown
Richmond[a]	4,628	22	58	6	6	1	5	0	3
Charleston[b]	4,042	50	0	4	14	1	22	1	8
Mobile[b]	2,450	60	5	4	8	1	17	0	5
Nashville[c]	877	38	5	23	11	3	10	0	9
Lynchburg[a]	962	31[d]	53	6	4	0	2	0	4

[a] Slaves listed by their employers.
[b] Slaves listed by their owners.
[c] Slaves listed in some wards by their employers, in some wards by their owners.
[d] Includes eighty-four slave men, about 8 percent of the male slaves, employed on the railroad.
SOURCE: Computed from U.S. Census MSS., RG 29.

income, and it gave slaves an added measure of control over their own lives. Slave hiring increased despite a variety of complaints from white workers fearful for their jobs and white residents fearful for their lives.[14] But slave hiring did not enlarge artisan employment of slaves in most cities. In Richmond and Lynchburg (where census takers noted slave employment rather than slave ownership), large tobacco manufacturers hired most of the slaves. When viewed from the perspective of employment rather than ownership, artisan control of slaves increased slightly. But throughout the urban South, merchants, professionals, and manufacturers (in factory towns like Richmond and Lynchburg) remained the largest employers of slave labor, and, for the most part, these employers required unskilled, rather than skilled, laborers.[15] (See Table 8.) While some merchants and manufacturers may well have employed slave artisans, some free artisans doubtless worked their slaves in menial roles. In any case, when slave artisans—estimated as all slave men owned by free white artisans—are placed within the context of the artisan class, their share of the skilled work force exceeds 8 percent in Charleston but nowhere else. Even when the estimated number of slave artisans is doubled (that is, every slave man owned by a white artisan plus an equal number owned by others), slaves still composed less than 15 percent of the artisan population in Mobile, Richmond, and Nashville. Thus, as a general rule, urban slaves appear to have toiled in either the most backward sector of the economy as domestic servants and day laborers or in the most advanced sector of the economy as factory hands. (See Table 9.)

Only in Charleston did slaves make up a large portion of the mechanic class. Charleston artisans owned slaves in numbers that proportionately nearly doubled the rate of artisan slave ownership in Mobile, Richmond, or Nashville. Moreover, unlike the pattern of artisan slave ownership in those cities, Charleston artisans held slave men in disproportionate numbers.[16] Those Charleston artisans who did not own slaves also had ample opportunity to hire them, since city-bound planters and white women owned a larger proportion of their city's slave population than in any of the other places investigated. Thus a tradition of slave artisanry reaching back into the eighteenth century—built upon the high level of skill demanded by the rice economy and sustained by a cultural milieu more akin to the West Indies than the mainland—existed in Charleston on the eve of the Civil War.[17] If every slave man owned by a Charleston artisan practiced his master's trade, Charleston's slaves

[14] For discussions of slave hiring, see Wade, *Slavery in the Cities*, 38–54; Starobin, *Industrial Slavery in the Old South*, 128–37, 211–12; Clement Eaton, "Slave-Hiring in the Upper South: A Step toward Freedom," *Mississippi Valley Historical Review*, 46 (1959–60): 663–78; and Richard B. Morris, "The Measure of Bondage in the Slave States," *ibid.*, 41 (1954–55): 219–40.

[15] For the best discussions of Southern tobacco manufacturing prior to the Civil War, see Joseph C. Robert, *The Tobacco Kingdom: Plantation, Market, and Factory in Virginia and North Carolina, 1800–1860* (Durham, N.C., 1938); and John O'Brien, "Black Richmond, 1850–1870" (Ph.D. dissertation, University of Rochester, 1978), chap. 1. Also see Starobin, *Industrial Slavery in the Old South*.

[16] In 1860, 51 percent of the slaves owned by Charleston's white men were women, but only 39 percent of the slaves owned by white artisans were women. See note 13, above.

[17] Artisan ownership of slaves was commonplace in post-Revolutionary Charleston, the largest slave city in the nation. In 1790, more than half of Charleston's artisans owned slaves, and their slaves amounted to nearly a quarter of the city's slave population. The nature of the available evidence makes it impossible to determine how many of the artisans' slaves were men, but the size of their holdings suggests that many used slaves in their shops as well as in their homes. For example, 60 percent of Charleston carpenters owned slaves. Almost three-quarters of these slaves were held in units of six or more, units large enough to extend beyond the domestic

TABLE 9
Skill Distribution among Free and Slave Workingmen, 1860

Using Minimal Estimate of Skilled Slaves

	Richmond[a]		Charleston[b]		Mobile[c]		Nashville[d]		Lynchburg[e]		Baton Rouge[f]	
	Skilled	Unskilled	Skilled	Unskilled	Skilled	Unskilled	Skilled	Unskilled	Skilled	Unskilled	Skilled	Unskilled
NUMBER	3,619	5,938	2,978	4,909	2,407	4,595	1,612	1,797	473	1,150	451	392
PERCENTAGE												
Southern-born White	45	6	31	3	23	7	43	20	63	9	33	10
Northern-born White	9	1	5	2	16	5	16	2	4	0	11	2
Foreign-born	33	12	32	21	50	36	31	28	16	5	41	16
Free Black	5	8	13	3	3	2	3	5	6	6	7	1
Slave	8	73	19	71	8	49	6	44	10	80	8	71

Using Maximal Estimate of Skilled Slaves

	Richmond[g]		Charleston[h]		Mobile[i]		Nashville[j]		Lynchburg[k]		Baton Rouge[l]	
	Skilled	Unskilled	Skilled	Unskilled	Skilled	Unskilled	Skilled	Unskilled	Skilled	Unskilled	Skilled	Unskilled
NUMBER	3,896	5,661	3,544	4,343	2,603	4,399	1,710	1,698	521	1,102	485	358
PERCENTAGE												
Southern-born White	41	6	26	4	21	8	41	21	58	9	31	11
Northern-born White	8	1	4	2	15	6	15	3	4	0	10	2
Foreign-born	31	13	27	24	46	37	29	30	14	5	38	18
Free Black	5	9	11	4	2	2	3	5	5	6	7	1
Slave	14	71	32	67	15	47	11	40	18	79	14	68

ASSUMPTION: The percentage of slaves who were skilled—that is, if x percent of slaves were skilled, then the skill distribution among workers by status, nativity, and race was as described in the corresponding table— a = 6 percent; b = 14 percent; c = 8 percent; d = 11 percent; e = 5 percent; f = 11 percent; g = 12 percent; h = 28 percent; i = 16 percent; j = 22 percent; k = 10 percent; and l = 22 percent.

SOURCE: Computed and estimated from the Census MSS., RG 29.

would have contributed nearly a fifth of the skilled workingmen in that city. If in addition to those owned by artisans, other slave men also engaged in skilled labor, the proportion of artisanal work performed by slaves would have been higher still. In Mobile, Richmond, and Nashville, all of which developed during the nineteenth century, far fewer slaves practiced skilled trades, and skilled bondsmen composed only a small proportion of the mechanic class. Although urban slaves everywhere enjoyed greater mobility and cultural autonomy than their counterparts in the countryside, only in Charleston—and cities where similar conditions existed—did large numbers of bondsmen practice skilled trades. Elsewhere, few seem to have escaped the dull, demeaning, and backbreaking work that also characterized slave labor in the countryside.

Although slaves were the single largest source of unskilled labor in Southern cities, many free men also worked at unskilled menial jobs. Assuming that all slave men not employed as artisans worked as laborers, slaves supplied slightly better than 70 percent of the unskilled and service workers in Richmond and Charleston, 50 percent in Mobile, and more than 40 percent in Nashville. In short, even where slaves performed most of the unskilled work, free workers still composed a substantial minority of the unskilled laborers. In some slave cities, like Nashville, free workers did most of the unskilled, menial work performed by men. (See Tables 7B and 9.)

Irish immigrants generally dominated the ranks of unskilled urban free men thoughout the urban South. In Charleston, fully 60 percent of the free unskilled laboringmen had been born in Ireland, and, although that proportion slipped substantially in Mobile, Richmond, and Nashville, it remained above 40 percent. In occupational terms, the nativist slander that an Irishman was a "nigger" turned inside out contained a considerable element of truth in such places. Immigrants of other nationalities, along with free Negroes, accounted for most of the remainder of the unskilled free workingmen. (See Tables 7B, 10.)

But, even more than among workingmen generally, native-born whites were conspicuous in their absence from the ranks of the unskilled; and, in the cities of the Lower South in particular, it would have been difficult to find a Southern-born white man shouldering a shovel or lifting a hod. Unskilled Southern-born whites constituted no more than 8 percent of the employed free men in the Southern cities studied. In Charleston, fewer than one Southern white man in fifty—compared to more than half of the Irishmen—did unskilled labor. (See Table 11.) While the structure of the urban laboring class confirmed the degraded status of blacks and identified the Irish with the slave, native-born Southern whites insulated themselves from such imputations.

---

needs of most households and to contain several slave men. Some Charleston carpenters held so many slaves that their number almost compelled commercial exploitation. A full 25 percent of slaveowning carpenters owned ten or more slaves. These estimates result from linking the 1790 Charleston manuscript federal census and the 1790 Charleston city directory. The directory lists occupations, and the census gives the number of slaves residing in individual households. Any computation of slave ownership (using the federal census before 1850), however, is compromised by the fact that some slaves within a given household may not have been owned by the head of the household; such computations must, therefore, be considered rough estimates. Jacob Milligan, comp., *The Charleston Directory* (Charleston, 1790); U.S. Bureau of the Census, *Heads of Families at the Time of the First Census of the United States, Taken in the Year 1790* (Washington, 1908), 31–34.

TABLE 10
Irish and Free Negro Men in the Free Work Force, 1860

City	All Free Workingmen (Percentage)		Unskilled Free Work-ingmen (Percentage)	
	Irish	Free Negro	Irish	Free Negro
RICHMOND	18	14	46	30
CHARLESTON	29	14	60	11
MOBILE	28	3	43	4
NASHVILLE	23	5	45	9
LYNCHBURG	—	14	23	27
BATON ROUGE	—	7	31	4

SOURCE: Computed from the U.S. Census MSS., RG 29.

As among the unskilled workers, color, status, and nativity sharply divided skilled workers. Except for the Irish, the vast majority of immigrant workingmen practiced artisanal trades, and immigrant artisans composed a disproportionate share of the skilled urban work force. (See Table 7A.) In Richmond, for example, nine out of ten British and German workingmen practiced skilled trades. Although immigrant workers could be found in almost every urban craft, they were especially important in urban service trades like tailoring and shoemaking. In Mobile and Charleston, four of five free shoemakers had been born outside the United States, a proportion only slightly smaller in Richmond and Nashville. Foreign-born workers similarly dominated blacksmithing in Lower South cities and composed a disproportionate share of the blacksmiths even in the urban Upper South.

Free Negro men contributed to the urban artisan class in a special way.[18] First, they were generally confined to one or two trades that whites had denominated "nigger work" and that were usually identified with servile, dirty, or distasteful labor. Although such trades differed from place to place, barbering and butchering typified such occupations. While free Negroes totaled 3 percent of the skilled free workingmen in Mobile and 16 percent of those in Charleston, they equaled, respectively, 20 and 78 percent of the free barbers in those two cities. Second, mulattoes generally composed a disproportionate share of the skilled freemen. This division between mulattoes and blacks was especially evident in the cities of the Lower South. Men of mixed racial origins composed over three-quarters of Charleston's free Negro barbers, one of the most lucrative and prestigious free Negro occupations, but less than one-quarter of the free Negro day laborers. Even in Upper South cities, Negro freemen of mixed racial origins enjoyed a higher skill level than those denominated black.

Southern-born white men also held a distinctive place within the ranks of the urban artisan class. They tended to congregate in a few occupations, most notably in the building trades and in crafts like piloting and printing in which native birth provided them with obvious advantages. Generally, over half the Southern-born

[18] Ira Berlin, *Slaves without Masters: The Free Negro in the Antebellum South* (New York, 1974), 217–49; and Leonard P. Curry, *The Free Black in Urban America: The Shadow of the Dream* (Chicago, 1981), 15–36.

TABLE 11
Unskilled Southern-Born White Workingmen, 1860

City	Number	Percentage of All Employed Free Men	Percentage of All Workingmen (Free and Slave)	Percentage of Free Workingmen
RICHMOND	324	4	3	7
CHARLESTON	158	2	2	4
MOBILE	342	5	5	8
NASHVILLE	360	8	11	14
LYNCHBURG	100	8	6	15
BATON ROUGE	38	4	4	7

SOURCE: Computed from the U.S. Census MSS., RG 29.

white artisans labored as printers and pilots and in the building trades. In some places this proportion reached three-quarters. Even in the building trades, however, Southern whites did not always predominate. While more than half the Southern-born white artisans in Charleston and Mobile worked in the building trades, they equaled no more than 40 percent of building-trade workers. In Charleston, about one in three skilled Southern-born white workingmen labored as carpenters, but the typical free Charleston carpenter was either a free Negro, a Northern white, or an immigrant. (See Table 12.) Outside of these trades, Southern-born whites were grossly underrepresented in the artisanal classes of Southern cities.

A work force with a disproportionately large immigrant artisanal sector and an overwhelmingly black and immigrant unskilled sector did not appear suddenly in Southern cities on the eve of the Civil War. Slave labor had characterized Southern urban life from the beginning of settlement, and the number of European immigrant workers had grown steadily during the middle decades of the nineteenth century. Indeed, in the Lower South, the evolution of an urban work force in which immigrants played a central role appears to have taken place well before mid-century. By 1850, immigrants already numbered almost half of the free workingmen of Charleston and three-fifths of those of Mobile—and an even larger proportion of the unskilled free workers in these cities. In both cities, two of three unskilled free men had been born outside the United States. In the Upper South cities of Richmond and Nashville, however, foreign-born workers still played a minority role in the free labor force at mid-century—although a substantial one. During the decade before the war, immigrant workers entered these Upper South cities in large numbers and increased their share of the working class not only at the expense of slaves—as scholars have emphasized—but also at the expense of native-born white workers.

While historians have focused their attention on the proportional decline of urban slavery, the most significant change in the composition of the urban work force was the increase of immigrant and the decline of native white workers. In Nashville, for example, the number of slave men increased by more than 50 percent between 1850 and 1860, but the number of immigrant workingmen

TABLE 12

Free Building-Trade Workingmen by Nativity and Race, 1860

City	Number	Percentage by Nativity and Race			
		Southern-Born White	Northern-Born White	Foreign-Born White	Free Black
RICHMOND	933	66	7	20	8
CHARLESTON	876	41	5	32	21
MOBILE	804	30	20	45	5
NASHVILLE	687	64	13	22	1
LYNCHBURG	160	84	2	9	5
BATON ROUGE	188	52	13	23	12

SOURCE: Computed by the U.S. Census MSS., RG 29.

increased threefold, with foreign-born artisans doubling and immigrant laborers increasing by some 500 percent. Meanwhile, the number of native-born white workingmen increased by less than 40 percent, lagging behind the allegedly declining slave population. In some artisanal trades, native-born whites suffered an absolute decline. A similar development took place in Richmond. There the slave population grew by about 20 percent as tobacco manufacturers scoured the countryside for hirelings. But the number of immigrant workers more than doubled, while native white workers increased at a pace akin to those in Nashville. In the Lower South ports of Charleston and Mobile, the composition of the work force changed less dramatically during the 1850s, because the central importance of immigrant workers had already been established. But, in the cities of both the Upper and the Lower South, immigrants made especially large gains in the skilled trades, so that their dominance of artisan work increased even faster than their prominence in unskilled labor. Throughout the urban South, foreign-born workers remained the most dynamic element in the working class and increased their dominant position. (See Table 13.)

Skilled free workers, unskilled slaves, immigrants of all sorts playing roles that historians have previously given over to others—this portrait of the composition of the urban work force brings Southern cities much closer to the description of a Charleston boardinghouse rendered by a British merchant in 1860: "Fully one-half the large number of guests in the House seemed as if they had just stepped out of Houndsditch, and remind me of what a friend in Mobile said, that 'I should meet more Jews in Charleston than I could see in Jerusalem.'"[19]

KNOWLEDGE OF THE COMPOSITION of the wage-earning population of the urban South has profound implications for comprehending the development of Southern

[19] W. Corsan, Two Months in the Confederate States, Including a Visit in New Orleans under the Domination of General Butler (London, 1863), 9–10.

society. Just as the new understanding of the role of immigrant workers in Southern cities forced a reconsideration of the structure of the entire work force (slave and free), so the new understanding of the South's urban work force necessitates a re-evaluation of the social order of the antebellum South. The reconsideration of urban laboring people raises questions about the development of Southern society, the character of slavery and the evolution of Afro-American culture, and the nature of politics in the urban South and the role of immigrants in

TABLE 13

Increase and Decrease of Urban Workingmen
between 1850 and 1860 by Race, Status, and Nativity

City	Percentage of Increase or Decrease				
	Southern-Born Whites	Northern-Born Whites	Foreign-Born Whites	Free Blacks	Slaves
RICHMOND	+37	+97	+166	+42	+27
CHARLESTON	+11	−24	+25	−11	−46
MOBILE	+73	+43	+81	+51	+17
NASHVILLE	+38	+106	+223	+162	+55

SOURCE: Computed by the U.S. Census MSS., RG 29.

the growing sectional controversy. The answers to these questions will ultimately rest on the results of investigations that have hardly begun. Based on this re-evaluation of the composition of the Southern urban working population, some suggestions can be made, if only to indicate the direction that those investigations might take.

First, this analysis of the composition of the urban working population raises questions about the culture of native Southern whites who remained in the countryside, despite opportunity in the city, and of those who migrated to cities but avoided manual work, skilled as well as unskilled. The answers to these questions suggest how the requirements of cotton agriculture and the great prosperity of the late antebellum countryside made yeoman farmers unlikely migrants to the cities. They also suggest the Southern yeomanry's deep attachment to the land and to its own unique culture as well as suggesting the strength of the unspoken entente between planters and yeomen, which guaranteed the security of the yeoman's separate world. It re-emphasizes the importance of understanding the history of rural plain people.[20]

[20] Steven Hahn, *The Roots of Southern Populism: Yeoman Farmers and the Transformation of the Georgia Upcountry, 1850–1890* (New York, 1983); Eugene D. Genovese, "Yeoman Farmers in a Slaveholders' Democracy," *Agricultural History*, 44 (1975): 331–42; and Frank L. Owsley, *Plain Folk of the Old South* (Baton Rouge, La., 1949).

The power of that distinctive way of life often survived the transfer to the city and shaped the lives of country folk in the urban South. As expanding centers of commerce, every Southern city housed a small army of clerks—young, generally unmarried men who boarded together and aspired to counting houses of their own. In overwhelming proportions, these young men had been born in the South, and (given the growth of Southern cities) probably in the countryside. In Charleston, for example, two-thirds of the clerical workers were native to the South and generally to the state of South Carolina, and a similar pattern could be found in other Southern cities.[21] Thus, differences between those who labored in clerical, commercial occupations and manual, industrial ones were compounded by distinctions of nationality throughout the urban South.

Second, understanding the composition of the work force of the urban South raises questions about the changing character of slavery and its development during the nineteenth century. Slaves had played a far different role in the post-Revolutionary urban South than in the mid-nineteenth century. It is not simply that there were proportionately fewer of them in the cities of the pre–Civil War period, a point that has consumed far too much of recent scholarly debate on the subject. More importantly, during the colonial period slaves had actively participated in almost all major artisanal trades; on the eve of the Civil War, except in a few cities with roots deep in the eighteenth century, they did not.[22]

The large number of slave artisans in the post-Revolutionary South helps explain how free Negroes came to enjoy a comparatively high level of skill during the nineteenth century, despite the early presence of politically active white artisans. Most free Negroes obtained their liberty during the period when slaves were still deeply involved in the artisanal economy. They maintained their skills through the antebellum years while slaves were systematically stripped of their crafts. A possible interpretation for the decline of slave skill argues that competition from newly arrived immigrants muscled slaves out of the artisan crafts. Yet, this explanation fails to account for the Negro freemen's ability to maintain their occupational position. In any three-way competition among white, slave, and free black workers, black freemen would probably be the most vulnerable. Yet, free Negroes maintained their occupational position, and the level of free Negro skill appears to have had little connection with the proportion of immigrants in any Southern city. It is possible, then, that the erosion of slave skill began before the great nineteenth-century European migrations and had far more to do with the expansion of the cotton economy than with the entry of foreign-born workers into the South. The opening of new lands to staple production required skilled labor to construct

[21] Clerical workers include accountants, agents, bookkeepers, clerks, and salesmen. Of the 890 clerical workers in Richmond, 83 percent were born in the slave states; of 1,146 in Charleston, 65 percent; of the 1,278 in Mobile, 71 percent; and, of the 554 in Nashville, 60 percent. This information was computed from the U.S. Census MSS., RG 29.

[22] Allan Kulikoff, "Tobacco and Slaves: Population, Economy, and Society in Eighteenth-Century Prince George's County, Maryland" (Ph.D. dissertation, Brandeis University, 1976), 235–39; Gerald W. Mullin, *Flight and Rebellion* (New York, 1972), chaps. 3–4; Philip D. Morgan, "Black Society in the Lowcountry," in Ira Berlin and Ronald Hoffman, eds., *Slavery and Freedom in the Age of the American Revolution* (Charlottesville, Va., 1983); and Louis Morton, *Robert Carter of Nomini Hall: A Virginia Tobacco Planter in the Eighteenth Century* (Williamsburg, Va., 1964). Also see the evidence cited in note 17, above.

quarters for master and slaves and to build and repair barns, carts, presses, and a variety of agricultural machinery. Slave artisans may have been the first to go west, pulled out of the cities in large numbers by the rapid spread of plantation agriculture across the South. In a time of great economic growth, artisan standing provided scant protection from sale. Indeed, it may have encouraged physical removal to distant rural workplaces, a process that reduced the number of slave artisans in cities, transformed urban skills into rural skills, and cut the generational lines by which slaves transferred their crafts. If a Richmond carpenter, who might otherwise pass his skill to his son in Richmond, was sold to Alabama, his son would be left without skill and he would be left without a son to reproduce his skill. The long-term loss of slave skill affected not only urban slaves but rural ones as well. In 1860, according to several estimates, well under 10 percent of rural slave men enjoyed artisanal status.[23]

The loss of skilled standing deeply affected the behavior and values of blacks, both slave and free, during the nineteenth century. In a variety of ways, it may have weakened black resistance to white domination. In almost all early working-class movements, the worldliness and confidence engendered by skill propelled artisans to positions of leadership.[24] Yet, the destruction of slave skill had other, less obvious—and perhaps even more insidious—effects. It appears to have slowed considerably the rate of self-purchase, a practice common among urban slaves elsewhere in the hemisphere. Without skills, even the most industrious slaves had difficulty buying their way out of bondage. Like the sharp decline of manumission at the beginning of the nineteenth century, the inability of slaves to purchase liberty severed the bonds that had existed between slaves and free blacks at the end of the eighteenth century when slaves moved into the free Negro caste in great numbers.[25] Already torn by differences in status, the black community faced still another obstacle to caste unity. Skill differences pushed black freemen and slaves further apart than they would have been if they had shared a common occupational experience.

After emancipation, the distinctive occupational traditions of former free and former slave blacks made those who had enjoyed freedom more important within the larger community yet, paradoxically, hampered their ability to act with authority. Free Negroes provided a disproportionate share of post–Civil War black leadership not only because they had been free but also because they carried the

---

[23] Roger Ransom and Richard Sutch, "The Impact of the Civil War and Emancipation on Southern Agriculture," *Explorations in Economic History*, 12 (1975): 1–28. In a study based on the mortality schedule of the U.S. Census (1850 and 1860), Michael P. Johnson has calculated the rate of slave skill to be about double the estimate of Ransom and Sutch; Johnson, "Slave Occupations and Marriages," unpublished essay courtesy of the author. For additional evidence on the scarcity of artisanal skills among exslaves during and just after the Civil War, also see Herbert G. Gutman, *The Black Family in Slavery and Freedom, 1750–1925* (New York, 1976), 39–41, 233, 479–83.

[24] The classic study of such leadership is E. P. Thompson's *The Making of the English Working Class* (New York, 1963). For the role of American artisans in developing working-class movements, see Alan Dawley, *Class and Community: The Industrial Revolution in Lynn* (Cambridge, Mass., 1976); and Paul G. Faler, *Mechanics and Manufacturers in the Early Industrial Revolution* (Albany, N.Y., 1981). For a cross-cultural comparison, see Bryan Palmer, "Most Uncommon Common Men: Craft and Culture in Historical Perspective," *Labor/Le Travailleur*, 1 (1976): 5–31.

[25] Berlin, *Slaves without Masters*, 15–50, 138–60.

artisanal tradition within the black community. Yet former slaves and former freepeople had not known each other well, particularly in the urban South. Fearful of the fate of slave craftsmen, free Negro artisans may well have hesitated to identify fully with the newly emancipated unskilled masses. That most of them took the risk says something about the dynamics of Reconstruction, but in the end their worst fears were realized.[26] Slaves did not lose skills as a result of emancipation; they had few to lose. Free Negroes suffered badly. An examination of the occupational structure of the black community in Mobile and Richmond in 1880 indicates that generational lines of craft transfer had been smashed within the black community. Although blacks maintained their pre–Civil War skill level through Reconstruction, the internal composition of the black artisan class changed dramatically. Compared to skilled white workers, black artisans—probably descendants of free Negroes—were top heavy with age in the major crafts. The vestiges of traditional black artisanal skills, which had reached a high point in the late eighteenth century and were maintained through the antebellum period by free Negroes, were liquidated in the last decades of the nineteenth century.[27] Artisanship and petty enterprise often went together, so that the decline in artisan skills also stifled small businesses. Booker T. Washington thrived in this constricted setting, but urban blacks migrating to Northern cities in the early decades of the twentieth century carried few skills and little business experience with them.

Finally, the composition of the work force of Southern cities raises questions about the immigrants who constituted so large an element in the free working population of Southern cities. Although a full understanding of their place as workers in Southern society requires close attention in particular cities to the ways immigrants lived, where they resided, what institutions they formed, and how they related to others, some preliminary probing suggests the dimensions of the issue.[28]

In the free states, immigrant workers stood at the center of the most important changes in economy, society, and politics during the late antebellum years. Newly arrived workers, particularly skilled ones, carried artisanal traditions from the Old World to the New, where they fused with the indigenous artisanal traditions of American mechanics and craftsmen. These beliefs, deriving in large measure from

[26] Thomas Holt, *Black over White: Negro Political Leadership in South Carolina during Reconstruction* (Urbana, Ill., 1977); David C. Rankin, "The Origins of Black Leadership in New Orleans during Reconstruction," *Journal of Southern History*, 40 (1974): 417–40; Charles Vincent, *Black Legislators in Louisiana during Reconstruction* (Baton Rouge, La., 1976); Loren Schweninger, *James T. Rapier and Reconstruction* (Chicago, 1978); Howard N. Rabinowitz, ed., *Southern Black Leaders of the Reconstruction Era* (Urbana, Ill., 1982); and especially David C. Rankin, "The Impact of the Civil War on the Free Colored Community of New Orleans," *Perspectives in American History*, 11 (1975): 379–416.

[27] Gutman, *Black Family in Slavery and Freedom*, 433–60, 476–519, 623–44. By 1880, the percentage of all skilled white workers under the age of thirty in Richmond was 46 percent and all skilled black workers under thirty 30 percent, and in Mobile in the same year the percentages, respectively, were 41 percent and 23 percent; the percentage of all white carpenters under the age of thirty in Richmond was 25 percent and of all black carpenters 9 percent; in Mobile the percentages respectively were 27 percent and 13 percent. This information was computed from the U.S. Census MSS., RG 29.

[28] The only book-length study of an antebellum Southern white immigrant and predominantly working-class community is Earl F. Niehaus's *The Irish in New Orleans, 1800–1865* (Baton Rouge, La., 1965). Also see Christopher Silver, "A New Look at Old South Urbanization: The Irish Worker in Charleston, South Carolina, 1840–1860," *South Atlantic Urban Studies*, 3 (1979): 141–72. John F. Nau's examination only begins at mid-century but contains material of interest; Nau, *The German People of New Orleans, 1850–1900* (Liedens, 1958). For a work that concentrates on German political leaders and intellectuals, see Dieter Cunz, *The Maryland Germans: A History* (Princeton, N.J., 1948).

40

the common character of artisan life and work throughout the Atlantic world, celebrated independence and emphasized a man's right to the fruits of his own labor as central to that independence. Such ideas mixed readily with republican notions about the rights of man and with nationalistic ideas about the rights of American citizens. Together these beliefs drew workers into the ongoing struggle against slavery, as an institution fundamentally opposed to those values that the artisanal experience taught guaranteed freedom. Artisans, some of them nascent manufacturers, played a large role in the rise of political antislavery in the free states, as they not only came to see slavery as a threat to their own liberty but also developed a deep sympathy for the plight of the slave. Such abstract beliefs did not, however, necessarily negate longstanding antipathy toward black people. Indeed, disdain for blacks persisted among Northern white workingmen, reinforced by the historic suspicion of small propertyholders toward the propertyless as well as fear of competition from the emancipated. To accommodate opposition to both slavery and the slave, the abolitionist movement frequently—though not always—advanced with opposition to blacks. Free soilism and Republicanism took both egalitarian and racist forms in the free states.[29]

Immigrant workers who arrived in the South carried ideas and traditions about the meaning of work and its relation to liberty similar to those carried by workers who migrated to the North. (In fact, many arrived first in the free states and then traveled south, and others moved back and forth between Northern and Southern cities.[30]) Deeply rooted beliefs about the connection between labor and liberty and cherished ideas about the connections of both to republicanism took on special meaning in a slave society. Although many quickly adopted Southern racial prejudices and some became slaveholders, immigrant workers generally remained suspicious of chattel bondage. Proportionately, immigrant workers owned or employed fewer slaves than did native-born workers. If some workers, skilled and unskilled, ultimately came to see black bondage as protection for white liberty and insurance for their own elevated position in a split labor market, others believed slavery to be an ever-present threat to their freedom. As in the North, this opposition to slavery took a variety of forms and did not necessarily assure sympathy for the slave. Hatred of slavery and the slave frequently became one.

Still, whatever the precise target, worker complaints about slave competition as a threat to their own liberty grew during the antebellum years. True to the proslavery argument, some of these complaints had no abolitionist import and sought only the removal of slaves from specific trades or from artisan work generally. Such petitions bespoke opposition not to slavery but to slaves. Frequently, they explicitly accepted slavery. Slaveholders generally found it easy to deflect these attacks and direct them to the most vulnerable element of the black population, the black

[29] Eric Foner, *Free Soil, Free Labor, Free Men: The Ideology of the Republican Party before the Civil War* (New York, 1970); Leonard L. Richards, *Gentlemen of Property and Standing* (New York, 1970); Dawley, *Class and Community*, chaps. 1–4; John Jentz, "The Antislavery Constituency in Jacksonian New York," *Civil War History*, 27 (1981): 101–02; David Montgomery, "Labor and the Republic in Industrial America," *Le Mouvement Social*, no. 111 (1980): 201–15; and Bruce Carlan Levine, "'In the Spirit of 1848': German-Americans and the Fight over Slavery's Expansion" (Ph.D. dissertation, University of Rochester, 1980).

[30] According to the historian of Charleston's Irish population, most of that city's Irish workers entered the U.S. in the North and then migrated to Charleston, and others, searching for work, migrated seasonally between Northern and Southern cities; Silver, "A New Look at Old South Urbanization," 145–46.

freemen. Attempts to proscribe free Negroes consistently met with greater success than did attempts to limit the use of slave workers. But some free workers, frustrated by the ability of slaveholders to preserve the widest range of opportunities for employing their valuable property, threatened to strike out at slavery. "In placing the negro in competition with white mechanics," noted a Charleston workingman in the city's leading daily, "you drag down the latter to a level with the former. This is well calculated to breed discontent and hatred on the part of the white mechanic, and make him an enemy of our institution."[31]

The everyday realities and necessities of working-class life may have reinforced disdain for racial bondage and increased sympathy for slaves among free workers, particularly immigrants. In the absence of residential segregation, workers of all sorts lived in close proximity. In Richmond, Frederick Law Olmsted found "a very considerable population of foreign origin," many of them "very dirty German Jews . . . thickly set in the narrowest and meanest streets, which seem otherwise inhabited by negroes."[32] Often neighbors practiced a common trade, as did free black carpenter Richard Washington and Irish carpenter George Mahone, who shared a house with their families in Richmond's second ward. Such men probably did not attend the same church, but they may well have shared in the conviviality of back-alley groceries and groggeries scattered throughout every Southern city. There free workers might strike a profitable bargain for some item of slave-stolen merchandise, or a fugitive slave might purchase a set of freedom papers. Much to the disgust of the leaders of Southern society, many white workers did not understand the niceties of Southern race relations or, if they did, did not seem to care. Few workingmen sold slaves liquor, rented them rooms, and aided them in eluding slavery.[33] "Not only free Negroes," complained a Richmond newspaper in 1860, "but ow white people can be found who will secret a slave from his master." Other acts of striking generosity punctuated these commonplaces to suggest how closely shared experience might bind workers together. In 1847, the First African Baptist Church of Richmond sent forty dollars overseas to assist victims of the Irish famine, and ten years later that same church donated a small sum to the city's Irish poor.[34]

---

[31] Berlin, *Slaves without Masters*, 229–33, 349–51; *Charleston Courier*, December 7, 1860, as quoted in Michael P. Johnson, "Wealth and Class in Charleston in 1860," in Walter J. Fraser, Jr., *et al.*, eds., *From the Old South to the New: Essays on the Transitional South* (Westport, Conn., 1981), 74, 80 n.

[32] Olmsted, *Journey in the Seaboard Slave States*, 55; and Curry, *Free Blacks in Urban America*, 49–80.

[33] The manuscript census schedules for the large Southern cities we have examined indicate that small shopkeepers were disproportionately foreign-born. These shopkeepers usually had started as wage earners, and they often became wage earners following business failure. Richard Wade has found much evidence of a traffic in petty theft between urban slaves and white shopkeepers. According to Earl Niehaus, Irish grocers were arrested for receiving sugar and flour stolen by New Orleans slaves. Liquor, apparently, was often traded for stolen goods. Wade, *Slavery in the Cities*; and Niehaus, *Irish in New Orleans*. The alliance between immigrant shopkeepers and black slaves often was simply a matter of convenience for both. But, with freedom, it became increasingly important and, in some places, served as the basis for the alliance between black and white Republicans. See, for example, the alliance between black editor John P. Mitchell, Jr., and Irish grocer James Bahen in Richmond; Michael P. Chesson, "Richmond's Black Councilmen," in Rabinowitz, *Southern Black Leaders of the Reconstruction Era*, 202–06, 216.

[34] *Richmond Daily Dispatch*, December 21, 1860; and Minutes of the First African Baptist Church, March 1847, October 1857, First African Baptist Church, Richmond, Virginia. Frederick Law Olmsted, visiting the Midlothian Coal Mines outside Richmond, recorded an incident that characterizes far more of the interchange between newly arrived immigrants and black slaves than historians have allowed. Olmsted observed, "Not long since, a young English fellow came to the pit, and was put to work with a gang of negroes. One morning, about

Of course, common conditions did not always promote common understanding or mutual respect. Often just the opposite resulted. Shared values and behavior evolved slowly, unevenly, and imperfectly among Southern urban workers during the antebellum years. Conflict among immigrant, native-born, and black workers divided working people, as did internal differences within each group—between British and Irish immigrants, native-born Northern and Southern whites, Catholic and Protestant immigrants, and black freemen and bondsmen. If white workers, immigrant and native, protested black competition and tried to push black craftsmen from their crafts, native-born workers joined the Plug Uglies, Rip Raps, Blood Tubs, and other nativist gangs to oust the immigrants. Slaves sought the protection of their masters and free Negroes their patrons to secure their jobs and protect their persons. The record of this intraclass hostility is full, and the presence of slavery aggravated and enlarged it.[35]

But, if free workers were pulled in all directions, their allegiance to the slave regime was never firm. Men and women who had fled the landlord-dominated societies of Western Europe were hardly predisposed to sympathize with the planter class. Slavery remained the linchpin of the Southern order, and the relationship of free workers to that institution continued to be ambiguous at best. Many were too newly arrived to understand it, and some found good reason to oppose it. Some foreign-born workers had been schooled in antislavery beliefs in Europe, including British artisans who had observed or participated in the abolitionist debates, and many others had learned to wield the phrase "wage slavery" to their advantage. The defenders of slavery, who sometimes argued that all work should be done by slaves and even that all workers should be slaves, alienated free workers by undervaluing their labor and, at times, slandering their persons. A whiggish Richmond newspaper's boast that the major advantage of slave labor was its "exclusion of a populace made up of the dregs of Europe" could not have won the approbation of most free workers in that city.[36]

---

a week afterwards, twenty or thirty men called on him, and told him that they would allow him fifteen minutes to get out of sight, and if they ever saw him in those parts again they would 'give him hell.' They were all armed, and there was nothing for the young fellow to do but to move 'right off.'

'What reason did they give him for it?'

'They did not give him any reason.'

'But what had he done?'

'Why I believe they thought he had been too free with the niggers; he wasn't used to them, you see, and he talked to 'em free like, and they thought he'd make 'em think too much of themselves.'" Olmsted, *Journey in the Seaboard Slave States*, 47–48.

[35] For hints of intraclass conflict, see William D. Overdyke, *The Know-Nothing Party of the South* (Baton Rouge, La., 1950). But the composition of the nativist movement (its leaders and its followers) awaits careful study. The class composition of nativist political "gangs" in places like Baltimore also needs study. Anti-immigrant political violence involved far more than minor electoral brawls. In the Louisville election day riot of August 1855 ("Bloody Monday"), twenty-two persons were killed, three in four of them foreigners. The election riots in New Orleans in both 1854 adn 1856 were nearly as violent. One of them lasted ten days. Afterward, the vote in Irish districts fell by two-thirds. Irish school teachers and policemen lost their jobs. Some Irish persons lost their lives. In 1856, some Irish residents of New Orleans petitioned the Mexican government, seeking land to colonize there. "The initiation of order," said the *New Orleans Delta* of native American violence, "is accompanied by murder." See Niehaus, *Irish in New Orleans*, 84–97. For evidence of clientage connections between free blacks and wealthy whites, see Berlin, *Slaves without Masters*, 316–40; and Michael P. Johnson and James L. Roark, "Charleston's Free Colored Elite and the Secession Crisis," unpublished essay courtesy of the authors.

[36] *Richmond Whig*, n.d., as quoted in Russell B. Nye, *Fettered Freedom* (East Lansing, Mich., 1959), 311; also see *ibid.*, chaps. 7–8. It would be useful to imagine what the immigrant English puddler and Irish drayman in Richmond thought when reading in the *Richmond Examiner* that the nation's first immigrants had fled "religious

The evolving defense of slavery, which left little room for free workers, suggests the deep distrust in which Southern slaveholders held free workers and their belief that free workers were not reliable allies. No doubt Southern leaders were hypersensitive to all opposition and apt to read antislavery sentiment into the most casual dissent. Still, as the sectional conflict escalated, their conviction deepened that a Southern counterpart to the Northern free soil movement was developing among Southern workingmen, a movement hostile not only to blacks but also to capitalized black labor—meaning slavery. In 1849, after touring Mobile, Savannah, and Augusta, a correspondent of John C. Calhoun observed that these cities had become unsound on the slavery issue and blamed the growing number of foreign-born workers. "The issue of Free Labour against Slave Labour," he predicted, "will soon be made in the South." Such concerns multiplied in the 1850s. A Charleston daily declared that alien mechanics were a "curse rather than a blessing to our peculiar institution." And, when Little Rock artisans protested against competition from free black and slave laborers, the *Arkansas True Democrat* warned that such a "movement, carried to its fullest extent, would abolish slavery in the South. If the mechanic can justly complain of the competition of slave labor, those engaged in every other industrial pursuit can complain of the negro on the farm."[37]

The slave masters' fear of subversion rested partly in the habits of artisanal and ethnic cohesion, which often overlapped and reinforced each other in ways that planters, like Northern capitalists, believed to be hostile to their rule. But slaveholders also feared that enfranchised and politically active white workingmen saw their interests as different from those of the planter class. In this context, the politics of the 1850s can be understood as an attempt by planters not only to counter subversion from without but also subversion from within.

Seeing the seeds of Southern free soilism among urban immigrant workers, the most astute planters resisted the movement to exclude black laborers, slave and sometimes even free. "Drive out negro mechanics and all sorts of operatives from our Cities, and who must take their place?" asked Christopher G. Memminger, the future Confederate secretary of the treasury, in 1849. "The same men who make the cry in the Northern Cities against the tyranny of Capital—there as here would drive before them all who interfere with them—and would soon raise the hue and cry against the Negro, and be hot Abolitionists—and every one of those men would have a vote."[38]

The fear of internal subversion laced Southern politics in the decade before the war and created knotty contradictions that not even the most sophisticated Southern politician could comb out. For example, while some planters argued that

---

and political persecution" but its new immigrants migrated "merely as animals in search of a richer and better pasture," lacked "moral, intellectual, or religious wants," and were ("the mass of them") "sensual, groveling, low-minded agrarians." Or when the same newspaper reminded its readers that, "while it is far more obvious that negroes should be slaves than whites, for they are fit only to labor, not to direct, yet the principle of slavery is itself right and does not depend upon differences of complexion." "Slavery black and white," the *Richmond Examiner* affirmed, "is necessary."

[37] Calhoun, as quoted in Shugg, *Origins of Class Struggle in Louisiana*, 144; Charleston *Standard*, June 18, 1853; and Little Rock *Arkansas True Democrat*, September 29, 1858.

[38] Memminger, as quoted in Starobin, *Industrial Slavery in the Old South*, 210.

reopening the African slave trade would secure nonslaveholder loyalty by allowing them to participate directly in slaveownership, others saw the influx of slaves as a means of ridding Southern cities of politically unreliable immigrant workers. Thus, what began as an attempt to unify the white South sharpened internal divisions and left planters and workers further apart than ever. A similar dynamic can be seen operating in the movement to re-enslave free blacks. Radical Southerners believed that re-enslavement provided greater security for the slave regime. Not only would it free the South of another subversive group, but, by selling enslaved free blacks to nonslaveholders, re-enslavement—like the reopening of the slave trade—would also garner nonslaveholder loyalty. Again, opposition came from a variety of quarters, and this time it not only enlarged the gulf between slaveholders and nonslaveholders but also divided the slaveholders among themselves. If some masters maintained that liquidation of the free Negro caste would secure slavery, others believed that the threat of re-enslavement would drive free Negroes out of the South and leave planters even more dependent on white workingmen. In the eyes of these slaveowners, white workers, not free blacks, offered the greatest threat to slavery. Thus, as slaveholders wrestled with the problems of internal division, they enlarged those divisions and also created new fissures in their own ranks. Little wonder the Confederacy came into the world amid contradictory calls for a white man's democracy and open attempts to disenfranchise some whites, particularly immigrant workers.[39]

FROM THE FIRST SHOT AT SUMTER, Southern leaders remained unsure of working-class loyalties. Just after the 1860 election, writing from New Orleans, politician John Slidell observed that in that city "seven-eighths at least of the vote for Douglas were cast by the Irish and Germans, who are at heart abolitionists."[40] While there were few Irish abolitionists among the workers in any Southern city, such doubts about the allegiance of the largely foreign-born work force only intensified with the onset of civil war. Some immigrants found themselves jailed for speaking their minds too freely on the subject of slavery. From New Orleans, the employer of one newly arrived Englishman appealed to the British government to have his employee released from jail; the immigrant worker had been charged with "using language hostile to slaveholding and introducing in the State [Louisiana] books and papers of similar character." Thirty months later, the British consul at Charleston reported to the Home Office that "labouring men"—immigrant workers surely prominent among them—"are frequently discharged from their employment and subjected to contumely for not taking up arms. They are frequently arrested and sent to gaol, as liable to conscription." In 1864, the president of an Alabama railroad conveyed to the Confederate secretary of war his suspicions about the

---

[39] Ronald Takaki, *A Pro-Slavery Crusade: The Agitation to Reopen the African Slave Trade* (New York, 1971); Berlin, *Slaves without Masters*, chap. 11; Michael P. Johnson, *Toward a Patriarchal Republic: The Secession of Georgia* (Baton Rouge, La., 1977), chap. 5; and Fred Siegal, "Artisans and Immigrants in the Politics of Late Antebellum Georgia," *Civil War History*, 18 (1981): 221-30.

[40] Slidell, as quoted in Peyton McCrary, *Abraham Lincoln and Reconstruction: The Louisiana Experiment* (Princeton, 1978), 56. Also see Johnson, *Toward a Patriarchal Republic*, 97.

skilled founders and puddlers at the huge Selma iron works. He observed that "all of these workmen are foreigners from Europe, or natives of the northern states, the majority being foreigners," and then made the common complaint: "These men do not feel identified in any great degree with the South and are not imbued with sentiments and feelings calculated to impress them so strongly in favor of our cause, as to induce them to make any great sacrifice of interest or feeling in its behalf." In spite of the Union noose tightening around the Confederacy, these foreign workers demanded higher wages and abandoned the Selma works even when their demands were met. Perhaps native-born workingmen would have ordered their loyalties in a similar fashion, but the beleaguered railroad executive doubted it.[41]

Dissaffected immigrant workers rallied to the Union flag at the first opportunity and, in places like New Orleans, which early fell to the Union army, provided the basis for a Unionist party. Elsewhere, immigrant workers had to wait until the war's end to demonstrate their political beliefs, but, when given the opportunity, many did so. In 1865, when the Union army occupied Charleston, federal officers promptly recruited two regiments among the loyal natives—one black, one Irish. A Union soldier, parading through Charleston, noted that the crowds who gathered to watch the column move through the city were "chiefly negroes and Irish, and their delight at seeing us was unbounded, the Irish being quite as enthusiastic in the expression of joy as the negroes."[42]

Estimates of the extent of antebellum free soilism, wartime disaffection and disloyalty, and postwar Republicanism among the immigrant workers of the urban South require much more refinement before they can go beyond the complaint of Slidell and others. But, whatever free workers thought about slavery, there can be no doubt that slave masters understood the demands of free workers for the elimination of slave competition as more than a conflict of interest with slaveholding; indeed, ultimately they saw it as a conflict of principles. This understanding held enormous importance in the hothouse of antebellum and reconstruction politics. While the full dimensions of this conflict remain to be explored, its partial outcroppings confirm that immigrant workers in the urban South cannot simply be incorporated into the extant understanding of the nature of Southern society, the evolution of slavery, or the character of antebellum politics. Instead, they demand reconsideration of all.

[41] Daniel Godwin to Newlop Ireland, n.d., enclosed in Ireland to Lord Russell, February 19, 1861, Public Record Office, London, Foreign Office 5/793; Consul Walker to Russell, August 21, 1863, *ibid.*, Foreign Office 5/907; and J. W. Lapsley to J. A. Seddon, February 15, 1864, National Archives, Washington, War Department Collection of Confederate Records, Secretary of War, Letters Received, ser. 5, Record Group 109, L-67 1864. In North Carolina cities, urban workers also played a role in the Unionist "Heroes of America." See William T. Auman and David D. Scarboro, "The Heroes of America in Civil War North Carolina," *North Carolina Historical Review*, 58 (1981): 350–51.

[42] McCrary, *Lincoln and Reconstruction*; General Rufus Saxton to E. M. Stanton, March 1, 1865, S-154 (1865), National Archives, Washington, Records of the Adjutant General's Office, Colored Troops Division, Letters Received, ser. 360, Record Group 94; and *War Letters, 1862–1865, of John Chipman Gray and John Codman Ropes* (Boston, 1927), 459.

THE IMPACT OF THE 'NEW IMMIGRATION' ON THE BLACK WORKER: STEELTON, PENNSYLVANIA, 1880-1920

by JOHN E. BODNAR

Northern industrial centers and large urban areas had been acquiring sizable Negro populations in the three decades before 1900. The Black population of Pittsburgh, for instance, more than tripled between 1880 and 1900. Buffalo doubled its Negro community in the same period, while Cleveland's grew from 2,000 to nearly 6,000. In smaller industrial centers the pattern was the same. In Pennsylvania steel towns such as Johnstown, the Negro community tripled in the last two decades of the nineteenth century. McKeesport, which had a mere fifteen Blacks in 1880, counted over 700 by 1900.[1]

This rising tide of Blacks, however, began to slow considerably in the first decade of this century. Pittsburgh, whose Black population had increased by one-hundred percent between 1890 and 1900, saw its Negro community grow by twenty-five percent in the decade after 1900. Industrial centers such as Lorain, Ohio gained only seventy-three Blacks in the ten years after 1900, after gaining over seven-hundred Negroes in the previous decade. Similar trends were evident in larger and smaller urban areas. McKeesport, which had gained 600 Blacks in the 1890s, gained only fifty between 1900 and 1910. Between 1890 and 1900 the Negro population of Homestead, Pennsylvania grew by over 500. In the subsequent decade Homestead gained only 150 Blacks. The Black population of Buffalo, which had increased by over 700 in the

---

[1] The population figures are computed from 47 Cong., 2nd Sess., H.R. Doc. 42, *Statistics of the Population of the United States at the Tenth Census* (Washington, 1883), 423-24. U.S. Census, *Eleventh Census, 1890*, Part I; *Twelfth Census, 1900, Population,* Part I.

48

1890s, grew by only seventy-three in the ten years prior to 1910. The Negro population of Erie, Pennsylvania did not grow at all between 1900 and 1910. Wilkes-Barre, Pennsylvania had fewer Blacks in 1910 than it had in 1900.[2]

What was salient in the experience of Pittsburgh, Buffalo, Erie, Wilkes-Barre, McKeesport, Lorain, and Johnstown and similar cities was that they all were industrial centers attracting a vast influx of Slavic and Italian immigrant labor, especially during the first decade of this century. The newcomers were largely unskilled workers and peasants, some with previous industrial experience. These immigrant workers, consequently, challenged the Negro worker for semiskilled and unskilled occupational opportunities. To date, however, except for some impressionistic accounts, the impact of Slavic and Italian immigrant labor upon the Negro worker has been relatively neglected by historical scholarship.[3] By concentrating on the impact immigrants had on Negro workers in a typical Pennsylvania steel town, I hope to suggest the complexity of factors which were tending to slow the growth of Black communities in numerous northern industrial centers immediately after 1900.

Steelton, Pennsylvania, lying just south of Harrisburg on the

---

[2] *Ibid.*, U.S. Census, *Thirteenth Census, 1910.*

[3] For a discussion of occupational background of immigrants in Europe see Jozo Tomasevich, *Peasants, Politics, and Economic Change in Yugoslavia* (Stanford, Cal., 1955) 160-180; Philip Taylor, *The Distant Magnet* (New York, 1971), 48-64; Josef John Barton, "Immigrants and Social Mobility in an American City: Studies of Three Ethnic Groups in Cleveland, 1890-1950," (unpublished Ph.D. diss., Univ. of Michigan, 1972), 306-333. Scholarship dealing with a comparison of the immigrant and Black experience includes Joseph S. Roucek and Francis J. Brown, "The Problem of the Negro and European Immigrant Minorities: Some Comparisons and Contrasts," *Journal of Negro Education.* XVIII (1939), 299-312. Roucek and Brown, in dealing with lower class aspirations, claimed that since Negroes could not escape their status so easily, they have less hope of climbing up the ladder of social mobility than the average immigrant. See also John J. Appel, "American Negro and Immigrant Experience: Similarities and Differences," *American Quarterly.* XVIII (1966), 95-103; Edward McDonagh and Eugene S. Richards, *Ethnic Relations in the United States* (New York, 1953), 295-96. Charles H. Wesley, *Negro Labor in the United States, 1850-1925* (New York, 1967), 75-76, 199. Some valuable insights can be gained in Judith R. Kramer, *The American Minority Community* (New York, 1970), 213; Timothy Smith, "Native Blacks and Foreign Whites; Varying Responses to Education Opportunity in America, 1880-1950," in *Perspectives in American History*, VI (1972), 309-311; John R. Commons, *Races and Immigrants in America* (New York, 1907), 147-52. The animosity of Irish immigrants toward Blacks, their chief rivals for unskilled jobs, has been discussed. See Oscar Handlin, *Boston's Immigrants, A Study in Acculturation* (Cambridge, Mass., 1959), 133, 205, 216. See especially Niles Carpenter, *Nationality, Color, and Economic Opportunity in the City of Buffalo* (Buffalo, 1927), 190-91. Carpenter declared that immigrants rose faster than Blacks. J. Iverne Dowie, "The American Negro: An Old Immigrant On a New Frontier," in O. Fritof Ander, ed., *In the Trek of the Immigrants*, (Rock Island, 1964), 241, 260. has called Negroes "America's oldest immigrants" and felt they were held down until they moved northward. See David Brody, *Steelworkers in America* (Cambridge, Mass., 1960), 185-267; Gilbert Osofsky, *Harlem, the Making of a Ghetto* (New York, 1969). 34-40.

east bank of the Susquehanna River, was a good example of a
northern industrial town where "new immigrants" and southern
Blacks met in direct competition for lower level jobs. Communities such as Steelton, in fact, were attracting Black laborers even
before they began employing Slavic and Italian newcomers. Steelton grew up around the works of the Pennsylvania Steel Company
which began erecting its mills in 1866. Within the next four
decades the community had attained a population of over 12,000.
Included in the population were some 1,200 Afro-Americans and
over 3,000 immigrants, mostly southern Slavs and a few Italians.[4]
The Black population numbered about 1,270 in 1900. Indeed, a
Negro community with three churches was flourishing in Steelton
by 1890, before the influx of Slavs and Italians began. The first
Slavic group did not organize until 1893 when Croatians and
Slovenes formed a fraternal lodge. The bulk of the Slavic immi-
gration, however, arrived after 1900. Thus, a Serbian Orthodox
Church was begun in 1903, while Bulgarians erected a church in
1909.[5]

The character of the immigrant population in Steelton had
changed markedly between 1880 and 1905. While the trickle of
Irish and English, and, to a lesser extent, Catholic Germans
slowed considerably, large numbers of Italians and Slavs entered
the mill town. These "new immigrants," however, found difficulties in achieving occupations above the low unskilled strata. Of
403 Slavic and Italian immigrants studied in 1905, some seventy-
nine percent were in unskilled occupations. This was nine percent
higher than the figure for "old immigrants" in 1880. Slavic and
Italian newcomers, moreover, had less of their members in semi-
skllled ranks in 1905 (thirteen percent to eight percent) and skilled
ranks (nine percent to zero percent), than the Germans, Irish, and
English immigrants had in 1880 (see Tables Ia and b).[6]

---

[4] William H. Egle, *History of Dauphin and Lebanon Counties* (Philadelphia, 1883), 400-404.
George P. Donehoo, *Harrisburg and Dauphin County* (Dayton, 1925), 210-211; "A History
of the Steelton Plant, Bethlehem Steel Corporation, Steelton, Pennsylvania," unpub. ms. in
Charles Schwab Memorial Library, Bethlehem, Pennsylvania.
[5] African Methodist Episcopal Church, *Historical Record* (Steelton, Penna., 1905).
Spomen-Knjiga 25 Godisnjica Hrvatsko-Radničko Podporno Društvo Sv. Louro, 1895-1920
(Steelton, 1920), 6-9. See my essay on, "The Formation of Ethnic Consciousness, Slavic
Immigrants in Steelton," in John Bodnar, ed., *The Ethnic Experience in Pennsylvania*
(Lewisburg, Penna., 1973).
[6] In addition to sources listed in Table I see Paul Worthman, "Working Class Mobility in
Birmingham, Alabama, 1880-1914," in T.K. Hareven, ed., *Anonymous Americans* (Engle-
wood Cliffs, N.J., 1971), 192.

TABLE Ia
OCCUPATIONAL DISTRIBUTION, IMMIGRANTS
1880-1915

	1880*	1905**	1915**
Unskilled	70%	79%	76%
Semiskilled	13%	8%	10%
Skilled	9%	0%	3%
Low Nonmanual	0%	12%	11%
High Nonmanual	8%	4%	1%
Number	58	403	616

*English, Irish, German
**Slavic-Italian

The list of German, English, and Irish immigrants for 1880 was compiled from the *Tenth Census*, 1880 for Steelton. The list of Slavic and Italian immigrants for 1905 and 1915 was compiled from the volumes of the *Naturalization Service: Petition and Record*, Prothonotary's Office, Dauphin County Court House; *Records of Internment* for St. Mary's Croatian Church and St. Nicholas Serbian Orthodox Church and from the lists of immigrants in the *Golden Jubilee of St. Ann'*. [*Italian*] *Catholic* Church (Steelton, 1953), *Consecration and Sixtieth Anniversary, Holy Annunciation Macedonian-Bulgarian Orthodox Church* (Steelton, 1970), *30th Anniversary of the Founding of St. Peter's Church* [Slovenian] (Steelton, 1939). The most complete listing of immigrants in Steelton, however, is to be found in the "Alien Lists" of the *Annual Enumeration and Assessment of All Persons, Property and Things* for Steelton in 1903 and 1905 located at the Dauphin County Court House, Harrisburg. These lists were special surveys of the immigrant population by assessors so that aliens could be properly enumerated and taxed. Once immigrants were identified they were traced in *Boyd's Directory of Harrisburg and Steelton* for 1905, 1915, and 1925. The total of 403 Slavs and Italians appearing in 1905 in the city directory, moreover, represented only about twenty-five percent of the more than 1600 Slavs and Italians appearing in the "Alien Lists." Unfortunately the "Alien Lists" did not indicate an immigrant's occupation while, of course, the city directories did. City directories tended to be less accurate in the coverage of unskilled and lower class workers. In fact, the number of unskilled immigrants, and Blacks used here was probably a conservative figure. See Peter Knights, "A Method for Estimating Census Under-Enumeration," *Historical Methods Newsletter*, III (Dec., 1969), 5-8; Charles M. Dollar and Richard Jensen, *Historian's Guide to Statistics* (New York, 1971), 12.

The classification of unskilled, semiskilled, and skilled was derived from published wage figures. A lawyer, doctor, or large merchant, for instance, would be put into a high nonmanual category since he was self employed. The low nonmanual ranks consisted of clerks who worked for someone else. Highly skilled machinists or patternmakers would be classed as skilled worker, while semiskilled occupations included a heater, a melter, a moulder, a blacksmith, or a crane operator. Common laborers formed the bulk of the unskilled. The following occupation ranking was drawn from much more extensive wage data provided in the *Reports of the Immigration Commission, Immigrants in Industry, Iron and Steel*, (Washington, 1911), I, 612-25.

By 1915 some two decades after the first Croatians and Slovenes had settled in Steelton, over three-fourths of the immigrants were still in unskilled endeavors. This was nearly three times the percentage for native whites and a slight increase from 1905. While the number of Slavs and Italians moving into semiskilled and skilled positions from 1905 to 1915 increased, the figure was small. The eight percent of the immigrants who were classed as semiskilled in 1905 became ten percent in 1915. Where no immi-

TABLE Ib
WAGE SCALE OF STEELTON PLANT
FOR SELECTED OCCUPATIONS, 1910

Skilled:

Machinist	$3.98	per day (salary)
Patternmaker	3.00	per day
Carpenter	.32	per hour
Heater	.29	"

Semiskilled:

Moulder	.26	"
Melter	.25	"
First Class Electrician	.24	"
Second Class	.22	"
Blacksmith	.22	"
Crane Operator	.20	"
Foreman (Labor gang)	.17½	."
Blower	.17	"
Engineer	.16	"
Keeper	.16	"
Charger	.16	"

Unskilled:

Ladleman	.13½	"
Helper	.13	"
Fireman	.13	"
Laborer	.11	"

For a more extensive discussion of categories used in this study, see Clyde Griffen, "Occupational Mobility in Nineteenth-Century America: Problems and Possibilities," *Journal of Social History,* "' (Spring, 1972), 310-30.

grants could be found in skilled trades in 1905, some three percent were skilled workers ten years later.

If immigrants experienced little advancement occupationally prior to World War I in Steelton, they could find a parallel in the experience of Black migrants from the southern United States. From the inception of steel production in 1866, Negroes had come or were, in some instances, brought to Steelton. They came largely from Maryland and Virginia in the decades before 1910 and from the deep South afterwards.[7]

[7] The origins of Steelton's early Negro population can be seen in the U.S. Census, *Tenth Census,* 1880 for Steelton. *Marriage Licenses Dockets* for Dauphin County, Pa., reveal their arrival from the deeper South after 1910. See also *Eleventh Census,* 1890, I, 553; *Twelfth Census,* 1900, I, 679. In studying another steel town in the first decade of this century, Margaret Byington noted that the break between Slavic immigrants and the rest of the community was more absolute than between whites and Negroes. See Byington, *Homestead, The Households of a Mill Town* (New York, 1910), 14-15.

TABLE II
OCCUPATIONAL DISTRIBUTION OF BLACKS, 1880-1915

	1880	1905	1915
Unskilled	95%	61%	70%
Semiskilled	3%	33%	26%
Skilled	0%	0%	0%
Low Nonmanual	0%	4%	3%
High Nonmanual	2%	3%	1%
Number	87	300	323

A group of Blacks was compiled by taking all black males from Steelton who appeared in the Dauphin County *Marriage Licenses Dockets* from 1890 to 1915 and *Twelfth Census*, 1900. Moreover, there were lists of Black members of the African Methodist Episcopal Church in the *A.M.E. Church*. The 1880 group was drawn from the *Tenth Census*, 1880.

In 1880 ninety-five percent of all Black workers in Steelton were unskilled. This ratio was substantially larger than for any other group. It compared poorly with the sixty-six percent of German, English, and Irish steelworkers who were unskilled and the sixty percent of native born whites. No Negroes at all were found among the skilled positions in 1880, a situation which Slavic immigrants encountered in 1905. Only three percent of all Afro-Americans were in semiskilled positions and only two percent in nonmanual ones. The latter category consisted of two Negro barbers (see Table II).

By 1905, however, Blacks had considerably improved their lot in Steelton's work force. The number of Negroes employed in unskilled tasks had dropped over thirty percent in the generation before 1905. Only sixty-one percent of all Blacks were now unskilled. Indeed, the percentage of Negroes in semiskilled jobs increased some ten times in the generation prior to 1905. While Blacks failed to make any incursions into the skilled ranks, moreover, five percent more were lodged in nonmanual positions in 1905 than in 1880. (See Table II).

What is peculiar and perhaps crucial to the Black-immigrants experience, however, is that the percentage of the former in unskilled positions was at its lowest point in 1905. The ratio of Negroes in semiskilled positions and nonmanual positions reached its peak in 1905 and declined thereafter. Blacks never entered the skilled trades such as the machinists.

The thirty-two percent of Black workers in semiskilled endeavors in 1905 had dwindled to twenty-six percent in 1915 and remained at that level past 1920 and 1930. In addition, the sixty-one percent of Black workers categorized as unskilled had never been lower prior to 1905 and would not be as low afterward. These facts are even more striking when one considers that the growing Negro population of Steelton tapered off after 1890 and actually declined between the turn of the century, when Slavic and Italian immigrants began to arrive in substantial numbers, and World War I, which largely terminated the immigration of Italians, Serbs, Croats, Slovenes, and Bulgarians.[8] The wave of Slavs and Italians sweeping into Steelton after 1895 halted the steady growth of the Black community which was five times larger in 1890 than it had been a decade earlier.[9]

Blacks had made significant advances in Steelton prior to 1900. They had established three churches and a newspaper *The Steelton Press*. Peter Blackwell, a Negro, was elected to town council in 1904 and several Black constables were employed during the 1890s. While ninety-four percent of Black laborers had been unskilled in 1880, as indicated above, only sixty-one percent were so engaged by 1905. Although their movements upward were only into semiskilled bluecollar jobs, Afro-Americans were advancing.[10]

---

[8] The Black population of Steelton was 202 in 1880. It reached 1,273 in 1890. In 1910 it had declined to 1,234. It did climb steadily after immigration was restricted and amounted to over 2,500 by 1930.

[9] See John J. Appel, "American Negro and Immigrant Experience: Similarities and Differences," 95-103; Joseph S. Roucek and Francis J. Brown, "The Problem of the Negro and European Immigrant Minorities: Some Comparisons and Contrasts," 299-312. Competition between Irish, Italian, Negro, and Jewish workers is treated briefly in Chapter I of Carolyn Golab, "The Polish Communities of Philadelphia, 1870-1920: Immigrant Distribution and Adaptation in Urban America, " (unpub. Ph.D. diss., Univ. of Pennsylvania, 1971). See also Stephan Thernstrom, and Elizabeth Pleck, "The Last of the Immigrants? A Comparative Analysis of Immigrant and Black Social Mobility in Late-Nineteenth Century Boston," unpublished paper for the 1970 meeting of the Organization of American Historians; Thernstrom, "Immigrants and WASPS: Ethnic Differences in Occupational Mobility in Boston, 1890-1940," Thernstrom and Richard Sennett, ed., *Nineteenth-Century Cities,* (New Haven and London, 1969), 125-64; Clyde Griffen, "Making It in America: Social Mobility in Mid-Nineteenth Century Poughkeepsie," *New York History,* LI (1970), 479-99. Griffen (485) argues that ethnic origin may be critical in explaining differences in social mobility. See also Richard J. Hopkins, "Occupational and Geographic Mobility in Atlanta, 1870-1896," *Journal of Southern History,* XXXIV (1968), 208. Hopkins found fewer unskilled workers in the ranks of immigrants than Blacks in 1870. Carl Oblinger has found Blacks being forced from certain building trades by Irish and German newcomers between 1840 and 1860. See Oblinger, "Alms for Oblivion: The Making of a Black Underclass in Southeastern Pennsylvania, 1780-1860," in Bodnar, ed., *The Ethnic Experience in Pennsylvania.*

[10] See Bodnar, "Peter C. Blackwell and the Negro Community of Steelton," *Pennsylvania Magazine of History and Biography,* XCVII (1973), 199-209.

TABLE III
EARNING OF LABORERS
IN STEELTON PLANT, 1910

	Number	%Earning Over $1.50 per day	%Earning Under $1.50 per day
Natives	1,450	79.4	20.6
Negro	149	59.1	40.9
Slovenian	57	47.4	52.6
Croatian	676	34.3	65.7
Serbian	273	14.3	85.7
Bulgarian	61	8.2	91.8

Immigrants in Industry, I, 707.

At the height of European immigration in 1905, Blacks actually held a stronger position in the labor force than did Croats, Slovenes, and Serbs. Only six out of every ten Negroes were classified as unskilled in 1905. In comparison, seventy-five percent of Slavic and Italian workers were in low level occupations. Afro-Americans enjoyed a higher proportion of semiskilled workers, thirty-two percent, than did the "new immigrant," eight percent. The federal immigration commission which studied Steelton in 1910 discovered that the average earnings of Negro laborers were higher than those for any other ethnic group except the native born whites (See Table III).[11]

In 1915 the differences between immigrants and Blacks had changed somewhat. The difference between the proportion of Negroes and immigrants in unskilled endeavors had narrowed. Afro-Americans, however, continued to have less of their numbers in unskilled categories than did immigrants. More Blacks, twenty-six percent, moreover, held semiskilled positions than Slavs, ten percent. Immigrants did hold more nonmanual positions than Blacks in 1905 and 1915. This was due primarily to a greater proliferation of neighborhood ethnic stores among Croats, Slovenes, and Bulgarians, than among Blacks. Neither Negroes nor immigrants made significant incursions into the skilled trades. No Blacks appeared at all in 1905 or 1915. Immigrants, however, finally made some inroads by 1915 but the skilled trades still

---

[11] Blacks in Steelton even had a lower rate of illiteracy (11 percent) than the foreign born (28 percent) according to the U.S. Census, *Fourteenth Census*, 1920, III, 872.

included only three percent of their ranks.

In a comparison of Black and immigrant workers after 1920, the stronger position Afro-Americans held over Slavs and Italians before 1920 was completely reversed. Whereas Blacks had a smaller proportion of their workers listed as unskilled in 1905 and 1915 than immigrants, only thirty-three percent of all immigrants were unskilled between 1920 and 1939 as compared to sixty-seven percent of the Blacks. The earlier dominance that Negroes enjoyed in semiskilled jobs had now given way to immigrant superiority—forty-seven percent to twenty-seven percent. Blacks, however, continued to be left out of skilled occupations. The relative preponderance of immigrants over Blacks in nonmanual fields continued at about the same rate (See Table IV).

The marked improvement of the Slav and Italian in relation to the Negro was modest in many respects. While the ratio of immigrants in unskilled jobs declined from seventy-eight percent in 1915 to only thirty-three percent after 1920, eight out of every ten immigrants were still in a blue collar job after 1920, exactly as

TABLE IV
OCCUPATIONAL DISTRIBUTION OF STEELTON'S WORK FORCE
1920-1939

	NBNP* (White)	FBFP** (Slavic-Italian)	Blacks	NBFP# (Slavic-Italian)	NBFP# (German, English, Irish)	Total
Unskilled	12%	33%	67%	16%	20%	30%
Semiskilled	50%	47%	27%	60%	45%	46%
Skilled	11%	9%	5%	4%	15%	6%
High Nonmanual	7%	3%	1%	7%	8%	6%
Low Nonmanual	20%	8%	2%	3%	12%	12%
Number	514	293	372	379	78	1,655

*Native born with both parents natives
**Foreign Born with foreign parents
#Native born with foreign born parents

This data was compiled from all males applying for marriage licenses from Steelton between 1920 and 1939. The 1,655 men represent every Steelton male listed in the Dauphin County *Marriage Licenses Dockets* between 1920 and 1939. These records, after 1920, gave the age, place of birth, and occupation of the applicant as well as the place of birth and occupation of the applicant's father.

they had been in 1905 and 1915. Immigrants shifted from un-skilled to semiskilled positions, but they were unable to escape blue collar positions. Tom Benkovic, a Croat, moved from the brutal heat of the open hearth to a position as a crane operator in a career that spanned over forty years.[12] Immigrants enjoyed up-ward mobility but on a limited and modest basis.

Although Blacks were surpassed by Slavs and Italians after 1920, both groups remained largely in unskilled and semiskilled positions throughout the first four decades of this century. As the semiskilled segment of the work force expanded, these positions were assumed at a more rapid rate by new immigrants rather than Negroes. Yet, neither Blacks nor immigrants ever escaped blue-collar work in any large numbers. More than eight out of every ten immigrants worked in blue-collar positions throughout their lifetimes. Blacks, while occupying lower positions at a higher rate, constantly found over nine out of every ten of their ranks in low level jobs (See Table V).

In addition to studying the occupational distribution of Steel-ton's ethnic groups, two other indicators reveal the impact immi-gration had upon the Black worker: occupational and geographical mobility rates. Between 1905 and 1915 only five percent of the Slavic and Italian immigrants were able to rise occupationally, largely from unskilled to semiskilled positions. In the next de-cade, the rate of upward mobility did increase substantially for Slavs and Italians, from five percent to twenty-nine percent. Yet, the most common experience by far remained no mobility at all for Slavs and Italians. An average of eight out of ten new immi-

TABLE V
PERCENTAGE OF IMMIGRANTS AND BLACKS
IN UNSKILLED AND SEMISKILLED JOBS, 1905-39

	1905	1915	1920-39	Average
Immigrants	83%	88%	80%	84%
	(Slavic-Italian)			
Blacks	93%	96%	94%	94%

[12] Taped interview with Thomas Benkovic, Steelton, July 11, 1971.

57

TABLE VI
BLACKS AND NEW IMMIGRANTS:
UPWARD MOBILITY FROM UNSKILLED POSITIONS
1905-1925

	Immigrants (Slavic-Italian)			Blacks			
Number	No Change	Up	Down	Number	No Change	Up	Down

				1905 Group			
1915: 95	91%	5%	—	67	71%	25%	—
1925: 46	71%	29%	—	(too small to compute)			
				1915 Group			
1925:214	76%	22%	—	35	87%	13%	—

grants remained immobile between 1905 and 1915 (See Table VI).

Blacks showed considerably more upward mobility between 1905 and 1915 than immigrants from southern Europe. Although it must be pointed out that out of seventeen Blacks who advanced in the decade after 1905 all moved from unskilled to only a semiskilled position. While the rate of Negro advancement was faster than that of the "new immigrant" before 1915, the pattern was reversed during the decade after 1915. Immigrants advanced more than twice as fast as Blacks between 1915 and 1925. During those years, Black mobility slowed from twenty-five percent to thirteen percent.[13]

Persistence rates, which have been defined as the proportion (usually expressed in a percentage) of a population remaining in a

---

[13]Paul Worthman's study of working class mobility in Birmingham, Alabama shows also that in the early twentieth century the large influx of white migrants—some of them Russians, "Hungarians," and Italians brought into Birmingham mills from the North—helped erode Black domination of some trades. See Worthman, "Working Class Mobility...," 185. He also states (179) that unfortunately he was not able to provide systematic examination of immigrant patterns of mobility since he could not find information about the place of birth of workers in 1890 and 1899. See also Stephan Thernstrom and Elizabeth Pleck, "The Last of the Immigrants? A Comparative Analysis of Immigrant and Black Social Mobility in Late-Nineteenth Century Boston," paper delivered at the 1970 annual meeting of the Organization of American Historians, 18-20. Thernstrom and Pleck found native born sons of Irish immigrants were much more successful in climbing to middle class positions. However, "Boston's [Irish] immigrants resembled Negroes in their occupational distribution rather more than they did old-stock Americans, though somewhat ahead of the Blacks; the least favored immigrants, the Irish, were virtually indistinguishable from Blacks, ranking a shade *behind* them in white-collar positions in 1880 and a *shade ahead* of them in 1890." The quotation is reproduced through the courtesy of Professor Thernstrom.

delimited area after a given time interval, provided another indication of the impact Slavs and Italians were having on the Black.[14]

Members of the "old immigration," English, Irish, and German, were exceptionally stable in their persistence patterns. Where only one-half the entire population remained in Steelton from 1880 to 1888, an incredible nine out of every ten English, Irish, and German immigrants did so. Moreover, these rates continued through the next seventeen years and ran over twenty percent higher than those for the population as a whole. In fact, among the semiskilled and skilled "old immigrants," all eleven persisted from 1888 to 1905. While the persistence rate was lower for the unskilled among these immigrants, it was still considerably higher than the rates for the rest of the population (See Table VII).

The pattern for the Slavs and Italians of the "new immigration" differed significantly from that of the newcomers from northern Europe. Whereas ninety percent of "old immigrants" stayed in Steelton during the eighties, only thirty-two percent of the Slavs and Italians persisted there from 1905 to 1915. As usual, the longer an immigrant remained in the town the less were his chances of leaving. Yet, even among those newcomers who had lived in Steelton from 1905 to 1915, over one-half still decided to seek other homes in the decade after 1915. The unskilled, newly arrived immigrant showed the greatest tendency to leave the borough from 1905 to 1915. Only twenty-seven percent of the unskilled immigrants who were in Steelton in 1905 could be found there ten years later. This compared unfavorably with the forty-four percent of nonmanual immigrants from the 1905 group who persisted throughout the ten year period (See Table VII).

Interestingly enough, after immigrants remained in Steelton for at least a decade, the persistence rates among the various skill categories were nearly the same. Although, it should be emphasized that more than half the immigrant population left Steelton during a given decade.

The immigrants who appeared in Steelton in 1915 were slightly more stable in the subsequent decade than Slavs and Italians from

---

[14]Peter R. Knights, "Population Turnover, Persistence, and Residential Mobility in Boston, 1830-1860," in Thernstrom and Sennett, 258.

TABLE VII
PERSISTENCE RATES OF IMMIGRANTS,
1880-1925

	Number	1880	1896	1905
		1880 Group (English, German, Irish)		
Unskilled	42	90%	86%	100%
Semiskilled	8	90%	100%	100%
Skilled	4	100%	100%	100%
Nonmanual	4	100%	100%	75%
Total	58	90%	90%	96%

	Number	1915	1925
		1905 Group (Slavic-Italian)	
Unskilled	303	27%	40%
Semiskilled	30	43%	46%
Skilled	0	0%	0%
Nonmanual	70	44%	45%
Total	403	32%	47%

	Number	1925
		1915 Group (Slavic-Italian)
Unskilled	479	37%
Semiskilled	61	59%
Skilled	20	30%
Nonmanual	76	53%
Total	616	42%

Persistence rates were obtained by tracing immigrants and Blacks through *Boyd's Directory of Harrisburg and Steelton* for 1888, 1896, 1905, 1915, and 1925.

the 1905 group. Yet, only four out of every ten could still be found after a decade as compared with three in ten for the 1905-1915 group. Again, persistence rates were considerably higher for nonmanual workers than for the unskilled immigrant.

While Blacks compared poorly in persistence rates with the

English, Irish, and Germans in Steelton during the 1880s, their rates were only slightly lower than that for the population as a whole. Forty-seven percent of the Negroes appearing in 1880 could still be found in Steelton eight years later. Characteristically, of those Blacks who remained in Steelton for most of the eighties, the chances were over eight in ten that they would remain throughout the nineties (See Table VIII).

What was salient was the tremendous decrease in the Black persistence rates during the years of the heavy Slavic immigration into Steelton. Croats, Slovenes, Serbs, and Bulgarians were slowly replacing Afro-Americans in semiskilled occupations. This disruption of the Black position in Steelton was also indicated in persistence rates. From a persistence rate of forty-seven percent

TABLE VIII
PERSISTENCE RATES FOR BLACKS, 1880-1925

	Numbers	1888	1896	1915	1925
		1880 Group			
Unskilled	82	45%	90%		
Semiskilled	3	33%	10%		
Skilled	0	0%	0%		
Nonmanual	2	100%	10%		
Totals	87	47%	85%		
		1905 Group			
Unskilled	183			33%	
Semiskilled	96			10%	
Skilled	0			0%	
Nonmanual	21			10%	
Totals	300			23%	
		1915 Group			
Unskilled	220				28%
Semiskilled	84				7%
Skilled	0				0%
Nonmanual	19				0%
Total	323				21%

Persistence rates were obtained by tracing immigrants and Blacks through Boyd's *Directory of Harrisburg and Steelton* for 1888, 1896, 1905, 1915, and 1925.

between 1880 and 1888, Negro rates fell to twenty-three percent between 1905 and 1915 and to twenty-one percent between 1915 and 1925. This was lower than the thirty-two percent (1905-1915) and forty-two percent (1915-1925) displayed by "new immigrants." Moreover, the downward trend in Black persistence rates compared poorly with Slavic and Italian rates which were slowly rising. It should be remembered, however, that among both groups the turnover in population remained substantially high (See Table VIII).

Even more striking in comparing the extent of geographical mobility between Blacks and Slavs and Italians was the greater persistence rates among immigrants after 1905. This is not to minimize the tremendous turnover in the immigrant population itself but immigrant persistence rates did substantially exceed those of the Afro-Americans. At a time when new immigrants were replacing Blacks in the semiskilled job categories, 1905-1939, they were also causing a greater degree of outward migration among blacks.[15]

The influx of Croats, Serbs, Slovenes, Bulgarians, and Italians into Steelton, especially after 1900, had a devastating impact upon the town's Black working force. Black upward mobility rates, which had been rising before 1915, began to slip after World War I. Of all the town's ethnic groups, only the Black witnessed a decline in population between 1890 and 1910. And the rising persistence rates displayed by Afro-Americans before 1905 began to erode when they were faced with immigrant competition. The moderation of Negro population rates in numerous northern industrial areas immediately after 1900 can be linked to the rising influx of Slavic and Italian labor. If Steelton is any indication, Negro workers were not only losing semiskilled occupations to Slavs and Italians but, consequently, being forced to leave their northern homes, presumably in search of work, at an increasing rate. World War I would terminate European immigration and

---

[15]In examining the Marriage License Dockets for Steelton between 1920 and 1939, it was found that of 332 Slavic immigrant sons applying for marriage licenses, 87 percent were born in Steelton. On the other hand of 372 Blacks applying for licenses, during the twenties and thirties, only 11 percent were natives of Steelton. The data suggested, of course, that immigrant children were tending to settle within the same community at a much larger rate than were Black children. The Blacks who were marrying in Steelton between 1920 and 1939 were not the children of Blacks who lived in the community in the first two decades of the century. Yet, the immigrant children were largely the sons of those who persisted in Steelton.

increase Negro migration northward *again*. The years just prior to the war, however, had assured the Negro worker that he would have to start his economic climb over again—from the bottom.[16]

---

[16]W. Lloyd Warner and Leo Scrole, *The Social System of American Ethnic Groups* (New Haven, 1945), 2, argue that an ethnic group's low socio-economic position stemmed from the fact that it had only recently arrived in an urban-industrial area. Inevitably, however, a group would climb through several generations and be replaced at the bottom of the "social heap" by a newer arrivals. Blacks in Steelton were pushed down and out, however, rather than upward by immigrants who followed them.

IMMIGRATION AND MODERNIZATION:
THE CASE OF SLAVIC PEASANTS
IN INDUSTRIAL AMERICA

The study of the impact of modernization upon traditional, preindustrial cultures has usually been based upon a dichotomous model. Traditional and modern societies have been described as distinct categories. Passage from the former to the latter was assumed to involve the destruction of traditional culture and the eventual embracement of the new with its emphasis on materialism, individualism, and progress. If manifestations of a traditional culture were found in modern societies, they were thought to be minor residues of premodern society which were able briefly to withstand the disintegrating effects of modernization.[1]

Recent scholars have made a strong case for the persistence of preindustrial values. Especially impressive has been the work on modernization and women. Joan Scott and Louise Tilly, in a study of nineteenth century Europe, argued that preindustrial values "rather than a new individualistic idealogy" justified the work of working-class women. What they posited was a model of "continuity or traditional values and behavior in changing circumstances." They explained that behavior was less a product of new ideas than of the effects of old ideas operating in a new or changing concept. Since women's work was already justified in terms of family survival in peasant Europe, Scott and Tilly concluded that no change in values was needed to allow lower class women to work outside the home during the nineteenth century — "peasant values and family interests sent them to work."[2]

Descriptions of immigrant groups and peasants moving to industrial society have also noted the tenacity with which preindustrial cultural preferences and familial arrangements resisted disintegration and change. Italian families in Buffalo, New York, resisted the assumed destructive tendencies of industrialization by selecting only jobs which would minimize the separation of parent and child. Italian associational life, communal ties, and other cultural traits were found flourishing in twentieth century Chicago.[3] A study of boarding and lodging in American families revealed that families were malleable and not broken by the weight of industrialization. Indeed, they cushioned the "shock of urban life" for newcomers.[4]

A conclusion that the impact of modernization was minimal and less than destructive, however, would be premature. Studies from the Philadelphia Social History Project confirm that modernization took its toll and was not always resisted successfully. Industrial and technological change in nineteenth century Philadelphia frequently altered work in various skills, reduced the income and refining our understanding of the impact modernization had upon immigrants from traditional societies.

It would admittedly be impossible to describe Slavic settlements in late nineteenth and early twentieth century America as devoid of old world traits. Familial relationships stand as prominent examples of elements resilient to the transformative nature of the urban-industrial milieu. Consider the roles assumed by various individuals in the Slavic family. An essentially hierarchical structure dominated by an authoritarian father characterized Slavic families in peasant Europe and America. An examination of Poles in Buffalo in the 1920's, for instance, found more than 90% of the Buffalo Poles believing that parents should exercise complete authority over their children.[10]

The expectation that children would contribute to the material support of the family was also characteristic of both European and American Slavs. In Pennsylvania mining districts Slavs not only exceeded all other ethnic groups in their use of child labor but routinely falsified their children's ages to obtain working permits. In Pittsburgh's South Side thousands of young Serbs spent their adolescent years working in glass factories until they could enter the steel mills. In Scranton 35% of Polish family income in 1911 was earned by children.[11]

Other characteristics of the Slavic peasant family were found long after settlement in America. The treatment of sexual attitudes continued without drastic change. Children were informed that erogeneous zones were repulsive, bad, or nonexistent. An examination of Slovak-American Catholics revealed that sex was seldom discussed. For Slavic women sex continued to be primarily for the purpose of procreation.[12] As in Europe, moreover, greater control was exercised over older children than younger ones. A gradual progression existed from older children who were "tightly controlled" to the youngest who were much more uninhibited.[13]

A classic example of the perpetuation of peasant family alignments was demonstrated by the South Slavs. The prevalent family structure among premodern Croats and Serbs was the *zadruga*. Its main components were a communal, joint family which rested upon the supremacy of the older male member and the belief that other males should never leave their home. Sons and their wives and children would remain within the homes of their fathers. Daughters would leave upon marriage to become members of the *zadruga* of their husbands. Sons remained to contribute to the support of the communal family.[14]

In an examination of Yugoslav family structure in the immigrant steel town of Lackawanna, New York, the *zadruga* form of kinship arrangement was found persisting after two decades of settlement in America. The South Slav households had the highest rate of extended families among the town's ethnic groups, including Poles and Slovaks. Grandparents, married children, and other relatives abounded in the Yugoslav households. Thirty-four% of Serbian and Croatian families were extended compared to only 20% of the Polish, Slovak, and Hungarian residents. Indeed, Yugoslavs lived in extended family households more than all other American immigrant groups according to studies conducted by the United States Immigration Commission. Moreover, over one out of every five Yugoslav households in Lackawanna had the families of married sons residing with the parents, an important feature of the *zadruga* pattern.[15]

If important aspects of family life continued in America, the religious practices of Slavic newcomers remained equally strong. The local parish continued to serve not only as a dominant center of religion but as a focus of community life.[16] Detroit Polish life, for instance, developed around St. Casimir's, St. Albertus, St. Josephats, and Sweetest Heart of Mary churches.[17] In Chicago early Poles identified their two largest communities by the names of their churches. "Stanislawowo," clustered around St. Stanislaus parish and "Wojciechowo" grew around the church of St. Adalbert. These communities were not only separated physically but seldom interacted. Jobs, schools, clubs, and churches were all located in these respective settlements and residents saw little need to extend their activities elsewhere.[18] "Stanislawowo" was an excellent example. It possessed a grade school, a high school, social clubs and religious societies. Organizations such as the "Macier z Polska" offered a variety of moral, cultural and "social training" activities for youth and adults. The parish continued its old world function as the cement of both religious and communal life.[19]

Slavs continued not only to practice their traditional religion and focus their social lives around their churches, but the spiritual orientation of peasant Europe with its emphasis upon non-secular rewards and religious values continued to influence Slavic attitudes. It was this residue of spiritual and religious values which explained the consistent anti-materialistic current which permeated Slavic-American thought. Throughout the first half-century of large scale Slavic settlement in America a consistent anti-materialism influenced the immigrant's mind. In the early 1890's, Polish newspapers were already mounting an assault upon the "Dollar God" of American culture. A Pole from Pennsylvania wrote *Dziennik Chicagoski* critizing the tendency of American society to strain parental-child relationships by stressing "excess and wantoness." "The struggle for the dollar facilitated the losing of religion and patriotism so dear to us," the Polish newspaper feared. Numerous editorials and articles emphasized the evil effects of the pursuit of material wealth. In an 1894 editorial, *Zgoda* told Poles that a "reasonable honest drive" to improve your material being was good. The "idolistic pursuit of money at the expense of your soul," however, "would bring hatred and desperation." *Zgoda* continued, "good character and work are the greatest wealth."[20]

It was precisely because of this skepticism of the promise of American life that Poles emphasized Polish over American schools. One Polish journal called Polish schools the "watch-tower" of the Polish spirit. American schools were felt to be a "horrible example" where children learned little but disrespect for their parents.[21] American schools were not considered "adequate" for Polish children not only because they were "irreligious" but because they were thought to be permeated with secularism.[22]

Slovaks invariably echoed the Polish sentiments. In a series of essays in *Jednota* by a Slovak writer, Ivan Kramoris, the Slovak immigrant situation was analyzed. Kramoris posed the question, "But what are we to do in America." He explained that such a choice would be made in the framework of economic versus moral standards. Kramoris argued that an individual's morality actually influenced his economic life. Little doubt existed in Kramoris' mind that the eventual emphasis should be placed upon morality. Other writers concurred. "So many are cursed with the lust of acquiring things that they see no further ahead than their own selfish self," a Slovak editor exclaimed, "those who measure success by the material things acquired are lost in the fog of life."[23]

Characteristically, the anti-materialistic bias influenced Slovak views on education. *Osadne Hlasy* illustrated the drawbacks of the public schools in 1929. Children were taught but not "reared" in American schools, according to the Slovak journal, "they educate the mind but not the heart." J.T. Porincak, a Slovak, clarified the argument:

> With a public school education they [children] go forth into the world, lost completely to the Slovaks. Their idea of life is a breezy and snappy novel, a blood curdling movie and lots of money.
> But our duty to our people commands us to save our youth from the moral catastrophe that is confronting them.[24]

The Slavic-American skepticism toward public school was clearly manifested in various studies of school attendance and progress. In a 1911 study released by the United States Immigration Commission, Poles and Slovaks ranked lowest among ethnic groups in the largest urban centers. The percentage of Slavic children in school beyond the sixth grade was lower than the rate for the progeny of Irish and Jewish newcomers and Negroes. Beyond grade six, the group with the smallest percentage of children in the public schools of Chicago and Cleveland in 1911 were the Slovaks (4%). Poles ranked lowest in Buffalo, New Britain and Scranton and next to last in Cleveland and Milwaukee.[25]

Not surprisingly, computations of public high school attendance in 1910 found Slavic children noticeably absent. In Chicago, while 5% of black children and 6% of Polish Jewish children were attending the secondary schools, only 1% of the Poles and Slavaks were doing so. In Cleveland only one-half of one percent of Slovak children were in high school in 1910 as compared with 11% of Irish immigrant children, and 7% of Polish Jews who arrived in America at the same time.[26]

Where parochial school attendance figures were available, Slavic attendance invariably ranked behind native-born and second generation Irish children. In Milwaukee parochial schools in 1910, 15% of the children of native-born Catholics were in school and 10% of the second generation Irish. Only 2% of the Poles were attending, however, and no Slovaks. Polish and Slovak representation in Cleveland's parochial schools was better but considerably behind the native-born and Irish. New Britain had 19% of its Irish youth in Catholic schools after the sixth grade but none of its Polish youth.[27] In Scranton 99% of all Polish immigrant children in parochial school were in grades one to five only. In Shenandoah, Pennsylvania, 32% of the children of native-born Catholics were beyond the fourth grade. No Poles had advanced that far despite having been in Shenandoah for over thirty years by 1910.[28]

Clearly, then, the arguments detailing widespread cultural persistence in the transition process from premodern to modern societies apply to the Slavic immigrant in America. Slavs were not completely staggered by the tremors of urban-industrial society and their traditional culture proved resilient. But to characterize Slavic immigrant communities in urban America as simply extensions of peasant communalism would be erroneous. The entire framework of peasant behavior in eastern Europe was within a context of work and survival. The exigencies of working class status in the United States would not alter this fact. Immigrant life in industrial towns and cities would evolve a preoccupation with survival also. This process would not lead to a destruction of peasant culture, but it did not simply perpetuate it either. Rather, while fundamental elements of the premodern world view would be reinforced in modern society, behavioral changes occurred that could best be explained not in terms of destruction or persistence but in terms of innovation. Slavs created their own strategies for survival which both drew from the traditional and embraced the new. What remained the same was the framework in which this was done — a framework where survival was the preoccupation. This framework was as much an element of working-class status as of peasant traditionalism.

The strategies for survival developed in America were often subtle. The Slavic family, for instance, which maintained much of its peasant character was not completely unaltered. While it was traditional for the family to support itself collectively, innovations such as the use of carefully prepared budgets nearly always administered by the Slavic women became widespread.[29] The female assumed the position of fiscal manager in the Slavic immigrant family. A Slovak in McKeesport, Pennsylvania recalled that as long as his father worked he turned his pay over to his mother along with all of his sons. Margaret Byington's famous survey of Homestead, Pennsylvania in 1910 found clear evidence of the extensive use of budgets by Slavs and their control by the immigrant woman. In the anthracite coal fields of Pennsylvania, Slavic mothers became the managers of smoothly functioning economic units where fathers and children automatically relinquished paychecks.[30]

Slavs in America also began to seek security in the peculiar context of working-class America. Denied opportunities for significant occupational mobility,[31] particularly since earlier arrivals such as the Irish and Germans already held skilled industrial jobs, Slavs turned intensely to home ownership as a means of solidifying their precarious economic status. In nearly every Slavic ethnic community in America immigrant savings and loan associations were established for the purpose of issuing home mortgages. Croatian immigrants organized the First Croatian Building and Loan Association in Chicago in 1910 in an immigrant's home. While it was difficult for some newcomers to relinquish their savings to an institution, deposits steadily increased. Loans were used predominantly to purchase homes and by 1935 the association had loaned over four million dollars for home mortgages.[32] Slovaks in Scranton, Pennsylvania, saved at the Bosak State Bank; Slovenes in southwestern Pennsylvania mining towns organized the Slovenian Savings and Loan Association in 1921 with branches in Strabane and Canonsburg. Croats in Gary, Indiana, initiated the America Savings and Loan Association for home mortgages. Before the Great Depression, Cleveland had five Polish savings and loan companies. Other representative institutions included the Croatian-American Building and Loan Association of Granite City, Illinois, the Pulaski Building and Loan Association and the Czecko-Slovak Building and Loan Association both of Chicago.[33] One Chicago real estate firm had eleven Poles to handle their "Polish business."[34] As one Croatian journal exclaimed, "a nation's basic wealth is its land and homes."[35]

Slavs exceeded nearly every ethnic group in urban America in purchasing homes. While the market value of their residences was consistently below native-born whites and other immigrant groups such as Germans, Irish, and Jews, seldom did anyone exceed their propensity to become homeowners.[36] In a nationwide survey conducted in 1930, the high rate of Slavic-American home ownership was dramatically revealed. In Akron, Bridgeport, Chicago and Cleveland, families originating from Czechoslovakia owned homes at a higher rate than all other immigrant groups. In Akron, Chicago, and Cleveland, Poles were second only to the Czechs and Slovaks. Polish families ranked highest in ownership rates in Buffalo, Toledo, Milwaukee, and Detroit. Slovaks were second in the later two cities. In all eight communities, Czechoslovak and polish rates exceeded the ownership rates for families from England and Ireland with the exception of the Irish in Toledo. In Milwaukee, while 70% of the Poles, 63% of the Czechoslovaks, and 52% of the Yugoslavs owned homes, only about one-third of the English and Irish were home owners. In Akron, while 68% of all foreign-born families owned their own residences, 84% of the Czechoslovaks were home owners.[37] In Chicago, the rate of Czechoslovak home ownership was about 2.5 times higher than that of Russian Jews, although the property of the Jews was valued considerably higher.[38]

If Slavic home ownership is studied in smaller industrial centers where they were concentrated, the pattern further reveals their quest for economic security. In Pennsylvania mill towns Slavic ownership rates exceeded even the families of native-born whites. Serbs and Croats dominated the rates in Aliquippa, Farrell, and Steelton. Slovaks were the leading owners in Braddock, Duquesne, Homestead, and Munhall. In Homestead, Slovaks bought homes twice as much as native-white families. In the coal towns of Shenandoah, Wilkes-Barre, Mount Carmel, and Nanticoke, native-born whites were far behind Poles in acquiring housing. While 23% of the natives obtained their own home in Nanticoke, 57% of the Poles decided to become owners. Not surprisingly, in 1930 the foreign-born owned homes at a higher rates than the statewide average for all families in Pennsylvania, a state whose immigrant population was primarily southern and eastern European.[39]

In other areas as well, Slavs emerged as leading home owners. In Cicero, Illinois, while 22% of the native whites possessed their own residence, 67% of the Czechs and Poles were owners. Similar trends were evident in Lorain, Ohio, Lackawanna, New York, and New Britain, Connecticut.[40]

In addition to developing new strategies in America to obtain a modest degree of economic security, Slavs also manifested an intensified concern for ethnic communalism. They created elaborate ethnic community structures which surpassed the regionalism of their European experience. Upon arrival in America Slavs seldom displayed powerful strains of ethnic identity. In Steelton, Pennsyl vania, Croatians were deeply divided for a number of years by village (Bjelovar and Voyvodina) loyalties which they brought with them. One second generation Croat recalled that his parents, who emigrated from Bjelovar, attempted to discourage him from ever marrying a "Voyvodincia." Indeed, the two groups often argued over church affairs and the practice of certain Old World customs. These regional differences were overcome, however, when Croats faced a common problem in America. In Steelton their dispute with Slovenes which led to the ouster of the Slovenes from the Croatian-Slovenian Church brought about the end of European regionalsim in favor of ethnic identity.[41]

The early attachment to village loyalties was certainly not unique to Steelton, neither was the triumph of ethnic nationalism over parochial interests. Slavs initially identified themselves by their place of birth, village, or region. Early immigrant fraternal lodges were usually begun along local lines. Slovak lodges in the coal fields of Pennsylvania were initially organized by counties of origin of Slovak newcomers, mostly from eastern Slovakia. Even in Steelton, Croats, had five different fraternal lodges which reflected generally their European village origins.[42]

Local divisions, however, gave way to immigrant communities which, although frequently troubled by persistent factionalism, became culturally unified in the face of economic and social turmoil in America. Local fraternal lodges and societies in mining and manufacturing centers gradually joined groups from other localities to form national associations. The Polish National Alliance, the First Catholic Slovak Union, and the Croatian Fraternal Union all welded scattered ethnic communities into organizations which provided some economic benefit and much social exchange. While this movement had just emerged in the premigration societies in the late nineteenth century, it was expanded in industrial society due to the need for a more formal basis for community and the fragile economic security provided by industrial work.[42] Premodern tribalism was not destroyed or simply perpetuated in modern society but embellished.

While the national fraternal societies were a powerful force in bringing local immigrant settlements into the mainstream of the new American-ethnic communities, they suffered from frequent dissension and competition for support. In 1890, Peter V. Rovnianek helped found the National Slovak Society in Pittsburgh. All Slovaks were welcome whether they were Catholics, Protestants, or Freemasons. Rovnianek's organization was openly nationalistic. On the other hand, the Reverend Stefan Furdek established a strictly Catholic fraternal organization, the First Catholic Slovak Union in 1890. Furdek's stated objectives included a desire to preserve the Catholic faith.[32] Since the success of different immigrant societies often depended upon the degree to which they purported to uphold Old World culture and language, their very competitiveness served to strengthen a sense of immigrant identity in America. As a perceptive observer has noted, moreover, the leadership of the societies was drawn from immigrants of disparate social backgrounds as well as regions; immigrants who may have had little chance for association in the Old World now acted in concert to establish new institutions.[33]

Poles were particularly driven to heightened ethnic consciousness by their experience within the Roman Catholic Church. Significant was the Polish

National Catholic Church movement which began in Scranton in 1897. Polish
workers in south Scranton began to argue for a greater voice in the management
of church affairs. When the Irish bishop of Scranton termed them "disobedient,"
they established their own church and invited a young Polish priest, Francis
Hodur, to guide them. By 1919 the Polish National Church movement, which
substituted Polish for Latin in church services after Latin had been accepted for
centuries in Poland, spread to over fifty congregations in America and eventually
to scores of parishes in Poland itself. The schismatic Poles also founded their
own fraternal union and publications.[34]

In Chicago, Poles that did not leave the Catholic church also began to assert
their ethnic identity. Disturbed at the lack of Polish bishops and the suggestion
of Chicago's Archbishop Mundelein that parishes would be based on territorial
rather than nationality grounds, Chicago Polonia, manifesting a growing concern
for their ethnic identity, issued its *I Polacci Negle Stati Uniti Dell' America Del
Nord* statement in 1920. The document, a collaborative effort on the part of the
General Union of Polish Clergy and the Polish Embassy to the Holy See,
outlined the grievances of America's Polonia. It called for more Polish bishops,
attacked the concept of territorial based churches — "churches of Poles were
meant for the exclusive use of Poles" — and defended Polish schools as necessary
for keeping family and language intact.[47]

Rising feelings of ethnicity seriously weakened and eventually divided the
Uniate or Byzantine Church in America as well. The church was composed
mostly of Rusins and Ukrainians. Resentment against the Ukrainian bishop,
however, prompted Rusin clergy and laymen to organize the Greek Catholic
Union in 1892.[48] The union, through its organ, *Amerikanskij Russki Viestnik*,
and the Rusin Civilian Church Council eventually clarified its objectives. They
included an attempt to halt the "Ukrainian policies" of the bishop. By 1918 the
church was officially divided into Ukrainian and Rusin branches. As H.R.
Niebuhr has pointed out, the immigrant church became more of a racial and
cultural institution than a religious one.[49]

Economic exploitation also forced immigrants to coalesce around an emerging consciousness which was a blend of working-class status and heightened
ethnic identity. Slavs were killed in a united labor protest at Lattimer, Pennsylvania, in 1897. The event evoked widespread criticism in the Slavic press against
American officials who fired upon the striking miners. Croatians in Chicago
contributed substantially to fellow Croats who struck mines in West Virginia,
Colorado and Pennsylvania.[50] In 1891, to cite a case in point, a guard was slain
at the Thompson Steel Works at Braddock, Pennsylvania, near Pittsburgh. Three
Slovaks, Andrew Toth, Michael Sabol, and George Rusnak were among sixty
persons charged with the murder. Most received light sentences, but Toth, Sabol,
and Rusnak were given the death penalty. Immediately Rovnianek's Slovak
Union and Slovak organizations throughout the company rallied to the cause
and sent petitions to the Pennsylvania Pardon Board requesting clemency be
shown the three Slavs for "a crime which they did not commit." A standard
petition form was printed in English and Slovak. Soon the forms, signed by
hundreds of immigrants, were arriving at the pardon board. Each petition

claimed that Slavic immigrants had been debarred from participation in public affairs and business in America:

A great majority of us became servants, hewers of wood, drawers of water, workers in the mills, the mines, the fields, and the shops for a compensation which barely allowed us the necessaries of life .... We are buying lands, building houses, educating our children .... The hanging of these men will be a terrible blow to our people.[51]

While Slovaks were not successful in freeing Toth, Sabol, and Rusnak immediately, such incidents served to bring Slovaks together in the face of what seemed to be a threat to Slovak immigrants collectively.

Slavs were carefully establishing working-class worlds in America by integrating old world traditions with pragmatic innovations necessitated by the constrictions and realities of their socioeconomic status. This process was illustrated in the attitude they assumed toward an industrial society and the results they found in it. Rather than embracing the "American dream" of personal advancement through education and a career, Slavs sought mainly secure employment. Conditions in urban and industrial America only served to strengthen the peasant view of work as an instrument of survival, not success.

And here we can turn from generalizations to specific, personal reactions. The Slavic arrivals studied in this investigation were peasants from the most underdeveloped areas of southern and eastern Europe who eventually settled industrial mills, factories, and mines. Of those immigrants interviewed all arrived between 1902 and 1914 from Croatia, Bosnia, Galicia, and and the eastern counties of Slovakia. All but one had been agricultural workers or laborers in Europe. Indeed, 82% of all Serbians and 70% of all Slovaks emigrating from Austria-Hungary were agrarian-peasant workers.[52]

Since most Slavs shared a premodern background, they arrived with the traditional east European peasant's conception of work. Work was central to the Slavic peasant's existance. All of life, indeed survival, revolved around the yearly cycle of farm duties. Parents and children learned the routine tasks of the farm thoroughly, as performances of such tasks often made the difference between survival and a catastrophe.[53]

Even though many Slavs in Europe were transient before they came to America, they moved only as means of survival. Alternative jobs were sought only out of necessity. Southern Slavs frequently went to sea before 1918 and worked as sailors. When a necessary sum of money was accumulated, they returned to their villages and did not attempt to increase their wealth further. Gospodars, the elder heads of Yugoslav extended families, viewed factory work as temporary. One village elder proclaimed that if factory employment were lost, peasants would be unable to eat. Yet it was important to retain the land as a means of security. A gospodar stated:

We work in the factory so that we can continue to hold onto the land and we hold onto the land because no one knows what is sure.[54]

The transient landless peasants who wondered throughout nineteenth-century Slovakia moved continuously in search of work as their only means of survival.[55]

Survival was always the preoccupation with the Slav and work was the

instrument of survival. The East European peasant viewed the world as a source
of "limited good." That is to say that no relationship existed between work and
the acquisition of wealth. Wealth — as well as land, health, and security — were
considered to exist in short supply and the peasant felt little could be done to
alter this situation. In Slavic Europe children were continually taught to work
hard; little else seemed available. Not surprisingly Russian peasants employed
one criterion in determining the suitability of their daughter's prospective
marriage partner: was the prospective son-in-law a "good worker."[57] Upward
social success seemed unobtainable and irrelevant as they searched only for
work. Zara Werlinich was a Serb who arrived in McKees Rocks, Pennsylvania in
1913. The seventh of thirteen children, he had little alternative but to leave his
father's farm after it was inherited by his oldest brother. Upon his arrival he
conceived a single goal: to get a job. "We all had to look for work," he recalled
"a job don't look for you." Werlinich was hired as a laborer in the Fort Pitt
Foundry and remained a laborer for twenty years until the depression forced
him out of work. He was gratified that the foundry provided a steady income.[57]

Werlinich's aims were shared by the majority of Slavic newcomers who sought
steady work as a course of security. Consider the orientation of Sam Vignovic, a
Serb who began working at a glass factory in Pittsburgh in 1914. "I was anxious
to make money and support myself," Vignovic recalled, "I didn't care about a
[particular] job even though it was hard." When Vignovic learned hourly wages
were fifteen cents higher at the nearby Jones and Laughlin Steel plant, he
changed positions. His reasoning was not based on a desire to raise his standard
of living but to improve his savings in the event he lost his job.[58]

Other Slavs displayed similar modest and characteristically working-class
intentions. A Serb (who requested anonymity) left the mountains of Bosnia in
1907 and arrived at the Carnegie Steel plant in Duquesne. He found his task of
filling wheel-barrows with gravel and sand for brick-layers dreadful but reasoned
that without work "they would put your plate upside down at the boarding
house." George Hudock, a Bethlehem Slovak, wanted to operate a crane and
rejected subsequent opportunities to earn more because those "opportunities"
seemed less "steadier."[59]

Slavs logically viewed industrial work as quite desirable. One Pittsburgh Slav
emphasized that many of his friends genuinely wanted to work in the steel mills
because they disliked outdoor work which was irregular and "time passed
quickly" in the steel plant. Another put the point more concisely, "the mill was
considered a good place to work."[60] One Polish newcomer considered his ten
hour day in America an improvement over the dawn to dusk routine he had
followed in Europe.

If the initial aspirations of Slavic newcomers were modest, subsequent behav-
iorial evidence suggested they seldom displayed any attempt at risk-taking or
attaining a higher position. If a steady job was the initial goal of Slavs, once
obtained it was not easily abandoned. Valerian Duda came from Poland to
McKeesport in 1906 at the age of seventeen. Along with other Poles he worked
at the National Tube Plant of United States Steel. He retired forty-eight years
later as a tester of galvanized pipe. Andrew Bodnar left Slovakia in 1913 and was

taken by an uncle to a Homestead mill. He retired forty-seven years later as a "piler" of steel beams.[61]

The reluctance of Slavs to leave steady work was a pervasive theme. Walter Balawajder, a Pole, had learned the trade of cabinet-making in Europe. Upon his arrival in McKeesport, however, he worked in a steel mill. A decade later when he learned that the Westinghouse Company in Pittsburgh was planning on fabricating radio cabinets, he was excited by the possibility of returning to his original trade. When Westinghouse quaranteed him higher wages but not permanent work he decided to remain in the mill. "Once you build up that seniority," he reasoned, "there was no use to go somewhere else for something you weren't sure of." Similarly John Urczyk, a Ukrainian from Galicia, came to America in 1913 and obtained work at the Pressed Steel Car Company in McKees Rocks. He recalled fellow immigrants at Pressed Steel unwilling to leave even their particular department. Urczyk revealed that this reluctance to change occupations stemed partially from a fear by Slavs that they would not know how to perform occupational tasks somewhere else.[62]

Most East European newcomers were forced to change occupations at one time or another but the moves were usually lateral rather than vertical, involuntary rather than voluntary. Economic dislocation influenced immigrant job changes more than a desire for social advancement.[63] Consider the experience of Valentine Bauer. Born in a Hungarian village, Bauer immigrated to Galitzin, Pennsylvania, at the age of nineteen where he worked for a decade in soft coal mines. When employment became sporadic at the mines Bauer contacted an uncle in Bethlehem and was hired as a blacksmith helper at the steel mill. Unable to sustain his family without an income during the 1919 steel strike, he began working at the Mack Truck Company in Allentown. He returned to the steel mill two years later. When employment became irregular during the 1930's, he was hired as a janitor for St. John's Hungarian Church and school. He occupied that position until his retirement in 1957. Bauer was emphatic in explaining his decision to remain as janitor, "The work was more steady." He elaborated:

> Well, we [immigrants] had to take what we got. I started in the mine. It used to be slack a lot so I would do farm work at Lorretto. I never wanted to leave Bethlehem. I was happy here and proud that I always lived in the fifth ward because my work is here and the church is hear.[64]

Even more important than the modest character of the aspirations and achievements of the first generation was the fact that the majority of the immigrant children displayed little advancement over their parents. In a quantitative assessment of intergenerational occupational mobility among South Slavic immigrants in Steelton, Pennsylvania, less than one out of four sons was able to attain an occupational status above his father between 1920 and 1940. While a modest amount of occupation advancement occurred,[65] the children were quite similar in their aspirations and accomplishments to their parents.

Most immigrant sons began their working career early. Of 115 immigrant children interviewed, all but two were working by the age of fourteen.[66] George Porvasnik was representative. Porvasnik, the son of a Slovak immigrant, was born in Pittsburgh in 1911. He left school at the age of fourteen to work in a plant which manufactured chains. The constant odor of banana oil on chains caused him to bleed frequently from the nose and he left after six months. Porvasnik became a rivet heater at Pressed Steel and remained there for forty years. Other young Slavs began employment in the "glass houses" of south Pittsburgh and in the silk mills of south Bethlehem. These jobs usually served as a prelude to a lifetime of toil at nearby steel plants.[67]

While the occupational careers of second generation Slavs were unspectacular, they fulfilled many of their original occupational expectations. Robert Milanovich, a Serbian-American, worked at a Pittsburgh glass factory only until an opening occurred at the Jones and Laughlin steel mill. Milanovich reasoned that the mill was better than most jobs around. Sam Mervosh's sole aim was to get a job. He began working in a rolling mill where his father knew the superintendent. The position particularly appealed to Mervosh because it was removed from the heat of the blast furnaces. And, as Milanovich, he claimed that pay in the mill was better than most wages in south Pittsburgh. Charles Jablonski simply "aspired" to get away from school. Frank Horvath, a Bethlehem Hungarian, wanted only a steady job. Horvath insisted that he never thought of having anything more than he had. "I just wanted a job," he affirmed, "whether it be a garbage man or an iceman."[68]

Once the second generation became established in their careers, they demonstrated, like their fathers, a reluctance to change positions. Occupational alterations were viewed with caution. Lewis Buchek and Joseph Wiatrak both declined positions with the postal service because they did not wish to jeopardize their seniority at a mill. Prior to a strike which temporarily put him out of work, Lewis Kozo never considered leaving Bethlehem Steel. A strike forced him to work temporarily as a salesman. While he enjoyed sales, he quickly returned to the mill so as not to jeopardize his pension. Sam Mervosh never thought of leaving a Pittsburgh mill because he felt unqualified for any other position.[69]

In addition to limited horizons, the working-class attitudes of many Slavic- and Magyar-Americans to their work was reinforced by traditional family and neighborhood associations. One Hungarian eschewed the higher wages of Brooklyn Ship Yards so as not to sever his family ties in Bethlehem. Another Pole remained in Bethlehem for the same reason. Michael Komernitski stayed at a screw and bolt factory in McKees Rocks. He not only feared the loss of his pension but genuinely liked living among Slovaks, Poles, and Ukrainians in the McKees Rocks "bottoms."[70]

It should not be surprising that the aims of the second generation were modest and similar to those of their fathers. The influence of the immigrant parent was crucial in shaping the aspirations of the child. The concepts of work which Slavs developed in industrial America did not weaken quickly. Indeed, the absence of social mobility in the immigrant generation assured a continuation of Slavic working-class status and, therefore, limited horizons. Work was still conceived as an instrument of survival rather than a means to a career or social advancement.

Immigrant parents influenced their children in subtle ways. Many children viewed their immigrant fathers as, above all else, hard workers. If sons had any image of their father it included manual work as an inevitable aspect of life. Indeed, the fathers served as "models of immobility." A Polish-American described his parents as individuals who believed in "work, work, work, and work." A Bethlehem Slovak recalled that his father never talked of changing jobs but only of doing a good days work for the company.[71] A Serbian son in Pittsburgh remembered his father as a man esteemed by fellow Serbs for his application to his job. The Serbian son claimed his father's characteristics were representative of most Serbs. He clearly explained his father's motives as fear of the loss of his job. He argued:

Those men were tireless. They did hard work. They stuck with their job; they didn't have to be driven. They were tireless and always feared the loss of their jobs since they had nothing to fall back on.[73]

Parents encouraged child labor as necessary for family survival. Sam Davich was required to work at age fourteen in a glass factory in Pittsburgh and turn over his earnings to his mother, as were most other immigrant children. Several Slovak girls went to work in Donora, Pennsylvania, when their father became ill and was able to work only part time in the mills. In Lyndora, Pennsylvania many Polish children were sent to Detroit in the late 1920's when news of jobs in the expanding automobile industry was received. One Ukrainian-American son explained that it was understood that a child helped his father because the parent "couldn't make out."[73]

Slavic children were not always sent to work randomly. In mining districts especially, but also in steel mills, fathers took their sons to work with them or at least secured for them their initial adult occupations.[74] More importantly, it was within these initial jobs that the second generation usually decided upon their career goals. Those who helped their fathers as coal loaders, for instance, usually viewed the position as "blaster," a less physically demanding task, as a job to work toward. Numerous young men were taught their first job skills by their fathers. Nick Kiak's first job was learning the operation of a crane from his father at the Bethlehem mill.[75] All but seven of over seventy second generation Slavs interviewed in southwestern Pennsylvania coal fields were taken into the mines by their fathers.[76] Premigration reliance on kinship helped to determine occupational patterns. But the industrial work situation itself was also influential in shaping career goals.

Slavic parents not only influenced their children by example and direct action but imparted definite views concerning education. A typical Slovak father stressed to his son that it was important to learn a manual skill than attend school. Michael Zahorsky was assured by his father that if he learned a trade he would never go hungry. Zahorsky became a blacksmith. Frank Horvath quit school at age sixteen to work in a Bethlehem furniture factory. His brothers had already started peddling milk to help pay the family milk bill. Horvath's parents questioned whether school helped anyone survive. They argued that an opportunity to leave school and make money should never be avoided.[77]

When Slavic newcomers did insist on education, religious vocation and ethnic cultures were usually stressed. Michale Labeka's father taught him the role of cantor in the Ukrainian church. A cantor was paid to sing religious responses in many Slavic churches. Labeka later supplemented his income as a mill worker in Monessen with his earnings as a cantor. Bernard Gorczyca's parents sent him to a Polish seminary in Michigan at age fourteen. Other parents admonished their children to study their native tongue and religious instruction.[78]

Slavic-American newspapers reinforced the disdain of American education. Immigrant children were told that America stressed education excessively and that intelligence was inborn anyhow. A slovak newspaper printed a letter from a student who argued that the aim of American-born Slovaks should be loyalty to home and parish "even though it doesn't help you make money." Another Slovak wrote to *Narodne Noviny* that Slovaks should strive only to be more religious and do their daily work. A Ukrainian periodical urged all Ukrainian-American mothers to see that 80% of their children's schooling was in Ukrainian subjects. The uneducated, according to *Svoboda*, were those who Americanized their names and forgot the immigrant culture. When *Amerikansko Slovenske Noviny* attacked American public schools in 1893 for "assimilating our children and turning them against their parents," it was only reflecting the pervasive distrust of most Slavs toward secular education. Not surprisingly a recent content analysis of Slovak-American newspapers concluded that Slovak editors praised education not as a source of social mobility but as a vehicle for cultivating morality and preserving the ethnic culture and language.[79] Clearly the anti-materialistic skepticism toward American schools cited earlier was reinforced by a socioeconomic status which valued steady work.

The plight of women in industrual society gave further evidence that different structural conditions were not necessarily effecting drastic change, which at the same time women's attitudes and work experience were not simply reflections of cultural persistence. The working-class world encountered by Slavic women was making demands quite similarr to those of their European homeland. If work on peasant farms required extensive participation of women, the Slavic women in industrial America were just as taxed. Caring for boarders, packing countless lunches, raising children, managing finances were familiar to most Slavic wives. Work outside the home was frequently necessary and, despite the findings of McLaughlin on Buffalo's Italians, "head on collision" with industrial society could not always be minimized let alone avoided. Jobs were necessary for survival. Considerations such as selecting jobs which involved minimal family strain were secondary to family survival. In eastern Pennsylvania textile mills. Slavic women chose jobs which offered quicker placements on wage-earnings scales and could be learned rapidly. For this reason cigar factories were preferred to silk mills. Often women either took what was available, followed friends to a particular factory, or looked for employment where language was not a barrier.[80] The following characterization of a Polish housewife in Johnstown, Pennsylvania in 1915 by a social investigator revealed that the demands of survival in industrial society evoked behavior which included a systhesis of tradition (child bearing methods, use of farm animals) and working-class devices (continued earning of wages through selling milk and caring for lodgers).

> Monday evening went to sister's to return wash board, having just finished day's washing. Baby born while there; sister too young to assist; women not accustomed to midwifery anyway, so she cut the cord herself. Got up and ironed the nextt

78

day .... She milked cows and sold milk the day after baby's birth. This woman keeps cows, chickens, and lodgers; also earns money doing laundry and char work. The husband deserts her at times; he makes $1.70 a day .... Mother thin and wiry; looks tired and worn. Frequent fights in home.[81]

The fatalism and "limited horizons" of peasant women was often noted and attributed to the high incidence of child deaths. Rudolph Bell, in his study of a South Slavic village, noted that burying one's own child was an expected tragedy which contributed to the image of the world as a source of "limited good."[82] But infant mortality rates continued at a high level for Slavs in America. Positioned in squalid mill towns and coal mining districts, Slavs suffered from poor diets, unsanitary conditions, and subsequently, dying children. The infant mortality rate in the United States (children under one year of age) in 1917 was 94 per 100,000 population. Among Poles in Shenandoah, Pennsylvania it was 187 per 100,000. The average annual death rate from "diarrhea and enteritis" among children under two years of age in Shenandoah was 365.8 per 100,000 compared to 104.8 for all of Pennsylvania and 71.4 for the United States.[83]

In Johnstown, Pennsylvania, a center for Slavic steel workers and miners, Serbs and Croats had an infant mortality rate of 263.9, in 1912 compared to a rate of 124 for all persons in America. Indeed, the rate surpassed the 149 per 100,000 rate for Serbia itself between 1901 and 1905.[84] The fact that Serbian or Croatian women seldom had either a Physician or a midwife was as much a result of their low economic resources as it was their ignorance of modern medical practices. In fact, midwives were not usually affordable to South Slavs in Johnstown.[85]

As a result of the squalor and conditions of working class life, child death remained an expected tragedy. The notes from the Johnstown study were graphic:

"Mother aged 31 years; 10 pregnancies in 10 years; 8 live born; 2 still born; 4 deaths in first year."

"Mother aged 30 years; 9 pregnancies in 11 years; 8 live births, 1 miscarriage reported; 3 deaths in first year due to pneumonia; malarial fever and rheumatism."

"Mother aged 35 years; 6 births in 12 years; 4 live births and 2 still births. All live born died in first year.... SAYS SHE HAD ALWAYS WORKED TOO HARD, KEEPING BOARDERS IN THIS COUNTRY AND CUTTING WOOD AND CARRYING IT AND WATER ON HER BACK IN THE OLD COUNTRY .... Father furious because all babies die; wore red necktie to funeral of last to show his disrespect for wife who can only produce children that die."[86]

The behavioral patterns exhibited by Slavic newcomers can best be described as neither innovations nor residues of a previous culture. They must be judged a systhesis. Modernization involved a clash of peasant culture and working-class pragmatism which resulted in a reinforcement of traditional behavior and perceptions. If a preoccupation with security and survival was necessary in eastern Europe, working-class conditions in America did little to alter that fact. The sources of immigrant behavioral patterns were found in both worlds. While the peculiar constellation of symbolic traits which derived from Europe, such as religion and ethnic identification, gave the appearance of vast ethnic differences among Slavs, on a structured level the behavior of all Slavic peasants in America was remarkably similar and revealed an ability to integrate their culture with an emerging working-class consciousness. Limited occupational mobility in America reinforced the limited horizons of peasant Slovakia, Croatia, and Poland. The economic need to cling to steady work reinforced the traditional familial ties which mitigated against seeking individual careers far from home and demanded contributions from children fro family sustenance. The increased desire to retain ethnic culture and the anti-materialistic thrust of peasant life butressed the working-class skepticism of public schooling. The high incidence of child death from industrial squalor insured the continuation of the relationship between infant death and fatalism from eastern Europe. Without extensive social mobility within modern society, the simple transfer from premodern to modern society would not in itself effect drastic change.

Modernization could also result in a different chemistry depending on the background of newcomers who were subjected to its impact and particular structural situations. In Britain the initial impact off industrialization on skilled artisans evoked elements of pride, political action, and "class combativity." It was not until the late nineteenth century that this agressive working-class view gave way to a "conservative and defensive culture" which resembled that of Slavic peasants in America.[87] While Slavs in America were involved in several labor protests for increased wages, generally their conservative, defensive posture was evidenced soon after their arrival in the industrial milieu. Arriving with a strong, traditionalist curtural bent, the tiresome burden of working-class life, sustained by limited mobility through two generations, hastened the emergence of a "defensive posture." Looking at the process of modernization, a recent scholar has noted the reconstruction of tradition in modern societies. He points out that the process whereby the various dimensions of tradition became institutionalized "are in continuously close relation to the organizational aspects of the social division of labor in general"[88] The Slavic peasant who emigrated to the lower levels of the American social structure reconstructed his own world by fusing old and new behavioral strategies to meet the continuing demands of survival.

Pennsylvania Historical and Museum Commission   John Bodnar

FOOTNOTES

Research for this essay was supported by grants from the American Council of Learned Societies, the Immigration History Research Center, University of Minnesota, and the Pennsylvania Historical and Museum Commission. The author would like to thank professor David Montgomery for his valuable criticisms.

1. William J. Goode, *The Family* (Englewood Cliffs, N.J., 1964) and Oscar Handlin, *The Uprooted* (New York, 1951).

2. Joan W. Scott and Louise A. Tilly, "Women's Work and the Family in Nineteenth Century Europe," *Comparative Studies in Society and History*, XVII (Jan., 1975), 41-43, 55. For an elaboration of this discussion see Peter Stearns, "Working Class Women in Britain, 1890-1914," in *Suffer and Be Still*, Ed. by Martha Vicinus (Bloomington, Ind.,

1972), p. 104. Teodor Shanin, "The Peasantry as a Political Factor" in *Peasants and Peasant Society: Selected Readings,* Ed. by T. Shanin (Baltimore, 1971), 241-44.

3. Virginia Yans McLaughlin, "Patterns of Work and Family Organizations: Buffalo's Italians," *Journal of Interdisciplinary History,* II (Autumn, 1971), 299-314; Rudolph Vecoli, "Contadini in Chicago: A Critique of the Uprooted," *Journal of American History* (Dec., 1964), 404-16.

4. John Modell and Tamara K. Hareven, "Urbanization and the Malleable Household: An Examination of Boarding and Lodging in American Families," *Journal of Marriage and the Family,* (Aug., 1973), 467-78.

5. Bruce Laurie, Theodore Hershberg and George Alter, "Immigrants and Industry: The Philadelphia Experience, 1850-1880," *Journal of Social History,* IX (Dec., 1975), 231-43.

6. Frank Furstenberg, Theodore Hershberg, and John Modell, "The Origins of the Female-Headed Black Family: The Impact of the Urban Experience," *Journal of Interdisciplinary History,* VI (Fall, 1975), 232.

7. Hershberg, "Free Blacks in Antebellum Philadelphia: A Study of Ex-Slaves, Freeborn, and Socioeconomic Decline," *Journal of Social History,* 5, (Winter, 1971-72), 194-204.

8. Scott and Tilly, "Women's Work and the Family in Nineteenth Century Europe," 436-37; Yans McLaughlin, "A Flexible Tradition," 441-42.

9. See Joel M. Halpern, "Peasant Culture and Urbanization in Yugoslavia," in *Contributions to Mediterranean Sociology,* Ed. by J.G. Peristiany (The Hague, 1968), 293.

10. Helen S. Zand, "Polish Family Folkways," *Polish-American Studies,* XIII (July-December, 1956). Niles Carpenter and Daniel Katz, "A Study of Acculturation in the Polish Group of Buffalo, 1926-1928," *University of Buffalo Studies,* VII (June, 1929), 128-29.

11. Interviews with Sam Davich, Pittsburgh, June 24, 1974, Pittsburgh Oral History Project (POHP), reel 35; Michael Komernitski, McKees Rocks, June 17, 1974, POHP, reel 16; Joe Rudiak, Pittsburgh, July 21, 1974, POHP, reel 19; John Wolota, Pittsburgh, June 14, 1974, POHP, reel 14. All tapes used in this study are on file at the Pennsylvania Historical and Museum Commission. *The Report on Conditions of Women and Child Wage Earners in the United States, IV: The Silk Industry,* 61 Cong., 2nd sess., sen. doc. 645 (19 vols.; Washington, 1911), presents data on over 800 immigrant family incomes in Pennsylvania and New Jersey.

12. Howard Stein, "An Ethno-Historic Study of Slovak-American Identity, McKeesport, Pennsylvania," (unpublished Ph.D. dissertation, Univ. of Pittsburgh, 1972), pp. 417-437. Peter Ostafin, "The Polish Peasant in Transition: A Study of Group Integration as a Function of Symbiosis and Common Definitions," (unpublished Ph.D. dissertation, University of Michigan, 1948), pp. 200-210.

13. Stein, "An Ethno-Historic Study of Slovak-American Identity," 430-37; Kazimierz Dobrowolski, "Peasant Traditional Culture," *Peasants and Peasant Societies,* ed. by Teodor Shanin (Baltimore, 1971), pp. 280-85.

14. Vera St. Erlich, *Family in Transition, A Study of 300 Yugoslav Villages* (Princeton, N.J., 1966), 32. On the evolution of the Zadruga see Emile Sicard, "La Zadruga Sud-Slave dans l'Evolution du Groupe Domestique," (published Ph.D. dissertation, University of Clermont-Ferrand, Parris, 1943), 373-76. See also v. Kriskovic, *Hrvatsko Pravo Kucnih Zadruga: Listorijskodogmatski Nacrt* (Zagreb, 1925); *Definitivni Rezultati, Popisa Stonovnistva OK 31 Januara, 1921 God,* 254-55, 375-76. Fran Vrbanic, "One Hundred

Years of the Development of the Population of Croatia-Slavonia," Yugoslav Academy of Science and Art, *Rad*, CXL (Zagreb, 1899), 17-58. While some dispute exists over the existence of the classic zadruga in Slovenia, Slovene family structure was still essentially based on a "patriarchal, extended family" headed by a "gospodar." It is true that zadruga never flourished in Moslem districts. These districts, however, did not supply any significant amount of immigrants to immigrant centers such as Lackawanna, Gary, Steelton, or Pittsburgh. See Irene Winner, *A Slovenian Village, Zerovnica* (Providence, 1971) pp. 58-78. Joel M. Halpern, *A Serbian Village* (New York, 1958), pp. 135-37.

15. See table I. U.S. Immigration Commission, *Immigrants in Industry*, Part 23: Summary Report on Immigrants in Manufacturing and Mining Canals.; (Wash., 1911), II, 502-12.

16. Joseph Parot, "The American Faith and the Persistence of Chicago Polonia," (unpublished Ph.D. dissertation, Northern Illinois University, 1971).

17. Thaddeus Radzialowski, "The View from a Polish Ghetto," *Ethnicity*, I (July, 1974), 125-32.

18. Edward R. Kantowicz, *Polish-American Politics in Chicago, 1888-1940* (Chicago, 1975), pp. 26-27; Joseph Parot, "Ethnic versus Black Metropolis: The Origins of Polish-Black Housing Tensions in Chicago," *Polish-American Studies*, 29 (Spring-Autumn, 1972), 8-12.

19. Parot, "The American Faith and the Persistence of Chicago Polonia, 1870-1920," pp. 107-112; John Bodnar, "Steelton's Immigrants: Social Relationships in a Pennsylvania Mill Town," (unpublished Ph.D. dissertation, University of Connecticut, 1975), Chapter II; Joze Zavertnik, *Ameriski Slovenci* (Chicago, 1925), 448-506; Imrich Mazar, *Dejiny Binghamton Tonskych* Slovakov, 1879-1919 (Binghamton, N.Y., 1919). Timothy Smith, "Lay Initiative in the Religious Life of American Immigrants, 1880-1950," *Anonymous Americans*, ed. by Tamara Harven (Prentice-Hall, 1971), pp. 215-21.

20. F. Majer to *Dziennik Chicagoski*, Aug. 27, 1892, Chicago Foreign Language Press Survey (CFLPS), reel 49. July 22, 1892, p. 4; Aug. 27, 1892, CFLPS, reel 49. *Zgoda*, Nov. 14, 1894, p. 4; Jan. 19, 1899, p. 6.

21. *Dziennik Chicagoski*, June 6, 1896; Sep. 1, 1908, CFLPS, reel 49.

22. *Ibid.*, Jan. 3, 1928. The overtones of anti-semitism which prevaded the Polish ethnic community often focused on the alleged materialistic aims of the Jews, although Polish anti-semitism had deeper historical roots in Europe. See *Narod Polski*, Aug. 6, 1919, CFLPS, reel 49.

23. Ivan Kramoris, "The Slovak Immigrant Situation," *Jednota*, Apr. 19, 1934; p. 3 *Jednota*, June 10, 1936, p. 9. Jane Addams related the distress of a visiting Czech professor in Chicago over the "materialism" of America including a few Bohemians; see *Twenty Years at Hull House* (New York, 1910), p. 171. Slovaks expressed attitudes similar to Poles in steroty ping Jews as materialistic; see *Jednota*, Sep. 8, 1937, p. 3.

24. *Jednota*, Apr. 22, 1936, p. 9; May 8, 1936, pp. 8-9.

25. See table V.

26. See table VI.

27. See table VII.

28. 61 Cong., 3rd Sess., serial 5875, *The Children of Immigrants in Schools* (5 vols. Washington, 1911), V, 95, 515, 909.

29. Scott and Tilly, "Women's Work and Family in Nineteenth Century Europe," 48-49. Scott and Tilly found evidence of fiscal management by women in some premodern families but reliance on budgets and their control by women were certainly innovative for east European peasants.

30. Stein, "An Ethno-Historic Study of Slovak-American Identity," p. 426; Margaret Byington, Homestead: The Households of a Mill Town (New York, 1910), pp. 152-57 contains valuable data on Slavic family budgets. Interviews from the Scranton Oral History Project (1973) on establish and financial role of the Slavic female. See also Peter Roberts, *Anthracite Coal Communities* (New York, 1904) and Bessie Pehotsky, *The Slavic Immigrant Woman* (Cincinnati, 1925).

31. The only two statistical studies of Slavic mobility are Barton, *Peasants and Strangers*, 107-112 and Bodnar, "Steelton's immigrants: Social Relationships in a Pennsylvania Mill Towns," (unpublished Ph.D. dissertation, University of Connecticut, 1975). The following table is based on material from Barton, p. 107-112 and Bodnar, p. 212 and shows occupational mobility in Steelton, Pennsylvania and Cleveland, Ohio between 1905 and 1925 for Slavic and Italian immigrants:

INTERCLASS MOBILITY	Cleveland 1910-1920	Steelton 1905-1915	Steelton 1915-1925
% of Manual Workers Climbing	9%	5%	5%
% of White Collar Skidding	22%	3%	10%
Number	300	127	261

Examinations of intergenerational mobility among Slavic-Americans are found in Bodnar, "Steelton's Immigrant's," Chapter VII and Barton, *Peasants and Strangers*, pp. 107-112. The following table is drawn from the works cited above. The ratios for the intergenerational occupational mob9lity of Slavic and Italian sons in Steelton and Cleveland between 1920 and 1950 are:

	Cleveland (born 1901-10)	Cleveland (born 1911-20)	Steelton (born 1900-15)
% of Lower Class Origins Climbing	25%	30%	22%
% of Middle Class Origins Skidding	70%	50%	43%
Number	81	92	180

The National Opinion Research Center has found that the percentage of Slavs in American white collar jobs was lower than the percentage for all Protestant groups, Orientals, Jews, and Irish, German, and Italian Catholics; Greeley, *Ethnicity in the United States* (New York, 1974), pp. 42-43.

32. *Memorial Book, 25th Anniversary First Croatian Building and Loan Association, 1910-1935* (Chicago, 1935).

33. *Wiadomosci Codzienne,* Jan. 28, 1938, p. 6; Feb. 9, 1938, p. 2; Marie Prisland, *From Slovenia to America* (Chicago, 1968), pp. 78-87; *Zajednicar,* Apr. 26, 1939, p. 11; Jozep Pauco, *Slovenski Prieko/pnic v Americke* (Cleveland, 1972), pp. 38-40.

34. *Zogda,* July 19, 1893, p. 8.

35. *Majski Glas* (May Herald) (May, 1937), p. 17; see also *The New American*, III (May 1936), p. 1.

36. For a comparison of real estate value see U.S. Census, *Fifteenth Census of the United States, 1930, Special Report on Foreign Born White Families by Country of Birth* (Washington, 1933), pp. 155-73.

37. See Table II.

38. U.S. Census, *Fifteenth Census of the United States, VI: Families*, pp. 658-712.

39. See Table III.

40. See Table IV.

41. Bodnar, "Steelton's Immigrants," Chapter VI.

42. Poles in Philadelphia always identified themselves by their villages of birth; see Caroline Golab, "The Polish Communities of Philadelphia, 1870-1920: Immigrant Distribution and Adaptation in Urban America," (unpublished Ph.D. dissertation, Univ. of Pennsylvania, 1971), pp. 233-34. See also Franciszek Bujak, *Zmiaca-Wies Powiatu Limanowskiego: Stosunki Gospodarcze i Spoleczne* (Krakow, 1903); Bodnar, "Steelton's Immigrants," Chapter VI.

43. Victor L. Greene, "For God and Country: The Origins of Slavic Catholic Self-Consciousness in America," *Church History*, XXXV (Dec., 1966), 446. Greene after a study of Chicago Poles, concluded that America made its immigrants ethnocentric. Similar conclusions are found in Timothy Smith, "Religious Denominations as Ethnic Communities: A Regional Case Study," *Church History*, XXXV (June, 1966), 226; Richard Kornblum, *Blue Collar Community* (Chicago, 1974), pp. 35, 187; Bodnar, "The Formation of Ethnic Consciousness, Slavic Immigrants in Steelton," *The Ethnic Experience in Pennsylvania* (Lewisburg, Pa., 1973), pp. 309-330.

44. Essential to studying the formation of the Slovak community is Konstantine Culen, *Dejiny Slovakov v. Amerike* (2 vols; Bratislava, 1942), I, 190-210; Jozef Pauco, *75 Rokov Prvej Katolicej Katolicej Slovensej Jednoty* (Middleton, Pa., 1970), pp. 5-15 and "Kratka Historia Pennsylvanskej Slov Jednoty," in *Pennsylvania Slovak Catholic Union Diamond Jubilee* (Pittson, Pa., 1968).

45. Barton, "Immigration and Social Mobility in an American City: Studies of Three Ethnic Groups in Cleveland, 1890-1950," (unpublished Ph.D. dissertation, Univ. of Michigan. 1971), pp. 146-47.

46. Theodore Andrews, *The Polish National Church in America and Poland* (London, 1953), pp. 29-44; Paul Fox, *The Polish National Catholic Church* (Scranton, n.d.), pp. 24-25, 119; Leo V. Zrzywkowski, "The Origin of the Polish National Catholic Church of St. Joseph County, Indiana," (unpublished Ph.D. dissertation, Ball State Univ., 1972).

47. Parot, "The American Faith and the Persistence of Chicago Polonia, 1870-1920," pp. 310-36.

48. Michael Roman, "Istorija Greko-Kaft Sojedenija," *Golden Jubilee, 1892-1942* (Munhall, Pa., 1942), pp. 39-74. Stephen Gulovich, "Rusin Exarchate in the United States," *Eastern Churches Quarterly*, VI (Oct.-Dec., 1946), 463-72; Walter C. Warzeski, *Byzantine Rite Rusins in Carpatho-Ruthenia and America* (Pittsburgh, 1971), pp. 113-17, Bohadan Ukrainian Catholic Church in America (unpublished Ph.D. dissertation, Univ. of Ottawa, 1964).

49. H. R. Niebuhr, *The Social Sources of Denominationalism* (New York, 1929), pp. 223-24. Marshall Sklare, "The Ethnic Church and the Desire for Survival," in Peter I. Rose, *The Ghetto and Beyond* (New York, 1969), pp. 101-17.

50. *Novi Svijet*, Jan. 19, 1928, p. 3.

51. Dept. of Justice Papers, Board of Pardons, Clemency File, R.G. 56, Pennsylvania Historical and Museum Commussion. See Greene, *The Slavic Community on Strike* (Notre Dame, Ind., 1968), for an account of the Lattimer Massacre.

52. Johann Chemlar, "The Austrian Emigration, 1900-1914," in *Perspectives in American History*, VII (1973), 291-92, 341.

53. Joel M. Halpern, *A Serbian Village* (New York, 1958), p. 64. Eric Wolf, *Peasants* (Englewood Cliffs, N.J., 1966), pp. 65-70. Mary Matossian, "The Peasant Way of Life," in *The Peasant in Nineteenth-Century Russia*, ed. by Wayne S. Vucinich (Stanford, Cal., 1968), p. 39.

54. Irene Winner, *A Slovenian Village: Zerovnica* (Providence, 1971), pp. 108, 120-121.

55. Rudolph M. Bell, "The Transformation of a Rural Village: Istria, 1870-1972," *Journal of Social History*, 7 (Spring, 1974), 251-252. Mark Stolarik, "Immigration and Urbanization, The Slovak Experience, 1870-1918," published Ph.D. diss., Univ. of Minnesota, 1974, Chapter I. Stolarik deals with Slovak peasant transiency in Europe.

56. The concept of "limited good" was developed by George Foster, "Peasant Society and the Image of Limited Good," *American Anthropologist* 67 (April, 1965), 293-315. Foster's views are substantiated by Bell, "The Transformation of a Rural Village," 256-258. Both Bell and Foster emphasize the peasant's perception of "limited good." Sula Benet, trans. and ed., *The Village of Viratino*, (Garden City, N.Y., 1970), p. 107.

57. Interview with Zara Werlinich, Pittsburgh, Aug. 16, 1974, Pittsburgh Oral History Project (POHP), reel 3. This and all interviews used in this study were taped in Pennsylvania and are on file at the Pennsylvania Historical and Museum Commission. In addition to the author, interviews were conducted by Peter Gottlieb, Lynda Nyden, and Major Mason, all of the University of Pittsburgh, and Carl Romanek of The Pennsylvania State University at McKeesport.

58. Interview with Sam Vignovic, Pittsburgh, Aug. 6, 1974, POHP, reel 8.

59. Interviews with Anonymous, West Mifflin, Aug. 16, 1974, POHP, reel 2. George Hudock, Bethlehem, July 16, 1974, Bethlehem Oral History Project (BOHP), reels 3-4.

60. Interviews with Mike Palovich, Pittsburgh, Aug. 7, 1974, POHP, reel 20; Nick Winovich, Pittsburgh, Aug. 7, 1974, POHP, reel 8. A similar aspiration was made by an Illinois steel worker, Steve Dubi. He recalled: "When we were kids we we thought the steel mill was it. We'd see the men comin out, all dirty, black . . . . We thought they were strong men. We just couldn't wait to get in there." See Studs Terkel, *Working* (New York, 1974), p. 552.

61. Interviews with Valerian Duda, McKeesport, July 8, 1974, POHP, reel 36; Andrew Bodnar, Munhall, June 3, 1974, POHP, reel 25.

62. Interviews with Walter Balawajder, McKeesport, July 11, 1974, POHP, reel 16, similar experiences were encountered by Mike Backer, Glassport, June 24, 1974, POHP, reel 33; John Urczyk, McKees Rocks, June 27, 1974, POHP, reel 10.

63. In two-hundred interviews used in the preparation of this paper only ten immigrants ever indicated an attempt to leave their industrial pursuits to enter business for themselves. Mike Pavlovich, for instance, left the Jones and Laughlin Steel plant in 1912 and opened a small saloon in Pittsburgh. His venture failed after one year, however, and he returned to a mill job. Of those who did enter private business, several did so only upon retirement from industrial work. See interview with Mike Pavlovich, Pittsburgh, Aug. 7, 1974, POHP, reel 20.

64. Interview with Valentine Bauer, Bethlehem, July 24, 1974, BOHP, reel 13. Additional explanations of Slavic geographic mobility are detailed in all interviews but see especially the interview with Peter Hnat, McKees Rocks, June 26, 1974, POHP, reel 9.

65. See footnote 31.

66. All but two of the 115 immigrant sons interviewed in this study were born between 1902 and 1914.

67. Interviews with George Porvasnik, McKees Rocks, July 12, 1974, POHP, reel 21; Sam Davich, Pittsburgh, June 24, 1974, POHP, reel 17; Charles Jablonski, Bethlehem, July 11, 1974, BOHP, reel 5. Davich worked at Jones and Laughlin plant for forty years. Jablonski spent his last forty-six working years at Bethlehem Steel. A similar experience is related by Michael Zahorsky, Aliquippa, July 31, 1974, POHP, reel 7.

68. Interviews with Robert Milanovich, Pittsburgh, Aug. 5, 1974, POHP, reel 3; Sam Mervosh, Pittsburgh, Aug. 12, 1974, POHP, reel 18; Charles Jablonski, Bethlehem, July 11, 1974, BOHP, reel 5; Frank Horvath, Bethlehem, July 16, 1974, BOHP, reel 3. Another Bethlehem worker wanted only a "job he would like." See interview with Francis Vadaz, July 11, 1974, BOHP, reel 6.

69. Interviews with Jouis Buchek, McKees Rocks, July 17, 1974, POHP; reel 12; Joseph Wiatrak, McKees Rocks, July 1, 1974, POHP, reel 1; Lewis Kozo, Bethlehem, July 15, 1974, BOHP, reel 2; Sam Mervosh, Pittsburgh, Aug. 8, 1974, POHP, reel 18.

70. Interviews with Frank Horvath, Bethlehem, July 16, 1974, reel 3; Charles Jablonski, Bethlehem, July 11, 1974, BOHP, reel 5; Michael Komernitski, McKees Rocks, POHP, reel 16.

71. Interviews with Bernard Gorczyca, Pittsburgh, June 20, 1974, POHP, reel 4; Frank Horvath, Bethlehem, July 16, 1974, BOHP, reel 3.

72. Interviews with Anton Cindrich, Pittsburgh, June 25, 1974, POHP, reel 17. Similar statements were made by Walter Klis, Pittsburgh, July 2, 1974, POHP, reel 15.

73. Interview with J. Wolota, Pittsburgh, June 14, 1974, POHP, reel 14. See Geoffrey H Steers, "Child-rearing Literature and Modernization Theory," The Family in Historical Perspective, Newsletter, (Winter, 1974), pp. 8-9. Benjamin Spock, Baby and Child Care (New York, 1968), p. 12; Philip Slater, The Pursuit of Lonliness (Boston, 1970), pp. 62-64.

74. Interviews with John Smitko, McKeesport, June 22, 1974, POHP, reel 34. Southwestern Pennsylvania Oral History Project, Pennsylvania Historical and Museum Commissions, reels 110-115.

75. Interviews with Joseph Slater, Dravosburg, July 2, 1974, POHP, reel 35. Nick Kiak, Bethlehem, July 11, 1974, BOHP, reel 9.

76. Interviews with Sam Davich, Pittsburgh, June 24, 1974, POHP, reel 17; Michael Komernitski, McKees Rocks, June 17, 1974, POHP, reel 16; Joe Rudiak, Pittsburgh, July 21, 1974, POHP, reel 19; John Wolota, Pittsburgh, June 14, 1974, POHP, reel 14. Southwestern Pennsylvania Oral History Project, reels 110, 112, 113, 129.

77. Interviews with Michael Zahorsky, Aliquippa, June 21, 1974, POHP, reel 7; Frank Horvath, Bethlehem, July 16, 1974, POHP, reel 3.

78. Interviews with Michael Labeka, McKees Rocks, June 18, 1974, POHP, reel 4; Bernard Gorczyca, Pittsburgh, June 20, 1974, POHP. reel 15; Joe Rudiak, Pittsburgh, July 21, 1974, POHP, reel 19.

79. *Svoboda*, Aug. 26, 1932, p. 3; *Narodne Noviny*, Apr. 16, 1930, p. 3; July 22, 1931, p. 5. Stolarik, "Immigration and Urbanization," pp. 161-173. This evidence contradicts T.L. Smith, "Immigrant Social Aspirations and American Education, 1880-1930," *American Quarterly*, 21 (Fall, 1969); p. 525, who claims that the immigration experience of southern and eastern Europeans intensified the concern for learning. A recent study of Greek-American immigrants found that hard work was stressed more than education. See Nicholas Tavushis, *Family and Mobility Among Greek Americans*, (Athens, 1972). Colin Greer argued that immigrant children attended school extensively only *after* economic stability was attained. "Public education was the rubber stamp of economic improvement," he claimed, "rarely has it been the boot strap;" see Greer, ed., *Divided Society: The Ethnic Experience in America*, p. 89.

80. Bessie Olga Pehotsky, *The Slavic Immigrant Women* (Cincinnati, 1925), pp. 10-37; Caroline Manning, *The Immigrant Woman and Her Job* (Washington, 1930), pp. 104-106.

81. U.S. Dept. of Labor, Children's Bureau, Publication 9 (Washington, 1915), p. 32.

82. Rudolph M. Bell, "The Transformation of a Rural Village: Istria, 1870-1920," *Journal of Social History*, 7 (Spring, 1974), 251-52; Irene Winner, *A Slovenian Village: Zerovnica* (Providence, 1971), pp. 230-39. Mary Matossian, "The Peasant Way of Life," in *The Peasant in Nineteenth-Century Russia*, ed. by Wayne Vucinich, (Stanford, Cal., 1968), p. 29.

83. U.S. Dept. of Labor, Children's Bureau, Publication 106 (Washington, 1922), p. 47.

84. U.S. Dept. of Labor, Children's Bureau, Publication 9 (Washington, 1915), pp. 11-12, 28.

85. *Ibid.*, pp. 13-16.

86. *Ibid.*, pp. 31-82. Similar findings can be found in studies of Gary, Indiana in Publication 12 (Washington, 1922), pp. 38-109. Emphasis is mine.

87. See E.P. Thompson, *The Making of the English Working Class* (New York, 1966), p. 832; Gareth Steadman Jones, "Working Class Culture and Working Class Politics in London, 1870-1900: Notes on the Remaking of a Working Class," *Journal of Social History*, 7 (Summer, 1974), 484.

88. S.N. Eisenstadt, "Post-Traditional Societies and the Continuity and Reconstruction of Tradition," *Daedalus*, 102 (Winter, 1973), 18.

Table 1. Family Structure in Selected Cities, 1880-1925[a]

	South Slavs, Lackawanna, 1925	North Slavs, Hungarians, Lackawanna, 1925	Southern Born Blacks, Boston, 1880	Italians New York City, 1905	Welsh, Scranton, 1880
Nuclear	30%	69%	56 %	59.9%	83%
Extended	34%	20%	10.6%	23.2%	3%
Augmented	60%	23%	33.3%	21.1%	14%
Number of Household	220	480		3,584	227

[a]Source: New York State Census for Lackawanna, 1925; Elizabeth Pleck, "The Two-Parent Household: Black Family Structure in Late-Nineteenth Century Boston," *Journal of Social History*, VI, (Fall, 1972), 21; Herbert Gutman, "Work, Culture, and Society in Industrializing America, 1815-1919," *American Historical Review*, LXXVIII (June, 1973), 588; John Bodnar, "Socialization and Adaptation: The Immigrant Families of Scranton," *Pennsylvania History*, XLIII (January, 1976).

Table 2[a]. Percentage of Foreign-Born Family Heads Owning Homes, Urban Areas, 1930

City	F = B Families	F = B % Owners: City	England	Ireland	Italy	Czechoslovakia	Poland	Yugoslav
Akron	13,014	68%	64%	—	68%	84%	70%	—
Bridgeport	18,109	35%	24%	40%	37%	39%	34%	—
Chicago	357,519	42%	31%	—	40%	54%	49%	41%
Cleveland	99,395	50%	38%	52%	—	65%	54%	49%
Buffalo	49,606	51%	37%	56%	45%	54%	58%	—
Toledo	14,399	69%	59%	75%	—	69%	81%	—
Milwaukee	47,393	58%	36%	33%	—	63%	70%	52%
Detroit	145,593	51%	41%	50%	—	59%	69%	54%

[a]Source: Fifteenth Census of the United States, 1930, Special Report on Foreign-Born White Families By Country of Birth (Washington, 1933), 155-73.

Table 3. Slavic Homeownership in Pennsylvania, 1930[a]

	Penna.	Aliquippa	Braddock	Duquesne	Farrell	Homestead	Johnstown
Families	2,235,620	5,271	4,081	4,473	2,973	4,346	15,042
% Owners	54%	45%	24%	42%	49%	31%	40%
% Native Owners (White)	54%	39%	18%	33%	34%	23%	35%
% Foreign-born Owners	60%	54%	33%	54%	63%	46%	51%
Largest F = B Group[b]	Slavic	Serbo-Croat	Slovak	Slovak	Serbo-Croat	Slovak	Slovak

	Shenandoah	Steelton	Wilkes-Barre	Mount Carmel	Munhall	Nanticoke
Families	4,438	2,974	18,718	3,760	2,963	5,378
% Owners	35%	49%	45%	47%	65%	45%
% Native Owners (White)	27%	43%	33%	37%	55%	23%
% Foreign-born Owners	41%	69%	57%	72%	78%	57%
Largest F = B Group	Polish	Serbo-Croat	Polish	Polish	Slovak	Polish

[a]Computed from U.S. Census, *Fifteenth Census of the United States, VI: Families*, 658-712.

[b]Slavs formed about 50 percent of the foreign-born population of Pennsylvania in 1930. Poles and Slovaks accounted for the largest number of Slavs.

89

Table 4. Homeownership in Selected Towns, 1930[a]

	Cicero, Ill.	Lorain, Ohio	Lackawanna, N.Y.	New Britain, Conn.
Families	16,255	10,167	4,357	15,534
% Owners	55%	58%	43%	35%
% Native Owners (White)	22%	48%	40%	32%
% Foreign-born Owners	67%	69%	53%	40%
Largest F = B Group	Czech-Polish	Slovak-Polish	Polish-Serbo-Croat	Polish-Italian

[a]Computed from U.S. Census, *Fifteenth Census of the United States, VI: Families*, 233, 366-78, 939.

Table 5[a]. Public School Attendance of Native & Immigrant Children Beyond Grade 6, 1910

	NBW	Negro	Hebrew German	Hebrew Polish	Irish	South Italian	Polish	Slovak	
Buffalo	31%	18%	40%	39%	32%	10%	6%	—	Croat 6% Slovene 8%
Chicago	24%	15%	26%	20%	19%	5%	6%	4%	Slovene 7%
Cleveland	26%	17%	31%	23%	24%	7%	7%	5%	
Milwaukee	23%	16%	—	—	25%	2%	10%	—	
New Britain	40%	—	—	—	61%	—	6%	—	
Scranton				22%		11%	4%	5%	
Shenandoah	16%	—	—	—	28%	—	1%	—	

[a]Statistics computed from 61 Cong., 3rd sess.; serial 5875, *The Children of Immigrants in Schools* (5 vols., Washington, 1911), II, 378, 648, 848, IV, 7, 477, V, 418, 508.

Table 6ª. High School Attendance, Native & Immigrant Children, 1910.

	NBW	Negro	Hebrew German	Hebrew Polish	Hebrew Russian	Irish	South Italian	Polish	Slovak
Buffalo	12%	8%	19%	16%	—	13%	3%	2%	—
Chicago	9%	5%	10%	6%	—	6%	1%	1%	1 %
Cleveland	12%	8%	13%	7%	—	11%	1%	2%	.5%
Milwaukee	10%	9%	—	—	3%	12%	1%	2%	—
New Britain	19%	—	—	9%	—	43%	—	1%	—

ªStatistics computed from 61 Cong., 3rd sess.; serial 5875 (5 vols., Washington, 1911), II, 378, 648, 848; IV, 77, 477; V, 418, 508.

Table 7ª. Parochial School Attendance by Ethnic Group Beyond Grade 6

	Native-born white	Irish	Polish	Slovak
Milwaukee	14.9%	10%	1.6%	0%
New Britain	22 %	26%	0 %	—
Cleveland	17 %	19%	5 %	10%

ª61st Cong., 3rd sess., serial 5875, *The Children of Immigrants in Schools* (5 vols.; Washington, 1911), pp. 95, 515, 909.

91

Migration, Kinship, and Urban Adjustment: Blacks and Poles in Pittsburgh, 1900-1930

John Bodnar, Michael Weber, and Roger Simon

The early decades of the twentieth century witnessed the initial confrontation on a large scale of Afro-Americans and European immigrants with the American city. Since both of these groups migrated primarily from rural to urban areas, historians and sociologists have compared their experiences. Many have concluded that any economic disadvantages endured by blacks took place simply because they were "the last of the immigrants." Eventually they would experience the same economic advancement all immigrant groups were assumed to have made. Like most generalizations, however, this one was seldom based on detailed, systematic analysis, especially at a disaggregate level. This view, moreover, did a disservice to the historical interpretation of both the black and immigrant encounters with urban life, for it obscured the variety of adaptive measures different ethnic groups assumed in the urban milieu and it underestimated the impact of established racial and ethnic stereotypes which affected both groups of newcomers.

Existing interpretations of urban migration and adaptation for blacks and immigrants usually fall between two extremes. For some historians the urban environment was essentially destructive and resulted in poverty, familial disorganization, a separation between work and family interests, and the abandonment of premigration behavioral patterns. The theory of "ethnic succession," a widely employed model in explaining the adaptation of various ethnic groups to urban America, rested partially upon this assumption. It saw a direct correlation between adaptation and length of residency in the city. Recent arrivals would fill the lower jobs and homes of older residents who moved upward and outward.[1] In time urbanization would inevitably eradicate

John Bodnar is chief, division of history, at the Pennsylvania Historical and Museum Commission. Michael Weber is associate professor of urban history at Carnegie-Mellon University. Roger Simon is associate professor of history at Lehigh University. Reginald Baker of the University of Pittsburgh provided assistance in computerizing census data. Research for this paper was supported by the Rockefeller Foundation and the Pennsylvania Historical and Museum Commission.

[1] The classic statement of this view is Paul Frederick Cressey, "Population Succession in Chicago: 1898-1930," *American Journal of Sociology*, LXIV (July 1938), 61. Cressey's view is

premigration cultures and effect an accommodation of the migrant with the urban society. This model implied that adjustment and integration were inevitable. Sociologists who accepted this model frequently noted the special difficulties of Afro-Americans but resorted to the recency of their arrival from preurban settings as an explanation. Some felt Afro-Americans would eventually experience the same accommodation that previous immigrants had. More recently, however, historians have suggested that the earlier immigrants benefited from the pervasive racism of society and advanced occupationally and socially in American cities only at the expense of Afro-Americans.[2] The findings of the Philadelphia Social History Project have especially emphasized the destructive impact of the urban experience as an explanation of black behavior and persistence in poverty. The project's publications have denied the significance of such variables as preurban culture. Black families suffered in the city, for instance, because of high mortality rates among males. Black workers, moreover, were unable to overcome racial hostility and pass job skills to their children. Urban racism and structural inequality were also found to have had a greater impact on blacks than the preindustrial legacy of slavery.[3]

An alternative interpretation of movement and adaptation to urban America rests upon the assumption that premigration culture and values persisted in the cities and withstood the disintegrating impact of city life. This widely held approach emphasized race and ethnicity as independent variables which accounted for dissimilar patterns of urban adaptation. Josef Barton, in a recent study of Cleveland, explained the divergent patterns of immigrant mobility among Slovaks, Rumanians, and Italians in terms of their respective ethnic backgrounds and orientations. Victor Greene's account of Poles in Chicago interpreted Polish behavior on the basis of a search for traditional objectives of religion and land. Helena Lopata argued that Polish behavior in America is to be understood in terms of status competition which originated in peasant Poland. Thus, young Poles would be eager to get a mill job because of the value placed upon hard work within the Polish community. Herbert Gutman has emphasized the continuity in the black family during migration from the rural South to the urban North. Gutman in particular stressed the persistence of black kinship ties, but neither he nor the others closely examined the manner in which immigrants and their families functioned during migration and initial settlement in the city. Similarly, a study of New York City concluded

modified by Thomas Kessner, *The Golden Door: Italian and Jewish Immigrant Mobility in New York City, 1880-1915* (New York, 1977), 156-60. Believing that Cressey's view of ethnic settlement was too static, Kessner stressed continual turnover within immigrant communities. See also Humbert Nelli, *The Italians in Chicago, 1880-1930: A Study in Ethnic Mobility* (New York, 1970), 45-48; W. Lloyd Warner and Leo Srole, *The Social Systems of American Ethnic Groups* (New Haven, 1945), 2; Stephan Thernstrom, *The Other Bostonians: Poverty and Progress in the American Metropolis, 1880-1970* (Cambridge, 1973), 176-77; Thomas Sowell, *Race and Economics* (New York, 1975), 149-50.

[2] See Thernstrom, *Other Bostonians*, 177-78, 186-87.

[3] Frank Furstenberg, Jr., Theodore Hershberg, and John Modell, "The Origins of the Female-Headed Black Family: The Impact of the Urban Experience," *Journal of Interdisciplinary History*, VI (Autumn 1975), 232; Theodore Hershberg, "Free Blacks in Antebellum Philadelphia: A Study of Ex-Slaves, Freeborn, and Socioeconomic Decline," *Journal of Social History*, 5 (Winter 1971-1972), 192-204.

that the cultural backgrounds of Italian and Jewish immigrants explained their differential patterns of mobility.[4]

A more balanced portrait of urban adaptation—one which acknowledges the complexity of the process—is found in the work of Robert L. Crain and Carol Sachs Weisman. Basing their analysis on detailed survey interviews, they found that the view of the unstable black family in northern ghettos was overly simplistic. To be sure, a high rate of marital instability was found among blacks, but no evidence of intergenerational transfer of such instability was discovered. For instance, daughters from broken homes were not more likely to initiate divorce in their own homes. In other words, the urban experience, at least for blacks, was not simply a question of destruction or cultural persistence but involved complex and specific reactions to particular circumstances. Data in recent historical works further suggests that adaptation was considerably more involved than the sweeping generalizations of the past have indicated. Research has demonstrated that Jews were more upwardly mobile than Italians, Rumanians manifested higher educational aspirations than Slovaks, and women were less likely to work outside the home in an Italian than in a Polish family. Dissimilarity was never more evident than when immigrants were compared with blacks. The intensity of racism directed toward blacks was unparalleled. Immigrants encountered a degree of hostility themselves. Precisely how both these groups interacted with a racially biased urban society is still unclear, however. Few examinations exist which attempt to go beyond "ethnic succession" or "premigration culture" as explanations for the process of urban adaptation and confront the complex interplay between migrants and the city they encountered.[5]

[4] Josef J. Barton, *Peasants and Strangers: Italians, Rumanians, and Slovaks in an American City, 1890–1950* (Cambridge, 1975), 54, 89–90; Victor Greene, *For God and Country: The Rise of Polish and Lithuanian Ethnic Consciousness in America, 1860–1910* (Madison, Wisc., 1975), 28–29, 35–36; Herbert G. Gutman, *The Black Family in Slavery and Freedom, 1750–1925* (New York, 1976), 450–52; Elizabeth Pleck, "The Two-Parent Household: Black Family Structure in Late Nineteenth-Century Boston," *Journal of Social History*, 6 (Fall 1972), 3–31; Sowell, *Race and Economics*, 144–45. See also Helena Znaniecki Lopata, *Polish Americans: Status Competition in an Ethnic Community* (Englewood Cliffs, N.J., 1976), 4; Kessner, *Golden Door*, 24–43; Virginia Yans-McLaughlin, *Family and Community: Italian Immigrants in Buffalo, 1880–1930* (Ithaca, N.Y., 1977), 55–81.

[5] Robert L. Crain and Carol Sachs Weisman, *Discrimination, Personality, and Achievement: A Survey of Northern Blacks* (New York, 1972), 10–18, 103–08, 120–23; Kessner, *Golden Door*, 111; Barton, *Peasants and Strangers*, 48–63, 125; Yans-McLaughlin, *Family and Community*, 203–10; Thernstrom, *Other Bostonians*, 176–77; John Bodnar, *Immigration and Industrialization: Ethnicity in an American Mill Town, 1870–1940* (Pittsburgh, 1977), 73, 136–37. For other comparisons of the black and immigrant experience, see Joseph S. Roucek and Francis J. Brown, "The Problem of the Negro and European Immigrant Minorities: Some Comparisons and Contrasts," *Journal of Negro Education*, 8 (July 1939), 299–312. Roucek and Brown argued that immigrants were more optimistic than blacks. See also John J. Appel, "American Negro and Immigrant Experience: Similarities and Differences," *American Quarterly*, XVIII (Spring 1966), 95–103; Charles H. Wesley, *Negro Labor in the United States, 1850–1925: A Study in American Economic History* (New York, 1927), 75–78, 199; Timothy L. Smith, "Native Blacks and Foreign Whites: Varying Responses to Educational Opportunity in America, 1880–1950," *Perspectives in American History*, VI (1972), 309–35; John R. Commons, *Races and Immigrants in America* (New York, 1907), 147–52. Comparisons of Irish and blacks can be found in Oscar Handlin, *Boston's Immigrants,*

This essay examines the differential pattern of urban adaptation by concentrating on the actual process of moving to the city and securing work. Premigration backgrounds and the harsh effects of lower-class urban life were certainly important, but until the actual mechanics of migration and settlement are clarified, dissimilar patterns of behavior and adjustment for various ethnic groups cannot be fully explained. Urban adaptation will be analyzed by comparing the migration experiences, socialization practices, and occupational mobility patterns of Poles and blacks in Pittsburgh between 1900 and 1930. Explanations for their respective patterns will be offered not only to explain the difference between immigrant and black patterns of adjustment but also to suggest the pernicious effects of urban racism.

This analysis is based upon ninety-four oral history interviews conducted among Polish immigrants and black migrants in Pittsburgh who came before 1917. In addition, we have taken a 20 percent random sample of Christian Polish and black families in Pittsburgh from the 1900 United States census manuscripts. All wards were sampled except for several with extremely small numbers of immigrants or blacks. Although the census did not give information on religion, it was possible to separate Jewish and Christian Poles by using first names and known information about wards which were heavily Jewish. Other sources clearly suggest that Jews did not name their children John, Stanislaus, Cazimir, or Thaddeus. Even more strikingly, Christian Poles did not name their children Abraham, Isaac, Moses, Rebecca, Miriam, or Ruth. A few names, such as Joseph, were common to both groups, but the manuscripts listed entire families. Thus it was not difficult to determine which were the Jewish families. This method is similar to that used by Thomas Kessner in his recent study of Jews and Italians in New York.[6]

Opinion concerning early black migration from the south is diverse. According to observers such as Carter Woodson, the initial wave of black migrants was composed mostly of "talented" blacks who were "higher" in education and aspirations than the mass of poor Afro-Americans who composed the bulk of migrants before World War I. A study of Detroit concluded that early migrants were primarily those disillusioned by the deprivation of black political rights in the South. Some investigators have modified Woodson's views, but nearly all have agreed with Gunnar Myrdal that a desire for economic and social betterment was the chief motive for migration.[7]

1790-1865: A Study in Acculturation (Cambridge, 1941), 137, 213, 221; Niles Carpenter, Nationality, Color, and Economic Opportunity in the City of Buffalo (Buffalo, 1927), 190–91; J. Iverne Dowie, "The American Negro: An Old Immigrant on a New Frontier," in In the Trek of the Immigrants: Essays Presented to Carl Wittke, ed. O. Fritiof Ander (Rock Island, Ill., 1964), 241–60; Gilbert Osofsky, Harlem, the Making of a Ghetto: Negro New York, 1890-1930 (New York, 1966), 34–40.

[6] Kessner, Golden Door, 179–80.

[7] Carter G. Woodson, A Century of Negro Migration (Washington, 1918), 36, 147–66; David M. Katzman, Before the Ghetto: Black Detroit in the Nineteenth Century (Urbana, Ill., 1973), 64; Florette Henri, Black Migration: Movement North, 1900-1920 (Garden City, 1975), 152–53, 352; Gunnar Myrdal, Richard Sterner, and Arnold Rose, An American Dilemma: The Negro Problem and Modern Democracy (New York, 1944), 191–97; U.S. Dept. of Labor, Negro Migrations in 1916-1917 (Washington, 1919).

Black movement from the South followed a classic migratory pattern of increasingly widening circles away from home in search of cash employment. At first the migration was brief; then it became seasonal, and eventually permanent, as the migrants strayed farther and farther from home. Clyde Kiser discovered that permanent migration from St. Helena Island, South Carolina, to New York City was preceded by temporary migration to nearby cities such as Savannah. Usually a father or other family member would seek temporary work outside the island in order to supplement agricultural income and allow most of the family to remain intact at home. These short-term movements not only provided additional income but familiarized blacks with wage labor and broader possibilities beyond farming.[8]

That early black migration is explained by the gradual movement of southern blacks from farms rather than an escape of the "talented tenth" was confirmed in oral interviews conducted between 1974 and 1976 among forty-seven migrants who came to Pittsburgh before 1917. Most Afro-Americans interviewed in Pittsburgh were raised on small farms in Alabama, Georgia, and Virginia. Migrants recalled their parents working as sharecroppers for larger farmers, who were in a few instances black. About one-fifth of the respondents came from farms owned by their fathers.

Common to most personal histories was the temporary departure of the male from the household in search of supplemental wages. Carrie J. recalled that a white owner frequently cheated her sharecropper father. Several times he was even denied his extra bale of cotton at Christmas. Such exploitation created economic difficulties which forced him to obtain a garbage collection job in Fitzgerald, Georgia.[9] The father of Olive W. first left sharecropping in Georgia to tap turpentine. Several years later he moved to a neighboring town to work in a sawmill. William H. recalled that his father, who owned his own farm, traveled from Alabama to a Georgia sawmill when farm work was "slack." Floyd T. had a father who left their family-owned Virginia farm to earn wages "driving" in Roanoke. Ben E. remembered his father leaving their Alabama farm to work on the railroad for "long periods of time." His father even spent some time in Pittsburgh before returning from one trip. It was no accident that Ben, who moved to the Steel City at age eighteen, or other respondents eventually came North. Their parents had already provided a glimpse of industrial wages and broader horizons.[10]

[8] Clyde Vernon Kiser, *Sea Island to City: A Study of St. Helena Islanders in Harlem and Other Urban Centers* (New York, 1932), 149–52.

[9] Carrie J. interview by Peter Gottlieb, July 23, 1976, tape recording, Pittsburgh Oral History Project (Pennsylvania Historical and Museum Commission, Harrisburg). The oral histories used in this study are drawn from a larger oral project on Poles, Italians, and Afro-Americans in the Pittsburgh area conducted between 1974 and 1978. A questionnaire developed by the project director, John Bodnar, was used in all interviews to insure the comparability of data. A copy of the questionnaire and all tapes are available at the Pennsylvania Historical and Museum Commission.

[10] Olive W. interview by Gottlieb, July 23, 1976, tape recording, Pittsburgh Oral History Project; William H. interview by Gottlieb, June 17, 1976, *ibid.*; Floyd T. interview by Gottlieb, May 11, 1976, *ibid.*; Ben E. interview by Gottlieb, July 31, 1974, *ibid.* A small stream of Pittsburgh blacks left Texas and Arkansas, moved to Gary and Chicago, and eventually secured work in Pittsburgh. See Florence W. interview by John Bodnar, July 27, 1976, *ibid.*; Walter M. interview by Bodnar, July 28, 1977, *ibid.*

Often temporary toil stretched into periods of longer duration. Hezikiah M. was born in Louisa County, Virginia, in 1886. His parents had been slaves in Louisa County and by 1880 had only twenty acres of "poor land" growing mostly vegetables for the consumption of their fourteen children. When his father heard of "higher and regular" wages in West Virginia coal mines, he temporarily left his wife and children. Hezikiah recalled that his father returned about twice annually to bring much needed wages. In the meantime, his mother raised the children and earned extra money by taking in laundry work. When he was thirteen, Hezikiah and his brothers were taken by their father to Sunswitch, West Virginia, to load coal. Living in shanties with older men, Hezikiah worked the mines for four years and then left for a series of jobs in hotel kitchens which eventually brought him to Pittsburgh.[11]

Essential to the process of migration was information on job availability and wages. As with other immigrant groups, blacks relied on informal networks of kin. This continued reliance on family supports Gutman's notion that various aspects of black kinship endured during slavery and later urbanization. He argued that the adversity which blacks faced during the late eighteenth and early nineteenth centuries continued to nurture a reliance on kin. A similar dependency upon kin was clearly evident in at least the initial phase of the migration process.[12]

The movement of friends and kin from southern farms generated informal dissemination of knowledge about industrial employment. As a teenager Jean B. began working at a sawmill near Mobile, Alabama, while living on his parents' farm. It was at the sawmill that he heard mention of Philadelphia, New York, and Chicago. Such conversation prompted him to come north. He decided upon Pittsburgh because of information supplied by two friends already living there. After saving forty-five dollars, he took a train from Mobile through Cincinnati to Pittsburgh, where his friends obtained a room for him.[13] William H. was working for a railroad in Alabama. His wife's uncle, who had worked in coal mines near Pittsburgh, informed him of higher wages. Although he initially intended to seek employment in the mines, a friend in Pittsburgh drew him to the Jones and Laughlin Steel plant where wages appeared even "better." Another black, who preferred to remain anonymous, told how his father became dissatisfied with his career of "hiring out" from farm to farm in Virginia. He decided to come to Pittsburgh in 1902, where he gained "permanent" work and later brought his family. Several relatives "on his mother's side" followed his father to Pittsburgh, lived with him until they found work, and then moved out.[14] Similar experiences were related by other migrants. James N. learned of larger opportunities and wages while periodically working as a "sawmill man" and in an Alabama steel mill. James eventually followed a younger brother to Pittsburgh's Hill District where he cor-

[11] Hezikiah M. interview by Gottlieb, Oct. 8, 1976, tape recording, Pittsburgh Oral History Project.

[12] Gutman, *Black Family*, 455.

[13] Jean B. interview by Gottlieb, June 29, 1976, tape recording, Pittsburgh Oral History Project.

[14] William H. interview. See also Edgar P. interview by Bodnar, August 14, 1977, tape recording, Pittsburgh Oral History Project.

rectly recalled a neighborhood teeming with Jews, Italians, and blacks. Another black woman recalled following brothers to Pittsburgh and settling in "Jewtown."[15] Olive W. settled in the Mount Washington section because her husband had relatives there. She eventually brought a sister to Pittsburgh to live with her in 1920.[16]

Kinship and friendship ties, however, were considerably less effective in helping newly arrived Negroes acquire industrial jobs. This is not to say that blacks were completely unable to offer assistance in getting work. The Pittsburgh Survey (1907-1908) described an exceptional cluster of black steelworkers at the Clark Mills of the Carnegie Steel Company. This group had worked as hod carriers or on the railroad before coming to Pittsburgh. The fact that over 61 percent of the group was from Virginia suggested the existence of a form of chain migration. However, these incidents were rare.[17]

In fact, a key role in hiring newcomers in Pittsburgh mills and plants, as elsewhere in American industry, was performed by white foremen, usually of English, Scottish, Irish, or German extraction. Furthermore, nearly every investigation of early-twentieth-century Pittsburgh depicted the stereotypical outlooks of these influential men. Southern-born blacks were particularly unwanted because they were thought to be "inefficient," "unstable," and unsuitable for the heavy pace of mill work.[18] By contrast, Slavs were actually preferred to both blacks and native whites because of their assumed docility and "habit of silent submission, their amenability to discipline, and their willingness to work long hours and overtime without a murmur." One foreman, interviewed by the Pittsburgh Survey, commented about Slavs: "Give them rye bread, a herring, and beer, and they are all right." Whether any validity could be attached to these views is not as important as their existence. Both groups were the objects of a condescending racism, but Slavic newcomers such as the Poles benefited from this discrimination in that they were able to secure work not only for themselves but for their children. By 1910 they were no longer depending on the American foremen for work; superintendents routinely allowed immigrants to hire their own relatives and friends.[19]

Largely as a result of the foremen's hostility, the black work force in Pittsburgh before 1917 was widely distributed throughout various industries and

[15] James N. interview by Gottlieb, June 28, 1976, tape recording, Pittsburgh Oral History Project; Queen W. interview by Gottlieb, Oct. 8, 1976, *ibid.*; Anonymous interview by John Bodnar, Aug. 11, 1977, *ibid.* Some black women found "day work" from Jewish families in the city.

[16] Olive W. interview; Walter M. interview. The importance of kinship in the urban migration process is discussed more fully in Charles Tilly and C. Harold Brown, "On Uprooting, Kinship, and the Auspices of Migration," *International Journal of Comparative Sociology*, 8 (Sept. 1967), 139-64. See also Arthur F. Raper, *Preface to Peasantry: A Tale of Two Black Belt Counties* (Chapel Hill, 1936), 71, for a discussion of black migration from Georgia in the 1930s. Although covering a later period than this study, Raper noticed the continuing relationship between kinship and migration.

[17] R. R. Wright, Jr., "One Hundred Negro Steel Workers," in *Wage Earning Pittsburgh*, ed. Paul Underwood Kellogg (New York, 1914), 97-104.

[18] Abraham Epstein, *The Negro Migrant in Pittsburgh* (Pittsburgh, 1918), 30-34; Emmett J. Scott, *Negro Migration during the War* (New York, 1920), 125.

[19] Peter Roberts, "Immigrant Wage-Earners," in *Wage Earning Pittsburgh*, ed. Kellogg, 37-41.

TABLE 1

Industrial Employment of Adult Males by Ethnicity, Pittsburgh, 1900

Industry	Southern-born Black	Russian Pole	Austrian Pole	German Pole
Labor	39.9%	54.8%	42.4%	34.8%
Metal	10.8%	19.1%	47.5%	43.7%
Commerce	1.4%	11.0%	1.0%	4.1%
Construction	2.6%	1.6%	2.0%	2.6%
Transportation	12.3%	3.6%	4.0%	2.6%
Public Service	7.2%	0.6%	1.0%	1.5%
Domestic Service	11.0%	0.5%	0.0%	0.7%
Other	14.8%	8.8%	2.1%	10.0%
N	1165	651	99	292

Source: U.S. Bureau of the Census, Manuscript Schedules of Population, 1900, Pittsburgh, RG 29 (National Archives). Sample data. All employed males age sixteen and over are included. The classification "labor" is taken from the manuscript census schedules. Some of these individuals probably worked in the metal industries. Other sources, however, indicate that few of them were black.

was not particularly concentrated, as were some immigrant groups, in a few occupations. Table 1, drawn from our 20 percent sample, shows that blacks were distributed more widely than the sample of Poles.

The failure of blacks to establish occupational networks in the steel industry was apparent. Only 10.8 percent of southern-born blacks were in the metal industries while nearly 40 percent were scattered through general labor occupations such as hod carrier or day laborer. Blacks were also found in substantial numbers in transportation (teamster, drayman), public service (barber, waiter), and domestic service (porter, janitor, servant). Poles, in contrast, were almost completely unrepresented in service and transportation jobs. Austrian and German Poles clearly funneled their incoming migrants into metal production. Not surprisingly, a federal survey several years after 1900 noticed that blacks in Pittsburgh had established themselves in a variety of occupational enclaves. The report noted "quite a hundred" blacks in business as printers, grocers, hairdressers, and restaurant owners. About one-half of the "drivers" in the city were black.[20]

By 1910 blacks remained scattered throughout the occupational spectrum and had still not permeated the steel industry. Only 507 blacks were found among 19,686 men working in Pittsburgh's blast furnaces and rolling mills. Of nearly 10,000 "clerks" in the city only 87 were black. Immigrants remained clustered in one specific category—laborers in blast furnaces and rolling mills. Blacks were widely distributed in occupations such as janitors, draymen,

[20] U.S. Congress, 62 Cong., 1 sess., Serial 6082, *Cost of Living in American Towns* (Washington, 1911), 338–39.

teamsters, and domestic servants.[21] One contemporary observer even thought such variety was encouraging and a sign of advancement.[22]

The hiring practices that closed blacks out of the large and highly organized industries meant that kin and friends were unreliable in aiding blacks in securing work once in the city. Being widely scattered through the work force, especially among numerous small-scale firms, meant blacks in Pittsburgh had little influence in procuring positions for kin back home. More than other groups, blacks were on their own in finding work. This is confirmed by the oral data.

Interviews revealed that Afro-American migrants to Pittsburgh usually had to procure work on their own and were only occasionally able to rely on kin or friends for employment. Ben E. followed his father to a coal mine, worked there for six months, and then decided to leave for Pittsburgh. Although he had friends in the city, he was forced to find work on his own as a limestone loader at the American Steel and Wire Company. When work was slack, he obtained employment himself in a Kentucky coal mine and, after returning to the city, at the Jones and Laughlin Steel plant's boiler department. His experience was not unique. Jean B. simply persisted in talking a foreman into hiring him on a labor gang. Some started businesses of their own. Gertrude D. testified that her husband began by contracting his own work as a plasterer. Another migrant hired himself out to contractors as a cement finisher, wallpaper hanger, and plasterer. Floyd T. started a small trucking and hauling concern with his brother. Hezikiah M. told of his brother who opened a small print shop.[23]

Without other means of assistance, black migrants developed strategies for dealing with white foremen, which frequently included boastful claims of work abilities. The fact that blacks were forced to resort to such practices is further evidence that foremen were reluctant to hire them and of the underlying racism they were forced to overcome. Harrison G. left Georgia for Pittsburgh and encountered a long line of potential employees at the Jones and Laughlin Steel plant. When his turn arrived, he told the foreman he could perform better than anyone else. Harrison explained that such boasting was

[21] U.S. Department of Commerce, Bureau of the Census, *Thirteenth Census of the United States Taken in the Year 1910*, Vol. IV: *Population 1910: Occupation Statistics* (Washington, 1914), 590–91. Although blacks had not made large incursions into the steel industry, their average wages in 1910 exceeded those of Polish and Italian workers in the mills. See U.S. Congress, Senate, *Reports of the Immigration Commission, Immigrants in Industry*, Part 2: *Iron and Steel Manufacturing* (2 vols., Washington, 1911) I, 63. Actually blacks had made greater inroads into manufacturing plants in Pittsburgh than in other northern cities such as Cleveland and New York. See Kenneth Kusmer, *A Ghetto Takes Shape: Black Cleveland, 1870–1930* (Urbana, Ill., 1976), 66–67. Thomas Sowell has called the period before 1910 a "promising" period for urban blacks because they established many small businesses. Sowell, *Race and Economics*, 120. For a discussion of Negro experience with iron manufacturing in the South, see Wesley, *Negro Labor in the United States*, 242–44.

[22] Helen A. Tucker, "The Negroes of Pittsburgh," *Charities and the Commons*, 21 (Jan. 2, 1909), 602.

[23] Ben E. interview; Olive W. interview; Jean B. interview; Gertrude D. interview by Gottlieb, tape recording, Pittsburgh Oral History Project; Anonymous interview; Floyd T. interview; Hezikiah M. interview.

part of his "strategy" for getting a job. Other blacks promised potential employers that they would "play it straight and go home when the job was done," "stay out of mischief," and remain on the job for a long time. Forced to project himself as an individual, a black such as James N. approached prospective employers and asserted he was "a good man whom the company could use." Ernest F. received no assistance at all in obtaining a job in a brick plant and simply approached the foremen on his own. Harrison G. secured a position at a South Side steel plant by showing a foreman he could load scrap even faster than a "bunch of hunkies."[24] Certainly this analysis casts doubt upon contemporary views that claimed black migrants were "idlers and loafers" who sought "easy money."[25]

Arriving at the same time as blacks, Polish immigrants also sought work in the industrial city. Most treatments of Polish immigration to America are not only fragmentary but blind to the various origins of Polish newcomers. Generally speaking, Poles entered Pittsburgh in successive waves from provinces under the control of Germany, Russia, and Austria. Beginning in the early 1870s, German Poles began settling in the "strip district" along Penn Avenue and further north in Lawrenceville. German Poles predominated in Herron Hill (Polish Hill) and the South Side before 1900. After the late 1890s, Austrian Poles from Galicia joined German Poles on the South Side and Russian Poles in the Lawrenceville section.[26]

Poles moving to Pittsburgh could be grouped into two categories. Those from Prussia moved to America almost entirely in family units and had little intention of returning to a country where German policies made it increasingly difficult for Poles to own land. Poles from the Austrian and the Russian sectors were more likely to arrive in Pittsburgh as single males and either return to Europe or reconstruct families in America. Like blacks, Poles were mobile before moving to Pittsburgh. Industrial Silesia and cities such as Poznan and Warsaw were attracting temporary wage earners as early as 1870. John S. and his father temporarily left their farm in Russian Poland to earn wages. While the children were growing up in Poland, Valerian D. recalled, his father had mined coal in Germany. Joseph B. was sent to Pittsburgh to earn

[24] Harrison G. interview by Gottlieb, Aug. 23, 1974, tape recording, Pittsburgh Oral History Project; Ben E. interview; James N. interview; William J. interview by Bodnar, Aug. 11, 1977, *ibid.*

[25] Louise Venable Kennedy, *The Negro Peasant Turns Cityward: Effects of Recent Migrations to Northern Centers* (New York, 1930), 122. Of course, discrimination kept blacks out of some jobs. In one glass plant "white workers 'ran them out'" and the company abandoned further attempts at hiring blacks. Epstein, *Negro Migrant in Pittsburgh*, 30-32. On the other hand, by 1910 hundreds of blacks were found as laborers, furnacemen, heaters, and pourers. Carnegie Steel employed about 1,500 blacks before 1916. *Wage Earning Pittsburgh*, ed. Kellogg, 112. In nineteenth-century Philadelphia blacks complained about their inability to get skilled jobs for their sons, a suggestion that black kinship ties were undermined. Hershberg, "Free Blacks in Antebellum Philadelphia," 192.

[26] *Historja Parafji SW. Wojciecha B.M.* (Pittsburgh, 1933); *Pamietnik of St. Adalbert's Parish* (Pittsburgh, 1915). Waclaw Kurszka, *Historya Polska w. Ameryce* (13 vols., Milwaukee, 1905-1913), II, 6-7. "Audit of International Institutes Material on Pittsburgh's Nationality Communities," American Council for Nationalities Services Papers, Shipment 4, Box 2, Archives of Industrial Society (University of Pittsburgh, Pittsburgh). Stanley E. interview by Bodnar, Sept. 9, 1976, tape recording, Pittsburgh Oral History Project.

wages for his family and eventually returned to Poland, only to see his own son leave for America.[27]

Characteristically, kinship was also crucial for Poles moving to the city. The mother of Joseph D. was brought from Gdańsk (Prussia) to "Polish Hill" by an uncle who ran a grocery store. Valerian D. was brought to McKeesport, Pennsylvania, by his father in 1906. Peter L. avoided service in the Russian army by following a brother to the Steel City. The parents of Joseph B. were brought from Russian Poland by relatives. With two sisters and a brother already working in the city, the father of Stephanie L. left German Poland in 1899 with his wife and daughter. Joseph B. sent passage for two brothers and a sister to join him on the South Side. Joseph Z. attracted two brothers to the Oliver Iron and Steel plant.[28]

Although blacks and Poles may have similarly relied on relatives during the migration process, there was a critical difference in the role of kin behavior of the two groups. Poles were clearly more effective in obtaining work for family and friends. They were particularly successful in establishing occupational beachheads at the steel mills of Jones and Laughlin and Oliver on the South Side, at Heppenstall's and the Pennsylvania Railroad yards in Lawrenceville, and at Armstrong Cork Company, the H. J. Heinz plant, and other large industrial plants. Thus, Poles were clustered in a few industries when compared to the more widely dispersed blacks. Valentine B. gained his first job in America on the railroad through his brother. Brothers also assisted Peter H. in obtaining employment in a foundry making castings for mines. Ignacy M. left Russian Poland in 1912 and relied on his brother to get him a position piling steel beams at the Jones and Laughlin plant. Joseph D. left Prussia for a job in a mill that was procured by his wife's uncle. A cousin found Edward R. work at a machine shop. John S. followed friends from Galicia in 1909 but needed relatives to acquire machinists work for him. Charles W. relied on relatives to gain him access to domestic work for Americans and boarding house tasks among the Poles.[29] The impact of these practices had implications for the families of newly arrived blacks and Poles. Partly because black families had difficulty in securing jobs for kin, their children were raised in a framework of

[27] See Stefan Kieniewicz, *The Emancipation of the Polish Peasantry* (Chicago, 1969), 58–63, 190–94; Celina Bobinska and Andrzej Pilch, eds., *Employment-Seeking Emigration of the Poles World Wide, XIX and XX C.*, (Krakow, 1975), 17–65; Witald Kula, Nina Assorodobraj-Kula, and Marcin Kula, *Listy Emigrantow z Brazylii I Stanow Zjednoczonych, 1880–1891* (Warsaw, 1973), 240–41, 251–52, 273–74; John S. interview by Bodnar, Sept. 30, 1976, tape recording, Pittsburgh Oral History Project; John B. interview by Bodnar, March 3, 1976, *ibid.*, Valerian D. interview by Gottlieb, July 8, 1974, *ibid.*; Stanley P. interview by Gregory Mihalik, Nov. 11, 1976, *ibid.*; Stanley E. interview; Walter K. interview by Gottlieb, July 2, 1974, *ibid.*

[28] Joseph D. interview by Mihalik, Sept. 17, 1976, tape recording, Pittsburgh Oral History Project; Valerian D. interview; Peter L. interview by Mihalik, Sept. 17, 1976, *ibid.*; Joseph B. interview by Mihalik, May 13 and 20, 1976, *ibid.*; Stephanie L. interview by Bodnar, March 24, 1976, *ibid.*; John B. interview; Francis P. interview by Bodnar, Jan. 10, 1976, *ibid.*

[29] Valentine B. interview by Bodnar, Sept. 22, 1976, tape recording, Pittsburgh Oral History Project; Stanley N. interview by Bodnar, Sept. 22, 1976, *ibid.*; Joseph B. interview; John B. interview; Helen M. interview by Bodnar, Jan. 17, 1976, *ibid.*; Peter H. interview by Gottlieb, June 26, 1974, *ibid.*; Ignacy M. interview by Gottlieb, July 2, 1974, *ibid.*; Joseph D. interview; Edward R. interview by Mihalik, Sept. 10, 1976, *ibid.*; John S. interview; Michael S. interview by Bodnar, Jan. 16, 1976, *ibid.*; Francis P. interview; Charles W. interview by Mahalik, Dec. 10, 1976, *ibid.*

self-sufficiency. An examination of the socialization process in migrant families revealed that blacks had clearly decided how children could secure their goals. Given the nature of class and racial subordination, young blacks emerged from their formative years with a sense of individualism, a realization that survival would ultimately depend upon their own personal resourcefulness.[30]

Strong individualism usually surfaced in black adolescents. Rather than emerging as adults fixed to the responsibilities of their families of origin, migrants prior to 1918 and their children looked toward a future that they alone would shape. Sally S. recalled that her brother left the family farm in Mississippi for a Florida sawmill "when he was big enough to work on his own." After several years her brother left Florida for Washington, D.C. Roy M. "had the urge to leave home" at age sixteen. He reasoned that if he could work in the fields of Arkansas he could surely work for his own wages. His move north, not uncharacteristically, was preceded by a period in an Arkansas sawmill. Before he was twenty, Grant W. had moved to Pittsburgh, obtained a job in a glass factory, worked at a steel foundry, and launched a semiprofessional baseball career. Several female respondents left home on their own at age twenty to attend school, perform domestic service, or hire out for "day work" in Pittsburgh. The father of William H. told his son at his twenty-first birthday, "you are your own man and you can go on your own." Ernest F. did not even tell his father when he left school to procure a job, although his father generally allowed him to make his own decisions.[31]

Often rising individual aspirations clashed with parental authority—a fact that suggested a certain tension between parents' emotional ties and their pragmatic conclusion about what was needed for adult survival. The resulting strain pushed some young blacks into a search for their own means of sustenance. Jasper A. left his family farm not only because he was tired of farming but because his father worked him "pretty hard." Roy M. expressed similar displeasure with "strict parents who would not allow him to pursue his own interests." Characteristically, both the brother and father of Olive W. had run away from home at age fourteen to work in Florida sawmills. One Pittsburgh respondent had the feeling that his father was "too repressive" and showed insufficient "trust" in his son. Grant W. argued with a stepmother over keeping his own wages and, although he felt "close" to his father, left home twice before age seventeen to work on his own.[32] A striking example of

[30] Eugene D. Genovese, Roll, Jordan, Roll: The World the Slaves Made (New York, 1974), 504–05. Genovese found a similar strong individualism in slave families. He argued that the relatively happy childhood of slave children resulted in "independent spirited adults."
[31] Sally S. interview by Clarence Turner, June 18, 1976, tape recording, Pittsburgh Oral History Project; Roy M. interview by Gottlieb, July 9, 1974, ibid.; William H. interview; Ernest F. interview by Gottlieb, April 20, 1976, ibid.; Anonymous interview; Grant W. interview by Gottlieb, July 12, 1976, ibid.
[32] Walter W. interview by Turner, Feb. 14, 1973, tape recording, Pittsburgh Oral History Project; Jasper A. interview by Gottlieb, July 12, 1976, ibid.; Roy M. interview; Olive W. interview; Ross P. interview by Bodnar, Aug. 10, 1977, ibid.; Grant W. interview. For the argument that during periods of rapid social change children achieved an increasing degree of independence, see Kenneth Soddy and Mary C. Kidson, eds., Men in Middle Life (London, 1967), 293. This movement toward independence may emanate from parents as well as children.

black individualism and self-reliance was Gertrude D., who, at age sixteen, lived alone in Nashville after her mother died. She acquired a job scrubbing laundry and became completely self-supporting. After several years she married and accompanied her husband to Pittsburgh.[33]

Early employment among children in working class families was certainly not unique. A recent study in Philadelphia concluded that "most urban American families were able to operate with a margin of comfort to the degree that they could count on a steady contribution from their laboring children of both sexes."[34] Such a pattern was not as evident among Pittsburgh's black migrant families. This is not to say that black children never contributed their wages to their parents. They sometimes did, although often for a specific purpose such as the education of a brother or sister. But black progeny were considerably more likely than immigrant children to retain their own wages rather than relinquish them to parents. Grant W., to cite a case in point, contributed part of his wages until he was sixteen so that his sister could finish high school. As soon as she graduated, he kept his earnings for himself. Floyd T. unloaded box cars as a teenager but discussed the matter of his wages with his parents and was allowed to "manage for himself." Jasper A. described his relationship with his parents as intimate but seldom sent money to them in the South. Queen W. kept her own wages at age fifteen when she went to Norfolk to do domestic work. A young worker, whose family moved from Virginia, did give some of his wages to his family but kept most for himself. James N. kept a similar portion of his early wages. Olive W. gave her parents occasional support but kept most of her wages for her own use. She did not recall her brothers and sisters turning anything over to her parents. Similarly, a survey of unmarried black migrants in Pittsburgh in 1917 found that less than 45 percent sent money to relatives.[35]

Unlike black youth who tended to launch careers of their own and retain wages, young Polish workers remained attached to their families of origin and contributed most of their earnings to their parents. Socialization in Polish

[33] Gertrude D. interview.

[34] John Modell, Frank F. Furstenberg, Jr., and Theodore Hershberg, "Social Change and Transitions to Adulthood in Historical Perspective," *Journal of Family History*, 1 (Autumn 1976), 29.

[35] Grant W. interview; Floyd T. interview; Jasper A. interview; Ernest F. interview; Queen W. interview; Anonymous interview; James N. interview; Olive W. interview; Epstein, *Negro Migrant in Pittsburgh*, 24. Recent studies have offered additional evidence that blacks were choosing an individual rather than a collective approach to survival. This does not imply an absence of emotional attachments or kinship assistance among blacks. But out of a deep concern for their children, black parents were nurturing attitudes of self-sufficiency. They were unable to offer material resources or social connections to assist their survival in adult life. Historian Crandall A. Shifflett in a study of rural black families in 1880 Virginia, found that they reduced the number of nonworking consumers in their household during the early years of marriage so that there would be fewer mouths to feed. As families progressed to middle years and children became old enough to work, Shifflett discovered the ratio of consumers (nonworkers) to workers gradually diminished. One explanation for Shifflett's declining consumer population in middle-aged black families was the possible departure of young black workers to pursue their own individual quests. See Crandall A. Shifflett, "The Household Composition of Rural Black Families: Louisa County, Virginia, 1880," *Journal of Interdisciplinary History*, VI (Autumn 1975), 244–45.

families functioned in a manner which insured both the inevitability of child labor and the relinquishing of earnings for family use at least until marriage. Before 1930, young Poles learned their lessons well. Ray C. expressed his reason for remaining in Lawrenceville as a young man. "I felt down deep I had an obligation to take care of my mother." Joseph D. never had to be told to assist his family. "I always thought dad had hard luck so I would stick with them [parents] until the other kids got old enough to work," he explained. The tendency of young Poles to consider family obligations was stated clearly by Edward R.: "We looked forward to the time when we got to the legal age. When we got to that point we quit school and got a job because we knew the parents needed money. . . . That's just the way we were raised."[36]

Carrying out the dictates of their upbringing, Polish youth nearly always gave their earnings to their mothers, the usual manager of Polish family finances.[37] Stanley N. "hustled newspapers" at mill gates and gave his three-dollar-per-week profit to his mother. Joseph B. and his brothers sold enough newspapers on Polish Hill to nearly equal his father's weekly salary of $12.50. After the father of John K. had his leg crushed at Carnegie Steel, John began working in a grocery store and giving his wages to his mother. Peter L. helped his parents by working in a butcher shop at age sixteen. In order to assist their families of origin, hundreds of young Poles found employment with glass manufacturers on the South Side by the age of fourteen, including many who worked at night.[38]

Young Polish girls were also expected to assist parents until marriage. In fact, it was not uncommon for Polish children to live in the same house with their parents for several years after marriage, something that was rarely found among blacks.[39] On the South Side Polish girls packed and inspected nuts and bolts at Oliver Iron and Steel. Stephanie W. recalled that all her sisters worked at either H. J. Heinz or the South Side Hospital and contributed their wages to their mother. At age sixteen Stephanie worked in a store that needed a "Polish girl" for its Polish clientele. Josephine B. left school after the eighth grade and did "day work" in Mount Lebanon, an upper-middle-class suburb. She and her brother who worked in a nearby coal mine relinquished all their earnings to

[36] Joseph D. interview; John K. interview by Bodnar, Sept. 12, 1977, tape recording, Pittsburgh Oral History Project; Ray C. interview by Mihalik, July 1, 1976, *ibid.*; Edward R. interview.

[37] Polish women, in contrast to black women, seldom worked after marriage unless their husbands were killed or incapacitated. In addition to managing finances they usually paid all bills and insurance. See interview with Francis P.

[38] Stanley N. interview; Joseph B. interview; John K. interview; Peter L. interview. Elizabeth Voltz, "The Child Labor Question," clipping in Civic Club of Allegheny County Records, 1846–1849, Box 3, Archives of Industrial Society.

[39] A contradiction in the data may seem evident when this statement is compared with Table 2 which shows that 0 percent of midstage Polish families were extended. The reason for the difference is that the census data was generated from a period in time—1900—when most Polish families had been in America for only about a decade and still had relatively few married children. The oral data revealed the dynamics of Polish family in the three decades after 1900 when the second generation began to initiate families of their own.

TABLE 2

Family Structure by Family Stage and Ethnicity, Pittsburgh, 1900

Family Structure	Southern-born Black	Russian Pole	German Pole
Young-Family Stage			
Nuclear	63.4%	72.6%	80.4%
Extended	13.4%	10.3%	9.8%
Augmented	23.3%	17.1%	9.8%
N	172	146	92
Mid-Stage			
Nuclear	52.2%	90.2%	93.2%
Extended	17.4%	0.0%	0.0%
Augmented	30.4%	9.8%	6.8%
N	46	41	44

Source: U.S. Bureau of the Census, Manuscript Schedules of Population, 1900, Pittsburgh, RG 29 (National Archives).

their parents. Joseph D. recalled that all of his sisters left school at age thirteen and worked in a cigar factory.[40]

Another way to evaluate the impact of the greater ability of Poles to provide jobs for kin is to examine family structure. In the 20 percent sample from the 1900 census, we can divide sample families into three groups according to family composition—nuclear, extended, and augmented—and into four groups according to stage in life cycle—newlyweds, young families, midstage, and mature. A nuclear family consisted of one or both parents and their children; an extended family included other relatives living in the home; an augmented family included nonrelative lodgers and boarders whose presence was intended to supplement the family income. Newlywed families were defined as childless couples; young families were those in which there were no working children and the wife was under age forty-five. Midstage families had employed children and/or a wife over age forty-five; mature families had children living outside the home[41] (Table 2).

The data reveal that, during the critical middle years when children attained working age, black families became less nuclear while Polish families became

[40] The employment of young girls at Oliver Iron and Steel was detailed in the *Pittsburgh Leader*, April 5, 1912, pp. 1, 16. See also John B. interview; Stephanie W. interview by Bodnar, March 21, 1976, tape recording, Pittsburgh Oral History Project; Francis P. interview; Stanley E. interview; Joseph D. interview; Peter L. interview; Josephine B. interview by Bodnar, March 3, 1976, *ibid.* Similar employment of young girls for family reasons in the early industrial revolution is discussed in Louise A. Tilly, Joan W. Scott, and Miriam Cohen, "Women's Work and European Fertility Patterns," *Journal of Interdisciplinary History*, VI (Winter 1976), 447-76; Tamara K. Hareven, "Laborers of Manchester, New Hampshire, 1912-1922: The Role of Family and Ethnicity in Adjustment to Industrial Life," *Labor History*, 16 (Spring 1975), 249-65.

[41] The life-cycle model is more accurate when tied to the age of the mother and more likely to reflect the childbearing and childrearing years. For further explanation of the model used in this essay, see Shifflett, "Household Composition of Rural Black Families," 242; Thomas K. Burch, "Comparative Family Structure: A Demographic Approach," *Estadistica*, XXVI (June 1968), 291-93; and Thomas K. Burch, "The Size and Structure of Families: A Comparative Analysis of Census Data," *American Sociological Review*, 32 (June 1967), 347-63.

TABLE 3

Mean Number of Unrelated Boarders in Household by Ethnicity
and Family Stage, 1900

	Young-Family	Mid-Stage
Southern-born Black	4.5	6.4
Russian Pole	4.9	3.5
German Pole	4.0	1.0

Source: U.S. Bureau of the Census, Manuscript Schedules of Population, 1900,
Pittsburgh, RG 29 (National Archives).

more nuclear. This suggests that growing children in Polish families were
contributing to family income so that paying boarders or relatives were
displaced. On the other hand, the increase in boarders and lodgers among
blacks at the same time as the children reached working age suggests that
those children were not contributing to the household economy.

The pattern is further substantiated by looking at the number of unrelated
boarders living with families in different stages (Table 3). Black families increased the number of unrelated boarders in their households from the young-
family to the middle-family stages. Polish families did just the opposite. The
average number of unrelated boarders among young southern-born black families was 4.5. This figure grew to 6.4 by the midstage. Between these two
periods in the family cycle Russian Poles lowered the mean number of
unrelated boarders from 4.9 to 3.5. German Poles reduced their average from
4 to 1. While the number of boarders in most households seemed high, it
should not be forgotten that these figures were drawn from a period of
widespread migration when boarders were not only commonplace but important sources of family revenue.

The post-1900 occupational mobility patterns of blacks and Poles revealed
the effects of their dissimilar responses to employment opportunities and racial
discrimination. Unable to insure jobs for kin and forced to rely on individual

TABLE 4

Occupational Mobility for Selected Male Ethnic Groups at
Five-Year Intervals, 1900–1915

Group	N 1900	% Upward 1905 1910 1915	% Downward 1905 1910 1915	% Same 1905 1910 1915
Southern-born Blacks	1165	24.3 32.7 30.2	14.9 16.8 21.3	60.9 50.5 47.7
Russian Poles	651	21.7 25.0 39.0	1.3 2.7 8.6	76.9 72.2 52.2
German Poles	292	14.1 21.2 21.4	6.4 9.0 14.3	79.5 69.7 64.3

Source: U.S. Bureau of the Census, Manuscript Schedules of the Population, 1900,
Pittsburgh, RG 29 (National Archives); *R. L. Polk Pittsburgh Directory*, 1905, 1910,
1915.

resourcefulness, blacks experienced both greater upward and greater downward occupational mobility between 1900 and 1915 (Table 4). Between 1900 and 1910, for instance, black upward movement was 32.7 percent while that of German Poles was only 21.2 percent. In the same period, however, blacks were almost twice as likely to slip downward. The high rates of mobility out of the city have resulted in dismayingly small sample cells. Admittedly the full extent of upward and downward mobility does not appear in the table. More detailed analysis of the career patterns of each group, however, revealed almost no movement from blue-collar to white-collar worker or vice-versa. In fact, nearly all movement occurred between unskilled and semiskilled cohorts. Thus, while blacks experienced more upward and downward mobility than Poles, the differences were generally insignificant. Black workers most often moved from unskilled to semiskilled and back to unskilled occupations. This greater movement of blacks, however, represents considerable movement from job to job—horizontal mobility—and reflects the lack of occupational security afforded to black workers. Poles, following kin into the workplace, failed to match either the upward or downward levels of black mobility. Rather, they moved routinely into blue-collar jobs, probably without actively pursuing alternatives, generally remained at the same occupational levels, and established clusters in various industries.

Clearly, not all newcomers to the city functioned the same way. The encounters of Poles and blacks with Pittsburgh effected dissimilar models of accommodation. These differences, however, were not simply the result of premigration cultures or the assumed disintegrating effects of the urban milieu. Both groups evidenced strong kinship attachments before and during the migration process. That they operated in somewhat different ways does not necessarily suggest that one was more dysfunctional than the other. In actuality both Polish and black families remained intact, and parents worked effectively to socialize their children in a manner which would facilitate their survival. What caused their adaptive courses to differ was the preference of employers for immigrants rather than blacks, which frustrated the implementation of black kinship in the procurement of work. In the face of urban conditions both blacks and Poles resorted to premigration traditions—blacks because they had to, Poles because they were able to. But neither premigration culture nor urban racism functioned independently. Adjustment was ultimately a product of the interaction of one with the other. Poles were objects of discrimination, but they actually benefited in a perverse way from their image as dull but steady workers by being allowed to rely on their traditional kinship ties. Neither Poles nor blacks moved rapidly up any ladder of succession. Poles, however, avoided intense racial hostility and planted their feet firmly on the lower rungs of the occupational hierarchy.

Explanations such as Gutman's analysis of the black family or Kessner's view of immigrants, which posit a basic continuity in the way kinship functioned in premigration and urban settings, must be modified to account for this interactional process which occurred between newcomers and the city. In reacting to the model of the city as a destroyer of social values and networks, historians too readily identified various ethnic values and behavior as residues of premigration cultures. But adaptation often involved strategic reactions to specific conditions. Black parents could not insist upon support from their progeny as frequently because they could not offer meaningful economic contacts in return. This was true in the rural South and urban North. Able to bring their sons into the workplace, however, Poles possessed greater leverage in demanding support from children and determining their occupational careers. When the transfer of land could no longer be used as a basis for family solidarity in peasant Poland, Poles found a surrogate in industrial America—jobs. The degree to which newcomers could rely on kinship, of course, could not entirely account for divergent patterns of adaptation, but it was certainly an important ingredient.

When European immigration declined and black migration from the South increased after 1917, racial hostility between immigrants and blacks became intense as blacks encountered emerging patterns of ethnic solidarity, especially in steel plants and among railroad workers.[42] At the Jones and Laughlin plant, for instance, Germans predominated in the carpenter shop, Poles in the hammer shop, and Serbs in the blooming mill. This was unfortunate since limited oral data suggested that the initial relations between Poles and blacks were considerably better before 1920, with visitations in each other's homes not uncommon. After being allowed to implement kinship ties in gaining jobs, however, immigrants were unwilling to welcome later arrivals into their established enclaves.

[42] See Kusmer, A Ghetto Takes Shape, 157, 175; Allan H. Spear, Black Chicago: The Making of a Negro Ghetto, 1890-1920 (Chicago, 1967), 34, 111, 150, 201; Osofsky, Harlem, 45-81; Emmett J. Scott, "Additional Letters of Negro Migrants of 1916-1918," Journal of Negro History, IV (Oct. 1919), 460-61; St. Clair Drake and Horace R. Cayton, Black Metropolis: A Study of Negro Life in a Northern City (New York, 1945), 91-93; Thaddeus Radzialowski, "The Competition for Jobs and Racial Stereotypes: Poles and Blacks in Chicago," Polish American Studies, XXXIII (Autumn 1976), 5-18.

Small Business and Japanese American Ethnic Solidarity

By Edna Bonacich

An important issue in the field of ethnic relations is the relationship between class and ethnicity or race. Is ethnicity a phenomenon that cross-cuts class divisions in a society and is independent of them? Is there a special bond, a primordial kinship-like tie, which leads people of putative common ancestry to join together in a shared "sense of peoplehood?" Or is ethnicity really a disguised form of class (in the Marxist sense of economic interest group), in which ethnic loyalties are only evoked when there are class interests to be pursued? In other words, is ethnicity a fundamental social force, or is it an epiphenomenon governed by more fundamental class forces?

To give a concrete example, the "black power" movement can be seen as a movement of national-cultural liberation, in which the principal theme is establishing the right of a "people" or ethnic group to determine their own destiny. Alternatively, it can be seen as an effort by a peculiarly oppressed class in American society to achieve some measure of equality and relief from oppression. In the second interpretation the "cultural" aspects of the movement would be seen as secondary, as means towards the end of altering the class position of the black community.

In this case ethnicity and class are so closely intertwined that it seems impossible, and perhaps trivial, to try to separate them. But the issue becomes important when we try to predict future alignments, especially when ethnicity and class are not so closely inter-

96

related. For example, if economic oppression ceased to fall along racial lines, would we still see a black power movement? Or if we are able to create a truly classless society, would ethnic divisions melt away? It is my central hypothesis that class is the more fundamental reality and that ethnic solidarity is most likely to be strong when rooted in shared class interests.

This paper explores the relationship between class and race for one ethnic group, the Japanese Americans. Unlike blacks, the predominant class position of Japanese Americans has not been that of a super-exploited proletariat, but rather that of a petit bourgeoisie. The Issei in particular came to concentrate heavily in this class. Thus in 1941 Bloom and Riemer (1949:20) found that, among male Japanese in the labor force in Los Angeles County, 47 percent were self-employed. For those over 45 years of age 60 percent were self-employed. These people worked as operators of small shops such as restaurants, grocery stores, or boarding houses, or as small farmers or market gardeners. These enterprises shared the features of not involving a large initial capital investment and of depending heavily on unpaid family labor. In essence, they were small businesses.

Miyamoto (1939:70-71) notes the same phenomenon in Seattle:

In speaking of the economic activities of the Japanese in Seattle, we must take special note of the overwhelming dominance in their lives of the

EDNA BONACICH 97

"small shop" . . . When we note the lack of any capitalist class or upper-middle class in this community, and when we see the vagueness and the relative smallness of a true working class, we can understand the remarkable predominance of a single class interest.

The reasons for this concentration are difficult to determine. Three possibilities which have received some attention are racism, culture, and sojourning.

a. *Racism.* The most common form of this thesis is to argue that blocked opportunities in the general economy forced the Issei into self-employment. For example, Daniels (1966:11-12) states:

> Because of the high degree of unionization in northern California and the anti-Oriental agitation which had been prevalent since the 1860s, no significant number of Issei were ever hired by white firms for factory or office work. The [immigrant], if he stayed in town, had to go into business for himself, or, more probably, go to work for an already established Issei.

There are problems with this approach. Specifically, it does not explain why Issei farmers, who could easily find work on white-owned farms, still pushed for self-employment. Furthermore, it does not explain why other groups whose opportunities have been limited (such as blacks) have not shown a similar concentration. Unless we assume a special kind of racism for different ethnic groups, this factor can only explain why Issei businesses were small as opposed to large, but not why they chose to become, and were able to get established as, independent entrepreneurs.

b. *Culture.* An alternative approach is to look for features in the culture the immigrants brought with them from Japan. There are a number of variants to this thesis. At one extreme is the belief that the small business idea was prevalent in Japan and simply transplanted here. Thus, among other factors Kitano (1969:19) mentions "the traditional expectation of many Japanese to run their own business." Alternatively, authors have selected particular features of Japanese culture, such as communal solidarity or a collectivist tradition, values supporting hard work and thrift, or particular institutions like the tanomoshi (rotating credit association), which would provide a more indirect link to small business concentration.

One problem with a cultural explanation is that it does not account for the many ways in which Japanese American economic forms are quite different from those of Japan. The Issei concentrated in only a few lines of endeavor (market gardening, fishing, commerce, and service firms) which hardly resemble the diversity of Japanese enterprise even at the time of emigration. The nation developed industrial corporations while the Issei on the whole did not. And the emigrants frequently altered their personal economic behavior on arriving in

98

this country, moving from the status of a peasantry to that of an entrepreneurial group.

c. *Sojourning*. I have developed this thesis elsewhere (Bonacich, 1973) in trying to account for some of the features of "middleman minorities" (groups that concentrate in the petit bourgeoisie) in general, but not the Japanese in particular. The basic idea is that sojourning provided a motive for thrift and risk-taking, both of which are necessary ingredients in entrepreneurship, and encouraged the retention of ethnic ties which could be used to support ethnic businesses.

I have some doubts about the validity of this interpretation now, though it still seems to me to tie a number of loose ends together. In particular it helps to explain why the Japanese would be more likely to enter business than either blacks or Anglos, both of whom are "settled" in this country. And it helps to explain the peculiar concentration in "liquidable" types of business as opposed to heavy industry. However, a more balanced view would take greater account of the racist environment into which the sojourners moved and of the culture of the original environment which prompted a sojourning emigration in the first place.

Regardless of its causes, concentration in small business provided a common class interest among the Issei which could find expression

EDNA BONACICH   99

in, and be fostered by, ethnic solidarity. There are at least three reasons for this link. First of all, small business lacks economies of scale and other forms of efficiency of large corporations. In competition with the corporations small business must make up for these deficiencies by other advantages. Issei small business was able to do this by using communal solidarity and trust to pass resources, such as capital, labor, patronage, jobs, and information, around the community more cheaply and to curb internal competition. Ethnic solidarity was a tool in the class conflict with big business.

Second, within Issei businesses, employers and employees tended to form a single class. Workers in Issei shops or on Issei farms would identify with the business because they were kin or from the same prefecture as the owner, or because they hoped to "learn the ropes" and set up a business for themselves later, often with the aid of their current employer. This class solidarity put Japanese American workers in conflict with employees in corporate firms, who saw their interests as distinct from the employer's and who wanted to improve wages and work conditions even if the employer objected. Small business drew Japanese American employer and employee together and placed them in class conflict with the working class in the surrounding society (see Modell, 1969).

Third, while the "small business economy" of the Issei was exclusively Japanese in composition, the corporate economy was ethnically diverse. Workers (or management) in a large factory would perceive joint interests which overrode ethnicity. No such experience was available in Issei enterprises. The small business economy was ethnically homogeneous, and as such promoted the alliance between class interest and ethnic solidarity.

Thus, concentration in small business supports a strong ethnic community. If Japanese Americans were to move out of small business and into the corporate economy, class bonds would be weakened. As a consequence, I would predict that ethnic bonds, too, would be weakened.

The data presented here come from the Japanese American Research Project at UCLA.[1] Part of the study entailed questioning a sample of 2304 Nisei from all over the United States mainland during the mid-1960s. The study was not designed to investigate small business concentration, so we had to use imperfect indicators, namely, self-employment and, for the non self-employed, ethnicity of the employer. This information was only collected for males.[2] We assumed that the self-employed and those who worked for other Japanese Americans were working in small business. Employees of non-Japanese American-owned businesses were assumed not to be in small business. It is granted that this assumption probably leads to some error, though we believe it has sufficient validity to study gross relationships.

100

In our sample 40 percent of the male Nisei were self-employed, a proportion three and one-half times as great as 1970 census figures show for all employed males in the United States. Another seven percent were working as employees of Japanese American businesses. This means that 47 percent of the Nisei in our sample worked in "ethnic firms" which we assume to be small businesses. The remaining 53 percent were employees in non-Japanese American businesses or worked for the public.

Small business cross-cuts the typical measures of class, such as occupational prestige. Table 1 shows how the ethnic firm is distributed according to occupation. It is evident that the occupations differ substantially on this dimension, but not in a linear way. Professionals, persons in clerical and sales occupations, and craftsmen and operatives, tend to concentrate in the non-ethnic economy, while proprietors, service workers and laborers (of whom 77 percent are gardeners), and especially farmers, cluster in ethnic small business. Almost half of the Nisei who are not in the ethnic economy are professionals, while most of those in ethnic firms are proprietors and farmers.

Small business is related to income in a striking way. Forty-two percent of the Nisei in ethnic firms earned $10,000 or less annually at the time of the study compared to 33 percent of those in the general economy. But at the other end of the scale 20 percent of those in small

TABLE 1.
NISEI MALE OCCUPATION AND TYPE OF FIRM

Occupation	Small Business	Non-Small Business	% Small Business
Professional, Technical, and Kindred	14%	48%	21% (640)
Managers, Officials, and Proprietors	30	12	69% (405)
Clerical, Sales, and Kindred	7	15	29% (218)
Farmers and Farm Workers	27	2	93% (275)
Craftsmen, Foremen, and Operatives	5	20	18% (249)
Service Workers and Laborers	18	4	82% (211)
	(949)	(1049)	

business earned $20,000 or more as compared with only eight percent of persons in non-Japanese American employ. The different income distributions suggest that the two economies have different meanings. The non-ethnic economy seems to promise security: a good income without too much risk, but with a financial ceiling. The ethnic economy is more of a gamble. One may strike it rich, but failure is costlier than would be the unadventurous life of a corporate employee. Undoubtedly this mirrors the fate of small business in general in America.

Table 2 gives us an indication that our distinction marks some sort of class difference insofar as this can be measured by political party affiliation. We find a greater proclivity on the part of those in small business to be members of the Republican Party, even if they are employees of these firms. This tendency increases with success, or income. In contrast, employees in the corporate economy tend not to join the Republicans, and this tendency is relatively independent of their income.

The division between small business and corporate economy among the Nisei is accounted for by a number of factors, including: year of birth (the younger, the less likely to be in small business), education (fewer of the more educated are in small business), work

102

TABLE 2.
MALE NISEI TYPE OF EMPLOYMENT BY POLITICAL PARTY, CONTROLLING FOR INCOME

Income	Percent Republican		
	Self-Employed	J.A. Employer	Non-J.A. Employer
To $10,000	37%	38%	31%
	(153)	(21)	(194)
To $20,000	46%	46%	33%
	(138)	(37)	(355)
$20,000 +	62%	----	38%
	(107)	(6)	(37)

EDNA BONACICH   103

history (those who start in small business occupations tend to remain there), and region (the Pacific coast harbors more Nisei in small business). In addition, legacy from one's parents plays an important role. Generally the less educated Issei (both in Japan and the U. S.) were more likely to enter farming than urban enterprise, and the farmers were less likely to send their sons to college, which would have propelled them into non-ethnic firm professions. Thus 60 percent of the Nisei who are in small business are the sons of Issei farmers, compared to only 41 percent of non-ethnic firm employees. Conversely 33 percent of the Nisei who are out of the ethnic economy have fathers who were proprietors as compared to 20 percent of those in the ethnic economy.

Given that the Nisei are almost evenly split between small business and non-small business, we can examine the impact of this class distinction on other social relations. We shall briefly examine four areas: family, informal associations, formal organizations, and religion. In general the hypothesis is that Nisei in small business retain retain closer ties with the ethnic community than do Nisei who work in the corporate world.

a. *Family.* Do Nisei who are in small business retain closer ties with their relatives? Nisei males were asked if they had any relatives living in the same city or county as themselves. For those in small business only nine percent said no, compared to 21 percent of those not working in small business.

Living in the same city or county with one's relatives may be a matter of chance or having a large number of relatives; it does not necessarily mean one has anything to do with them. But living in the same neighborhood cannot be construed as accidental. It indicates a much stronger desire to maintain kinship ties. Sixty-six percent of the Nisei in small business report having relatives living in the same neighborhood compared to 48 percent of those out of small business.

We controlled for income as a factor which might limit one's choices. It is conceivable that Nisei in small business are forced to live in the same neighborhood as relatives because they cannot afford to move away. Table 3 dispels this contention. Wealthier Nisei in small business continue to live near relatives, while those who are not in small business move away when they can afford to.

So far we have only examined the sheer physical presence of relatives. The JARP survey asked a question concerning more active involvement with the family: "About how many times in the past month have you visited with or been visited by relatives living in the same neighborhood or metropolitan area or county as you?" The measure purposefully excludes those with no relatives in the same city or county; we want to look at family interaction under the

TABLE 3.
MALE NISEI TYPE OF FIRM BY RELATIVES LIVING IN THE
SAME NEIGHBORHOOD, CONTROLLING FOR INCOME

| | Percent Any Relatives | |
Income	Small Business	Non-Small Business
To $10,000	71%	57%
	(195)	(206)
To $20,000	60%	44%
	(186)	(369)
$20,000+	64%	29%
	(117)	(38)

condition that there is an opportunity for it. Even within this restriction, Nisei in small business have more to do with their relatives: 21 percent had not visited within the last month, 40 percent had visited one to four times, and 40 percent had visited five times or more. In contrast, 33 percent of those out of small business had not visited relatives in the past month, and only 29 percent had visited more than four times.

In sum, it appears that small business somehow encourages the maintenance of closer ties with one's family, and/or that closer family ties help to support ethnic small business.

b. *Informal Associations*. Four types of informal association were measured: work associates, neighborhood of residence, close friendship, and the reading of ethnic newspapers. In all cases we wanted to see whether small business was associated with a more "ethnic" set of contacts.

The Nisei were asked what proportion of the people they usually meet at work were Japanese Americans. Those in small business reported meeting a higher proportion. Thus 47 percent in small business said that at least a quarter of the people they meet at work are Japanese Americans, compared to 13 percent of those not in small business.

There were some marked occupational differences on this measure. Farmers were most likely to meet Japanese Americans at work, while professionals and service workers and laborers (largely gardeners) were least likely to. Table 4 shows the effect of both occupation and small business on the ethnicity of work contacts. In all cases people in ethnic businesses, regardless of occupation (with the exception of gardeners), have much more contact with the ethnic community. Especially noteworthy is the professional category. Independent professionals are quite different from professionals who work for corporations, even though they are equally well-educated.

One's place of work is only one of many contexts in which social relations develop. Another is one's place of residence or neighborhood. The Nisei were asked: "Would you say that this neighborhood is made up mostly of Japanese Americans, mostly of non-Japanese Americans, or is it mixed?" Since only four percent described their neighborhood as mostly Japanese American, we combined this category with "mixed" and treated them both as an indicator of a more ethnic neighborhood. Those who are in small business are more likely to live in such neighborhoods: 47 percent do, compared to 36 percent of those not in small business.

The Nisei were asked about the ethnicity of their two closest friends outside of their relatives. Fifty-nine percent of those in small business listed exclusively Japanese Americans among their two closest friends, compared to 43 percent of those working outside of small

106

TABLE 4.
ETHNIC COMPOSITION OF PEOPLE NISEI MALES MEET AT
WORK, BY OCCUPATION AND TYPE OF FIRM

| | Percent 1/4 + J.A. | |
Occupation	Small Business	Non-Small Business
Professional, Technical, and Kindred	42%	8%
	(132)	(504)
Managers, Officials, and Proprietors	47%	12%
	(208)	(122)
Clerical, Sales, and Kindred	56%	24%
	(62)	(151)
Farmers and Farm Workers	51%	33%
	(241)	(18)
Craftsmen, Foremen, and Operatives	67%	15%
	(43)	(201)
Service Workers and Laborers	20%	14%
	(169)	(37)

EDNA BONACICH

business. Within the ethnic firm, employees (as opposed to the self-employed) are especially likely to have friends within the ethnic community (71 percent, versus 57 percent of the self-employed). The wives of men in small business also have their friendship patterns affected by their husbands' economic activity. Thus, 54 percent of these wives have exclusively Japanese American best friends, while only 38 percent of the wives of people working outside of the ethnic community have such a grouping of friends.

The fourth measure of informal affiliation within the ethnic community is the regularity with which Nisei read the ethnic press. Forty-three percent of small business people reported that they read such a press regularly, compared to 26 percent of those not engaged in small business. Table 5 shows the effect of occupation on the propensity to read ethnic newspapers regularly, within each "economy." Regardless of occupation, those in small business always read more. However, it is the gardeners who are most likely to follow the ethnic press.

Based on all four indicators of informal associations within the ethnic community, it appears that those in small business retain closer ties.

TABLE 5.
PROPORTION OF MALE NISEI WHO READ ETHNIC
NEWSPAPERS REGULARLY, BY OCCUPATION AND
TYPE OF FIRM

Occupation	Small Business	Non-Small Business
Professional, Technical, and Kindred	38%	23%
	(72)	(316)
Managers, Officials, and Proprietors	46%	31%
	(145)	(65)
Clerical, Sales, and Kindred	46%	32%
	(39)	(94)
Farmers and Farm Workers	38%	----
	(149)	(6)
Craftsmen, Foremen, and Operatives	42%	29%
	(24)	(119)
Service Workers and Laborers	51%	20%
	(88)	(20)

108

c. *Formal Organizations.* The Nisei were asked if they belonged to any organizations, other than church-related ones, the majority of whose membership was Japanese American. For those outside of small business only 39 percent belonged to such organizations, compared to 61 percent of those in small business.

Surprisingly on the other end of the scale, belonging to non-ethnic organizations was not related to small business. Forty-eight percent of both small business and non-small businessmen belonged to at least one non-ethnic organization. This suggests that, while small business encourages the joining of ethnic organizations, it does not particularly encourage exclusiveness.

Table 6 shows how the two types of organizational affiliation are combined for people in different types of firms and occupations. Nisei in the ethnic economy are most likely to belong to both types of organization, followed by exclusively ethnic ones. They are unlikely to belong to non-Japanese American associations exclusively. Nisei who are not in small business, in contrast, are more likely to be non-affiliated, with over one-third falling into this category. When they do join, they are most likely to join non-ethnic organizations exclusively. Their least preferred pattern is to join exclusively ethnic organizations.

TABLE 6.
MALE NISEI MEMBERSHIP IN ORGANIZATIONS,
BY TYPE OF FIRM, AND OCCUPATION

Type of Firm	No Orgs.	Only J.A. Orgs.	Only Non-J.A. Orgs.	Both	
Small Business	25%	28	15	33	(510)
Non-Small Business	34%	18	26	21	(619)
Occupation					
Professional, etc.	27%	12	34	27	(387)
Managers, etc.	30%	25	17	28	(206)
Clerical, etc.	40%	27	15	18	(131)
Farmers, etc.	20%	24	14	41	(152)
Craftsmen, etc.	41%	25	14	20	(146)
Service, etc.	25%	47	6	21	(108)

EDNA BONACICH

Occupational type is also related to organizational patterns. Clerical and sales workers, and craftsmen and operatives, are most likely to be affiliated. These two occupational types can be seen as the "lower" non-ethnic economy occupations. They are starkly different from the "lower" ethnic economy lines of work, farming and gardening. The latter show a marked preference for belonging to exclusively ethnic organizations and stand out in this regard. The farmers, on the other hand, are most likely to belong to both ethnic and non-ethnic organizations. It appears that, while maintaining membership in ethnic organizations, they have joined the local farm bureau, etc.

The modal membership for professionals is in exclusively non-ethnic organizations, while they are least likely to belong solely to Japanese American associations. If they belong to ethnic organizations at all, they are likely to do so in concert with membership in non-ethnic organizations. The pattern for proprietors and managers is less clear, probably reflecting the heterogeneity of the category (combining both ethnic firm proprietors and non-ethnic firm managers and executives).

Despite the details of variation in membership patterns by different occupational groups, the overall finding is that small business supports ethnic organizations.

d. *Religion*. The Nisei were asked about their religious affiliation. Unfortunately they were not asked about the ethnic composition of their congregation; many of the Christians may belong to churches with a high proportion of Japanese Americans and thus retain ties with the community. Still religion itself marks a difference in small business, with Buddhists more likely to operate this type of firm than Christians or non-affiliates. Fifty-eight percent of Buddhists are in small business compared to 42 percent of Christians and 38 percent of non-affiliates.

Religion is a declining differentiator in the Japanese American community, as shown in Table 7. Among the earliest born Nisei, Buddhists are 32 percent more likely than Christians to be in ethnic firms. This declines to 10 percent for the middle age group and is slightly reversed for the most recent-born.

We can interpret this finding in two ways. It could mean that the younger Nisei have not yet fulfilled their potential and that religious differences will manifest themselves later in their lives. Or it could mean, and this seems more likely, that religion was once an important differentiator of economic behavior but is less significant as time passes.

In any case, the fact that religion is associated with type of business is one more indicator of a link between economy and community. Those Nisei who are affiliated with a more traditional "ethnic" religion are more likely to concentrate in small business.

110

TABLE 7.
MALE NISEI RELIGION BY TYPE OF FIRM,
CONTROLLING FOR YEAR OF BIRTH

| | Percent in Small Business | | |
	Buddhist	Christian	None
Born before 1925	73%	47%	41%
	(189)	(292)	(39)
Born 1925-1934	45%	35%	44%
	(160)	(208)	(45)
Born after 1934	25%	31%	23%
	(53)	(79)	(58)

The evidence presented in this paper has a number of weaknesses, but the tendency it suggests is unambiguous. This is that small business and ethnic solidarity are linked together. The direction of causality in this relationship is not clear from the evidence. It could be that communal solidarity fosters the entrance into small business, or that those who enter small business, for non-communal reasons, find themselves drawn closer to the community as a result. Indeed both processes may be operating simultaneously.

On the other hand, when Nisei work in the corporate economy, their ties to the ethnic community appear to be weakened. Again this could work both ways: those with weaker ties are more likely to leave the ethnic economy, or corporate employment weakens community solidarity. Regardless of the direction of causality, our data reveal a link between class and ethnicity. For the Japanese Americans, a breakdown in the petit bourgeois class concentration spells a breakdown in the manifestations of ethnic solidarity.

NOTES

*This paper is a modified and much condensed version of some of the themes dealt with in Edna Bonacich and John Modell, *The Economic Basis of Ethnic Solidarity: A Study of Japanese Americans* (unpublished manuscript). It is a lengthened version of a paper delivered at the Pacific Sociological Association Annual Convention in Victoria, August, 1975.

1. The study received financial support from the Japanese American Citizens League, the Carnegie Corporation of New York, and the National Institute of Mental Health.

EDNA BONACICH   111

2. The JARP survey did not ask married females about their own economic activity. On some items they reported on their husbands, in which case we could derive a picture of male Nisei behavior based on male self-reports and female reports on their husbands. On items where females were not asked about their husbands, the number of respondents is reduced to the males alone.

REFERENCES

Bloom, Leonard and Ruth Riemer. *Removal and Return*. Berkeley: University of California Press, 1949.

Bonacich, Edna. "A theory of middleman minorities." *American Sociological Review*, 38 (October 1973): 583-594.

Daniels, Roger. *The Politics of Prejudice*. Gloucester, Mass.: Peter Smith, 1966.

Kitano, Harry H. L. *Japanese Americans: The evolution of a subculture*. Englewood Cliffs, N. J.: Prentice-Hall, 1969.

Miyamoto, Shotaro Frank. "Social Solidarity among the Japanese in Seattle." Seattle: *University of Washington Publications in the Social Sciences*, 11 (December 1939): 57-130.

Modell, John. "Class of ethnic solidarity: The Japanese American company union." *Pacific Historical Review*, 38 (May 1969):193-206.

112

JOHN J. BUKOWCZYK

"Polish Rural Culture and Immigrant Working Class Formation, 1880-1914"

In 1964, Rudolph Vecoli's "*Contadini* in Chicago: A Critique of *The Uprooted*" overturned a long standing orthodoxy in the field of immigration history, namely, that America's immigrants had been cut off from their cultures when they immigrated. Vecoli showed that, instead of being uprooted, South Italian immigrants were *transplanted* into cultural soil they carried with them from the old country.[1]

The image of transplanted immigrants which Vecoli portrayed guided immigration and labor historiography toward the examination of immigrant backgrounds and, in the process, established culture both as a category of explanation and as a subject in need of further close investigation. Immigration and labor historians, however, have since been unable to agree what effect transplanted rural culture has had on immigrant behavior and the process of immigrant working class formation. The majority have stressed the positive effects of immigrant culture. In *The Slavic Community on Strike* (1968), Victor R. Greene showed that, for many immigrant miners in the Pennsylvania anthracite fields, transplanted rural culture provided an indispensable basis for working-class solidarity and labor militance during some most trying and turbulent years.[2] Greene's was a powerful attack on the John R.

Versions of this article were presented at the 1980 Social Science History Association meeting in Rochester, New York, and at SUNY-Buffalo in the History Department's 1981 Colloquium Series. I would like to thank Herbert Gutman and Edward Thompson, whose work has influenced the research for this paper enormously. I would also like to thank Alan Dawley, David Gerber, Chris Johnson, Ed Kantowicz, Ted Radzialowski, and Bob Zieger for their helpful discussion and comments at various stages in its preparation. They, of course, bear no responsibility for the outcome.

1 Rudolph V. Vecoli, "*Contadini* in Chicago: A Critique of *The Uprooted*," *Journal of American History*, 51 (1964), 404-417.

2 Victor R. Greene, *The Slavic Community on Strike: Immigrant Labor in Pennsylvania Anthracite* (Notre Dame, Indiana: University of Notre Dame

Commons school of labor historiography with its anti-immigrant bias, but it awaited Herbert G. Gutman's seminal article, "Work, Culture, and Society in Industrializing America, 1815-1919," to broaden Greene's provocative findings. Drawing upon cultural anthropology as well as the pathbreaking work of the English Marxist historian E. P. Thompson, Gutman promulgated a concept of culture as a *resource* which immigrant working people actively retained. While Vecoli's immigrants simply displayed transplanted cultural forms and were influenced by them, Gutman's consciously and actively used those cultural forms to alter their social environment. Thus not only did transplanted rural culture often serve as a critical alternative to the logic of the factory system, but immigrants invoked transplanted cultural values, practices, and forms in order to claim rights and articulate grievances.[3]

Despite widespread acceptance of the position that immigrant cultures were a powerful resource which enhanced community solidarity and worker resistance, some historians have been less sure. In *Immigrant Workers: Their Impact on American Labor Radicalism*, for example, Gerald Rosenblum observed that immigrants were willing recruits to American industry who easily accepted employee status, in part because they could not know to defend craft traditions which they had never experienced, in part because their cultural frame of reference remained outside of the American social system. The formation of ethnic communities— "ethnic subsystems"—perpetuated the latter situation.[4] Rosenblum's negative view of immigrant workers, though somewhat modified, was largely sustained by Gabriel Kolko. In *Main Currents in Modern American History*, Kolko contended that emigrants formed "the most miserable segments of the industrial reserve army" in Europe and behaved accordingly once in America. Divided among themselves by language, cultural practices, and values, some immigrants meekly accepted oppressive conditions both because they were long inured to the hardships of European subsistence economies and because they appreciated the relative improvement over their former lot. Other immigrant workers were submissive, meanwhile, because they regarded themselves as temporary sojourners, interested in maximizing their earnings in the short run

Press, 1968), 207-216.

[3] Herbert G. Gutman, "Work, Culture, and Society in Industrializing America, 1815-1919," in *American Historical Review*, 78 (June, 1973), 531-588.

[4] Gerald Rosenblum, *Immigrant Workers: Their Impact on American Labor Radicalism* (New York: Basic Books, 1973), 30-39, 96.

and in eventually re-emigrating.[5]   The conclusion that emerged
from Rosenblum's and Kolko's research thus questioned the findings of Greene, Gutman, and others: immigrants were the bane of
working-class militance precisely because of their social backgrounds and their persistent cultural values.

While one side may have been a bit romantic and the other a
bit nativistic, each adduced valid evidence to support its respective
position in the debate, so that a curious problem thus emerged:
how could transplanted immigrant culture have had such dichotomous and contradictory effects?   The answer lay in the concept
of culture shared by the protagonists.   The monolithic notion of
a "pre-modern" or "traditional" culture, on which both sides relied,
was somewhat flat and static and did not take full account of the
historical process.   In fact, transplanted immigrant cultures were
volatile and internally contradictory systems whose effects were
ofttimes contradictory and dichotomous. Those cultures, moreover,
were gripped by the throes of change on *both* sides of the Atlantic.

In order to examine how transplanted rural culture helped
channel the behavior of immigrant workers in contradictory directions, perhaps attention should turn to a specific group—Polish immigrants in Gilded Age and pre-war America—with a view toward
seeing what they can tell us.   We find at the outset that turn-of-
the-century Polish immigrants were not an undifferentiated mass
but a highly variegated group.   The economic emigration from
Poland between the 1880's and the First World War occurred in
three phases, each involving different segments of the Polish population.   Emigration from the German-held territories of western
Poland—including artisans, shopkeepers, intellectuals, scions of
the Polish lower gentry, and agriculturalists—began in the 1870's
and crested between 1880 and 1893, after which an economic depression in the United States and an amelioration of conditions in
the German-Polish countryside caused it to slacken.   By this time,
however, Poles began to leave the Russian-held territories of the
Polish Congress Kingdom, which incorporated central and eastern
Poland.   While this emigration included small-town dwellers and
non-agriculturalists, the majority of the Russian-Polish emigrants
were agriculturalists—small holders and agricultural wage laborers.
Emigration from the Austrian-held territory of Galicia began in the
1880's also, but only snowballed after 1900.   Most depressed in

5 Gabriel Kolko, *Main Currents in Modern American History* (New York: Harper and Row, 1976), 67-99.

terms of social composition, between 1902 and 1911 it included 25% independent farmers ("peasants"), 35% agricultural day laborers, 15% servants, and only 10% skilled tradesmen. Many of these planned eventually to re-emigrate.[6]

Most Polish immigrants, it is true, came from the countryside. But that emigrants from the Polish countryside were not a homogeneous mass of rural cultivators but were divided into small farmers, skilled artisans, agricultural day laborers (compensated with wages or in kind), and servants suggests a cultural corollary. The culture which Polish emigrants undeniably possessed when they left rural Poland was not just rural culture (or traditional, pre-industrial, premodern, or Polish culture), but several *class cultures*. These were shaped by the social relations of serfdom and manorialism in dissolution, of agricultural capitalism, of a self-sufficient household economy, and of their manifold permutations and combinations. They were also colored by the cultural influence of the partitioning powers. That the culture of the Polish immigrants was not a monolith thus already may account for its contradictory effects on immigrant working-class behavior: an *assortment* of class cultures guided Polish immigrant behavior in an assortment of directions.

Amidst this diversity, however, a few aspects of the Polish immigrants' cultural legacy did provide common ground. The first involved common motivations shared by many immigrants. It will be recalled that few Galician and Russian Poles, who made up the great bulk of the emigration after the 1880's, ever envisioned a career in the mines or the factories of distant America. This does not imply, however, that they were upwardly mobile workers, the Horatio Algers of social mobility fame who painstakingly inched their way from rags to respectability, if not riches, up the American "ladder of success." To the contrary, Polish immigrants faced challenges to survival in the industrial world that were strikingly similar to the ones they had known in the Polish countryside. Not

6 Russia, Prussia, and Austria had divided Poland into three partitions, wiping that troubled country from the map of Europe. See Stefan Kieniewicz, *The Emancipation of the Polish Peasantry (Chicago: University of Chicago Press, 1969)*, 192-223; Victor Greene, "Poles," in S. Thernstrom, ed., *Harvard Encyclopedia of American Ethnic Groups* (Cambride, Mass.: Harvard University Press, 1980), 787-803; Johann Chmelar, "The Austrian Emigration, 1900-1914," Thomas C. Childers, trans., in *Perspectives in American History*, 7 (1973), 319, 321-324, 341. For an accessible summary of these differences, see Caroline Golab, *Immigrant Destinations* (Philadelphia: Temple University Press, 1977), chapter 3.

surprisingly, as recent research has argued, they thus remained preoccupied "with survival strategies and family welfare . . . " as " . . . part of a larger cultural system which focused its energies on the maintenance of the family unit."[7] Yet this explanation might be usefully amplified by suggesting that the larger, family-centered cultural system arose from the specific social, economic, and class relationships associated with a household economy that seems to have been prevalent throughout rural Poland. Understanding that Poles emigrated not from a "rural" economy or a "traditional" economy but, more specifically, from a family-centered, self-sufficient household economy to which they planned eventually to return goes a long way toward explaining immigrant behavior here, especially the behavior of those who migrated from that land of small holdings, Eastern Galicia. Rural Poles thus often tried to avoid labor unions and strikes because these threatened to upset their fundamental goals.[8] Instead, many accepted factory labor as a short-term means to earn money which would serve their long-range cultural goals—acquiring or expanding self-sufficient agricultural holdings back in Poland and thereby sustaining the rural household economy.[9]

A second aspect of the Polish immigrants' cultural legacy, meanwhile, also provided another sort of common ground. The vast majority of Polish immigrants, those from Austrian and Russian Poland, came from lands which were still very recently engulfed by the institution of serfdom. Though serfdom ended in the German-held territories of western Poland quite early in the nineteenth century, it lasted until 1848 in Galicia and until 1864 in the Russian-held Polish Congress Kingdom. Thereafter, quasi-feudal elements persisted on an extra-legal or customary basis in both partitions.[10] Into the twentieth century, the Polish countryside from which many Poles migrated retained its manorial cast with

7 John Bodnar, "Immigration, Kinship, and the Rise of Working-Class Realism in Industrial America," *Journal of Social History*, 14 (Fall, 1980): 56.

8 William I. Thomas and Florian Znaniecki, *The Polish Peasant in Europe and America*, 2 vols. (New York: Knopf, 1927), 1:336, 385.

9 Helen Stankiewicz Zand, "Polish Family Folkways in the U.S.," *Polish American Studies*, 13 (1956), 83; Helen Znaniecki Lopata, "The Polish American Family," *Ethnic Families in America: Patterns and Variations*, ed. Charles H. Mindel and Robert W. Habenstein (New York: Elsevier, 1976), 18. Also cf. John Bodnar, "Immigration and Modernization: The Case of Slavic Peasants in Industrial America," *Journal of Social History*, 10 (1976), 54, 56.

10 Kieniewicz, *Emancipation*, 45, 58-59, 70, 131, 190-193.

a diverse panoply of surviving feudal trappings—the labor dues and feudal tenancies, the servitudes and use rights, and the aristocratic families that still dominated vast expanses of land and that claimed the privileges and power, prerogatives and immunities arrogated by their class. The fact that the quasi-feudal social relations of serfdom survived in much of Poland well into the nineteenth century suggests important ramifications for the issue of cultural transplantation. Not only did rural lower-class culture in Poland bear the marks of the manorial system, but transplanted immigrant culture in America continued to retain the manorial imprimatur.

Despite regional and local variations in Polish serfdom, the essential social relations remained very similar and exerted a formative influence both on rural popular culture in Poland and on rural culture transplanted in the immigrant districts of America. Curiously, however, that common cultural core had a rather complicated and ambiguous effect on peasant behavior in Poland and immigrant behavior here. From the work of both Eugene Genovese and E. P. Thompson, we have become familiar with the suppressive, hegemonic effect that relationships of paternalism and deference have had upon lower-class popular cultures.[11] Manorialism in Poland embodied a similar social and ideological dynamic which either diffused or contained class conflict in the countryside and which sapped the independence and vitality of lower-class rural popular culture. Yet contradictions in manorial society produced contradictions in that culture which guided Polish lower-class behavior in many, often conflicting directions. Even when transplanted, a Polish rural culture which had been shaped by the manorial system worked the same way. Rather than having a single behavioral effect on Polish immigrants, this transplanted culture also guided immigrant behavior in contradictory directions.

Victor Greene may have convincingly dispelled the stereotype that Polish industrial workers were invariably docile and submissive in the work place, but Greene's success should not blur the fact that strong grounds actually had existed for the original negative stereotype of the immigrants and that their behavior was influenced by the cultural traditions of the manorial system. At times, it is true, Polish workers' willingness meekly to submit to the dic-

---

[11] Cf. E.P. Thompson, ''Patrician Society, Plebian Culture,'' *Journal of Social History*, 7 (1974), 382-406; Eugene Genovese, *Roll, Jordan, Roll: The World the Slaves Made* (New York: Random House, 1976).

tates of their employers must have represented calculated defensive behavior. Yet the habit of docility and submissiveness, often remarked to be Polish characteristics, undeniably were embodied in the rural lower-class culture of manorial Poland which was transplanted in American factory districts.

One such pattern involved the diffusion of rural popular protest. Class sentiments which surfaced in the Polish countryside often were diffused through the so-called "Church-and-King" phenomenon, a common feature in European rural society in which aggrieved country folk looked to royal beneficence for relief from the social injustices perpetrated by local landlords.[12] In 1811, for example, Polish peasants in Upper Silesia erroneously believed that compulsory estate labor had been abolished by the Prussian king and that the Junkers and local officials concealed the royal decree.[13] A variant of the "Church-and-King" phenomenon may have survived among some Poles in Brooklyn. Theodore Havemeyer, the industrial baron of Brooklyn's largest sugar refining concern, mingled benevolence with power by cultivating a reputation of affection for his men. " . . . Boss Theodore," a company source wrote, "would shake every man by the hand at Christmas time and wish him well . . . ." Perhaps it was not intended as a joke, as union organizers claimed, when one unidentified refinery worker suggested that Havemeyer himself be elected treasurer of a newly established union in 1886.[14] If this indicates that Brooklyn Poles may have retained a deferential attitude toward authority, they were not alone. During the 1915 oil refinery strike in nearby Bayonne, New Jersey, striking Polish workers gave the nickname "*Kresni Ocec*" [sic]—godfather—to a county sheriff who had tried to settle their dispute.[15]

A wide range of secular elements in Polish gentry culture, meanwhile, also penetrated popular culture in the Polish countryside in insidious and subtle ways. Throughout Poland, peasant cultivators adopted the aristocratic affectation of hand-kissing, a

12 Cf. Herbert Gutman, "Work, Culture, and Society," 571-572.

13 Kieniewicz, *Emancipation*, 62. Also cf. Jan Słomka, *From Serfdom to Self-Government: Memoirs of a Polish Village Mayor, 1842-1927*, tr. William John Rose, English shortened edition (London: Minerva Publishing Co., 1941), 159-160.

14 *American Sugar Family*, 1 (1920), 4; *New Yorker Volkszeitung*, 3 April 1886.

15 George Dorsey, "The Bayonne Refinery Strikes of 1915-1916," *Polish American Studies*, 33 (1976), 27.

gesture which survived the transatlantic crossing.[16] Significantly, other such practices emulative of gentry forms also persisted even after immigration. One Polish custom saw Polish peasant men douse peasant women with pails of water on Easter Monday (*Dingus*)—probably a fertility rite. In America, however, Polish immigrants adopted upper-class practice for "spilling day," sprinkling immigrant women with bottles of perfume. Similarly, Polish immigrants in America adopted a hobby that had been considered a "caprice of the upper classes" in Poland, keeping rabbits or pigeons.[17] Finally, a third adaptation involved name-changing. Traditional Polish peasant names typically have ended with a consonant, whereas gentry names, since the fifteenth century, usually have ended in "-ski," an adjectival suffix denoting an estate, village, or region.[18] Through the 1700's, this difference often underscored the social and economic disparity between the classes.[19] By the 1800's, the period of the partitions, however, such marks of social distinction had grown far more tenuous, as foreign political oppression stripped the lower gentry of its political rights while economic change impoverished more and more of the so-called "village nobility,"[20] leaving increasing numbers of otherwise undistinguished peasants clinging to their surnames, the last vestige of their once superior social status in the Polish countryside. In

16 Walter J. Slowiak, "A Comparative Study of the Social Organization of the Family in Poland and the Polish Immigrant Family in Chicago" (M.A. thesis, Loyola University, 1950), 24; Sr. Mary Adele Dabrowska, "A History and Survey of the Polish Community in Brooklyn" (M.A. thesis, Fordham University, 1946), 47.

17 Although in an industrial economy cyclically riddled by depression and unemployment, it is equally true that this "idle" pursuit might have served a practical purpose: it was an inexpensive source of food. Stories of both practices come to me from my grandparents via the oral tradition. See also Louis E. Van Norman, *Poland: The Knight Among Nations* (New York: Fleming H. Revell Co., 1907), 307; Słomka, *From Serfdom*, 44-45.

18 Frank R. Walczyk, "The Walczyk Family in America," *Polish American Studies*, 18 (1961), 45; Thomas and Znaniecki, *Polish Peasant*, 1:480.

19 Sometimes, of course, it did not. According to Piotr Wandycz, "... great distinctions ... based on wealth and tradition" divided Poland's gentry. Polish "noblemen," or *szlachta*, enjoyed a hereditary status and customary legal rights, but not necessarily large landholdings and great wealth. Thus, while virtually all wealthy Polish landholders could claim gentry status, not all of Poland's very numerous gentry — about 25% of the Polish population — were wealthy. See Piotr S. Wandycz, *The Lands of Partitioned Poland, 1795-1918* (Seattle, Wash.: University of Washington Press, 1974), 4-5.

20 Wandycz, *Lands of Partitioned Poland*, 20.

this state of social flux, low-born Poles began to lengthen their names by appending the honorific "-ski," probably to the resentment and consternation of their social betters. In America, too, while few Polish immigrants legally changed their names to simpler American forms (judging by change-of-name records), Thomas and Znaniecki, the noted Chicago sociologists, reported that "so many fools" had followed the example of one Jan Król, who changed his name to Królikowski, a Polish gentry form.[21]

Emulation of the Polish upper class was significant for what it revealed about the popular cultural values of immigrants from rural Poland. The proliferation of gentry cultural forms suggested a dilution of class sentiments. Polish immigrants might accept subservience in the American factory more readily when they could still win social status borrowed from an older manorial world. At once, the adoption of gentry cultural forms and the internalization of gentry values and norms undermined the independent vitality of transplanted lower-class culture, upon which class mobilization traditionally has been based.

The borrowing of norms from Polish upper-class culture thus shaped immigrant working-class attitudes, but it was the pervasiveness of religious values and forms which more clearly deflected class sentiments among rural immigrants. Despite the record of schism and conflict within Polish Roman Catholic parishes in America, the religion of manorial Poland nonetheless stamped immigrant hearts and mind with persistent habits of deference and docility, submission and obedience. Unlike white American Protestantism, Polish Roman Catholicism did not impart a sense of guilt and a longing for forgiveness among its communicants, nor had it tried to express the pathos of impersonalized bondage and, conversely, a thirst for Divine recognition, dominant themes in antebellum Black Christianity.[22] The reality which Polish Roman Catholicism articulated was suffering; its central mood was a longing for mercy. Not surprisingly, the figure of the Blessed Virgin Mary loomed large in Polish popular religion, for Mary became the quintessential expression of this leitmotif. The compassionate, meek, mild Mary singularly represented the Divine mediatrice and

---

21 Had he accepted American norms of status mobility, Król might simply have taken the English translation of his ironically regal surname: "king." He insisted, however, upon Polish rural practice. See Thomas and Znaniecki, *Polish Peasant*, 2:1155.

22 Paul Radin's introduction to Fisk University, *God Struck Me Dead*, viii, cited in Genovese, *Roll, Jordan, Roll*, 254.

comforting Mother.

Polish Roman Catholicism thus confirmed the peasants' view of their own reality. The marginality of subsistence in an agricultural economy dominated by large land holders and the static class relations of feudalism and manorialism bred a sense of futility summed up well in one Polish proverb: "The wind blows in a poor man's eyes." The fatalism which this sense of futility produced was suitably incorporated in the peasants' religion which replicated this doleful world-view. But if Roman Catholicism confirmed the peasants' view of their own reality, it also conformed to the needs of Poland's landed classes, whose sons and daughters occupied high places in the ecclesiastical hierarchy. When transplanted in American soil, Roman Catholicism exercised an unintended, though similar effect. The world portrayed in Roman Catholicism remained a field neither for spiritual challenge nor for material conquest, but a temporary burden which fallen humanity had to suffer. In short, the world was "a vale of tears," as the commemorative journal of one Polish fraternal benevolent association in Brooklyn pointedly observed.[23]

This view helped preserve a steady obedience to the Church, to be sure, but also something more. Surely, if a Protestant work ethic were ever important as an economic ethos, this rural Polish Roman Catholic ethos must have had important implications for work too. Consider, that during a 1910 cordage strike in northern Brooklyn, the proprietor of a local saloon implored striking jute mill workers—most of them Polish women—to "go back to work and be law abiding, as God does not allow men to strike."[24] Though we cannot know whether the saloonkeeper's plea perfectly resonated with the religious sensibilities of her working-class customers, her comment is nonetheless illuminating. The Polish Roman Catholic ethos transplanted from the manorial Polish countryside fostered habits of docility and obedience not just to ecclesiastical authority, but to civil and industrial authority as well.

The ensemble of transplanted cultural values, attitudes, and

23 Thomas and Znaniecki, *Polish Peasant*, 2:156-206; Helen Stankiewicz Zand, *Polish Proverbs* (Scranton, Pa.: Polish American Journal, 1974), 27; Thaddeus Radzialowski, "The View From a Polish Ghetto: Some Observations on the First One Hundred Years in Detroit," *Ethnicity*, 1 (1974), 131; *Golden Jubilee, St. Stanislaus B. & M. Society, 1903-1953, Group 126, Polish Union of the U.S. of N.A.* (n.p., n.d.), 1, in New York Polonia Box 3, Immigration History Research Center, University of Minnesota, St. Paul, Minnesota.

24 *New York Call*, 18 June 1910.

patterns just reviewed provided Polish immigrant working people with a structure of meaning through which they comprehended, sometimes seemingly unpragmatically and inappropriately, new class relations and a new work environment on this side of the Atlantic. Transplanted culture with its manorial stamp proved remarkably resilient, and it limited the range of actions available to Polish immigrant workers in a curious way. Polish immigrant working people could do only what they knew or could conceive of as possible. That fact exerted a profound impact on the process of immigrant working class formation. Along the way, it produced a host of examples which seemed to credit the negative immigrant stereotype of docility and submissiveness.

While the cultural legacy from manorial Poland thus inhibited immigrant labor militance, sometimes it had the opposite effect. The reason for this lay in the contradictory nature of that culture and the society which spawned it. One picturesque vignette of peasant rusticity clearly illustrates the conflicting tendencies which strained social relations within the Polish manorial world. At harvest time, an early twentieth-century traveler recorded, the estate master and mistress would make their annual visit to the fields. In a mock ceremony, "they are waylaid by the peasants, who tie their hands with bands of straw, the lady and gentleman only regaining their liberty after paying a fine."[25] The metaphor of the "theater," which Thompson used to describe the pull-and-tug of paternalism and deference in rural England, also fits the Polish case.[26] Pageants like these were meaningful rituals with a menacing content. They showed that within the web of paternalism and deference, a rough reciprocity obtained: landlords exploited, peasants extorted. Peasants dutifully called upon the manor at weddings, harvest time, Christmas, and Easter and by their physical presence lent credibility to the landowners' claim that a unity of classes prevailed. But through these visits, peasants also recovered some of the surplus value of their own labor, in the form of treats, tips, and gifts.[27] When lord and lady visited their fields, allowed peasants to bind them with straw, and purchased their own release, perhaps all implicitly understood the unstated relationship which formed the real nexus of classes: bribes and threats.

Class tensions thus also formed a part of the cultural legacy of manorialism in Poland. In Galicia and in the Russian-held Pol-

25 Van Norman, *Poland*, 308.
26 Cf. Thompson, ''Patrician Society, Plebian Culture.''
27 Slowiak, ''Comparative Study,'' 68; Van Norman, *Poland*, 239-242.

ish Congress Kingdom, where quasi-feudal social relations obtained well into the nineteenth century, the rural populace nourished a long and deep tradition of resistance to the landlord class. Often that resistance was subterranean. Sometimes, however, it was quite overt. In the 1840's, for example, discontent among the peasantry in the Polish countryside was widespread; significantly, it mingled anti-landlord themes with Polish nationalism. While some of the rural leaders were themselves wealthy landlords like Henryk Kamieński (1813-66) or intellectuals like Edward Dembowski (1821-46), a grassroots peasant leadership also developed. Thus one Russian Polish priest, Piotr Ściegienny (1800-90), a peasant's son, urged rural Poles to rise up against the landlords and to resist the Russian tsar as well. In Austrian Poland, peasant hostility to the land-owning class far surpassed their resentment of Austrian rule, as gentry nationalists in the Tarnów district of Galicia rudely discovered in 1846 when, at the instigation of Austrian officials, peasants rose up to crush a gentry-led Polish insurrection in the winter of that year. According to Stefen Kieniewicz, the historian of the Polish peasantry, in one week's time peasants plundered about 400—or 90%—of the district's manors and killed about 1200 persons—landowners, members of landowning families, and estate officials.[28] Though the Galician jacquerie and accompanying peasant movement soon subsided, anti-landlord sentiments did not disappear from the Polish countryside. In the 1880's and 1890's—the period, it should be recalled, of mass emigration—a peasant populist movement, replete with vehement anti-landlord rhetoric, erupted in the turbulent Galician partition. Though some of its prominent leaders included well-born Poles—viz., Rev. Stanisław Stojałowski (1845-1911) and Bolesław Wysłouch (1847-1937) —others like Jakub Bojko (1857-1944) and Jan Stapiński (1867-1946) had roots in the peasantry.[29]

Long familiar with exploitation and resistance, immigrants from the highly stratified Polish countryside must have possessed a sharper and deeper understanding of the concept of class than native-born working people who had been reared in the comparatively democratic and egalitarian American society. This understanding, moreover, doubtless influenced the way they understood and expressed class relations once in the United States. Re-

[28] Kieniewicz, *Emancipation*, 111-112, 121-122. Wandycz, *Lands of Partitioned Poland*, 134-135. On the Polish peasant uprising in Galicia, also see Thomas W. Simons, Jr., "The Peasant Revolt of 1846: Recent Polish Historiography," *Slavic Review*, number 30 (December, 1971), 795-817.

[29] Kieniewicz, *Emancipation*, 208-209, 215.

grettably though predictably, evidence here is sparse, but fragments do seem to substantiate the latter claim. In the Polish countryside, for example, cattle were sometimes used as draft animals in plowing, probably by the poorest cultivators.[30] Perhaps for this reason landlords sometimes referred to the overworked and submissive peasants as "cattle."[31] Significantly, when one Polish immigrant in Brooklyn described his work experience in America in a letter to Poland, he drew upon the language of class imported from rural Poland:

What people from America write to Poland is all bluster; there is not a word of truth. For in America Poles work *like cattle*. Where a dog does not want to sit, there the Pole is made to sit, and the poor wretch works because he wants to eat. [Italics added][32]

Like transplanted secular culture, the religious tradition carried over from manorial Poland was not always a conservative influence. Its values curiously ambiguous and its symbols remarkably malleable, Polish Roman Catholicism sometimes helped propel the immigrants toward assertive and even militant behavior. Poles were doubtless present in 1910, for example, when Slavic steelworkers in Hammond, Indiana, knelt before a crucifix and lighted candle as each swore in turn not to scab, and when Slavic coal miners in Avelia, Pennsylvania, reportedly crucified a despised foreman during another strike that year.[33] Similarly, in another strike in the Pennsylvania anthracite fields in 1902, striking miners signed the following eulogy to UMW president John Mitchell, which seems worth quoting at length:

Mr. President—We, the undersigned committee representing the anthracite coal region, of Polish, Ruthenian, Lithuanian, and Slavic descent, feeling the most sincere appreciation and deepest gratitude for your manly, energetic, disinterested, self-sacrificing and vigorous conducting of the last anthracite strike . . . do hereby express

---

30 Louise A. Boyd, *Polish Countryside*, American Geographical Society Special Publication No. 20 (New York, 1937), 36, 163.

31 W.I. Thomas, in Herbert Blumer, *An Appraisal of Thomas and Znaniecki's The Polish Peasant in Europe and America* (New York, 1939), 104-105, quoted in Paul Wrobel, *Our Way: Family, Parish, and Neighborhood in a Polish-American Community* (Notre Dame, Ind.: University of Notre Dame Press, 1979), 18.

32 Anonymous letter, quoted in *Listy Emigrantów z Brazylii i Stanów Zjednoczonych*, ed. W. Kula, et. al. (Warsaw: Ludowa Spóldzielnia Wydawnicza, 1973), 88.

33 Gutman, "Work, Culture, and Society," 578.

our most sincere thanks for protecting our interests and
for the hard struggle you undertook for us.

Blessed be the moment when you, as salvator of
our troubles . . . arrived in our midst and . . . boldly and
courageously stood like a hero against . . . adverses . . .

Receive, dear leader, a thousand-fold blessing of all
the poor, hard working and struggling people, who shall
teach their children, that the embodiment of everything
that is pure, just, right and sublime is our president, John
Mitchell.[34]

Indeed, the style was "pompous and labored," as our source notes,
but compare it with that of the following transplanted excerpts
from the text of the Roman Catholic mass:

Accept, O Holy Father, Almighty and Eternal God,
this spotless host, which I your unworthy servant, offer
to you, my living and true God . . .

It is fitting indeed and just, right and helpful to
salvation, for us always and everywhere to give thanks
to You, O Holy Lord, Father Almighty, Everlasting
God . . . [35]

It was also decidedly liturgical.

Though Polish priests sometimes had raised consecrated
Hosts in order to submerge popular protest, immigrants now showed that they themselves also could invoke a wide inventory of religious symbols and devices for their own more radical ends. While
appropriating its symbols and styles, Polish immigrants also found
in Roman Catholicism a shared value system, a focus for community solidarity, and a source of human worth impervious to
degradation.   Taken together, these powerfully enhanced their
capacity for collective self-assertion.

Transplanted Roman Catholicism provided immigrant workers with another benefit as well, however. If Polish Roman Catholicism counseled submissiveness and docility in the Polish countryside, it also had served as a bulwark against exploitative excesses.
Industrialists in Poland found that their power was circumscribed
by the fact they had to accommodate peasant religiosity. Polish
rural folk believed, for example, that unless a house were blessed
by a priest it would be haunted, and Poland's factory owners reportedly had difficulty securing workers unless their buildings also

[34] Greene, *Slavic Community*, 201-202.

[35] Rev. Hugo H. Hoever, S.O. Cist., *Saint Joseph Daily Missal* (New York:
1961), 659, 669. Cf. *Manualik Dzieci Marji* (Cracow: Ks. Misjonarzy na Kleparzu,
1926), which gives a Polish translation of the second example cited.

first had been blessed.[36] Rural religion also reinforced "preindustrial" cultural values and work habits. Consider one remarkable Polish statistic. In ethnically mixed Eastern Galicia, both Roman Catholic and Orthodox holidays interrupted work, so that in the 1870's, 34 Galician districts had 100 to 120 non-working days, 22 districts had 120 to 150 non-working days, and 16 districts had a staggering 150-200 non-working days per year.[37] In America, when the immigrants' transplanted "Catholic work ethic" encountered a capitalist factory system, which emphasized managerial control and efficiency, and nativist employers committed to tighter work discipline, the outcome was revealing. Sometimes the system simply bent, like in one Glen Lyon, Pennsylvania, coal mine that closed on three Polish holidays—Three Kings' Day, St. Joseph's Day, and Christmas, presumably to avoid heavy absenteeism among its labor force.[38] At other times, managerial attempts to obliterate rural cultural carryovers in the interests of stricter discipline snapped the delicate calm that prevailed in many American factories. Here a 1910 strike by Polish laborers and Lithuanian firemen at the American Sugar Refining Company's giant Brooklyn plant takes on special significance. One of the strikers' chief grievances protested a company order requiring them to work on Easter Sunday, the holiest day of the liturgical year.[39] By reinforcing "preindustrial" values and work rhythms, Roman Catholicism thus also provided a potent resource against the regimentation of factory discipline. Clearly, the Poles' Roman Catholic ethos cut both ways. It did not always suit the interests of effective social control or of efficient factory management.

Polish rural culture, stamped by the social relations of the manorial system and transplanted in America, thus helped guide immigrant behavior simultaneously toward assertive as well as toward deferential patterns. But the effects of that culture were not always even as clearcut as this simple dichotomy might suggest. A second grievance in the strike cited above shows that an easy categorization of the effects of culture is sometimes impossible and that culture often operated in ways which were dismayingly convoluted. The Polish workers who balked at Easter Sunday work also protested a new company policy which henceforth would ban con-

36 Van Norman, *Poland*, 306.

37 Chmelar, "Austrian Emigration," 327.

38 John Bodnar, *Workers' World: Kinship, Community, and Protest in an Industrial Society, 1900-1940*, Studies in Industry and Society, No. 2 (Baltimore, Md.: Johns Hopkins University Press, 1982), 85.

39 *Brooklyn Daily Times*, 29 March 1910.

sumption of alcohol during the working day and inside the plant.[40] It is, of course, significant that Polish immigrant workers were not so easily stripped of a cultural practice, but instead fought to protect it against capitalist predations. It is doubly significant that, by doing so, they advanced a positive alternative to the imposition of factory work discipline. But that the issue of drinking was a point of contention is particularly significant for us here because it intimately involved class relations not only in the factory districts of Brooklyn but also in the Polish countryside.[41]

Alcohol consumption in the Polish countryside began to climb in the 1820's as the popularity of vodka surpassed that of hydromel, a mead-like liquor. Improvement in production techniques combined with a fall in export prices for grain had led to increased vodka production and thus to a steady decline in vodka prices. In the subsequent decade, this price movement was enhanced as an increasing amount of vodka was now distilled from potatoes, absorbing about 25% of the Polish potato crop. The effect of this was literally numbing. Calorie for calorie, the price of vodka became a mere one fortieth of that for bread and the problem of drunkenness grew to epidemic proportions. In fact, per capita annual consumption of vodka in the Polish Congress Kingdom climbed to a staggering three gallons of 100% spirits, i.e., six times the present rate![42]

Clearly, drunkenness had become firmly established as a prominent feature of rural Polish lower-class culture, but what concerns us here is that class issues were implicated in this meteoric rise in alcohol consumption. Traditionally, the Polish gentry enjoyed a *de jure* monopoly over distilling and selling alcohol on their estates and later acquired a *de facto* monopoly over alcohol sales in towns. This monopoly was called the *propinacja*. Custom, however, also entitled upper-class landowners to a feudal right, called the *propinacja* compulsion, by which peasants were obligated to buy a certain volume of vodka from the gentry-owned liquor-selling establishments. This served a two-fold purpose—providing a market for the gentry-produced alcohol and creating a means by which the gentry could extract agricultural surplus from an otherwise uncooperative peasantry who used it as payment for the drink.

The abolition of serfdom often nominally ended the *propinacja*,

40 # *Ibid.*

41 Cf. Hillel Levine, "Gentry, Jews, and Serfs: The Rise of Polish Vodka," *Review*, 4 (Fall, 1980), 223-250.

42 Kieniewicz, *Emancipation*, 90-92, 116-117, 207-208.

but usually only changed its form, as landowners began to pay peasants in manor-house vouchers redeemable at the village inn which, incidentally, these very same landowners supplied with alcohol. Normally, the vouchers circulated like money, but, as one peasant autobiographer recorded:

> When they got used up, so that folk did not want to take them, they would go with them to the licensed liquor place and use them to pay for vodka. The proprietor then, knowing the manor people well, would have no trouble in changing them for new ones.

Lasting longest in Galicia, where in modified form it did not expire until 1910, the *propinacja* well served the class interests of Polish landowners as a means of capital accumulation. "Some eighteenth-century estate accounts," the historian of the Polish peasantry reports, "show an accurate balance between the cost of wages and *propinacja* income." By the mid-nineteenth century, those *propinacja* revenues skyrocketed, and, "in many estates, the net income from the inn was equal to one half of the gross cash income."[43]

A clergy-led temperance movement with anti-landlord overtones in the 1840's only succeeded temporarily in cutting alcohol consumption in the Polish countryside,[44] and thus a taste for strong drink was included among the cultural traditions of the lower-class Polish immigrants who settled in Brooklyn's factory district. Yet while rural Poles had consumed large volumes of vodka while still in Poland, in Brooklyn's sugar refineries they acquired a taste for beer, probably from their German co-workers who, like English agricultural workers, coal whippers, and miners in the early 1880's, traditionally may have regarded the brew as a restorative.[45] At any rate, consumption of beer became a time-honored custom in the giant refineries, practiced as a means to mitigate the debilitating effect of the searing sugar house heat.[46]

At this point, Polish immigrant sugar refinery workers may have experienced a sense of *déjà vu*, for in the early days of that industry, beer consumption was not only tolerated but condoned by refinery owners, who sold beer checks to the men, redeemable at a bar in the refinery basement. Laxness and largesse did not account for this peculiar managerial practice, but rather unbridled

---

43 *Ibid.*, Słomka, *From Serfdom*, 84.

44 Kieniewicz, *Emancipation*, 116-117.

45 Słomka, *From Serfdom*, 117. Cf. E.P. Thompson, *The Making of the English Working Class* (New York: Random House, 1963), 317.

46 *New York Call*, 24 June 1908.

self-interest. Beer sales benefited Brooklyn industrialists by making refinery employment more attractive, reportedly recovering a staggering *forty* percent of the wages paid out to the men, and thus further proletarianizing immigrant laborers.[47]   In short, this Brooklyn version of the *propinacja* compulsion enhanced the control over the work force and aided in capital accumulation.   It may be, indeed, anomalous that immigrant workers doggedly fought to retain a cultural practice so clearly detrimental to their welfare, health, and own best interests, but that they did suggests that their beer grievance represented both a problematical and an important moment in a long history of class relations.

Transplanted rural culture from manorial Poland was thus the indispensable prism through which immigrant perceptions, experience, and behavior were variously refracted.   That it was not monolithic and that the common cultural legacy which they did possess itself was internally contradictory together help explain why immigrant workers should have behaved so variously.   Yet these reasons do not alone suffice to account for a second problem. Between the 1880's and the War, the contradictory effects of transplanted immigrant culture we have discussed were not distributed entirely at random.   The docility of Polish immigrant workers was most often observed in the 1880's, and their comparative assertiveness, most frequently noted after 1900. Indeed, it was Polish workers who staged some of the epic strikes of the latter period— e.g., the Lawrence textile strike of 1912, the Brooklyn sugar refinery and cordage strikes of 1910, the Bayonne oil refinery strikes

---

[47] Charles M. Skinner, "The Sugar Trust and Its Employees," *Workers for the Trusts*, Brooklyn Eagle Library, Series 14, Vol. 15 (May, 1900): 51; *Brooklyn Daily Times*, 3 May 1886; 29 March 1910; *Eagle*, 30 August 1893; Słomka, *From Serfdom*, 84; Kieniewicz, *Emancipation*, 116-117. Also cf. Charles van Onselen, *Chibaro: African Mine Labour in Southern Rhodesia, 1900-1933* (London: Pluto, 1976), 168-169, which describes conditions in the Rhodesian mining compounds in the early twentieth century:

> The extensive brewing of beer within the compound had been encouraged in the first place not only because it cut out the peasant producer but because it helped to stabilise the labour force. The Civil Commission in Salisbury talked in 1908 of beer brewing being encouraged in the mines, "the object of course being to make the mine popular and induce the boys to remain." And in a very diffuse way, beer drinking as a form of recreation no doubt did contribute to the popularity of the compound. But the Attorney General had a more specific understanding of the economic forces operating when he pointed out that mine owners encouraged beer brewing because "if a labourer can find means of spending money he is likely to remain for a longer period." At one level, then, beer was simply one further way of reducing labour turnover and assisting the process of proletarianisation in Rhodesia.

of 1915 and 1916, and the Great Steel Strike of 1919.[48] If the effects of transplanted rural culture were so diverse and often so contradictory, why should this obvious pattern have emerged?

In part the pattern may be related to the changing composition of the emigration from Poland. In the 1880's, most Polish immigrants were German Poles, while after 1900 the vast majority came from the Russian and Austrian partitions. Yet the reason for the pattern may also relate, once again, to our hitherto incomplete explication of culture. Not only was immigrant culture not monolithic, but it was not static; nor was the society that surrounded it. As culture and society changed, so too did immigrant working-class responses change in this volatile period.

The changing pattern of effects, which transplanted Polish rural culture helped produce, can be attributed in part to the changing context into which it was introduced in America. Between the 1880's and the World War, American capitalism underwent a sweeping consolidation, while the organization of capitalist production was rationalized. These profound developments in the American economy produced a polarization of classes in the United States which gave rise to a militant industrial union movement and which spawned an assortment of radical ideologies among American working people. These changing events and conditions dialectically intersected with transplanted immigrant culture, and the result influenced immigrant behavior. Even when their culture remained the same, introduced into a radically different context it thus helped produce a different historical outcome and responses among immigrant working people, e.g., greater militance, more strike activity, and increased participation in labor unions. But, indeed, the immigrants' transplanted culture—values, attitudes, symbols, forms, practices, and consciousness—was often altered by situations and events. Not static but dynamically changing, the immigrants' evolving culture helped order immigrant behavior and pattern immigrant choices toward increasing labor

48 See Donald B. Cole, *Immigrant City: Lawrence, Massachusetts, 1845-1921* (Chapel Hill, N.C.: University of North Carolina Press, 1963); John J. Bukowczyk, ''Steeples and Smokestacks: Class, Religion, and Ideology in the Polish Immigrant Settlements in Greenpoint and Williamsburg, Brooklyn, 1880-1929'' (Ph.D. diss., Harvard University, 1980); George Dorsey, ''The Bayonne Refinery Strikes of 1915-1916,'' *Polish American Studies*, 33 (Autumn, 1976), 19-30; David Brody, *Steelworkers in America: The Nonunion Era* (Cambridge, Mass.: Harvard University Press, 1960) In John J. Bukowczyk, ''The Transformation of Working-Class Ethnicity: Corporate Control, Americanization, and the Polish Immigrant Middle Class in Bayonne, New Jersey, 1915-1925,'' *Labor History*, 25 (Winter, 1984), 53-82.

militance by the early years of the twentieth century.

Polish immigrant culture was thus in flux, but it is wrong to suppose that change only began when that culture was transplanted to this side of the Atlantic. Already in Poland, rural culture was not static, but in constant transformation as nascent capitalist social realities eroded the Polish manorial system with its veneer of gentry paternalism. The result was to fracture the rural cultural world, efface deferential behavior among the Polish peasantry, and render more obvious the issues of class.

Our stereotype of a static "traditional" peasant society thus collapses before the tempestuous social history of nineteenth-century rural Poland. Though rural discontent ran rampant in both the Russian and Austrian partitions, it was in the latter, where so much rural conflict had occurred earlier in the century, that the peasantry first became politically organized. Already in 1893, a small Peasant Party Union (*Związek Stronnictwa Chłopskiego*) formed in Galicia; but it soon was eclipsed by the appearance, in 1895, of the Polish Populist Party (*Polskie Stronnictwo Ludowe*), the first peasant party in Eastern Europe.[49] The populists' program called for political rights and justice for the peasantry and tended to represent the interests of the small-holders and not the landless rural proletariat. Nonetheless, the populists' rhetoric was decidedly class-conscious. Populist rhetoric included threats that village streets would be "paved with gentlemen's skulls instead of cobblestones," while one traveler's account noted a frequent complaint among Galician landlords during the period, that peasants were "losing their old-time respectful manners, and, with the modern ideas of democracy, . . . acquiring an offensive manner of independence."[50] Growing class-consciousness among the peasantry sometimes manifested itself in graphic ways. In Galicia, for example, where the peasants' class sentiments were often said to be unusually pronounced, peasants eschewed the practice of emulating the gentry by appending a "-ski" to their surnames.[51]

Alongside the peasant populist movement, meanwhile, a rural

[49] Wandycz, *Lands of Partitioned Poland*, 294-295.

[50] Kieniewicz, *Emancipation*, 137, 139, 182, 206-207, 217, 224-229, 231-232; Van Norman, *Poland*, 238.

[51] Thomas and Znaniecki, *Polish Peasant*, I:480. There exists a large literature on the subject of Polish populism. See, for example, Peter Brock, *Nationalism and Populism in Partitioned Poland: Selected Essays* (London: Orbis Books, 1973), 181-212; Olga A. Narkiewicz, *The Green Flag: Polish Populist Politics, 1867-1970* (London: Croom Helm and Totowa, N.J.: Rowman and Littlefield, 1976); and the older work by Aleksander Świętochowski, *Historia chłopów polskich w zarysie*, 2 vols. (Lwów: Nakł. Wydawnictwa Polskiego, 1928).

socialist movement also flourished in the Polish countryside at the turn of the century, especially among the landless agricultural laborers whose concerns went unaddressed by the Polish Populist Party. In Galicia and in Russian Poland, the Polish Socialist Party recruited local activists from among the peasantry and championed the demand for a parcelling of estate lands. In Russian Poland, another socialist group, the Social Democracy of the Kingdom of Poland and Lithuania, also appealed for peasant support, although less successfully as it opposed parcelling.[52] Not surprisingly, such organizational efforts had weighty repercussions in a land fraught with deep social and economic grievances. When the 1905-1906 insurrection against the Russian tsar touched off action in the towns and cities of the Polish Congress Kingdom, Polish rural socialists also rebelled. During the revolutionary activities in Russian Poland in 1906, 300 agrarian strikes took place during spring planting and 400 at harvest time, with sixty of eighty-five counties hit by disturbances. Austrian-held Galicia remained quiet during this time, but it had been hit by a similar wave of rural protest a few years earlier, in 1898, 1900, and 1902.[53] Back in Russian Poland, tsarist repression soon did stamp out the flames of agrarian and urban revolution, but sparks continued to fly. The post-1906 political exodus from the Congress Kingdom brought socialist exiles across the Atlantic to America where they soon helped ignite Polish working-class discontent here.[54]

By the early twentieth century, the years of peak emigration, the Galician and Russian Polish countryside was thus a turbulent place indeed. And it was this turbulent place from which Polish immigrants migrated. Of course, it is impossible to know whether the most politicized segments of the Polish rural population chose migration. Comparative evidence from the South Italian case suggests that it was actually the least politicized who are most likely to have left.[55] Yet *all* rural Poles had lived in a cultural context that was informed by the radical social movements of the period, and those who emigrated could not have escaped its influence. That influence was profound indeed, for the movements introduc-

[52] Kieniewicz, *Emancipation*, 216-217, 230.

[53] *Ibid.*, 209, 216, 231.

[54] See Wiktor Tylewski, *"Materialy do dziejów Polskiego Socjalizmu w Stanach Zjednoczonych . . . ,"* *Problemy Polonii Zagranicznej*, 2 (1961), 210-216.

[55] John S. MacDonald and Leatrice MacDonald, "Institutional Economics and Rural Development: Two Italian Types," *Human Organization*, 23 (Summer, 1964), 117.

ed into Polish rural culture an ideology of rights and a language of class which powered popular unrest. This dynamic cultural change, as much as anything else, certainly helps account for increasing immigrant militance by the end of our period.

This fact in turn may help explain why industrialists, civic leaders, and other Americanization fanatics were so intent upon Americanizing immigrant workers in the 1910's and early 1920's. The immigrants' transplanted rural culture not only posed an obstacle to industrial efficiency, but also formed a potent threat in its own right. Radical ideologies were not simply an urban industrial phenomenon, but erupted from Polish country districts seething with economic change, social unrest, and angry class strife. Labor radicalism may have failed to take hold in America's immigrant districts. But that failure is more the story of repression and cooptation, not the absence of potential.

AN ARISTOCRACY OF LABOR:
The Irish Miners of Butte, 1880–1914

by
David Emmons

It has been more than 30 years since Eric Hobsbawn first reminded historians that the working class was in fact a loose fraternity of working classes, and that atop the pyramidal heap of classes that worked was a clearly defined aristocracy. In most instances these workers were "natural" aristocrats, set off from others in the working class by artisanal skills acquired through long apprenticeships. There were times, however, when elite status could be maintained only through contrivance, usually job exclusivity insured by trade union membership. These "contrived aristocrats" were the minority; most of the elite workers had earned their status and their right to keep it.[1]

They had also, however, as with all aristocrats, to be able to afford the life befitting and required of that status, including the obligation to reproduce themselves. This meant controlling the size of the work force in the interest of higher and more regular wages. "The test," says Hobsbawm, "was the ability to exclude, *never mind how.*" Steady if not guaranteed employment with the resultant chance to accumulate some savings was both source and object of the working-class elite. Only steady employment permitted them to marry, sustain their families, acquire property, and as a consequence, bring a necessary stability and respectability to both their own and the larger community.[2]

---

[1] *Labouring Men* (London, 1964), ch. 15. This chapter was based on a paper delivered in 1954. Hobsbawm's ideas are conveniently summarized in his "Debating the Labour Aristocracy" (1979), "The Aristocracy of Labour Reconsidered" (1978), and "Artisan and Labour Aristocrats?" (1983) in Hobsbawm, *Workers: Worlds of Labor* (New York, 1984), 214–226; 227–251; 252–272.

[2] "Debating," 215, 220–221; "Aristocracy Reconsidered," 229, 234–236, 239, 250–251; "Artisan," 256, 264–267. The quote is from "Aristocracy Reconsidered," 234, emphasis mine.

There were not many aristocrats in the English working class
of the 19th century. Hobsbawm assumes that no more than 15%
of the wage workers qualified. Their institutions — churches,
cooperatives, sporting clubs, ethnic friendly associations, and craft
trade unions — were traditional, communal, socially leveling, in
other words, strikingly unlike the modern and individualistic world
of the middle class. Politically, as long as their privileged status
was recognized, they belonged on the side of moderate labor reformism. Their very presence insured that the working class would
remain if not divisive at least divided between the skilled and unskilled, the respectable element and the "rough."[3]

The American experience was different. In the first place, as
Hobsbawm points out, no "permanent, proletarian labor aristocracy" developed anywhere "if the way out of the working class
was relatively open, as I think was the case for white Protestant
19th century Americans."[4] A significant percentage of this nation's unskilled workers, however, was neither white nor Protestant nor, except by residency, American. Obviously, this is not
the place for an extended discussion of the full consequences of
immigrant Catholics and Southern blacks in an industrializing
work force.[5] Still, assuming the absence of a working class elite

---

[3]"Debating," 215-219; "Artisan," 252, 267-268; "Aristocracy Reconsidered," 243. See also Hobsbawm's "The Formation of British Working-Class Culture," in *Workers*, 184-185.
[4]"Debating," 221.
[5]The literature on this subject is vast and growing. That part of it of greatest use in the preparation of this paper includes John Bodnar, *Workers' World: Kinship, Community, and Protest
in an Industrial Society, 1900-1940* (Baltimore, 1982); David Brody, *Workers in Industrial
America: Essays on the 20th Century Struggle* (New York, 1980), 3-48; Brody, "Workers
and Work in America: the New Labor History," in James B. Gardner and George R. Adams,
eds., *Ordinary People and Everyday Life: Perspectives on the New Social History* (Nashville, 1983), 139-160; Alan Dawley, *Class and Community: The Industrial Revolution in Lynn*
(Cambridge, 1976); Eric Foner, "Class, Ethnicity, and Radicalism in the Gilded Age: the
Land League and Irish-America," in Foner, *Politics and Ideology in the Age of the Civil
War* (New York, 1980), 150-200; Herbert Gutman, *Work, Culture and Society in Industrializing America: Essays in American Working-Class and Social History* (New York, paperback edition, 1976), particularly the title essay, 3-78; David Montgomery, "The Irish and
the American Labor Movement," in David N. Doyle and Owen D. Edwards, eds., *America
and Ireland, 1776-1976: The American Identity and the Irish Connection* (Westport, Conn.,
1980), 205-218; Daniel Walkowitz, *Worker City, Company Town: Iron and Cotton Worker
Protest in Troy and Cohoes, New York, 1855-1884* (Urbana, Ill., paperback edition, 1981);
Robert Sean Wilentz, "Industrializing America and the Irish: Towards the New Departure,"
Labor History, 20 (1979), 579-595. Four excellent anthologies are Milton Cantor, ed., *American
Workingclass Culture: Explorations in American Labor and Social History* (Westport, CT,
1979); Richard Ehrlich, ed., *Immigrants in Industrial America, 1850-1920* (Charlottesville,
VA, 1979); Michael Frisch and Daniel Walkowitz, eds., *Working-Class America: Essays on
Labor Community and American Society* (Urbana, paperback edition, 1983); Daniel Leab,
ed., *The Labor History Reader* (Urbana, Ill., 1985). This last collection includes Melvyn
Dubofsky's "The Origins of Western Working-Class Radicalism, 1890-1905." (230-253).

among Protestants, we come nearer an understanding of the immigrant Catholic working class by seeing if it ever constituted an elite and, if so, whether it functioned as Hobsbawm's did prior to World War I, as a force for political and ideological moderation.

Once again, Hobsbawn provides a model. "Any group of workers," he writes, skilled or unskilled "which could establish the economic advantages of the artisan, notably an institutionalized scarcity on the labor market and some control over its own work was assimilated to artisan status."[6] To be sure, these were "contrived aristocrats," but their claim to and defense of aristocratic privileges were no less determined for being "unearned." Specifically, this means that immigrant workers in American industry, assuming they met the other criteria for aristocratic status, including stability and respectability, could, by controlling the work force, be elevated to the rank of labor aristocracy.

Whether this aristocracy also served to cool the fires of labor radicalism is a more difficult question for historians of American workers than it is for students of the English and European working class. At least four factors underscore the differences between old and new world workers. The American working class, unlike its English and continental counterparts was ethnically mixed, possessed considerable political influence, had greater opportunities to move up or, failing that, to move on, and, perhaps as a consequence of all of the above, may have been more susceptible to the ideology of the dominant native and non-working class culture. Each of these considerations was thought to have exercised a moderating influence on the American working class.[7]

This is not the place for a detailed discussion of those factors but a couple of points should be made. As John Bodnar and Aileen Kraditor have recently pointed out, each of these explanations for the failure of American workers to move much beyond labor reformism suffers from the assumption that the workers *should* have been radical and would have been had it not been for *external* forces. In Kraditor's words, the workers were seen as "either Victims (read exploited) or Battlers for Freedom,"

---

[6]Hobsbawm, "Debating," 220.
[7]Brody, "Workers and Work," 155; Walkowitz, *Worker City*, 13, 101, 137–138, 164–165, 253–255; Cantor, "Introduction," in *American Workingclass Culture*, 18; Richard Lingenfelter, *The Hardrock Miners: A History of the Mining Labor Movement in the American West* (Berkeley, paperback edition, 1974), 103–104, 186–190; Dawley, *Class and Community*, 235–241.

(read radicals, true to their class) but seldom, as Bodnar puts it, as "culture bearing individuals." The idea that the workers' conservatism may have been *internal* has not been considered. Similarly, as James Henretta has shown, moving up socially is a criterion of success only for those for whom social mobility was important. To use it as an indicator of the openness of the system or as a test of individual initiative with a people for whom it might have had scant if any significance is patently unfair and historically unrewarding. Like the assumption that worker rejection of radicalism was somehow "unnatural," the unexamined belief that workers wanted, sometimes desperately, to be something else, distorts rather than informs the historical record.[8]

Bodnar, however, goes beyond criticism of what the "Workers' World" was not to a persuasive discussion of what it was. Central to that world was what he calls the enclave, "a complex phenomenon" that arose from the blending of obligations to family, ethnicity, religion, and work. Membership in the enclave gave meaning to the workers' world, but work was only one (and perhaps the least) of its components. "Family obligations," he writes, "dominated working-class predilections . . . family security and stability" were "preeminent" in the workers' world. Men worked to maintain the enclave. Indeed, as Bodnar notes, "regular employment was the foundation of the enclave itself." The key word, however, was "regular." It was steady work they required at a wage that permitted them to save enough to buy the "small piece of property" necessary to family security and the maintenance of the community. There were times, of course, when this security could only be insured by "cooperating with those who were more powerful," but this need not, in fact should not, be seen as evidence of worker victimization, or as some kind of "sweetheart" deal and hence a violation of abstract laws of worker solidarity. It makes more sense to view it as it was viewed, as an effort to control a part (one's own) of the work place in the interest of the larger community.[9]

[8] Bodnar, *Workers' World*, 4–9, 165–185; Kraditor, *The Radical Persuasion, 1890–1917: Aspects of the Intellectual History and the Historiography of Three American Radical Organizations* (Baton Rouge, LA paperback edition, 1981), 2; see also 372n56; James Henretta, "The Study of Social Mobility: Ideological Assumptions and Conceptual Bias," in Leab, ed., *Labor History*, 28–41.
[9] Bodnar, *Workers' World*, 1–2, 63–65, 177–179, 185.

These are hardly the values of the upwardly mobile middle class but neither are they those of the revolutionary proletariat. And so to that earlier list of influences that tended to moderate the protests of American workers must be added this other and far more persuasive one: the conservatism internal to the workers' world, the result of the "meeting of the industrial with the family-based economy," an economy, moreover, that "socialized its children to accept . . . steady, industrial jobs; seldom challenging the industrial system." As for the enclave, that kind of extended family, it "fostered community rather than class-based behavior . . . based on the knowledge that limitations existed on what was obtainable from the larger society."[10]

Protests could and did occur; and they were protests made easier, perhaps even made possible, by the support of the enclave. But they were also protests in defense of that enclave. The community, in other words, offered both support system and "ultimate objective" for worker protest.[11] As for the idea that worker acceptance of the prevailing ideology of the dominant class was a contributing factor in labor's conservatism, Bodnar sees little evidence that workers were influenced by any part of that ideology. Individualism and the promise of social mobility were viewed with considerable skepticism by men for whom collective action and occupational stability were preeminent.[12]

Bodnar is discussing unskilled, principally immigrant Catholic workers, the "lower ranks of the industrial proletariat," but there are interesting similarities between his worker enclaves and Hobsbawm's aristocracy of labor. Both were manifestly of the working class, both sought to control the work force in the interests of steady employment, and both had a moderating influence on their respective labor movements. Each developed societies — craft trade unions, ethnic associations, church organizations — which gave institutional expression to their separateness. Neither was without resources in its dealings with the industrial world and, though it would be too much to claim that each was

---

[10]*Ibid.*, 165-166, 63. F. S. L. Lyons argues that the demographics of Ireland, particularly late marriages and large families, was a "recipe for conservatism." *Culture and Anarchy in Ireland, 1890-1939* (Oxford, 1979), 52.
[11]Bodnar, *Workers' World*, 165-166. See also Walkowitz, *Worker City*, 101-138, particularly 110-128.
[12]Bodnar, *Workers' World*, 167.

autonomous, it would be further yet from the truth to see them as helpless victims of external forces.[13]

It is in this context of enclave as aristocracy that I deal with the Irish miners of Butte. Butte was typical of hundreds of industrializing cities with predominately immigrant working classes. Its Irish miners were conscious of their ethnic, occupational, and class responsibilities and the enclave they built, the community of stable and "respectable" Irish miners, reflected each of these components. The values and institutions of the enclave were familial and collective and bore little resemblance to those of either an acquisitive bourgeoisie or a revolutionary proletariat. The most direct challenge to the enclave came from within the working class, from men — workers not miners — who did not share the enclave's deep commitment to stability and industrial peace.

These were features characteristic of the working class of many of America's medium-sized industrializing cities, but it is the ways in which Butte was different from these other places that give it a special significance and make the story of its Irish miners even more instructive. First, Butte was western and hence new. The place was not formless, but neither was it tightly structured socially. Worker stability was important everywhere but it commanded a premium in a city like Butte in the late 19th century.[14] Second, Butte was a hardrock mining town; there were occupational hazards in every industry but quartz mining was arguably the most dangerous occupation of the era and Butte's mines were certainly among the most dangerous in the world. Early death and preparation for it produced demographic and psychological problems for the Irish. In addition to this most obvious kind of mine danger, there were the less deadly hazards of cyclical unemployment caused by mine shut-downs and the seemingly constant stream of transient workers; that these itinerants, often untrained

[13]*Ibid.*, 165; Hobsbawm, "Artisans," 250–251.
[14]On the point of community stability and the important role workers played in building it see Ralph Mann, *After the Gold Rush: Society in Grass Valley and Nevada City, California, 1849–1870* (Stanford, 1982); Donald Harrison Doyle, *The Social Order of a Frontier Community: Jacksonville, Illinois, 1825–1870* (Urbana, paperback edition, 1983); Michael Katz, *The People of Hamilton, Canada West: Family and Class in a Mid-Nineteenth Century City* (Cambridge, paperback edition, 1975). For contemporary views of Butte's social instability see Linus Brockett, *Our Western Empire, or the New West Beyond the Mississippi River. . . .* (Philadelphia, 1882), 1003; William Thayer, *Marvels of the New West. . . .* (Norwich, CT, 1888), 341–344, 521, 714.

and uncaring, also increased the dangers of working underground made them doubly unacceptable to the settled Irish miners.[15]

Third, the Irish Catholics arrived early in Butte and in considerable numbers. By 1900, counting both immigrant and second generation, the Irish population of Silver Bow County (Butte) was 17,282 out of 47,635, or 36%. That figure made Butte, 2500 miles from the nearest eastern port, the most overwhelmingly Irish city in the U.S. Of 5369 working men in that Irish total, 3589, or 68%, worked underground in the mines; another 1200 worked for mining companies, increasing the percentage of Irish mine workers to 90% of the working adult males.[16]

The enclave of Irish miners, obviously, did not consist of the entire 4700. Many in that number were unmarried transients of marginal if any value to a community based as surely on steadiness and family responsibilities as on ethnicity or occupation. The enclave required more for inclusion than merely being Irish and a miner. The problem, of course, is determining which of the mine workers, at any given time, *intended* to stay and make Butte and its Irishtown his home. Questions of intent do not lend themselves to the usual quantitative analysis. For the moment, however, the point is simply that Butte's Irish, settled and itinerant, mined for a living, and that, to the extent that enclaves reflected occupation, the Butte Irish displayed a remarkable occupational homogeneity.

The other features of the enclave were also in place. There was little significant association with the non-Irish world. Most of the Irish lived in Dublin Gulch or Corktown, either in family homes or in one of a dozen boarding houses operated by and

---

[15]For mine mortality figures see Mark Wyman, *Hard Rock Epic: Western Miners and the Industrial Revolution* (Berkeley, 1979), 115. Figures for the years from 1893 to 1908 for selected Butte mines are given in U.S., Immigration Commission, "Metalliferous Mining in Montana," in *Immigrants in Industries*, S. Doc. 633, 61st Cong., 2nd sess., 1911, vol. III, part 25, 122. Hereafter cited as Immigration Commission, *Immigrants in Industry, 1911*. See also U.S., Commission on Industrial Relations, *Mining Conditions and Industrial Relations at Butte, Montana*, S. Doc. 415, 64th Cong., 1st sess., 1915, *Final Report and Testimony*, vol. IV, 3681-4095. Hereafter cited as Commission, *Industrial Relations, 1915*. On mine shutdowns and transiency see Lingenfelter, *Hardrock Miners*, 130, 173, 176; Wyman, *Epic*, 58-60; Ronald C. Brown, *Hard-Rock Miners: The Intermountain West, 1860-1920* (College Station, TX, 1979), 3-7. For a discussion of both types of hazards as they affected Butte see David M. Emmons, "Immigrant Workers and Industrial Hazards: The Irish Miners of Butte, 1880-1919," *Journal of American Ethnic History*, 5 (Fall, 1985), 41-64.

[16]U.S., Bureau of the Census, *12th Census of the U.S., 1900*, vol. I, *Population*, part I, 768, 798, 875. Occupational statistics are drawn from U.S., Bureau of the Census, *1900 Census Population Schedules, Montana*, vols 8-9, Silver Bow County. Hereafter cited as *MS Census, 1900*.

for Irish miners. Of the married Irish, only 7% had selected a partner from outside the Irish Catholic community. The extended family system attained a near perfected form; almost 500 Irishmen lived with and probably owed their jobs to an uncle, a brother-in-law, or a sibling. The first two Catholic churches in Butte had as their patrons St. Patrick and St. Lawrence O'Toole, and a third parish, St. Mary's, with 400 Irish families (398 of them economically dependent on the mines) was the only exclusively Irish parish in the U.S.[17] There were three divisions of the Ancient Order of Hibernians (AOH), with a combined membership in 1906 of over 1000 men, over 700 of whom were miners. Each division had a Ladies' Auxiliary, and the three together sponsored a corps of the Hibernian Knights and a Hibernian Band. In addition there were Gaelic League and Gaelic Athletic Association chapters as well as the Robert Emmet Literary Association (RELA), the second largest Clan-na-Gael camp in the U.S. with a peak membership in 1905 of over 600 men (approximately 450 of whom were miners), and a well-armed division of the para-military Irish Volunteers.[18]

Both the Hibernians and the Emmets had what can only be called a full social schedule in addition to their cultural, political, and revolutionary responsibilities. They sponsored picnics, parades, gala balls, anniversary celebrations, wakes, athletic competitions, debates, song fests, dances, a kind of informal dating service, and poetry readings. But their most significant service was worker related. Both offered sick and death benefits to their members, including informal nursing care, paid at the rate of $3.50 per day, provided by the fraternal associates of the afflicted

[17]Data regarding residence, marriage, and extended families are from *MS Census, 1900* and *MS Census, 1910.* For a general discussion of some of these points see Robert E. Kennedy, Jr., *The Irish: Emigration, Marriage, and Fertility* (Berkeley, 1973), 13, 149, 198. Rev. Michael J. Hannan, *Father English and St. Mary's Parish, Butte, Montana: The Miners' Catholic Church and Parish* (Butte, 1917), copy in Diocese of Helena Office, Helena, MT. Interview with Fr. Sarsfield O'Sullivan, Whitehall, MT, Nov. 19, 1984.
[18]Information on these and other Irish organizations in Butte is found in the Irish Collection, World Museum of Mining, Butte. Microfilm of this collection, 12 reels, is in the K. Ross Toole Archives, Mansfield Library, Univ. of Montana, Missoula. Hereafter cited as IrC. R. L. Polk's *Directories . . . Butte* (St. Paul and Butte, published yearly) for individual years list the Ancient Order of Hibernians and the Ladies' Auxiliaries with membership totals and officers for each. The secret and revolutionary Robert Emmet Literary Association (Clan-na-Gael) is not listed in Polk's. Reference to the RELA as the second largest in the United States is in Sunburst Club (Helena, Montana Clan-na-Gael), "Minute Books," Sept. 18, 1897. Irish Volunteers, "Minute Books," both in IrC.

members. Given that memberships consisted overwhelmingly of miners, these were important services.[19]

In brief, the ethnic, occupational, demographic, religious, and associational bases of Bodnar's enclave were unmistakeably evident. Like all enclaves, the community of Irish miners required a stable working class, men of steady habits and steadier employment, to sustain it. This was not easy under the best of industrial circumstances; it may have seemed unattainable, given the realities of the American quartz mining industry. Mines played out, markets collapsed, labor violence was met by the forced deportation of rebellious workers.[20] The result was men on the move, a vagabond proletariat as sensitive to the exigencies of cyclical economies as any chairman of the board.

Butte's Irish were drawn from that roaming working class. An analysis of the Irish populations of America's mining regions, the birthplace of the adult second generation Irish, and the birthplaces of the children of both the immigrant and second generations indicates the pattern. Between 1870 and 1890 the Irish were the most numerous European immigrant group in the anthracite and bituminous fields of Pennsylvania, the copper districts of Michigan, and the hardrock mining regions of the West. By 1900 many of these Irish and their children were in Butte. Based on the birthplace of second generation adults, Michigan was the most common state of previous residence, followed by Pennsylvania, New York, and the western mining states. The list of birthplaces of Irish children — of both immigrant and second generation parents — is headed by Michigan; then, in order, come Pennsylvania, California, Nevada, and Colorado.[21]

Data regarding county of origin for those born in Ireland does not come as easily. Census enumerators asked only for nation of birth, but specific, if not entirely exact information on Irish county of birth can be had be determining Butte's most numerous Irish surnames and tracing them to the counties with which they

---

[19]RELA, "Minute Books," passim; AOH, Divisions 1, 2, and 3, "Minute Books," passim. The sick and death benefits of both organizations are discussed in Emmons, "Immigrant Workers."
[20]For an example of the movement of Irish miners into Butte as a result of a mine closure see RELA, "Minute Books," Dec. 13, 1900. On mobility as a consequence of forced deportation see Executive Board, Western Federation of Miners, "Minute Books," May 25, Dec. 12, 1903; June 14, 1904 in Western History Collection, Univ. of Colorado, Boulder (hereafter cited as WHC). The three examples are from Anaconda, Montana; Telluride and Victor, Colorado.
[21]MS Census, 1900 and MS Census, 1910.

are most commonly associated. Based on City Directories for six representative years between 1886 and 1914, nine of the ten most commonly encountered Irish surnames were from County Cork. Corroborating evidence for this Cork connection is provided by Riobard O'Dwyer who traced the family histories of over 6000 men and women from the Eyeries parish in West Cork. Over 1700 people from that tiny corner of Ireland emigrated to the United States between 1870 and 1915 and of that total almost 1200 made their way to Butte. The occasion of this remarkable emigration was the failure of the copper mines of the Eyeries district.[22]

A number of related factors are indicated by this analysis of origins. Many of Butte's Irish were, in the language of one of them, "broken in." This meant a couple of things, among them an acute awareness of the ethno-centrism of their world. In the copper mines of West Cork, Cornishmen were brought in to assume supervisory positions; in Pennsylvania, Cornish and Welsh were arrayed against Irish Molly Maguires; in Michigan, the Finns were among their early rivals; in the western regions, the Cornish, the Chinese, and the Italians competed with them for jobs. But if a certain prickly Irishness accompanied them, so did the well-developed habits of protest that were a part of that Irishness. From the Land Leagues in Ireland, the Molly Maguires in Pennsylvania, the Miners' Unions of California, Nevada, and Colorado, the Irish learned the language and organization of worker protest.[23]

But they knew also the language and rhythm of work. Hardrock mining, particularly before the introduction of new tools

---

[22]The names were drawn from Polk's *Directories*. For a discussion of the close association of Irish surname with region see Edward MacLysaght, *Irish Families: Their Names, Arms and Origins* (New York, 1972), 38–39. Riobard O'Dwyer, *Who Were My Ancestors?* (Astoria, IL, 1976).

[23]The "broken in" miner was John Daly. See his testimony in Commission, *Industrial Conditions, 1915*, 3947. See also U.S., Bureau of Mines, "Metal Mine Accidents in the United States During 1918," by Albert Fay, Technical Paper 252 (Washington, DC, 1920). For the Irish-Cornish rivalry in the mines of West Cork see Daphne du Maurier, *Hungry Hill* (Cambridge, MA, 1943), 13–14, 23, 26. The best account of the Molly Maguires is Wayne Broehl, *The Molly Maguires* (Cambridge, 1964). The issue with the Finns is discussed by Jacob Oliver, a "neutral" Butte miner in Commission, *Industrial Conditions, 1915*, 3785–3786. See also Al Gedicks, "Ethnicity, Class Solidarity and Labor Radicalism Among Finnish Immigrants in Michigan Copper Country," *Politics and Society*, 7 (1977), 127–156. On ethnic rivalries in the Western hardrock districts see Lingenfelter, *Hardrock Miners*, 103–105, 186, 190, 195, 226; Brown, *Hard-Rock Miners*, 132–133; Wyman, *Epic*, 32–33, 42, 44, 45, 158, 167. The background in labor protest is dealt with by Lingenfelter, *Hardrock Miners*, 132–133 and Dubofsky, "Origins." See also the letter from "Kilmainham" to the *Miners Magazine*, Jan., 1901.

and machinery in the 1890s, was skilled work; the emerging Irish "aristocracy of labor," in other words, did have an artisanal element. The point is not that they worked faster or harder than the less experienced; the contrary was the case. At issue, however, was not production—"putting the rock in the box"—but safety. Good miners, "practical" miners as they were known, made fewer mistakes. Here was one instance where Irish workers possessed the necessary skills as well as the willingness to do the hard work. They were experienced miners for whom the pace of industrial mining can have held few surprises.[24]

This is not the same as saying it held few terrors. There were scant differences between broken in and broken down and nothing interrupted the steady employment they sought more quickly or with such devastating consequences as accident- or work-related illness. This, too, was a part of the Irish miner's remembered past It is true, as Hobsbawm notes, that a miner above ground was just another unskilled laborer. It is equally true, however, that a willingness to assume risks was as rare and hence as valuable a commodity as craft skills. Both were in demand. This willingness to assume the occupational hazards of their trade enhanced both the respect miners were paid by the middle class and the closeness of their working class enclave.[25] Like skilled tradesmen, and many of them were that as well, men who took uncommon risks were accorded uncommon status and a sense of personal superiority undoubtedly was a part of their consciousness of self. Unfortunately, this was an instance of rank without privilege;

---

[24]The U.S., Commissioner-General of Immigration counted immigrant miners as "skilled labor." See *Annual Report to the Secretary of the Treasury*, H. Doc. 758, 58th Cong., 2nd sess., 1903, 24. On this same point see Immigration Commission, *Immigrants in Industries, 1911*, 100, 101; James A. MacKnight, *The Mines of Montana . . . Prepared for the National Mining Congress* (Helena, 1892), 21–22; *Butte Mining Journal*, Feb. 25, 1891. Since the Irish miners in Cork were not allowed to use dynamite for reasons of political security, immigrants from there may have had little experience with explosives. See du Maurier, *Hungry Hill*, 76. The American labor leader, John Brophy spoke of his father's sense of pride in being a good miner. His comments are in Brody, *Workers in Industrial America*, 3–4. Brown, *Hard-Rock Miners*, 70–71, 78.

[25]Hobsbawm, "Aristocracy Reconsidered," 231. Reference to skilled miners is in U.S., Bureau of Mines, "A Preliminary Report of an Investigation of Miners' Consumption in the Mines of Butte, Mont., Made in the Years 1916–1919," by Daniel Harrington and A. J. Lanza, Technical Paper 260 (Washington, DC, 1921), 7–9, 11; *Butte Bystander*, Mar. 16, 1895; Executive Board, Western Federation of Miners, *Report, Dec. 16, 1906*, WHC. On middle class respect for those willing to assume risks see Paul Frisch, "'Gibralter of Unionism': The Development of Butte's Labor Movement, 1878–1900," unpublished paper, copy in Butte/Silver Bow Archives. Cantor, "Introduction," 16; Walkowitz, *Worker City*, 130; Brody, *Workers in Industrial America*, 4.

status gave them few if any means to minimize the risks and, even had it, the elimination of the risks would also have eliminated the special consideration that went with being a hardrock man.

Their work experience had also demonstrated their essential powerlessness in controlling the events which forced them to take to the road. But powerlessness, in this instance, bred resentment not resignation, deepening the wandering Irishman's determination to make Butte a permanent home. There are hundreds of entries in the Manuscript Census for Butte of Irish-born miners with children born in three or four different states. Assuming that a peripatetic life was not their first choice, Butte's Irish miners can be expected to have placed a premium on steadiness and stability, on becoming part of a settled Irish community.[26] To be sure, not many succeeded; there were over 2800 single Irish miners in Butte's boarding houses in 1900 and of the almost 6000 Irish in Butte in 1900, fewer than 1,000 were still there in 1910, a persistence rate of only 17%.[27]

The miners among that 17% constituted the heart of the enclave. The rewards of their steadiness determined the Irish standard of success. Those rewards were real, immediate, and compelling. They had families, they were part of a larger associational and religious community, they did honest work, many owned their homes. These were hard earned privileges; the men had paid their dues and they would do what was necessary to hold the enclave and their place in it.

The key element was persistence. They had to stay in one place long enough to accumulate a psychological and economic stake in the town. They had, in other words, to become an active part of the enclave. Persistence in this case, as in others, was its own reward. Using home ownership as a reasonable indicator of a settled Irish mining community provides an instructive lesson in working-class success. Of the entire number of Irish miners in 1900, 56% of those who had been in Butte four to seven years owned their homes; if eight or more years becomes the determinant

---

[26] *MS Census, 1900* and *MS Census, 1910.*
[27] *MS Census, 1900* and *MS Census, 1910.* This persistence rate is about the same as that for other industrializing towns at this time. See Mann, *After the Gold Rush,* 266.
[28] *MS Census, 1900.* See also Kathleen N. Conzens, "The New Urban History: Defining the Field," in *Ordinary People,* 75, 76. For miners, "upward" mobility was often the result of injuries that forced them to work "topside," often as a saloon keeper or police or fireman. See AOH, Division 1, "Minute Books," Aug. 17, 1892, Sept. 21, 1904, Jan. 11, 1905, April 5, 1905.

of persistence, the figure jumps to 73%. As in other parts of industrializing America, this level of persistence did not come easily and regular employment, of course, was a particular luxury in the hardrock regions. Occupational mobility, the alternative path to the security of property, would have required leaving the enclave; it had little meaning and less allure.[28]

The settled Irish miner was skilled in his craft, aware of his Irishness, aware, too, of his rights as a worker and practiced in the defense of both. He knew the dangers of his work, the cyclical nature of his industry — and that he was essentially helpless to influence either. He sought, above all other things, steady work. Butte provided it. There were, of course, periodic mine shut downs that reminded the Irish that they held their jobs on sufferance, that their "place in the community" was "at risk." But these hard times also had the effect of separating the stable and rooted Irish miners from the itinerant. The stable survived the shut downs, if not intact at least in place, another signal to the Irish and non-Irish communities alike of the steadiness of the Irish work force.[29] Two other sources of job insecurity, managerial innovation and technological change, did not appreciably affect the number or steadiness of jobs.[30]

Worker initiative, however, also played a role in smoothing out some of the unpredictability in the employment pattern by influencing, to the extent that circumstances would permit, the hiring and retention practices of the major employers. It is almost enough to point out that the first four managers of the huge Anaconda Company were Marcus Daly, William Scallon, John D. Ryan, and Cornelius F. Kelley. Not only was each an Irishman, each was also a member of the Irish Catholic Ancient Order of Hibernians; Scallon was a member of the RELA and Daly was proposed for RELA membership. But the Irish connection within the Anaconda Company did not stop with the highest office. The

---

[29]For early mine production statistics see *Engineering and Mining Journal*, Jan. 7, 1888; Michael Malone, *The Battle for Butte: Mining and Politics on the Northern Frontier, 1864–1906* (Seattle, 1981), 52–54, 149. By 1909 the copper production of the Butte district was over 40,000,000 tons, almost 20% of the world's production. MT., Dept. of Publicity, Bureau of Agriculture, Labor and Industry, *Report . . . 1911* (Helena, 1912), 153. The reference to the Irish place in the community is in AOH, Division 3, "Minute Books," Dec. 9, 1907. Mine shut downs occurred in 1891, 1893, 1903, 1907, and 1914.

[30]The consolidation of the Butte mines between 1899 and 1906 did not involve managerial changes. Those came in 1914 when various forms of "Taylorism" were tried.

general manager of Anaconda mines was usually an Irishman, as were the general superintendent and most of the hiring officers, the foremen and shift bosses, including such long time foremen as James Brennan, James Higgins, "Rimmer" O'Neill, Pat Kane, Mike O'Farrell, and John Sullivan. Indeed, one of the largest and certainly one of the most influential Irish "clubs" in Butte was the Anaconda Copper Mining Company.[31]

The Irish miner enclave understood the benefits implied by Irish run mines. Both the RELA and the AOH had active job committees, usually three prominent and influential members who were either mine foremen, and thus in a position to hire, or knew closely someone who was. There can have been few Irish miners who did not know someone in the enclave. During flush times this policy occasioned little comment from the non-Irish community. The mine shutdown of 1907, however, must have brought charges of influence peddling and one Hibernian suggested that "matters" of this sort "should be kept very secret so as not to get abroad and place some people in an embarrassing position." As for grumblers who were not placed through "this organization . . . we are better off without them . . . let them join the 'Birds and Animals' organizations and see how many jobs they will secure for them."[32]

---

[31] AOH, "Membership and Dues Ledgers, 1882–1914"; RELA, "Membership Ledgers, 1881–1919." Daly's nomination for membership in the revolutionary RELA is in "Minute Books," July 29, Aug. 5, 1886. IrC. No one was proposed for membership unless known to be sympathetic to the goals of the Clan-na-Gael. See H. B. C. Pollard, *The Secret Societies of Ireland: Their Rise and Progress* (London, 1922), 307–311. For a partial list of Anaconda hiring officers see WPA, *Copper Camp: Stories of the World's Greatest Mining Town, Butte, Montana* (New York, 1943), vii–viii, 3, 8, 209–210; John Lindsay, *Amazing Experiences of a Judge* (Philadelphia, 1939), 81–82; Isaac Marcosson, *Anaconda* (New York, 1957), 22, 41, 61; Polk's *Directories* often listed the names of shift bosses and foremen; see for selected years, *passim*. The "Irish" mines included the Anaconda, the St. Lawrence, the Neversweat, and the Mountain Consolidated. Two of Marcus Daly's and the Anaconda Company's most determined enemies also claimed to be Irish. F. Augustus Heinze said his mother was of Norman Irish descent and, more tangibly, gave $500 to a fund to construct a monument to an Irish hero, *The Reveille*, (Butte), Oct. 11, 1902; P. J. Brophy to Heinze, June 19, 1903 in Brophy Papers, Montana Historical Society, Helena. William Andrews Clark, during a heated political campaign, claimed to be a descendant of Robert Emmet and a fluent Gaelic speaker. *Missoula Gazette* in *Butte Intermountain*, Sept. 26, 1888. Clearly, Prof. Mark Wyman's point that the mine workers in the West were immigrants and the mine managers native does not apply to Butte. See *Epic*, 57.

[32] Both organizations were required by their by-laws and oaths to give job preference to other members. AOH, *Ritual and Manual of the AOH in America* (Oshkosh, Wisc., 1901), 5. The secret Clan-na-Gael oath was "exposed" in the *Examiner* (Butte), Dec. 21, 1895. Reference to Job or Employment committees appears regularly in the "Minute Books" of both the AOH and the RELA. The two references quoted are from AOH, Division 3, Nov. 16, 1908 and April 19, 1913. For similar stories from other cities see Walkowitz, *Worker City*, 95–96,

There is no record of how successful the Irish associations were in finding employment. There can be no question, however, that the AOH and the RELA appealed to the most work experienced, careful, and skilled members of the Irish labor force. In the first place, prospective members had to have been known by the men proposing them for at least three years; there are hundreds of entries in the membership ledgers of new men with "known for 10 (or more) years" or "knew him in Ireland" next to the name of his proposer. There were other checks on casual membership. Only members in good standing for six months were eligible for sick and death benefits; the initiation fees, yearly dues, and assessments of both organizations were in excess of a week's wages, further discouraging the itinerant. The result was even greater distance between the settled and the unsettled Irish miners, perhaps reaching the point, as Bodnar writes, "that workers with . . . connections . . . were actually held in higher esteem than 'unattached' employees, who were presumed to be more transient." There is no question that these Irish associations exercised a considerable influence in the "stabilization" of Butte.[33]

Of equal significance, however, is that the Irish had an advantage over the non-Irish, of whatever social status, particularly in the Anaconda mines. One member of the territorial legislature, for example, noted that it was ". . . a matter of common report that the laborers of (the) Anaconda were almost exclusively Irish. . . ." "Clannishness," he went on, "was characteristic of the human race," but it was unfair that ". . . of two men equally competent to fill a position, the Irishman invariably got it." Butte's mines were as ethnically identified as its neighborhoods.[34]

152–153; Dennis Clark, *The Irish in Philadelphia: Ten Generations of Urban Experience* (Philadelphia, 1973), 68.

[33]AOH, *By-laws, revised and adopted . . . Jan. 26, 1887*; AOH, "Black Book" (untitled, pocket-sized summary of rules), copies in IrC. RELA, "Membership and Dues Ledgers"; "Minute Books." Both contain reference to how many years the proposed members were known. It was never fewer than three. It is difficult to track names from year to year in the membership ledgers but an unscientific survey indicates beyond question that both organizations had a stable core of more than 100 men who had been in Butte for five or more years. Father Michael Hannan spoke for the community when he said that members of Irish associations "towered above the average Irishman, morally, socially, and economically. . . ." AOH, Division 3, "Minute Books," Dec. 21, 1908. Father Michael Kennedy congratulated the Hibernians for holding their jobs during the shut down of 1907. It "spoke well for their sobriety and ability." *Ibid.*, Sept. 23, 1907. See also P. J. Brophy to Conor O'Kelley, June 20, 1904, Brophy Papers, and the comments of Con Kelley to the Commission, *Industrial Conditions, 1915*, 3695. The Bodnar quote is from *Workers' World*, 174.

[34]*Helena Independent*, Feb. 20, 1889. See also *Butte Mining Journal*, Feb. 20, 1889. Some mines

More was involved than ethnocentrism. At a time when two man drills were the rule, men worked in pairs. Drill teams tended to consist of men of like ethnicity and shift crews may have reflected a similar ethnic homogeneity. One result, sought by worker and mine owner alike, was safer mines. Put simply, Irish were more considerate of the safety of other Irish. This does not mean that mine owners were unaware of the usefulness of ethnic rivalries in boosting production or combating worker solidarity.[35] But those were objects that required mixing the entire work force of a district; they were not served by mixing drill teams or shift crews.

The anti-Catholic and anti-immigrant American Protective Association, was not moved by the arguments for safety. There were Irish mines, said the APA newspaper, because "soulless corporations prefer those they can control." In Butte, with its Irish-run mines, that meant that "'NO MAN OF ENGLISH BIRTH NEED APPLY' was virtually posted on the doors of the Anaconda syndicate of mines." These charges came within a year of the formation of the potentially radical Western Federation of Miners, during a particularly severe economic depression, and immediately after the violent strikes in the mining districts of Idaho and Colorado. The point was made that the APA was using religion and ethnicity to split the working class. The point was credible.[36]

But so were some of the APA charges. Nativists may have been right when they claimed that "suspicion of A.P.A. affiliation" led to immediate discharge from Anaconda mines. Marcus Daly made no effort to hide his Irishness or his distaste for "Orangemen and A.P.As." In addition to his AOH affiliation and

were known as Irish. WPA, *Copper Camp*, 173; Wayland Hand, "Songs of the Butte Miners," *Western Folklore*, 9 (Jan., 1950), 7; Father Patrick Brosnan to his mother Kilflynn, Co. Kerry, June 19, 1917, Brosnan Letters. I am indebted to Prof. Kerby Miller of the University of Missouri for making these letters available to me.
[35]Evidence of the use of this practice in Butte is found in William Read to Walker Bros., July 18, 1878, Alice Gold and Silver Mining Co. Records, Letter Press Books, Montana Historical Society. See also Immigration Commission, *Immigrants in Industry 1911*, 156–157; Commission, *Industrial Conditions, 1915*, 3747. The *Montana Socialist* commented on how the "Babel of Tongues" hurt the cause of worker solidarity. Nov. 13, 1915. The AOH complained that hardline Protestants refused "to enter into an agreement with Catholics for a strike." John O'Dea, *History of the AOH in America*, 4 vols. (Philadelphia, 1926), III: 1108. See also Lingenfelter, *Hardrock Miners*, 225; Cantor, "Introduction," 15–18.
[36]For the APA charges see the *Examiner*, June 15, 1895, Feb. 27, Mar. 19, April 19, Oct. 31, 1896. The charge that the APA was trying to prevent labor solidarity was made by the *Butte Bystander*, April 6, June 29, July 16, 1895; May 24, 1896. See also Lingenfelter, *Hardrock Miners*, 190–194.

RELA sympathies, he was a close reader of Patrick Ford's *Irish World and American Industrial Liberator*. Both halves of Ford's newspaper's title might have affected his hiring policy. It would certainly not have been out of character for him to aid the Irish world by hiring the Irish industrial worker. Whatever the cause, and AOH and RELA influence may have been considerable, there were 1251 Irish-born and 365 English-born miners among the 5534 men working in Daly's mines in 1894, and this at a time when the English outnumbered the Irish in Butte.[37]

The active involvement of the enclave in job placement undoubtedly eased the "recruiting" chores of the foremen and shift bosses. These hiring officers had only to maintain ties with the ethnic community, in most instances a natural consequence of their membership in that community, to insure a supply of steady and Irish workers. In partial return, the foremen and shifters, with the approval of the mine managers, allowed AOH and RELA members free access to the mines for fund-raising purposes ranging from the Boer Ambulance Corps Fund to the Thomas Francis Meagher Memorial Fund. They provided day shift work for association officers, practice time off for the association bands. Most significantly, they closed the mines on such exclusively Irish holidays as St. Patrick's Day and Robert Emmet's birthday. The response of the non-Irish miner to the loss of a day's pay was not recorded; neither was the reaction of the Butte Miners' Union, faced with holidays that rivalled its own Miners' Union Day and, to a theoretical extent, mocked its very pretensions of union.[38]

There had to have been times when this fraternal goodwill verged perilously close to union manipulation and graft. The Irish-born labor leader Edward Boyce, in fact, made this charge, excoriating Daly for playing upon ethnicity and ethnic rivalries to

[37]The *Examiner*, June 15, 1895; *Butte Bystander*, July 16, 1895. On Daly's habit of reading the *Irish World* see Hugh Daly, *Biography of Marcus Daly* (Butte, 1934), 2–3. The 1894 statistics are taken from Anaconda Copper Mining Co., General Office, Subject File 522, Montana Historical Society. On the percentage of English see Bureau of the Census, *12th Census, 1900*, 798. Note the Daly-like Irish mine owner in Clyde Murphy's novel of Butte, *The Glittering Hill* (Cleveland, 1944).

[38]The "Minute Books" of both organizations are filled with references like "Mr. Daly to close the mines on the day of the pic-nic," (RELA, June 13, 1889), ". . . assurances that the syndicate mines would close down that day for repairs," (RELA, July 5, 1900), ". . . all the managers . . . promised that the mines would close down on that occasion." (AOH, Division 1, March 3, 1900), IrC; Walkowitz discusses the consequences of the competition between ethnic and union sponsored social activities. *Worker City*, 157.

control the unions, a control Boyce thought so complete that he removed the Western Federation of Miners' headquarters from Butte to Denver. On another occasion a member of the AOH stated that newer men sometimes hesitated to speak freely at AOH meetings, fearing that what they said would be repeated "on the sixth floor," a reference to the Hennessy Building where the Anaconda Company had its corporate headquarters.[39]

In addition to these perhaps imaginary fears of collusion was the fact that the Hibernians and the Emmets were performing the duties usually reserved for labor organizations. Irish associations found their members jobs, helped them to keep those jobs in hard times, paid sick and death benefits, even determined worker holidays. They became what Hobsbawm called "informal unions," as important to the worker in his search for stability as the formal unions. Their members seemed to understand this. In 1910 Thomas Kealy of Division 3 of the Hibernians said he wanted no "fallen away Hibernians" around him: "They were *scabs, worse than scabs*" (an interesting choice of words).[40]

A usual question asked about working-class enclaves — whether in the process of serving as informal unions they usurped formal union power and deflected worker allegiance or supplemented the union's power and broadened the workers' allegiance — has little meaning in this context. In Butte enclave and union were part of one another. Butte's mines were operated on a closed shop basis until 1914. The entire mine work force, or at least those the union's officers could catch, including the mine foremen and shift bosses, paid dues to the Butte Miners Union, making it the largest local in the United States with a membership in 1910 of almost 7000 men. The vast majority of that membership, however, limited its participation in union affairs to paying dues and celebrating Miners' Union Day. This left the management of the BMU to officers who were often chosen in elections in which fewer than 25% of the total membership

---

[39]Boyce's attacks on Daly are in the *Miners Magazine*, May, Aug., and Dec., 1900. For Boyce's account of why he moved the WFM offices see his Travel Diary, May 24, 1897; June 1, 1897; Edward Boyce Papers, Eastern Washington State Historical Society Library, Spokane. See also WFM, *Proceedings, 11th Annual Convention, 1903*, (Denver, 1903), 185-186. The remark about the sixth floor is from AOH, Division 3, "Minute Books," Oct. 30, 1915, IrC.
[40]Hobsbawm, "Aristocracy Reconsidered," 239. The Kealy quote is from AOH, Division 3, "Minute Books," July 9, 1910, IrC, emphasis mine. See also Brody, *Workers in Industrial America*, 22-23.

bothered to vote. The BMU, in other words, was run by the older, established miners selected by those who wished to become the same. In Butte, that meant the Irish.[41]

The first president of what became the Butte Miners' Union was A. C. Witter, a native of Indiana, but the four officers who served with him were Pat Shovlin, Ed Rooney, John Sullivan, and William Larkin. Between 1883 and 1896, the BMU elected 23 Irishmen to the 26 highest Union offices, president and secretary; in 1897 all 14 of the Union's offices went to Irishmen. Nothing changed in the 1900s. The president in 1901 was John J. Quinn. He was followed, successively, by Ed Hughes, William McGrath, Ed Long, Francis O'Connor, P. J. Duffy, James Shea, P. W. Flynn, Dan Holland, Dan Sullivan, George Curry, Dennis Murphy, and, in 1914, Bert Riley.[42]

As important as the Irishness of the leadership was the fact that many of the officers of the BMU were also active members of the AOH and/or the RELA. A check of Union officers against the Irish associations' membership ledgers turned up 62 different names between 1882 and 1914. In 1905, to cite just one specific example, the AOH hired a "solicitor," a member whose responsibility it was to bring lapsed Hibernians back to good standing. The man selected was Daniel J. McCarthy. He was the ideal choice; he worked at the Mountain Con, known as one of the "Irish" mines, lived in Dublin Gulch, and, most significantly, was the Treasurer of the BMU.[43]

---

[41]Foner, "Class, Ethnicity, and Radicalism," 176, 195–197; Walkowitz, *Worker City*, 124, 164–165. Wilentz, "Industrial America," 586. Some claimed the BMU was the largest local in the world. *Butte Mining Journal*, Sept. 5, 1888; Frank Bohn, "Butte Number One," *The Masses*, 5, (August, 1914), 9. William Haywood claimed it was the largest in the US. *The Autobiography of Big Bill Haywood* (New York, 1929), 83. As a general rule, between 75–80% of the miners were paid up members. *Butte Bystander*, Mar. 17, 1894; L. O. Evans, *Address to Missoula (Montana) Chamber of Commerce, 1917*, 16. In the election of 1910 1825 votes were cast for the presidency of a union with more than 7000 members. *Butte Independent*, June 4, 1910. See also the remarks in the *Butte Mining Journal*, April 25, June 9, 1888.

[42]The *Butte Bystander* of June 7, 1896 listed the presidents of the union from its founding in 1878, along with the men who served with Witter. The 1897 officer list is from *ibid.*, Mar. 7, 1897. Polk's *Directories* list all the officers from 1901 to 1914. BMU delegates to Western Federation of Miners conventions also were overwhelmingly Irish. See, for example, the names O'Connor, James O'Neill, Malloy, McCarthy, Jeremiah O'Neill, O'Leary, Kelleher, Lowney, and Duffy—the Butte delegates from 1906. WFM, *Proceedings . . . 14th Annual Convention* (Denver, 1906), 210–211. The leadership of the BMU was more overwhelmingly Irish than that of the other WFM locals. *Butte Bystander*, Nov. 15, 1896; Immigration Commission, *Immigrants in Industry, 1911*, 145, 211.

[43]AOH, "Membership and Dues Ledgers," RELA, "Membership and Dues Ledgers." The McCarthy story is in AOH, Division 1, "Minute Books," August 16, 1905, IrC. McCarthy's position with the BMU was noted in Polk, *Directory, 1906*.

This close association between Union officers and Irish associations was to be expected. The result, however, was a Union that appeared to its critics an extension of the Irish enclave, an enclave that, though based solidly in the working class, did not represent all the components of that class. The division was not entirely ethnic. The BMU spoke to the needs of the stable and persistent of whatever nationality. As one contemporary put it, the BMU was "made up of a splendid body, many of whom were heads of families and owners of their own homes."[44] Whatever the reason, on every important issue that faced it from 1902 until internal dissension destroyed it in 1914, the BMU took the position best calculated to enhance the security of the established miners by stabilizing the work force and insuring steady employment.

It strongly supported the eight hour day not because it sought a duel with the owners over workplace authority but because it would increase by 20% the number of years a miner could work. The 10 hour work day meant a career of about 15 years; many miners were unable to work beyond their mid-40s. Guy Miller, a veteran of many mines and many miner battles, put the matter as directly as it could be put. The eight hour work day "not only *lengthened the years of men's service in the mines* . . . it multiplied the opportunity to live during their years."[45]

Of equal significance was the guarantee of a wage that made those years tolerable. Everywhere in the western mining districts the "Butte scale," $3.50 per day, obtained. The BMU, however, paid less attention to the daily wage and more to the yearly incomes those wages produced, incomes which, by 1905, were said to give Butte one of the highest payrolls per capita in the world and Butte's miners among the highest incomes in the industry. As Dan Lynch, a BMU officer, told the AOH, a "man could make as much money in Ireland as in America — except in Butte." No one could have missed Lynch's point. Certainly the BMU did not and, in direct violation of WFM policy, sought to make perma-

[44]C. P. Connolly, "The Labor Fuss in Butte," *Everybody's Magazine* 31 (August, 1914), 207. For a discussion of the stabilizing influence of women see Elizabeth Pleck, "Women's History: Gender as a Category of Historical Analysis," in *Ordinary People,* 51; Mann, *After the Gold Rush,* 44–46, 56–67, passim, 107–114, 160–168.

[45]On the question of workplace authority see Bodnar, *Workers' World,* 65. On a miner's life expectancy see Commission, *Industrial Relations, 1915,* 3916. Guy Miller's remarks are from WFM, *Proceedings . . . 21st Biennial Convention* (Denver, 1914), 132, emphasis mine.

nent those wages by negotiating time contracts with the mining companies in 1907 and 1912.[46]

These contracts, moreover, were based on sliding scales that reflected the price of copper, a provision that both stabilized the work force if prices fell and tied the workers to the long term success of the companies. This was not, however, an association the Miners' Union found compromising. In 1901, BMU bought $50,000 worth of Anaconda Company stock; three years later, it supported the consolidation of Butte's mines, a consolidation that stabilized the work force, producing, among other direct consequences, dramatic increases in AOH and RELA memberships.[47]

Finally, the union did not protest the hiring or work place transfer practices of the mines. Foremen hired, shift bosses and foremen could fire. Either could reassign individuals or drilling teams to different parts of the mine or to different mines. But the men who held both of these offices were also members of the BMU. It was natural to expect that "conservatives" would be given preferential treatment in hiring and retention, and that they would be assigned safer jobs. Joseph Shannon, for example, an untiring if not convincing critic of BMU conservatism, insisted

[46]For Butte payrolls see WPA, *Copper Camp*, 291. The Census Bureau compiled statistics showing that Montana's wages were the highest paid in the U.S.; *12th Census, 1900*, Part II, *Manufacturers*, 500, 504, 505. In 1900 Montanans had the highest per capita income in the U.S. See E. S. Lee, et al, *Population Redistribution and Economic Growth, US., 1870-1950*, vol. I, *Methodological Considerations and Reference Tables* (Philadelphia, 1957), 753. National figures are in Philip Taylor, *The Distant Magnet: European Emigration to the U.S.A.* (New York, paperback edition, 1973), 188. Evidence that workers—and merchants—were more interested in yearly rather than daily wages is found in Commission, *Industrial Relations, 1915*, 3701, 3742-43, 3831; Lynch's remarks are from AOH, Division 3, "Minute Books," July 15, 1907. IrC. Railroads promoted the emigration of industrial workers to Montana using payrolls as one lure. See, for example, Union Pacific RR., *Resources of Montana, 1890* (Chicago, 1891), 78-79. The contract issue is discussed in Mt., Dept. of Labor and Industry, *First Biennial Report* (Helena, 1914), 24; WFM, *Proceedings . . . 20th Annual Convention* (Victor, CO, 1912), 256ff, 307. The WFM prohibition against time contract was repeated in 1907. See *Proceedings . . . 15th Annual Convention* (Denver, 1907), 261. See also Vernon H. Jensen, *Heritage of Conflict: Labor Relations in the Nonferrous Metals Industry up to 1930* (Ithaca, 1950), 71, 304-05.

[47]Mt., Dept. of Labor and Industry, *First Report*, 24-26; Commission, *Industrial Relations 1915*, 3692, 3715, 3854; the stock purchase deal is discussed in *ibid.*, 3853-54, 3866; *Miners Magazine*, August, 1901. Consolidation and its effects on employment are mentioned in Malone, *Battle*, 140, 155, 188. For the effects of corporate consolidation in another city see Walkowitz, *Worker City*, 27-29. The charge that the BMU supported consolidation was made in WFM, *Proceedings*, 1914, 56-57. For AOH and RELA membership jumps see the "Minute Books" of both organizations for the years from 1904-1906. It is worth noting that the Cornish miners responded to consolidation by leaving town; they preferred the freedom and leasing privileges possible with decentralized mine ownership. See Immigration Commission, *Immigrants in Industry, 1911*, 111-113, 115; Haywood, *Autobiography*, 58; Raphael Samuel, (ed.), *Miners, Quarrymen and Saltworkers* (London, paperback edition, 1977), 48-49, 58-60.

that these "fine day miners . . . got an easy place in the mine, where the air is good and they always have a good word for the company. . . ." The dangerous jobs went to "the men that are not inclined to be company men . . . strong men, . . . weak in the head."[48]

Such union policies were bound to provoke criticism. The BMU was universally judged one of the most conservative in the nation, its own officers noting that ". . . for fair employers, this union will at times strain a point to be more than just. . . ." Guy Miller later argued that the "conservative, who, finding things pretty fair and wages pretty fair, . . . *if left alone,*" was not a likely candidate for social revolution. Like all members of an enclave, he had too well developed a sense of the limits on what was possible to "engage constantly for (what) cannot be granted."[49] The man who spoke those last lines was Con Kelley, boss of the Anaconda mines. His office, however, does not disqualify him. Kelley was Irish, a member of the AOH, and a former hardrock miner; he knew well the enclave and its values. John C. Lowney, another Butte Irishman and one-time BMU president said essentially the same thing: Lowney was commenting on William Haywood's 1910 Butte speech which promised that the radical IWW "would nail the red flag to the mast of #1 and that Amalgamated officials would climb up there every morning and get down on their knees to it. . . ." Lowney asked, "see if you can imagine the Amalgamated officials going up to kiss a red flag every morning." There was no sycophancy to Lowney's remarks; he was simply stating the obvious to men who shared his understanding of it.[50]

It was not just BMU conservatism, however, that outraged the insurgents but also the distinct brogue with which that conservatism was expressed. Joe Shannon claimed that the Irishmen who negotiated the 1907 contract for the BMU "went over and

---

[48]Commission, *Industrial Relations, 1915*, 3857-58. The same charge was made in 1917 by another radical, Thomas Campbell. MT., Council of Defense, "Minute Books," July 26, 1917; Montana Historical Society.

[49]The statement from the BMU is in *Miners Magazine*, Dec. 10, 1903; Guy Miller's remarks are in WFM, *Proceedings*, 1914, 135, emphasis mine. The last reference is from Commission, *Industrial Relations 1915*, 3860. One of the earliest references to BMU conservatism and company control of its officers is in *Butte Mining Journal*, June 3, 1891; the point was repeated endlessly until 1914.

[50]Kelley's background in the mines is in Marcossen, *Anaconda*, 67-77. A summary of Haywood's remarks and Lowney's response is in WFM, *Proceedings*, 1914, 154.

bought real estate in Ireland. . . . They went back home." To the oft-repeated charge that the Anaconda Company controlled the conservative leadership of the BMU was added the more specific charge that the "great majority of the members are conservatives, that the Catholic Irish have been the leading factions among the conservatives. . . ." One sure way of discrediting radicalism, it was pointed out in 1914, would be for the "copper barons" to disguise someone as a radical "soap box orator . . . and have him start by killing Jesus and damning the pope. You fellows in Butte want to watch for this type."[51]

The point is not that the Irish were inherently conservative or that they had succumbed to the temptations of lace curtains. Neither is it that their Catholicism had befuddled their awareness of class. In their own minds the Irish miners were simply protecting the enclave by protecting their jobs, their families, and their health, goals that appeared conservative only to those for whom the enclave had no meaning.[52]

Change overtook the Irish miner enclave between 1910 and 1914. New technology eroded the usefulness of old skills. The experienced hand no longer had an advantage over the tyro. Anyone could be a hardrock man. In addition, the search for new ores — zinc and manganese — as well as the enormously acceler-

---

[51]Commission, *Industrial Relations, 1915*, 3854; WFM, *Proceedings, 1912*, 260. For the same point see *ibid. 1914*, 137. Bill Haywood burlesqued the brogue in his "The Battle of Butte," *International Socialist Review*, 15 (Oct. 1914), 223. The "killing Jesus" remark is in the *Butte Miner*, Oct. 16, 1914. Shannon, although Irish and a long time Butte resident, was not in the enclave. He did not live in Dublin Gulch, mined only intermittently, was not a member of either of the Irish associations, had "stirred up the foreign element" in the lumber camps outside of Butte, and, as a final rejection of the enclave, stated publicly that "this soul business is a kind of myth with me . . . I believe in looking after the body . . . we have enough to do to take care of the body." Polk, *Directories*, 1908–1914; Commission, *Industrial Relations, 1915*, 3856; Evans, *Address*, 1917, 7. The AOH application forbidding any association with societies "the Catholic Church is opposed to" would alone have disqualified him. Copy of 1893 application in IrC.

[52]For the dedicated Irish nationalists, harmonious industrial relations in Butte may have seemed to favor the cause. Certainly the interclass nature of the Irish associations strengthened the ethnic community. For most Irish, however, there can have seemed little direct relationship between events in Butte and developments in Ireland. The church, to be sure, was conservative; Irish-American Bishop of Montana John Carroll delivered a scathing sermon on the evils of socialism — but this is most assuredly not the same as saying Catholics were conservative. For these and related matters see Irish Volunteers, Co. A, "Minute Books," Oct. 11, 1914; RELA, "Minute Books," June 24, 1914; *Butte Independent* (the city's Irish newspaper), April 2, 1910; Bishop John Carroll, "Sermon, St. James Cathedral, Nov. 16, 1913," typescript copy in Carroll Papers, Diocese of Helena Office. See also the response to a previous anti-socialist pastoral letter in the *Montana Socialist*, Aug. 31, 1913. For a very instructive discussion of the limits of clerical influence see James Carroll, "On Not Skipping the Sermon," *Commonweal*, III (Nov. 2–16, 1984), 603–05.

ated demand for copper after World War I, created a demand for these new men. Failed strikes in Michigan, South Dakota, and Colorado as well as a new wave of immigration from Southern and Eastern European countries put thousands of unattached men on the road. Butte, as always, was a common destination.[53] Further increasing the attractiveness of these new immigrants was the promise and eventual passage of state Workmen's Compensation. There is considerable irony in the fact that this law, designed to make the work place safer, encouraged the mining companies to hire inexperienced foreign nationals who were either unmarried or whose wives and parents lived in Europe and were thus ineligible for compensation benefits. The result of these developments was a mine work force different from, and infinitely more dangerous than, any the Irish had known in Butte.[54]

Making the matter worse was the fact that the Irish miner enclave, unlike most aristocracies of labor, was not reproducing itself. The second generation of Butte Irishmen, as well as the later immigrants, showed considerably less interest in the Hibernians and the Emmets and both organizations began to age appreciably. Neither did the members of this second generation go into the mines, at least not at the rate their fathers had. In 1910 three out of every four Irish immigrants worked underground; fewer than half the second generation Irish joined them. The reasons had nothing to do with status. The second generation did not move into white collar jobs. Most only moved above ground — horizontally in terms of occupational mobility. Many of those who did advance did so within the miner enclave; by 1911 19% of the second generation Irish were in supervisory positions in the mines. This was a remarkably high percentage, attesting to their skills, the pull of tradition, and the strength and

---

[53]See the statistics from the Butte Free Employment Office for 1913. The demand for work far exceeded the supply of jobs. MT Dept. of Labor and Industry, *1st Biennial Report, 1913-14*, 55. Malone, *Battle*, 4-5; Commission, *Industrial Relations, 1915*, 3782, 3855-56; *Montana Socialist*, June 28, 1914.

[54]Workmen's Compensation was passed in 1911 but struck down by the state courts. It was passed again in 1915. For its effects on hiring practices see *Montana Socialist*, Jan. 8, 1916; "Butte-Anaconda Joint Strike Bulletin," June 11, 1917; *Butte Bulletin*, Sept. 10, Sept. 30, 1918. By 1918 Butte had the fourth largest Local Exemption Board in the United States with 8677 registered resident aliens. J. H. Rowe, Local Board Chairman, to John S. Smith, Chief Naturalization Examiner, Seattle, Jan. 31, 1918, Record Group 60, Dept. of Justice Files, 186233-61, microfilm, Univ. of Montana. There is a "No Smoking" sign from this era at the World Museum of Mining in Butte. The warning is in 15 languages.

reach of the enclave; but attesting, too, to the dangers, including the delayed hazard of miners' consumption, inherent in working in the deep mines.[55]

The so-called Bohunk invasion of 1910 was the first indication that the social order was changing. Three thousand East European immigrants were said to have arrived in Butte; all were men, none was married. They bought jobs from foremen who then rented them cabins. The reputation of these Slovaks, however, had preceded them. From every mining camp had come the stories: they depressed wages, drove out the steady men with families ("white men," said one newspaper, "good old miners of the Marcus Daly days."), sent their wages back to Europe, embraced all manner of radical theories yet were impossible to organize, were surly and unmanageable and a hazard to themselves and those with whom they worked. The enclave was not, of course, the only community affected by these East Europeans; it responded to the threat, however, with characteristic directness. Peter Breen, a prominent Irish attorney, spoke for the enclave when he commented simply that Marcus Daly would not have let the "Bohunks" into Butte, a remark that says more than Breen probably intended.[56]

Two years later another instance of ethnic rivalry presented an even greater challenge to the Irish dominated Butte Miners' Union. In March 1912, 500 Finnish Socialists were fired from their

---

[55]Of 1037 applications for membership in AOH, Division 1, only 281 are identified as "Irish by descent." IrC. There was considerable concern on this point. See for example, Division 3, "Minute Books," Nov. 29, 1910, Dec. 24, 1910; O'Dea, AOH, vol. III, 1381, 1390, 1502. By 1910, of the adult male population, 73 percent of the immigrant Irish and only 44 percent of the second generation worked underground. MS Census, 1910. The 19 percent figure for second generation mine supervisors is from Immigration Commission, Immigrants in Industry, 1911, 563; see also 115, 150.

[56]The Butte Evening News, July 24, 1910 had the first story on the "invasion." See also the issues of July 17, July 18, July 23, July 31 and Aug. 1, 1910; WPA, Copper Camp, 133-136. For other references to these new immigrants see Butte Bystander, Oct. 16, 1897; The Reveille (Butte), Aug. 28, 1902; Immigration Commission, Immigrants in Industry, 1911, 97, 109, 122, 123, 151; Thomas Meagher to Ed Boyce, Dec. 26, 1913, Boyce Papers; WFM, Proceedings, 1914, 50-51, 193; Montana Socialist, March 6, 1915. Data on the decrease in individual worker production and the increase in worker turnover are in Paul F. Brissenden, "The Butte Miners and the Rustling Card," American Economics Review, 10 (1920), 770, 771. Sick and death benefits from the BMU averaged $7,700 per year from 1878 to 1899; in 1910 the total was $78,000. WFM, Proceedings . . . 18th Annual Convention (Denver, 1910), 200-203. On the background of these new men nationally see Brody, Workers in Industrial America, 16-18. Breen's comments and the reference to the Marcus Daly days are in Butte Evening News, July 24, 1910. There was trouble of some kind between the Irish and the East Europeans. See AOH, Division 3, "Minute Books," Aug. 13, 1910, Mar. 22, 1913.

jobs in the mines. They went to the BMU and demanded that
the union avenge them, even to the point of calling a strike to
recover their jobs. The BMU had never in its 34 year history called
a strike; it was not going to call one now. A strike vote was held;
the fired miners losing by more than 3000 votes. The Finns claimed
discrimination by both the companies and the union; in fact, they
hardly distinguished between the two. The leadership of the BMU,
they said, was controlled by the Anaconda Company, and both
union and company felt threatened by recent Socialist victories
in Butte and Silver Bow County. Firing Socialists was the first
step in their joint counter offensive.[57]

The Finns were for the most part unmarried, unsettled, and
had a reputation for carelessness in the mines. They were said
to be opposed to time contracts and individual leases and to consider sabotage a legitimate weapon in the conduct of class war.
Each of these positions, said the editor of a Finnish language
newspaper, was the result of their experiences with the Finnish
labor movement. There the distinctions between worker and political action were not as clearly drawn as in Butte, but the policies that arose from that unwillingness to separate the two were
anathema to security conscious Irish miners. If this were not
enough, the availability of the Finns and other "new immigrants,"
as the Federal Immigration Commission of 1911 noted, "has tended
to prevent the advance of wages." In Montana, the Commission
went on in a revealing statement, "this tendency has been resisted
. . . by the activity of the union which has been largely responsible for . . . *the retention in the industry of a considerable number
of the native-born and north Europeans now employed in it.*"[58]

These were significant issues, but to this list must be added
another more personal one. As Jacob Oliver, a close observer,
put it, ". . . there was a good deal of race feeling in connection"
with the Finns' charge of company dominance of the union. In

---

[57]WFM, *Proceedings, 1912,* 20, 22, 259, 319; Commission, *Industrial Relations, 1915,* 3744.
[58]On alien status see Commission, *Industrial Relations, 1915,* 3725-26, 4006. The point was made
   that the Socialists wanted to incorporate Anaconda property into the city and tax it accordingly. The company retaliated. WFM, *Proceedings, 1914,* 154-155. The Finns' experiences
   in Finland are discussed by Frank Aaltonen in *ibid.,* 190-191; see also 125-127, 269, 281-82;
   Gedicks, "Ethnicity," pp. 133, 136. The BMU constitution forbade "the introduction of anything of a political nature." *Miners Magazine,* Aug. 1902. The influence of the BMU in "retaining" jobs for north Europeans (read Irish) is from Immigration Commission, *Immigrants
   in Industry, 1911,* 211, emphasis mine.

other words, the Finns noticed, as they could hardly have not, the Irish ties. Nor did the Irish miss the point. While the strike vote was being taken, "throngs was [sic] yelling, 'they are all Socialists, Finlanders.' 'To hell with them'" And, as the vote showed, the enclave was determined that the Finns, as Oliver went on, were "not going to drive (the Irish) out of Butte."[59]

This can only have been a reference to jobs and to the Finns' and other new immigrants' growing ability to influence BMU policy regarding them. Hostility to time contracts made those jobs less secure; sabotage and other forms of what the radicals called "direct action" destroyed jobs as surely as mines. In addition, wages had the disconcertingly bad habit of going down in those regions where "new immigrants" dominated. These were the reasons, according to one Finn, "why Butte #1 eliminated those Finlanders from that organization," why, according to a contemporary, the firings "had the sanction of union officials." Further evidence that the companies had less to do with the dismissals than the union is found in the fact that most of the Finns were offered their jobs back; the companies, it seemed, had discovered that "over zealous foremen," many of them Irish and all of them union men, had fired more Finns than the political situation required.[60]

Obviously the old hiring system based on the ethnic community had broken down by 1912. But the problems were not just ethnic. The supply of job seekers was greater than the number of jobs, always a concern of the BMU, and the new men, Irish included, were less settled, less safety conscious, and less productive. A sign on North Butte Mining Company property, for example, warned "Be Careful! Don't Get Hurt. There are TEN MEN Waiting for YOUR JOB!" The surplus ten were also more radical, or at least more riotous. Radical organizations, particularly the Industrial Workers of the World, played to these men. They were the "most miserable of America's workers," as Bill Haywood called them. But, according to another radical, they constituted,

[59]Commission, *Industrial Relations, 1915*, 3785–86; WFM, *Proceeding, 1914*, 151, 170; *ibid., 1912*, 170, 258, 313, 329. The Finns "lost all interest in the BMU" after this incident. *Ibid*, 261, 265; WFM, Local Unions, "Financial Records, 1907–1932", WHC.
[60]WFM, *Proceedings, 1914*, 190–91; Connolly, "Labor Fuss," 207; Commission, *Industrial Relations, 1915*, 3718.

as a consequence of their misery, "the advance guard of the labor movement."[61]

They may, in fact, have been that, but this was a labor movement different in purpose and rhetoric from that of the BMU and its Irish Catholic leadership. It can only have been with utter amazement that old time Butte miners heard the remarks of Arturo Giovannitti, an IWW advocate of direct action. He was in Butte in the summer of 1914, immediately after dissidents within the BMU had dynamited and destroyed the Miners' Union Hall. Giovannitti proposed, as an epitaph for the BMU, the words, "Here Lies the Remains of 36 Years of Peace and Prosperity"; the workingmen of Butte, he went on, "should be ashamed of those thirty-six years."[62]

It was this openness of industrial unions to itinerant workers and the apparently mindless radicalism of that class that made those unions so threatening. To the settled miners, the older men who had homes as well as long memories, it must have seemed that the days of wandering and rebellious miners had returned. But Butte was no longer a mining camp. It and its established Irish had outgrown those years of social anarchy and neither was eager to see them return. The mining camp had become an industrializing city; itinerant workers had become, or been replaced by, more stable and conservative men. The enclave was based on the resulting family and associational ties, and the new men, Irish as surely as non-Irish, were literally unattached. Far from constituting an advance guard these new workers were a ". . . foraging aggregation of transient hoodlums, sweatless vagrants and proletarian parasites." The division clearly was more social than ethnic; it separated the settled Irish from the unsettled, the enclave from those who threatened it.[63]

---

[61]The "Don't Get Hurt Sign" was reported in the *Montana Socialist*, Oct. 23, 1915; Brody, *Workers in Industrial America*, 37, 39; WFM, *Proceedings, 1912*, 278, 326, 346; the "advance guard" statement was made by Tom Campbell. *Ibid.*, 278. See also *ibid.*, *1914*, 57.

[62]Giovannitti's remarks are in the *Miners Magazine*, July 9, 1914. The Immigration Commission attributed the higher wages in Butte to the "dominance of the union." *Immigrants in Industry, 1911*, 119.

[63]The "conservatives," whether representatives of the Anaconda Company or in the BMU, insisted on distinguishing between the "real" miners and the transients. Evans, *Address*, 9; *Miners Magazine*, July 9, July 16, 1914; Commission, *Industrial Relations, 1915*, 3740; WFM, *Proceedings, 1914*, 143-145. The rebel leaders, with the exception of Joe Shannon, were all residents of boarding houses, presumably unmarried, and/or recently arrived in Butte. See Polk, *Directories, 1910-14* for Muckie McDonald, George Tompkins, John McGrew, John

Obviously the enclave and the union were as affected by the changes in the work force as the companies — and as determined to recover a measure of stability in that work force. The solution hit upon was the so-called rustling card system, implemented by the Anaconda Company at the urging of an Irish mine foreman, William Daly, in December 1912. This new hiring system required all prospective miners to secure a card allowing them to look for or "rustle" a job. The system had been used previously in the mines of the Coeur d'Alene region and in the Anaconda Company smelters in Great Falls and Anaconda, Montana.[64]

The card system with its implications of blacklisting became eventually the source of enormous worker unhappiness. Even at the time of its passage a small majority of the 3400 men voting in a BMU referendum on the new hiring system expressed disfavor with it, but 3600 BMU members did not vote and the union leadership took no action. Worker unhappiness, whatever its extent, cannot have arisen from the actual questions on the card. The company did want to know place of birth and citizenship status, but the only question that outwardly addressed the issue of "sweatless vagabonds" was the one that asked "If married, where does your family reside?" Even this can hardly be made to seem conspiratorial or discriminatory.[65]

Neither can the company explanations for the adoption of the policy. The card was implemented, said Con Kelley, to protect the safety of the miners, make simpler the compilation of statistics for federal and state governments, help local merchants track down "deadbeats," ease the problems of a 30% job turn-

Niva, John Muzevich, John Sullivan, Mick Sullivan, Peter Marchando, John Gabbert, Theodore Stepanovich, Robert Noble, Fred Mignardot, Joseph Guelfi, Joseph Bradley, Joseph Little, and William Powell. See also Immigration Commission, *Immigrants in Industry, 1911*, 88, 116–117, 555. WFM, *Proceedings, 1914*, 166. The AOH even charged that some of these "submerged tenth of society" were adopting Irish names "for the concealment of their actual nationality and identity." O'Dea, *AOH*, vol. III, 1372.

[64]Commission, *Industrial Relations, 1915*, 3699, 3797; Immigration Commission, *Immigrants in Industry, 1911*, 173. There was a far larger percentage of East Europeans at the Anaconda smelters which may explain why the rustling card was first used there in 1903. *Ibid.*, 601. See also WFM, *Proceedings, 1914*, 198.

[65]On the vote see WFM, *Proceedings, 1914*, 156; *Anaconda Standard*, Dec. 22, 1912. Copies of the card and the application for it appear in Evans, *Address*, 18–19 and Commission, *Industrial Relations, 1915*, 3797. For the later, i.e., post-1914, protest see WFM, *Proceedings, 1914*, 57; Metal Mine Workers Union to Sec. of Labor, W. B. Wilson, June 23, 1917, Record Group 60, Dept. of Justice File 33-493, microfilm. See also Brissenden, "Butte Miners," 756–770; John A. Fitch, "A Union Paradise at Close Range," *Survey*, 32 (Aug. 1914), 538–539.

177

over rate — William Daly by 1913 was identified as an "Efficiency Engineer" — and help the company give preference to local men when job opportunities arose.

As for the union leaders, evidence that they were not disposed to contest the issue was provided by L. O. Evans, general counsel for the company, who recalled in 1917 that "there was even a request . . . from the officials of the Butte Miners' Union, as they were meeting difficulties . . . in keeping track of their members and collecting their monthly dues. . . ." In fact, and contrary to the earlier practice, the BMU leaders refused to allow unemployed miners to "rustle" a job *before* joining the union and paying their dues, an instance where the closed shop, so favored by unionists generally, was used in defense of a conservative status quo. Without a job, union dues could not be paid; without a paid up union membership, a job could not be had.[66]

As far as grievances against the Company were concerned, however, radical discontent with the system had to have arisen from unwritten questions and unstated understandings. As much was implied by a disclaimer issued by the radicals of 1914. Rebelling against "discrimination and organized greed," insurgents destroyed the Miners' Union Hall, and with it the Miners' Union, in June 1914. The Butte Mine Workers' Union, a new organization formed by and for the rebels, in a vigorous defense of its actions, stumbled over the charge of discrimination: "To explain this to those of you who have not worked in Butte will, we know, be a difficult task. But those of you who have worked here will readily understand our repudiation" of the BMU.[67]

The Mine Workers' Union was more specific as it framed its constitution and by-laws. Great emphasis was placed on company hiring practices. The language of these sections was categorical. "No shift boss or foreman shall be admitted to this union

---

[66]Kelley's testimony is in Commission, *Industrial Relations, 1915,* 3700–03, 3716, 4065. See also WFM, *Proceedings . . . 11th Annual Convention* (Denver, 1903), 188; Evans, *Address,* 15–18, 28; Brissenden, "Butte Miners," 765–66. Daly was referred to as an "Efficiency Engineer" in Polk, *Directory, 1913.* On the curious use of the closed shop principle see Bohn, "Butte Number One," 11; Haywood, "The Revolt," 93. Part of the problem may have been that fewer and fewer men were willing to assume the risks of working underground, particularly as the ethnic character of the work force changed. The only solution to this was safer mining techniques, in this instance, an open pit rather than underground shafts. See Joseph Kinsey Howard, "Wonderful Butte," *The American Mercury,* Mar. 1947, 301–307.
[67]"List of Grievances of Butte Mine Workers' Union, June 30, 1914, in WFM, *Proceedings, 1914,* 56. The other reference is from *ibid.,* 175. See also *Miners Magazine,* July 16, 1914.

under any circumstances. It shall be *incumbent* upon members
to *handle the boss on the job.* Any discrimination against any
group . . . shall be resented by the men on the job." Later, in
a public announcement, the new union admonished its men to
"treat the boss like a man . . . do not, under any circumstances,
tolerate in the future, as in the past, . . . any bulldozing, brow-
beating, bamboozeling or abuse of any kind. . . ."[68]

Taken together, the by-laws and the announcement make clear
that the bosses were discriminating in both hiring and the assignment of duties (that, in Hobsbawm's language, the aristocracy
was "protecting itself through job monopoly secured by trade
unions and workshop control"). At issue is the nature of that discrimination. The *Montana Socialist,* official newspaper of the
party and a conspicuous opponent of the Anaconda Company,
the Catholic Church, Butte's Irish newspaper, and the BMU,
offered a judgment. Rustling cards were denied, said the *Socialist,*
to two groups of men, those with socialist leanings and those *"an-
tagonistic to the Knights of Columbus,* and/or "belonging *to the
A.P.A. or the Guardians of Liberty."* In other words, the rustling
card had replaced RELA and AOH control of hiring! This was
a remarkable charge made the more so by its striking likeness
to one made 20 years earlier by the APA. Obviously the idea that
the Irish Catholic enclave enjoyed preferential treatment from
the Anaconda Company was both durable and widely held.[69]

For more than 30 years the Butte Miners' Union, supported
by the larger Irish miner enclave with which it was at times indistinguishable, pursued policies designed to insure, in Giovannitti's
unintended compliment, peace and prosperity. The union enjoyed
remarkable success, bringing an important element of stability
to both work place and community. Its power derived from its
source in the enclave, but its affairs were not conducted entirely

---

[68]Butte Mine Workers' Union, "Constitution and By-laws," in *Miners Magazine,* July 16, 1914,
emphasis mine; BMWU, "Announcement, August 17, 1914," in Mt. Dept. of Labor and
Industry, *1st Biennial Report,* 1913–1914, 31. WFM officials emphasized these points. See
President Charles Moyer's reference to them as "syndicalism, direct action, and sabotage."
Proceedings, 1914, 68.
[69]Hobsbawm, "Artisan," 267. The *Montana Socialist* article appeared Sept. 11, 1915, emphasis
mine. For other attacks on the BMU, the Catholic clergy, and Butte's Irish newpaper, the
Butte Independent see *Montana Socialist,* March 16, August 31, 1913; March 1, July 12,
Nov. 21, Nov. 28, Dec. 5, 1914. The rustling card application used in the Coeur d'Alene re-
gion was said to have asked "Do you believe in the religion of the Catholic Church?" WFM,
Proceedings . . . 13th Annual Convention (Salt Lake City, 1905), 310.

in defense of that world. Raised in uncertainty and disorder, the Irish miners of Butte sought some small measure of predictability. They were not the only beneficiaries of their success. If their values arose from the collective, almost communal world in which they lived, the whole community benefited from the Irish defense of those values. If the enclave required permanence and stability, so did the industry and the city.

Perhaps the Irish were too successful. New men, including new Irishmen, wanted more — and less — than security, particularly as they came to understand at what cost that security was obtained. The enclave had not only moderated the labor movement, it had redefined the goals thought to be inherent in that movement. That, however, says more about the intellectual rigidity of those who assign definite, and often revolutionary, responsibilities to the working class than it does about the class itself. The important point is that not until 1914, and then in part because of their unwillingness to send their sons underground, did the stable Irish miners of Butte lose the privileges of the labor aristocracy. They were convinced of the usefulness and dignity of their work but even had they not been, they understood that only steady work permitted them to hold their place in Butte. They became, as Hobsbawm writes, the "superior ins," distinguished by their respectability as much as their Irishness from the "inferior outs." It was not a status easily surrendered.

To protect it Dan Crowley suggested that new Hibernian job committees be formed. This in 1915, less than a year after the destruction of the BMU! Crowley, however, may only have wanted to take advantage of what Patrick Kenny had learned; that, after the distractions of the previous year, "it was intended that we would be given the preference in Butte once more."[70] By whom intended was not stated. But then Pat Kenny was a better historian than prophet anyway, a common enough failing among the aristocracy.

---

[70]AOH, Division 3, "Minute Books," Jan. 23, Feb. 27, 1915.

CLYDE GRIFFEN

OCCUPATIONAL MOBILITY IN NINETEENTH-CENTURY AMERICA: PROBLEMS AND POSSIBILITIES

Sooner or later historians who take up the study of occupational mobility in the United States face two disturbing discoveries. The first discovery is that the data available, even in the period after 1850 when the federal census becomes most useful, pose more serious problems in classification than we anticipated. We knew that we lacked means of duplicating the sociologists' precise ranking of occupations using systematic data on income, educational attainment and prestige.[1] But we hoped that the occupational designations in census schedules and city directories when supplemented by property information from tax lists would disclose a clearly differentiated hierarchy. Instead, the more we refine our analyses, the more complex the problem of classification becomes. Since we know that the classification scheme we choose will determine the amount of mobility we find, this complexity threatens confidence in the results of our studies.[2]

The second discovery is that the particular interest which prompted our studies has biased our approach in ways that limit their usefulness. As the pioneering works of Merle Curti and of Stephan Thernstrom suggest, most of us began with the desire to learn how fluid American society was in the nineteenth century.[3] We did *not* begin with a primary interest in understanding the occupational universe and how it changed with industrialization and urbanization. Our preoccupation with stratification and mobility made us more attentive initially to the sociologists who developed this field than to economic or labor historians pursuing changes in the composition and experience of the work force in

Professor Griffen is in the history department of Vassar College. The thinking in this essay owes most to Sarah D. Griffen, his collaborator in investigating occupational and residential mobility in Poughkeepsie, New York, 1850-80. The author has benefited from the criticism of Stephan Thernstrom and Stanley Coben of UCLA and of Lawrence Levine and Richard Abrams of the University of California at Berkeley.

particular occupations or in the economy as a whole.

To facilitate comparison of our results with other studies of mobility, past and present, most of the time we used the same or similar occupational classifications as the sociologists, modifying them where they obviously did not work for nineteenth-century data.[4] For the same reason we emphasized movement from blue-collar to white-collar work as the chief measure of upward mobility. In the beginning, our interest in the complexities of occupational designation tended to be limited to the problems they posed for classification and to their possible effects upon our measures of mobility.

Yet, as it turns out, our difficulties in classifying particular designations by skill level for this century of rapidly increasing specialization soon raise fundamental doubts about our schemes and measures. Whether one turns for help to the older work in American labor history by John Commons and Norman Ware or to the recent, fine-grained studies for England and America by Eric Hobsbawm, Sidney Pollard and Herbert Gutman, he comes away skeptical about how accurately any classificatory scheme can represent the marked variations in the progress of specialization within traditional crafts.[5] In some crafts the level of skill required of most workers remained largely unchanged long after that level in other crafts approximated that of factory operatives. Within particular crafts at one census, a researcher frequently finds such differences between cities and sometimes between firms in the same city. Hand-loom carpet weavers in Philadelphia, at the expense of a reduced standard of living, delayed conversion to power looms for carpeting in that city until after the Civil War although major firms elsewhere had adopted them as early as 1845.[6]

We lack systematic studies of white-collar workers in the nineteenth century, but we know that their universe also was being transformed by specialization. Thus, clerks previously performed a variety of functions differing in skill and responsibility. These functions had an increasing tendency in larger enterprises to be divided among different persons. Ultimately, occupational nomenclature would distinguish between men who keep accounts, work in shipping rooms or wait on customers, but in the nineteenth century the job names were so nondescriptive that it is very difficult to determine how far this white-collar specialization had advanced in a city and within which enterprises.

This variation in the progress of specialization is only the most obvious reason for raising now the question of whether our problems in classification are so serious as to require changing our approach to them. My own experience in investigating Poughkeepsie, New York, has altered radically my earlier views on how far we should try to refine our schemes of classification. It also has changed my views on the uses and limitations of our quantitative results on frequencies of career and intergenerational mobility.

Students of the subject knew that the qualitative significance of mobility frequencies would not be self-evident, that they could not show what occupational mobility meant subjectively to those who experienced it. To that extent, we always assumed that quantitative analysis at best narrows and clarifies our options in interpretation. But we did believe that our percentages by themselves would show the direction and extent of occupational mobility. I now question how well the frequencies we are computing describe movements up and down the occupational hierarchies of the nineteenth century.

My experience does not, however, suggest that our present measurements are of little use. Although I question how faithfully they represent certain types of movement, I also believe they are a major step forward in narrowing our options in interpretation. Qualified and supplemented by kinds of analyses not yet employed routinely, they greatly improve our understanding of the dimensions of occupational mobility.

My hope is that the limitations we now discover will redirect our research in ways which will be far more revealing of the interaction between mobility, industrialization and urbanization. In the end I think we may conclude that our early, understandable preoccupation with studying social fluidity *per se* carried us too far in the direction of isolating our subject from the specific contexts essential to explaining its meaning to the Americans who experienced it. The purpose of the present paper, however, is not to anticipate the future but to offer an example of the kind of assessments I think we must make, assessments based on our experiences in investigating occupational mobility in particular communities.

The first problem all of us face is the difficulty, often the impossibility, of determining the exact meaning of occupational designations. At the outset, changes in the federal census' instructions to enumerators indicate that we cannot assume a constant meaning or comparable specificity to designations even within a short period of time. Thus, the new instructions for 1870 called for more specificity, including the distinguishing of wholesalers from retailers in merchandising and of apprentices and bosses from other workers in manufacturing.[7]

When one turns to the manuscript schedules for a particular community, one discovers that the enumerators sometimes were more precise than their instructions required before 1870. More important, they often were less precise than those instructions subsequently. In Poughkeepsie, the illustration for this essay, Frank Hengstebeck, for example, appears successively as a locksmith in 1850, a hardware merchant in 1860, a locksmith again in 1870 and as "Keeps Tin Store" in 1880.[8] In each of these years he was, in fact, a hardware merchant who also produced locks and tinware. His sons who also worked in the store appear as tinsmiths.

Inadequate census designations for proprietors can usually be clarified in city directories or their difference in importance determined by property data. But for clerical and sales workers, lack of consistency in both sources poses a serious problem. The tracing of career patterns for those workers who are distinguished as grocery, dry goods, drug and bank clerks, bookkeepers and accountants all indicate differences in level of skill.[9] Yet a majority of the enumerations in both census and directory in Poughkeepsie use the unqualified designation "clerk." Since the occupation, usually transitional, was dominated by younger workers, one cannot rely on property data to determine differences in level.

Lack of specificity is even more serious for manual workers since city directories prove less helpful in clarifying inexact designations than for any group of white-collar workers. The change in instructions in 1870 notwithstanding, the census enumerators in Poughkeepsie rarely indicated whether skilled craftsmen were foremen or master workmen, whether they were employers, self-employed workmen without assistants, or employees in small shops and factories. Only the employers can be identified with any consistency in the city directory.

Laborers regularly employed in factories and furnaces rarely were distinguished from day laborers.[10] And factory employees are not specified consistently. The Buckeye Mower and Reaper Works, one of Poughkeepsie's largest employers, illustrates the problem. Buckeye paid consistently high average wages as reported in the federal manufacturing census, but required a wide range of skills—from patternmakers through blacksmiths, grinders and polishers to teamsters and ordinary laborers.

Contemporary sources show that Buckeye employed about 200 male workers in the years around 1880.[11] Yet the federal census of that year designates only 30 men as Buckeye workers and only 12 of these are so designated in the city directory. The directory yields another 25 names as workers at the plant, making a grand total of little more than a fourth of the work force which can be identified by name (see Table 1). While the 1880 census specifies a plant superintendent and two foremen, no such designations appear for 1870. Yet a newspaper description in 1866 when the plant numbered 125 workers mentions four departments with foremen for each.

Table 1. Previous and Subsequent Occupations of Workers at Buckeye Mower and Reaper Company in 1880

	BUCKEYE	Laborer	Other Low	Skilled Metal	Other Skilled	White Collar	Total Cases
Previous	10%	35%	8%	25%	10%	12%	49
Subsequent	32%	14%	9%	27%	16%	2%	44

NOTE: The totals are less than all workers identified as Buckeye in 1880; some workers could not be found employed in Poughkeepsie previous or subsequent to that year. Of the 13 workers identified as Buckeye only through the City Directory, 6 were listed as laborers, 3 as other low manual, 3 as skilled metal, and 1 as other skilled in the 1880 census.

Even those workers identified lack exact occupational designation since the factory name and not the nature of their work is given. One might assume that they were largely unskilled or semiskilled operatives and service workers; the listing of some of these men at previous censuses as laborers, boatmen and teamsters would seem to support that assumption. Other workers at Buckeye appear previously as machinists, moulders and blacksmiths, which suggests they performed more highly skilled tasks within the factory.

If the 55 workers identifiable as Buckeye employees in 1880 automatically are classified as semiskilled factory operatives, then those appearing previously at unskilled designations will be tabulated as downwardly mobile. In reality, the level of skill required by their work may not have changed at all; they may even have been employed at Buckeye continuously. Whether the census designations for the 150-odd unidentified employees accurately reflect the level of their work remains a complete mystery.

Supposedly skilled craft designations present similar problems. Manufacturing census reports on number of workers per firm suggest that at least one-third of those enumerated as bakers in Poughkeepsie must have been employed by a cracker factory. Newspaper reports describe the process of production as mechanized except for the preparation of the dough.[12] The factory's employees apparently were not skilled craftsmen nor were they as well rewarded as workers in the city's smaller bakeries; but there is no sure way of distinguishing the two groups. Carpet weavers in Poughkeepsie pose the same problem. Most of them must have been employed by Pelton's factory, but there is clear evidence that a minority worked for themselves or in small shops using hand looms, presumably doing specialized work not yet profitable enough for power looms.

This difficulty in distinguishing types of employment among carpet weavers, bakers and Buckeye workers or of separating day laborers from those with regular and perhaps semiskilled employment in furnaces may, of course, go largely undetected by the investigator. If he simply relies on his census occupational designations without attempting to check them against city directories or to follow leads found in newspapers, manufacturing censuses and other sources to clarify their meaning, he might plausibly assume that all Buckeye workers should be classified as semiskilled factory operatives, all bakers and carpet weavers as skilled craftsmen and, without any awareness of what he was doing, all semiskilled iron workers at Fallkill as laborers. But should this happen, he has already biased his mobility frequencies in the direction of blurring any usual differences in traits between these levels.

This blurring may seriously distort an interpretation of social fluidity. Thus, if workers first classified as unskilled and semi-skilled achieve white-collar employment subsequently about as often as those first classified skilled, one plausible inference is that skilled workers did not have superior opportunities.[13] But our willingness to accept this inference depends upon our confidence that individual manual occupations can and have been classified accurately as unskilled, semiskilled or skilled.

My own tendency is to question such an inference in any study of an American city in the nineteenth century which is based on census or directory data. I do so primarily because of my experience with that data for Poughkeepsie in which many of the finer but important gradations in the occupational structure are seriously underrepresented because of inexact designation. Where I could distinguish individuals within these gradations, I usually found corresponding differences in careers. But in the absence of fairly complete payroll records, the gradations are not clear and thus we cannot separate the more highly skilled workers from the less skilled for the purpose of tracing and comparing their careers.[14]

No scheme for occupational classification employed by historians so far escapes the problems inherent in inexact designation. Consider the seemingly most objective criterion for ranking occupations in the nineteenth century—wealth.[15] If, as we have seen, foremen and skilled workers in factories are not distinguished consistently from less skilled operatives, then averaging the wealth of factory employees will simply blur the usual gap between these positions and result in a misleading ranking of the occupation. But there are other important objections to using wealth by itself as the basis for ranking. And since wealth is the only criterion we have which seems to permit a precise ranking, these objections call into question the whole effort to refine our schemes of classification.

First, the only systematic indications we have of wealth for the nineteenth century are self-reporting of property in the censuses and assessments on tax lists; we do not have any comprehensive data on incomes for most communities.[16] Quite apart from questions about the reliability of census reports or about the bases and inclusiveness of evaluation in tax lists,[17] there are certain inherent problems in using property alone as a means of ranking.

Some occupations which we know rank high in skill and reward, notably the more responsible kinds of clerkships, are normally transitional, dominated by young men in their twenties or early thirties who subsequently will become owners or managers of firms in various lines of finance, merchandising and manufacturing. Their incomes if known normally would place them in the upper fourth of the labor force, but they rarely report property and when they do the amounts tend to be small. Any ranking of these occupations by property, whether the mean or median is chosen as the average, will underestimate their standard of living, their position in society and their future prospects. The greater this underestimation of their starting point, the greater will be the overestimation of their actual mobility subsequently.[18]

There are comparable problems in using property data for many manual occupations. The majority of workers in most crafts report no property, but the size of that majority differs among crafts.

Some crafts with the highest proportion of workers reporting property, such as cabinet-making, coopering, and shoemaking in Poughkeepsie in 1870, turn out on closer examination to be crafts affected adversely by a withering skill dilution.[19] In all three cases the work force was contracting because of diminishing opportunities in these occupations in Poughkeepsie and a corresponding decline in the number of young men entering them. This contraction meant an increasingly older and, therefore, typically more propertied work force. Age distribution alone largely explains the proportion of the propertied. The amounts reported reflect previous prosperity in these trades more than their present condition; the going wage rates for coopers and shoemakers were no longer much above those for unskilled workers.[20]

The use of property, as distinguished from current income, skews any ranking of occupations in favor of those which have been most prosperous in the immediate past whether they continue to be so or not. Since property is not very useful as an index to the position of most employees in an occupation at the time the ranking is made, and especially not for workers just beginning their careers, there is no advantage to treating it as more than one among many variables. And there are at least two strong disadvantages in using property alone as a means of ranking besides those already mentioned. First, it results in rankings which almost inevitably will differ widely from city to city and from period to period within the same city, thereby increasing our problems in comparison. Second, it suggests too much precision, tending to discourage the use of additional, less precise variables to help us interpret occupational patterns and changes.

The frustration of attempts to develop more refined schemes of classification has radically changed my view of what we should do about ranking occupations for the purpose of computing mobility frequencies. For the time being, at least, I think we ought to stick to fairly simple schemes which divide the occupational hierarchy into commonly recognized levels which are broad enough to minimize agonizing over ambiguous designations like "clerk." My own preference for comparability with other studies is five levels—unskilled, semiskilled, skilled, low and high white-collar— with possible functional subgroupings at some levels, such as the separation of professionals from proprietors and managers within high white-collar, or of service workers from factory operatives within the semiskilled class. This scheme will obscure, temporarily, many of the gradations we know exist, but I think it more useful for the present to refine our pictures *after* rather than before our classification and computation of mobility frequencies.

Our tendency has been to worry about the characteristics of an occupation while we were trying to group it with other occupa- tions as a skill level, but then to forget it thereafter and concentrate on the characteristics of skill levels and the patterns of movement among them. I am suggesting that we reverse this tendency, that we do most of our worrying about the crudeness of skill-level assignments for occupational designations after we have obtained mobility frequencies. I do so because the supposed result of our studies, the frequencies themselves, turn out to be among our most useful clues to the meaning of the designations given. In theory and method there is a clear distinction between the study of occupational structure and the study of occupational mobility. The former is concerned with the experience of bakers as an occupational group, the latter, only with the careers of individuals who may happen to be bakers. The deficiencies of nineteenth- century data, however, require us to move back and forth between these two types of studies to improve either of them.[2 1]

Thus, most investigators would classify craftsmen who achieve employer status within their crafts with white-collar or, if you prefer, nonmanual workers. But especially for a period of increasing specialization one immediately wonders how much the achievement of employer status within crafts represents not only upward mobility for the employer himself, but also improved opportunities for his children. One also wonders whether those opportunities are as frequent as for children of white-collar fathers generally. Separate analyses of mobility by individual craft and by industry prove very useful here, as examination of the building trades suggests.

More frequently than in most crafts, the census and directories for Poughkeepsie distinguish employers in these trades as boss carpenters, masons or painters. Although a majority of their sons pursued the same trade, only a minority of the sons became employers. Even after those sons who entered other white-collar occupations are added, less than half of all these sons of bosses, builders and contractors sustain their fathers' achievement[22] (see Table 2).

Table 2. Status at Last Listing of Sons of Non-Manual Fathers (selected occupations)

	Saloon Keepers	Peddlers Hucksters	Ship Captains	Builders Contractors Bosses	Merchants (Lumber, Dry Goods, Commission)
Number of Sons	36	9	21	36	36
% Non-Manual	42	44	33	39	89

By contrast, well over two-thirds of all sons of white-collar fathers ended their own careers in white-collar work. Given this difference, it might be tempting to reclassify these employers in the building trades at the top of the blue-collar hierarchy. But some further comparison of mobility frequencies suggests that this resort also obscures important differences. First, in Poughkeepsie the overall rate of achievement of white-collar status by sons of blue-collar fathers was less than one-quarter, compared to nearly one-half for the sons of employers in the building trades. Even when one confines the comparison to sons of skilled workers only, a marked difference remains.

Second, and more important, the pattern of intergenerational mobility for these building-trades sons is practically identical with that for the sons of certain small proprietors and vendors, notably saloonkeepers and peddlers. The latter cannot, without even more violence to consistency in terminology, be reclassified as blue collar or manual, yet their mobility patterns do differ somewhat from those of grocers and variety-store owners and dramatically from dry goods, lumber and coal, and flour merchants.

Separate analysis of mobility patterns for each of the occupations named above is preferable to any attempt at refining their classification. One can then estimate how differences in their patterns influence grosser measurements of mobility in which these occupations are grouped together as a skill level.

The more one plays with the possibilities of analyzing occupations separately, the more one discovers the variety of manipulations which can be used to probe differences in condition and opportunity.[23] This is true not only of differences among workers bearing the same designation, but also among those bearing different designations but normally classified at the same skill level. Thus, in interpreting the achievement of some groups of petty proprietors it proves as useful to look at their first occupations as it did to look at the careers of their sons.

This inflow or recruitment analysis will show that less than a fifth of those who ended their careers as saloonkeepers in Poughkeepsie had begun in any form of white-collar work; indeed, another one-fifth had been first listed as "laborers." And of the remainder, the largest group were first designated in crafts injured by skill dilution in this period, notably shoemaking and the wood trades (see Table 3). Comparison with men who ended their careers as grocers suggests caution about regarding the two designations as always comparable. A minority of the grocers also began in white-collar work, but the proportion was different. A third of them had been listed previously at white-collar work, primarily as clerks, and, unlike the saloonkeepers, a minority of them had parents or siblings who were grocers before them.

Other variables reinforce suspicion that the designations grocer and saloonkeeper do not always represent the same level of achievement. Although the majority in both occupations had little or no property, were not located in the heart of the business district, and frequently went out of business, a minority of the grocers who seem to have ·been wholesalers as well as retailers and centrally located show substantially more property and annual income than the most prosperous saloonkeepers.[24] Their firms also had longer lives as determined by tracing the yearly entries in the city directory.

Table 3. Previous Status of Workers Listed Subsequently in
Selected Occupations*

	Laborer	Other Low	Injured Skilled	Other Skilled	Non-Manual	Total	Total first listed at these occupations
Saloon Keeper	18%		39%	24%	18%	33	
Peddler	29%	36%	7%	14%	14%	14	
Machinist/ Engineer	35%	12%	7%	40%	7%	43	87
Moulder	54%	8%	15%	15%	8%	13	31
Carpenter	20%	15%	15%	31%	19%	59	199
Mason	63%	17%		17%	4%	24	106
Painter	22%	27%	5%	32%	14%	37	69
Butcher	16%	21%	16%	16%	32%	19	40

*Table includes only workers employed in Poughkeepsie in at least two censuses.

The tracing of occupational origins which suggested differences in status between the designations grocer and saloonkeeper is only one among many ways of refining our notions of an occupation. One can analyze the flow out of a designation as well as into it, which proves particularly helpful in identifying occupations where opportunities are numerically decreasing or less attractive, whether through contraction in work force or reduction in reward or both. Thus, in most skilled crafts four-fifths or more of those who first appear in a trade also end their careers in it or in a closely related trade where skills can be transferred directly, but, in declining trades, shifts into unrelated occupations usually are more frequent. The differences in such shifts between generations are dramatic. In many skilled trades no more than half of the sons who remained in Poughkeepsie followed their fathers' occupations, but the contrast between trades already hurt by skill dilution and those still relatively unaffected is striking. Only about one-fifth of the sons of shoemakers followed their fathers' trade compared to two-thirds of the sons of machinists and engineers.

One refinement in the analysis of occupational shifts provides an important caution against generalizing the condition of all workers in a trade from its overall condition. Controlling for the age at which shifts occurred discloses that in each of three successive decades in Poughkeepsie one-third or more of the changes from unskilled to skilled designations occurred after age forty. Entry into a craft so late in life raises doubts about how much increase in skill and reward occurred, even when average wages were high, as they were for machinists and engineers before 1880.

The doubts about improvement in skill and reward are reinforced by comparing crafts for proportion of workers first listed at other occupations. Among the machinists and engineers, these late listings prove nearly half as frequent as initial listings, a higher ratio than in most crafts. One-fifth of these latecomers had worked in related metal trades previously, primarily black-smithing, and another fifth transferred from the wood trades where they might have had previous experience with machine construction, repair and maintenance. But nearly half began their careers in low manual jobs, primarily as laborers, and in a few cases appeared again at last job as laborer or in specialized metal work like grinding and steel polishing. Presumably these workers remained marginal to the trade, never developing the range and mastery of skills expected of journeymen who apprenticed in it.

Whether or not these variations in skill, specialization, and probable reward justify the notion of an aristocracy among machinists and engineers, it seems clear that these designations overlap with the semiskilled below and the low white-collar above. To cite the extremes, in 1860 both John Silvernail, age 50, and Thomas Brown, age 34, are designated simply as "machinist," neither reporting any real estate but $50 and $500 personal property respectively. Silvernail had been listed in Poughkeepsie in 1850 as a laborer, making him one of the latecomers to skilled status, and he would be listed in 1870 as a steel polisher and in 1880 at age 70 as a laborer again. The English-born Brown, by contrast, was not listed in the city previously, but given his age in 1860, probably had apprenticed in the trade. By 1870 he is designated as patent maker and in 1880 appeared as inventor and superintendent of Buckeye. Actually by 1866 when he was 40 years old, Brown not only had become superintendent of Buckeye but also reported an income of nearly $2,000 annually, placing him among the top 200 incomes in the city.[25]

The range in competence and reward we discover even *within* a craft with high average wage rates like machinist reinforces my conviction that little is to be gained at the moment by trying to refine our assignment of occupations to skill levels. Rather, what we need are subsequent analyses which point up the ranges within occupations classified under each skill level and the clustering within that range. Then we can estimate the amount of overlapping between adjacent skill levels and determine whether our mobility frequencies based on movements between these levels are biased seriously by the overlapping. Indeed one of the strongest arguments for keeping classification schemes as simple and identical as possible is that one can then compare the extent of distinctiveness or overlapping between levels in different times and places. Thus, assume that all the traditionally skilled crafts of 1800 also are classified as skilled in 1900. Differences in the amount of overlapping in career patterns between these crafts and occupations classified with the adjacent semiskilled and white-collar levels then will be one useful index of the progress of skill dilution or skill intensification during the century.

Analysis of individual occupations is particularly important for that middle area in the occupational hierarchy which most affects the usual gross measure of mobility, movement from manual to nonmanual work. For it is in the range between skilled blue-collar work and the lower paid white-collar occupations (including petty proprietorships, supervisory positions and low-paid sales and office clerks) that the meaning of occupational designations is most ambiguous and the amount of apparent overlapping in competence and reward most evident.

Contrary to C. Wright Mills' colorful stereotypes, this overlapping of upper blue-collar workers with lower white-collar workers does not seem to be a twentieth century development.[26] Although I am not sure that most clerks in Poughkeepsie were as superior to the best paid blue-collar workers at mid-century as Eric Hobsbawm suggests for England, I do think Hobsbawm's general description of long-run tendencies at the middle level of the hierarchy is relevant to America, too.

195

Socially speaking the best-paid stratum of the working class merged with what may be loosely called the 'lower middle class. ' . . . In the earlier part of the century this would mean mainly small shopkeepers, some independent masters, foremen and managers (who were also generally promoted workers). Towards the end of the century it would also mean clerks and the like . . . skilled labor aristocrats, being, if anything, superior in social status to many white-collar workers.[27]

Change in the relative importance of various occupational groups within the lower middle class in American cities, as in England, seems to have varied according to the scale and diversification of their economies. In Poughkeepsie between 1850 and 1880 small shopkeepers—in craft-related even more than in purely retail or service ventures—predominated. Toward the end of the period the situation changed, for clerkships rather than apprenticeships in crafts became increasingly important as entry occupations to subsequent proprietorships, reflecting an increase in the scale and internal specialization in some types of manu-facturing and merchandising.

Difference between cities in the timing of this change is one more reason why mobility studies, for the present, should emphasize analysis of shifts among specific occupations. Com-paring frequencies of mobility in Poughkeepsie with those Thernstrom found for Boston for a slightly later period suggest to me the crucial importance for rapid upward mobility, especially for immigrants and their children, of differences between urban economies in the proportion of manufacturing still carried on in small shops where employers and workers shared a common craft.[28]

The spectacular achievement of white-collar status by first-generation Germans in Poughkeepsie is due primarily to the frequency with which they became employers in craft-related shops, notably in the food and apparel trades but also in the more specialized wood and metal manufactures. The Irish in Boston, by contrast, more often provided labor for much larger enterprises where skills were more diluted and where opportunities for achieving employer status were far less frequent. Quite apart, then, from the advantages German immigrants had over the Irish in skill, capital or entrepreneurial propensity, there is evidence for believing that the small city, in which small craft-related shops still dominated much of the manufacturing, held obvious advantages for European newcomers.

The problem of interpreting the significance of becoming an employer, apparently so simple and clearcut a realization of the American dream, illustrates the limitations of occupational mobility studies at present. But it also suggests how useful these studies are potentially for deepening our understanding of the related processes of industrialization and urbanization.

Some doubts about the significance of the achievement of becoming an employer, even in a small city in the Civil War era, are evoked by discovery that in the low-paying food and apparel trades the ratio of shops to workers tends to increase and in no trade does the ratio decline significantly. The growing frequency of small shops owned by first- and second-generation Americans, especially of German origin, seems to account for this increase.

By contrast, in the expanding and well-paid trades of machinist, engineer and moulder, the ratio of employers to employees declines between the censuses of 1850 and 1880. In foundries, furnaces and agricultural implement factories the number of workers per firm increases. The widening gap in capital required between owning a small food shop or owning a factory explains the difference; but the critical question remains, how does this difference affect the significance of achieving employer status?

Whether the proprietor of a small bakery, tailoring or shoe-making shop was usually better off economically than a machinist, moulder, engineer or blacksmith—even if the latter worked for a large foundry or a factory like Buckeye—can be questioned on several grounds. The frequency of failures in small businesses was notoriously high, then as now.[29] Hours of work were as long and frequently longer than in factories and the immediate returns often less and certainly precarious. Since the wages of journeymen in the food and apparel trades were low, saving from them even the small capital needed to start a small shop probably meant real sacrifice for an uncertain and often marginal reward.[30]

One can argue, of course, that economic reward and even security was less important to nineteenth-century men than the independence and sense of achievement that presumably came from being self-employed or employing others. Certainly the literature of success until very late in the century had a

preindustrial and highly moralistic bias. It emphasized respectability rather than riches, very often urging the reader to take up
trades like carpentry and blacksmithing in which it was easiest to
start a business. This literature did assume, however, that such
independence was still a good way to achieve a modest but
comfortable and secure standard of living.[31]

What we do not know is how self-employed men at mid-century
perceived and valued their independence when—by the limited
objective data we have—it seemed both precarious and no more
remunerative than employment by others. My own tentative
conclusion is that most men gave more weight to economic
reward—the standard of living and the security it provided—than
to occupation in comparing their own status with that of their
peers. Self-employment more often than not meant superior
economic reward. But when it did not, Americans were under no
illusion that being a shopkeeper automatically entailed a position
superior to that of any blue-collar worker. Applying this evaluation within the limited range of their own experience, I am
persuaded that most Americans compared their position with that
of their peers quite accurately. Thus, an English-born weaver like
Thomas Lumb may have preferred running a grocery in his home
in one of the poorer districts of the city to his previous
employment in Pelton's carpet factory. But he probably would
not have regarded his situation as superior in status to that of his
neighbor and fellow countryman on Hoffman Street, John Ogden,
a railroad engineer with an annual income of nearly $1,000 in
1866.

We ignore contemporary perception at important points, I fear,
if we simply take our mobility frequencies—especially the gross
measure of movement between blue collar and white collar—as a
faithful reflection of the underlying realities of occupational
change. We attribute to Lumb a degree of improvement he seems
unlikely to have discovered in comparing himself with some
blue-collar workers like Ogden in his immediate acquaintance.
Perhaps more important, we neglect the potential usefulness of
marginal but perhaps quite numerous cases of this kind in probing
the complexity of the nineteenth-century occupational universe.

In the present, relatively undeveloped state of mobility studies
we should worry also about whether our interest in comparing

frequencies for patterns of similarity and dissimilarity between communities tends to be more concerned with explaining apparent dissimilarities than with asking the critical question of whether similarities in frequencies have the same meaning for communities which differ in size and character, especially in degree of industrialization. The locksmith-become-hardware-merchant, like the German immigrant Frank Hengstebeck, had made an obvious step upward in the context of Poughkeepsie's economy by 1870, but this step would have been invisible to the larger manufacturers of Boston. Hengstebeck or any other craftsman-become-employer could seem of some consequence in the smaller city as late as 1870 to a degree improbable in the more specialized and already bureaucratizing metropolitan economy. Yet he would be classified in a mobility study for the metropolis as well as for the small city as having satisifed the same basic measure of upward mobility, movement from blue collar to white collar.

These cautions point up the importance for the immediate future of a tentative, exploratory attitude toward the frequencies of occupational mobility we are now computing. It is entirely possible that the dimensions of movement our present results describe will require little modification after the kinds of refinement in analysis suggested in this essay. But we would be foolish, I think, either to view them now as essentially final answers about the state of opportunity in America at given points in time or to dismiss them as of dubious value pending the development of more precise schemes of classification. Rather we should regard them as extremely useful *clues* in our attempts to understand the interaction of mobility, industrialization and urbanization in our past.

FOOTNOTES

1. See especially Otis Duncan and Peter Blau, *The American Occupational Structure* (N.Y., 1967); also Duncan's "A Socioeconomic Index for All Occupations" in Albert Reiss, Jr., *et al, Occupations and Social Status* (N.Y., 1961) and R. W. Hodge, P. M. Siegel, and P. H. Rossi, "Occupational Prestige in the U.S., 1925-63," *American Journal of Sociology,* 70 (1964).

2. The last section of Stephan Thernstrom, "Notes on the Historical Study of Social Mobility," *Comparative Studies in Society and History,* 10 (Jan., 1968) anticipates this complexity; Michael Katz, "Occupational Classification in History" (forthcoming in the

Journal of Interdisciplinary History) concludes that the historical study of occupational mobility requires at least three systems of classification: by personal wealth, by occupation as ranked by mean wealth, and by occupation as ranked by imputed prestige; Stuart Blumin, "The Historical Study of Vertical Mobility," *Historical Methods Newsletter*, 1 (Sept., 1968) discusses the difficulties of these three types of classification and suggests that only one of them, ranking occupations by mean wealth, is both feasible empirically and a way through subsequent analysis of occupational mobility to a reliable inference of economic mobility.

3. Merle Curti, *The Making of an American Community* (Stanford, Calif., 1959); Stephan Thernstrom, *Poverty and Progress* (Cambridge, Mass., 1964).

4. See Richard Hopkins' explanation of his choice of measures in footnote 6, "Occupational and Geographic Mobility in Atlanta, 1870-1896," *Journal of Southern History*, 34 (May, 1968), 201-2. A major exception is Stuart Blumin's five-level scheme based on mean wealth for each occupation, adopted after experimentation with alternative schemes of classification. See his "Mobility and Change in Antebellum Philadelphia" in Stephan Thernstrom and Richard Sennett, eds., *Nineteenth-Century Cities* (New Haven, Conn., 1970), especially 172-4.

5. John R. Commons, *et al.*, *History of Labour in the United States*, 4 vols. (N. Y., 1918-35); Norman Ware, *The Industrial Worker, 1840-1860* (N. Y., 1924); Eric Hobsbawm, *Labouring Men* (N. Y., 1964); Sidney Pollard, *A History of Labour in Sheffield* (Liverpool, 1959); Herbert Gutman, "The Reality of the Rags-to-Riches Myth," in *Nineteenth-Century Cities*, "Class, Status, and Community Power" in Frederic Jaher, ed., *The Age of Industrialism in America* (N. Y., 1968), and especially his unpublished essay on Standard Oil's relations with its coopers.

6. Sam Bass Warner, Jr., "Innovation and the Industrialization of Philadelphia, 1800-1850" in Oscar Handlin and John Burchard, eds., *The Historian and the City* (Cambridge, Mass., 1963), 66-9; for variation in the adoption of new manufacturing methods in other nineteenth-century industries, see Paul Strassmann, *Risk and Technological Innovation* (Ithaca, N. Y., 1959).

7. Carroll Wright and W. C. Hunt, *History and Growth of the U.S. Census* (Washington, D.C., 1900).

8. Some preliminary results from this project appear in Clyde Griffen, "Workers Divided: Craft and Ethnic Differences in Poughkeepsie, N. Y., 1850-1880" in *Nineteenth-Century Cities* and "Making It in America: Social Mobility in Mid-Nineteenth Century Poughkeepsie," *New York History*, 51 (Oct., 1970).

9. Thus, of 28 Poughkeepsie men paying tax on incomes of more than $600 in 1866 who were listed at clerical occupations, there were eight bookkeepers, three bank clerks, two dry goods clerks and two salesmen. Of the 31 remaining unspecified clerks, six were sons or relatives of rich merchants and probably employed by them. None were listed as grocery clerks. Among 58 clerks of native parentage in 1870 who remained white-collar workers in 1880, there were eight dry goods, six bank, and four grocery clerks; whereas in the 20 who became blue collar by 1880, there were one dry goods, one bank, and three grocery clerks. Suggestively, among native-born clerks of Irish parentage in 1870, one-third were specified "grocery" but none were in dry goods or banks.

10. The manuscript schedules of the federal manufacturing census and other sources indicate that between 150 and 200 workers were employed by the city's furnaces from the mid-1850s onward. But the unskilled or semiskilled, the vast majority of these furnace workers, appear in the census simply as "laborer." Not until the late 1870s does the city directory specify place of employment for some groups of laborers and then we discover more than 150 names, predominantly Irish, with the listing, "Laborer, Fallkill Iron Works."

11. Poughkeepsie *Daily Eagle*, April 11, 1866, and Sept. 9, 1879; James Smith, *History of Dutchess County* (New York, 1883), 388.

12. Poughkeepsie *Daily Press*, Nov. 1, 1863. Individual data on wealth is little help in distinguishing cracker factory employees from apprentice or journeymen bakers in small shops. With the exception of proprietors, most "bakers" in the city report no real estate and negligible personal property.

13. Stephan Thernstrom draws this inference from such results for Boston and contrasts the apparent fluidity with the labor aristocracy which Eric Hobsbawm describes for England. Melvin Richter, ed., *Essays in History and Theory* (Cambridge, Mass., 1970), 231-2. The classification schemes used in the Boston and Poughkeepsie studies are very similar and my frequencies, unlike Thernstrom's, do show a marked difference between low manual and skilled workers in subsequent achievement of white-collar jobs. But this difference in result is not the source of my suspicion that certain manual workers in America as in England had superior prospects for advancing themselves and their children.

14. Even when we cannot place individuals within these gradations, we can estimate the proportion of the work force within them from the manufacturing census, accounts of individual firms and other sources which suggest the type of work done and the skills required.

15. For a systematic and favorable analysis of wealth as a means of ranking occupations, see Blumin, "The Historical Study of Vertical Mobility."

16. There was a federal income tax during the decade after 1863, but the large majority of incomes were exempted. In Poughkeepsie males reporting taxable income in 1866, the year of the lowest exemption ($600), comprised less than one-fifth of the male labor force. This income data can be extremely useful in determining which movements into white-collar employment brought the greatest reward and, more generally, reinforces the inference drawn from property tax lists that the American rich even in the mid-nineteenth century were very rich indeed by comparison with the mass of workers. But it does not shed any light on variations in reward among the mass.

17. The reliability of reports by property owners themselves to census enumerators obviously is open to question. But so are tax lists prepared by local assessors. Generally, even tangible assets like real estate were undervalued and tax officials constantly complained about the gross underreporting of personal property. Furthermore, property owned outside the city limits officially was beyond the assessors' inquiry and, in some cities, the assessments within the city did not distinguish between owners and users. See Edward Pessen, "The Egalitarian Myth and the American Social Reality: Wealth, Mobility, and Equality in the "Era of the Common Man,' " *American Historical Review* (Oct. 1971), 989-1034.

18. Thus, clerks rank lower than carters in Blumin's scale.

19. Skill dilution within a craft—the reduction of the level of skill required whether by specialization of work process, displacement by machine or both—is described in Blanche Hazard's classic *Organization of the Boot and Shoe Industry* (N. Y., 1921); for useful summaries of the impact of skill dilution in several trades see John H. G. Laslett, *Labor and the Left* (N. Y., 1970), *passim*.

20. *Nineteenth-Century Cities*, 82-3.

21. Since the focus of the present inquiry is *mobility* studies, however, it should be clear that the classification scheme adopted must subordinate any functional similarities or relations between occupations to their rank in a skill-level hierarchy. Because of the breadth of the levels suggested here, some subgrouping by function or industry within levels is feasible. Conversely, a classification scheme for the study of occupational structure may include subgrouping by skill level within an industry, but that ranking must be subordinate to the primary grouping by functional relation.

22. On the separation between the speculative builder who supplied capital and the master carpenter-become-labor contractor, see Robert A. Christie, *Empire in Wood* (Ithaca, N. Y., 1956), ch. 2.

23. These manipulations must be regarded as clues which need to be supplemented by other evidence. Otherwise the analyses suggested here run the danger of circular reasoning. The fact that sons of employers in certain industries show a low frequency of achievement of employer status for themselves does not by itself diminish their fathers' achievement.

24. Based upon advertisements in local newspapers and directories, the manuscript population schedules for 1860 and 1870, the city tax list for 1865, and the list of those paying federal tax on incomes of $600 or more in 1866, published in *Daily Eagle*, July 14, 1866.

25. The proportion of iron moulders whose first job in Poughkeepsie was not in that trade was even higher than for machinists and more than half of these latecomers previously were day laborers. The significance of differences in skill and responsibility within a trade is further pointed up by the case of a moulder whose true status, unlike that of Thomas Brown, the machinist, was never clarified in the census. Almost from the time of his arrival in the city in 1865, James Carroll acted as foreman of one of the larger foundries, reporting $9,000 property in 1870. Only three of the 31 iron moulders designated in Poughkeepsie in at least two censuses subsequently achieved white-collar status. Carroll, as a meat-market owner after 1880, and James Luckey, the only other moulder reporting more than $3,000 before he left his craft, account for two of the three. Of 29 sons of moulders reported employed in Poughkeepsie, Luckey and Carroll account for three of the five who rose to high white-collar status. See *Commemorative Biographical Record of Dutchess County, New York* (Chicago, 1897), 790.

26. See Mills' contrast between "old" and "new" middle classes in his *White Collar* (N.Y., 1956); historians also have tended to assume a wide gulf between manual and non-manual callings in the nineteenth century. See Thernstrom, *Poverty and Progres.* 91.

27. Hobsbawm, *Labouring Men*, 273-4.

28. Even by 1860 the ratio of shops listed in the business directory to workers in the trade was about 1 to 4 among shoemakers, tailors and bakers whereas less than 1 in 10 of the machinists and engineers were employers or self-employed. Yet the distribution of reported wealth in the census is similar in each of these trades; not surprisingly, therefore, in the apparel and food trades a number of self-employed workers report no property whereas a number of machinists and engineers employed by others report as much property as small employers in the former trades. In the same census one-fourth of the grocers, one-third of the proprietors of petty retail and service ventures and one-half of the saloonkeepers report no property showing that a fair number of these ventures were as marginal as the smaller shops in the crafts. A number of the craftsmen who shifted to such ventures during this period reported no property subsequently so that wealth itself provides no way of determining whether they improved their condition.

29. R. G. and A. R. Hutchinson and Mabel Newcomer, "A Study in Business Mortality: Length of Life of Business Enterprises in Poughkeepsie, New York, 1843-1936," *American Economic Review*, 28 (Sept., 1938).

30. In 1875 daily wage rate in Poughkeepsie for tailors, shoemakers, butchers and bakers ranged from $1.75 to $2.50; in contrast machinists, moulders and engineers received between $3.00 and $4.00.

31. Richard Weiss, *The American Myth of Success* (N. Y., 1969), 100-1.

Work, Culture, and Society
in Industrializing America, 1815-1919

HERBERT G. GUTMAN

THE WORK ETHIC remains a central theme in the American experience, and to study this subject afresh means to re-examine much that has been assumed as given in the writing of American working-class and social history. Such study, moreover, casts new light on yet other aspects of the larger American experience that are usually not associated with the study of ordinary working men and women. Until quite recently, few historians questioned as fact the ease with which most past Americans affirmed the "Protestant" work ethic.[1] Persons much more prestigious and influential than mere historians have regularly praised the powerful historical presence of such an ethic in the national culture. A single recent example suffices. In celebrating Labor Day in 1971, the nation's president saluted "the dignity of work, the value of achievement, [and] the morality of self-reliance. None of these," he affirmed, "is going out of style." And yet he worried somewhat. "Let us also recognize," he admitted, "that the work ethic in America is undergoing some changes."[2] The tone of his concern strongly suggested that it had never changed before and even that men like Henry Ford and F. O. Taylor had been among the signers of the Mayflower Compact or, better still, the Declaration of Independence.

It was never that simple. At all times in American history—when the country was still a preindustrial society, while it industrialized, and after it had become the world's leading industrial nation—quite diverse Americans, some of them more prominent and powerful than others, made it

Earlier versions of this paper were delivered at the Anglo-American Colloquium in Labour History sponsored by the Society for the Study of Labour History in London, June 1968; and at the meeting of the Organization of American Historians in Philadelphia, April 1969. Several friends and colleagues made incisive and constructive criticisms of these drafts, and I am in their debt: Eric Foner, Gregory S. Kealey, Christopher Lasch, Val Lorwin, Stephan Thernstrom, Alfred F. Young, and especially Neil Harris and Joan Wallach Scott. So, too, it has profited much from comments by graduate seminar students at the University of Rochester. My great debt to E. P. Thompson should be clear to those who even merely skim these pages.

[1] See especially the splendid essays by Edmund S. Morgan, "The Labor Problem at Jamestown, 1607–18," *AHR*, 76 (1971): 595–611, and C. Vann Woodward, "The Southern Ethic in a Puritan World," in his *American Counterpoint, Slavery and Racism in the North-South Dialogue* (Boston, 1971), 13–46.

[2] Quoted in the New York *Times*, Apr. 2, 1972.

531

clear in their thought and behavior that the Protestant work ethic was
not deeply engrained in the nation's social fabric. Some merely noticed
its absence, others advocated its imposition, and still others represented
an entirely different work ethic. During the War of Independence a
British manufacturer admitted that the disloyal colonists had among
them many "good workmen from the several countries of Europe" but
insisted that the colonists needed much more to develop successful manufactures. "It is not enough that a few, or even a great number of people,
understand manufactures," he said; "the spirit of manufacturing must
become the general spirit of the nation, and be incorporated, as it were,
into their very essence. . . . It requires a long time before the personal, and
a still longer time, before the national, habits are formed." This
Englishman had a point. Even in the land of Benjamin Franklin, Andrew
Carnegie, and Henry Ford, nonindustrial cultures and work habits regularly thrived and were nourished by new workers alien to the "Protestant" work ethic. It was John Adams, not Max Weber, who claimed that
"manufactures cannot live, much less thrive, without honor, fidelity,
punctuality, and private faith, a sacred respect for property, and the moral
obligations of promises and contracts." Only a "decisive, as well as an
intelligent and honest, government," Adams believed, could develop such
"virtues" and "habits." Others among the Founding Fathers worried about
the absence of such virtues within the laboring classes. When Alexander
Hamilton proposed his grand scheme to industrialize the young republic,
an intimate commented, "Unless God should send us saints for workmen
and angels to conduct them, there is the greatest reason to fear for the
success of the plan." Benjamin Franklin shared such fears. He condemned
poor relief in 1768 and lamented the absence among contemporaries of
regular work habits. "Saint *Monday*," he said, "is as duly kept by our
working people as *Sunday;* the only difference is that instead of employing their time cheaply at church they are wasting it expensively at the
ale house." Franklin believed that if poorhouses shut down "Saint Monday
and Saint Tuesday" would "soon cease to be holidays."[3]

Franklin's worries should not surprise us. The Founding Fathers, after
all, lived in a preindustrial, not simply an "agrarian" society, and the
prevalence of premodern work habits among their contemporaries was
natural. What matters here, however, is that Benjamin Franklin's ghost
haunted later generations of Americans. Just before the First World
War the International Harvester Corporation, converted to "scientific

[3] "A Manufacturer," London *Chronicle*, Mar. 17, 1778, quoted in *Pennsylvania Magazine of History and Biography*, 7 (1883): 198–99. John Adams to Tench Coxe, May 1792, quoted in *National Magazine*, 2 (1800): 253–54, in Joseph Davis, *Essays in the Earlier History of the American Corporation* (New York, 1917) 1: 500; Thomas Marshall? to Alexander Hamilton, Sept./Oct. 1971, in Harold C. Syrett, ed., *The Papers of Alexander Hamilton*, 9 (New York, 1965): 250–52; Benjamin Franklin, *Writings, 1767–1772*, ed. A. H. Smith (New York, 1907), 5: 122–27, 534–39.

management" and "welfare capitalism," prepared a brochure to teach its Polish common laborers the English language; "Lesson One," entitled "General," read:

> I hear the whistle. I must hurry.
> I hear the five minute whistle.
> It is time to go into the shop.
> I take my check from the gate board and hang it
>   on the department board.
> I change my clothes and get ready to work.
> The starting whistle blows.
> I eat my lunch.
> It is forbidden to eat until then.
> The whistle blows at five minutes of starting time.
> I get ready to go to work.
> I work until the whistle blows to quit.
> I leave my place nice and clean.
> I put all my clothes in the locker.
> I must go home.

This document illustrates a great deal. That it shows the debasement of the English language, a process closely related to the changing ethnic composition of the American working population and the social need for simplified English commands, is a subject for another study. Our immediate interest is in the relationship it implies between Americanization, factory work habits, and improved labor efficiency.[4]

Nearly a century and a half separated the International Harvester Corporation from Benjamin Franklin, but both wanted to reshape the work habits of others about them. Machines required that men and women adapt older work routines to new necessities and strained those wedded

---

[4] Gerd Korman, "Americanization at the Factory Gate," *Industrial and Labor Relations Review*, 18 (1965): 402. See also his *Industrialization, Immigrants, and Americanization: The View from Milwaukee* (Madison, 1967). These instructions should be compared to those issued in February 1971 by LaGrange, Illinois, General Motors officials to engine division supervisory personnel: "BELL TO BELL POLICY: It is the policy of the [electomotive] division that all employe[e]s be given work assignments such that all will be working effectively and efficiently during their scheduled working hours except for the time required for allowable personal considerations. EACH EMPLOYEE WILL BE INSTRUCTED ON THE FOLLOWING POINTS: 1. Be at their work assignment at the start of the shift. 2. Be at their work assignment at the conclusion of their lunch period. 3. All employe[e]s will be working effectively and efficiently until the bell of their scheduled lunch period and at the end of their scheduled shift. 4. Employe[e]s are to work uninterrupted to the end of the scheduled shift. In most instances, machines and area clean-up can be accomplished during periods of interrupted production prior to the last full hour of the shift." These instructions came to my attention after I read an earlier version of this paper to students and faculty at Northern Illinois University. Edward Jennings, a student and a member of Local 719, United Automobile Workers, delivered the document to me the following day. See also the copy of the work rules posted in 1888 in the Abbot-Downing Factory in Concord, New Hampshire, and deposited in the New Hampshire Historical Society. Headed "NOTICE! TIME IS MONEY!" the rules included the following factory edict: "There are conveniences for washing, but it must be done outside of working hours, and not at our expense." I am indebted to Harry Scheiber for bringing this document to my attention.

to premodern patterns of labor. Half a century separated similar popular laments about the impact of the machine on traditional patterns of labor. In 1873 the Chicago *Workingman's Advocate* published "The Sewing Machine," a poem in which the author scorned Elias Howe's invention by comparing it to his wife:

> Mine is not one of those stupid affairs
> That stands in the corner with what-nots and chairs ...
> Mine is one of the kind to love,
> And wears a shawl and a soft kid glove ...
> None of your patent machines for me,
> Unless Dame Nature's the patentee!
> I like the sort that can laugh and talk,
> And take my arm for an evening walk;
> And will do whatever the owner may choose,
> With the slightest perceptible turn of the screws.
> One that can dance—and possibly flirt—
> And make a pudding as well as a shirt;
> One that can sing without dropping a stitch,
> And play the housewife, lady, and witch ...
> What do you think of my machine,
> Ain't it the best that ever was seen?
> 'Tisn't a clumsy, mechanical toy,
> But flesh and blood! Hear that my boy.

Fifty years later, when significant numbers of Mexicans lived in Chicago and its industrial suburbs and labored in its railroad yards, packing houses, and steel mills (in 1926, thirty-five per cent of Chicago Inland Steel's labor force had come from Mexico), "El Enganchado" ("The Hooked One"), a popular Spanish tune, celebrated the disappointments of immigrant factory workers:

> I came under contract from Lorelia.
> To earn dollars was my dream,
> I bought shoes and I bought a hat
> And even put on trousers.
> For they told me that here the dollars
> Were scattered about in heaps
> That there were girls and theatres
> And that here everything was fun.
> And now I'm overwhelmed—
> I am a shoemaker by trade
> But here they say I'm a camel
> And good only for pick and shovel.
> What good is it to know my trade
> If there are manufacturers by the score
> And while I make two little shoes
> They turn out more than a million?
> Many Mexicans don't care to speak
> The language their mothers taught them

> And go about saying they are Spanish
> And denying their country's flag . . .
> My kids speak perfect English
> And have no use for Spanish,
> They call me "fadder" and don't work
> And are crazy about the Charleston.
> I am tired of all this nonsense
> I'm going back to Michogan.

American society differed greatly in each of the periods when these documents were written. Franklin personified the successful preindustrial American artisan. The "sewing girl" lived through the decades that witnessed the transformation of preindustrial into industrial America. Harvester proved the nation's world-wide industrial supremacy before the First World War. The Mexican song served as an ethnic Jazz Age pop tune. A significant strand, however, tied these four documents together. And in unraveling that strand at particular moments in the nation's history between 1815 and 1920, a good deal is learned about recurrent tensions over work habits that shaped the national experience.[5]

The traditional imperial boundaries (a function, perhaps, of the professional subdivision of labor) that have fixed the territory open to American labor historians for exploration have closed off to them the study of such important subjects as changing work habits and the culture of work. Neither the questions American labor historians usually ask nor the methods they use encourage such inquiry. With a few significant exceptions, for more than half a century American labor history has continued to reflect both the strengths and the weaknesses of the conceptual scheme sketched by its founding fathers, John R. Commons and others of the so-called Wisconsin school of labor history.[6] Even their most severe critics, including the orthodox "Marxist" labor historians of the 1930s, 1940s, and 1950s and the few New Left historians who have devoted attention to American labor history, rarely questioned that conceptual

[5] "The Sewing Machine," *Workingman's Advocate* (Chicago), Aug. 23, 1873; "El Enganchado," printed in Paul Taylor, *Mexican Labor in the United States: Chicago and the Calumet Region* (Berkeley, 1932), vi–vii.

[6] Helpful summaries of recent scholarship in American labor history are Thomas A. Kruger, "American Labor Historiography, Old and New," *Journal of Social History*, 4 (1971): 277–85; Robert H. Zieger, "Workers and Scholars: Recent Trends in American Labor Historiography," *Labor History*, 13 (1972): 245–66; and Paul Faler, "Working Class Historiography," *Radical America*, 3 (1969): 56–68. Innovative works in the field that have broken away from the traditional conceptual framework include especially Richard B. Morris, *Government and Labor in Early America* (New York, 1946); David Brody, *Steelworkers in America: The Non-Union Era* (Cambridge, 1960); Stephan Thernstrom, *Poverty and Progress: Social Mobility in a Nineteenth Century City* (Cambridge, 1964); David Montgomery, *Beyond Equality: Labor and the Radical Republicans, 1862–1872* (New York, 1967); Montgomery, "The Working Class of the Preindustrial American City, 1780–1830," *Labor History*, 9 (1968): 1–22; Montgomery, "The Shuttle and the Cross: Weavers and Artisans in the Kensington Riots of 1844," *Journal of Social History*, 5 (1972): 411–46; Alfred F. Young, "The Mechanics and the Jeffersonians: New York, 1789–1801," *Labor History*, 5 (1964): 247–76; and Alexander Saxton, *The Indispensable Enemy: Labor and the Anti-Chinese Movement in California* (Berkeley, 1971).

framework.[7] Commons and his colleagues asked large questions, gathered important source materials, and put forth impressive ideas. Together with able disciples, they studied the development of the trade union as an institution and explained its place in a changing labor market. But they gave attention primarily to those few workers who belonged to trade unions and neglected much else of importance about the American working population. Two flaws especially marred this older labor history. Because so few workers belonged to permanent trade unions before 1940, its overall conceptualization excluded most working people from detailed and serious study. More than this, its methods encouraged labor historians to spin a cocoon around American workers, isolating them from their own particular subcultures and from the larger national culture. An increasingly narrow "economic" analysis caused the study of American working-class history to grow more constricted and become more detached from larger developments in American social and cultural history and from the writing of American social and cultural history itself. After 1945 American working-class history remained imprisoned by self-imposed limitations and therefore fell far behind the more imaginative and innovative British and Continental European work in the field. In Great Britain, for example, the guideposts fixed by Sidney and Beatrice Webb have been shattered by labor and social historians such as Asa Briggs, Eric Hobsbawm, Henry Pelling, Sidney Pollard, George Rudé, E. P. Thompson, and Brian, J. F. C., and Royden Harrison, among other scholars who have posed new questions, used new methods, and dug deeply into largely neglected primary materials.[8] As a consequence, a rich and subtle new history of the British common people is now being written. Much of value remains to be learned from the older American labor historians, but the time has long been overdue for a critical re-examination of their

---

[7] The best example of orthodox "Marxist" labor history is Philip S. Foner, *History of the Labor Movement in the United States,* (New York, 1947–65). Emphasis in so-called New Left history on the relationship between "corporate liberalism" and American labor is found in James Weinstein, *Corporate Ideal in the Liberal State, 1900–1918* (Boston, 1968), and in Ronald Radosh, *American Labor and United States Foreign Policy* (New York, 1969). A different approach is found in Jesse Lemisch, "Jack Tar in the Streets: Merchant Seamen in the Politics of the American Revolution," *William and Mary Quarterly,* 25 (1968): 371–407.

[8] This essay draws especially on the methods of analysis in the following works: E. P. Thompson, *Making of the English Working Class* (London, 1963); Thompson, "Time, Work-Discipline, and Industrial Capitalism," *Past and Present,* 38 (1967): 56–97; Thompson, "The Moral Economy of the English Crowd in the Eighteenth Century," *Past and Present,* 50 (1971): 76–136; Sidney Pollard, *Genesis of Modern Management* (Cambridge, 1965); Pollard, "Factory Discipline in the Industrial Revolution," *Economic History Review,* 16 (1963): 254–71; Eric Hobsbawm, *Primitive Rebels and Social Bandits* (Manchester, 1959); Hobsbawm, *Labouring Men* (London, 1964) and especially the essay on "Custom Wages and Workload," 344–70; George Rudé, *Crowd in History* (New York, 1964); George Rudé and Eric Hobsbawm, *Captain Swing* (New York, 1968); Brian Harrison, "Religion and Recreation in Nineteenth Century England," *Past and Present,* 38 (1967): 98–125; Harrison, *Drink and the Victorians* (Pittsburgh, 1971); Asa Briggs, ed., *Chartist Studies* (New York, 1954); Royden Harrison, *Before the Socialists* (London, 1965); J. F. C. Harrison, *The Quest for the New Moral World: Robert Owen and the Owenites in Britain and America* (New York, 1969).

framework and their methodology and for applying in special ways to the particularities of the American working-class experience the conceptual and methodological break-throughs of our colleagues across the ocean.

The pages that follow give little attention to the subject matter usually considered the proper sphere of labor history (trade-union development and behavior, strikes and lockouts, and radical movements) and instead emphasize the frequent tension between different groups of men and women new to the machine and a changing American society. Not all periods of time are covered: nothing is said of the half century since the First World War when large numbers of Spanish-speaking and rural Southern white and black workers first encountered the factory and the machine.[9] Much recent evidence describing contemporary dissatisfactions with factory work is not examined.[10] Neither are bound workers (factory slaves in the Old South) or nonwhite free laborers, mostly blacks and Asian immigrants and their descendants, given notice. These groups, too, were affected by the tensions that will be described here, a fact that emphasizes the central place they deserve in any comprehensive study of American work habits and changing American working-class behavior.

Nevertheless the focus in these pages is on free white labor in quite different time periods: 1815–43, 1843–93, 1893–1919. The precise years serve only as guideposts to mark the fact that American society differed

[9] The best recent work is Robert Coles, *South Goes North* (Boston, 1972).

[10] The publication in late 1972 of "Work in America" by the Upjohn Institute for Employment Research, a study financed by the U.S. Department of Health, Education, and Welfare, revealed widespread dissatisfactions with work among contemporary blue- and white-collar workers and even their supervisors. The dispute over this finding in government circles is described in *Newsweek*, Jan. 1, 1973, pp. 47–48, and Howard Muson, "The Ranks of the Discontent," New York *Times*, Dec. 31, 1972. Other evidence of dissatisfaction among factory workers with work routines is reported in the New York *Times* Jan. 23, Apr. 2, and Sept. 3, 1972. The April dispatch reported that a University of Michigan survey team described twenty-five aspects of their jobs to factory workers and then asked the workers to rank them in order of importance. Interesting work ranked first; pay was listed second. Absenteeism, the three large Detroit automobile manufacturers reported, had doubled between 1965 and 1972, "increasing from two to three percent . . . to 5 to 6 percent." In some plants, up to fifteen per cent of the workers were absent "on Fridays and Mondays." Quite interesting discussions of contemporary work dissatisfactions are found in Bennett Kremen, "No Pride in This Dust. Young Workers in the Steel Mills," *Dissent* (Winter 1972), 21–28, and Steve Kline, "Henry and His Magic Kabonk Machine," *Boston Globe Magazine*, July 16, 1972, pp. 8–10, 20–24. See also Rochester *Times-Union* (N.Y.), Nov. 29, 1971, for a discussion of obstinate work and leisure habits among Southern white workers fresh to Northern-owned factories. And a brief feature story in the Rochester *Democrat and Chronicle* (N.Y.), Apr. 30, 1972, told about an artisan Santo Badagliacca who seemed to belong to another era. He had moved to Rochester from Sicily in 1956 with his wife and five-year-old daughter. He was then forty and worked for nearly twelve years as a "tailor" for the National Clothing Company, Timely Clothes, and Bond Clothes, Inc. He quit the clothing factories in 1968 and opened a small custom tailoring shop in his home. In four years, not a single order came for a custom-made suit. Three or four persons visited his place weekly but only to have alterations made. Badagliacca explained his decision to quit the factory: "Each day, it's just collars, collars, collars. I didn't work forty years as a tailor just to do that." See also Richard Sennett and Jonathan Cobb, *The Hidden Injuries of Class* (New York, 1972), and William Serrin, *The Company and the Union: The 'Civilized Relationship' of the General Motors Corporation and the United Auto Workers* (New York, 1973).

Fig. 1. Tagging immigrants in railroad waiting room. Ellis Island, 1926. This family's tags, marked "P.R.R." and "L.V.R.R.," for Pennsylvania Railroad and Lehigh Valley Railroad, suggest they are headed for the anthracite coal region of Pennsylvania. Photograph by Lewis W. Hine. (A fuller collection of Hine's work together with a critical biography and analysis of his place as an artist can be found in Judith Mara Gutman, *The Eyes of Lewis Hine* [scheduled for publication in the fall of 1973] and *Lewis W. Hine and the American Social Conscience* [New York, 1967].) Photograph courtesy George Eastman House Collection.

Fig. 2. Jewish immigrant. Photograph by Lewis W. Hine.
Courtesy George Eastman House Collection.

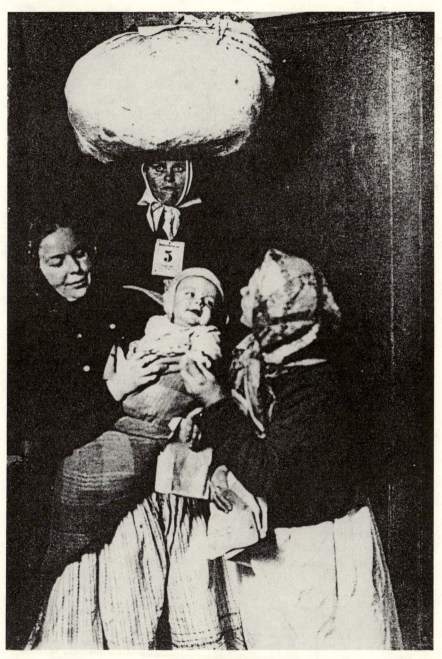

Fig. 3. Italian immigrants, Ellis Island, 1905. Photograph by Lewis W. Hine.
Courtesy George Eastman House Collection.

greatly in each period. Between 1815 and 1843 the United States remained a predominantly preindustrial society and most workers drawn to its few factories were the products of rural and village preindustrial culture. Preindustrial American society was not premodern in the same way that European peasant societies were, but it was, nevertheless, premodern. In the half century after 1843 industrial development radically transformed the earlier American social structure, and during this Middle Period (an era not framed around the coming and the aftermath of the Civil War) a profound tension existed between the older American preindustiral social structure and the modernizing institutions that accompanied the development of industrial capitalism. After 1893 the United States ranked as a mature industrial society. In each of these distinctive stages of change in American society, a recurrent tension also existed between native and immigrant men and women fresh to the factory and the demands imposed upon them by the regularities and disciplines of factory labor. That state of tension was regularly revitalized by the migration of diverse premodern native and foreign peoples into an industrializing or a fully industrialized society. The British economic historian Sidney Pollard has described well this process whereby "a society of peasants, craftsmen, and versatile labourers became a society of modern industrial workers." "There was more to overcome," Pollard writes of industrializing England,

than the change of employment or the new rhythm of work: there was a whole new culture to be absorbed and an old one to be traduced and spurned, there were new surroundings, often in a different part of the country, new relations with employers, and new uncertainties of livelihood, new friends and neighbors, new marriage patterns and behavior patterns of children within the family and without.[11]

That same process occurred in the United States. Just as in all modernizing countries, the United States faced the difficult task of industrializing whole cultures, but in this country the process was regularly repeated, each stage of American economic growth and development involving different first-generation factory workers. The social transformation Pollard described occurred in England between 1770 and 1850, and in those decades premodern British cultures and the modernizing institutions associated primarily with factory and machine labor collided and interacted. A painful transition occurred, dominated the ethos of an entire era, and then faded in relative importance. After 1850 and until quite recently, the British

11 Pollard, "The Adaptation of the Labour Force," in *Genesis of Modern Management*, 160–208. Striking evidence of the preindustrial character of most American manufacturing enterprises before 1840 is found in Allen Pred, "Manufacturing in the American Mercantile City, 1800–1840," *Annals of the American Association of Geographers*, 56 (1966): 307–25. See also Richard D. Brown, "Modernization and Modern Personality in Early America, 1600–1865: A Sketch of a Synthesis," *Journal of Interdisciplinary History*, 2 (1972): 201–28.

working class reproduced itself and retained a relative national homogeneity. New tensions emerged but not those of a society continually busy (and worried about) industrializing persons born out of that society and often alien in birth and color and in work habits, customary values, and behavior. "Traditional social habits and customs," J.F.C. Harrison reminds us, "seldom fitted into the patterns of industrial life, and they had . . . to be discredited as hindrances to progress." That happened regularly in the United States after 1815 as the nation absorbed and worked to transform new groups of preindustrial peoples, native whites among them. The result, however, was neither a static tension nor the mere recurrence of similar cycles, because American society itself changed as did the composition of its laboring population. But the source of the tension remained the same, and conflict often resulted. It was neither the conflict emphasized by the older Progressive historians (agrarianism versus capitalism, or sectional disagreement) nor that emphasized by recent critics of that early twentieth-century synthesis (conflict between competing elites). It resulted instead from the fact that the American working class was continually altered in its composition by infusions, from within and without the nation, of peasants, farmers, skilled artisans, and casual day laborers who brought into industrial society ways of work and other habits and values not associated with industrial necessities and the industrial ethos. Some shed these older ways to conform to new imperatives. Others fell victim or fled, moving from place to place. Some sought to extend and adapt older patterns of work and life to a new society. Others challenged the social system through varieties of collective associations. But for all—at different historical moments—the transition to industrial society, as E. P. Thompson has written, "entailed a severe restructuring of working habits—new disciplines, new incentives, and a new human nature upon which these incentives could bite effectively."[12]

Much in the following pages depends upon a particular definition of culture and an analytic distinction between culture and society. Both deserve brief comment. "Culture" as used here has little to do with Oscar Lewis's inadequate "culture of poverty" construct and has even less to do with the currently fashionable but nevertheless quite crude behavioral social history that defines class by mere occupation and culture as some kind of a magical mix between ethnic and religious affiliations.[13] Instead

· [12] J. F. C. Harrison, *Learning and Living* (London, 1961), 268; Thompson, "Time, Work-Discipline, and Industrial Capitalism," 57.

[13] Valuable and convincing theoretical criticisms of the culture of poverty construct appear in detail in Eleanor Burke Leacock, ed., *The Culture of Poverty: A Critique* (New York, 1971). See also William Preston's withering comments on the faulty application of the culture of poverty to a recent study of the Industrial Workers of the World: William Preston, "Shall This Be All? U. S. Historians versus William D. Haywood *et al.*," *Labor History*, 12 (1971): 435-71. The use of crude definitions of class and culture in otherwise sophisticated behavioral social history is as severely criticized in James Green, "Behavioralism and Class Analysis," *Labor History*, 13 (1972): 89-106.

this paper has profited from the analytic distinctions between culture and society made by the anthropologists Eric Wolf and Sidney W. Mintz and the exiled Polish sociologist Zygmunt Bauman. Mintz finds in culture "a kind of resource" and in society "a kind of arena," the distinction being "between sets of historically available alternatives or forms on the one hand, and the societal circumstances or settings within which these forms may be employed on the other." "Culture," he writes, "is *used*; and any analysis of its use immediately brings into view the arrangements of persons in societal groups for whom cultural forms confirm, reinforce, maintain, change, or deny particular arrangements of status, power, and identity." Bauman insists that for analytic purposes the two (culture and society) need always be examined discretely to explain behavior:

Human behavior, whether individual or collective, is invariably the resultant of two factors: the cognitive system as well as the goals and patterns of behavior as defined by culture systems, on the one hand, and the system of real contingencies as defined by the social structure on the other. A complete interpretation and apprehension of social processes can be achieved only when both systems, as well as their interaction, are taken into consideration.

Such an analytic framework allows social historians to avoid the many pitfalls that follow implicit or explicit acceptance of what the anthropologist Clifford Geertz calls "the theoretical dichotomies of classical sociology— *Gemeinschaft* and *Gesellschaft*, mechanic and organic solidarity, [and] folk and urban cultures." Too often, the subtle historical processes that explain particular patterns of working-class and other behavior have been viewed as no more than "the expansion of one at the expense of the other."[14] An analytic model that distinguishes between culture and society reveals that even

14 Eric Wolf, "Specific Aspects of Plantation Systems in the New World: Community Sub-Cultures and Social Class," in *Plantation Systems of the New World* (Washington, 1949), 142; Sidney W. Mintz, "Foreword," in Norman Whitten and John F. Szwed, eds., *Afro-American Anthropology: Contemporary Perspectives* (New York, 1970), 1–16 but especially 9–10; Zygmunt Bauman, "Marxism and the Contemporary Theory of Culture," *Co-Existence*, 5 (1968): 171–98; Clifford Geertz, *Old Societies and New States* (Glencoe, 1963), 32–54, 109–10, 154–55. See also Emilio Willems, "Peasantry and City: Cultural Persistence and Change in Historical Perspective, A European Case," *American Anthropologist*, 72 (1970): 528–43, in which Willems disputes the proposition that "peasant culture is incompatible with industrialization" and shows that in the German Rhineland town of Neyl there existed significant "cultural continuity of urban lower class and peasantry rather than cultural polarity between the two segments." A brilliant article which focuses on West Indian slaves but is nevertheless methodologically useful to students of all lower-class cultures is S. W. Mintz, "Toward an Afro-American History," *Journal of World History*, 13 (1971): 317–33. The confusion between race and culture greatly marred early twentieth-century American labor history, and no one revealed that more clearly than John R. Commons in *Races and Immigrants in America* (New York, 1907), 7, 11–12, 153–54, 173–75, *passim*. "Race differences," Commons believed, "are established in the very blood and physical condition" and "most difficult to eradicate." Changes might take place in language and other behavioral patterns, "but underneath all these changes there may continue the physical, mental, and moral incapacities which determine the real character of their religion, government, industry, and literature." The behavior of the recent immigrants confused historians like Commons. His racial beliefs and the crude environmentalism he shared with other Progressive reformers encouraged that confusion. "Ireland and Italy," he could write, "have nothing to compare to the trade-union movement

in periods of radical economic and social change powerful cultural continuities and adaptations continued to shape the historical behavior of diverse
working-class populations. That perspective is especially important in examining the premodern work habits of diverse American men and women and
the cultural sanctions sustaining them in an alien society in which the factory and the machine grew more and more important.

Men and women who sell their labor to an employer bring more
to a new or changing work situation than their physical presence. What
they bring to a factory depends, in good¯part, on their culture of origin,
and how they behave is shaped by the interaction between that culture
and the particular society into which they enter. Because so little is yet
known about preindustrial American culture and subcultures, some caution
is necessary in moving from the level of generalization to historical
actuality. What follows compares and contrasts working people new to
industrial society but living in quite different time periods. First, the
expectations and work habits of first-generation predominantly native
American factory workers before 1843 are compared with first-generation
immigrant factory workers between 1893 and 1920. Similarities in the
work habits and expectations of men and women who experienced quite
different premodern cultures are indicated. Second, the work habits and
culture of artisans in the industrializing decades (1843–93) are examined
to indicate the persistence of powerful cultural continuities in that era
of radical economic change. Third, evidence of premodern working-class
behavior that parallels European patterns of premodern working-class
behavior in the early phases of industrialization is briefly described to
suggest that throughout the entire period (1815–1920) the changing composition of the American working class caused the recurrence of "premodern" patterns of collective behavior usually only associated with the
early phases of industrialization. And, finally, attention is given to some
of the larger implications resulting from this recurrent tension between
work, culture, and society.

THE WORK HABITS and the aspirations and expectations of men and women
new to factory life and labor are examined first. Common work habits
rooted in diverse premodern cultures (different in many ways but never-

---

of England, but the Irish are the most effective organizers of the American unions, and the
Italians are becoming the most ardent unionists. Most remarkable of all, the individualistic
Jew from Russia, contrary to his race instinct, is joining the unions." "The American unions,
in fact," Commons concluded, "grow out of American conditions, and are an American
product." But he could not explain how these "races" so easily adapted to American conditions.
How could he when he believed that "even the long series of crimes against the Indians,
to which the term 'Century of Dishonor' seems to have attached itself with no protest, must
be looked upon as a mob spirit of a superior race bent on despoiling a despised and inferior
race"?

Herbert G. Gutman

theless all ill fitted to the regular routines demanded by machine-centered factory processes) existed among distinctive first-generation factory workers all through American history. We focus on two quite different time periods: the years before 1843 when the factory and machine were still new to America and the years between 1893 and 1917 when the country had become the world's industrial colossus. In both periods workers new to factory production brought strange and seemingly useless work habits to the factory gate. The irregular and undisciplined work patterns of factory hands before 1843 frustrated cost-conscious manufacturers and caused frequent complaint among them. Textile factory work rules often were designed to tame such rude customs. A New Hampshire cotton factory that hired mostly women and children forbade "spirituous liquor, smoking, nor any kind of amusement . . . in the workshops, yards, or factories" and promised the "immediate and disgraceful dismissal" of employees found gambling, drinking, or committing "any other debaucheries." A Massachusetts firm nearby insisted that young workers unwilling to attend church stay "within doors and improve their time in reading, writing, and in other valuable and harmless employment." Tardy and absent Philadelphia workers paid fines and could not "carry into the factory nuts, fruits, etc.; books or paper." A Connecticut textile mill owner justified the twelve-hour day and the six-day week because it kept "workmen and children" from "vicious amusements." He forbade "gaming . . . in any private house." Manufacturers elsewhere worried about the example "idle" men set for women and children. Massachusetts family heads who rented "a piece of land on shares" to grow corn and potatoes while their wives and children labored in factories worried one manufacturer. "I would prefer giving constant employment at some sacrifice," he said, "to having a man of the village seen in the streets on a rainy day at leisure." Men who worked in Massachusetts woolen mills upset expected work routines in other ways. "The wool business requires more man labour," said a manufacturer, "and this we study to avoid. Women are much more ready to follow good regulations, are not captious, and do not clan as the men do against the overseers." Male factory workers posed other difficulties, too. In 1817 a shipbuilder in Medford, Massachusetts, refused his men grog privileges. They quit work, but he managed to finish a ship without using further spirits, "a remarkable achievement." An English visitor in 1832 heard an American complain that British workers in the Paterson cotton and machine shops drank excessively and figured as "the most beastly people I have ever seen." Four years later a New Jersey manufacturer of hats and caps boasted in a public card that he finally had "4 and 20 good, permanent workmen," not one infected with "the brutal leprosy of blue Monday habits and the moral gangrene of 'trades union' principles." Other manufacturers had less good fortune. Absenteeism occurred frequently among the Pennsylvania iron workers at the rural Hopewell Village forge: hunting, harvesting, wedding parties, frequent "frolicking" that sometimes lasted for days, and uproarious Election and Independence Day celebrations plagued the mill operators. In the early nineteenth century, a New Jersey iron manufacturer filled his diary with notations about irregular work habits: "all hands drunk"; "Jacob Ventling hunting"; "molders all agree to quit work and went to the beach"; "Peter Cox very drunk and gone to bed. Mr. Evans made a solemn resolution any person or persons bringing liquor to the work enough to make drunk shall be liable to a fine"; "Edward Rutter off a-drinking. It was reported he got drunk on cheese."[15]

Employers responded differently to such behavior by first-generation factory hands. "Moral reform" as well as what Sidney Pollard calls carrot-and-stick policies meant to tame or to transform such work habits. Fining was common. Hopewell Furnace managers deducted one dollar from Samuel York's wages "for getting intoxesitated [*sic*] with liquer [*sic*] and neglecting hauling 4 loads wash Dird at Joneses." Special material rewards encouraged steady work. A Hopewell Village blacksmith contracted for nineteen dollars a month, and "if he does his work well we are to give him a pair of coarse boots." In these and later years manufacturers in Fall River and Paterson institutionalized traditional customs and arranged for festivals and parades to celebrate with their workers a new mill, a retiring superintendent, or a finished locomotive. Some rewarded disciplined workers in special ways. When Paterson locomotive workers pressed for higher wages, their employer instructed an underling: "Book keeper, make up a roll of the men . . . making *fulltime*; if they can't support their families on the wages they are now getting, they must have more. But the other men, who are drunk every Monday morning, I don't want them around the shop under any circumstances." Where factory work could be learned easily, new hands replaced irregular old ones. A factory worker in New England remembered that years before the Civil War her employer had hired "all American girls" but later shifted to immigrant laborers because "not coming from country homes, but living as the Irish do, in the town, they take no vacations, and can be relied on at the mill all year round." Not all such devices worked to the satisfaction of workers or their employers. Sometime in the late 1830s

---

[15] *Mechanic's Free Press* (Philadelphia), Jan. 17, 1829; Edith Abbott, *Women in Industry* (New York, 1910), 374–75; Silesia Factory Rules, Germantown *Telegraph*, Nov. 6, 1833, reprinted in William Sullivan, *Industrial Worker in Pennsylvania* (Harrisburg, 1955), 34; letters of Smith Wilkinson and Jedidiah Tracy to George White, n.d., printed in George White, *Memoir of Samuel Slater* (Philadelphia, 1836), 125–32; Carroll D. Wright, *Industrial Evolution of the United States* (New York, 1901), 296; Rowland T. Berthoff, *British Immigrants in Industrial America* (Cambridge, 1953), 146; Card of H. B. Day, 1836, printed in Paterson *Guardian* (N.J.), Aug. 6, 1886; J. E. Walker, *Hopewell Village* (Philadelphia, 1966), 115–16, 256, 265–68, 282–83, 331, 380–84; "The Martha Furnace Diary," in A. D. Pierce, *Iron in the Pines* (New Brunswick, 1957), 96–105; Sidney Pollard, "Factory Discipline in the Industrial Revolution," *Economic History Review*, 16 (1963): 254–71.

merchant capitalists sent a skilled British silk weaver to manage a new mill in Nantucket that would employ the wives and children of local whalers and fishermen. Machinery was installed, and in the first days women and children besieged the mill for work. After a month had passed, they started dropping off in small groups. Soon nearly all had returned "to their shore gazing and to their seats by the sea." The Nantucket mill shut down, its hollow frame an empty monument to the unwillingness of resident women and children to conform to the regularities demanded by rising manufacturers.[16]

First-generation factory workers were not unique to premodern America. And the work habits common to such workers plagued American manufacturers in later generations when manufacturers and most native urban whites scarcely remembered that native Americans had once been hesitant first-generation factory workers.[17] To shift forward in time to East and South European immigrants new to steam, machinery, and electricity and new to the United States itself is to find much that seems the same. American society, of course, had changed greatly, but in some ways it is as if a film—run at a much faster speed—is being viewed for the second time: primitive work rules for unskilled labor, fines, gang labor, and subcontracting were commonplace. In 1910 two-thirds of the workers in twenty-one major manufacturing and mining industries came from Eastern and Southern Europe or were native American blacks, and studies of these "new immigrants" record much evidence of preindustrial work habits among the men and women new to American industry. According to Moses Rischin, skilled immigrant Jews carried to New York City town and village employment patterns, such as the *landsmannschaft* economy and a preference for small shops as opposed to larger factories, that sparked frequent disorders but hindered stable trade unions until 1910. Specialization spurred anxiety: in Chicago Jewish glovemakers resisted the subdivision of labor even though it promised better wages. "You shrink from doing either kind of work itself, nine hours a day," said two observers of these immigrant women. "You cling to the variety . . . , the mental luxury of first, finger-sides, and then, five separate leather pieces, for relaxation, to play with! *Here* is a luxury worth fighting for!" American work rules also conflicted with religious imperatives. On the eighth day after the birth of a son, Orthodox Jews in Eastern Europe held a festival, "an occasion of much rejoicing." But the American work

16 Walker, *Hopewell Village, passim;* Walker, "Labor-Management Relations at Hopewell Village," *Labor History,* 14 (1973): 3–18; *Voice of Industry* (Lowell), Jan. 8, 1847; New York *Tribune,* June 29, July 4, Aug. 20, 1853; Paterson *Guardian,* Sept. 13, 1886; Massachusetts Bureau of Labor Statistics, *First Annual Report, 1869–1870* (Boston, 1870), 119; Paterson *Evening News,* Nov. 21, 1900.
17 Fining as means of labor discipline, of course, remained common between 1843 and 1893. See, for examples, *Illinois Bureau of Labor Statistics, Fourth Annual Report, 1886* (Springfield, 1887), 501–26; Pennsylvania Bureau of Labor Statistics, *Fourteenth Annual Report, 1886* (Harrisburg, 1887), 13–14.

week had a different logic, and if the day fell during the week the celebration occurred the following Sunday. "The host . . . and his guests," David Blaustein remarked, "know it is not the right day," and "they fall to mourning over the conditions that will not permit them to observe the old custom." The occasion became "one for secret sadness rather than rejoicing." Radical Yiddish poets, like Morris Rosenfeld, the presser of men's clothing, measured in verse the psychic and social costs exacted by American industrial work rules:

> The Clock in the workshop,—it rests not a moment;
> It points on, and ticks on: eternity—time;
> Once someone told me the clock had a meaning,—
> In pointing and ticking had reason and rhyme. . . .
> At times, when I listen, I hear the clock plainly;—
> The reason of old—the old meaning—is gone!
> The maddening pendulum urges me forward
> To labor and still labor on.
> The tick of the clock is the boss in his anger.
> The face of the clock has the eyes of the foe.
> The clock—I shudder—Dost hear how it draws me?
> It calls me "Machine" and it cries [to] me "Sew"![18]

Slavic and Italian immigrants carried with them to industrial America subcultures quite different from that of village Jews, but their work habits were just as alien to the modern factory. Rudolph Vecoli has reconstructed Chicago's South Italian community to show that adult male seasonal construction gangs as contrasted to factory labor were one of many traditional customs adapted to the new environment, and in her study of South Italian peasant immigrants Phyllis H. Williams found among them men who never adjusted to factory labor. After "years" of "excellent" factory work, some "began . . . to have minor accidents" and others "suddenly give up and are found in their homes complaining of a vague indisposition with no apparent physical basis." Such labor worried early twentieth-century efficiency experts, and so did Slavic festivals, church holidays, and "prolonged merriment." "Man," Adam Smith wisely observed, "is, of all sorts of luggage, the most difficult to be transported." That was just as true for these Slavic immigrants as for the early nineteenth-century native American factory workers. A Polish wedding in a Pennsylvania mining or mill town lasted between three and five days. Greek and Roman Catholics shared the same jobs but had different holy days, "an annoyance to many employers." The Greek Church had "more than eighty festivals in the year," and "the Slav religiously observes the days on which the saints are commemorated and invariably takes a holiday." A celebration of the

[18] Moses Rischin, *Promised City: New York's Jews, 1870–1914* (Cambridge, 1962), 19–33, 144–99 but especially 181–82; New York *Tribune*, Aug. 16, 1903; William Herd and Rheta C. Dorr, "The Women's Invasion," *Everybody's Magazine*, Mar. 1909, pp. 375–76; Melech Epstein, *Jewish Labor in the United States* (New York, 1950), 280–85, 290–91.

Fig. 4, above. Italian canal construction workers in western New York playing cards in a shack. Photograph by Lewis W. Hine. Courtesy George Eastman House Collection.

Fig. 5, below. Native white textile-mill worker in the South, 1912. Photograph by Lewis W. Hine. Courtesy George Eastman House Collection.

Fig. 6, above. Italian workers in a New York tenement-house sweatshop, 1909. Photograph by Lewis W. Hine. Courtesy George Eastman House Collection.

Fig. 7, below. Shaping rods under a trip hammer in an iron or steel mill in the Pittsburgh area. Note the absence of machine processes. Photograph by Lewis W. Hine. Courtesy George Eastman House Collection.

American Day of Independence in Mahanoy City, Pennsylvania, caught the eye of a hostile observer. Men parading the streets drew a handcart with a barrel of lager in it. Over the barrel "stood a comrade, goblet in hand and crowned with a garland of laurel, singing some jargon." Another sat and played an accordion. At intervals, the men stopped to "drink the good beverage they celebrated in song." The witness called the entertainment "an imitation of the honor paid Bacchus which was one of the most joyous festivals of ancient Rome" and felt it proof of "a lower type of civilization." Great Lakes dock workers "believed that a vessel could not be unloaded unless they had from four to five kegs of beer." (And in the early irregular strikes among male Jewish garment workers, employers negotiated with them out of doors and after each settlement "would roll out a keg of beer for their entertainment of the workers.") Contemporary betters could not comprehend such behavior. Worried over a three-day Slavic wedding frolic, a woman concluded: "You don't think they have souls, do you? No, they are beasts, and in their lust they'll perish." Another disturbed observer called drink "un-American, . . . a curse worse than the white plague." About that time, a young Italian boy lay ill in a hospital. The only English words he knew were "boots" and "hurry up."[19]

More than irregular work habits bound together the behavior of first-generation factory workers separated from one another by time and by the larger structure of the society they first encountered. Few distinctive American working-class populations differed in so many essentials (their sex, their religions, their nativity, and their prior rural and village cultures) as the Lowell mill girls and women of the Era of Good Feelings and the South and East European steel workers of the Progressive Era. To describe similarities in their expectations of factory labor is not to blur these important differences but to suggest that otherwise quite distinctive men and women interpreted such work in similar ways. The Boston Associates, pioneer American industrialists, had built up Lowell and other towns like it to overcome early nineteenth-century rural and village prejudices and fears about factory work and life and in their regulation of working-class social habits hoped to assure a steady flow of young rural women ("girls") to and from the looms. "The sagacity of self-interest as well as more disinterested considerations," explained a Lowell clergyman in 1845, "has led to the adoption of a strict system of moral police." Without "sober, orderly, and moral" workers, profits would be "absorbed by cases of irregularity, carelessness, and neglect." The Lowell capitalists

19 William M. Leiserson, *Adjusting Immigrant and Industry* (New York, 1924), ch. 1; R. J. Vecoli, "Contadini in Chicago: A Critique of 'The Uprooted'," *Journal of American History*, 51 (1964): 404–27; Phyllis H. Williams, *South Italian Folkways in Europe and America* (New Haven, 1938), 30–32; A. Rosenberg, *Memoirs of a Cloak Maker* (New York, 1920), 42, quoted in Louis Levine, *Women's Garment Workers* (New York, 1924), 42; Peter Roberts, *New Immigration* (New York, 1912), 79–97, 118–19; Roberts, *Anthracite Communities* (New York, 1904), 49–56, 219, 236, 291, 294–95.

thrived by hiring rural women who supplemented a distant family's income, keeping them a few years, and then renewing the process. Such steady labor turnover kept the country from developing a permanent proletariat and so was meant to assure stability. Lowell's busy cotton mills, well-ordered boarding houses, temples of religion and culture, factory girls, and moral police so impressed Anthony Trollope that he called the entire enterprise a "philanthropic manufacturing college." John Quincy Adams thought the New England cotton mills "palaces of the Poor," and Henry Clay marveled over places like the Lowell mills. "Who has not been delighted with the clock-work movements of a large cotton factory?" asked the father of the American System. The French traveler Michel Chevalier had a less sanguine reaction. He found Lowell "neat and decent, peaceable and sage," but worried, "Will this become like Lancashire? Does this brilliant glare hide the misery and suffering of the working girls?"[20]

Historians of the Lowell mill girls find little evidence before 1840 of organized protest among them and attribute their collective passivity to corporation policing policies, the frequent turnover in the labor force, the irregular pace of work (after it was rationalized in the 1840s, it provoked collective protest), the freedom the mill girls enjoyed away from rural family dominance, and their relatively decent earnings. The women managed the transition to mill life because they did not expect to remain factory workers too long. Nevertheless frequent inner tension revealed itself among the mobile mill women. In an early year, a single mill discharged twenty-eight women for such reasons as "misconduct," "captiousness," "disobedience," "impudence," "levity," and even "mutiny." The difficult transition from rural life to factory work also caused tensions outside the mills. Rural girls and women, Harriet Robinson later recalled, came to Lowell in "outlandish fashions" and with "queer names," "Samantha, Triphena, Plumy, Kezia, Aseneth, Elgardy, Leafy, Ruhamah, Almaretta, Sarpeta, and Florilla . . . among them." They spoke a "very peculiar" dialect ("a language almost unintelligible"). "On the broken English and Scotch of their ancestors," said Robinson, "was engrafted the nasal Yankee twang." Some soon learned the "city way of speaking"; others changed their names to "Susan" or "Jane"; and for still others new clothing, especially straw hats, became important. But the machines they worked still left them depressed and with feelings of anxiety. "I never cared much for machinery," Lucy Larcom said of her early Lowell years. "I could not see into their complications or feel interested in them. . . . In sweet June weather I would lean far out of the window, and

[20] Anthony Trollope, quoted in Howard Gitelman, "The Waltham System and the Coming of the Irish," *Labor History*, 8 (1967): 227–54; John Quincy Adams and Henry Clay quoted in Seth Luther, *An Address to the Workingmen of New England* (Boston, 1832), title page; Michel Chevalier, *Society, Manners, and Politics in the United States* (Boston, 1939; reprinted New York, 1969), 133–44; Henry Miles, *Lowell As It Is and Was* (Lowell, 1845), 128–46.

try not to hear the unceasing clash of sound inside." She kept a plant beside her and recollected an overseer who confiscated newspaper clippings and even the pages of a "torn Testament" some women had slipped into the factory. Years after she had left the textile mills, Lucy Larcom ridiculed her mill-girl poems: "I continued to dismalize myself at times quite unnecessarily." Their titles included "The Early Doomed" and "The Complaint of a Nobody" (in which she compared herself to "a weed growing up in a garden"). When she finally quit the mill, the paymaster asked, "Going where you can earn more money?" "No," she remembered answering, "I am going where I can have more time." "Ah, yes!" he responded, "time is money."[21]

Even the *Lowell Offering* testified to the tensions between mill routines and rural rhythms and feelings. Historians have dismissed it too handily because the company sponsored it and refused to publish prose openly critical of mill policies. But the fiction and poetry of its contributors, derivative in style and frequently escapist, also often revealed dissatisfactions with the pace of work. Susan, explaining her first day in the mill to Ann, said the girls awoke early and one sang, "Morning bells, I hate to hear./Ringing dolefully, loud and clear." Susan went on:

You cannot think how odd everything seemed to me. I wanted to laugh at everything, but did not know what to make sport of first. They set me to threading shuttles, and tying weaver's knots and such things, and now I have improved so that I can take care of one loom. I could take care of two if I only had eyes in the back of my head. . . . When I went out at night, the sound of the mill was in my ears, as of crickets, frogs, and Jew-harps, all mingled together in strange discord. After, it seemed as though cotton-wool was in my ears. But now I do not mind it at all. You know that people learn to sleep with the thunder of Niagara in their ears, and the cotton mill is no worse.

Ellen Collins quit the mill, complaining about her "obedience to the ding-dong of the bell—just as though we were so many living machines." In "A Weaver's Reverie," Ella explained why the mill women wrote "so much about the beauties of nature."

Why is it that the delirious dreams of the famine-stricken are of tables loaded with the richest viands? . . . Oh, tell me why this is, and I will tell you why the factory girl sits in the hours of meditation and thinks, not of the crowded, clattering mill, nor of the noisy tenement which is her home.

Contemporary labor critics who scorned the *Lowell Offering* as little more than the work of "poor, caged birds," who "while singing of the roses . . . forget the bars of their prison," had not read it carefully. Their

---

[21] Roll Book of the Hamilton Company, 1826–27, printed in Carolina Ware, *Early New England Cotton Manufacture* (Boston, 1924), 266–67; Harriet Robinson, *Loom and Spindle* (New York, 1898), 62–69; Lucy Larcom, *A New England Girlhood* (Boston, 1889), 138–43, 152–55, 174–76, 180–85, 209–19, 226–31.

attachment to nature was the concern of persons working machines in a society still predominantly "a garden," and it was not unique to these Lowell women. In New Hampshire five hundred men and women petitioned the Amoskeag Manufacturing Company's proprietors in 1853 not to cut down an elm tree to allow room for an additional mill: "It was a beautiful and goodly tree" and belonged to a time "when the yell of the red man and the scream of the eagle were alone heard on the banks of the Merrimack, instead of two giant edifices filled with the buzz of busy and well-remunerated industry." Each day, the workers said, they viewed that tree as "a connecting link between the past and the present," and "each autumn [it] remind[s] us of our own mortality."[22]

Aspirations and expectations interpret experience and thereby help shape behavior. Some Lowell mill girls revealed dissatisfactions, and others made a difficult transition from rural New England to that model factory town, but that so few planned to remain mill workers eased that transition and hampered collective protest. Men as well as women who expect to spend only a few years as factory workers have little incentive to join unions. That was just as true of the immigrant male common laborers in the steel mills of the late nineteenth and early twentieth centuries (when multi-plant oligopoly characterized the nation's most important manufacturing industry) as in the Lowell cotton mills nearly a century earlier. David Brody has explained much about the common laborers. In those years, the steel companies successfully divorced wages from productivity to allow the market to shape them. Between 1890 and 1910, efficiencies in plant organization cut labor costs by about a third. The great Carnegie Pittsburgh plants employed 14,359 common laborers, 11,694 of them South and East Europeans. Most, peasant in origin, earned less than $12.50 a week (a family needed fifteen dollars for subsistence). A staggering accident rate damaged these and other men: nearly twenty-five per cent of the recent immigrants employed at the Carnegie South Works were injured or killed each year between 1907 and 1910, 3,723 in all. But like the Lowell mill women, these men rarely protested in collective ways, and for good reason. They did not plan to stay in the steel mills long. Most had come to the United States as single men (or married men who had left their families behind) to work briefly in the mills, save some money, return home, and purchase farm land. Their private letters to European relatives indicated a realistic awareness of

[22] William Scoresby, *American Factories and Their Mill Operatives* (Boston, 1845), 21-23, 58-66, *passim;* Norman Ware, *Industrial Worker, 1840–1860* (New York, 1924), 85; "New York Industrial Exhibition," *Sessional Papers* (Commons) 1854, vol. 26, p. 10; Ray Ginger, "Labor in a Massachusetts Cotton Mill," *Business History Review,* 28 (1954): 67–91 (a brilliant study of mobility among New England factory women). Useful works on the early New England cotton mills and their female workers include Ware, *Early New England Cotton Manufacture;* Hannah Josephson, *Golden Threads, Mill Girls and Magnates* (New York, 1949); Vera Shlakman, "Economic History of a Factory Town: A Study of Chicopee, Massachusetts," *Smith College Studies in History,* 20, nos. 1–4 (1934–35); Edith Abbott, *Women in Industry.*

their working life that paralleled some of the Lowell fiction: "if I don't earn $1.50 a day, it would not be worth thinking about America"; "a golden land so long as there is work"; "here in America one must work for three horses"; "let him not risk coming, for he is too young"; "too weak for America." Men who wrote such letters and avoided injury often saved small amounts of money, and a significant number fulfilled their expectations and quit the factory and even the country. Forty-four South and East Europeans left the United States for every one hundred that arrived between 1908 and 1910. Not a steel worker, a young Italian boy living in Rochester, New York, summed up the expectations of many such immigrant men in a poem he wrote after studying English just three months:

> Nothing job, nothing job,
> I come back to Italy;
> Nothing job, nothing job,
> Adieu, land northerly....
>
> Nothing job, nothing job,
> O! sweet sky of my Italy;
> Nothing job, nothing job,
> How cold in this country....
>
> Nothing job, nothing job,
> I return to Italy;
> Comrades, laborers, good-bye;
> Adieu, land of "Fourth of July."[23]

Immigrant expectations coincided for a time with the fiscal needs of industrial manufacturers. The Pittsburgh steel magnates had as much good fortune as the Boston Associates. But the stability and passivity they counted on among their unskilled workers depended upon steady work and the opportunity to escape the mills. When frequent recessions caused recurrent unemployment, immigrant expectations and behavior changed. What Brody calls peasant "group consciousness" and "communal loyalty" sustained bitter wildcat strikes after employment picked up. The tenacity of these immigrant strikes for higher wages amazed contemporaries, and brutal suppression often accompanied them (Cleveland, 1899; East Chicago, 1905; McKees Rock, 1909; Bethlehem, 1910; and Youngstown in 1915 where, after a policeman shot into a peaceful parade, a riot caused an estimated one million dollars in damages). The First World War and its aftermath blocked the traditional route of overseas outward mobility, and the consciousness of immigrant steel workers changed. They sparked the 1919 steel strike. The steel mill had become a way of life for

23 David Brody, *Steelworkers in America: The Non-Union Era* (Cambridge, 1960), 26–28, 36, 96–111, 119–20, 125–46, 180–86, *passim*; Brody, *Labor in Crisis* (Philadelphia, 1965), 15–45; "Song of an Italian Workman," Rochester *Post-Express* (N.Y.), n.d., reprinted in *Survey*, 21 (1908): 492–93.

them and was no longer the means by which to reaffirm and even strengthen older peasant and village life-styles.[24]

LET US SHARPLY shift the time perspective from the years before 1843 and those between 1893 and 1919 to the decades between 1843 and 1893 and also shift our attention to the artisans and skilled workers who differed so greatly in the culture and work-styles they brought to the factory from men and women bred in rural and village cultures. The focus, however, remains the same—the relationship between settled work habits and culture. This half century saw the United States (not small pockets within it) industrialize as steam and machinery radically transformed the premodern American economic structure. That so much attention has been given to the Civil War as a crucial divide in the nation's history (and it was, of course, for certain purposes) too frequently has meant neglect by historians of common patterns of behavior that give coherence to this period. Few contemporaries described these large structural changes more effectively if indirectly than the Boston labor reformer Jennie Collins in 1871:

If you should enter a factory and find the water-wheels in the garret, the heaviest machinery in the seventh story, and the dressing and weaving in the basement, you would find the machinery and system less out of joint than at present it seems to be in this strange country of ours. The structure of our society is like a building for which the stones were carefully designed and carved, but in the construction of which the masons seized upon whatever block came handiest, without regard to design or fitness, using window-sills for partition walls, capstones for the foundation, and chink-pieces for the corner-stone.

The magnitude of the changes noticed by Collins cannot be understated. In 1869 half of the country's manufacturing enterprises still managed on water power. The nation in 1860 counted more slaves than factory workers. In his unpublished study of six upstate New York counties Richard L. Ehrlich has found that in five counties during that same year employment in manufacturing plants having at least fifty workers accounted for thirty-seven per cent or less of their respective labor forces. In the six counties (Albany, Erie, Monroe, Oneida, Onondaga, and Rensselaer) the average number of persons employed by firms engaging fewer than fifty employees was less than nine. In the year of Abraham Lincoln's election as president, the United States ranked behind England, France, and Germany in the value of its manufactured product. In 1894 the United States led the field: its manufactured product nearly equalled in value that of Great Britain, France, and Germany together. But such profound economic changes did not entirely shatter the older American social structure and the settled cultures of premodern native and immigrant American artisans.

[24] Brody, *Steelworkers in America, passim;* Brody, *Labor in Crisis,* 15-45.

"There is no such thing as economic growth which is not, at the same time, growth or change of a culture," E. P. Thompson has written. Yet he also warns that "we should not assume any automatic, or over-direct, correspondence between the dynamic of economic growth and the dynamic of social or cultural life." That significant stricture applies as much to the United States as to England during its Industrial Revolution and especially to native and immigrant artisans between 1843 and 1893.[25]

It is not surprising to find tenacious artisan work habits before the Civil War, what Thompson calls "alternate bouts of intense labour and of idleness wherever men were in control of their working lives." An English cabinetmaker shared a New York City workplace with seven others (two native Americans, two Germans, and one man each from Ireland, England, and France), and the readers of *Knight's Penny Magazine* learned from him that "frequently . . . after several weeks of real hard work . . . a simultaneous cessation from work took place." "As if . . . by tacit agreement, every hand" contributed "loose change," and an apprentice left the place and "speedily returned laden with wine, brandy, biscuits, and cheese." Songs came forth "from those who felt musical," and the same near-ritual repeated itself two more times that day. Similar relaxations, apparently self-imposed, also broke up the artisans' work day in the New York City shipyards, and a ship carpenter described them as "an indulgence that custom had made as much of a necessity in a New York shipyard as a grind-stone":

In our yard, at half-past eight a.m., Aunt Arlie McVane, a clever kind-hearted, but awfully uncouth, rough sample of the "Ould Sod," would make her welcome appearance in the yard with her two great baskets, stowed and checked off with crullers, doughnuts, ginger-bread, turnovers, pieces, and a variety of sweet cookies and cakes; and from the time Aunt Arlie's baskets came in sight until every man and boy, bosses and all, in the yard, had been supplied, always at one cent a piece for any article on the cargo, the pie, cake and cookie trade was a brisk one. Aunt Arlie would usually make the rounds of the yard and supply all hands in about an hour, bringing the forenoon up to half-past nine, and giving us from ten to fifteen minutes "breathing spell" during lunch; no one ever hurried during "cake-time."

Nor was this all:

After this was over we would fall to again, until interrupted by Johnnie Gogean, the English candyman, who came in always at half-past ten, with his great board, the size of a medium extension dining table, slung before him, covered with all sorts of "stick", and several of sticky candy, in one-cent lots. Bosses, boys and men —all hands, everybody—invested one to three cents in Johnnie's sweet wares,

[25] Jennie Collins, *Nature's Aristocracy* (Boston, 1871), 4; Richard L. Ehrlich, "The Development of Manufacturing in Selected Counties in the Erie Canal Corridor, 1815-1860," (Ph.D. dissertation, State University of New York, Buffalo, 1972); Stuart Bruchey, *Roots of American Economic Growth* (New York, 1965), 139; George Rogers Taylor, *Transportation Revolution, 1815-1860* (New York, 1951), 249; Thompson, *Making of the English Working Class*, 97, 192.

and another ten to fifteen minutes is spent in consuming it. Johnnie usually sailed out with a bare board until 11 o'clock at which time there was a general sailing out of the yard and into convenient grog-shops after whiskey; only we had four or five men among us, and one apprentice—not quite a year my senior—who used to sail out pretty regularly ten times a day on the average; two that went for whiskey only when some one invited them to drink, being too mean to treat themselves; and two more who never went at all.

In the afternoon, about half-past three, we had a cake-lunch, supplied by Uncle Jack Gridder, an old, crippled, superannuated ship carpenter. No one else was ever allowed to come in competition with our caterers. Let a foreign candy-board or cake basket make their appearance inside the gates of the yard, and they would get shipped out of that directly.

At about five o'clock p.m., always, Johnnie used to put in his second appearance; and then, having expended money in another stick or two of candy, and ten minutes in its consumption, we were ready to drive away again until sundown; then home to supper.

Less well-ordered in their daily pleasures, the shoemakers in Lynn, Massachusetts, nevertheless surrounded their way of work with a way of life. The former cobbler David Johnson recorded in minute detail in *Sketches of Old Lynn* how fishermen and farmers retained settled ways first as part-time shoemakers in small shops behind their homes. The language of the sea was adapted to the new craft:

There were a good many sea phrases, or "salt notes" as they were called, used in the shops. In the morning one would hear, "Come Jake, hoist the sails," which simply was a call to roll up the curtains. . . . If debate ran high upon some exciting topic, some veteran would quietly remark, "Squally, squally, today. Come better *luff* and bear away."

At times a shoemaker read from a newspaper to other men at work. Festivals, fairs, games ("trolling the tog"), and excursions were common rituals among the Lynn cobblers. So was heavy drinking with the bill often incurred by "the one who made the most or the fewest shoes, the best or the poorest." That man "paid 'the scot.'" "These were the days," Johnson reminded later and more repressed New England readers, "when temperance organizations were hardly known."[26]

Despite the profound economic changes that followed the American Civil War, Gilded Age artisans did not easily shed stubborn and time-honored work habits. Such work habits and the life-styles and subcultures related to them retained a vitality long into these industrializing decades.

26 Thompson, "Time, Work-Discipline, and Industrial Capitalism," 73; "A Workingman's Recollections of America," *Knight's Penny Magazine*, 1 (1846): 97–112; Richard D. Trevellick, in *Fincher's Trades Review*, n.d., reprinted in George E. McNeill, ed., *The Labor Movement: the Problem of To-day* (New York, 1887), 341–42; David Johnson, *Sketches of Old Lynn* (Lynn, 1880), 30–31, 36–49. The relationship between drink, work, and other artisanal communal activities was described inadvertently in unusual detail for dozens of British crafts and trades on nearly every page of John Dunlop's *The Philosophy of Artificial and Compulsory Drinking Usage in Great Britain and Ireland* (6th ed.; London, 1839), a 331-page temperance tract. There is good reason to believe that the craft customs described in this volume were known to American artisans and workers, too.

Not all artisans worked in factories, but some that did retained traditional craft skills. Mechanization came in different ways and at different times to diverse industries. Samuel Gompers recollected that New York City cigarmakers paid a fellow craftsman to read a newspaper to them while they worked, and Milwaukee cigarmakers struck in 1882 to

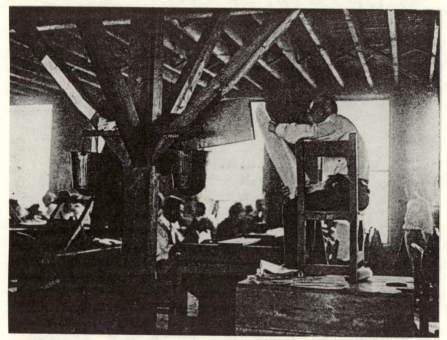

Fig. 8. "Reader" in a cigar factory (probably in New York City), 1909. Photograph by Lewis W. Hine. Courtesy George Eastman House Collection.

retain such privileges as keeping (and then selling) damaged cigars and leaving the shop without a foreman's permission. "The difficulty with many cigarmakers," complained a New York City manufacturer in 1877, "is this. They come down to the shop in the morning; roll a few cigars and then go to a beer saloon and play pinnocio or some other game, . . . working probably only two or three hours a day." Coopers felt new machinery "hard and insensate," not a blessing but an evil that "took a great deal of joy out of life" because machine-made barrels undercut a subculture of work and leisure. Skilled coopers "lounged about" on Saturday (the regular pay day), a "lost day" to their employers. A historian of American cooperage explained:

Early on Saturday morning, the big brewery wagon would drive up to the shop. Several of the coopers would club together, each paying his proper share, and one of them would call out the window to the driver, "Bring me a Goose Egg," meaning a half-barrel of beer. Then others would buy "Goose Eggs," and there

230

would be a merry time all around. . . . Little groups of jolly fellows would often sit around upturned barrels playing poker, using rivets for chips, until they had received their pay and the "Goose Egg" was dry.

Saturday night was a big night for the old-time cooper. It meant going out, strolling around the town, meeting friends, usually at a favorite saloon, and having a good time generally, after a week of hard work. Usually the good time continued over into Sunday, so that on the following day he usually was not in the best of condition to settle down to the regular day's work.

. Many coopers used to spend this day [Monday] sharpening up their tools, carrying in stock, discussing current events, and in getting things in shape for the big day of work on the morrow. Thus, "Blue Monday" was something of a tradition with the coopers, and the day was also more or less lost as far as production was concerned.

"Can't do much today, but I'll give her hell tomorrow," seemed to be the Monday slogan. But bright and early Tuesday morning, "Give her hell" they would, banging away lustily for the rest of the week until Saturday which was pay day again, and its thoughts of the "Goose Eggs."

Such traditions of work and leisure—in this case, a four-day work week and a three-day weekend—angered manufacturers anxious to ship goods as much as it worried sabbatarians and temperance reformers. Conflicts over life- and work-styles occurred frequently and often involved control over the work process and over time. The immigrant Staffordshire potters in Trenton, New Jersey, worked in "bursts of great activity" and then quit for "several days at a time." "Monday," said a manufacturer, "was given up to debauchery." After the potters lost a bitter lockout in 1877 that included torchlight parades and effigy burnings, the *Crockery and Glass Journal* mockingly advised:

Run your factories to please the crowd. . . . Don't expect work to begin before 9 a.m. or to continue after 3 p.m. Every employee should be served hot coffee and a boquet at 7 a.m. and allowed the two hours to take a free perfumed bath. . . . During the summer, ice cream and fruit should be served at 12 p.m. to the accompaniment of witching music.

Hand coopers (and potters and cigarmakers, among others) worked hard but in distinctly preindustrial styles. Machine-made barrels pitted modernizing technology and modern habits against traditional ways. To the owners of competitive firms struggling to improve efficiency and cut labor costs, the Goose Egg and Blue Monday proved the laziness and obstinacy of craftsmen as well as the tyranny of craft unions that upheld venerable traditions. To the skilled cooper, the long weekend symbolized a way of work and life filled with almost ritualistic meanings. Between 1843 and 1893, compromise between such conflicting interests was hardly possible.[27]

[27] Samuel Gompers, *Seventy Years of Life and Labor*, (New York, 1925), 1: 42–53, 63–82; Thomas Gavett, *Development of the Labor Movement in Milwaukee* (Madison, 1965), 43 ff.; New York *Herald*, Nov. 17, 1877; Franklin E. Coyne, *The Development of the Cooperage Industry in the United States* (Chicago, 1940), 7–26 but especially 21–22; *Crockery and Glass Journal*, n.d., reprinted in *Labor Standard* (N.Y.), Sept. 9, 1877; Frank Thistlethwaite, "Atlantic Migration of the Pottery Industry," *Economic History Review*, 10 (1957–58): 264–73.

Settled premodern work habits existed among others than those employed in nonfactory crafts. Owners of already partially mechanized industries complained of them, too. "Saturday night debauches and Sunday carousels though they be few and far between," lamented the *Age of Steel* in 1882, "are destructive of modest hoardings, and he who indulges in them will in time become a striker for higher wages." In 1880 a British steel worker boasted that native Americans never would match immigrants in their skills: " 'adn't the 'ops, you know." Manufacturers, when able, did not hesitate to act decisively to end such troubles. In Fall River new technology allowed a print cloth manufacturer to settle a long-standing grievance against his stubborn mule spinners. "On Saturday afternoon after they had gone home," a boastful mill superintendent later recollected, "we started right in and smashed a room full of mules with sledge hammers. . . . On Monday morning, they were astonished to find that there was not work for them. That room is now full of ring frames run by girls." Woolen manufacturers also displaced hand-jack spinners with improved machinery and did so because of "the disorderly habits of English workmen. Often on a Monday morning, half of them would be absent from the mill in consequence of the Sunday's dissipation." Blue Monday, however, did not entirely disappear. Paterson artisans and factory hands held a May festival on a Monday each year ("Labor Monday") and that popular holiday soon became state law, the American Labor Day. It had its roots in earlier premodern work habits.[28]

The persistence of such traditional artisan work habits well into the nineteenth century deserves notice from others besides labor historians, because those work habits did not exist in a cultural or social vacuum. If modernizing technology threatened and even displaced such work patterns, diverse nineteenth-century subcultures sustained and nourished them. "The old nations of the earth creep on at a snail's pace," boasted Andrew Carnegie in *Triumphant Democracy* (1886), "the Republic thunders past with the rush of an express." The articulate steelmaster, however, had missed the point. The very rapidity of the economic changes occurring in Carnegie's lifetime meant that many, unlike him, lacked the time, historically, culturally, and psychologically, to be separated or alienated from settled ways of work and life and from relatively fixed beliefs. Continuity not consensus counted for much in explaining working-class and especially artisan behavior in those decades that witnessed the coming of the factory and the radical transformation of American society. Persistent work habits were one example of that significant continuity. But these elements of continuity were often revealed among nineteenth-century American workers cut off by birth from direct contact with the

28 *Age of Steel*, Aug. 5, 1882 (courtesy of Lynn Mapes); Berthoff, *British Immigrants in Industrial America*, 54–55, 146; announcement of "Great Festival" on "Labor Monday," Paterson *Labor Standard*, May 29, 1880.

preindustrial American past, a fact that has been ignored or blurred by the artificial separation between labor history and immigration history. In Gilded Age America (and afterwards in the Progressive Era despite the radical change in patterns of immigration), working-class and immigration history regularly intersected, and that intermingling made for powerful continuities. In 1880, for example, 63 of every 100 Londoners were native to that city, 94 coming from England and Wales, and 98 from Great Britain and Ireland. Foreign countries together contributed only 1.6 per cent to London's massive population. At that same moment, more than 70 of every 100 persons in San Francisco (78), St. Louis (78), Cleveland (80), New York (80), Detroit (84), Milwaukee (84), and Chicago (87) were immigrants or the children of immigrants, and the percentage was just as high in many smaller American industrial towns and cities. "Not every foreigner is a workingman," noticed the clergyman Samuel Lane Loomis in 1887, "but in the cities, at least, it may almost be said that every workingman is a foreigner." And until the 1890s most immigrants came from Northern and Western Europe, French- and English-speaking Canada, and China. In 1890, only three per cent of the nation's foreign-born residents—290,000 of 9,200,000 immigrants—had been born in Eastern or Southern Europe. (It is a little recognized fact that most North and West European immigrants migrated to the United States after, not before, the American Civil War.) When so much else changed in the industrializing decades, tenacious traditions flourished among immigrants in ethnic subcultures that varied greatly among particular groups and according to the size, age, and location of different cities and industries. ("The Irish," Henry George insisted, "burn like chips, the English like logs.") Class and occupational distinctions within a particular ethnic group made for different patterns of cultural adaptation, but powerful subcultures thrived among them all.[29]

Immiserization and poverty cut deeply into these ethnic working-class worlds. In reconstructing their everyday texture there is no reason to neglect or idealize such suffering, but it is time to discard the notion that the large-scale uprooting and exploitative processes that accompanied industrialization caused little more than cultural breakdown and social anomie. Family, class, and ethnic ties did not dissolve easily. "Almost as a matter of definition," the sociologist Neil Smelzer has written, "we associate the factory system with the decline of the family and the onset of anonymity." Smelzer criticized such a view of early industrializing England, and it has just as little validity for nineteenth-century industrializing America. Family roles changed in important ways, and strain was widespread, but the immigrant working-class family held together.

[29] Andrew Carnegie quoted in Henry Pelling, *America and the British Left* (New York, 1957), 52; Samuel Lane Loomis, *Modern Cities and Their Religious Problems* (New York, 1887), 68–73; Henry George quoted in Carl Wittke, *Irish in America* (Baton Rouge, 1956), 193.

Examination of household composition in sixteen census enumeration districts in Paterson in 1880 makes that clear for this predominantly working-class immigrant city, and while research on other ethnic working-class communities will reveal significant variations, the overall patterns should not differ greatly. The Paterson immigrant (and native white) communities were predominantly working class, and most families among

TABLE 1. MALE OCCUPATIONAL STRUCTURE AND HOUSEHOLD COMPOSITION
BY ETHNIC GROUP, PATERSON, NEW JERSEY, 1880,
ENUMERATION DISTRICTS 150–53, 161–72[a]

	British	German	Irish	Native White
Total Males 20 and Older	2090	927	2841	1461
Total Females 20 and Older	1941	804	3466	1689
Male Occupational Structure				
Unskilled Laborer	8.2%	9.8%	43.6%	20.8%
Skilled Worker	75.5%	64.3%	44.8%	62.5%
Nonlaborer	16.3%	25.9%	11.6%	16.7%
Household Composition				
Number of Kin-related Households	1402	686	2142	905
Number of Subfamilies[b]	117	41	158	125
Nuclear Households	73.9%	78.1%	73.1%	65.7%
Extended Households	13.5%	10.3%	13.6%	18.7%
Augmented Households[c]	14.6%	13.1%	15.3%	19.0%
Per cent of Households and Subfamilies with a Husband and/or Father Present	87.2%	91.6%	81.1%	78.9%

[a] I am indebted to Carol W. Allison for gathering the raw Paterson data from the 1880 federal manuscript census schedules.
[b] A subfamily is defined as a complete or incomplete nuclear family residing with another nuclear family.
[c] Augmented households include lodgers. The sum of nuclear, augmented, and extended households is greater than 100 per cent because some households included both relatives and lodgers and have been counted twice.

them were intact in their composition. For this population, at least (and without accounting for age and sex ratio differences between the ethnic groups), a greater percentage of immigrant than native white households included two parents. Ethnic and predominantly working-class communities in industrial towns like Paterson and in larger cities, too, built on these strained but hardly broken familial and kin ties. Migration to another country, life in the city, and labor in cost-conscious and ill-equipped factories and workshops tested but did not shatter what the anthropologist Clifford Geertz has described as primordial (as contrasted to civic) attachments, "the 'assumed' givens . . . of social existence: immediate contiguity and kin connections mainly, but beyond them, the givenness that stems from being born into a particular religious community, speaking a particular language, and following particular social patterns." Tough familial and kin ties made possible the transmission and adaptation of European working-class cultural patterns and beliefs to industrializing America. As late as 1888, residents in some Rhode Island mill villages still figured their wages in British currency. Common rituals and festivals bound together such communities. Paterson silk weavers had their Macclesfield wakes, and Fall River cotton-mill workers their Ashton wakes. British immigrants "banded together to uphold the popular culture of the homeland" and celebrated saints' days: St. George's Day, St. Andrew's Day, and St. David's Day. Even funerals retained an archaic flavor. Samuel Sigley, a Chartist house painter, had fled Ashton-under-Lyne in 1848, and built American trade unions. When his wife died in the late 1890s a significant ritual occurred during the funeral: some friends placed a chaff of wheat on her grave. Mythic beliefs also cemented ethnic and class solidarities. The Irish-American press, for example, gave Martin O'Brennan much space to argue that Celtic had been spoken in the Garden of Eden, and in Paterson Irish-born silk, cotton, and iron workers believed in the magical powers of that town's "Dublin Spring." An old resident remembered:

There is a legend that an Irish fairy brought over the water in her apron from the Lakes of Killarney and planted it in the humble part of that town. ... There were dozens of legends connected with the Dublin Spring and if a man drank from its precious depository ... he could never leave Paterson [but] only under the fairy influence, and the wand of the nymph would be sure to bring him back again some time or other.

When a "fairy" appeared in Paterson in human form, some believed she walked the streets "as a tottering old woman begging with a cane." Here was a way to assure concern for the elderly and the disabled.[30]

Much remains to be studied about these cross-class but predominantly working-class ethnic subcultures common to industrializing America. Relations within them between skilled and unskilled workers, for example, remain unclear. But the larger shape of these diverse immigrant communities can be sketched. More than mythic beliefs and common work habits sustained them. Such worlds had in them what Thompson has called "working-class intellectual traditions, working-class community patterns,

[30] Neil Smelzer, *Social Change in the Industrial Revolution* (Chicago, 1959), 193; Clifford Geertz, *Old Societies and New States* (Glencoe, 1963), 109–10; Lillie B. Chace Wyman, "Studies in Factory Life," *Atlantic Monthly*, 62 (1888): 17–29, 215–21, 605–21 and 63 (1889): 68–79; Berthoff, *British Immigrants in Industrial America*, 147–81, *passim*; Paterson *Labor Standard*, Oct. 2, 1897; Thomas N. Brown, *Irish-American Nationalism* (Philadelphia, 1966), 32; Paterson *Evening News*, Oct. 27, 1900. Except for the fact that nuclear households declined greatly at the expense of households containing lodgers (augmented households), examination of the household composition among immigrant Jews and Italians in Lower Manhattan in 1905 shows that powerful familial and kin ties bound together later immigrant communities, too. The data are summarized briefly in table 3 (see appendix).

and a working-class structure of feeling," and men with artisan skills powerfully affected the everyday texture of such communities. A model subculture included friendly and benevolent societies as well as friendly
local politicians, community-wide holiday celebrations, an occasional
library (the Baltimore Journeymen Bricklayer's Union taxed members
one dollar a year in the 1880s to sustain a library that included the collected
works of William Shakespeare and Sir Walter Scott's Waverley novels),
participant sports, churches sometimes headed by a sympathetic clergy,
saloons, beer-gardens, and concert halls or music halls and, depending
upon circumstance, trade unionists, labor reformers, and radicals. The
Massachusetts cleric Jonathan Baxter Harrison published in 1880 an
unusually detailed description of one such ethnic, working-class institution, a Fall River music hall and saloon. About fifty persons were there
when he visited it, nearly one-fourth of them young women. "Most of
those present," he noticed, were "persons whom I had met before, in the
mills and on the streets. They were nearly all operatives, or had at some
time belonged to that class." An Englishman sang first, and then a black
whose songs "were of many kinds, comic, sentimental, pathetic, and silly.
. . . When he sang 'I got a mammy in the promised land,' with a strange,
wailing refrain, the English waiter-girl, who was sitting at my table, wiped
her eyes with her apron, and everybody was very quiet." Harrison said
of such places in Fall River:

All the attendants . . . had worked in the mills. The young man who plays the
piano is usually paid four or five dollars per week, besides his board. The young
men who sing receive one dollar per night, but most of them board themselves.
. . . The most usual course for a man who for any reason falls out of the ranks
of mill workers (if he loses his place by sickness or is discharged) is the opening
of a liquor saloon or drinking place.

Ethnic ties with particular class dimensions sometimes stretched far
beyond local boundaries and even revealed themselves in the behavior of
the most successful practitioners of Gilded Age popular culture. In 1884,
for example, the pugilist John L. Sullivan and the music-hall entertainers
Harrigan and Hart promised support to striking Irish coal miners in the
Ohio Hocking Valley. Local ties, however, counted for much more and
had their roots inside and outside of the factory and workshop. Soon after
Cyrus H. McCormick, then twenty-one, took over the management of his
father's great Chicago iron machinery factory (which in the early 1880s
employed twelve hundred men and boys), a petition signed by "Many
Employees" reached his hands:

It only pains us to relate to you . . . that a good many of our old hands is not
here this season and if Mr. Evarts is kept another season a good many more will
leave. . . . We pray for you . . . to remove this man. . . . We are treated as though
we were dogs. . . . He has cut wages down so low they are living on nothing but

bread. . . . We can't talk to him about wages if we do he will tell us to go out side the gate. . . . He discharged old John the other day he has been here seventeen years. . . . There is Mr. Church who left us last Saturday he went about and shook hands with every old hand in the shop . . . this brought tears to many mens eyes. He has been here nineteen years and has got along well with them all until he came to Mr. Evarts the present superintendent.

Artisans, themselves among those later displaced by new technology, signed this petition, and self-educated artisans (or professionals and petty enterprisers who had themselves usually risen from the artisan class) often emerged as civic and community leaders. "Intellectually," Jennie Collins noticed in Boston in the early 1870s, "the journeymen tailors . . . are ever discussing among themselves questions of local and national politics, points of law, philosophy, physics, and religion."[81]

Such life-styles and subcultures adapted and changed over time. In the Gilded Age piece rates in nearly all manufacturing industries helped reshape traditional work habits. "Two generations ago," said the Connecticut Bureau of Labor Statistics in 1885, "time-work was the universal rule." "Piece-work" had all but replaced it, and the Connecticut Bureau called it "a moral force which corresponds to machinery as a physical force." Additional pressures came in traditional industries such as shoe, cigar, furniture, barrel, and clothing manufacture, which significantly mechanized in these years. Strain also resulted where factories employed large numbers of children and young women (in the 1880 manuscript census 49.3 per cent of all Paterson boys and 52.1 per cent of all girls aged eleven to fourteen had occupations listed by their names) and was especially common among the as yet little-studied pools of casual male laborers found everywhere. More than this, mobility patterns significantly affected the structure and the behavior of these predominantly working-class communities. A good deal of geographic mobility, property mobility (home ownership), and occupational mobility (skilled status in new industries or in the expanding building trades, petty retail enterprise, the professions, and public employment counted as the most important ways to advance occupationally) reshaped these ethnic communities as Stephan Thernstrom and others have shown. But so. little is yet known about the society in which such men and women lived and about the cultures which had produced them that it is entirely premature to infer "consciousness" (beliefs and values) only from mobility rates. Such patterns and rates of mobility, for example, did not entirely shatter working-class capacities for self-protection. The fifty-year period between 1843 and 1893 was not conducive to permanent, stable trade unions,

[81] Thompson, *Making of the English Working Class*, 194; Richard T. Ely, *Labor Movement in America* (New York, 1886), 125; Jonathan Baxter Harrison, *Certain Dangerous Tendencies in American Life and Other Essays* (Boston, 1880), 178–88; *National Labor Tribune* (Pittsburgh), Dec. 13, 1884; Robert Ozanne, *Century of Labor-Management Relations at McCormick and International Harvester* (Madison, 1967), 10–28; Collins, *Nature's Aristocracy*, 94.

but these decades were a time of frequent strikes and lockouts and other forms of sustained conflict.[32]

Not all strikes and lockouts resulted in the defeat of poorly organized workers. For the years 1881 to 1887, for example, the New Jersey Bureau of Labor Statistics collected information on 890 New Jersey industrial disputes involving mostly workers in the textile, glass, metal, transportation, and building trades: six per cent ended in compromise settlements; employers gained the advantage in forty per cent; strikers won the rest (fifty-four per cent). In four of five disputes concerning higher wages and shorter hours, New Jersey workers, not their employers, were victorious. Large numbers of such workers there and elsewhere were foreign-born or the children of immigrants. More than this, immigrant workers in the mid-1880s joined trade unions in numbers far out of proportion to their place in the labor force. Statistical inquiries by the Bureau of Labor Statistics in Illinois in 1886 and in New Jersey in 1887 make this clear. Even these data may not have fully reflected the proclivity of immigrants to seek self-protection. (Such a distortion would occur if, for example, the children of immigrants apparently counted by the bureaus as native-born had remained a part of the ethnic subcultures into which they had been born and joined trade unions as regularly as the foreign-born.) Such information from Illinois and New Jersey suggests the need to treat the meaning of social mobility with some care. So does the sketchy outline of Hugh O'Donnell's career. By 1892, when he was twenty-nine years old, he had already improved his social status a great deal. Before the dispute with Andrew Carnegie and Henry Clay Frick culminated in the bitter Homestead lockout that year, O'Donnell had voted Republican, owned a home, and had in it a Brussels carpet and even a piano. Nevertheless

TABLE 2. ORGANIZED WORKERS, MALE WHITES IN NONAGRICULTURAL PURSUITS, ILLINOIS (1886) AND NEW JERSEY (1887)

Nativity	Illinois 1886		New Jersey 1887	
	Breadwinners	Organized	Breadwinners	Organized
Number				
Native-born	423,290	25,985	243,093	24,463
Foreign-born	308,595	57,163	137,385	26,704
Per cent				
Native-born	57.8%	31.3%	63.9%	47.8%
Foreign-born	42.2%	68.7%	36.1%	52.2%

[32] *Connecticut Bureau of Labor Statistics, First Annual Report, 1885* (Hartford, 1885), 70–73; Stephan Thernstrom, *Poverty and Progress, Social Mobility in a Nineteenth Century City* (Cambridge, 1964), *passim;* and Thernstrom and Richard Sennett, eds., *Nineteenth Century Cities* (New Haven, 1969), *passim.*

this Irish-American skilled worker led the Homestead workers and was even indicted under a Civil War treason statute never before used. The material improvements O'Donnell had experienced mattered greatly to him and suggested significant mobility, but culture and tradition together with the way in which men like O'Donnell interpreted the transformation of Old America defined the value of those material improvements and their meaning to him.[33]

Other continuities between 1843 and 1893 besides those rooted in artisan work habits and diverse ethnic working-class subcultures deserve brief attention as important considerations in understanding the behavior of artisans and other workers in these decades. I have suggested in other writings that significant patterns of opposition to the ways in which industrial capitalism developed will remain baffling until historians re-examine the relationship between the premodern American political system and the coming of the factory along with the strains in premodern popular American ideology shared by workers and large numbers of successful self-made Americans (policemen, clergymen, politicians, small businessmen, and even some "traditional" manufacturers) that rejected the legitimacy of the modern factory system and its owners.[34] One strain of thought common to the rhetoric of nineteenth-century immigrant and native-born artisans is considered here. It helps explain their recurrent enthusiasm for land and currency reform, cooperatives, and trade unions. It was the fear of dependence, "proletarianization," and centralization, and the worry that industrial capitalism threatened to transform "the Great Republic of the West" into a "European" country. In 1869, the same year that saw the completion of the transcontinental railroad, the chartering of the Standard Oil Company, the founding of the Knights of Labor, and the dedication of a New York City statue to Cornelius Vanderbilt, some London workers from Westbourne Park and Notting Hill petitioned the American Ambassador for help to emigrate. "Dependence," they said of Great Britain, "not independence, is inculcated. Hon. Sir, this state of things we wish to fly from . . . to become citizens of that great Republican country, which has no parallels in the world's history." Such men had a vision of Old America, but it was not a new vision. Industrial transformation between 1840 and 1890 tested and redefined that vision.

[33] Table on New Jersey and Illinois trade union membership in Isaac Hourwich, *Immigration and Labor: The Economic Aspects of European Immigration to the United States* (New York, 1912), 524; Leon Woolf, *Lockout: the Story of the Homestead Strike of 1892* (New York, 1965), 187–88.

[34] See, for examples, H. G. Gutman, "The Worker's Search for Power: Labor in the Gilded Age," in H. Wayne Morgan, ed., *The Gilded Age: A Reappraisal* (Syracuse, 1963), 38–68; Gutman, "Protestantism and the American Labor Movement: The Christian Spirit in the Gilded Age," *American Historical Review*, 72 (1966–67): 74–101; Gutman, "Class, Status, and Community Power in Nineteenth Century American Industrial Cities: Paterson, New Jersey, a Case Study," in Frederic C. Jaher, ed. *Age of Industrialism: Essays in Social Structure and Cultural Values* (New York, 1968), 263–87.

Seven years after their visit, the New York *Labor Standard*, then edited by
an Irish socialist, bemoaned what had come over the country: "There was
a time when the United States was the workingman's country, . . . the land
of promise for the workingman. . . . We are now in an *old country.*" This
theme recurred frequently as disaffected workers, usually self-educated
artisans, described the transformation of premodern America. "America,"
said the Detroit *Labor Leaf*, "used to be the land of promise to the poor.
. . . The Golden Age is indeed over—the Age of Iron has taken its place.
The iron law of necessity has taken the place of the golden rule." We
need not join in mythicizing preindustrial American society in order to
suggest that this tension between the old and the new helps give a coherence to the decades between 1843 and 1893 that even the trauma of
the Civil War does not disturb.[35]

As early as the 1830s, the theme that industrialism promised to make
over the United States into a "European" country had its artisan and
working-class advocates. Seth Luther then made this clear in his complaint
about "gentlemen" who "exultingly call LOWELL the Manchester of
America" and in his plea that the Bunker Hill monument "stand *unfinished,* until the time passes away when aristocrats talk about mercy to
mechanics and laborers, . . . until our rights are acknowledged." The
tensions revealed in labor rhetoric between the promises of the Republic
and the practices of those who combined capital and technology to build
factories continued into the 1890s. In 1844 New England shoemakers
rewrote the Declaration of Independence to protest that the employers
"have robbed us of certain rights," and two years later New England
textile workers planned without success a general strike to start on July
4, 1846, calling it "a second Independence Day." The great 1860 shoemakers' strike in Lynn started on George Washington's birthday, a celebration strikers called "sacred to the memory of one of the greatest men
the world has ever produced." Fear for the Republic did not end with the
Civil War. The use of state militia to help put down a strike of Northeastern Pennsylvania workers in 1874 caused *Equity*, a Boston labor
weekly, to condemn the Erie Railroad as "the George III of the workingman's movement" and "the Government of Pennsylvania" as "but its
parliament." ("Regiments," it added, "to protect dead things.")[36]

Such beliefs, not the status anxieties of Progressive muckrakers and New
Deal historians, gave rise to the pejorative phrase "robber baron." Dis-
contented Gilded Age workers found in that phrase a way to summarize
their worries about dependence and centralization. "In America," exploded

   [35] *Reynold's Newspaper* (London), Mar. 28, 1869; *Labor Standard* (N.Y.), May 6, 1876;
Detroit *Labor Leaf*, Sept. 30, 1885.
   [36] Luther, *Address to the Workingmen of New England, passim;* Ware, *Industrial Worker,
1840–1860,* 38–48; Philip S. Foner, *History of the Labor Movement in the United States*
(New York, 1947), 1: 202–09, 241–45, 292; *Equity* (Boston), 1 (1874), quoted in James Dombrowski,
Early Days of Christian Socialism (New York, 1936), 81.

the *National Labor Tribune* in 1874, "we have realized the ideal of republican government at least in form." "America," it went on, "was the star of the political Bethlehem which shone radiantly out in the dark night of political misrule in Europe. The masses of the old world gazed upon her as their escape." Men in America could be "their own rulers"; "no one could or should become their masters." But industrialization had created instead a nightmare: "These dreams have not been realized. . . . The working people of this country . . . suddenly find capital as rigid as an absolute monarchy." Two years later, the same Pittsburgh labor weekly asked, "Shall we let the gold barons of the nineteenth century put iron collars of ownership around our necks as did the feudal barons with their serfs in the fourteenth century?" The rhetoric surrounding the little-understood 1877 railroad strikes and riots summed up these fears. Critics of the strikers urged repressive measures such as the building of armories in large cities and the restriction of the ballot, and a few, including Elihu Burritt, even favored importing "British" institutions to the New World. But the disorders also had their defenders, and a strain in their rhetoric deserves notice. A radical Massachusetts clergyman called the strikers "the lineal descendants of Samuel Adams, John Hancock, and the Massachusetts yeomen who began so great a disturbance a hundred years ago . . . only now the kings are money kings and then they were political kings." George McNeill, a major figure in the nineteenth-century labor movement and later a founder of the American Federation of Labor, denied that the Paris Commune had come to America: "The system which the pilgrims planted here has yet a residue of followers. No cry of 'commune' can frighten the descendants of the New England commune. This is the COMMONWEALTH, not the *Class* wealth, of Massachusetts." A discharged Pittsburgh brakeman put it differently in blaming the violence on a general manager who treated the railroad workers "no better than the serfs of Great Britain, sir, . . . introduced into this country a lot of English ideas and customs, [and] made our men wear uniforms and traveling bags." "A uniform," he worried, "constantly reminds them of their serfdom, and I for one would rather remain out of work than wear one." An amazed reporter wondered how this man could "assert his rights as a free born American, even if in so doing himself and family starved."[37]

This Pittsburgh brakeman revealed values that persisted throughout the decades of industrialization, that expressed themselves most commonly in the rhetoric and behavior of artisans and skilled workers, and that worried other influential Americans besides railroad magnates and industrial manufacturers. In 1896 an army officer won a prize for writing

37 *National Labor Tribune* (Pittsburgh), Dec. 12, 1874, and Oct. 14, 1876; Jesse Jones, "Railroad Strike of 1877," and George McNeill, "An Address," *Labor Standard* (N.Y.), Aug. 26, and Sept. 30, 1877; Robert, Pittsburgh dispatch, Chicago *Inter-Ocean*, Sept. 11, 1877.

the best essay submitted to the *Journal of the Military Service Institutions of the United States*. Theodore Roosevelt helped to judge the contest. The officer insisted that "discipline" needed to be more rigorous in an American as opposed to a European army. Even though he knew little about European societies, his insistence that "means of discipline are entirely artificial productions of law" in the United States counted as a profound insight into a social condition that plagued industrialists and sparked frequent discontent among skilled and other workers in industrializing America:

> Discipline should be as a rod of iron. It may seem hopelessly illogical to claim that the army of a free people needs to be kept in stricter discipline than any other army, with wider space between the officers and the enlisted men, yet there are natural reasons why it should be so. The armies of Europe are drawn from people who for countless generations have lived under monarchical institutions and class government, where every man is born and bred to pay homage to some other man, and the habit of subordination to the will of another is a matter of heredity. It is natural that when such a man finds himself in the army he is not only amenable to discipline, but any relaxation on the part of the officer would be accepted as a matter of grace.
>
> With us these conditions are reversed. Every man is born and bred in the idea of equality, and means of discipline are entirely artificial productions of law, not only without support from traditional habit, but they have that habit to overcome, and familiarity on the part of the officer would breed contempt of authority.

Two decades earlier, the London editor of the *Industrial Review* and increasingly conservative British trade-union leader, George Potter, posed the same problem somewhat differently. The disorders incident to the 1877 railroad strikes convinced him that Americans then lived through an earlier stage of English history, before "habit" had "begotten" men to "use their combinations peaceably and wisely." "The state of things that existed then in England," Potter insisted, "exists now in the United States. It was at one time believed that this was impossible within the borders of the great Republic, but it has proved itself wrong." Potter believed that the widespread violence in 1877 had been caused by men "suddenly or newly brought together to defend an interest" and therefore lacking "that wisdom of method that time and experience develop." But Potter was wrong. The men who quit work in 1877 (and before and after that) included many deeply rooted in traditional crafts and worried that the transformation of the American social and economic structure threatened settled ways of work and life and particular visions of a just society. Their behavior—in particular the little-understood violence that accompanied the strikes (including the burning and destruction of the Pennsylvania Railroad's Pittsburgh yards and equipment)—makes this clear. It had specific purposes and was the product of long-standing grievances that accompanied the transformation of Old America into New America.[38]

QUITE DIVERSE PATTERNS of collective working-class behavior (some of them disorderly and even violent) accompanied the industrialization of the United States, and certain of them (especially those related to artisan culture and to peasant and village cultures still fresh to factory labor and to the machine) deserve brief attention. Characteristic European forms of "premodern" artisan and lower-class protest in the United States occurred before (prior to 1843), during (1843–93), and after (1893–1919) the years when the country "modernized." The continuing existence of such behavior followed from the changing composition of the working-class population. Asa Briggs's insistence that "to understand how people respond to industrial change it is important to examine what kind of people they were at the beginning of the process" and "to take account of continuities as well as new ways of thinking," poses in different words the subtle interplay between culture and society that is an essential factor in explaining working-class behavior. Although their frequency remains the subject for much further detailed study, examples of premodern working-class behavior abound for the entire period from 1815 to 1919, and their presence suggests how much damage has been done to the past American working-class experiences by historians busy, as R. H. Tawney complained more than half a century ago, "dragging into prominence forces which have triumphed and thrusting into the background those which have been swallowed up." Attention is briefly given to three types of American artisan and working-class behavior explored in depth and with much illumination by European social historians ("church-and-king" crowds, machine-breaking, and food riots) and to the presence in quite different working-class protests of powerful secular and religious rituals. These occurred over the entire period under examination, not just in the early phases of industrial development.[39]

Not much is yet known about premodern American artisan and urban lower-class cultures, but scattered evidence suggests a possible American variant of the European church-and-king phenomenon. Although artisan and lower-class urban cultures before 1843 await their historians, popular street disorders (sometimes sanctioned by the established authorities) happened frequently and increasingly caused concern to the premodern

[38] Major George Wilson, "The Army: Its Employment During Times of Peace and the Necessity for Its Increase," *Journal of the Military Service Institution of the United States,* 18 (1896): 8–9; George Potter, "The American Labour Riots," *Industrial Review* (London), Aug. 4, 1877, p. 9.
[39] Asa Briggs, review of Thompson, *Making of the English Working Class,* in *Labor History,* 6 (1965): 84–91; R. H. Tawney, *Agrarian Problem in the Sixteenth Century* (London, 1912), 177.

elite classes. Street gangs, about which little is yet known except the
suggestion that some had as members artisans (not just casual or day
laborers) and were often organized along ethnic lines, grew more important in the coastal and river towns after 1830. New York City, among
other towns, had its Fly Boys, Chichesters, Plug Uglies, Buckaroos, and
Slaughterhouse Gangs, and their violence against recent immigrants provoked disorderly counterthrusts. Political disorders on election days, moreover, were apparently well-organized and may have involved such gangs. The
recurrence of such disorders through the pre-Civil War decades (including
the nativist outbursts in nearly all major Northern and Southern cities
in the 1850s) may have meant that local political parties, in their infancy,
served as the American substitute for the King and the Church, a third
party "protecting" artisans and even day laborers from real and imagined
adversaries and winning clanlike loyalty. Although the testimony of
Mike Walsh, a Tammany leader and later the publisher of the *Police
Gazette,* must be read with care, he suggested an interesting relationship
between the decline of premodern lower-class entertainments and the
rise of modern political "machines." Election politics, Walsh noted in
the *Subterranean,* saw "the Goth-and-Vandal-like eruption of the shirtless
and unwashed democracy" which Walsh connected to the disappearance
of popular lower-class entertainments. A "gloomy, churlish, money-wor-
shipping . . . spirit" had "swept nearly all the poetry out of the poor
man's sphere," said the editor-politician. "Ballad-singing, street danc-
ing, tumbling, public games, all are either prohibited or discountenanced,
so that Fourth of July and election sports alone remain." Workers flocked
to political clubs and labored hard for a party to "get a taste of the
equality which they hear so much preached, but never, save there, see
even partially practiced." If Walsh's insight has merit, political parties
quite possibly competed with early craft unions in adapting older forms
of popular entertainment and ritual to changing needs. That process,
once started, had a life beyond the early years of the premodern political
party and continued as the composition of the working-class changed.
The ethnic political "boss" created a new dependence that exploited
well-understood class feelings and resentments but blunted class consciousness. The relationship, however, was not simple, and in the 1880s
the socialist Joseph P. McDonnell exploited that same relationship to
convince local New Jersey politicians to respond to pressures from predominantly immigrant workers and thereby to pioneer in the passage of
humane social legislation, a process that began well before the stirring
of the middle- and upper-class conscience in Progressive America.[40]

[40] Mike Walsh, *Subterranean* (N.Y., n.d.), quoted in M. R. Werner, *Tammany Hall* (New
York, 1932), 49–51 (courtesy of Paul Weinbaum). On gangs, nativism, politics, and antebellum
street violence, see A. F. Harlow, *Old Bowery Days* (New York, 1931), *passim; Protestant
Crusade, 1800–1860* (New York, 1938), *passim;* and McNeill, *Labor Movement,* 344. The ways
in which McDonnell used machine politics and politicians to push social reform in the 1880s

Available evidence does not yet indicate that machine-breaking of the "Luddite" variety was widespread in the United States. There are suggestive hints in reports that Ohio farm laborers burnt and destroyed farm machinery in 1878 and that twenty years later in Buffalo a crowd of Polish common day laborers and their wives rioted to break a street-paving machine, but the only clear evidence found of classic machine-breaking occurred early in the Civil War among rural blacks in the South Carolina Sea Islands, who resisted Yankee missionary and military efforts to make them plant cotton instead of corn and therefore broke up cotton gins and hid the iron work. "They do not see the use of cotton," said a Northern female school teacher, and a Yankee entrepreneur among them added that "nothing was more remote from their shallow pates than the idea of planting cotton for 'white-folks' again." (Some time later, this same man ordered a steam-run cotton gin. "This engine," he confided, "serves as a moral stimulus to keep the people at work at their hand-gins, for they want to gin all the cotton by hand, and I tell them if they don't by the middle of January I shall get it by steam.") If white workers rarely broke machines to protest their introduction, they sometimes destroyed the product of new technology. In the early 1830s Brooklyn ropemakers paraded a "hated machine" through town and then "committed to the flames" its product. Theirs was not an irrational act. They paid for the destroyed hemp, spun "a like quantity" to allow the machine's owner to "fulfill his engagement for its delivery," and advertised their product in a newspaper, boasting that its quality far surpassed machine-made rope "as is well known to any practical ropemaker and seaman." Silk weavers in the Hudson River towns of New Jersey broke looms in 1877 but only to prevent production during a strike. A more common practice saw the destruction of the product of labor or damage to factory and mining properties to punish employers and owners. Paterson silk weavers regularly left unfinished warps to spoil in looms. Crowds often stoned factories, burned mine tipples, and did other damage to industrial properties (as in the bitter Western Pennsylvania coke strikes between 1884 and 1894) but mostly to protest the hiring of new hands or violence against them by "police." Construction gangs especially in railroad work also frequently destroyed property. In 1831, between two and three hundred construction workers, mostly Irish, punished an absconding contractor by "wantonly" tearing up track they built. Similar penalties were meted out by Italian construction gangs between 1880 and 1910 and by unorganized railroad workers, mostly native-born repairmen and trainmen, between 1850 and 1880, who

---

are described in Gutman, "Class, Status, and the Gilded Age Radical: The Case of a New Jersey Socialist," in a work currently in press, Gutman and Gregory S. Kealey, eds., *Many Pasts: Readings in American Social History* (Englewood Cliffs, 1973), vol. 2.

tore up track, spiked switches, stole coupling links and pins, and did other damage to protest changing work rules or to collect back wages.[41]

"Luddism" may have been rare, but classic "European" food riots occurred in the United States, and two in New York City—the first in 1837 and the second in 1902—that involved quite different groups of workers are briefly examined to illustrate the ways in which traditional cultural forms and expectations helped shape working-class behavior. (Other evidence of similar disorders, including the Confederate food riots led by white women in Mobile, Savannah, and Richmond, await careful study.) In February 1837, thousands gathered in City Hall Park to protest against "monopolies" and rising food prices. Some months before that park had witnessed yet another demonstration against the conspiracy trial of twenty-five striking journeymen tailors. In their rhetoric the protesters identified the trial with the betrayal of the premodern "Republic." "Aristocrats" had robbed the people of "that liberty bequeathed to them, as a sacred inheritance by their revolutionary sires" and "so mystified" the laws that "men of common understanding cannot unravel them." "What the people thought was liberty, bore not a semblance to its name." Resolutions compared the tailors to that "holy combination of that immortal band of

[41] *Labor Standard* (N.Y.), Sept. 28, 1878; Edward S. Abdy, *Journal of a Residence and Tour in the United States from April 1833 to October 1834* (London, 1838), 1: 77–79; Gutman, "Class, Status, and Community Power"; Pennsylvania Bureau of Labor Statistics, *Fifteenth Annual Report, 1887* (Harrisburg, 1888), F1–F18 and *Nineteenth Annual Report, 1891* (Harrisburg, 1892), D1–D18; *Niles' Weekly Register,* 40 (1831): 338–39; New York *Tribune,* May 2, 1857; *John Swinton's Paper* (N.Y.), Feb. 24, 1884; New York *Tribune,* Oct. 21, 1893; *New York State Board of Mediation and Arbitration, Eleventh Annual Report, 1898* (New York, 1899), 139–42; Gutman, "Trouble on the Railroads in 1873–1874." *Labor History,* 2 (1961): 215–35. The materials on the Sea Island blacks are found in Laura Towne, *Letters and Diaries of Laura S. Towne 1862–1884, Written from the Sea Islands of South Carolina,* ed. Rupert S. Holland (Cambridge, Mass., 1910), 16–17, 20–21; Elizabeth Ware Pearson, ed., *Letters from Port Royal, 1862–1868* (Boston, 1906), 221–22, 236–37, 250; Willie Lee Rose, *Port Royal Experiment: Rehearsal for Reconstruction* (Indianapolis, 1964), 141; Jane and William Pease, *Black Utopias* (Madison, 1963), 134, 143, 149–50. Although American blacks are not included in these pages, the behavior and thought of rural and urban blacks fits the larger patterns suggested here in a special way. Their experiences first as slaves and then as dependent laborers in the rural South as well as in the industrial North (where most manufacturing industries remained closed to them until the First World War) distinguished most lower-class blacks from all immigrant and native white workers. In still little-understood but profoundly important ways enslavement followed by racial exclusion sustained among blacks a culture that despite change remained preindustrial for more than merely two or three generations. Despite this significant difference, similarities in behavior between blacks and native and immigrant white workers can be noticed. Visitors to the Richmond tobacco factories in the 1850s found industrial slaves there who practiced "Blue Monday." Joseph C. Roberts, *The Story of Tobacco in America* (New York, 1949), 86–91. Blacks themselves made comparisons to whites who shared difficult premodern rural experiences: "I have never heard any songs like those [slave songs] anywhere since I left slavery, except when in Ireland. . . . It was during the famine of 1845–1846." Frederick Douglass said that. Quoted in Harriet Beecher Stowe, *Men of Our Times* (Hartford, 1868), 395. Contemporary observers who noticed black work habits after emancipation rarely told of "laziness" but nearly always noticed irregularity, and in 1909 W. E. B. Du Bois quoted approvingly a writer who suggested that "what is termed Negro 'laziness' may be a means of making modern workingmen demand more rational rest and enjoyment rather than permitting themselves to be made machines." W. E. B. Du Bois, *Negro-American Family* (Atlanta, 1909), 42. See also Du Bois's discussion of the same matter in *World's Week,* 103 (1926), quoted in Asa H. Gordon, *Sketches of Negro Life and History in South Carolina* (Industrial College, Ga., 1929), 10–11.

Mechanics who . . . did throw into Boston Harbor the Tea." In 1837 a crowd dumped flour, not tea, and in its behavior revealed a commonplace form of premodern protest, a complaint against what Thompson calls "the extortionate mechanisms of an unregulated market economy." The crowd in City Hall Park heard protests about the high price of rent, food, and especially flour and denunciations of "engrossers," and the New York *Herald* called the gathering "a flour meeting—a fuel meeting—a rent meeting—a food meeting—a bread meeting—every kind of a meeting except a political meeting." But a New York newspaper had printed advice from Portland, Maine, that "speculating" flour dealers be punished with "some mark of public infamy," and after the meeting adjourned a crowd (estimates range from two hundred to several thousand) paraded to Eli Hart's wholesale flour depot. A speaker advised it to "go to the flour stores and offer a fair price, and if refused take the flour." Crowd members dumped two hundred barrels of flour and one thousand bushels of wheat in the streets, broke windows, did other minor damage, and chased the city's mayor with stones and "balls of flour." At first, little looting occurred, and when wagons finally appeared to carry home sacks of flour "a tall athletic fellow in a carman's frock" shouted: "No plunder, no plunder; destroy as much as you please. Teach these monopolists that we know our rights and will have them, but d–n it don't rob them." The crowd moved on to other flour wholesalers and continued its work. It smashed the windows of B. S. Herrick and Son, dumped more flour, and finally stopped when "a person of respectable appearance" came from inside the building to promise that what remained untouched would be distributed gratis the next day to the "poor." The crowd cheered and melted away. More than twenty-eight persons were arrested (among them "mere boys," a few "black and ignorant laborers," a woman, and as yet unidentified white men), but the *Herald* found "mere humbug . . . the unholy cry of 'It's the foreigners who have done all this mischief'." The daily press, including the *Herald*, denounced the crowd as "the very canaille of the city," but the *Herald* also pleaded for the reimposition of the assize of bread. "Let the Mayor have the regulation of it," said the *Herald*. "Let the public author-ities regulate the price of such an essential of life." (In 1857, incidentally, New Yorkers again filled the City Hall Park to again demand the restora-tion of the assize of bread and to ask for public works.)[42]

More than half a century later different New York City workers re-

[42] John R. Commons and others, eds., *Documentary History of American Industrial Society* (Cleveland, 1910), 5: 314–22; New York *Herald*, Feb. 13–16, 1837; New York *Evening Post*, Feb. 14, 16, 1837; New York *Sun*, n.d., quoted in Thomas Brothers, *United States of America as They Are* (London, 1840), 374–76; E. P. Thompson, "The Moral Economy of the English Crowd in the Eighteenth Century," *Past and Present*, 50 (1971): 76–136 but especially 134. On the Confederate bread riots, see Paul Angle and Earl S. Miers, eds., *Tragic Years, 1860–1865* (New York, 1960), 1: 526–28; William J. Kimball, "The Bread Riot in Richmond," *Civil War History*, 7 (1961): 149–54. Early American patterns of price regulation involving foodstuffs and the disputes over them are detailed splendidly in Richard B. Morris, *Government and Labor in Early America* (New York, 1946), *passim*, and Sam Bass Warner, *The Private City* (Philadelphia, 1968), ch. 1.

enacted the 1837 food "riot." Unlike the rioters of 1837 in origins and rhetoric, the later rioters nevertheless displayed strikingly similar behavior. In 1902, and a few years before Upton Sinclair published *The Jungle*, orthodox New York City Jews, mostly women and led by a woman butcher, protested the rising price of kosher meat and the betrayal of a promised boycott of the Meat Trust by retail butchers. The complaint started on the Lower East Side and then spontaneously spread among Jews further uptown and even among Jews in Brooklyn, Newark, and Boston. The Lower East Side Jews demanded lower prices. Some called for a rabbi to fix for the entire New York Jewish community the price of meat, as in the East European *shtetl*. Others formed a cooperative retail outlet. But it is their behavior that reveals the most. The nation's financial metropolis saw angry immigrant women engage in seemingly archaic traditional protest. Outsiders could not understand its internal logic and order. These women did not loot. Like the 1837 demonstrators, they punished. Custom and tradition that reached far back in historical time gave a coherence to their rage. The disorders started on a Wednesday, stopped on Friday at sundown, and resumed the following evening. The women battered butcher shops but did not steal meat. Some carried pieces of meat "aloft on pointed sticks . . . like flags." Most poured kerosene on it in the streets or in other ways spoiled it. "Eat no meat while the Trust is taking meat from the bones of your women and children," said a Yiddish circular apparently decorated with a skull and crossbones. The New York police and the New York *Times* came down quite hard on these Jewish women. A "dangerous class . . . very ignorant," said the *Times*, explaining:

They mostly speak a foreign language. They do not understand the duties or the rights of Americans. They have no inbred or acquired respect for law and order as the basis of the life of the society into which they have come. . . . The instant they take the law into their own hands . . . they should be handled in a way that they can understand and cannot forget. . . . Let the blows fall instantly and effectively.

Two days later, the *Times* reflected on a British Royal Commission then examining the effects of Jewish immigration on British society. "Stepney," the *Times* of New York noted, also was "becoming a foreign town. . . . Perhaps when the Royal Commission reports on what England should do about its un-English Londoners we shall learn what to do about these not yet Americanized New Yorkers whose meat riots were stranger than any nightmare." The *Times* found comfort in what it felt to be a "fact." Immigrant Jews had sparked the 1902 troubles. "The attempted incendiarism," it believed, "could not happen in an American crowd at all." The New York *Times* had done more than idealize a world that had never been lost in suggesting that premodern Americans had been little more than ordered and expectant entrepreneurs. In comparing its response in 1902 to that of the New York *Herald* in 1837, we measure some of the distance that proper Americans had travelled from their own, premodern American roots.[43]

Even though American society itself underwent radical structural changes between 1815 and the First World War, the shifting composition of its wage-earning population meant that traditional customs, rituals, and beliefs repeatedly helped shape the behavior of its diverse working-class groups. The street battle in 1843 that followed Irish efforts to prevent New York City authorities from stopping pigs from running loose in the streets is but one example of the force of old styles of behavior. Both the form and the content of much expressive working-class behavior, including labor disputes, often revealed the powerful role of secular and religious rituals. In 1857 the New York City unemployed kidnapped a musical band to give legitimacy to its parade for public works. After the Civil War, a Fall River cotton manufacturer boasted that the arrival of fresh Lancashire operatives meant the coming of "a lot of greenhorns here," but an overseer advised him, "Yes, but you'll find they have brought their horns with them." A few years later, the Pittsburgh courts prevented three women married to coal miners from "tinhorning" nonstrikers. The women, however, purchased mouthorgans. ("Tin-horning," of course, was not merely an imported institution. In Franklin, Virginia, in 1867, for example, a Northern white clergyman who started a school for former slave children had two nighttime "tin horn serenade[s]" from hostile whites.) Recurrent street demonstrations in Paterson accompanying frequent strikes and lockouts nearly always involved horns, whistles, and even Irish "banshee" calls. These had a deep symbolic meaning, and, rooted in a shared culture, they sustained disputes. A Paterson manufacturer said of nonstrikers: "They cannot go anywhere without being molested or insulted, and no matter what they do they are met and blackguarded and taunted in a way that no one can stand . . . which is a great deal worse than actual assaults." Another manufacturer agreed:

All the police in the world could not reach the annoyances that the weavers have at home and on the street that are not offenses—taunts and flings, insults and remarks. A weaver would rather have his head punched in than be called a "knobstick," and this is the class of injury they hate worst, and that keeps them out more than direct assault.

But the manufacturers could not convince the town's mayor (himself a British immigrant and an artisan who had become a small manufacturer) to ban street demonstrations. The manufacturers even financed their own

[43] *New York Herald*, Apr. 21, 23, May 15–30, 1902; *New York Tribune*, Apr. 19, 21, May 11, 16–27, June 15, 1902; *New York World*, May 16–19, 1902; *New York Commercial Advertiser*, May 15, 17, 24, 26, 1902; *New York Times*, May 23–26, June 7, 1902; *New York Journal*, May 15, 1902; *People* (N.Y.), May 14, 15, 20, 23, 26, 1902. Food riots occurred again among immigrant New York City Jews in the spring of 1917.

private militia to manage further disorders, but the street demonstrations continued with varying effectiveness until 1901 when a court injunction essentially defined the streets as private space by banning talking and singing banshee (or death) wails in them during industrial disputes. In part, the frequent recourse to the courts and to the state militia after the Civil War during industrial disputes was the consequence of working-class rituals that helped sustain long and protracted conflicts.[44]

Symbolic secular and, especially, religious rituals and beliefs differed among Catholic and Jewish workers fresh to industrial America between 1894 and the First World War, but their function remained the same. Striking Jewish vestmakers finished a formal complaint by quoting the Law of Moses to prove that "our bosses who rob us and don't pay us regularly commit a sin and that the cause of our union is a just one." ("What do we come to America for?" these same men asked. "To bathe in tears and to see our wives and children rot in poverty?") An old Jewish ritual oath helped spark the shirtwaist strike of women workers in 1909 that laid the basis for the International Ladies' Garment Workers Union. A strike vote resulted in the plea, "Do you mean faith? Will you take the old Jewish oath?" The audience responded in Yiddish: "If I turn traitor to the cause, I now pledge, may this hand wither and drop off at the wrist from the arm I now raise." (Incidentally, during this same strike a magistrate who advised troublesome Jewish women that "you are on strike against God" provoked Bernard Shaw's classic quip, "Delightful, medieval America always in the most intimate personal confidence of the Almighty.") Immigrant Catholic workers shared similar experiences with these immigrant Jews. A reporter noticed in 1910 at a meeting of striking Slavic steel workers in Hammond, Indiana: "The lights of the hall were extinguished. A candle stuck into a bottle was placed on a platform. One by one the men came and kissed the ivory image on the cross, kneeling before it. They swore not to scab." Not all rituals were that pacific. That same year, Slavic miners in Avelia, Pennsylvania, a tiny patch on the West Virginia border, crucified George Rabish, a mine boss and an alleged labor spy. An amazed journalist felt their behavior "in the twentieth century . . . almost beyond belief":

Rabish was dragged from his bed and driven out into the street amid the jeers of the merciless throng. . . . Several men set about fashioning a huge cross out of mine timbers. They even pressed a crown of thorns upon his temples. After they had nailed him to the cross, the final blasphemy was to dance and sing about the still living man.

44 Billington, *Protestant Crusade*, 196; New York *Herald*, Nov. 12, 1857; Fall River *Weekly News*, Jan. 21, 1875; L. H., Pittsburgh, to the editor, *John Swinton's Paper* (New York), Sept. 28, 1884; A. B. Corliss, Franklin, Va., to the editor, *American Missionary*, 11 (1867): 27-28; Paterson *Press*, Aug. 2, 1877; Paterson *Guardian*, Aug. 2, 1877; Gutman, "Class, Status, and Community Power"; 283-87; Gutman, "Social Structure and Working-Class Life and Behavior in an Industrial City, Paterson, New Jersey, 1830-1905," unpublished manuscript.

Fig. 9. Striker argues with a strikebreaker in New York City. Photograph by Lewis W. Hine. Courtesy George Eastman House Collection.

That event was certainly unusual, but it was commonplace for time-honored religious symbols as well as American flags to be carried in the frequent parades of American workers. Western Pennsylvania Slavic and Italian coal miners in a bitter strike just east of Pittsburgh (eighteen of twenty thousand miners quit work for seventeen months when denied the right to join the United Mine Workers of America) in 1910 and 1911 carried such symbols. "These rural marches," said Paul Kellogg, "were in a way reminiscent of the old time agrarian uprisings which have marked English history." But theirs was the behavior of peasant and village Slavs and Italians fresh to modern industrial America, and it was just such tenacious peasant-worker protests that caused the head of the Pennsylvania State Police to say that he modeled his force on the Royal Irish Constabulary, not, he insisted, "as an anti-labor measure" but because "conditions in Pennsylvania resembled those in strife-torn Ireland." Peasant parades and rituals, religious oaths and food riots, and much else in the culture and behavior of early twentieth-century immigrant American factory workers were cultural anachronisms to this man and to others, including Theodore Roosevelt, William Jennings Bryan, Elbert Gary, and even Samuel Gompers, but participants found them natural and effective forms of self-assertion and self-protection.[45]

THE PERSPECTIVE emphasized in these pages tells about more than the behavior of diverse groups of American working men and women. It also suggests how larger, well-studied aspects of American society have been affected by a historical process that has "industrialized" different peoples over protracted periods of time. Fernand Braudel reminds us that "victorious events come about as the result of many possibilities," and that "for one possibility which actually is realized, innumerable others have drowned." Usually these others leave "little trace for the historian." "And yet," Braudel adds, "it is necessary to give them their place because the losing movements are forces which have at every moment affected the final outcome." Contact and conflict between diverse preindustrial cultures and a changing and increasingly bureaucratized industrial society also affected the larger society in ways that await systematic examination. Contemporaries realized this fact. Concerned in 1886 about the South's "dead"—that is, unproductive—population, the Richmond *Whig* felt the "true remedy" to be "educating the industrial morale of the people." The

[45] Rischin, *Promised City*, 144–94; Levine, *Women's Garment Workers*, 154; Graham Adams, *Age of Industrial Violence, 1910–1915* (New York, 1966), 105–16, 188–94; Chicago *Socialist*, Jan. 31, 1910, quoted in Brody, *Steelworkers in America*, 125–46; Cleveland *Plain Dealer*, Apr. 24, 1910 (courtesy of Robert D. Greenberg); Paul Kellogg and Shelby M. Harrison, "The Westmoreland Strike," *Survey*, 25 (1910), 345–66; *Report on the Miners' Strike in the Bituminous Coal Fields in Westmoreland County, Pennsylvania, in 1910–1911* (Washington, 1912), *passim*. A recent work which convincingly disputes earlier views that Slavic coal miners were difficult to organize into trade unions is Victor H. Greene, *Slavic Community on Strike* (Notre Dame, 1968).

Whig emphasized socializing institutions primarily outside of the working class itself. "In the work of inculcating industrial ideas and impulses," said the *Whig*, "all proper agencies should be enlisted—family discipline, public school education, pulpit instruction, business standards and requirements, and the power and influence of the workingmen's associations." What the *Whig* worried over in 1886 concerned other Americans before and after that time. And the resultant tension shaped society in important ways. Some are briefly suggested here. In a New York *Times* symposium ("Is America by Nature a Violent Society?") soon after the murder of Martin Luther King, the anthropologist Clifford Geertz warned: "Vague references to the frontier tradition, to the unsettledness of American life, to our exploitative attitude toward nature or to our 'youthfulness' as a nation, provide us with prefabricated 'explanations' for events we, in fact, not only do not understand, but do not want to understand." More needs to be said than that Americans are "the spiritual descendants of Billy the Kid, John Brown, and Bonnie and Clyde." It has been suggested here that certain recurrent disorders and conflicts relate directly to the process that has continually "adjusted" men and women to regular work habits and to the discipline of factory labor. The British economic historian Sidney Pollard reminds us that this "task, different in kind" is "at once more subtle and more violent from that of maintaining discipline among a proletarian population of long standing."[46]

The same process has even greater implications for the larger national American culture. Hannah Arendt has brilliantly suggested that the continual absorption of distinctive native and foreign "alien" peoples has meant that "each time the law had to be confirmed anew against the lawlessness inherent in all uprooted people," and that the severity of that process helps explain to her why the United States has "never been a nation-state."[47] The same process also affected the shaping and reshaping of American police and domestic military institutions. We need only realize that the burning of a Boston convent in 1834 by a crowd of Charlestown truckmen and New Hampshire Scotch-Irish brickmakers caused the first revision of the Massachusetts Riot Act since Shays' Rebellion, and that three years later interference by native firemen in a Sunday Irish funeral procession led to a two-hour riot involving upwards of fifteen thousand persons (more than a sixth of Boston's population), brought militia to that city for the first time, and caused the first of many reorganizations of the Boston police force.[48] The regular contact between alien work

[46] Richmond *Whig*, June 15, 1886 (courtesy of Leon Fink); Clifford Geertz, "We Can Claim No Special Gift for Violence," New York *Times Magazine*, Apr. 28, 1968, pp. 24–25; Pollard, "Factory Discipline in the Industrial Revolution," 254–71.
[47] Hannah Arendt, "Lawlessness Is Inherent in the Uprooted," New York *Times Magazine*, Apr. 28, 1968, pp. 24–25.
[48] Oscar Handlin, *Boston's Immigrants* (New York, 1968), 186–91; Roger Lane, *Policing the City: Boston* (Cambridge, Mass., 1967), chs. 1–2.

cultures and a larger industrializing or industrial society had other consequences. It often worried industrialists, causing C. E. Perkins, the president of the Chicago, Burlington, and Quincy Railroad to confide in a friend in the late nineteenth century, "If I were able, I would found a school for the study of political economy in order to harden men's hearts." It affected the popular culture. A guidebook for immigrant Jews in the 1890s advised how to make it in the New World: "Hold fast, this is most necessary in America. Forget your past, your customs, and your ideals. . . . A bit of advice to you: do not take a moment's rest. Run, do, work, and keep your own good in mind."[49] Cultures and customs, however, are not that easily discarded. So it may be that America's extraordinary techno-

Fig. 10. Jewish peddler in Chicago. ca. 1910. Photograph by Lewis W. Hine.
Courtesy George Eastman House Collection.

logical supremacy—its talent before the Second World War for developing labor-saving machinery and simplifying complex mechanical processes—depended less on "Yankee know-how" than on the continued infusion of prefactory peoples into an increasingly industrialized society.[50] The same

[49] Sidney Fine, *Laissez Faire and the General Welfare State* (Ann Arbor, 1956), 54. 56, 103; Rischin, *Promised City*, 75.

[50] John Higham, in C. Vann Woodward, ed., *Comparative Approaches to American History* (New York, 1968), 101; H. J. Habakkuk, *American and British Technology in the Nineteenth Century* (Cambridge, 1967), *passim.*

process, moreover, may also explain why movements to legislate morality and to alter habits have lasted much longer in the United States than in most other industrial countries, extending from the temperance crusades of the 1820s and the 1830s to the violent opposition among Germans to such rules in the 1850s and the 1860s and finally to formal prohibition earlier in this century.[51] Important relationships also exist between this process and the elite and popular nativist and racist social movements that have ebbed and flowed regularly from the 1840s until our own time, as well as between this process and elite political "reform" movements between 1850 and the First World War.[52]

The sweeping social process had yet another important consequence: it

[51] Although the literature on American temperance and prohibition movements is vast, nothing yet written about them approaches in clarity of analysis and use of evidence Brian Harrison, *Drink and the Victorians: The Temperance Question in England, 1815–1872* (Pittsburgh, 1971). Much information on the relationship between temperance and late nineteenth-century American factory labor is found in the little-used *U.S. Commissioner of Labor, Twelfth Annual Report, 1897* (Washington, 1897), a detailed analysis of the replies about working-class drinking habits from the owners of more than seven thousand establishments which together employed about 1,750,000 workers. For the later period see (but with great care), Herman Feldman, *Prohibition: Its Economic and Industrial Aspects* (New York, 1927), especially pages 200–12. Feldman, who surveyed representative manufacturing firms about the impact of Prohibition on work patterns, learned that "many plants in pre-Prohibition days had the five-day week long before Henry Ford ever thought of it, because so many workers were absent after pay-day." Employers used "considerable ingenuity" to cut down Monday absenteeism. Some had shifted pay-day from Saturday to a mid-week work day, and others paid wages less frequently. Feldman received replies from 287 firms. Two-thirds said improved attendance at work followed Prohibition. A New Hampshire shoe manufacturer no longer had to "reckon with the after-effects of celebrations, holidays, and weekends" as he did "years ago." And a St. Louis metal manufacturer told that the Saturday paycheck no longer meant "the usual 'Blue Monday.'" "Now," he explained, "we have changed to Friday, and as we are paying by the check system this enables the men to deposit their checks in one of the local banks that stay open on Friday evenings. We have no Saturday absences." Not all sounded so optimistic. "The stuff available to labor," said an employer of Delaware River tugboat and barge workers, "and there is plenty of it, is so rotten that it takes the drinking man two to three days to get over his spree." And a Connecticut manufacturer feared that new technology threatened regular attendance at work more than traditional or spurious spirits. "Cheap automobiles," he said, "make more employees tardy than does liquor."

[52] Detailed local studies are badly needed here, and these should focus on the clear continuities between antebellum municipal "reform" movements and the issues that dominated much of local politics in the Gilded Age. Such studies will reveal neglected elements of continuity in political issues, patterns of elite reform, and patterns of political centralization that started before the Civil War and continued into the Progressive Era. Few saw this more clearly than President Andrew D. White of Cornell University who reminded delegates to the First Lake Mohonk Conference on the Negro Question in 1890 that "in 1847" New York had "sank back toward mobocracy." "We elected judges on small salaries for short terms," said White; "we did the same thing with the governors. We have swung backward or forward . . . out of that. We now elect men for longer terms. In many ways, we have returned to more conservative principles." Isabel Barrows, ed., *First Lake Mohonk Conference on the Negro Question* (Boston, 1890), 120. See also Samuel P. Hays, "The Politics of Reform in Municipal Government in the Progressive Era," *Pacific Northwest Quarterly*, 55 (1964): 157–69. The pattern Hays uncovered for Progressive Pittsburgh was not new because its roots rested in elite fears of immigrant and working-class domination of municipal governments (and especially the influence of those groups on local fiscal and educational policies), fears that revealed themselves powerfully before the Civil War and retained much importance during the Gilded Age. The focus on municipal corruption has hidden such important social and political processes from historians. See the original and convincing study by Douglas V. Shaw, "The Making of an Immigrant City: Ethnic and Cultural Conflict in Jersey City, New Jersey, 1850–1877" (Ph.D. dissertation, University of Rochester, 1972), that demonstrates conclusively (for that city at least) that antebellum elite nativism did not end with the Civil War but continued into the postwar decades.

reinforced the biases that otherwise distort the ways in which elite observers perceive the world below them. When in 1902 the New York *Times* cast scorn upon and urged that force be used against the Jewish women food rioters, it conformed to a fairly settled elite tradition. Immigrant groups and the working population had changed in composition over time, but the rhetoric of influential nineteenth- and early twentieth-century elite observers remained constant. Disorders among the Jersey City Irish seeking wages due them from the Erie Railroad in 1859 led the Jersey City *American Standard* to call them "imported *beggars*" and "*animals*", "a mongrel mass of ignorance and crime and superstition, as utterly unfit for its duties, as they are for the common courtesies and decencies of civilized life." (According to their historian Earl Niehaus, the antebellum New Orleans Irish fared so bady in the "public" view that many non-Irish criminals, Germans and even blacks among them, assumed Irish names.) Although the Civil War ended slavery, it did not abolish these distorted perceptions and fears of new American workers. In 1869 *Scientific. American* welcomed the "ruder" laborers of Europe but urged them to "assimilate" quickly or face "a quiet but sure extermination." Those who retained their alien ways, it insisted, "will share the fate of the native Indian." Elite nativism neither died out during the Civil War nor awaited a rebirth under the auspices of the American Protective Association and the Immigration Restriction League. In the mid-1870s, for example, the Chicago *Tribune* called striking immigrant brickmakers men but "not reasoning creatures," and the Chicago *Post-Mail* described that city's Bohemian residents as "depraved beasts, harpies, decayed physically and spiritually, mentally and morally, thievish and licentious." The *Democratic Chicago Times* cast an even wider net in complaining that the country had become "the cess-pool of Europe under the pretense that it is the asylum of the poor." Most Chicago inhabitants in the Gilded Age were foreign-born or the children of the foreign-born, and most English-language Chicago newspapers scorned them. The Chicago *Times* told readers that Slavic Chicagoans were descended from "the Scythians," "eaters of raw animal food, fond of drinking the blood of their enemies whom they slew in battle, and [men] who preserved as trophies the scalps and skins of enemies whom they overthrew." "The old taste for the blood of an enemy has never been obliterated," said this proper Chicago newspaper. And the Slavs had now "invaded the peaceful republic." In words echoed differently in the New York *Times* fifteen years later, the Chicago *Times* advised: "Let us whip these slavic wolves back to the European dens from which they issue, or in some way exterminate them." Here, as in the Jersey City *American Standard* (1859) and the New York *Times* (1902), much more was involved than mere ethnic distaste or "nativism." In quite a different connection and in a relatively homogeneous country, the Italian Antonio Gramsci concluded of such evidence that "for a social elite the features of subordinate groups always display something barbaric and pathological." The changing composition of the American working class may make so severe a dictum more pertinent to the United States than to Italy. Class and ethnic fears and biases combined together to worry elite observers about the diverse worlds below them and to distort gravely their perceptions of these worlds. Few revealed these perceptual difficulties and genuine fears more clearly than John L. Hart in 1879:

About one half of our poor can neither read nor write, have never been in any school, and know little, positively nothing, of the doctrines of the Christian religion, or of moral duties, or of any higher pleasures than beer-drinking and spirit-drinking, and the grossest sensual indulgence. . . . They have unclear, indefinable ideas of all around them; they eat, drink, breed, work, and die; and while they pass through their brute-like existence here, the rich and more intelligent classes are obliged to guard them with police and standing armies, and to cover the land with prisons, cages, and all kinds of receptacles for the perpetrators of crime.

Hart was not an uneducated "nativist." He had been professor of rhetoric, the English language, and literature at the College of New Jersey and also the principal of the New Jersey State Normal School. These words appeared in his book entitled *In the School-Room* (1879) where he argued that "schoolhouses are cheaper than jails" and that "teachers and books are better security than handcuffs and policemen." We have returned to Lesson One.[53]

THESE PAGES have fractured historical time, ranging forward and backward, to make comparisons for several reasons. One has been to suggest how much remains to be learned about the transition of native and foreign-born American men and women to industrial society, and how that transition affected such persons and the society into which they entered. "Much of what gets into American literature," Ralph Ellison has shrewdly observed, "gets there because so much is left out." That has also been the case in the writing of American working-class history, and the framework and methods suggested here merely hint at what will be known about American workers and American society when the many transitions are

[53] Jersey City *American Standard*, Sept. 20, 1859 (courtesy of Douglas V. Shaw); Earl Niehaus, *Irish in New Orleans* (Baton Rouge, 1965), 186; *Scientific American*, June 19, 1869, pp. 393–94; *Chicago Tribune*, May 11, 1876; *Chicago Post and Mail*, n.d., reprinted in *Chicago Tribune*, July 25, 1876; *Chicago Times*, Apr. 25, 1874; *Chicago Times*, May 6, 1886 (courtesy of Steven Hahn); Antonio Gramsci, quoted in Charles Tilly, "Collective Violence in European Perspective," in Hugh D. Graham and Ted R. Gurr, eds., *Violence in America* (New York, 1969), 12; John L. Hart, *In The School-Room* (Philadelphia, 1879), 252–57 (courtesy of Barbara Berman). See also John Kober, *Capone, The Life and World of Al Capone* (New York, 1972), 344, for an extraordinary description of Alcatraz prison routine in the 1930s: "Midmorning. Bell. Recess. Bell. Work. 11:30. Bell. Prisoners Counted. Bell. Noon. Bell. Lunch. 1 P.M. Bell. Work. Midafternoon. Bell. Recess. Work. 4:30. Bell. Prisoners Counted. Bell. 6:30. Bell. Lockup. 9:30. Bell. Lights Out."

studied in detail. Such studies, however, need to focus on the particularities of both the group involved and the society into which they enter. Transitions differ and depend upon the interaction between the two at specific historical moments. But at all times there is a resultant tension. Thompson writes:

There has never been any single type of "the transition." The stress of the transition falls upon the whole culture: resistance to change and assent to change arise from the whole culture. And this culture includes the systems of power, property-relations, religious institutions, etc., inattention to which merely flattens phenomena and trivializes analysis.

Enough has been savored in these pages to suggest the particular importance of these transitions in American social history. And their recurrence in different periods of time indicates why there has been so much discontinuity in American labor and social history. The changing composition of the working population, the continued entry into the United States of nonindustrial people with distinctive cultures, and the changing structure of American society have combined together to produce common modes of thought and patterns of behavior. But these have been experiences disconnected in time and shared by quite distinctive first-generation native and immigrant industrial Americans. It was not possible for the grandchildren of the Lowell mill girls to understand that their Massachusetts literary ancestors shared a great deal with their contemporaries, the peasant Slavs in the Pennsylvania steel mills and coal fields. And the grandchildren of New York City Jewish garment workers see little connection between black ghetto unrest in the 1960s and the Kosher meat riots seventy years ago. A half century has passed since Robert Park and Herbert Miller published W. I. Thomas's *Old World Traits Transplanted*, a study which worried that the function of Americanization was the "destruction of memories."[54]

Not all fled such a past. Born of Croatian parents in McKeesport, Pennsylvania, in 1912 (his father and brother later killed in industrial accidents), Gabro Karabin published a prize-winning short story in *Scribner's Magazine* (1947) that reflected on the experiences replayed in different ways by diverse Americans and near-Americans:

Around Pittsburgh, a Croat is commonplace and at no time distinctive. As people think of us, we are cultureless, creedless, and colorless in life, though in reality we possess a positive and almost excessive amount of those qualities. Among ourselves, it is known that we keep our culture to ourselves because of the heterogeneous and unwholesome grain of that about us. . . . We are, in the light of general impression, just another type of laboring foreigner . . . fit only as industrial fuel.

[54] Ralph Ellison and James Alan McPherson, "Indivisible Man," *Atlantic*, 226 (1970): 57; Thompson, "Time, Work-Discipline, and Industrial Capitalism," 89; Park and Miller, *Old World Traits Revisited*, 281. I am indebted to Leon Stein, the editor of *Justice*, for calling to my attention the fact that W. I. Thomas, whose great study of the Polish immigrant leaves us all in his debt, was the author of *Old World Traits Revisited*.

The native-born American poet William Carlos Williams made a similar point. He lived near the city of Paterson and grasped its tragic but rich and deeply human interior textures far more incisively than temporary visitors such as Alexander Hamilton and William D. Haywood and illustrious native sons such as William Graham Sumner and Nicholas Murray Butler. The poet celebrated what gave life to a city in which men, women, and children made iron bars and locomotives and cotton and silk cloth:

> It's the anarchy of poverty
> delights me, the old
> yellow wooden house indented
> among the new brick tenements
>
> Or a cast iron balcony
> with panels showing oak branches
> in full leaf. It fits
> the dress of the children
>
> reflecting every stage and
> custom of necessity—
> chimneys, roofs, fences of
> wood and metal in an unfenced
> age and enclosing next to
> nothing at all: the old man
> in a sweater and soft black
> hat who sweeps the sidewalk—
>
> his own ten feet of it—
> in a wind that fitfully
> turning his corner had
> overwhelmed the entire city.

Karabin and Carlos Williams interpreted life and labor differently from the Chicago *Times* editor who in the Centennial Year (1876) boasted that Americans did not enquire "when looking at a piece of lace whether the woman who wove it is a saint or a courtesan."[55]

[55] Gabro Karabin, quoted in George J. Prpic, *Croatian Immigrants in America* (New York, 1971), 331–32; William Carlos Williams, "The Poor," in Louis Untermyer, ed., *Modern American and Modern British Poetry* (rev. ed.; New York, 1955), 132; Chicago *Times*, May 22, 1876.

APPENDIX

TABLE 3. MALE OCCUPATIONAL STRUCTURE AND HOUSEHOLD COMPOSITION,
SELECTED JEWS AND ITALIANS, NEW YORK CITY, 1905

	Jews	Italians
Total Males 20 and Older	6250	4518
Total Females 20 and Older	4875	3433
Male Occupational Structure		
Unskilled Laborer	7.7%	39.1%
Clothing Worker	44.7%	18.0%
Skilled Worker (Nonclothing)	21.5%	29.2%
Nonlaborer	26.1%	13.7%
Household Composition		
Percentage of All Households with a		
Nuclear Kin-related Core	96.6%	94.5%
Number of Kin-related Households	3584	2945
Number of Subfamilies	159	262
Nuclear Households	48.6%	59.9%
Extended Households	11.8%	23.2%
Augmented Households	43.1%	21.1%
Percentage of Households and Subfamilies		
with a Husband and/or Father Present	93.2%	92.9%

Note: As in 1880 the percentages again total more than 100 per cent because a small number
of households that included both lodgers and relatives are counted twice.

The data are drawn from the New York State 1905 manuscript census schedules,
and I am indebted to Mark Sosower, Leslie Neustadt, and Richard Mendales for
gathering this material. As with the 1880 Paterson data, they cast grave doubts
on the widely held belief that working-class family disruption commonly occurred as the by-product of immigration, urbanization, and factory work. The
1905 Jews studied lived on the Lower East Side (Rutgers, Cherry, Pelham,
Monroe, Water, Pike, Jefferson, Clinton, Madison, Livingston, Henry, Division,
Montgomery, Delancey, Rivington, Norfolk, Suffolk, and East Third Streets,
East Broadway, and Avenue B). The Italians resided on Hancock, Thompson,
Mulberry, Bayard, Mott, Canal, Baxter, Elizabeth, Spring, Prince, Grand, Hester,
McDougal, Sullivan, West Houston, Bleecker, Bedford, Downing, and Carmine
Streets, and the Bowery. The table above deserves another brief comment. Cloth-
ing workers are listed as a separate occupational category because census job
descriptions make it impossible to determine their skill levels. A large percentage
of those listed as nonlaborers engaged in petty enterprise (including peddling):
10.9 per cent of all the Jewish males and 8.3 per cent of all the Italian males. On
early twentieth-century immigrant households and family behavior, see
Virginia Yans McLaughlin, "Patterns of Work and Family Organization Among
Buffalo's Italians," *Journal of Interdisciplinary History*, 2 (1971): 299–314, and
McLaughlin, "Like the Fingers of the Hand: The Family and Community Life
of First-Generation Italian-Americans in Buffalo, New York" (Ph.D. dissertation,
State University of New York, Buffalo, 1970).

The Padrone and the Immigrant
ROBERT F. HARNEY

The Padrone is a stock figure in North American immigrant studies, the image of an alien boss or labour agent exploiting alien workers widespread. For turn-of-the-century nativists, the existence of 'padrone systems' ranked high among the proofs that the 'new' immigrants from the Mediterranean had no aptitude for American freedom, and for a long time the aura of padronism clung to many ethnic businessmen; more recently, historians have viewed the padrone system as a natural bridge between the greenhorn immigrant and American capitalism's voracious appetite for cheap labour. It comes as a shock, therefore, to realize that, despite a rich primary literature and an apparent consensus about the padrone's role,[1] the word *padrone* remains more pejorative than definitional. This paper looks at some of the contradictions and misconceptions that surround 'padronism.'

'Padronism' went through several phases in the nineteenth century, each phase marked by semantic as well as historical and moral problems. The first padroni were the traditional Italian street entertainers and hustlers who, wandering about western Europe and North America, employed boys as shills, beggars, and apprentices. The word *padrone*, as applied to these men, meant something between master and patron.[2] Behind the word stood a system of recruiting and indenturing the excess children of the rural Italian poor. "These children were collected by the padrone . . . from the hillsides of Italy, and practically in the condition of slaves were carried from Europe to America."[3] The practice of indenturing young children was common in Southern Europe. The family often saw it as alleviation of their burden and as a chance for upward mobility for the child.[4] Yet it was natural that others regarded the practice as immoral and the indentured children as catamites or slaves.

By the 1840s, the padrone had assumed Fagin-like proportions, with the indentured children being viewed as corrupted innocents. The great Italian revolutionary, Mazzini, who found his exile in London tarnished by the presence of a padrone system, wrote to his mother about his attempts to destroy it:

The society for the Protection of Italian Lads will do good you may be sure, and will also give a favorable idea of us to the English. I have no time to tell you all the horrors that some of the masters commit towards the poor boys, and that they bear in silence because they do not know to whom to appeal and because terror had made them more abject than nigger-slaves.[5]

Mazzini's letter set the moral tone of much later comment on the system. For example, Francisco Nitti, the Italian statesman, labelled these exploiters not *padroni* but *negriere*,[6] slave-traders. Padronism, in its many different forms, continued to lend itself to comparisons with slavery. In 1905, an editorial in *Charities* magazine described a West Virginia camp to which Italian immigrants had been shanghaied:

Armed guards were frequent. A man turned over to the boss after a fight was locked up in a shanty under a guard of negroes. In the night a shot was heard. The man was not seen again . . . A gatling gun on a hill overlooked the camp. The Contractors and their men carried revolvers and some rode with rifles in their hands.[7]

The padrone, then, was not just a capitalist but a white-slaver as well. If he no longer enslaved children, he became an exploiter of 'child-like' and helpless peasant workers.

As instances of padrone control over children declined among Italian migrants, abuses concerning adult Italian workers grew. Two facts kept alive the high level of moral indignation and consequent definitional confusion about 'padronism.' One was the easy and often racist analogy between childhood and peasant naivete. Baron Fava, Italian Ambassador to the United States, saw the padrone system as a product of South Italian gullibility – "so long as a large part of our Italian emigration comes from the southern provinces, represented mainly by the agricultural or rural classes. PROVERBIAL FOR THEIR SIMPLICITY, there will always be those . . . who are ready to take advantage of them."[8] The second fact that prompted moral outrage (sometimes a facade for nativism) was that other Mediterranean peoples, particularly Greeks and Syrians, continued the traditional form of padronism, child exploitation. It was government officials and social agencies in the receiving country who applied the Italian word padrone to the Greek and Syrian situations, but it seemed an apt enough phrase for strings of juvenile peddlers, shoeshine boys, and beggars who, like their earlier Italian counterparts, seemed to be in servitude to their importers and employers.[9]

Despite rhetoric about slavery and brutality to minors, the padrone system as it developed after the Civil War bore little resemblance, beyond the ethnicity of the participants, to the earlier practice. At his worst, the padrone imported workers under contract to him at a certain rate and sold their labour to the highest bidders.[10] Obviously such a system went beyond the moral limits of capitalism and was dangerous to a free economic system. Even the most unscrupulous native employers and labor

102

bureaux, Americans thought, did not so totally control their workers. It was apparent that 'foreigners' made the practice possible; it was assumed that such a system so inimical to personal freedom was more common to the Old World than the New, and again the residual moral fervor of the crusade against child labour and against slavery added to the outcry.

The word 'padrone' seems to have been much more current among the native American observers than among the immigrants. Like the English describing syphilis as a French disease, Americans employed 'padrone,' the Italian word, to suggest the alien nature of the institution itself. Just as one can remember the uniquely American pronunciation of Mafia favored by Senator Estes Kefauver during crime hearings, one can almost hear the members of the Ford Committee or the Industrial Commission rolling the foreignness of 'padrone' over their tongues.[11] Both contemporaneous observers and historians, in fact, used the term to imply criminality. For example, Jane Addams described the "Sinister aspect of this exploitation" – by "agents in Palermo"; a recent historian has written that "within the immigrant colony, bankers and padroni, blackhanders and other lawbreakers realized small but important profits by swindling or terrorizing compatriots."[12]

Italian newcomers and educated Italian observers rarely used *padrone* to describe agents or employers. Newcomers quickly learned the dialect of Italo-America, and in that tongue the padrone was a *boss* or *bossa*; such a term could be applied to anyone from a foreman to the owner of a labour bureau or of a factory. While an Italo-American boss may have been addressed as *padrone,* it is difficult to tell at this distance whether that was a mock or a real civility; at any rate, it was a neologism. For newly arrived Italians, the word *padrone* made little sense in its North American context. Constantine Panunzio, recounting his first days in the North End of Boston, illustrates some of this linguistic confusion. Panunzio called his first landlady, *la padrona,* in the traditional sense. She was the owner of a boarding house, a substantial establishment, and deserved the title. He was more at a loss when he met his first local notable.

One morning we were standing in front of one of those infernal institutions which in America are permitted to bear the name of 'immigrant banks' when we saw a fat man coming toward us . . . ." Buon giorno, padrone," said one of the men. "Padrone?" said I to myself. Now the word 'padrone' in Italy is applied to a proprietor, generally a respectable man, at least one whose dress and appearance distinguish him as a man of means. This man not only showed no signs of good breeding in his face, but he was unshaven and dirty and his clothes were shabby. I could not quite understand how he could be called 'padrone.'[13]

Perhaps encountering the same North End 'padrone,' the educated Italian traveler Amy Bernardy described the establishment of the *banchista,* the so-called immigrant banker. A notice written in bad Italian

103

by that worthy, affixed to the bank window, reminded his fellow countrymen of his 'modesta opera di banchiere e di contrattore' and that he was
known as a man who never charged a 'bossatura.'[14] The word padrone did
not appear. Nitti and Fortunato, two of the most important political
writers on the emigration from the Italian South, also bypassed the word
padrone in favor of 'banchiste,' the "ultimate expression of human
degradation,"[15] and 'improvvisati banchieri.'[16]

The truth is that, if the earlier indenture of children did fit certain Old
World patterns, the new padronism was not familiar to Italian greenhorns
or to travelers. Certainly there were exploited day labourers, crooked
foremen, and usurious moneylenders in Italy. Baron Sonnino, in his
inquest on life in Sicily, encountered a number of 'padrone-like' institutions and even used padrone to describe the campiere's (field guard or
steward) control over the landless peasant.[17] Luigi Villari found a type of
padrone system at work in the Sicilian mines and in the Massa-Carrara
quarry country,[18] but in neither case was the phenomenon widespread.
This is one reason why confusion surrounds the social origins of the
padroni who appeared in North American Little Italies. Were they
common immigrants who learned to exploit their paesani or were they a
separate middle class in the immigration itself?

In testimony before the Industrial Commissioners in 1901 the editor
of a Chicago Italian paper could not make up his mind.

For truths sake it must be said also that from the class of Italian peasants in American
towns, bosses or padroni often develop, just as from a group of slaves there sometimes springs a most inhuman overseer. . . . As a swarm of crows or wolves and
buzzards invariably follows a fighting army to prey upon the dead, these individuals
follow the endless stream of Italian immigration wherever it is directed.[19]

One of the best modern scholars on the subject is equally uncertain about
the social origins of the exploiters. R. J. Vecoli, writing about Chicago,
remarks that the padroni were often "men who had risen from the ranks
of the unskilled" while others "were members of the gentry who sought
to make an easy living."[20] Educated Italian observers, noting the rough
dialect of the 'bosses' and bankers, saw them as cafoni arrivati (parvenu
peasants); humbler migrants were inclined to credit the boss with middle
class origins, or at least to humor his pretensions.[21] One study of Croatian
immigrants showed that the development of railroads from the interior
to the Dalmatian ports made innkeepers and certain kinds of go-betweens
obsolete in their homeland, causing them to emigrate. Did some sort of
natural harmony in the stages of world industrialization provide a new
role for these men as bosses, boardinghouse owners, and saloonkeepers
in the New World?[22] A Roman cartoon suggests another source. A
cashiered army officer is pictured meeting a dishonest politician emerging
from prison:

104

264

Army Officer: 'What is the game now? An honest life?'

Late Office-holder: 'No I think I shall open an immigrant bank in New York.'

Army Officer: 'Indeed! I had thought of that myself.'[23]

There is little we can say, without more study, about the social origins of the *padroni*. Luigi Villari saw Little Italies as plagiarisms, colonies without traditional Italian elites. If that is so, then *padrone* and *bossa*, both the words themselves and the reality, were linguistic devices which recognized the prestige of new men without granting them Old World titles of rank.[24] The 'padrone' was clearly a man to be propitiated. Like a *latifondista* or local politician of past experience, this New World labor agent had monopolistic power to give or withhold work. And work, immediate and for cash, was the rationale for much of the migration. Still the man was not *signore*, and, as with Mastro-Don Gesualdo, the upwardly mobile hero of Verga's novel, it was not easy for the Italian immigrant to categorize the padrone's social class in traditional terms.[25]

One stereotype about 'padroni,' that at first seems sound, is that they were successful exploiters because of their links to the immigrants' culture and society. That is, that they often had real or ritualized family ties with the worker; they spoke dialect, and generally gained their ascendancy because of the financial and language problems of the greenhorn. They fed on the peasants' need to deal with men and not institutions when job-seeking and facing the outside world.

At one extreme one finds patterns in Italy, Greece, and Syria where the family itself served as a massive and knowledgeable labour bureau, or where exigent godparents were named for migration purposes, or where family members were commissioned by employers to hire more family members.[26] Among all the peoples engaged in the padrone system, the line between the expedient use of kinship systems and business practice was too obscure for the North American observer to understand. The Syro-Lebanese idea of the 'wastah,' the kinsman as go-between, appeared to the authorities to be padronism. Yet it may have simply meant an uncle overworking his nephews as peddlers. For the Syrians, it was an aspect of the integrity of their family structure during the migration process.[27] The Immigration Commission claimed that many Greek boys landed with 'pseudo-fathers' and then were passed on to the padroni. Further on, though, the Commission mentioned the great and legitimate stress laid by Greeks on godfathership but added that "the padrone have shrewdly used this to their advantage."[28]

The Commissioner-General of Immigration's Report of 1907 introduces another complication in the relationship between familism, the padrone, and the needs of North American capitalism. "An influence of great importance," he wrote, "is the letter to the homefolks written by the alien temporarily or permanently domiciled here. These letters constitute the most extensive method of advertising that can be imagined."[29] The Dillingham Commission saw this as a deceitful use of kinship by the padrone who "brought over all their youthful kinsmen . . . who naturally regarded them as guardians and protectors."[30] Family and village chains of migration interwove with the work of labour agents. A study of Chicago Italians which claims that the bulk of prepaid tickets were bought by relatives for relatives and not by labour agents or padroni is simplistic. For, at the same time, foremen and contractors were sending some of their better workers back to the European villages to recruit relatives and friends and were arranging the appearance of family sponsorship where only hard business relations existed.[31] Typically, "they had no contract in writing, merely the letter of an uncle of one of them promising work if they would come. He was not to employ them, but he would turn them over to men who would."[32]

After kinship ties, the highest values of rural society were those of friendship and local identity. When we move beyond family to establish the reasons for the scale and power of the 'padrone system' in terms of these rural values, we encounter more problems. Exclusionists and assimilationists alike were certain that they knew the causes of padronism: "Under the system persons have taken advantage of their better knowledge of our language and conditions to control the labour of the new immigrant of the same race."[33] Ignorance of English and of American mores put the immigrant in the hands of the padrone. The assumption though begs questions about the scale of padronism. Vecoli is of the opinion that, "bewildered by the tumult of the city, the newcomers sought out a townsman who could guide them." Much earlier, Amy Bernardy wrote that the success of an immigrant banker in the North End of Boston was epitomized in the expression, u paesano. Vecoli adds that the padrone made a "business of the ignorance and necessities of his countrymen," while Bernardy reproduced an open letter sent by the 'banker' to his worker/clients that began with the term 'Connaizionali.'[34]

If we look back, we find three marvelously vague definitions of the 'ethnic' relationship between padrone and migrant; the Dillingham Commission used the word 'race,' Vecoli, the neutral and ambivalent English term, 'countrymen,' and Bernardy didn't notice the contradiction in scale and identity between paesano and connazionale. In these interpretations, men who defined paese as home town and forestiere (strangers) as people from adjacent towns, do business with someone from the same province or even the same country as a paesano and thus trustworthy. Dialect is confused with the national language, and one more facet about the padrone is assumed rather than explained. If campanilismo (the social nexus which had as its perimeter the range of the local church bell) were

106

at work, only a fellow townsman could be trusted and the consequent scale of padrone power could not usually transcend groups larger than small work gangs. And *campanilismo* was real. For example, a Bureau of Labor Bulletin showed that some foremen preferred Mexican gangs to Italian ones since "they don't have feuds and disorders like the Italians who are always fighting unless the whole gang is from the same town in Italy."[35]

This question of scale confused government investigators too. Ex-Commissioner of Immigration Stump tried to explain the labour system used by the railways to the Industrial Commission: When the workers "go to the banker to whom they belong," he sends them to the railroad accompanied by "what is called a 'boss.' . . . They arrive there under the charge of the boss, they speak no English, and will have nothing to do with anybody but that boss. . . . When payday comes the boss receives the wages, and he accounts to the 'padrone.' . . . The padrone lately call themselves bankers."[36] Yet other sources describe the interpreters and subforemen themselves as padroni.

A foreman could perhaps be a fellow townsman or second cousin to a track section gang of twenty or thirty men, but was 'paesanism' the basis of the relationship between turn-of-the-century bosses and those they hired by the hundreds for sewer, railroad, and street work? What of the immigrant bank, what were the limits of its paesanism? Here the nature of the padrone is badly entangled with the more difficult question of the changing ethnic perceptions of the arriving immigrant himself.[37] Frank Zotti, a Croat banker, steamship agent, and newspaper publisher, defaulted on 8,000 Croat depositors. Antonio Cordasco and Alberto Dini of Montreal signed up hundreds of men, Northern and Southern Italians, for work on the Canadian Pacific Railroad and Grand Trunk. One Italian padrone was in trouble with Illinois authorities because of his sharp practice with Armenian and Roumanian labourers.[38] When men labelled padroni operated on such a scale, what did family ties, dialect, or paesanism have to do with the matter?

Whatever the semantic difficulties with our stock figure, we should be able to hammer out a functional definition of padronism. There have been attempts at precision about the role of the 'padrone.' Charlotte Erickson claims that "the difference between the padrone and the unscrupulous type of intelligence [labour] bureau agent was that the padrone hired the immigrant at a fixed rate and stood to profit from whatever wage he could get above the rate."[39] Definitions such as this permit the historian to see the padrone system as short-lived and dead by the end of the 1880s. Unfortunately this view revives the questionable moral distinction between indenture of a sort and capitalist exploitation and also ignores the fact that government agencies, social workers, and exclusionists continued to use the word padrone for a number of other forms of exploitation. For example, one of the richest sources on the subject, John Koren's study for the Department of Labour in 1897, was titled *The Padrone System and Padrone Banks.*[40]

In fact, the list of occupations allegedly tied to 'padronism' makes a definition by function nearly impossible. Tainted with 'padronism' would be labour recruiters (employment agencies), immigrant bankers, steamship and travel agents, contractors, saloon keepers, boardinghouse proprietors, interpreters, private postal agents, food importers, ethnic newspaper publishers, foremen (work gang bosses), commissary and bunkhouse agents, and finally that most hated institution of the isolated worker, the company store. The survival of the earlier forms of padronism (among Greeks, Syrians, and Italians) adds to the list the proprietors of confectionary and ice cream parlours, of shoeshine shops, and organized peddling – anything that called for the labour-intensive use of young immigrants.[41] Almost every occupation other than labourer, factory worker, or priest in an ethnic settlement area has been identified with padronism.

This paper can only suggest the width and depth of the definitional morass.[42] Attempts at a distinction between the immigrant banker and the so-called padrone have been particularly tortured. Efforts to distinguish crime from capitalist exploitation – to draw a line between that which was alien and that which was good 'American' business practice – continue to plague the definition. Charlotte Erickson refers to 'immigrant bankers' as "next in respectability" to steamship agents and padrone.[43] The Dillingham Commission in 1911 claimed that "the padrone system has substantially disappeared." A few pages later, the Commission remarked that the term "bank as applied in most cases is a misnomer," for "the bankers are usually . . . labor agents." These bankers "because of superior intelligence [sic] and a better knowledge of conditions in the country became the general advisors of newly arrived immigrants of the same race."[44] As the variety of mediation between exploiter and exploited increased, observers of the situation became more confused about the nature of the relationship.

The Industrial Commission betrayed the semantic strain – "but if by the padrone we understand that Italians are still controlled after they come here . . . by these same bankers or padrones . . . if this is what is considered the padrone system, it still exists."[45] The modus operandi of immigrant bankers, while it may have been a caricature of 'American' enterprise, was more complex than the earlier practice of labour agents.

When he reaches Ellis Island he is met by his 'cousin' the bank's representative, and is duly discharged to him in N.Y. or shipped to him by rail. If he has any money of his own, he deposits it in the bank; the bank lends him more money if he needs it;

108

the bank finds his place to sleep and eat, the bank sees that he has a doctor if he needs one; and in a day or two the ignorant peasant with others of his kind is despatched to work in the subway.[46]

Nuances between words like padrone, immigrant banker, ethnic merchant, innkeeper, 'legitimate' employment agency, and saloon keeper depended on prejudice not fact. Amy Bernardy described a Boston immigrant bank with a sign in the window offering work to two hundred railway workers. "The bank included a notarial service, a travel agency, a printing press for throw away advertising, an employment agency, Italian patent medicines and imported foods and newspapers."[47] Descriptions of Slovene and Croat saloon keepers of the time mention the variety of services they offered; one was even informal hiring agent for International Harvester, should we believe the recent authority who solemnly adds that Slavs, unlike Italians, were too individualistic to tolerate a padrone.[48]

The American courts offered little guidance in differentiating between crime and exploitation. A Keystone-Cop example was the case of the Greek candy store owner who swindled forty-two Albanians at $10 a head by promising them work at a railroad station, work which he had seen advertised in the newspaper. The jobs never came through. When the Albanians appealed to the Immigrant's Protection League, the case was dismissed on the grounds that the Greek could not be said to be running an employment agency without a license since he had no employment agency sign on his candy store. (The judge added that since the Albanians were Muslims, they couldn't understand the oath anyway.) Was that Greek candyman a padrone, a crook, an employment agent, some or all of the foregoing?[49]

The same source notes that licensed employment agencies when dealing with unskilled workers charged as high a 'registration' fee as they could get. Yet many men who were immigrant bankers/padroni charged no fee. This description of an Italian business man in the coal fields well sums up the new 'padronism':

An Italian conducts ... a steamship agency, and employment agency in connection was a large mercantile establishment. His employment agency is quite extensive, and he has numerous connections through which he meets the demands of contractors in various states for unskilled labor to be used on railroad and other construction work. ... No compensation, it is claimed, is received from the men for whom he secures work, but profits are received from the contractor or construction company to whom labor is furnished. In return for the right to maintain a commissary or store, and collect all bills for supplies and lodging through the construction company's paymaster, the employment agency agrees to send or bring to the scene of the work the required number of men at specified wages and to pay the contractor or construction company 5% of the bills collected to cover the trouble and expense of collection.[50]

The new 'padrone' owned shanties and was a slum landlord at the work site; in the slack season, he provided crowded, unsanitary boarding houses at exorbitant rates for workers. Both on the job and in the boarding house, the 'padrone' controlled the price and quality of the food supply, and there is no doubt that the worker was gouged.

The Industrial Commission heard one witness claim that "hotel keepers ... tried to get hold of Italian immigrants in order to speculate upon them; because, you see, many keepers of lodging houses here are a set of speculators on our own people by engaging them for some kind of work in which the padrone system is exercised."[51] The Dillingham Commission reproduced a typical contract between a 'padrone' and the company he served as labour agent. It included an agreement that the 'padrone' would run the 'company store' and the workers' shanties. The Company would subtract the store bills and boarding cost from the workers' pay.[52] As one victim put it, "We began to do some simple figuring and discovered that when we had paid for our groceries at the 'storo' for the privilege of sleeping in the shanty, and the fifty cents to the 'padrone' for having been so condescending as to employ us we would have nothing left but sore arms and backs."[53] One thing becomes clear from our discussion of padrone activities. The only workable definition of the padrone is ascriptive. The Padrone was a man whom other people called padrone. Those other people may as often have been government investigators or social workers as immigrants, for *bossa*, not *padrone*, as we noted earlier, was one of the first words newcomers learned.[54] Men with such ascribed status came in many shapes and sizes. The padrone could be the only one at a street car construction site without a *zappa* (shovel), an old Greek cobbler surrounded by his indentured nephews, or the man with diamond stick pin and sharp American suit at the roll top desk in an immigrant banker's office. Perhaps one had to be 'ethnic' to be a padrone; perhaps not. Let me cite the testimony of Mortimer Waller when he appeared before the Royal Commission that looked into the activities of Italian labour agents in Montreal. Mr. Waller himself ran an employment agency.

QUESTION. Is there anything else you would like to state in connection with the investigation Mr. Waller?
ANSWER. No sir, I do not think so. Only I think myself that Englishmen should have as fair a chance of supplying this Italian labour as the Italians themselves.[35]

Obviously, Mr Waller did not see ethnicity as a qualification for padronism. If he did succeed in trading in Italians, would we label Mr. Mortimer Waller a padrone?

Residual moralism and the tricks of ethnocentric language have obscured our understanding of what Francesco Nitti saw as the workings of 'intermediarismo' in Italian rural society.[56] Despite the scale of operations of immigrant bankers and labour agents, there is a quality of immanence, and of the personal, that touches upon an important aspect of the role of the ethnic go-between in North America. If there were differences

110

between the ethnic agent and the American labour agency, those differences had to do with the Old World village where a traditional monopoly over the distribution of employment was exercised by the landed classes and the literate. In this sense, the use of padrone to mean patron/protector, while it may verge on the grotesque when one knows the number of swindlers involved, came naturally enough to migrants from the Mediterranean. There is very little humor, for example, in the CPR hiring agent, Antonio Cordasco, being crowned "King of Italian Laborers" in Montreal; it was forced tribute. "Intermediarismo," as Nitti called it, thrived in the limbo between the world of feudal patronage on the one hand and the capitalist/individualist system on the other. What was true for the peasant in the Old World, was truer in New York, Boston or Montreal. One needed protectors and access to and defense from the outside world.

Hints of this frame of mind may be found in both anthropological writing and contemporaneous accounts. The arriving migrant worker was accustomed to a world of face-to-face encounters, where status was ascriptive, where employment was no one's right.[57] The padrone's monopoly on work opportunities and his often fey command of English made him a notable. Like the new middle class of villages and small towns in the Mediterranean World, "the index of success [lay in] the number and complexity of [his] affairs or interesse. For example, gabellotti in Sicily were money lenders, rentiers, and employment agents. Owners of taverna in Greece had a variety of functions. Such men mediated for people caught between traditional and modern society."[58] The padrone, with his many roles as broker, simply took up where they left off. One expected to buy the right to work. For it was "not a question here of considering that one may be entitled to these things by right for between what is one's right and what is possible lie a thousand indifferent shrugs of the shoulder."[59] Migrant workers almost seemed to want to trust 'bosses,' bankers, and agents. Trust did not mean affection or the cessation of class hostility; it was a compound of habit and predictability. If one could see boss or banker as a patron, one could know the limits of exploitation. The consequences of the disequilibrium of the patron-client relationship were measurable. After all, what was a patron without clients, and in that fact lay some protection. Values were clearly in flux. As the migrant tried to recreate his Old World in America, the returnee brought more capitalism home to his village. One Italian banker told the Industrial Commission that workers did not keep receipts on their deposits because they accepted the balance he recorded without question. At the same time, in Italy, an observer lamented the passing of oral contracts for short term work between employer and laborer and blamed the American experience.[60]

It is in the light of this relationship to the Old World that one begins to notice one more distortion about the padrone. Contemporary observers

111

and modern historians have conceived of padronism in terms of its relevance to immigration and assimilation. The padrone was seen as villainous, not just because he exploited his countrymen, but perhaps more because he impeded their flow into the melting pot. In this view, the padrone kept his men from contact with the host country: he helped to perpetuate the congested conditions of the ghetto,[61] and he was either a cause or a symptom of the failure of 'Americanization' among the 'new immigrants.' Even as that view of the padrone has been shaken, underlying assumptions about assimilation have gone uncontested. In recent articles, Iorizzo and Nelli have both offered the revisionary view that, unpleasant as it was and limited as it was, the padrone system was a necessary step in the assimilation of Italo-Americans and others.[62] In a more complicated analysis, the Macdonalds show how the padrone system was tied to chain immigration.[63] It follows, for all of these writers, that the decline of the system was in direct proportion to the success of the immigrants in Americanizing enough to do without intermediaries.

There is, of course, considerable truth in that view, but it continues the traditional picture of the migrant as a slave without volition and powerless before the padrone. In the Dillingham Commission report, for example Greek shoeshine boys were depicted as prisoners: "In nearly all instances the boys refuse to answer questions concerning their ages and their work in the presence of the padrone or his spies.... Many padrone insist on reading, or having their managers read, all letters the boys receive while in their employ and likewise examine letters they send out."[64] Even the high rate of return to the old country by Mediterranean bachelor migrants was seen as the fault of padroni and travel agents who, having milked the greenhorns, sent them back to replace them with others.[65]

To suggest that the 'victims' of padronism approved of and in some ways created the system because they were fundamentally migrant, concerned with temporary work, cash income, hostile to the North American environment, and anxious to return to their villages, alters the easy moral tale in which the padrone was a slaver and the worker a slave. It suggests that America did not appeal only to the uprooted who wished to immigrate but also to sojourners. The newcomers in this sense were often not uprooted but, rather, deeply committed to returning and improving the family's status in the Old World. In other words, in an understanding of 'padronism' lie the answers to questions about the newcomer's purpose and his mental frame vis-a-vis migration and immigration.

Although I will make no attempt at quantification,[66] a glance at the sources suggests that, despite contrary myths, large numbers of newcomers saw themselves as sojourners. (Given the demands of survival, that state of mind can never be fully measured in returnees or remittance rates.) The mind-set of migrants was crucial in the question of assimila-

112

tion.[67] Since many were far less uprooted than North American observers assumed, they had little desire to break free from the ethnic environment created by the labour system. At one extreme, the migrants had the feeling that they "were temporizing here; that they had come to America to make a few hundred dollars to send or take back to Italy; and that it did not make much difference what they ate, wore or did, just so long as they got the money and got back."[68]

As early as 1906, John Foster Carr realized "that the same inborn conservatism that risks nothing makes of southern Italians the most mobile supply of labour that this country has even known."[69] Carr almost perceived what Italian writers knew, that what appeared to be uprootedness often proved the strength of roots. Young Italian migrants described trips to America as *campagne*, military campaigns.[70] America had become for many villages an extension of the local society and economy. In order for migration to work properly, a highly efficient system of providing short term full employment was necessary.[71] Short term may be misleading since, for the true sojourner, not years in America but the strength of continuing ties to the hometown — economic and familial, not just nostalgic — was the true measure of time. B. T. Sung claims that Chinese laundry workers often referred to their stay in America "as a temporary interval" even if they had been here over twenty years.[72] Among the Sicilians in New York there was great anxiety about the state of their reputation in the home village because "they expect to return. Whole families have a date fixed."[73] On the CPR work gangs, men who had been almost ten years in New York, Boston, or Portland comported themselves as much like sojourners as the greenhorns did.[74].

The role of the ethnic brokers in North America had its roots in the crisis of the European village. The padrone is understood better in terms of the socio-economic needs of the emigrating country than in terms of assimilation, for seeking entry into the North American economy did not mean knocking at the door of acculturation. Migration, as well as immigration, was an acquired tradition by which villages and families in southern Europe tried to avoid the dislocation born of overpopulation and the impact of the money economy.

An Italian partisan of emigration said that "it vanquished usury ... and it has helped and helps many now not to succumb to hunger ... even the payment of taxes is possible only because of the work of emigrants."[75] In many places, stability came to depend on despatching the most mobile men of working age, delaying the marriage age, and paying everything from dowries to taxes with money from migrants. This was so in Italy, Greece, Syria, and probably parts of Eastern Europe as well.[76] The relevance of this system to the question of 'padronism' is clear. Towns and villages were composed of families; young men migrated as family members, and their concern, at least initially in America, was the Old World

113

family. The centrality of the padrone as postal drop, ticket agent, and banker followed from this. Prpic estimates that bachelor Croats sent home 80% of their earnings; other groups had similar patterns. Over time and after some 'campagne' that money led to the family immigrating and settling in America, but it is clear that a very large amount of money initially was earmarked for the improvement of the village and family economy, or was invested at home for the migrant.[77]

Remarking on the uncertainty of the southern peasant economy, one of Verga's characters says that "property doesn't belong to those that have got it, but to those who know how to acquire it."[78] Despite models of peasant life and economy that suggest pre-modern harmony, the reality in Southern Europe was that brothers had to go to America to provide their sisters' dowries, that husbands had to go in order to free their land from mortgages and taxes, especially after periodic natural disasters. The family had to keep moving to stand still. "In 1881 ... it was a great storm and the crops were entirely ruined. We knew of no America then and we nearly starved." Weather, taxes, dowries, the intrusion of outside capital made land tenure and stability nearly impossible in the village. Time was brought and a social system endured by using the labour intensive possibilities of North America to make hard cash, but the man digging the ditch or shining the shoes had his eyes turned to a homeland. A Syrian migrant wrote to his brother, "Please tell me about the house and our land property, also let me know what happened to the fig tree which I planted near the fence wall." Another migrant wrote home asking his parents to buy for him his brother's share of the land.[80] For such people, the padrone who served as job provider and link with home, was both patron and exploiter. He, like them, lived between two worlds.

This paper, even as it has struggled to free itself from some of the myths, has been forced to use the language of the myth: padrone, assimilation, and immigration, words straightforward enough, but coined amidst ethnocentric misconception. They impose upon us too limiting a view of the migrant's relationship to old world institutions and to American myths. One wonders how many other stock figures such as the padrone can survive a new and more skeptical approach to the history of immigration.

NOTES

1 The chief primary sources are U.S. Senate *Reports of the Immigration Commission* (Doc. #747), 61st Congress 3rd Session, Washington, 1911, 42 volumes, henceforth cited as *Dillingham Commission*; Volume XV of U.S. Congress *Reports of the Industrial Commission*, Washington, 1901, cited as *Industrial Commission*; John Koren, "The Padrone System and Padrone Banks," U.S. Dept. of Labor *Bulletin #9* (March, 1897); F. J. Sheridan, "Italian Slav and Hungarian Unskilled Immigrant Laborers in

114

the United States," U.S. Bureau of Labor *Bulletin* #72 (Sept. 1907). Two earlier government committee reports, the Ford Committee on Contract Labor Violations (1889) and the U.S. Immigration Commission Report on European Immigration (1893) are useful. Finally the *Royal Commission appointed to inquire into the Immigration of Italian Labourers to Montreal and the alleged Fraudulent Practices of Employment Agencies* (Ottawa, Dept. of Labour, 1905), though less well-known, is very valuable, cited henceforth as *Royal Commission (Italians)*.

2 *Dizionario Enciclopedia Italiana* does not include the North American use and meaning of the word padrone. Under the entry *negriere* (slavetrader) are *datore di lavoro* and *padrone*.

3 *Industrial Commission* (1901), XV: xxxix.

4 *Dillingham Commission* II: 403; C. Cronin, *The Sting of Change: Sicilians in Sicily and Australia* (Chicago, 1970), p. 58; H. P. Fairchild, *Greek Immigration to the United States* (New Haven, 1911) p. 172.

5 Letter from Giuseppe Mazzini to his mother (London, 6 Jan. 1845) in *G. Mazzini's Letters* (London, 1930), p. 96.

6 Francesco Nitti, "La Nuova Fase dell'Emigrazione d'Italia" in *Scritti sulla questione meridionale* (Bari, 1958), I: 387. Nitti used the word padrone to refer to proprietors of larger properties for whom the peasants worked. See *Scritti IV, Inchiesta sulle condizioni dei contadini in Basilicata e in Calabria* (Bari, 1968).

7 "The Italian in America," in *Charities* XII (1905), reproduced in L. Tomasi (ed), *The Italian in America. The Progressive View, 1891–1914* (N.Y., 1972). The frequency with which Italian contract labour replaced black slave labour in Brazil and in the U.S. requires further study.

8 Baron Fava quoted in L. Iorizzo, "The Padrone and Immigrant Distribution," in S. M. Tomasi and M. H. Engel (eds), *The Italian Experience in the United States*, (Staten Island, 1970), p. 46.

9 See "The Greek Padrone System," in *Dillingham Commission* II: 391–408.

10 C. Erickson, *American Industry and the European Immigrant, 1860–1885* (Cambridge, 1957), p. 92 and pp. 85–86.

11 See *Industrial Commission* XV: 156 and 158. Dr. Egisto Rossi, Chief of Italian Bureau, Port of New York, referred to it as a 'boss' system, adding that "The padrone system has its principal origin here." That did not slow up the Commissioners. One attempt has been made to see the system as an American tradition. See M. Lipari, "The Padrone System an Aspect of American Economic History," *Italy-American Monthly* #2 (April, 1935).

12 J. Addams, "Immigration: A Field Neglected by the Scholar," in P. Davis (ed), *Immigration and Americanization* (Boston, 1920), p. 8; H. Nelli, "Italians and Crime in Chicago: The Formative Years," *American Journal of Sociology*, LXXIV: 3 (Jan., 1969), p. 383.

13 C. Panunzio, *The Soul of An Immigrant* (N.Y., 1921), pp. 78–79.

14 A. Bernardy, *Italia randagia attraverso gli Stati Uniti* (Torino, 1913), pp. 104–108; A. Bernardy, *America Vissuta* (Torino, 1911), pp. 323–324.

15 G. Fortunato, *Il Mezzogiorno e le Stato Italiano, Discorsi Politici, 1880–1910* (Bari, 1911).

16 Nitti, *Scritti*, II: 492; A. Mosso, *Vita Moderna degli Italiani* (Milan, 1906), uses the word 'bosses' in English in his Italian text, p. 34.

17 Baron S. Sonnino and Franchetti, *La Sicilia nel 1876* (Florence, 1925), pp. 202, 135–139.

18 L. Villari, *Italian Life in Town and Country*, p. 207.

19 Testimony of A. Mastro-Valerio, Editor of *La Tribuna Italiana* (Chicago), in *Industrial Commission (1901)*, XV: 496.

20 R. J. Vecoli, "Contadini in Chicago: A Critique of the Uprooted," *Journal of American*

115

History, LI (Dec., 1964), p. 412. *Dillingham Commission* II: 381–382 sees them all as 'risen from the ranks.'

21 Cusumano, "Study of the Colony of Cinisi in N.Y.C.," in R. Park and H. Miller, *Old World Traits Transplanted* (N.Y., 1921), p. 151, sees them as well-born. Bernardy, *America Vissuta*, pp. 322–323, scoffs at their arriviste pretensions.

22 G. Prpic, The *Croatian Immigrants in America* (N.Y., 1971), pp. 92–93. Such people were more likely to be immigrants than migrants.

23 Broughton Brandenburg, *Imported Americans* (N.Y., 1903), p. 23.

24 L. Villari, "L'Emigrazione italiana negli Stati Uniti," *Nuova Antologia*, CXLIII: 298.

25 G. Verga, *Mastro-Don Gesualdo* (London, 1970 [first published in 1888]), p. 24.

26 C. Tilly and C. Brown, "On Uprooting, Kinship and the Auspices of Migration," *International Journal of Comparative Sociology*, VIII: 2 (Sept., 1967), p. 442, admit that the line between family and business in the 'auspices of migration' may be too complex to dissect. J. S. Macdonald and L. D. Macdonald, "Urbanization, Ethnic Groups, and Social Segmentation," *Social Research*, 29: 4 (Winter, 1962), p. 444, show best understanding of this problem.

27 S. I. Farsoun, "Family Structure and Society in Modern Lebanon," in A. Shiloh (ed), *People and Culture of the Middle East* (N.Y., 1960), pp. 269–270.

28 *Dillingham Commission*, II: 401 and 405; L. W. Moss and S. C. Cappannari, "Patterns of Kinship, Comparaggio and Community in the South Italian Village," *Anthropological Quarterly*, 33: 1 (Jan., 1960), pp. 24–32.

29 Quoted in Fairchild, *Greek Immigration*, p. 88.

30 *Dillingham Commission*, II: 399.

31 H. Nelli, *Italians in Chicago, 1880–1930: A Study in Ethnic Mobility*, pp. 55–87, and H. B. Nelli, "The Italian Padrone System in the United States," *Labor History* 5: 2 (Spring, 1964), p. 155; *Industrial Commission* (1901) XV:43–44. See Prpic, The *Croatian Immigrants*, pp. 107–108, on how foremen sent workers back to recruit relatives and fellow villagers. This process would be too complex for Nelli's distinctions.

32 Brandenburg, *Imported Americans*, p. 112. On the same ship, he met a man being sent to his home village at contractor's expense to hire workers, p. 33.

33 *Dillingham Commission*, I: 29; G. Abbott, *The Immigrant and the Community* (N.Y., 1921), p. 31; Iorizzo, "Padrone and Immigrant Distribution," p. 75; Macdonald, "Urbanization," p. 155.

34 Vecoli, "Contadini in Chicago," p. 411; Bernardy, *America Vissuta*, p. 323 and Bernardy, *Italia randagia*, p. 104.

35 Park and Miller, *Old World Traits*, p. 181. Campanilism, extreme localism, was obviously breaking down, although very slowly, in the Italian South. Since the scale of group identity was itself in flux in the period of migration, the historian can only hint at the variables of loyalty.

36 Testimony of Herman Stump, Ex-Commissioner of Immigration, in *Industrial Commission (1901)*, XV, pp. 7–8.

37 J. F. Carr, "The Coming of the Italian," in P. Davis (ed), *Immigration and Americanization*, p. 151. This article first appeared in *Outlook* in 1906. Carr noted that, while new neighbourhoods looked very Italian to the receiving society, arriving Italian greenhorns had difficulty distinguishing between older Italian immigrants and native Americans.

38 Prpic, *Croatian Immigrants*, pp. 210–212; *Royal Commission (Italians)*, *passim*; Abbott, "*The Immigrant and the Community*," pp. 45–46.

39 Erickson, *American Industry*, pp. 85–86; *Industrial Commission (1901)*, XV: 431–432, described this as "the padrone par excellence" but added "the character of the padrone has changed."

40 John Koren, "The Padrone System and Padrone Banks," *Bulletin* of the Dept. of Labor #9 (March, 1897). The Industrial Commission usually identified the banker or boss as a padrone. The Dillingham Commission used the term "immigrant banker," preferring to use padrone for the Greek and Syrian system of importing and indenturing minors.

41 Both Nelli, "The Italian Padrone System," and Iorizzo, "The Padrone and Immigrant Distribution," give interesting accounts of the various aspects of 'padronism' at work. G. Abbott, "The Chicago Employment Agency and the Immigrant Worker," *American Journal of Sociology,* XIV, 3 (Nov. 1908), is also very useful.

42 The extremes of inclusive and exclusive definition may be found in Nelli and Iorizzo. Nelli prefers to think that the 'padrone par-excellence' died out in the 1880s and that flagrant cases of exploitation after that centered only on railroad work. Iorizzo, in criticizing another account for stating that there was no padrone system in Columbus, Ohio, betrays a remarkably inclusive definition. "Apparently she meant a highly formalized one [padrone system]," he writes, "for she spoke of many Italian saloons, railroad laborers, organ grinders and many other elements connected with the padrone," p. 74.

43 Erickson, *American Industry,* pp. 84–85.

44 *Dillingham Commission,* I: 29–31. For a breakdown of the multiple businesses run by 100 immigrant banks that the Commission studied, see *Dillingham Commission,* II: 415 and 419; Brandenburg, *Imported Americans,* p. 21.

45 *Industrial Commission (1901),* XV, 88.

46 Brandenburg, *Imported Americans,* pp. 22–23.

47 Bernardy, *America Vissuta,* pp. 323–324.

48 E. Balch, *Our Slavic Fellow Citizens* (N.Y., 1910), p. 308–309; Prpic, *Croatian Immigrants,* p. 159; T. Smith, "New Approaches to the History of Immigration in 20th Century America," *American Historical Review,* LXXI, 4 (July, 1966).

49 Abbott, *The Immigrant and the Community,* pp. 44–45.

50 *Dillingham Commission,* VI, 554.

51 *Industrial Commission (1901),* XV, pp. 157 and 435. Besides the profit from supplying food to the men, the padrone charged from $1.00 to $3.00 a head for the shanties in which the men slept, p. 433. "In such cases he finds it convenient to go to the boarding house of the boss or banker where he remains until Spring, when it is understood that he shall enter the employ of the boss." See *Royal Commission (Italians).* Cordasco made 150% profit on a can of sardines for CPR track workers and the railroad collected for him, p. 24–25 and 62–63; for complicated relationship of boarding houses to the system see the testimony of various foremen and subbosses.

52 Dillingham Commission, VIII, 333–334.

53 Panunzio, *Soul of An Immigrant,* p. 80.

54 T. Cyriax, *Among Italian Peasants* (Glasgow, 1919), p. 9. Cyriax records the English vocabulary of a man who had spent four years in the U.S. "He could say: eight hour and no 'more, job, boss, dog, bread and cheese, beans, drink, go'ome, sleep, shoot, and of course, dollar and cent."

55 *Royal Commission (Italians),* pp. 47–48.

56 Nitti, *Scritti,* II, p. 147.

57 A. Smith, *Theories of Nationalism* (London, 1971), p. 42; E. Gellner, *Thought and Change,* (London, 1964), pp. 155–157. Both emphasize face-to-face contact and ascriptive status. Gellner juxtaposes 'structure and culture.' See also A. Kyrakidou-Nestoros, "The Theory of Folklore in Greece," *East European Quarterly,* V, 4, p. 499.

58 J. Schneider, "Family Patrimonies and Economic Behavior in Western Sicily," *Anthropological Quarterly,* 42: 3 (July, 1969), pp. 42–43 and 126–129.

117

59 Michael Kenny, "Patterns of Patronage in Spain," *Anthropological Quarterly*, 33: 1 (Jan., 1960), p. 19. See also J. Boissevain, "Patronage in Sicily," *Man*, I (1966), p. 18.
60 *Dillingham Commission*, II, 417; V. di Somma, "L'Emigrazione nel Mezzogiorno," *Nuova Antologia*, CCXIII: 5 (May, 1907), p. 513.
61 G. Speranza, "Italians in Congested Districts," in L. Tomasi (ed.), *The Italian in America*, p. 56.
62 Iorizzo, "The Padrone and Immigrant Distribution," pp. 73–74, and Nelli, "The Italian Padrone," p. 164.
63 J. S. & L. Macdonald, "Urbanization," pp. 444–445.
64 *Dillingham Commission*, III, 395.
65 Brandenburg, *Imported Americans*, p. 23 and Testimony of T. Powderly, Commissioner General of Immigration, Feb. 1899 in *Industrial Commission (1901)*, XV, 44.
66 See *Dillingham Commission*, VI, 273. Among coal miners, South Italians and Croats had the highest return rates; F. Thistlethwaite, "Migration from Europe Overseas in the 19th and 20th Centuries," in H. Moller (ed.), *Population Movements in Modern European History* (N.Y., 1964). See N.Y.U. Ph.D. thesis on Italian repatriation and remittances by Betty Caroli. F. Cerase, "Nostalgia or Disenchantment: Considerations on Return Migration," in S. Tomasi and M. Engel (eds), *The Italian Experience*; I. Ferenczi, "An Historical Study of Migration Statistics," *International Labor Review*, XX (1929), p. 380, shows that the highest return rates were among those groups with the highest percentage of male immigrants.
67 S. Eisenstadt, *The Absorption of Immigrants* (London, 1954), p. 4; J. Gulick, "Conservatism and Change in a Lebanese Village," *American Anthropologist*, Vol. 55: 318, claims that most Syrian emigrants intended to make money and return home.
68 Brandenburg, *Imported Americans*, p. 32.
69 Carr, "The Coming of the Italian," p. 145.
70 L. Villari, "L'Opinione pubblica americana e i nostri emigrati." *Nuova Antologia*, CCXXXII (1910), p. 503.
71 Mosso, *Vita Moderna*, pp. 36–37.
72 B. L. Sung, *Mountain of Gold: The Story of the Chinese in America* (N.Y. 1967), p. 195.
73 Park and Miller, *Old World Traits*, p. 150, and Cyriax, *Among Italian Peasants*, p. 90.
74 *Royal Commission (Italians)*, pp. 29–40 and 65–72.
75 Fortunato, *Discorsi*, II: 501.
76 L. W. Moss and S. C. Cappannari, "Estate and Class in South Italian Hill Village," *American Anthropologist*, 64:2 (April, 1962), p. 300; V. Vasilikos, *Outside The Walls* (N.Y., 1973), p. 24, "I'm thinking of following my island tradition. What tradition? Leave. Be a stewie on a ship and go to America."
77 Louise Sweet, "The Women of Ain ad Dayr," *Anthropological Quarterly*, V. 40, p. 170; Cyriax, *Among Italian Peasants*, pp. 76–77; Brandenburg, *Imported Americans*, pp. 53–54, gives some idea of the amounts of money returning to Italy that never appear in the statistics. One man had $3,500 on his person jointly sent by a father and three sons working in the mills in Birmingham, Alabama.
78 G. Verga, "Property," in *Little Novels of Sicily* (N.Y., 1953), p. 102.
79 Quoted in Cyriax, *Among Italian Peasants*, p. 43. It is clear that models like that of Chayanov work poorly for the villages of south-eastern Europe. Village and peasant life was under constant assault from the larger economy and its values. I hope in another place to pursue the relationship of the village economy, the dowry system, and the new value of cash to North American migration.
80 A. I. Tannous, "Emigration, a Force of Social Change in an Arab Village," in A. Lutiffiyya and C. Churchill (eds), *Readings in the Arab Middle Eastern Societies and Cultures* (The Hague, 1970), p. 308.

OCCUPATION AND ETHNICITY IN FIVE NINETEENTH-CENTURY CITIES: A COLLABORATIVE INQUIRY*

Theodore Hershberg, University of Pennsylvania—*Philadelphia, Pennsylvania*
Michael Katz, York University—*Hamilton, Ontario*
Stuart Blumin, Cornell University—*Kingston, New York*
Laurence Glasco, University of Pittsburgh—*Buffalo, New York*
Clyde Griffen, Vassar College—*Poughkeepsie, New York*

Much of the new historical social research has not focused on the outcomes of particular events.[1] Instead, it has sought to discover the relationships among past socioeconomic and demographic patterns. In shifting from the study of the specific to the study of the general, as in placing the case study within a broader context, historians face the intellectual problems, both analytic and methodological, posed by the requirements of comparability. Confidence in historical generalization, after all, grows as theory and explanation fit many independent bodies of empirical evidence.

While comparability is by no means confined to quantitative research—for example, constructing analytic categories for classifying internal conflicts would aid in the comparative study of civil wars—the increasing use of quantification offers historians a uniquely valuable opportunity to make detailed and direct comparisons between their studies.[2] Yet despite the widespread adoption of quantitative methods, the similarity of subjects studied, and the use of identical data sources (especially Population Manuscript Census Schedules), nothing has been done to ensure direct comparability.[3] This should not be surprising; there is nothing inherent in quantitative method which operates to generate directly comparable results. To the contrary, a conscious and quite deliberate effort is required if advantage is to be taken of the opportunity for comparison made available by quantification.

Without such an effort the ability to synthesize the results of new research will be severely limited. Two important examples of the problems posed by comparability can be seen in the spate of mobility studies sparked by the publication a decade ago of Stephan Thernstrom's *Poverty and Progress*.[4] Comparability in these studies depends upon the use of identical techniques of *record linkage*, or the means by which individual careers are reconstructed, and *occupational classification*, or the means by which cross-sectional as well as analyses of change over time are made. Record linkage, most often expressed as "rates of persistence," tells how many people after a lapse of time remained in the study area and enables the description of their socioeconomic characteristics (as distinct from those who left). Occupational classification reduces the welter of individual occupations to manageable analytic categories and makes possible the evaluation of occupational change (upward or downward). When different techniques are used to link an individual at two points in time, and when identical jobs are placed in different occupational categories, comparability is seriously compromised.

Recognizing these and other problems associated with the comparison of disparate

*The authors wish to thank for their financial support the Center for the Study of Metropolitan Problems, National Institute of Mental Health (MH16621), and the Ontario Institute for Studies in Education.

174

studies, we decided to explore the possibilities of working together on directly comparable research. With each of us having in common machine-readable data describing a nineteenth-century city, our paths crossed frequently at professional meetings. In fact, the origins of this paper can be traced to the Yale Conference on the Nineteenth-Century Industrial City organized by Stephan Thernstrom and Richard Sennett (November, 1968),[5] but it was not until January, 1972, that we met at the offices of the Philadelphia Social History Project (PSHP)for the purpose of determining the precise nature of our collaborative undertaking.

We were aware that our five cities did not represent a scientific sample collected to meet specified requirements, but we decided to maximize the precision of the comparisons that inevitably would be made between our individual studies. Moreover, the considerable variation among our five cities justified our asking: *To what extent were there similar socio-structural and demographic characteristics in five cities which differed in size, history, location, economy, and rate of growth?*[6] The decisions reached at our first meeting moved us far along the road to answering this question. We agreed on three basic elements: the variables, their definition, and the relationships among them to be studied.

Our initial comparisons were confined to males above the age of 18. The year 1860 was chosen because the data for all the cities in that year was available in its "cleanest" form. Three different censuses were used in the comparisons. The data for Kingston, Philadelphia, and Poughkeepsie came from the Federal Population Manuscript Schedules of the United States Census for 1860, the data for Buffalo from the New York State Population Manuscript Schedules for 1855, and the data for Hamilton from the Canadian Population Manuscript Schedules for 1861 linked to the Hamilton assessment rolls of the same year.

The variables selected to describe the adult male workforce in the five cities were age, real property holding, ethnicity, and occupation. *Age* was defined in six categories: 18-19, 20-29, 30-39, 40-49, 50-59, and 60 and above. *Real property holding* was defined simply as holding real property or not. *Ethnicity* was defined in seven categories as Irish, English-Scottish, Canadian, German, white American, non-white American, and "Other." *Occupation* was defined to include only those occupations which constituted the first three-quarters of the male workforce in each city. Each occupation was assigned a unique number code as well as a vertical (hierarchical) and horizontal (sector of the economy) code.[7]

Occupation was by far the most complex variable with which we had to deal. To determine the cities, each historian followed an identical set of procedures. First, for each city the number of workers in each occupation was totaled and a list constructed for each city showing the number in each occupation and the percentage they constituted of the entire workforce (see Table 1). The list was arranged in descending number order with the occupation with the greatest number of workers listed first. The cumulative percentage of workers was then added at each successive occupation until 75 percent of the total workforce was accounted for. The number of occupations required to reach this percentage in each city varied from as few as 30 in Buffalo to as many as 80 in Philadelphia.

The list of occupations for each city was then forwarded to the PSHP where they were collated; that is, the lists were combined and a new list compiled containing a total of 113 different occupations, or the total number of distinct occupations appearing in the five lists (see Table 2). The new combined list was then returned to each of us. Working independently a unique vertical code was assigned to each occupation (see Table 3). The vertical codes consisted of five levels and each historian determined which code he would assign to each of the 113 occupations. The rankings were then forwarded to the Canadian project. In

175

Table 1
Workforce by City

BUFFALO—Rank Order

Rank	Occupation	No.	%	Cum. %
1	Laborer	127	16.8	16.8
2	Carpenter	61	8.1	24.9
3	Servant	49	6.5	31.4
4.5	Brickmason	26	3.4	34.8
4.5	Tailor	26	3.4	38.2
6	Shoemaker	22	2.9	41.1
7	Clerk	20	2.6	43.7
8.5	Sailor	17	2.2	45.9
8.5	Farmer Laborer	17	2.2	48.1
10.5	Merchant-Retail	16	2.1	50.2
10.5	Painter	16	2.1	52.3
12	Furnaceman	13	1.7	54.0
13.5	Cooper	12	1.6	55.6
13.5	Blacksmith	12	1.6	57.2
16	Teamster	11	1.5	58.7
16	Butcher	11	1.5	60.2
16	Grocer	11	1.5	61.7
18.5	Cabinet Maker	9	1.2	62.9
18.5	M.D.	9	1.2	64.1
21	Yardman	7	0.9	65.0
21	Ship Carpenter	7	0.9	65.9
21	Piano Maker	7	0.9	66.8
24.5	Commission Merchant	6	0.8	67.6
24.5	Agent	6	0.8	68.4
24.5	Cigar Maker	6	0.8	69.2
24.5	Baker	6	0.8	70.0
28.5	Sales, Agent	5	0.7	70.7
28.5	Peddler	5	0.7	71.4
28.5	Tinsmith	5	0.7	72.1
28.5	Lawyer	5	0.7	72.8

HAMILTON—Rank Order

Rank	Occupation	No.	%	Cum. %
1	Laborer	1485	19.8	19.8
2	Carpenter	528	7.0	26.8
3	Clerk	303	4.0	30.8
4	Shoemaker	260	3.5	34.3
5	Merchant	207	2.7	37.0
6	Tailor	205	2.7	39.7
7	Grocer	150	2.0	41.7
8	Blacksmith	144	1.9	43.6
9	Gentleman	121	1.6	45.2
10	Tavern Keeper	120	1.6	46.8
11	Porter	110	1.5	48.3
12	Painter	108	1.5	48.3
13	Cabinetmaker	99	1.3	51.0
14.5	Attorney	97	1.3	52.3
14.5	Mason	97	1.3	53.6
16	Moulder	93	1.2	54.8
17	Machinist	83	1.1	55.9
18	Plasterer	81	1.1	57.0
19	Sailor/Mariner	80	1.1	58.1
20	Engineer	74	1.0	59.1
21	Tinsmith	73	1.0	60.1
22	Printer	71	0.9	61.0
23	Baker	69	0.9	61.9
24	Gardener	63	0.8	62.7
25	Physician	60	0.8	63.5
26.5	Peddler	57	0.8	64.3
26.5	Clergy	57	0.8	65.1
28	Servant (M)	56	0.7	65.8
29	Teamster	53	0.7	66.5
30	Agent	52	0.7	67.2
31	Salesman	51	0.7	67.9
32	Builder	48	0.6	68.5
33	Butcher	47	0.6	69.1
34	Harness/Saddlemaker	44	0.6	69.7
35	Carriage Maker	43	0.6	70.3
36	Chemist	42	0.6	70.9
37	Farmer	42	0.6	71.5
38	Hotel Keeper	38	0.5	72.0
39	Student	37	0.5	72.5
40	Barber	36	0.5	73.0
41.5	Railroad Worker	35	0.5	73.5
41.5	Teacher	35	0.5	74.0
43	Joiner	31	0.4	74.4
44.5	Bricklayer	30	0.4	74.8
44.5	Cigar Maker	30	0.4	75.2
46	Stone Cutter	22	0.3	76.3
47	Innkeeper	20	0.3	76.6
48	Stage Driver	6	0.1	76.7

176

Table 1 Continued

POUGHKEEPSIE—Rank Order

Rank	Occupation	No.	%	Cum. %	Rank	Occupation	No.	%	Cum. %
59	Storekeeper	391	.32	70.06	1	Laborer	578	14.7	14.7
60	Dyer	380	.31	70.37	2	Carpenter	223	5.7	20.4
61	Saddler	368	.30	70.67	3	Clerk	220	5.6	26.0
62	Agent	362	.29	70.96	4	Shoemaker	124	3.1	29.1
63	Plumber	357	.29	71.25	5	Cooper	123	3.1	32.2
64	Paper Hanger	356	.29	71.54	6	Merchant	115	2.9	35.1
65	Stone Mason	347	.28	71.82	7	Farm Laborer	112	2.8	37.9
66	Boatman	346	.28	72.10	8	Carriage Maker	95	2.4	40.3
67	Seaman	337	.27	72.37	9	Mason	93	2.4	42.7
68	Brewer	334	.27	72.64	10	Tailor	90	2.3	45.0
69	Lawyer	333	.27	72.91	11	Chair Factory	89	2.3	47.3
70	Servant	312	.25	73.16	12.5	Teamster/Carter	87	2.2	49.5
71	Watchman	286	.23	73.39	12.5	Gentleman	87	2.2	51.7
72	Turner	279	.23	73.62	14	Boatman	84	2.1	53.8
73	Gas Fitter	277	.22	73.84	15.5	Painter	76	1.9	55.7
74	Hostler	258	.21	74.05	15.5	Gardener	76	1.9	57.6
75	Broker	256	.21	74.26	17	Blacksmith	73	1.9	59.5
76	Fisherman	250	.20	74.46	18	Grocer	70	1.8	61.3
77	Upholsterer	241	.19	74.65	19	Lawyer	64	1.6	62.9
78	Dentist	214	.17	74.82	20	Machinist	60	1.5	64.4
79	Liquor Dealer	207	.17	74.99	21	Farmer	53	1.3	65.7
80	Carman	195	.16	75.15	22	Baker	51	1.3	67.0
					23	Driver/Coachman	41	1.0	68.0
					24	Cigar Maker	40	1.0	69.0
					25	Doctor/Dentist	39	1.0	70.0
					26	Tinsmith	38	1.0	71.0
					27.5	Cabinet Mar	36	0.9	71.9
					27.5	Printer	36	0.9	72.8
					29	Engineer	35	0.9	73.7
					30	Butcher	31	0.8	74.5
					33	Clergy	30	0.8	75.3
					33	Teacher	30	0.8	76.1
					33	Jeweler	30	0.8	76.9
					33	Moulder	30	0.8	77.7
					33	Tanner	30	0.8	78.5
					36	Saddler	29	0.7	79.2
					37.5	Weaver	28	0.7	79.9
					37.5	Agent	28	0.7	80.6
					39	Manufacturer	24	0.6	81.2
					40.5	Captain/Pilot	23	0.6	81.8
					40.5	Bookkeeper	23	0.6	82.4
					42	Peddler	22	0.6	83.0
					43	Barber	20	0.5	83.5
					44.5	Stonecutter	19	0.5	84.0
					44.5	Turner	19	0.5	84.5
					46.5	Hostler	17	0.4	84.9
					46.5	Sash & Blind Maker	17	0.4	85.3
					48	Brewer	16	0.4	85.7
					49	Saloonkeeper	14	0.4	86.1
					50	Waiter	11	0.3	86.4

177

Table 1 Continued

KINGSTON—Rank Order

Rank	Occupation	No.	%	Cum.%
1	Laborer	1026	21.8	21.8
2	Boatman	511	10.9	32.7
3	Farm Laborer	253	5.4	38.1
4	Farmer	220	4.7	42.8
5	Clerk	190	4.0	46.8
6	Quarryman	182	3.9	50.7
7	Carpenter	139	3.0	53.7
8	Cooper	117	2.5	56.2
9.5	Stone Cutter	105	2.2	58.4
9.5	Teamster	105	2.2	60.6
11	Blacksmith	102	2.2	62.8
12	Shipwright	91	1.9	64.7
13	Shoemaker	90	1.9	66.6
14	Grocer	85	1.8	68.4
15	Mason	81	1.7	70.1
16	Brickmaker	78	1.7	71.8
17	Merchant	75	1.6	73.4
18	Painter	61	1.3	74.7
19	Tailor	55	1.2	75.9
20	Innkeeper	49	1.0	76.9
21	Butcher	47	1.0	77.9
22	Peddler	37	0.8	78.7
23	Wagon Maker	34	0.7	79.4
24.5	Attorney	33	0.7	80.1
24.5	Gardener	33	0.7	80.8
26	Saddler	28	0.6	81.4
27.5	Cigar Maker	27	0.6	82.0
27.5	Ostler	27	0.6	82.6
29	Cabinet Maker	26	0.6	83.2
30	Engineer	23	0.5	83.7
31.5	Printer	22	0.5	84.2
31.5	Tinsmith	22	0.5	84.7
33	Physician	21	0.4	85.1
34	Baker	20	0.4	85.5
36	Clothier	19	0.4	85.9
36	Factory Overseer	19	0.4	86.3
36	Machinist	19	0.4	86.7
38.5	Barber	15	0.4	87.1
38.5	Stage Driver	15	0.4	87.5
41.5	Dealer	12	0.4	87.9
41.5	Clergyman	12	0.4	88.3
41.5	Mfr.—Other	12	0.4	88.7
41.5	Packer	12	0.4	89.1

PHILADELPHIA—Rank Order

Rank	Occupation	No.	%	Cum.%
1	Laborer	17,488	14.12	14.12
2	Clerk	5363	4.33	18.45
3	Carpenter	5045	4.07	22.52
4	Shoemaker	4246	3.42	25.94
5	Tailor	3135	2.53	28.47
6	Weaver	2990	2.41	30.88
7	Merchant	2375	1.92	32.80
8	Mariner	2325	1.88	34.68
9	Cordwainer	2130	1.72	36.40
10	Blacksmith	2066	1.67	38.07
11	Machinist	1923	1.55	39.62
12	Painter	1698	1.37	40.99
13	Farmer	1526	1.23	42.22
14	Baker	1427	1.15	43.37
15	Grocer	1424	1.15	44.52
16	Dealer	1395	1.13	45.65
17	Gentleman	1285	1.04	46.69
18	Waiter	1236	1.00	47.69
19	Carter	1235	1.00	48.69
20	Bricklayer	1147	.93	49.62
21	Salesman	1140	.92	50.54
22	Porter	1106	.89	51.43
23	Printer	987	.80	52.23
24	Cabinet Maker	963	.78	53.01
25	Innkeeper	937	.76	53.77
26	Gardener	922	.74	54.51
27	Butcher	901	.73	55.24
28	Engineer	864	.70	55.94
29	Victualler	850	.69	56.63
30	Moulder	831	.67	57.30
31	Brickmaker	815	.66	57.96
32	Driver	800	.65	58.61
33	Farm Laborer	723	.58	59.19
34	Coachman	686	.55	59.74
35	Cigar Maker	683	.55	60.29
36	Waterman	623	.50	60.79
37	Barber	622	.50	61.29
38	Physician	591	.48	61.77
39	Cooper	578	.47	62.24
40	Plasterer	572	.46	62.70
41	Wheelwright	570	.46	63.16
42	Druggist	569	.46	63.62
43	Bookbinder	566	.46	64.08
44	Jeweler	533	.43	64.51
45	Stonecutter	525	.42	64.93
46	Tinsmith	514	.41	65.34
47	Bookkeeper	511	.41	65.75
48	Hatter	494	.40	66.15
49	Conductor	490	.40	66.55
50	Bartender	489	.39	66.94
51	Tobacconist	481	.39	67.33
52	Hotel Keeper	460	.37	67.70
53	Operator	447	.36	68.06
54	Drayman	442	.36	68.42
55	Confectioner	425	.34	68.76
56	Lab Man	409	.33	69.09
57	Tavern Keeper	403	.33	69.42
58	Manufacturer	399	.32	69.74

178

51 cases there was complete agreement on the vertical code assigned by each historian; in 26 cases one among us disagreed with the others; and in only 11 cases was there disagreement which was not confined to an adjacent category. In the cases where disagreement was found, the majority ranking was adopted. In this manner, each of the 113 occupations was assigned a vertical rank on the five point scale.

The vertical codes are neither purely "intuitive," that is, based on skill or prestige, nor "derived," that is, based on empirical data such as wealth or wages. In fact, we deliberately avoided the discussion of such points because we wished to see how closely the occupational rankings made individually resembled those made by our colleagues. When the pattern of common agreement emerged, we decided to proceed with the assigned codes. The five vertical categories which resulted can be characterized briefly as follows. *Category One* includes the professional and high white-collar occupations. *Category Two* includes the proprietors and low white-collar occupations. *Category Three* includes the skilled artisans. *Categories Four and Five* include all unskilled workers with the division between the categories, however, coming along the line of "specified" occupations such as carter or treamster and "unspecified" occupations such as laborer[8] (see Table 4).

The horizontal or "sector-of-the-economy" categories presented far less of a problem than did the vertical categories. To compare the differences which existed between the structure of the economy in each of the five cities, a very basic horizontal code was agreed upon. It consists (see Table 5) of three simple breakdowns: *Primary* (such as agriculture and extractive), *Secondary* (such as manufacturing and construction), and *Tertiary* (such as commerce and services). Each of these categories, in turn, were sub-divided where further detail was considered necessary: for example manufacturing was divided into wood and wood products, apparel, food, and beverages. Each occupation was then coded for its horizontal position in the economy.

Next we each prepared a computer tape containing all the variables describing each worker whose occupation was one of the 113 agreed upon. Since 75 percent of the workforce in each city was accounted for in less than 80 occupations, the actual proportion of the workforce for each city represented in 113 occupations was considerably greater. The format for the tapes, that is, the precise column location and the code values for each variable was *identical*: each record contained the age, real property holding, ethnicity, and occupation for each individual.

The tapes were first forwarded to the Canadian project where, using SPSS,[9] a series of cross-tabulations were generated, copied, and mailed to the rest of the group. We met at the PSHP for the second time in December, 1972, discussed the newly generated data, and decided what further tables, especially those using specific occupations, we desired. Once again the additional tables were run, copied, and forwarded to the group. The initial version of the paper (presented at a session of the Organization of American Historians, Chicago, 1973) consisted of distinct sections written by each of us. The current version of the paper represents a synthesis of the sections in the earlier draft.

The five cities ranged in size from the smallest, the river towns of Kingston and Poughkeepsie, through the lakeports of Hamilton and Buffalo, to the metropolis of Philadelphia. Kingston, New York, was a small commercial city (more accurately, a town containing two nearly contiguous villages) on the west bank of the Hudson River, just under 100-

179

Table 2: Workforce in Five Cities

OCCUPATION	Buffalo No. in Occ.	Buffalo % of Total Workforce	Buffalo Rank in City	Buffalo Cum. % of Rank	Hamilton No. in Occ.	Hamilton % of Total Workforce	Hamilton Rank in City	Hamilton Cum. % of Rank	Kingston No. in Occ.	Kingston % of Total Workforce	Kingston Rank in City	Kingston Cum. % of Rank
Agent	6	0.8	24.5*	68.4	52	0.7	30	67.2				
Baker	6	0.8	24.5*	70.0	69	0.9	23	61.0				
Barber					36	0.5	40	73.0				
Bartender												
Blacksmith	12	1.6	13.5*	57.2	144	1.9	8	43.6	102	2.2	11	62.8
Boat Cpt./Pilot												
Boatman									511	10.9	2	32.7
Boiler												
Bookbinder												
Bookkeeper												
Brewer												
Bricklayer	26	3.4	4.5*	34.8	30	0.4	44	74.8	78	1.7	16	71.8
Brickmaker												
Broker												
Builder												
Butcher	11	1.5	16*	60.2	48	0.6	32	68.5				
Cabinet Maker	9	1.2	18.5*	62.9	47	0.6	38	69.1				
Carman					99	1.3	13	51.0				
Carpenter	61	8.1	2	24.9	528	7.0	2	26.8	139	3.0	7	53.7
Carriage Maker					43	0.6	35	70.3				
Carter												
Chair Factory												
Clergy	6	0.8	24.5*	69.2	57	0.8	26.5*	65.1				
Chemist					42	0.6	36	70.9				
Chair Maker					30	0.4	45	75.2				
Clerk	20	2.6	7	43.7	303	4.0	3	30.8	190	4.0	5	46.8
Coachman												
Commission Merchant	6	0.8	24.5*	67.6								
Conductor												
Confectioner												
Cooper	12	1.6	13.5*	55.6					117	2.5	8	56.2
Cordwainer												
Dealer												
Dentist												
Drayman												
Driver												
Druggist												
Drygoods/Fancy												
Dyer												
Engineer												
Farmer	17	2.2	8.5*	48.1	74	1.0	20	59.1	220	4.7	4	42.8
Farm Laborer					42	0.6	37	71.5	253	5.4	3	38.1
Ferryman												
Fisherman												
Furnaceman												
Gardener	18	1.7	12	54.0	63	0.8	24	62.7				
Gas Fitter												
Gentleman					121	1.6	9	45.2				
Glass Blower/Former												
Grocer	11	1.5	16*	61.7	150	2.0	7	41.7	85	1.8	14	68.4
Harness/Saddle Maker					44	0.6	34	69.7				
Hatter												
Hostler												
Hotel Keeper					38	0.5	38	72.0				

Occupation	I n	I %	I r	I %	II n	II %	II r	II %	III n	III %	III r	III %
Innkeeper												
Joiner												
Lab Man					31	0.4	43	74.4				
Laborer	127	16.8	1	16.8	1485	19.8	1	19.8	1026	21.8	1	21.8
Lawyer	5	0.7	28.5*	72.8	97	1.3	14.5*	52.3				
Liquor Dealer					83	1.1	17	55.9				
Machinist												
Manufacturer												
Mariner	16	2.1	10.5*	50.2	97	1.3	14.5*	53.6				
Mason					207	2.7	5	37.0	81	1.7	15	70.1
Merchant	16	2.1	10.5*	52.3	93	1.2	16	54.8	75	1.6	17	73.4
Moulder												
Nail Maker/Cutter												
Operator					108	1.4	12	49.7	61	1.3	18	74.7
Painter												
Paper Hanger					57	0.8	26.5*	64.3				
Pattern Maker												
Peddler	5	0.7	28.5*	71.4	60	0.8	25	63.5				
Piano Maker												
Physician	7	0.9	21*	66.8	81	1.1	18	57.0				
Plasterer	9	1.2	18.5*	64.1	110	1.5	11	48.3				
Plumber					71	0.9	22	61.0				
Porter												
Printer									182	3.9	6	50.7
Puddler												
Quarryman	17	2.2	8.5*	45.9	35	0.5	41.5*	73.5				
Railroad Worker	5	0.7	28.5*	70.7	80	1.1	19	58.1				
Saddler					51	0.7	31	67.9				
Sailor/Mariner												
Sales. Agent												
Salesman												
Seaman	49	6.5	3	31.4	56	0.7	28	65.8				
Servant	7	0.9	21	65.9	260	3.5	4	34.3				
Ship Carpenter												
Shipwright									91	1.9	12	64.7
Shoemaker	22	2.9	6	41.1					90	1.9	13	66.6
Stonecutter									105	2.2	9.5*	58.4
Stonemason												
Storekeeper					37	0.5	39	72.5				
Student	26	3.4	4.5*	38.2	205	2.7	6	39.7	55	1.2	19	75.9
Tailor					120	1.6	10	46.8				
Tanner												
Tavern Keeper												
Teacher	11	1.5	16*	58.7	35	0.5	41.5*	74.0	105	2.2	9.5*	60.6
Teamster	5	0.7	28.5*	72.1	53	0.7	29	66.5				
Tinsmith					73	1.0	21	60.1				
Tobacconist												
Turner												
Typesetter												
Upholsterer												
Victualler												
Waiter												
Waterman												
Watchman												
Weaver												
Wheelwright												
Yardman	7	0.9	21*	65.0								

Table 2 continued

OCCUPATION	Philadelphia				Poughkeepsie			
	No. in Occ.	% of Total Work-force	Rank in City	Cum. % of Rank	No. in Occ.	% of Total Work-force	Rank in City	Cum. % of Rank
Agent	362	.39	62	70.96	51	1.3	22	67.0
Baker	1437	1.15	14	43.37				
Barber	632	.50	37	61.29	73	1.9	17	59.5
Bartender	489	.39	50	66.94				
Blacksmith	2066	1.67	10	38.07	84	2.1	14	53.8
Boat Cpt./Pilot								
Boatman	346	.28	66	72.10				
Boiler	566	.46	43	64.08				
Bookbinder	511	.41	47	65.75	31	.8	30	74.5
Bookkeeper	334	.27	68	72.64	36	.9	27.5*	71.9
Brewer	1147	.93	20	49.62				
Bricklayer	815	.66	31	57.96				
Brickmaker								
Brickmason								
Broker	256	.21	75	74.26				
Builder	901	.73	27	55.24				
Butcher	963	.78	24	53.01				
Cabinet Maker	195	.16	80	75.15				
Carman	5045	4.07	3	22.52	223	5.7	2	20.4
Carpenter					95	2.4	8	40.3
Carriage Maker								
Carter	1235	1.00	19	48.69				
Chair Factory					89	2.3	11	47.3
Chemist					30	.8	33*	75.3
Clergy								
Cigar Maker	683	.55	35	60.29	40	1.0	24	69.0
Clerk	5363	4.33	2	18.45	220	5.6	3	26.0
Coachman	686	.55	34	59.74				
Commission Merchant								
Conductor	490	.40	49	66.55				
Confectioner	425	.34	55	68.76				
Cooper	578	.47	39	62.24	123	3.1	5	32.2
Cordwainer	2130	1.72	9	36.40				
Dealer	1395	1.13	16	45.65				
Dentist	214	.17	78	74.82				
Drayman	442	.36	54	68.42				
Driver	800	.65	32	58.61	41	1.0	23c	68.0
Druggist	569	.46	42	63.62				
Drygoods/Fancy								
Dyer	380	.31	60	70.37				
Engineer	864	.70	28	55.94	35	.9	29	73.7
Farmer	1526	1.23	13	42.22	53	1.3	21	65.7
Farm Laborer	723	.58	33	59.19	112	2.8	7	37.9
Ferryman								
Fisherman	250	.20	76	74.46				
Furnaceman								
Gardener	922	.74	26	54.51				
Gas Fitter	277	.22	73	73.84				
Gentleman	1285	1.04	17	46.69				
Glass Blower/Former								
Grocer	1424	1.15	15	44.52	76	1.9	15.5*	57.6
Harness/Saddle Maker								
Hatter	494	.40	48	66.15	87	2.2	12.5*f	51.7
Hostler	258	.21	74	74.05				
Hotel Keeper	488	.37	52	57.70	70	1.8	18	61.3

Occupation	N	%			N	%		
Innkeeper	937	.76	25	53.77	30	.8	33	76.9
Jeweler	533	.43	44	64.51				
Joiner								
Lab Man	409	.33	56	69.09				
Laborer	17,488	14.12	1	14.12	578	14.7	1	14.7
Lawyer	333	.27	69	72.91	64	1.6	19	62.9
Liquor Dealer	207	.17	79	74.99				
Machinist	1923	1.55	11	39.62	60	1.5	20	64.4
Manufacturer	399	.32	58	69.74				
Mariner	2325	1.88	8	34.68				
Mason	2375	1.92	7	32.80	93	2.4	9	42.7
Merchant	831	.67	30	57.30	115	2.9	6	35.1
Moulder					30	.8	33*	77.7
Nail Maker/Cutter								
Operator	447	.36	53	68.06	76	1.9	15.5*	55.7
Painter	1698	1.37	12	40.99				
Paper Hanger	356	.29	64	71.54				
Pattern Maker								
Peddler								
Piano Maker	591	.48	28	61.77	39	1.0	25[1]	70.0
Physician	572	.46	40	62.70				
Plasterer	357	.29	63	71.25				
Plumber	1106	.89	22	51.43				
Porter	987	.80	23	52.23	36	.9	27.5*	72.8
Printer								
Puddler								
Quarryman								
Railroad Worker	368	.30	61	70.87				
Saddler								
Sailor/Mariner								
Sales. Agent								
Seaman	1140	.92	21	50.54	124	3.1	4	29.1
Servant	337	.27	67	72.37				
Ship Carpenter	312	.25	70	78.16				
Shoemaker	4246	3.42	4	25.94	90	2.3	10	45.0
Stonecutter	525	.42	45	64.93	30	.8	33*	78.5
Stonemason	347	.28	65	71.82				
Storekeeper	391	.32	59	70.06				
Student								
Tailor	3135	2.53	6	28.47	30	.8	33*	76.1
Tanner								
Tavern Keeper	403	.33	57	69.42	87	2.2	12.5*	49.5
Teacher								
Teamster								
Tinsmith								
Tobacconist	514	.41	46	65.34	38	1.0	26	71.0
Turner	481	.39	51	67.33				
Typesetter	279	.23	72	73.62				
Upholsterer	241	.19	77	74.65				
Victualler	850	.69	29	56.63				
Waiter	1236	1.00	18	47.69				
Waterman	623	.50	36	60.79				
Watchman	286	.23	71	73.39				
Weaver								
Wheelwright	2990	2.41	6	30.88				
Yardman	570	.46	41	63.16				

Table 2 continued

Notes: Occupations not found on the chart were beyond the 75% cutoff point, and may appear in the individual city listings (following pages).

† The total "No in Occ." includes the actual number of Blacks, Irish, and Germans in each occupation, and a figure for the Native-White Americans adjusted for a one-in-six sample (actual number times six).

a. Carpenter/Joiner
b. Drayman/Hackman
c. Driver/Coachman
d. Farmer/Farm Laborer
e. Ferryman/Bargeman
f. The category of "Gentleman" includes
   (1) those who listed "Gentleman" as their occupation and
   (2) those who listed "no occupation" but had $5000 worth of real property or $3000 in personal property.
g. Grocer/Grocery Clerk
h. Machinist/Mechanic
i. Doctor/Dentist
j. Shoemaker/Bootmaker
k. Teamster/Carter
l. Tinsmith/Tinner

* Tied Ranks

Sources: See sample sheet.

184

Table 3

Vertical Categories: Composite Scores

Occupation	Glasco	Blumin	Hershberg	Griffin	Katz	Composite
Agent	2	2	2	2	2	2
Baker	3	3	3	3	3	3
Barber	2	3	3	3	4	3
Bartender	4	4	4	4	4	4
Blacksmith	3	3	3	3	3	3
Boat Captain	3	3	3	2	3	3
Boatman	4	4	4	5	4	4
Boiler	3	4	3	-	3	3
Bookbinder	3	3	3	3	3	3
Bookkeeper	2	3	2	2	2	2
Brewer	3	2	3	3	3	3
Bricklayer	3	3	3	3	3	3
Brickmaker	3	3	3	3	3	3
Brickmason	3	3	3	3	3	3
Broker	2	2	2	2	2	2
Builder	3	2	2	2	2	2
Butcher	3	3	3	3	3	3
Cab Maker	3	3	3	3	3	3
Carman	4	5	4	4	4	4
Carpenter	3	3	3	3	3	3
Carriage Maker	3	3	3	3	3	3
Carter	4	5	4	4	4	4
Chair Factory	-	4	4	4	4	4
Clergy	1	2	1	1	1	1
Chemist	1	2	2	1	2	2
Cigar Maker	3	3	3	3	3	3
Clerk	2	3	2	2	2	2
Coachman	4	5	4	4	4	4
Commission Merchant	1	1	1	1	1	1
Conductor	3	4	4	2	3	3
Confectioner	3	3	3	3	3	3
Cooper	3	3	3	3	2	3
Cordwaiver	3	3	3	3	3	3
Dealer	2	3	3	2	4	3
Dentist	1	2	2	1	2	2
Drayman	4	5	4	4	4	4
Druggist	1	2	2	1	2	2
Dry Goods/Fancy	-	2	2	1	2	2
Dyer	3	4	3	3	3	3
Engineer	1	2	3	3	3	3
Farmer	2	2	3	2	3	2
Farm Laborer	5	5	5	5	5	5
Ferryman	4	4	4	-	4	4
Fisherman	4	4	4	5	4	4
Furnaceman	3	4	4	4	4	4
Gardener	4	3	4	4	3	4
Gas Fitter	3	4	3	3	3	3
Gentleman	-	1	1	1	1	1
Glass Blower	3	3	3	3	3	3
Grocer	2	3	2	2	2	2
Saddle Maker	3	3	3	3	3	3
Hatter	3	3	3	3	3	3
Hostler	2	5	4	5	4	4
Hotel Keeper	2	3	2	1	1	2
Innkeeper	2	3	2	1	1	2
Jeweler	3	2	2	3	2	2
Joiner	3	3	3	3	3	3
Lab Man	5	4	5	-	5	5
Laborer	5	5	5	5	5	5
Lawyer	1	1	1	1	1	1
Liquor Dealer	2	3	2	2	1	2

185

Table 3 Continued

Occupation	Glasco	Blumin	Hershberg	Griffin	Katz	Composite
Machinist	3	3	3	3	3	3
Manufacturer	2	2	1	1	2	2
Mariner	4	5	4	5	4	4
Mason	3	3	3	3	3	3
Merchant	2	1	1	1	1	1
Moulder	3	3	3	-	3	3
Nail Maker	3	4	3	4	3	3
Operator	2	4	3	-	3	3
Painter	3	3	3	-	3	3
Paper Hanger	3	3	3	-	3	3
Pattern Maker	3	3	3	3	3	3
Peddler	2	4	3	2	4	3
Piano Maker	3	3	3	3	3	3
Physician	1	1	1	1	1	1
Plasterer	3	3	3	3	3	3
Plumber	3	3	3	3	3	3
Porter	4	5	4	5	4	4
Printer	3	3	2	3	2	3
Puddler	3	4	3	3	3	3
Quarryman	4	5	4	5	4	4
Railroad Worker	5	5	4	5	4	4
Saddler	3	3	3	3	3	3
Sailor	4	5	4	5	4	4
Sales Agent	2	3	2	2	2	2
Salesman	2	3	2	2	2	2
Seaman	4	5	4	5	4	4
Servant	4	5	4	5	4	4
Ship Carpenter	3	3	3	3	3	3
Shipwright	3	3	3	3	3	3
Shoemaker	3	3	3	3	3	3
Stonecutter	3	3	3	3	3	3
Stonemason	3	3	3	3	3	3
Storekeeper	2	3	2	2	2	2
Student	-	-	2	-	2	2
Tailor	3	3	3	3	3	3
Tanner	3	3	3	3	3	3
Tavern Keeper	4	3	2	2	2	2
Teacher	1	3	2	1	2	2
Teamster	4	4	4	4	4	4
Tinsmith	3	3	3	3	2	3
Tobacconist	2	3	2	2	2	2
Turner	3	3	3	3	3	3
Typesetter	3	4	3	3	3	3
Upholsterer	3	3	3	3	3	3
Victualer	2	3	2	2	2	2
Waiter	4	5	4	4	4	4
Waterman	5	5	4	5	4	5
Watchman	2	5	4	4	4	4
Weaver	3	4	4	3	3	3
Wheelwright	3	3	3	3	3	3
Yardman	4	5	4	5	4	4

Number of Cases:

    (1) in which all raters agree 51
    (2) in which only one rater disagrees . . . 26
    (3) in which there is a disagreement
        not in an adjacent category 11

186

Table 4

Vertical Categories: Five Rankings

I	II	III	IV	V
Clergy	Agent	Baker	Bartender	Farm Laborer
Commission Merchant	Bookkeeper	Barber	Boatman	Lab Man
Gentleman	Broker	Blacksmith	Carman	Laborer
Lawyer	Builder	Boat Captain	Carter	Railroad Worker
Merchant	Chemist	Boiler	Chair Factory	Waterman
Physician	Clerk	Bookbinder	Coachman	
	Dentist	Brewer	Drayman	
	Druggist	Bricklayer	Driver	
	Dry Goods/Fancy	Brickmason	Ferryman	
	Farmer	Butcher	Fisherman	
	Grocer	Cab Maker	Furnaceman	
	Hotel Keeper	Carpenter	Gardener	
	Innkeeper	Carriage Maker	Hostler	
	Jeweler	Cigar Maker	Mariner	
	Liquor Dealer	Conductor	Porter	
	Manufacturer	Confectioner	Quarryman	
	Sales Agent	Cooper	Sailor	
	Salesman	Cordwaiver	Seaman	
	Storekeeper	Dealer	Servant	
	Student	Dyer	Teamster	
	Tavern Keeper	Engineer	Waiter	
	Teacher	Gas Fitter	Watchman	
	Tobacconist	Glass Blower	Yardman	
	Victualer	Hatter		
		Joiner		
		Machinist		
		Mason		
		Moulder		
		Nail Maker		
		Operator		
		Painter		
		Paper Hanger		
		Pattern Maker		
		Peddler		
		Piano Maker		
		Plasterer		
		Plumber		
		Printer		
		Puddler		
		Saddle Maker		
		Saddler		
		Ship Carpenter		
		Shipwright		
		Shoemaker		
		Stonecutter		
		Stonemason		
		Tailor		
		Tanner		
		Tinsmith		
		Turner		
		Typesetter		
		Upholsterer		
		Weaver		
		Wheelwright		

187

Table 5

Horizontal Categories: Sectors of the Economy

I. Primary

(a) Agriculture

Farmer
Farm Laborer

(b) Extractive

Fisherman
Mariner
Quarryman

II. Secondary

(a) Manufacturing

1. Textile and
   Leather
   Tanner
   Weaver

2. Apparel
   Cordwaiver
   Dyer
   Hatter
   Pattern Maker
   Saddler
   Tailor
   Shoemaker

3. Wood and Wood
   Products
   Cabinet Maker
   Carriage Maker
   Chair Factory
   Turner
   Wheelwright

4. Metal and Metal
   Products

   Boiler
   Cooper
   Engineer
   Furnaceman
   Gas Fitter
   Machinist
   Moulder
   Puddler
   Tinsmith
   Nail Maker

5. Food and
   Beverage
   Brewer
   Butcher
   Confectioner
   Baker

6. Luxury Items
   Book Binder
   Glass Blower
   Jeweler
   Piano Maker
   Upholsterer

7. Other
   Cigar Maker
   Manufacturer
   Operator
   Printer
   Stonecutter
   Typesetter

(b) Construction

Brickmaker
Bricklayer
Brickmason
Builder
Carpenter
Joiner
Mason
Painter
Paper Hanger
Plasterer
Plumber
Ships Carpenter
Shipwright
Stonemason

(c) Labor

Lab Man
Laborer

188

Table 5 Continued

III. Tertiary

(a) *Commerce*

Agent
Bookkeeper
Broker
Chemist
Clerk
Commission
  Merchant
Dealer
Druggist
Dry Goods/
  Fancy
Grocer
Hotelkeeper
Innkeeper
Liquor
  Dealer
Merhcant
Peddler
Sales Agent
Dalesman
Storekeeper
Tavern
  Keeper
Tobacconist
Victualler

(b) *Transportation*

Blacksmith
Boat Captain/
  Pilot
Boatman
Carman
Carter
Conductor
Drayman
Driver
Ferryman
Hostler
Railroad
  Worker
Sailor/
  Mariner
Seaman
Teamster
Waterman
Yardman

(c) *Public Service*

Barber
Bartender
Waiter
Watchman

(d) *Domestic Service*

Coachman
Gardener
Porter
Servant

(e) *Profession*

Clerg;
Dentist
Laywer
Physician

(f) *Education and Government Profession*

Student
Teacher

IV. Unclassifiable

Gentleman

miles north of New York City. Settled in the 1650s as a farming community and an outlet for Esopus Valley grain, Kingston remained small, rural, and predominantly Dutch until slightly beyond the first quarter of the nineteenth century. Then, in 1828, the completion of the Delaware and Hudson Canal from the anthracite fields of northeastern Pennsylvania to tidewater at Kingston set in motion a series of economic developments which transformed the town into a small but fairly diverse city. The canal itself brought a number of unskilled Irish immigrants to the town, and stimulated the growth of limestone and bluestone quarrying, lime and cement manufacturing, freighting, and other industries requiring large numbers of unskilled and semi-skilled workers. This demand was also met by Irish immigrants, as well as by immigrants from Germany and, in smaller numbers, by native-born migrants from other towns in the Hudson Valley. Other migrants from the Valley, New England, and Germany, recognizing Kingston's new importance as both a local market and a commercial center for west shore farmers, opened a wide variety of retail stores and craftsmen's shops. By 1860 Kingston contained 16,640 inhabitants, only half of whom were native Americans. Fully one-third of the population was Irish, and a sixth consisted of Protestant, Catholic, and Jewish Germans. Of course, the farms and even many of the descendants of the seventeenth-century settlers lent continuity with Kingston's past, but no longer did they dominate the town's economic and social life. By 1860, coal, not wheat, was Kingston's staple and an Irish dock worker her most typical citizen.

No more than a hamlet early in the eighteenth century, Poughkeepsie, New York, had become a village of more than 1000 by 1800 and an incorporated city of nearly 15,000 by 1860. Midway between New York City and Albany on the east bank of the Hudson River, it prospered through superior water transportation. Always a trading and shipping center for an agricultural hinterland, it participated in the regional market which extended from Albany to Long Island by the beginning of the nineteenth century. Soon after 1800 manufacturing developed along a local stream. Many of the early firms had disappeared by the Civil War, but the city's industry grew and diversified, tapping regional and national markets by water. In 1860 Poughkeepsie ranked thirty-fifth in population among the 50 largest Northeastern cities and twentieth in ratio of manufacturing workers to total labor force. Six firms had more than 50 employees and twenty-four had more than 20 employees, comprising 15 and 30 percent respectively of the male labor force. The coincidence of the Irish famine emigration and construction of the Hudson River Railroad spurred transformation of the city's ethnic composition. By 1860 the native-born accounted for nearly 60 percent, the Irish 20 percent, the Germans 12 percent, and the British 6 percent of the male labor force.

Hamilton, Ontario, was a lakeport about 40 miles west of Toronto. A commercial city, with no industry to speak of, Hamilton emerged as an important regional center in the 1840s after the completion of the Burlington Canal, growing from a few thousand in the middle of the decade to 14,000 in 1851 and 19,000 in 1861. However, in the late 1850s, before the depression which hit the city extremely hard, the population had climbed to well over 25,000. During the depression the city went bankrupt because of its over-investment in railroads and waterworks, and the population fell rapidly, starting to rise once again around 1860. By 1861 the worst of the depression had ended and the city's recovery had begun. What is of special note about Hamilton, and other Canadian cities at this time, is their immigrant character. In both 1851 and 1861 only about 9 percent of the adult male workforce had been born in Canada; the rest were immigrants, mainly from England, Ireland, and Scotland.

190

Located in the western end of New York State, Buffalo was directly in front of the wave of German and Irish immigration which hit the eastern coast of the United States in the 1840s and 1850s. The impact on the city was twofold. First, between 1845 and 1855 its population more than doubled from 30,000 to over 70,000 making it one of the fastest growing cities in the nation. Second, by the time the wave began to recede, the city was no longer "American" in terms of population. By 1855 three-quarters of its adult population was foreign-born. Native-born whites made up less than a quarter of its inhabitants; Irish comprised a fifth; and both were overshadowed by the German-speaking element, which made up almost half of the adult population. Those who remained in Buffalo generally found their lives bound up with the city's two principal activities—commerce and manufacturing. Situated at the end of the Erie Canal, the nation's major water route, Buffalo was the place where cargoes from the agricultural hinterland of the Old Northwest—Ohio, Michigan, Indiana, Illinois, and Wisconsin—were taken off lake boats and then floated on barges down the Canal to New York City. The major item in this trade was wheat, and by 1855 Buffalo had surpassed Chicago, Galatz, and Odessa to become the leading grain port in the world. Although primarily a commercial city with some farming, Buffalo's economy included a rapidly growing manufacturing component. Manufacturing was done in small firms, and included ship building, iron making, agricultural machinery, edge tools, white lead, copper and brass, cabinets, and pianos.

A sprawling urban giant on the Delaware River, Philadelphia was among the world's leading industrial concentrations. Job opportunities were abundant, and the city attracted tens of thousands of Irish and German immigrants, as well as native-born stock from the countryside. Although blacks comprised only a small portion of the city's total population (565,000 in 1860), Philadelphia was home, too, for the largest free black population outside the South. After a decade of rapid growth, Philadelphia remained America's second biggest city and port-of-entry, with about one-third of its inhabitants foreign-born. Although its machine-tool, foundry, and locomotive shops were on the cutting edge of innovation, the city's phase of industrialization in 1860 is better characterized by rationalization and reorganization of work especially evident in the shoe and textile industries than by advances in technology. With investment capital plentiful, political boundaries recently expanded from a small, rectangular plot to a vast area of 130 square miles, and a transportation network consolidated so that by 1860 twenty-seven million passengers rode the horse-drawn street railways, Philadelphia's future on the eve of the Civil War seemed bright indeed.

Despite the remarkable variations between these five cities in terms of their history, location, size, and local flavor, they shared a number of distinct social, structural, and demographic characteristics. These shared characteristics or patterns provide us with some idea of what is typical in a nineteenth-century city and the outline of a backdrop against which to pick out what is deviant or idiosyncratic as well.

Very little in these comments should prove surprising or startling. The results, by and large, are about what one would expect to find. They gain their importance by their repetition in place after place, that is, from the uniformities in social and demographic structure which they indicate.

Specifically, there were similarities in the overall distribution of features in (1) occupational structure considered in functional terms; (2) occupational ranking, which, in a loose sense, serves as a proxy for class; (3) age structure; and (4) property ownership.

191

Additionally, there were distinct similarities in some of the relationships between social features: (1) occupational function and ethnicity; (2) class and ethnicity; (3) property ownership and class; (4) property ownership and ethnicity; and (5) age, ethnicity, and occupational rank.

First of all the similarity in occupational structure is considered functionally: this is portrayed in tabular and graphic form in Graph 1. Here we have collapsed the categories to six: agriculture and extractive; manufacture and labor; construction; transport; commerce and professions; and other. The most striking similarity is in the percentage of the workforce engaged in manufacturing and laboring occupations, between 41 and 49 percent in each of the five cities. In four of the five cities the proportion in commerce and professions is quite similar as well, varying between 18 and 23 percent, the deviant case, Kingston, accounted for by the substantial proportion there engaged in farming. The total proportion in each city working in transport and construction combined is likewise quite similar, ranging from 19 to 29 percent, with emphasis on one or the other industry in each city. Thus it is safe to assume that in a mid-nineteenth-century city without a large agricultural component included in the population about 48 percent of the workforce will be engaged in manufacturing and laboring occupations, about 20 percent in commerce and the professions; about 25 percent in construction or transport (with a 20-5 or 18-7 split between the two) and the remaining 7 percent scattered.

Similar patterns exist when occupations are ranked vertically (Graph 2). In the top group the percentage varies between 5 and 10. In the lowest two combined between 30 and 32 percent in four of the cities. It is probably accurate to say that, combining the rankings into three groups which we can call classes for short, the highest class comprises between 15 and 25 percent of the working population; the middling one slightly less than half and the lowest just under one-third.

With the exception of Philadelphia—whose distinctiveness here may reflect its size—property ownership is also quite uniform, varying between 24 and 31 percent. Perhaps we can assume that in a middle sized city roughly a quarter of the workforce owned their own houses.

Except for Hamilton, which had a quite different pattern of settlement, the cities' workforces were remarkably similar in age composition. (Part of the difference in the Hamilton data is due to the almost total absence of 18 and 19 year olds on the assessment to which the census data used here is linked [Graph 3].) Between 35 and 40 percent were between the ages of 18 and 29, between 25 and 33 percent in their thirties, just under 20 percent in their forties and 12-20 percent over that age of 50. There was less uniformity, however, in ethnicity. In two of the cities—Buffalo and Hamilton—native whites made up a rather small fraction of the workforce, just over 20 percent and about 9 percent, respectively. In the other three cities the fraction of natives varied between slightly less than 45 and just over 55 percent. The proportions of Irish and Germans also varied, though, as the graph shows, roughly in inverse proportion to each other. The differences in ethnic composition make the similarities in occupational structure, class, and age all the more striking.

Location may explain part but not all of the ethnic variation between the five cities. Let us focus briefly on Poughkeepsie and Kingston. Both towns were located on the Hudson River, one about 75 miles and the other about 90 miles from New York City. Both, in other words, were inland regional subcenters, with essentially the *same access to the same pool of*

192

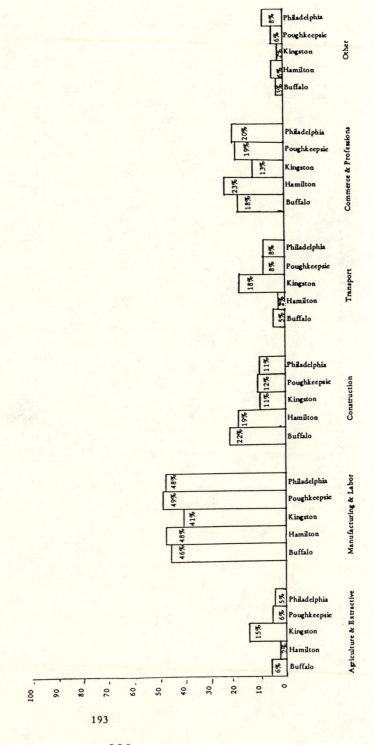

Graph 1: Occupational Structure: Horizontal
5 Cities, 1860-1861

Percent

100
90
80
70
60
50
40
30
20
10
0

Agriculture & Extractive

Buffalo 6%
Hamilton 2%
Kingston 15%
Poughkeepsie 6%
Philadelphia 5%

Manufacturing & Labor

Buffalo 46% 48%
Hamilton 48%
Kingston 41%
Poughkeepsie 49%
Philadelphia 48%

Construction

Buffalo 22%
Hamilton 19%
Kingston 11%
Poughkeepsie 12%
Philadelphia 11%

Transport

Buffalo 5%
Hamilton 2%
Kingston 18%
Poughkeepsie 8%
Philadelphia 8%

Commerce & Professions

Buffalo 18%
Hamilton 23%
Kingston 13%
Poughkeepsie 19% 20%
Philadelphia 20%

Other

Buffalo 1%
Hamilton 6%
Kingston 7%
Poughkeepsie 6%
Philadelphia 8%

193

299

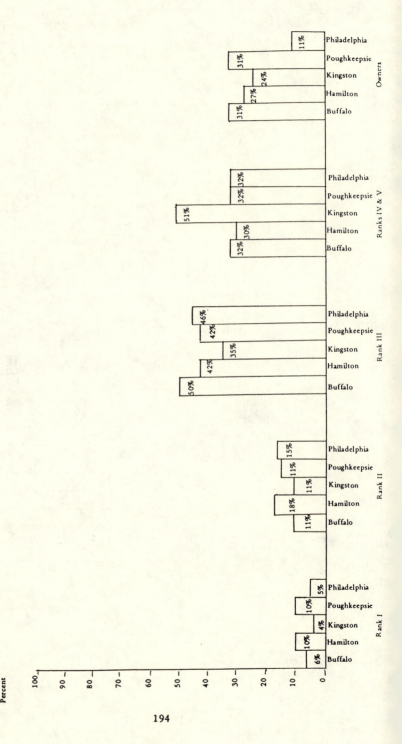

Graph 2: Occupational Rank and Property Ownership Distribution

194

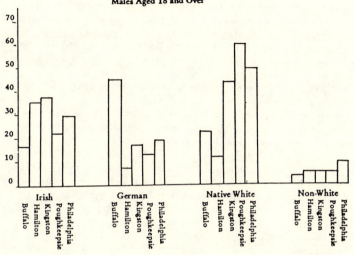

Graph 3: Ethnic and Age Distributions in 5 Cities, 1861:
Males Aged 18 and Over

Ethnicity

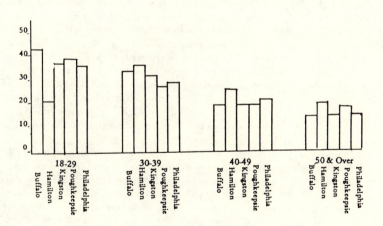

Age

195

301

foreign immigrants, almost all of whom were entering the region through its major port at the mouth of the Hudson. Why, then, did Poughkeepsie remain 57 percent native, while Kingston's native proportion shrank to 44 percent? (The two towns were about the same size, and grew at similar rates during the decades preceding 1860.) Why was Poughkeepsie's Irish proportion only 20 percent while Kingston's was 35 percent? Why were the differences in the proportions of the German-born in the two towns much closer, at 12.5 percent for Poughkeepsie and 15 percent for Kingston?

The conventional answer seems to be the accurate one. Kingston and Poughkeepsie did, after all, have rather different economies, and this difference does seem to explain why one town became mostly immigrant while the other remained mostly native. Our functional occupational categories only partly reveal the economic differences. Poughkeepsie's work force was quite diversified, resembling in this respect the three cities we are slighting here, except for slightly greater proportions of men (in Poughkeepsie) working in the manufacture of wood and wood products, metal and metal products, and luxury and miscellaneous items, slightly higher proportions in farming and the professions, and a somewhat lower proportion in unskilled labor. Kingston, on the other hand, was rather less diversified, with great numbers of men working in back-breaking "dollar a day" jobs on the coal docks and stone-hauling wagons, and in the quarries and lime and cement plants. The difference between the two towns (indeed, between Kingston and the other four) is clearest among the vertical occupational categories. The proportion of Poughkeepsie's workers contained in the lowest category is 32 percent (almost exactly the same as in Philadelphia, Buffalo, and Hamilton). Kingston's proportion is a resounding 51 percent.

In short, Kingston's economic development made available those sorts of jobs which drew immigrants, mostly unskilled Irishmen, up from New York City, while Poughkeepsie's development was of the sort which offered jobs that the Irish had less hope of filling. But why, then, did Hamilton, Buffalo, and Philadelphia, whose economies were so similar to Poughkeepsie's, develop ethnic proportions so different from that city and indeed from each other? Here we must return to the question of location, and perhaps in the process exceed the conventional. Location within the region—access to a given pool of immigrants—combines with the structure of local economic development to shape the ethnic structure of a given local population. These two factors, we argue, provide between them a necessary and sufficient explanation of local ethnic variation. Economically, Hamilton, Ontario, was much like Poughkeepsie, but because of its location drew on an entirely different pool of immigrants. The latter factor, in this case, explains their differing ethnic mixtures, just as the former explains the difference between Poughkeepsie and Kingston. The ethnic differences between Kingston and Hamilton are a function of both.

The argument may be restated in this way: within a given region, it is possible to associate the internal migrations of ethnic minorities (and, indeed, majorities) with the development of specific local economies, once sufficient evidence has established the association of specific ethnic groups with specific types of employment.

There were, as indicated earlier, similar patterns in the relations between occupation, ethnicity, age, and property in these five cities. The first of these is the extent to which people of similar ethnic backgrounds distributed themselves in different sorts of work (Table 6 and Graph 4). To highlight the distributions we have developed an index, which will be used in the display of other relations as well. The purpose of the index is to provide a way of comparing distributions which takes into account the varying ethnic composition of

196

Manufacturing: Apparel	Buffalo	Hamilton	Kingston	Poughkeepsie	Philadelphia	Composite
Irish	- 3	1	- 2	- 2	1	- 1.4
English-Scot.	1	1	- 2	+3	—	+ .25
Native White	- 3	- 2	1	- 2	- 2	- 1.8
German	+3	1	+5	+5	+5	+3.6
Non-White Native	- 4	1	- 5	- 2	- 4	- 3

Manufacturing: Metal						
Irish	- 2	- 2	- 2	- 2	- 2	- 2
English-Scot.	1	+2	1	1	—	+ .5
Native White	1	+2	1	1	+2	+ .8
German	1	- 3	+2	+3	1	+ .5
Non-White Native	- 5	- 5	- 5	- 5	- 5	- 5

Construction						
Irish	1	- 2	- 2	1	- 2	- 1.2
English-Scot.	1	+2	+5	1	—	+1.7
Native White	1	—	+2	1	+3	+1
German	1	- 2	—	- 3	- 3	- 1.6
Non-White Native	- 3	1	- 5	- 4	- 3	- 3

Labour						
Irish	+4	+5	+4	+5	+5	+4.6
English-Scot.	- 2	- 3	- 3	- 3	—	- 2.7
Native White	- 4	- 3	- 3	- 3	- 3	- 3.2
German	+2	- 2	1	1	- 2	- .50
Non-White Native	1	+2	+2	+5	+2	+2.2

Commerce and Professions						
Irish	- 2	- 2	- 3	- 3	- 2	- 2.4
English-Scot.	- 2	1	+2	- 3	—	- .7
Native White	+5	+3	+3	+2	+2	+3
German	- 3	1	1	- 3	- 2	- 1.6
Non-White Native	- 3	- 2	- 3	- 3	- 4	- 3

* 1. Divide % of Ethnic Group in occupation by % of Ethnic Group in Population and multiply by 100.

2. Score the figure that results as follows:

201 and over = +5
176 - 200 = +4
151 - 175 = +3
126 - 150 = +2
75 - 125 = 1
50 - 74 = - 2
25 - 49 = - 3
1 - 24 = - 4
0 = - 5

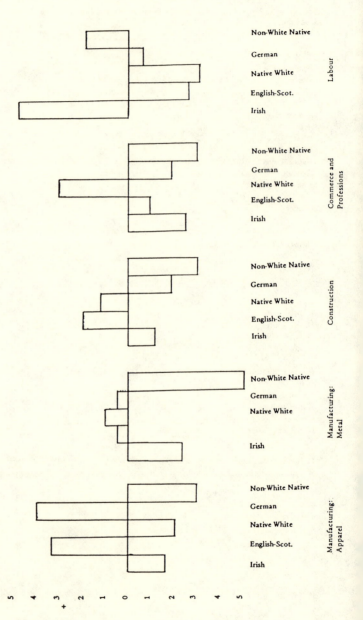

Graph 4: Ethnicity and Occupation in 5 Cities, 1860-61: A Composite-Index

198

304

the cities. That is, if the workforce of one city is 30 percent Irish but those engaged in laboring occupations are 45 percent Irish while, in another city, the workforce is 20 percent Irish and those engaged in laboring occupations are 30 percent Irish, then there is actually no difference in the clustering or disproportionate representation of Irish among the laboring people. In each case they are over-represented by about 50 percent, compared to their proportion of the workforce as a whole. In order to express this sort of disproportion, we have, first, divided the percentage of each ethnic group in an occupational category by the percentage of the ethnic group in the entire population and multiplied the result by 100. The index figures that result are arranged on a scale from -5 to +5, as indicated in Table 9. A +5 indicates an over-representation of five units, a -5 an under-representation of five units; a 1 means that the representation is not considered disproportional, and so on.

The results show a strong and consistent dominance of native whites in commercial and professional occupations (+2 to +5); of Irish in laboring (+4 or +5 in all five cities); and, except for Hamilton, of Germans in the apparel trades (+3 to +5). At the same time they show a pronounced absence of certain ethnic groups in some occupations: of Irish in the metal trades and commercial and professional occupations; of non-whites in everything except laboring; of English and Scottish in laboring; of Germans, generally, in construction and in commercial and professional occupations and, as would be expected, of native whites in laboring. In sum: Germans dominated the apparel trades; construction and metals were generally mixed; Irish and non-whites dominated in laboring; and native whites in commerce and the professions. The results are so consistent that it is possible to form a composite score composed of a rough average of the ranking of ethnic clustering in each trade in each city. If there had been much variation between cities, the composite scores would have been near zero and varied little from each other. In fact there are strong patterns, represented graphically in Table 10. These point out, unmistakably, the ethnic variation in occupational structure.

Similar ethnic variations can be seen in class structure as well. In Table 7 we have combined the vertical occupational groups into three categories which stand as surrogates for classes and derived an index score for the degree of ethnic concentration in each. The results are strikingly similar for the three groups considered in the table: Irish, native whites, and non-whites. In the highest class the scores for the Irish are all negative, varying from -2 to -4, whereas for the native whites the scores are positive, ranging from +3 to +5. Among the non-whites the scores, with the puzzling exception of Buffalo, are all negative, as might be expected. At the bottom of the scale the findings are exactly reversed: the concentration of Irish in the lowest class is strong, varying from +2 to +5; that of non-whites is also uniformly positive, from +3 to +5 and of native whites it is negative throughout, either -2 or -3.

The similarities remained when we refined the analysis, examining individual occupations rather than horizontal or vertical groupings of them. We chose eleven occupations, four of them customarily classified as white collar (lawyer, merchant, grocer, and clerk), five as skilled crafts (machinist, carpenter, baker, shoemaker, and tailor), and the remaining two as less skilled employments (teamster and ordinary laborer). As seen in the composite scores on the accompanying Index of Ethnic Concentration (Table 8), eight of these occupations show dramatic over-representation of one ethnic group and, with a few exceptions, under-representation of the other four ethnic groups.

199

Table 7: Index of Ethnic Concentration in Social Classes

	Irish	Native White	Non-White
Highest Class			
Buffalo	- 3	+5	+2
Hamilton	- 2	+4	- 4
Kingston	- 3	+3	- 3
Poughkeepsie	- 4	+3	- 2
Philadelphia	- 4	+3	- 5
Middle Class			
Buffalo	- 2	1	1
Hamilton	- 2	1	- 2
Kingston	- 2	1	- 3
Poughkeepsie	- 2	1	- 3
Philadelphia	1	1	- 3
Lowest Class			
Buffalo	+4	- 3	+3
Hamilton	+4	- 3	+3
Kingston	+2	- 2	+3
Poughkeepsie	+5	- 2	+5
Philadelphia	+3	- 2	+5

Table 8: 1860 Index of Ethnic Concentration *

	Buffalo	Hamilton	Kingston	Poughkeepsie	Philadelphia	Composite
Lawyer						
Native White	+5	—	+5	+3	+4	+4.3
English-Scot.	1	—	- 5	- 3	—	- 2.6
German	- 4	—	- 5	- 5	- 4	- 4.5
Irish	- 4	—	- 4	- 5	- 4	- 4.3
Non-White	- 5	—	- 5	- 5	- 4	- 4.8
Merchant						
Native White	+5	+5	+3	+2	+4	+3.8
English-Scot.	1	1	+5	- 2	—	+ .6
German	- 4	- 3	- 4	- 3	- 3	- 3.4
Irish	- 3	- 2	- 4	- 3	- 4	- 3.2
Non-White	- 5	- 2	- 5	- 5	- 4	- 4.4
Clerk						
Native White	+5	+4	+4	+3	+4	+4.0
English-Scot.	1	+2	- 2	- 4	—	- 1.0
German	- 3	- 5	- 3	- 3	- 4	- 3.6
Irish	- 3	- 2	- 4	- 4	- 3	- 3.2
Non-White	- 3	- 5	- 5	- 5	- 4	- 4.4
Grocer						
Native White	1	+2	1	1	1	+ .4
English-Scot.	- 3	1	+4	- 2	—	- .2
German	1	- 5	1	- 2	1	- 1.4
Irish	1	1	1	1	+2	+ .4
Non-White	- 5	- 2	- 5	- 5	- 4	- 4.2

200

Table 8 continued

Machinist	Buffalo	Hamilton	Kingston	Poughkeepsie	Philadelphia	Composite
Native White	+3	- 5	+3	+2	+2	+1.0
English-Scot.	+4	+2	+5	1	—	+3.0
German	- 2	- 5	1	- 3	1	- 2.0
Irish	- 2	- 2	- 5	- 4	- 3	- 3.2
Non-White	- 5	- 5	- 5	- 5	- 5	- 5.0
Carpenter						
Native White	1	1	+3	+2	+2	+1.4
English-Scot.	1	+2	+5	1	—	+2.3
German	1	- 2	1	- 3	- 2	- 1.4
Irish	- 2	- 2	- 3	- 2	- 2	- 2.2
Non-White	- 3	1	- 5	- 4	- 3	- 3.0
Baker						
Native White	- 3	—	- 2	1	- 3	- 2.3
English-Scot.	+2	—	- 5	+5	—	+ .7
German	+3	—	+5	+2	+5	+3.8
Irish	- 3	—	- 4	- 2	- 3	- 3.0
Non-White	- 5	—	- 5	- 5	- 4	- 4.8
Shoemaker						
Native White	- 2	- 4	1	1	- 2	- 1.6
English-Scot.	- 2	1	- 3	1	—	- 1.3
German	+2	1	+5	+5	+5	+3.4
Irish	- 3	1	1	1	1	- .6
Non-White	- 5	+2	- 5	- 3	- 3	- 2.8
Tailor						
Native White	- 3	1	- 2	- 3	- 3	- 2.2
English-Scot.	- 2	+2	1	+5	—	+1.3
German	+3	+2	+5	+5	+5	+4.0
Irish	- 3	1	- 3	- 2	- 2	- 2.0
Non-White	- 3	- 2	- 5	- 2	- 4	- 3.2
Teamster						
Native White	1	- 5	+2	1	- 2	- 1.0
English-Scot.	+2	- 2	- 2	1	—	- .8
German	- 3	- 5	- 2	- 2	- 2	- 2.8
Irish	+5	+4	- 2	1	+3	+2.0
Non-White	1	- 5	+5	+5	+1	+1.0
Laborer						
Native White	- 4	- 4	- 3	- 3	- 3	- 3.4
English-Scot.	- 2	- 3	- 3	- 3	—	- 2.8
German	+2	- 2	1	1	- 2	- .4
Irish	+4	+5	+3	+5	+5	+4.4
Non-White	1	+2	+2	+5	+2	+2.2

* For the method of computation see Katz, Table 11.

201

Among lawyers, merchants, and clerks, native-born whites have the expected advantage, with the English and Scottish suffering least in comparison. By contrast, ethnic representation among grocers is relatively balanced, with the single exception of non-whites. The two groups with the most similar and even representation—the native-born whites and the Irish—also were at opposite poles in public esteem, suggesting that no ethnic group had a decided advantage in this occupation. Rather this result seems to reinforce what historians of immigration long have said about the significance of the grocer of foreign birth or extraction who extended credit to his fellow countrymen, catered to their special tastes in food, and provided a place for conviviality.

Among the skilled trades, the English and Scottish, coming from the most advanced industrial nation, show an expected over-representation among machinists. Their advantage over the United States-born in this highly skilled trade was slighter than our index suggests, however. Native-born whites in Hamilton were Canadian-born and sharply under-represented among machinists, skewing the composite score. The United States-born in Hamilton do display their usual over-representation in the trade so that a recomputation substituting them nearly eliminates the preeminence of the English and Scottish.

The pattern among carpenters is broadly similar. A ranking of the five ethnic groups from most over-represented to most under-represented is identical with the ranking for machinists. But the range in scores is generally narrower for the carpenters and the representation more balanced than in any of the other four crafts we examined. Whether Irish, German, and non-white carpenters had comparable skill, reward, and opportunity for advancement remains in question; in a building trade which may fluctuate greatly in size of work force, members of less well-represented ethnic groups may have been marginal to the trade.

In our three food and apparel trades, the balance swings decisively in favor of the foreign-born. With one exception in the composite scores, native-born whites and non-whites show a lower level of representation than any foreign-born group. The Germans make the great difference in these skilled crafts, being almost as sharply over-represented among bakers, shoemakers, and tailors as thee native-born whites were among lawyers, merchants, and clerks. At the bottom of the ladder, the Irish and non-whites alone are over-represented among teamsters and laborers; the more responsible employment, teamstering, also shows the more balanced representation.

As the indices of ethnic concentration for these five cities show, there are individual variations which do not conform nicely to this general description of the composite scores. Some of these variations raise intriguing questions. Thus, the sharp over-representation of the English and Scottish among merchants and grocers in Kingston is unique for the five cities; that immigrant group also happens to constitute a somewhat smaller proportion of the labor force of Kingston than of the other cities. Non-whites have a more favorable representation in skilled and white collar occupations in Canadian Hamilton than in any United States city which makes one wonder whether the small non-white population of that city was made up largely of fugitive slaves. In both cities this better showing of one ethnic group may involve selective migration.

In some senses it is thus possible to consider ethnicity and class as synonymous: Irish birth usually brought a low ranking as did non-white birth; native white birth much more often meant high status. However, the relations between property, class, and ethnicity show that birth and rank sometimes acted independently of each other (Table 9).

202

Table 9: Index of Property-Owning by Class and Ethnicity

		Class	
	High	Mid	Low
Buffalo	- 2	1	- 2
Hamilton	1	1	- 2
Kingston	- 5	1	- 2
Poughkeepsie	- 5	1	- 2
Philadelphia	——	1	- 2

		Ethnicity	
	Irish	Native White	Non-White
Buffalo	- 2	1	- 2
Hamilton	1	1	1
Kingston	1	1	1
Poughkeepsie	1	1	- 3
Philadelphia	1	- 2	- 3

		Property Ownership among Labourers %	
	Irish	Native White	Non-White
Buffalo	12	15	29
Hamilton	18	9	38
Kingston	14	9	10
Poughkeepsie	32	9	8
Philadelphia	6	4	4

203

As might be expected, people in the highest class generally had a disproportionate amount of property; people in the middling class had an amount proportional to their share of the population, and people in the lowest class most often lacked property. However, the same distinctions cannot be made between Irish, native whites, and non-whites. There are few indications of disproportionate property holding among them. With the exception of non-whites, property appears to have been distributed among ethnic groups roughly in proportion to their share of the population. This is accounted for, largely, by the greater propensity of Irish than of native white laborers to hold property. With the exception of Buffalo, considerably fewer native white laborers owned property than did Irish ones. Perhaps, given the bias of opportunity in their favor, only the least ambitious and least capable native whites became laborers, while lack of opportunity and discrimination kept many hard-working and able Irish and non-whites—among whom there is a similar pattern of substantial property ownership by laborers—from rising out of laboring occupations. Or the explanation might lie in cultural values and the differing ways in which Irish, blacks, and native whites chose to spend their money. Certainly the relations between class, ethnicity, and property—though consistent—remain nonetheless intricate.

If the interrelationship of ethnicity, occupation, and property is explored in greater detail, however, we see that more was involved than a process of occupational self-selection. In Tables 10 and 11, we have listed the percentage of property owners for twelve major occupations in each of the five cities, and constructed an Index for each of them. That Index shows that *regardless of occupational rank*, the immigrants and blacks outdid their native-born counterparts in acquiring real property. The differences, while not dramatic in most cases, were consistent. Out of the twelve occupations, the Irish bested their native-born counterparts in seven (clerks, lawyers, merchants, and grocers among the non-manual occupations; laborers, shoemakers, and teamsters among the manual occupations). In turn the Irish were bested by the native-born in only three occupations (machinists, tailors, and "others"), and they did about the same in two (bakers and carpenters). The results are similar for the Germans. Even for the blacks, clearly the most disadvantaged group occupationally, the pattern holds. In no city were there sufficient blacks in non-manual occupations to permit comparison with whites, and only in Philadelphia were there sufficient blacks in artisanal trades to permit comparison along lines other than that of unskilled laborers. Out of six occupations in Philadelphia in which comparisons were possible, however, blacks had a higher rate of property ownership than their native-born white counterparts in four (carpenters, tailors, teamsters, and laborers), did as well among shoemakers, and fell below the native-born white rate only among the miscellaneous "other" classification.

From this evidence, then, it seems clear that we are dealing with a situation in which property ownership was related to class considerations, but in which it was substantially modified by ethnicity and culture.

The same can be said, finally, of the relations between age, ethnicity, and occupational rank (Table 12 and Graph 5). (The following comments infer life-cycle from cross-sectional analysis, and for that reason, must be considered tentative.) It is striking—and perhaps the most unexpected finding here—that the proportions of the workforce in occupational ranks III and IV declined with age. This holds true for each city. The relations between these middling occupational ranks and age are perfectly inverse in each case. In Buffalo 66 percent of the 20-29 year olds were in the middle ranks of the workforce compared to 48

Table 10: Percentage Owning Property, by Ethnicity and Occupation

	Kingston					Poughkeepsie					Philadelphia					Hamilton					Buffalo				
	Overall	Irish	German	White	Black	Overall	Irish	German	White	Black	Overall	Irish	German	White	Black	Overall	Irish	German	White	Black	Overall	Irish	German	White	Black
Baker	20	na	9	na	na	22	na	na	29	na	15	9	17	12	na	na	na	na	na	na	29	na	33	10	na
Carpenter	36	25	29	37	na	30	32	14	32	na	15	14	7	16	32	52	58	53	43	na	40	38	44	35	na
Clerk	5	0	13	4	na	10	na	14	8	na	5	7	3	5	na	15	23	16	8	na	16	21	14	16	na
Grocer	57	63	79	45	na	74	75	na	74	na	30	34	32	26	na	25	35	20	11	na	55	51	53	53	29
Laborer	14	15	16	7	18	25	33	15	13	12	6	6	5	4	4	17	18	15	10	38	22	12	27	15	na
Lawyer	64	na	na	66	na	56	na	na	56	na	21	33	na	21	na	na	na	na	na	na	50	na	na	56	na
Machinist	6	na	na	8	na	25	na	na	20	na	10	8	9	11	na	17	na	13	na	na	30	33	39	34	na
Merchant	75	na	na	74	na	75	na	na	78	na	38	45	34	38	na	27	36	30	19	na	54	54	53	46	na
Shoemaker	21	22	11	29	na	27	26	37	22	na	8	7	7	8	7	25	32	23	na	na	24	67	32	32	na
Tailor	15	25	10	21	na	29	25	28	39	na	9	9	8	13	15	30	20	35	na	na	37	22	40	14	na
Teamster	16	20	30	14	na	41	50	43	38	na	12	14	11	9	12	36	47	11	na	na	28	38	38	6	na
"Other"	27	24	24	30	17	30	21	26	33	13	12	11	11	14	4	28	37	28	22	11	31	21	35	32	14
Overall	24	20	22	29	16	31	32	25	33	15	11	10	10	14	4	27	28	29	23	22	31	20	34	33	20

205

311

Table 11: Comparison of Irish, Germans and Blacks with Native-Born Whites
in Terms of Percentage Owning Real Property—by Specified Occupation
(Derived from Table I)

	Ratio of Percentages					Index of Concentration					
	Kingston	Poughkeepsie	Philadelphia	Hamilton	Buffalo	Kingston	Poughkeepsie	Philadelphia	Hamilton	Buffalo	Average
Baker	x	x	75	x	x	x	x	1	x	x	0.0
Carpenter	68	100	88	135	109	-2	1	1	2	1	0.0
Clerk	0	x	140	288	131	-5	x	2	5	2	1.0
Grocer	140	101	131	318	96	2	1	2	5	1	1.8
Laborer	214	254	150	180	80	5	5	2	4	1	3.2
Lawyer	x	x	157	x	x	x	x	3	x	x	3.0
Machinist	x	x	73	x	97	x	x	-2	x	1	-1.0
Merchant	x	x	118	189	102	x	x	1	4	1	1.3
Shoemaker	76	118	88	x	479	1	1	1	x	5	1.3
Tailor	119	64	69	x	58	1	-2	-2	x	-2	-1.5
Teamster	143	132	156	x	633	2	2	3	x	5	3.0
Other	80	64	79	168	66	1	-2	1	3	-2	-0.2
Baker	x	x	142	x	330	x	x	2	x	5	3.5
Carpenter	78	44	44	x	126	1	-3	-3	x	2	-1.0
Clerk	325	175	60	x	88	5	3	-2	x	1	1.5
Grocer	176	x	123	x	100	4	x	1	x	1	1.3
Laborer	229	115	125	x	180	5	1	1	x	4	2.3
Lawyer	x	x	x	x	x	x	x	x	x	x	x
Machinist	x	x	82	x	115	x	x	1	x	1	0.0
Merchant	x	x	89	x	87	x	x	1	x	1	0.0
Shoemaker	38	168	88	x	229	-3	3	1	x	5	1.3
Tailor	48	72	62	x	105	-3	-2	-2	x	1	-1.8
Teamster	214	113	122	x	600	5	1	1	x	5	2.5
Other	80	79	79	x	109	1	1	1	x	1	0.0
Baker	x	x	x	x	x	x	x	x	x	x	
Carpenter	x	x	200	x	x	x	x	4	x	x	
Clerk	x	x	x	x	x	x	x	x	x	x	
Grocer	x	x	x	x	x	x	x	x	x	x	
Laborer	x	x	100	x	x	x	x	x	x	x	
Lawyer	x	x	x	x	x	x	x	x	x	x	
Machinist	x	x	x	x	x	x	x	x	x	x	
Merchant	x	x	x	x	x	x	x	x	x	x	
Shoemaker	x	x	88	x	x	x	x	x	x	x	
Tailor	x	x	115	x	x	x	x	x	x	x	
Teamster	x	x	133	x	x	x	x	x	x	x	
Other	x	x	29	x	x	x	x	x	x	x	

Irish: Percentage Owning Property Divided by Percentage Native-Born Whites of Same Occupation Owning Property. Index Computed as Described by M. B. Katz.

German: Calculation Same as Above.

Blacks: Calculation Same as Above, but only for City of Philadelphia.

"x" = insufficient number of cases for valid comparison.

206

Table 12: Age and Occupational Rank in 5 Cities, 1861

	20-29	30-39	Percentages 40-49	50-59	60 and over
I & II					
Buffalo	13	18	21	22	28
Hamilton	28	28	27	27	26
Kingston	8	14	21	26	38
Poughkeepsie	22	21	27	33	38
Philadelphia	21	20	23	26	32
III & IV					
Buffalo	66	58	52	48	39
Hamilton	52	49	48	46	40
Kingston	65	53	48	42	37
Poughkeepsie	61	54	53	47	38
Philadelphia	64	60	55	52	47
V					
Buffalo	21	25	28	31	33
Hamilton	20	23	24	26	34
Kingston	27	32	31	33	25
Poughkeepsie	17	26	21	20	23
Philadelphia	15	21	21	22	22

207

313

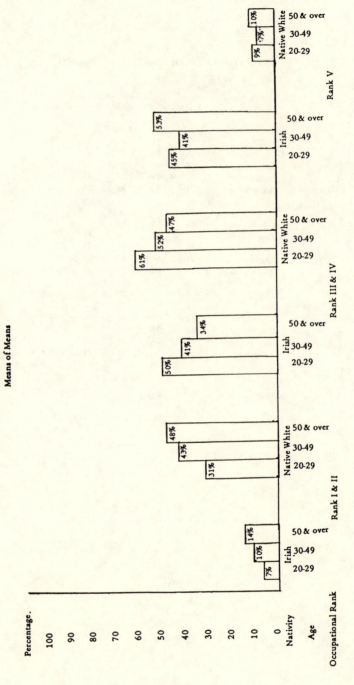

Graph 5:

Ethnicity, Occupational Rank, and Age, 5 Cities, 1861:

Means of Means

percent of the 50-59 year olds and 39 percent of the men 60 and over. In Philadelphia the percentage dropped, with each cohort, from 64 to 60 to 55 to 52 to 47. The figures are similar for the other cities. The men who left the middling ranks, it appears, split, some falling and some rising, for the proportion in ranks I-II and V generally increased with age. All of this suggests a bifurcation of experience. Nearly 60 percent of each cohort started off its occupational career in a skilled trade. With time about one-third or one-half of those who remained alive moved to a new sort of occupation, somewhat more increasing their rank than declining. However, this general pattern appears somewhat different when Irish and native whites are compared as in Graph 5, which displays a chart and graph based on the mean of means in the five cities—a measure designed to give an approximate idea of the central tendency in the cities looked at as a group. The proportion of Irish and native whites in the middling ranks both declined. But the proportion of native whites in the highest categories rose far more than the proportion of Irish, while the proportion of Irish in the lowest class increased steadily with age and the percentage of native whites there remained relatively steady and very low. The Irish thus more often declined in occupational rank as they got older; the natives more frequently improved. As an Irish worker slipped in skill and strength, his hold on his class position became more tenuous. Over time the initial advantage of the native white over the Irish born man became even more marked. Social stratification, this argues, was uniformly wider among the aged than among the young.

In order to explore this pattern a little more thoroughly, let us draw upon some of the material for Buffalo. We use the Buffalo data because it was based on the New York State census rather than the Federal census. The former asked a very useful question of the population—how many years have you been in the city?—and thus provides us with an important additional variable with which to investigate the interrelationship of ethnicity, occupation, and age.

Graph 6 displays the relationship between age, length of residence, and percentage of each ethnic group who had unskilled occupations. The table shows two clear patterns. First, regardless of age, the more recently an immigrant had migrated to the city, the more likely he was to be in an unskilled occupation; conversely, the longer he had been in the city the less likely he was to be unskilled. Second, although an older immigrant (in his forties, say) was more likely to be unskilled, the longer he remained in the city, the more his representation among unskilled workers converged toward that of his younger counterpart.

These two patterns help explain why older immigrants concentrated in unskilled occupations. The mechanism, apparently, was the act of migration, and in particular the *timing* of migration in terms of the individual's life cycle. For the foreign-born, picking up and moving to a new country and city gave a decided edge to the younger, more flexible worker in adjusting to an unfamiliar work environment. For the older worker the adjustment process was much slower; only after 10 to 20 years did he match his younger counterpart in being ready and able to leave the ranks of unskilled labor (in which he was more likely to work strictly among people of his own ethnic background) for the semi-skilled and skilled ranks (in which he was more likely to be in an ethnically mixed situation). For the native-born, there were so few unskilled workers in Buffalo that the patterns, while still observable, are not so striking. Often born in New York State, their migration was of a much shorter distance, they more easily adapted to the environment, and consequently, as the illustration shows, the expected inverse relationship between age and percentage unskilled emerges—in contrast to the immigrant pattern.

209

Graph 6

Buffalo, N.Y., 1855

Percentage of Family
Heads with Unskilled
Occupations, for
Specified Age and
Persistence Groups

Native-Born Whites

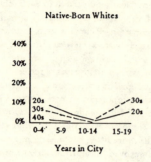

Years in City

Irish

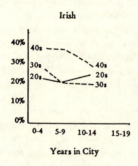

Years in City

Germans

Years in City

210

These findings provide two additional processes—migration and persistence—which not only were interrelated with age and occupation, but also were peculiarly filtered through the prism of ethnicity.

These similarities in the distribution of social and demographic features and in their relationships with each other do not exhaust the common patterns in even the rough and schematic data which we have managed to put into comparable form. They do point to some of the major ways in which nineteenth-century cities might be said to have similar internal structures. They point at once to an answer to the ever present question that historians who focus on one city must answer: how do you know your results are representative? We know that studying a single city has validity, in part, because there were common structural features, i.e., relatively similar social and demographic patterns, among them. At the same time these similarities point to the critical importance of continuing and expanding collaborative inquiries, which are the only way in which we can with certainty isolate the particular from the common.

In this comparison of five North American cities in 1860, we have confined our attention to the relationship between ethnicity and occupation. Our analysis of that relationship has the limitations of any comparison at one point in time; it does not tell us how temporary or how stable that relationship is for the ethnic and occupation groups studied, much less describe the careers of individual members of those groups. The first limitation is important because the massive influx of Irish and Germans in the late 1840s and '50s may have altered a previous distribution of ethnic groups among occupations; the pattern we find in 1860, in turn, may reflect short-run more than long-run effects of that immigration. Fortunately, a number of aggregate studies for the nation and for individual cities provides some perspective here.

The second limitation is more serious. Because we are not ready yet to compare the careers of the individuals comprehended in our analysis for 1860, we can at best speculate from the situation of the group what the prospect for the individual may have been. The analysis of the lesser representation of skilled occupations among the aged infers a career pattern or life cycle, a "bifurcation of experience," for those who begin as skilled and semi-skilled workers from an age distribution at one point in time. Within that bifurcation, we suggest a greater tendency toward upward mobility among native-born artisans and toward downward mobility among Irish artisans.

The analysis for Buffalo of the relationship between this bifurcation and length of residence in the city makes a comparable inference. Discovering that the gap between the older and younger foreign-born in percentage at unskilled work narrows with longer residence in the city, we suggest that migration gave the younger, presumably more flexible immigrant the edge in adjusting to an unfamiliar environment. This inference about adjustment, about occupational change, is plausible and probably will be confirmed by tracing studies. But lacking that confirmation, it can only be a presumption. The possibility remains, for example, that the greater proportion of skilled workers among younger than among older recent arrivals in 1860 represents no difference in adjustment in the New World but rather a difference in occupational level at the time of emigration.

Recognizing these limitations in our comparison at one point in time, we believe that this description of relationship between ethnicity and occupation is important in illuminat-

211

ing a time of both massive immigration and industrialization. We have discovered more similarity in that relationship than we anticipated, given the differences between our cities in location, length of settlement, size, rate of growth, and ethnic composition. Once controlled for the differences in ethnic composition, the characteristics of each ethnic group proved remarkably similar from Philadelphia to Hamilton, with occasional marked deviation in a single city.

Pursuit of local variation is of more concern to the five of us than to social historians at large unless we discover a wider significance. We thought initially that we saw that wider significance in some differences between the newer of our five cities, Buffalo and Hamilton, and the three older ones. In both cities the frequency of ownership of real estate is higher, suggesting the greater opportunity so often postulated for newer settlements. Also, both cities have a much higher proportion of the foreign-born, suggesting greater chances for their social acceptance and upward mobility. And in absolute numbers Buffalo did provide greater opportunity for the foreign-born and especially for the Germans who constituted two-fifths of the labor force. But the occupational structures of Buffalo and Hamilton and the ethnic representation within them do not differ from the older cities. It still may be true that newer cities farther west which had as high proportions of the foreign-born as Buffalo and Hamilton also will show a more favorable occupational representation. But for our five cities recency of settlement and a more rapid rate of growth did not make the difference expected.

It also is possible that some fundamental differences between our cities even in the relationship between ethnicity and occupation may be disclosed by information we could not compare at this time. In our present analysis the category of skilled workers includes all those designated in the census by their trade, whether or not they were self-employed or employers. It is possible that the scale of shops and factories in particular industries varies little between cities so that a comparison of the frequency of proprietorship within them would show little difference. But if that does not prove true and the prospects for achieving proprietorship in particular industries do differ substantially between cities, then the relationship between ethnicity and occupation may vary in a way we have not explored. Thus, Germans may be greatly over-represented among shoemakers, tailors, and bakers in all five cities, but the frequency with which they became owners might differ radically. For the increase in capital required by major differences in scale might also shift the balance of opportunity between ethnic groups, favoring native-born, English, and Scottish entrepreneurs especially. But this possible difference is pure speculation at this point in our analysis.

What wider significance then does our limited inquiry seem to have so far? First, and most obviously, it reinforces and refines the nation-wide picture of ethnic specialization in Edward Hutchinson's classic *Immigrants and Their Children* and in treatments of individual cities like Robert Ernst's *Immigrant Life in New York City* and Donald Cole's *Immigrant City*. It does so by showing that the relative concentration of ethnic groups in particular trades does not vary greatly between five otherwise dissimilar cities.

Second, the striking over-representation of the native-born whites in the upper ranks and of the Irish and the non-whites in the lower ranks of the occupational hierarchy confirms the conventional impression that ethnicity and class were synonymous in some senses. It also reinforces the idea of an uplifting effect in immigration in which aliens moving into the bottom of the occupational hierarchy boost native white workers upward.

212

However, the more balanced representation of the Germans and of the English and Scottish in the three occupational classes which we defined also reminds us of the limitation of this identification of ethnicity with class even at mid-century and perhaps of the limitation of the uplifting effect as well. Their patterns do suggest the more novel conclusion that each ethnic group had its characteristic adaptation in the New World, relating in very similar fashion to the occupational structures of different cities even when those structures differed as they did in neighboring Kingston and Poughkeepsie. Despite (or perhaps in part due to) the volatility of population in these years, the influx of newcomers into cities from foreign countries, native farms, and other cities and towns sorted itself out with remarkable uniformity.

Because our comparison is a cross-section at one point in time and not a tracing of individual careers, we cannot exhibit the process of job improvement for the native-born whites. Nor can we be sure whether the occupational distribution of groups like the Germans and the English and Scottish represent primarily the levels at which they entered the American economy or represent instead significant career mobility after they entered it. But the striking similarity we find between cities in the relation of ethnicity and occupation does seem to complement the finding of Stephan Thernstrom in his recent comparison of tracing studies covering a wide range in time. In the concluding chapter of *The Other Bostonians*, Thernstrom argues that rates of persistence and of career and intergenerational occupational mobility do not differ much between cities.[10] He did not attempt in this comparison to break down these rates for individual ethnic groups; what limited disaggregation has been done so far suggests similarity here also, as in the tendency of initially higher native-born and initially lower foreign-born rates of persistence to converge from 1850 to 1880.

The challenge of all these similarities is that they are beginnings only. They raise a multitude of fundamental questions and, for the moment, answer only rather low-level descriptive questions, such as, among unskilled workers did the Irish have a greater propensity than other ethnic groups to own real estate? The Irish did, and we are left to speculate why. We are likely in this case to ask about the possible influence of the culture the Irish brought with them and not to assume necessarily that economic considerations alone determined their New World economic adaptation.

We stress the importance of this kind of questioning because our usual tendency is to try to explain nation-wide or regional similarities in urban patterns through the operations of the marketplace, a marketplace which by 1860 was relatively well-integrated. This does seem the most sensible approach to the discovery that the occupational structure of American cities of various types and sizes differs much less than conventional urban biography has suggested. As Thernstrom has pointed out, the rapid population turnover we find must have minimized local variations in structure and correspondingly in career mobility rates between different cities. Ethnic over- or under-representation in certain occupations also seems most easily explained by narrowly economic considerations. Thus, if the majority of the famine Irish in cities can be presumed to have been agricultural laborers, then their concentration among ordinary laborers here is not surprising.

But some of the relationships between occupation and ethnicity we find suggest a more complicated interaction between economic and cultural variables. A case in point is the dramatic under-representation of non-whites among grocers in our cities in 1860. One might conjecture that the blacks lacked capital and easy access to credit, but the Irish were

213

similarly handicapped. So one tends to infer that the injury caused by slavery and discrimination and the corresponding lack of a tradition of self-employment in the New World account for this early lack of engagement by non-whites in a kind of business which has offered immediate opportunities for most ethnic minorities. Culture rears its complicated head.

Analysis of German over-representation in the food and apparel trades we compared has the same outcome. A variety of explanations, economic and cultural, suggest themselves. Shoemaking and tailoring already had been modified by specialization in the Northeast by 1860; did the low wages invite immigrant craftsmen willing to work for less? Certainly native artisans often made that complaint. On the other hand, as Hutchinson's analysis for the nation reveals, the Germans also showed high concentration in other skilled trades in the food, apparel, and also woodworking industries. Was there something about these industries that made them particularly inviting to immigrants from a country less advanced in industrition than England was in 1860?

Small shops did remain more frequent in the food and apparel industry, if not in woodworking, than in many lines of manufacturing. The opportunities for self-employment and shop ownership would seem to have been greater. Was there some stronger predilection for self-employment among the Germans than among the Irish or the English and Scottish? Such a predilection might be primarily inertia among those raised in an artisan culture; artisans often managed to survive on the margins of an industrializing economy as handloom weavers did by pursuing specialities in manufacturing or as shoemakers did in many localities by pursuing what remained of the custom trade.

But this explanation of German concentration in small shop manufacturing in the United States presumes that the concentration had more to do with the timing of industrialization in the German states and, correspondingly, with the condition of handicrafts there rather than with any traits of German culture. That presumption may not be warranted. And perhaps the emphasis here on broad stages in the evolution of industrialization may be misplaced. As Herbert Gutman has noted, we know too little still about the occupational culture of the individual trades and professions during this process; we know even less about the variations which different immigrant groups may have brought. There is, for example, evidence suggesting differences between ethnic groups in their regard for particular crafts even before emigration.

The Irish in America at mid-century are over-represented in masonry and in foundry work. It has been urged that this concentration reflects the nature of the work—comparatively arduous and dirty—and a prejudicial view of the Irish as best suited for that work. The affinity may be more complex: From medieval times the Irish honored construction, especially masonry, and metal-working more than most crafts; similarly, the question of standards of workmanship among craftsmen, so interesting to American employers for economic reasons, may depend significantly upon culture, as the tendency to prefer German to French workers long has suggested.

There is nothing original in this kind of speculation; its purpose is to encourage us to begin exploring through more systematic comparative investigation what correspondence there may be between the places immigrants found for themselves in the American occupational structure and the places they held in the Old World. We need comparison, for instance, of German representation in employments in North American cities with the occupational distribution in the areas of heaviest emigration in Germany to see how different the patterns are.

214

This aggregate comparison will be a useful beginning, but necessarily crude. For it will not differentiate within the homeland between the more stable occupations and those experiencing the greatest emigration. And it will not tell us anything about occupational change occurring during the emigration, i.e., the extent to which occupational selectivity an the point of departure was altered by change in occupation upon arrival in North America. Ultimately there is no substitute for systematic studies tracing individuals between the Old and New Worlds, arduous and limited in success as such studies will be.

It seems fitting—perhaps by now it is expected—that an exercise in comparative social history like this one should conclude by urging a widening of the field of comparison.

NOTES

1. See the review of several new volumes by Samuel P. Hays, "Historical Social Research: Concept, Method and Technique," *Journal of Interdisciplinary History*, 4 (Winter, 1974), 475-483.

2. William Aydelotte, "Lee Benson's Scientific History: For and Against," *Ibid.*, 263-273.

3. This is in no small part due to the ways in which our profession prepares us to do research. In choosing a topic we do not ask, "What are the pressing intellectual questions facing our discipline?" and respond with the appropriate research organization. Instead, our selections are constrained, consciously and unconsciously, by these considerations: avoid collaborative and interdisciplinary ventures because they complicate hiring, tenure, and promotion decisions; avoid topics that require resources beyond the means of the individual researcher because funds are not easily available. Many questions which historians posed long ago remain unanswered and others have not yet been asked because they cannot be approached within our present highly individualistic research framework. They will remain unasked and unanswered until we recognize the limitations of the organization of traditional research.

4. Cambridge, 1964.

5. Stephan Thernstrom and Richard Sennett, eds. *Nineteenth-Century Cities* (New Haven, 1969).

6. The actual hypotheses posed at our initial meeting were: "Ethnic differences between occupations are a function of (a) age; (b) length of residence; and (c) household status." The second, which we considered more likely to be true, was "The ownership of real property is a function of both ethnicity and occupation. Within occupations the ownership of real property is a function of ethnicity."

7. Length of residence and household status were dropped because in the former it was not available in all our studies, and in the latter the information, although included in all our individual studies, was not ready for analysis. The choice of 18-19 year olds as a separate age category reflects the fact that some of the studies did not collect data on males under the age of 18. Possible variation in land values between the five cities made it unwise for us at this stage of research to do more than make a simple distinction between ownership and non-ownership. However, our individual studies had each indicated the importance of this distinction. Throughout the discussion of results in this paper native white refers, in the case of Hamilton, to men born in Canada and, in the case of the other four cities, to men born in the United States.

8. These rankings are appropriate to the year 1860. We have not yet considered how they should be altered to account for the impact of industrialization. Many important questions about the classification of the nineteenth-century occupational universe remain unanswered. Hence, we would not recommend that anyone uncritically use these rankings in the study of social mobility between the mid- and latter-nineteenth century. A working conference on occupational classification is a logical and valuable next step. For individual views on occupational classification see Stuart Blumin, "The Historical Study of Vertical Mobility," *Historical Methods Newsletter*, 1 (September, 1968), 1-13; Laurence Glasco, "Ethnicity and Social Structure: Irish, Germans and Native-Born of Buffalo, New York, 1850-1860," (unpublished doctoral dissertation, State University of New York at Buffalo, 1973); Clyde Griffen, "Occupational Mobility in Nineteenth-Century America: Problems and Possibilities," *Journal of Social History*, 5, (Spring, 1972), 310-330; Michael Katz, "Occupational Classification in History," *Journal of Interdisciplinary History*, 3 (Summer, 1972), 63-88; Bruce Laurie, Theodore Hershberg, and George Alter, "Immigrants and

215

Industry: The Philadelphia Experience, 1850-1880," prepared for the Conference on "Immigrants in Industrial America," sponsored by The Eleutherian Mills Historical Library and the Balch Institute, November 1-3, 1973; and Theodore Hershberg, "The Philadelphia Social History Project: A Methodological History," (unpublished doctoral dissertation, Stanford University, 1973).

9. Norman Nie, D. Bent, and C. Hull, *S P S S: Statistical Package for the Social Sciences*, (New York, 1970).

10. These comparisons are hampered by the lack of comparability in occupational classification and record-linkage procedures to which we referred earlier.

IN SEARCH OF
A NORWEGIAN-AMERICAN WORKING CLASS

John R. Jenswold

THIS ARTICLE, here translated, annotated, and slightly adapted for American readers, was commissioned by the Norwegian magazine *Samtiden*. When first published in a 1984 issue on "The Dream of America: Norway in America—America in Norway," it introduced Norwegian readers to recent concepts in American social history. While such themes as social mobility and the American success ideology have long interested American historians, they had not been applied to the Norwegian immigrant experience.

Drawing upon examples from Minnesota and the East Coast, the article is a general survey of Norwegian participation in industrializing and urbanizing the United States. The author hopes that the new interest in urban Scandinavian immigration—recently expressed on both sides of the Atlantic—will uncover the sources needed to illuminate the lives of these immigrants of an overlooked class and era.

AMERICA in the last decades of the 19th century, Knut Hamsun observed, was "a society in the making." In the turmoil of transition from a land of serene farms to a nation of industrial cities, the Norwegian author found "the feverish rush and to-do that comes of people on the move" in a culture in which "every day is moving-in day for a newcomer."[1] All this activity created a great deal of cultural noise, which Hamsun criticized in his 1889 book, *Fra det moderne Amerikas*

Aandsliv. The sojourner in American history in the 1980s has the same task as the European observer of American society in the 1880s—to cut through the promotional noise to find some substance in the din.

Like Hamsun, foreign visitors and native critics found in American culture of the restless 19th century a penchant for selling, a commerce that was not limited to the hawking of land and peddlers' goods. The commodities of human aspirations and dreams were added to the stock. Their advertisements were myths. To speak of a Norwegian-American working class is to challenge two historical myths. One concerns the popular conception of the Norwegian immigrant experience. The other is the formidable American myth of success.

The popular image of Norwegian immigrants grew out of the circumstances surrounding the celebration in the 1920s of their past. To commemorate the centennial of the beginning of organized emigration from Norway, ethnic leaders called for a widespread program to preserve the group's past, "to assess that event accurately, in all its bearings," as Judge Andreas Ueland of Minneapolis demanded.[2]

Desperation as well as commemorative nostalgia colored the effort. These early patrons of ethnic history envisioned nothing less than the end of Norwegian-American life. The rate of immigration had dropped dramatically with the onset of World War I and failed

[1] Hamsun, *The Cultural Life of Modern America*, trans. Barbara G. Morgridge (Cambridge, Mass.: Harvard University Press, 1969), 5.
[2] Ueland, *Recollections of an Immigrant* (New York: Milton, Balch & Co., 1929), 193.

John R. Jenswold is Curator/Editor of the University Art Museum, University of Minnesota. The author of several articles on Scandinavian immigration, he is currently at work on a study of Norwegian immigrant life, 1880-1930, in Brooklyn, Chicago, and Minneapolis.

to recover during the short depression of the early 1920s. Economic constraints were supplemented by legislation with the passing of the immigration acts of 1921 and 1924. Although intended mainly to stem the tide of industrial immigrants from Southern and Eastern Europe, these laws marked the end of the "open door" tradition. While no one could have envisioned the effects of the Great Depression of the 1930s and World War II in further curtailing European immigration, the message seemed clear enough to the ethnic leaders of 1925: The great migration was over, and they and their children were the sole custodians of Norwegian culture in America.

There was also some doubt that the younger generation would carry on the traditions. By 1925 the "American transition" was thought to be largely complete. Scholars cited the abandonment of regional dialects, the increased use of English in worship and conversation, and a declining interest in ethnic institutions among the young as indexes of Americanization. "The societies, immigrant journals, and other Norwegian-American institutions appeared hopelessly outdated and obsolete to a majority of the children of the immigrants," historian Odd S. Lovoll noted.[3] Members of the older generation, who believed that their Norwegianness had helped give them a personality distinct from the homogeneity of America, looked on in alarm. There was a sense of impending loss, that the rich heritage of the group would be devoured by the new commercial culture represented by assembly lines and department stores, radio and motion pictures.

The patricians responded with a flurry of historical activities then unmatched among America's ethnic groups. In 1925 a group of scholars, businessmen, and clergy founded the Norwegian-American Historical Association. Under its aegis immigrant papers were collected, translated, and published. Scholarship appeared in books by such historians as Theodore C. Blegen and Knut Gjerset and a journal, Norwegian-American Studies and Records, was launched. In succeeding decades, a wealth of letters, reminiscences, family histories, and church records have been collected and published by the association, the state historical societies of Minnesota and Wisconsin, and independent scholars.[4]

The picture of Norwegians that has emerged from 60 years of history writing has been one of hearty, hard-working, and pious farmers. Keeping with the temperament of the times, writers have celebrated the persistence of sturdy pioneers and the successful rise of great men to positions of power and prominence in the new world. In contrast to the non-Protestant "new immigrants" from Southern and Eastern Europe, Norwegians were not blamed for the complex problems of the urban and industrial society. They were said to have migrated to midwestern farms before America industrialized. Once here, they fought the Civil War for the Union and against slavery, organized politically, and in the process assimilated easily into American life. On the farms, according to this view, Norwegians achieved a modest level of comfort and economic independence upon which their children could build prosperity. While other immigrants huddled in improverished ghettos in the city, the Norwegians, it was believed, were fulfilling the American Dream of success quietly.

TO SIMPLIFY the Norwegian experience in this manner is to overlook the dynamics of the social and economic forces that transformed rural immigrant Norwegians of the mid-19th century into rural, urban, and suburban Americans of the mid-20th. A survey of the full scope of the migration reveals how closely Norwegians resembled other industrial immigrants.[5] Most Norwegians entered the United States during the industrial era: three times as many of them emigrated to America in the 60 years between 1880 and 1940 than had left Norway in the previous six more-celebrated decades of migration. The immigrants of this later era were different from those of the earlier period of family emigration from Norway. Most were men—60 percent of the 308,270 newcomers who arrived between 1880 and 1915. Two-thirds of these men were between the ages of 15 and 30, and a large majority of immigrants of both sexes were unmarried. (Many married men, who emigrated alone, planned to bring their wives and children over to the new country after a couple of years of earning and saving.) Like other immigrants of the period, not all Norwegian newcomers had an ironclad commitment to endure all hardships in America; hard times sent large numbers of them home. It has been estimated that as many as a quarter gave up on the American Dream and returned to the port cities of Mother Norway.[6]

Most Norwegian immigrants were a part of the great migration of peoples from all parts of Europe to industrializing America. While overshadowed in raw numbers by those coming from Eastern and Southern Europe, the flow of workers from Western and Northern

[3] Lovoll, A Folk Epic: The Bygdelag in America (Boston: Twayne Publishers, 1975), 144, 174-175.
[4] Odd S. Lovoll and Kenneth O. Bjork, The Norwegian-American Historical Association, 1925-1975 (Northfield: The Association, 1975).
[5] Arnfinn Engen, ed., Utvandringa: det store oppbrotet (Oslo: Samlaget, 1978). 36; Norway, Departementet for Sociale Saker (Services), Utvandringsstatistikk (Kristiania, 1921); Ingrid G. Semmingsen, "Norwegian Emigration to America During the Nineteenth Century," Norwegian-American Studies and Records 11 (1940): 78-80.
[6] Norway, Statistik Sentralbyrå (Central Bureau of Statistics), Ekteskap, fødselsr, og vandring (Oslo, 1975), 218.

Europe did not merely continue, but increased. And for many the lure was the new America of industrial cities. While many newcomers sought out their country cousins at first, they turned increasingly to urban and industrial occupations afer 1880. The number of Norwegian and Swedish men engaged in manufacturing tripled in the 1880s, and similar dramatic increases were reported in such untraditionally Norwegian immigrant occupations as the building trades and iron and steel production. Similarly, the number of employed women (excluding farm wives) tripled between 1880 and 1890, the majority of them migrating to cities and towns to work in trades, transportation, and domestic service, a trend not uncommon among other immigrant groups of the time.[7]

These Norwegian immigrants were, in the words of Einar Haugen, "children of a new age in Norway."[8] They had witnessed vast changes in everyday life wrought by forces of industrialization and urbanization in their homeland. As the 19th century wore on, a great number of Norwegians had experience in the growing cities of Kristiania (Oslo) or Bergen or the seaports or farm-trading towns. In the period from 1880 to 1915, nearly one-third of the emigrants had departed Norwegian towns, compared with one-tenth in the period before the Civil War. Even if many of these emigrants were originally from farms and valleys, they arrived not totally unfamiliar with urban life.[9]

Norwegian America became increasingly urban after 1880. The percentage of Norwegians residing in four major urban centers—Brooklyn, Chicago, Minneapolis, and Seattle—grew from 6 to 13 percent in 1900, to 20 percent in 1920. Chicago served as the first major urban center for the group, to be rivaled by Minneapolis and Seattle in the 1890s. These three cities became the cultural centers for Norwegians in their respective

regions: Chicago for the Great Lakes states, Minneapolis for the Upper Midwest and the Great Plains, and Seattle for the transplanted midwesterners in the Pacific Northwest. After the turn of the century, greater numbers of Norwegians made it no farther into the new land than New York City. There they found residence and work among their compatriots in Brooklyn, the emerging center of Norwegian culture on the Atlantic coast.[10]

In these four places immigrants joined the descendants of the rural pioneers who were leaving the farm settlements of the Midwest to seek work in the rising industrial centers. Visible evidence of ethnic community life appeared among the urban Norwegians— churches and their subsidiary charitable and social associations, fraternal and athletic clubs, singing societies, Norwegian-language newspapers, and ethnic business ventures. Smaller *kolonis* (settlements) sprang up in the port cities of Boston, Philadelphia, and San Francisco. In addition, Norwegians appeared in smaller industrial cities in Massachusetts, New Jersey, and Pennsylvania. By 1930, most Norwegian Americans, like most Americans in general, were classified as urban. Within a century of migration and settlement, they had made the transition from the countryside to the city.[11]

THE AMERICA that the new Norwegian immigrants encountered in such large numbers was a land held in thrall by an ideology of success. Native and newcomer alike were bombarded with sermons, political speeches, biographies, popular songs, and novels celebrating the "self-made man" and prescribing ways of achieving upward social mobility.

The ideology of success was stamped into American culture from the time of its founding. Benjamin Franklin, for example, was a major popularizer of this ideology. In his *Advice to Young Tradesmen*, *Autobiography*, and *Poor Richard's Almanack*, Franklin advised his countrymen on "the Way to Wealth" through hard work, frugality, and good character. In the 19th century, Russell H. Conwell, a Baptist minister who founded Temple University in Philadelphia, traveled from city to town, preaching that there were "acres of diamonds"—financial rewards—everywhere for the taking. But novelist Horatio Alger was the ideology's most prolific propagandist. In his many popular novels, which sold over twenty million copies, Alger passed the ideology of success on to America's youth.[12]

So pervasive was the idea in American culture that the immigrant press parroted it back to its readers. As vehicles for Americanization (which was often thought to be synonymous with upward mobility), the newspapers saw it their duty to educate the newcomers in ways of succeeding in the new land. *Skandinavan* of Chicago

---

[7] E. P. Hutchinson, *Immigrants and their Children, 1850-1950* (New York: John Wiley & Sons, 1956), 135, 150-151; United States, *Census*, 1890, *Population*, 2: 484-518. In the 19th century U.S. census reports made no distinction between Norwegians and Swedes. Census statistics from this period, when applied to either group, therefore lack precision, but are still useful to illustrate a general trend.

[8] Einar Haugen, *The Norwegian Language in America: A Study in Bilingual Behavior* (Bloomington, Ind.: Indiana University Press, 1969), 29.

[9] Ingrid G. Semmingsen, "Family Emigration from Bergen, 1874-92: Some Preliminary Results of a Statistical Study," *Americana-Norvegica III* (Oslo: Universitetsforlaget, 1971), 38-63; Rolf Kåre Østrem and Peter Rinnan, "Utvandring fra Kristiania, 1880-1917: en studie i urban utvandring" (Hovedoppgave i historie, Universitetet i Oslo, 1979).

[10] U.S., *Census*, 1920, *Population*, 2:926, 928, 934, 940, 942, 947, 959, 961, 963.

[11] U.S., *Census*, 1930, *Population*, 2:232.

[12] On Conwell, see *Encyclopedia Americana* 7 (Danbury, Conn.: Grolier, Inc., 1982): 713.

325

filled the pages of its English handbooks with samples of business letters that stressed politeness and punctuality. *Nordisk Tidende* of Brooklyn went further, from prescribing the proper methods of success to encouraging the proper attitudes. Early in 1920 the paper printed "The Business of Making a Living, or Ten Steps to Economic Success," by Arthur M. East of the Young Men's Christian Association. The ten keys were: work and earn, budget, record expenses, get a bank account, buy life insurance, prepare a will, own your own home, pay bills promptly, invest in government securities, share with others. Intended to secure the immigrant a place in the mainstream of American middle-class life, East's ten commandments repeated the success ethic that young Benjamin Franklin had penned nearly two centuries earlier. But for most Norwegians, as for most urban Americans, the first commandment was the key to the other nine. In order to procure insurance, government securities, or a home, one first had to be able to "work and earn." And education, skills, and luck in the wild boom-and-bust fluctuations of immature American capitalism were more responsible for success or failure than an individual's character.[13]

But according to the ideology of success, the American economy was a neutral and constant environment, an open arena that offered a fresh start to hard-working and innovative people from the farms and towns of the Old World. "For two hundred years America has made human beings out of Europe's worst spawn," Knut Hamsun paraphrased the belief. "[I]t has turned idlers from every corner of the earth into steady workers. We have been told wondrous tales about people who went shuffling about in wooden shoes here suddenly becoming light-footed there," Hamsun wrote.[14] America, it was promised, freed the immigrants from the old bounds of class and status and allowed them to succeed on their own individual character traits. This view is reflected in Agnes M. Larson's study of John A. Johnson. She describes that Norwegian-American industrialist's success as having occurred "[i]n a fluid society and in a dynamic country where notable individual achievement was possible."[15]

The shattering of old class systems, the myth acknowledged, did entail the development of new class systems. Racism and the course of Southern agriculture had created a permanent American subclass, the black slaves, whose poverty and lack of civil rights were passed on from one generation to the next. And there was an upper class whose status was established by wealth and reinforced by visible consumption. The acceptance and admiration of these people by those less prosperous stem in large part from the belief in the accessibility of success. America's aristocracy was supposed to have risen from rags to riches through good

character, shrewdness, or luck. Besides, it was further preached, the land of unlimited resources and technological marvels ensured that "there is always room at the top." In the early 1920s *Nordisk Tidende* published a series of laudatory profiles of Brooklyn's prosperous Norwegian Americans. Though vague concerning the skills and advantages these men had begun with, the newspaper assured its readers that most had started *"med tomme hander"*—with empty hands. The message to the working people was clear.[16]

THE INTERACTION of the success ideology with economic and social realities can be seen by examining Minneapolis and St. Paul at the turn of the century. In the 1890s the Twin Cities seemed to symbolize the promise of America, a new world where new cities sprang from the wilderness in the course of a few years. Immigrants whose previous urban lives were led in the shadows of Kristiania's Akershus Fortress or Bergen's Rosenkrantz Tower encountered in Minneapolis and St. Paul cities which a half century earlier had been dirt paths lined by ramshackle mills, taverns, and cabins. Expansion of the flour-milling and lumber industries linked by railroads to the rest of the country attracted masses of Yankees and immigrants to the young towns after the Civil War. From 2,500 persons in 1860, the population of Minneapolis soared to 13,000 in 1870, and to almost 47,000 in 1880. St. Paul experienced a parallel growth, doubling from approximately 20,000 in 1870 to 41,000 in 1880.[17] The industrializing decade of the 1880s brought even wilder expansion. By 1890 Minneapolis had some 165,000 inhabitants, while St. Paul had over 133,000. A large portion of these residents were immigrants—60,588 of the Minneapolitans and 53,177 of the St. Paulites. Over 16,000 Norwegian immigrants lived in the two cities in 1890—3,521 in St. Paul and 12,624 in Minneapolis.[18]

This was the setting for Olof Nickolaus Nelson's two-volume book, *History of the Scandinavians and Successful Scandinavians in the United States*. Published in Minneapolis between 1893 (volume I) and 1897 (volume II), the book contains nearly 300 biographies of men in the fields of business, education, law, medicine,

---

[13] *Norsk-Amerikansk Haandbog* (Chicago: John Anderson Publishing Co., 1883, 1889); *Nordisk Tidende*, Jan. 8, 1920, p. 6.

[14] Hamsun, *Cultural Life*, 6.

[15] Larson, *John A. Johnson: An Uncommon American* (Northfield: Norwegian-American Historical Association, 1969), 273.

[16] *Nordisk Tidende*, Oct. 13, 1921-June 22, 1922, p. 1. (The articles did not appear in every issue.) See also "Hvem er Hvem?" (Who's Who?), *Nordisk Tidende*, Sept. 7, 1922, p. 1.

[17] U.S., *Census*, 1870, *Population*, 1:178; 1880, *Population*, 1:538-541. Figures have been rounded off.

[18] U.S., *Census*, 1890, *Population*, 1:370, 670-671.

and politics in the Midwest. Eighty-two of the subjects were Norwegians residing in Minneapolis or St. Paul.

Although Nelson did not define precisely what he meant by "successful Scandinavians," he attempted to explain the success of the men whose stories he told through ethnological determinism. He invited his readers to recall the Vikings, whom he characterized as stubborn, firm, and determined, but courageous, honest, and hospitable. The noblest Viking trait to Nelson was a strong sense of individual self-reliance. Armed with this quality, Nelson thought, it was inevitable that those with the "Scandinavian personality" would succeed in America, a new fluid society that allowed men of good character to accomplish whatever they set out to do. Believing that Scandinavian institutional life in America was very poorly developed, Nelson concluded that "Whatever is accomplished in the political, social, or financial spheres by any Scandinavian-American, is accomplished by the individual." In other words, the successful men in his book were self-made men whose success was neither aided nor hindered by society.[19]

Most of the successful Norwegians Nelson found in Minneapolis and St. Paul could hardly be considered self-made. Nine were born in America, and 19 had emigrated at an age too early for a career. The remaining 54 had hardly begun with empty hands. Ten had had private tutoring and 17 had attended the university in Kristiania. Eleven had gone abroad—to Copenhagen, Paris, or Germany—for further education, while 12 had had professional training. While many young immigrants had benefitted from an elementary education in Norway, most did not begin the contest for success in America with the educational head start of most of Nelson's heroes.

Their previous status, education, and skills set the "successful" apart from their neighbors in the Minnesota cities. One such fortunate person was Andreas Ueland. Son of Ole Gabriel Ueland, liberal leader in the Norwegian parliament in the mid-19th century, young Ueland became a prominent lawyer and judge in Minneapolis. K. Kortgaard from the Hamar region had a wealthy father who "gave his son a liberal education." He had been sent to Fredrikstad to learn the lumber business, to England to learn the English language, and to Germany and Holland to learn business practices. Shortly after arriving in Minneapolis, he became a banker, city official, and consul for Portugal. John H. Field brought a commercial education and business experience with him from Kristiania. Arriving in Minne-

apolis during the boom period of the 1880s, he "at once found employment in Scandia Bank." Within ten years he was a bank president and prominent citizen.[20]

Occasionally individuals appeared who, from the information available, seemed to have been self-made men. Banker A. C. Haugan was "accustomed from childhood to hard labor" on a farm near Trondheim. "Haugan had not enjoyed the advantages of an extensive education," Nelson reported, "but, being diligent and energetic, it was his ambition to enter upon a business career." From his start as a common laborer in a Minneapolis lumberyard, Haugan somehow rose to become a proprietor of a grocery store, member of the city council, and president of a local bank. Here, indeed, was the dream of America. The biography of attorney Henry J. Gjertsen tells the story of a young man who left his parents' farm to study law and achieved professional and economic success. "For a young man he has come to the front rapidly," Nelson concluded.[21]

So mobility, rags-to-riches or rags-to-respectability, was possible in the maelstrom of American industrialization. But it was exceptional, even in the boom years of the new cities of the New World. Nelson's group of successful Norwegians included 14 ministers, 10 lawyers, 9 bankers, 9 doctors, 8 journalists, 5 government officials, 2 artists, 2 engineers, and 2 businessmen, as well as a dentist and an architect. By contrast, most urban immigrants did not enjoy such a high-bourgeois status. Of the 16,310 Scandinavian men in Minneapolis in 1890, only 151 were engaged in the professions, a category that included law, clergy, and medicine. The largest number, 6,382, were in domestic and personal service, a group dominated by laborers. A nearly equal number, 6,124, were engaged in the manufacturing and mechanical industries. Nelson also overlooked immigrant women. Of the 5,363 Scandinavian women counted in Minneapolis and St. Paul in 1890, a remarkably high number—3,731—were listed as "servants." Others were identified as dressmakers and laundresses. All of these people, who did not qualify for inclusion among Nelson's "successful Scandinavians," comprised the majority of the Norwegians in Minneapolis and St. Paul. They were a Norwegian-American working class.[22]

SCANDINAVIANS across America in 1890 worked in the same occupations as their countrymen in the Minnesota cities—domestic and personal service, and the manufacturing and mechanical industries. Although farming, fishing, and mining formed the largest single category of work in the census reports, more than half of all Scandinavian workers were engaged in urban or industrial labor. Of approximately a half-million total workers only 5,000 were in the professions.[23] As in the case of Minneapolis and St. Paul, it is the professional

[19] Nelson, *History of Scandinavians*, 1:19-22, 2:x.
[20] Nelson, *History of Scandinavians*, 1:624, 462, 396.
[21] Nelson, *History of Scandinavians*, 1:424, 406.
[22] U.S. *Census*, 1890, *Population*, 2:694-695.
[23] U.S., *Census*, 1890, *Population*, 2:484-489.

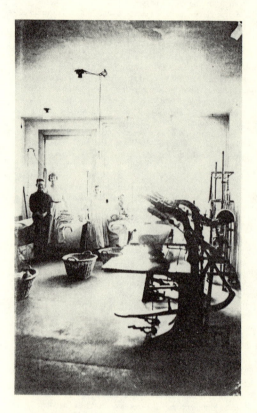

LAUNDRY workers, Minneapolis, about 1920

one percent of whom so much is known, and the huge majority about whom we know so little. Few working-class Norwegians, like their neighbors and coworkers of other ethnic groups, have had biographers and journalists to celebrate their lives and careers. They did not leave a profusion of personal papers to archives. The little that is known about their lives has been gleaned from a few letters and diaries and through a careful reading of elite writings. From these scant sources a picture of the majority immigrant experience begins to emerge.

Workers' institutions were one means of expression for the urban majority. Abandoning the ideology of

success, immigrant workers developed their own radical responses to American capitalism when they realized that their status might be permanent. There is every indication that Norwegians participated in working-class organizing. Norwegian workers, for example, were employed at the Pullman factory south of Chicago in the 1890s; unfortunately, very little is known of their role in the 1894 strike that, in drawing the battle lines between management and government on one side and industrial unionists on the other, set the pattern for industrial conflict up to World War II. In the beginning of the 20th century, such unions as the Industrial Workers of the World (IWW) and the International Seamen's Union of America included thousands of Norwegian lumbering and shipping workers. Norwegian-American labor leader Andrew Furuseth's crusade for seamen's protective legislation is well known, but the role of Norwegians in the more radical IWW is a largely unwritten chapter of American labor history.

Every city with a large Norwegian population had ethnic socialist organizations, such as Chicago's Scandinavian-American Workers' Society Karl Marx. Each major urban center also produced radical newspapers in the Norwegian language. One of the longest lived was Minneapolis' Gaa Paa (Go Forth), edited and published by Emil Lauritz Mengshoel and his wife Helle from 1903 to 1914. The role these organizations and publications played in binding Norwegians to American radicalism has yet to be analyzed adequately.[24]

When the history of Norwegian-American labor radicalism is written, it will probably be discovered that most members of the working class did not participate in the organizations. Like the American working class of which they were a part, Norwegian workers were a class on the move. A lack of residential permanence has been documented by a generation of historians studying rates of persistence—the ability of people to stay in one place from one decennial census to the next. Surveying the results of studies in over 30 cities, historian Stephan Thernstrom calculated that persistence averaged between 40 and 60 percent. In other words, roughly one-half of the people in industrializing America were on the road, without stable work or residence during any ten-year period. The image of the static small town, the timeless family farm, and the stable ur-

[24] But see Odd-Stein Granhus, "Scandinavian-American Socialist Newspapers with Emphasis on the Norwegian Contribution and E. L. Mengshoel's Gaa Paa/Folkets Røst," in Essays on the Scandinavian-North American Radical Press, 1880s-1930s, ed. Dirk Hoerder (Bremen, Germany: Labor Newspaper Preservation Project, University of Bremen, 1984), 78-99, published after this article originally went to press.

328

ban neighborhood dims in importance when confronted with these studies. American workers, Thernstrom concluded, constituted a floating proletariat.[25]

This mobility is reflected in documents from the Norwegian working class in America. The diary of an anonymous immigrant has found its way into the Norwegian-American Historical Association archives in Northfield. Throughout the second half of 1901, this unknown worker stopped to record in a small pocket notebook the events of his daily life and his reactions to the American working milieu. In search of factory work, he traveled up and down the East Coast, across New Jersey, New York, and Pennsylvania: "12 Aug. Have been around all morning, first in Elizabeth [New Jersey]; before there I went to New York and to Newark to look for work, but none was to be found. 13th [Aug.] Today I was in Brooklyn and New York, but with the same result."[26]

The search for work was the paramount concern for such immigrants as this diarist. It took precedence over family, friends, or a hospitable Norwegian *koloni* in the

decision of where to settle in America. It determined the conditions of life for the immigrant, as well as his temperament. Finding a job was a satisfying event. "Have today been to work again," the anonymous diarist penciled in his notebook on July 29, 1901. "I am now beginning to enjoy myself better in my new place." Worker J. Håland expressed a similar satisfaction in a letter home from Brooklyn in 1896: "When I have work, I'm in better humor and time goes faster."[27]

The short and precarious terms of employment the immigrant worker faced were determined not so much by his character as by the changing state of the American economy. These conditions were expressed in everyday life: strikes, conflicts with foremen, workplace conditions, health, and the seasonal nature of hiring. A good job took six days of the worker's week, occasionally seven for some factory and household workers. Largely unregulated by forces outside of the corporation, factories lacked minimal protection against accidents and health hazards. In the absence of widespread unionization and arbitration, the worker had to approach all dealings with management gingerly. "4th Sept. 1901. Began in my new job today and did pretty well with it. My foreman looks tough but was almost moderate after I understood him. Everything is of steel, so it is hard to work with, but one does what one can. The air is gruesome here in the workplace—one finds one's nose and mouth both full of slag." Accidents and poor health conditions caused workers to lose jobs,

[25] Thernstrom, *The Other Bostonians: Poverty and Progress in the American Metropolis, 1880-1970* (Cambridge, Mass.: Harvard University Press, 1973), 220-225.
[26] Anonymous diary, 1901, Norwegian-American Historical Association Archives, Northfield, (hereafter cited as Diary, NAHA).
[27] Håland to Berthe Gurine Olsen, April 6, 1896, Grimsted Letters, Aust-Agder Archives, Arendal, Norway.

PREDOMINANTLY *female textile workers at North Star Woolen Mills, Minneapolis, about 1905*

or at least miss valuable work hours while seeking medical treatment: "21st Sept. I didn't work today; laid around for most of the whole day." "28th Sept. Didn't work. Laid in most of the whole day. Everything is the same."[28]

The lives of immigrant workers were made more precarious by the seasonal nature of much of their work. Factories would be shut down during periods when orders were scarce, throwing employees back into the search for work. Unemployment insurance would not appear until the 20th century, and then slowly on a state-by-state basis. "Times are tough here," Jacob Olsen Fevig wrote to his parents from Philadelphia in April, 1896, "but it should soon get a little better when the summer sets in here."[29] Konrad Knudsen, a young construction worker in New Jersey, reflected on the impact of the seasons and the health of the economy on his work. "I have been promised several jobs, but nothing has come of them," he wrote home to the Agder region. "Here it has been a really bad winter since New Year's but I think a little work has been begun."[30] Like their countrymen in the construction trades, Norwegians in the maritime industries spent several months each year without work. For these workers, the annual cycles of hiring and laying-off meant living part of every year in poverty.

Although the seasonal idleness of the "seafolk" was considered an annual occurrence in the Brooklyn *koloni*, extended joblessness during the short depression of the early 1920s brought confusion and panic. Readers of *Nordisk Tidende* read weekly reports of life among their jobless and homeless countrymen. "There are now over 1000 jobless Scandinavian seamen in Brooklyn and New York," the paper reported in February, 1921. "Many of them have been inland for several months without being able to find work." They had spent their meager savings and there was simply no work to be had. Churches opened their doors at night and charities placed desperate advertisements in the newspapers,

asking for cast-off clothing and blankets, and beseeching the *koloni's* businessmen to create inconsequential jobs for destitute seamen.[31]

The crisis of the Brooklyn seafolk in 1920-21 underscores the position of the working people at the mercy of minor fluctuations of the immature American industrial economy. The experience of most working people did not allow them to find the kind of success Franklin and Alger promised in their books and banker Hansen and lawyer Gjertsen lived in Minneapolis. For most of those who remained in America, success probably meant mere survival, perhaps a modest home, and some savings from a secure job. If these things could be retained and passed on, the grandchildren of the Norwegian worker might advance into business and the professions. But then one must ask whether they made that kind of advancement as Norwegian Americans or as Americans.

The immigrant generation heard the promise of success touted everywhere, but the promise of failure was equally loud. "The same family that lived on two crowns a day here needs a dollar and a half a day there," Knut Hamsun told Norwegians in 1889, "and for the great majority it takes considerable doing to get hold of this dollar and a half; it really keeps you whirling to earn that money," he added.[32] Perched precariously on the edge of success or failure in the emerging industrial economy, the Norwegian-American workers were whirling continuously. They were a small and little documented part of that noisy "society in the making" that has become modern America.

---

[28] Diary, NAHA.
[29] Fevig to Ole Knudsen, April 6, 1896, Grimsted Letters.
[30] Konrad Knudsen to Ole Knudsen, April 2, 1896, Grimsted Letters.
[31] *Nordisk Tidende*, Feb. 10, 1921, p. 1.
[32] Hamsun, *Cultural Life*, 6.

ALL photographs are in the MHS audio-visual library.

GORDON W. KIRK, Jr.

CAROLYN TYIRIN KIRK

MIGRATION, MOBILITY AND THE TRANSFORMATION OF THE OCCUPATIONAL STRUCTURE IN AN IMMIGRANT COMMUNITY: HOLLAND, MICHIGAN, 1850-80

Alterations in the size and composition of a community's labor force may be viewed as the function of three factors—migration, natural or vital processes and vertical mobility. Two of these processes serve to alter the size of the labor force: net-migration—the differential between in- and out-migration—and net natural processes, that is, the balance between those entering the labor force for the first time as a result of achieving adulthood and those leaving through either death or retirement. While these processes account for changes in the size of the labor force, they also provide channels through which a community can fulfill its fluctuating occupational needs and thus transform its occupational structure. A third factor, net occupational mobility, although not affecting the size of the labor force, offers another avenue by which a community can meet its varying occupational needs and consequently is an additional source of change in the composition of the labor force.

In recent years, numerous nineteenth-century communities ranging from large urban centers to small frontier settlements have been examined to determine their patterns of occupational mobility and/or persistence. While these studies have greatly expanded our understanding of the American social order, they have left questions unanswered. In particular, little effort has been made to gauge systematically the effects of migration and occupational mobility on the occupational structure of these communities, and the impact of net natural processes has been totally ignored. In other words, a key question involves the relationship among these three processes in meeting the occupational needs of a community and thus transforming its structure.[1] Moreover, it is still unresolved whether persistence or migration was the more viable avenue for upward mobility in the nineteenth century. Did those who migrate tend to be more occupationally mobile than those who did not? The following examination of the impact of migration, occupational mobility and natural processes will indicate the relative importance of these processes in transforming the occupational structure in one nineteenth-century community. The further analysis of both the sources of increase in various occupational groups and the occupational characteristics of in- and

Gordon Kirk is in the history department of Western Illinois University; Carolyn Tyirin Kirk is in the sociology department of Monmouth College and a graduate student in sociology at Michigan State University.

out-migrants will help to answer the question of whether persistence or migration was the more viable avenue for upward mobility.[2] Finally, this type of study will aid scholars and readers, in determining to what extent findings of occupational mobility studies based on city directories and census manuscripts may either inflate or underestimate actual rates of vertical mobility.

Unit of Analysis

The community chosen for this case study is Holland, Michigan, from 1850 to 1880. This area differs from those communities whose patterns of persistence and occupational mobility have been examined heretofore. Unlike both the ethnically heterogeneous large and medium sized cities of the North and South and other rural communities of the Middle West that have been studied, Holland was an ethnically homogeneous frontier settlement that increasingly came to rely upon light industry rather than agriculture. The importance of this type of community in one respect has been underscored by Page Smith who delineates two major types of towns historically: those that were the result of no prior planning and those that were colonized by relatively homogeneous ethnic and religious groups. Although largely ignored, this second type of community, Smith argues, was far more numerous and important than is commonly assumed.[3]

The Holland community, a western Michigan settlement, was founded in 1847 by a group of Dutch immigrants, primarily Seceders from the State Church in the Netherlands who sought to establish a homogeneous Christian community. Although religious considerations served as the primary organizing mechanism for the settlement, economic conditions in the Netherlands provided the major impetus for migration. The origins of the Holland community can be traced to the depression of the early 1840s in the Netherlands when two Secessionist ministers, Antonie Brummelkamp and Albertus C. Van Raalte, organized a group to emigrate to Java and, upon being refused permission by the Dutch government, changed their destination to the United States. After a trip to America during which he selected the Holland site, Van Raalte brought the first group of settlers in 1847. In order to promote a strong Christian community, others were encouraged to migrate, and a number of groups, frequently led by Secessionist clergymen, soon followed.[4]

By 1880 the population of the Holland community had grown to 8,399, over four and one-half times larger than in 1850 (see Table 1). The settlement included Holland township, the city of Holland, Zeeland township and the village of Zeeland (a part of the latter township). The expansion of the population, although almost four-fold, can be divided into two periods: very rapid growth characterized the period to 1870 while the next decade witnessed a more modest growth rate. At the same time more concentrated centers were established. In 1867 the city of Holland was incorporated and by 1880 the village of Zeeland was noted in the census. A comparison of the three major divisions indicate, however, that the city of Holland expanded at a lower rate than the two townships in the 1870s although by 1890, ten years beyond this study, the population of the townships increased only slightly while the city began a period of rapid expansion.

Table 1—Population growth of
the Holland Community, 1850-90.

	City* of Holland	Zeeland† Township	Holland Township	Total Holland Community
1850:				
Population			1,829	1,829
1860:				
Population		1,466	1,891	3,357
Percentage Increase			3.4	83.6
1870:				
Population	2,319	2,343	2,353	7,015
Percentage Increase		59.8	24.4	108.9
1880:				
Population	2,620	2,715	3,064	8,399
		(484)**		
Percentage Increase	13.0	15.9	30.2	19.7
1890:				
Population	3,945	2,834	3,086	9,865
		(785)**		
Percentage Increase	50.6	4.4	0.7	17.5

*The city of Holland was incorporated in 1867.
†Zeeland township became legally separated from Holland township in 1851.
**Zeeland village; also included in totals for Zeeland township.

While experiencing rapid population growth, the Holland community underwent even greater economic development in the years from 1850 to 1880. During this period both the industrial and the agricultural sectors grew much more rapidly than the population. There were, however, differences in the two sectors—specifically, the agricultural sector of the community's economy grew much more rapidly before 1870 than in the decade following, as indicated by data supplied in the state of Michigan censuses relating to amount of improved acreage and crop production. In contrast, the industrial sector grew more rapidly than agriculture throughout the period with its highest rate of per capita growth coming in the 1870s. Not only did the industrial sector grow rapidly, but also manufacturing gradually turned from the processing of natural resources and agricultural products for local consumption to producing more goods for export from the community. In the first two decades under consideration the milling of lumber and grain dominated the community's industrial activity. Although milling remained important and the area maintained various farm-related industries, e.g., wagon-making, cooperage, harness-making, etc., for local rural consumption, industries producing goods for local non-farm residents and for export became increasingly important. Food processing firms—other than grain mills which continued to increase—including several meat packing firms, a cheese and butter factory and a bread factory were established while leather processing came to dominate the economy. By 1880 the tanneries of the community had a combined total product of $621,795 accounting for almost 60 percent of all industrial output, the bulk of which found markets outside the community.[5]

These economic developments produced major alterations in the occupational structure of the community. The proportion of people directly involved in agriculture as either farm operators or rural workers declined (see Table 2). In 1850, the federal census placed 45.9 percent in farm occupations. This appears to be a very low estimate of the actual number involved since the vast majority of the 35.6 percent of the labor force classified as laborers in 1850 more than likely worked in agriculture. At this time the primitive state of the community's industry limited employment possibilities for this unskilled labor group to agriculture, where they performed such menial work as clearing land and tilling the soil for other farmers. Assuming that most of those enumerated as laborers in 1850 were actually involved in some type of agricultural pursuit, changes in the community's occupational structure indicate a marked trend away from agricultural employment. The proportion of the labor force involved in farming declined from slightly over 70 percent in 1860 to slightly more than 50 percent in both 1870 and 1880.

Methodology

Data for this study are drawn from the manuscripts of the federal census from 1850 to 1880. These records contain the name, age, birthplace and occupation of everyone in the community as well as listing those who were retired. Included in the 1850 enumeration of Holland was territory that would eventually become Zeeland Township (1851) and the city of Holland (1867). Thus, this study of the Holland community includes all members of the male labor force of the city of Holland, Zeeland Township and Holland Township.

The first step in setting up this study was to develop a two-page "questionnaire" for all members of the male labor force that would encompass all relevant data from the census manuscripts such as name, birthplace, occupation, wife's and children's names and birthplaces and ages of all household members which were converted to birth dates for convenience.[6] Then two major comparative methods were employed to link individuals both intra- and inter-generationally. First, after recording all data

Table 2—Changing Occupational Structure
of the Holland Community, 1850-80.

Occupation	1850 No.	1850 %	1860 No.	1860 %	1870 No.	1870 %	1880 No.	1880 %
White-Collar Workers	23	4.2	67	6.5	204	13.5	316	14.9
Professional	10	1.8	20	1.9	36	2.4	64	3.0
Big Businessmen*	1	0.2	7	0.7	34	2.2	44	2.1
Small Businessmen†	11	2.0	29	2.8	111	7.3	150	7.1
Clerical & Sales	1	0.2	11	1.1	23	1.5	58	2.7
Blue-Collar Workers	281	50.0	234	22.7	511	33.8	678	32.0
Skilled Workers	80	14.2	125	12.1	208	13.7	275	13.0
Semiskilled Workers	1	0.2	36	3.5	99	6.5	288	13.6
Unskilled Workers	200	35.6	73	7.1	204	13.5	115	5.4
Farmers	50	8.8	321	31.1	649	42.9	690	32.6
Over $5,000	0	0.0	0	0.0	26	1.7	61	2.9
$1,001-$5,000	8	1.4	115	11.2	416	27.5	462	21.8
$501-$1,000	8	1.4	133	12.9	156	10.3	129	6.1
Under $500	34	6.0	73	7.1	51	3.4	38	1.8
Rural Workers	208	37.1	409	39.6	149	9.8	432	20.4
Gardeners	2	0.4	8	0.8	7	0.5	5	0.2
Tenants & Sharecroppers**	0	0.0	0	0.0	0	0.0	19	0.9
Farmers Without Farms	195	34.7	277	26.9	89	5.9	172	8.1
Farm Laborers	11	2.0	124	12.0	53	3.5	236	11.2
Total	562	100.1	1,031	99.9	1,513	100.0	2,116	99.9

*This category includes businessmen listed in the industrial census as being the owner or partner in a concern with a capitalization in excess of $1,000.

†This category includes all those listed in the general census as public officials, merchants, proprietors, and managers, and who are not listed in the industrial census as being the owner or partner in a concern with a capitalization of $1,000 or more.

**None listed in either the census of 1850 or 1860.

Source: Manuscripts of the Seventh Census of the United States, 1850: Population of the United States; Manuscripts of the Eighth Census of the United States, 1860: Population of the United States; Manuscripts of the Ninth Census of the United States, 1870: Population of the United States; Manuscripts of the Tenth Census of the United States, 1880: Population of the United States; (Microfilmed), Michigan State Library.

from each of the censuses from 1850 to 1880, the forms were put in alphabetical order by census years in preparation for matching both individuals and fathers with sons. In order to solve the problem of surname variations encountered in this process, a list of such variations was compiled to serve as a guide (i.e., Dykema and Diekema). Furthermore, to confirm matches, name, birthdate and birthplace of both those in the labor force and all members of their families were checked. For sons who left home during the decade, the problem of linkage was more difficult. Matching these individuals with their fathers was accomplished by keeping a record of the last census a son lived at home and then searching the following census to see if he was listed. Age was the major determinant for distinguishing between similar names. Part of the problem of tracing sons was alleviated since they often continued to live with their parents after entering the labor force. Furthermore, sons who left home to raise a family frequently named their first-born after the mother or father. Lastly, many of those who left home set up their new residences next door to their parents.

The second comparison utilized the "addresses" of the residents. Each census taker numbered each household in order of enumeration. This information made it possible to make additional linkages by retracing the census takers' tracks. For example, all those linked between 1850 and 1860 were listed numerically by their 1860 number while all those listed in 1850 only and 1860 only were arranged in two other files by their respective enumeration numbers. When a pattern was found for a section of the 1850-60 linked names between routes taken by the two census takers—for example, numbers 576-90 in 1850 corresponded closely to numbers 248-234 in Zeeland Township in 1860—gaps within that range would be checked in the 1850-only and 1860-only files to determine if another linkage could be made at that "address." As in the first method involving only names, family information was utilized here. Both types of comparisons were done several times in order to make as many matches as possible. There were a few cases, however, in which linkages seemed possible but dubious; in these cases the two forms were not matched. The number of such cases, however, was extremely small and does not affect the general patterns found.[7]

By tracing the careers of all these individuals through the federal censuses, it is possible to determine rates of net occupational mobility, net natural processes and in-, and out- and net-migration. The rate of net occupational mobility for each occupational classification is obtained by subtracting the number of occupationally mobile out of that category from the number of occupationally mobile into that category and dividing the result by the total number in that category at the end of the decade.

Rates of net natural processes for this study are determined by the following procedures.[8] In addition to tracing the careers of all adult males, the father's name (where applicable) has also been recorded which makes it possible to determine the number of new entrants into the labor force as a result of achieving adulthood. A new entrant is one whose father was listed in a census preceding one in which the son is listed as having an occupation. Data on death rates are based on estimates derived from the manuscripts of the federal census reporting social statistics, which list all who die during the census year. Thus, the deaths in the labor force have been estimated for a given decade by dividing the number of deaths reported in both the census immediately preceding that decade and the census concluding that decade by two. The resulting figure multiplied by ten gives an estimate of the number who died in a decade. Furthermore, for part of the analysis the total estimated number of deaths has been apportioned among the occupations within the labor force using the occupational distribution existing at the beginning of the decade. Net natural processes has been calculated by subtracting the estimated number of deaths and those listed as retired for the first time from the total number of new entrants into the labor force. This procedure may overestimate the number of deaths since it includes newcomers who died in the decade of their in-migration. In addition, it assumes that the census years are representative of other years in a given decade. Because no other data on deaths exist, such a procedure is necessary; evidence from the community found in local histories, memoirs and newspapers, moreover, does not indicate that the years between censuses exhibited extremely high or low death rates.

Number of out-migrants has been determined by subtracting the estimated number of deaths from the number appearing at the beginning of a decade but not present at the end of the decade. Likewise, subtracting the number of new entrants from the number not present at the beginning of a decade but enumerated in the following census indicates the number of in-migrants. Net-migration represents the differential between in- and out-migration. For part of the analysis similar calculations have been made for each occupational group in the Holland community. The figures resulting from these procedures serve as the basis for calculating various rates of migration.

Growth of the Labor Force

The thirty-year period between 1850 and 1880 witnessed a spectacular expansion of the Holland community's labor force as the number of employed males increased almost four-fold, jumping from 562 to 2,116 (see Table 3). A net gain of this magnitude, moreover, involved a turnover of more than 4,000 people based on decennial census data.[9] Accounting for almost 85 percent of the increase, net-migration was the most important source of increase in the size of the labor force. By contrast, net natural forces represented only 15 percent of the expansion in the labor supply.

Although migration by far supplied the largest proportion of the gain in the number of employed males in this thirty-year period, its influence waned after 1870. In the two decades prior to this date, combined gains through net-migration not only equalled total increments in the labor force but also offset losses resulting from the deficit through net natural processes. In the 1850s, net gains from migration numbered 443 while similar increases from natural forces totaled only 26, and the following decade saw gains through net-migration exceed the expansion of the labor force by 37.

With increases through net natural processes exercising a more positive role in the growth of the labor force than before, the 1870s marked a turning point in the migration history of the community. The differential between new adults entering the labor force and those leaving through either death or retirement constituted 246 persons or about 40 percent of the total expansion of the labor force. By contrast, increases emanating from migration, although continuing to be the largest source of change, were relatively less important than earlier. In this decade, expansion due to net-migration decreased in absolute terms from 519 the previous decade to 357 and in relative terms from over 100 percent to just under 60 percent of the total increase.

Table 3—Sources of Increase in the Labor Force
of the Holland Community, 1850-80

	1850-1860	1860-1870	1870-1880	Total
In-Migration	590	814	823	2,227
Out-Migration	147	295	466	908
Net-Migration	443	519	357	1,319
New Adults	104	77	492	673
Deaths	75	105	210	390
Retirement	3	9	36	48
Net Natural Processes	26	−37	246	235
Total	469	482	603	1,554
Net-Migrations % of Increase	94.5	107.7	59.2	84.9
Net Natural Processes % of Increase	5.5	−7.7	40.8	15.1

Changes in the Composition of the Labor Force

Although net-migration rather than net natural processes most fully explains gains in the size of the labor force, an analysis of the changing composition of the occupational structure must also consider internal changes resulting from occupational movement. That is, one may have a situation where net-migration greatly enlarges the size of the labor force but where new occupational needs are met by members of the existing community as a result of either occupational mobility or new adults entering the labor force.

From a different perspective. every community has its occupational needs. The degree to which newly created occupational openings are not filled through net occupational mobility and net natural processes represents the failure of a community to meet its occupational needs internally and is manifested by changes resulting from net-migration. That is, to the extent that a community cannot satisfy its own demands, it must meet them by attracting a sufficient number of migrants who possess the needed occupational skills. Likewise, those members of the labor force who fail to adjust to the changes in the economy may have to leave the community and go elsewhere in search of employment.

The role of these processes in altering the occupational structure of the Holland community varied from decade to decade as well as among occupational groups. In spite of these fluctuations, net-migration was the most dynamic element in altering the composition of the labor force. Out of twelve cases, drawn from four broad occupational groups over three decades, net-migration accounted for the greatest change in size seven times between 1850 and 1880 (see Table 4). Net occupational mobility, by contrast, was the major source of change in two occupational groups in the 1850s and one in the 1860s, and net natural processes was the most dynamic force in two groups in the 1870s.

More specifically, within the urban labor force, net-migration played a more important role than the other two processes in supplying increases to blue-collar positions. In every decade it provided the main source of growth to this category representing at least 20 percent of this group. In contrast, net occupational mobility made negative contributions to the blue-collar group in every decade and only in the 1870s did net natural processes yield an increase.

Gains among white-collar workers due to net-migration were relatively less important. Although increases to the white-collar labor force from net-migration in the first two decades under consideration exceeded those provided by the other two sources of change, the magnitude of these differences failed to equal similar differentials in the blue-collar category in all three decades. Such increases, representing over half of the white-collar workers in 1860, fell to almost 13 percent by 1880. On the other hand, growth from the two internal processes (net occupational mobility and net natural processes) became increasingly important, and by the 1870s their combined contribution provided the major source of expansion within the white-collar group. These developments in the white-collar group, furthermore, were a result not only of the decrease in net-migration but also of an increase due to net natural processes from 0.0 to 13.9 percent between 1860 and 1880, which more than offset the decline in the net occupational mobility rate from close to 20 percent in the 1850s and 1860s to just under 8 percent in the 1870s. Thus, net-migration, insofar as it fulfilled the changing occupational needs of the non-agricultural labor force, tended to be relatively more important in the least economically desirable positions.

Similarly, net-migration tended to supply a disproportionately larger increase or smaller decrease to the economically less prestigious agricultural category. That is, the difference between net-migration and the two internal processes combined was more positive for the rural workers group than for the farm operator category except for the period of the 1870s, when net natural processes became the largest contributor to change in the rural workers category. Subtracting the combined contribution of the internal processes from that of net-migration for the farm operators group yields differences of -11.5, 12.7, and 19.5 percent for the 1850s, 1860s and 1870s respectively. Similar calculations for the rural workers category provide figures of 55.0, 75.2, and -26.1 percent for the same three decades.

Despite this similarity in the role of net-migration, changes in the composition of the agricultural labor force deviated in a number of respects

Table 4—Components of Change in the Labor Force
of the Holland Community
Based on Broad Occupational Categories
by Decades, 1850-80.*

Occupation	Net-Migration		Net Occupational Mobility		Net Natural Processes	
	No.	%	No.	%	No.	%
1850-60†						
White-Collar	31	52.2	13	19.4	0	0.0
Blue-Collar	82	35.0	−104	−44.4	−25	−10.7
Farm Operators	117	36.4	150	46.7	4	1.2
Rural Workers	213	52.1	−59	−14.4	47	11.5
1860-70						
White-Collar	91	44.6	40	19.6	6	2.9
Blue-Collar	300	58.7	−17	−3.3	−6	−1.2
Farm Operators	202	31.1	141	21.7	−15	−2.3
Rural Workers	−74	−49.7	−164	−110.1	−22	−14.8
1870-80						
White-Collar	43	13.6	25	7.9	44	13.9
Blue-Collar	138	20.4	−36	−5.3	65	9.6
Farm Operators	91	13.2	16	2.3	−66	−9.6
Rural Workers	85	19.7	−5	−1.2	203	47.0

*See Appendix I for a more detailed breakdown by occupation.
†All percentages based on the size of the labor force at the end of each decade.

from the patterns delineated in the examination of urban occupations. As in white-collar positions, the proportion of farm operators due to either net-migration or net occupational mobility declined. In contrast to the white-collar positions, net occupational mobility showed the steepest decline, and net natural processes declined rather than increased.

Even though net-migration made a more positive contribution to the rural workers group than did the two internal processes combined during the first two decades, an analysis of all three components taken separately reveals a somewhat different pattern. In the 1850s, the three components of change played the same relative role in the rural workers category as they did in the blue-collar category throughout the entire period. In addition, net occupational mobility had the greatest negative effect on the rural workers group in every decade. In contrast to the blue-collar category, however, after 1860 net natural processes was the most positive factor and net-migration followed a middle path between the other two forces in altering the composition of the rural workers category.

The different patterns of change exhibited by the agricultural labor force could have been due to its decline in relative terms. Within the farm operators category, all three components came to play increasingly diminishing roles in increasing the size of this group. This indicates that entrance into the farm operators category was becoming more restrictive over time to new adults, newcomers and members of other occupational groups alike. In the 1870s, such a trend corresponds to a decrease in the proportion of farm operators in the labor force although the wealthiest sub-category continued to increase proportionately. This suggests that perhaps it became less feasible to subsist as a small farm operator. It also points to the possibility that land (particularly good farm land) became increasingly scarce as a result of population growth and thus made it more difficult for those outside of the farm operator category to gain entrance into that group. Such explanations may also account for the patterns of change among rural workers where net occupational mobility made the greatest negative or the least positive contribution (1870s), and net natural processes increasingly made the most positive contribution. Such trends reflect the fact that a large proportion of rural workers were farmers' sons who would ultimately take over all or part of the family farm.[10]

Patterns of In- and Out-migration

The ease with which changes in the size and composition of the labor force resulting from migration can be sketched obscures the complexity of this process. That the net-gain of 1,319 working males between 1850 and 1880 involved the movement of over 3,000 people, a figure one and one-half times the size of the labor force in 1880, indicates that migration is an extremely complex phenomenon having a greater impact on a community than is expressed by its net contribution to the growth of the labor force. Thus a clearer understanding of the relationship between migration and occupational mobility requires a detailed examination of both in- and out-migration by occupational groups. In the following analysis, percentage rates of in- and net-migration will be based on the size of the labor force in the last year of the decade and out-migration rates will be based on the size of the labor force at the beginning of the decade.

During the years under consideration rates of out-migration remained relatively constant, rising only about 2 percent per decade from 26 to 31 percent. By contrast, rates of in-migration varied more and decreased steadily from 57 to 39 percent between 1850 and 1880 (see Table 5). Given the constancy of out-migration rates, this also means that net-migration varied widely and declined. Thus, during these years Holland experienced substantial population turnover, in every decade between one-fourth and one-third of the male adult labor force departed and an even larger number of newcomers entered the labor force.

More important for an understanding of the relationship between migration and the occupational structure is the fact that these gross changes in the in- and out-migration rates camouflage wide variations among occupational groups. That is, not only did the Holland community experience substantial population turnover, but also patterns of in- and out-migration tended to be related to occupational class. In general, rates of both in- and out-migration were highest in the less economically remunerative positions.

Table 5—Migration Rates for the Holland Community
Based on Broad Occupational Categories
by Decade, 1850-80.*

Occupation	In-Migration No.	%	Out-Migration No.	%	Net-Migration No.	%
1850-60	590	57.2	147	26.2	443	43.0
White-Collar	40	59.7	9	39.1	31	49.2
Blue-Collar	166	70.9	84	29.1	82	35.0
Farm Operators	128	39.9	11	22.0	117	36.4
Rural Workers	256	62.6	43	20.7	213	52.1
1860-70	814	53.8	295	28.7	519	34.3
White-Collar	109	53.4	18	26.9	91	44.6
Blue-Collar	381	74.6	81	34.6	300	58.7
Farm Operators	241	37.1	39	12.1	202	31.1
Rural Workers	83	55.7	157	38.4	−74	−49.7
1870-80	823	38.9	466	30.8	357	16.9
White-Collar	113	35.8	70	34.3	43	13.6
Blue-Collar	366	54.0	228	44.6	138	20.4
Farm Operators	183	26.5	92	14.2	91	13.2
Rural Workers	161	37.3	76	51.0	85	19.7

*See Appendix II for a more detailed breakdown by occupation.

With the exception of the 1850s, the highest rates of out-migration occurred at the bottom of the occupational structure. In this first decade, little variation existed between occupational groups. Excluding the sales and clerical group and gardeners (who numbered three people in 1850), only the out-migration rate of 60 percent for professionals deviated by more than 8 percent from the community average of 25 percent.

In contrast to the 1850s, rates of departure in the two succeeding decades corresponded closely to occupational levels. Out-migration rates for rural workers in both decades were more than three times greater than those for farm operators. Moreover, none of the rates for specific occupations within the farm operators category approached those for any occupational group within the rural workers classification. A similar pattern prevailed for non-agricultural occupational groups. Although in the first decade white-collar rates of departure exceeded by 10 percent those for blue-collar workers, the following two decades found the pattern reversed, with blue-collar rates being 7 and 10 percent higher respectively.

While patterns of departure were similar for both the agricultural and urban labor forces, the differential in out-migration rates between farm operators and rural workers far exceeded the differential between white- and blue-collar workers. One explanation for these developments might be that as the community's occupational needs changed as a result of the economy's greater reliance on light industry rather than agriculture there was a greater scarcity of economic resources for those at the bottom of the agricultural labor force than for blue-collar workers. That is, between 1860 and 1870 the absolute number of rural workers declined. The increase in the absolute number in the 1870s, furthermore, coincided both with a decrease in small yeoman farmers and an increase in large farm operators, suggesting that small farms were becoming less feasible while positions working for large farm operators, although presenting little opportunity for advancement into the farm operator category, were becoming more numerous. That out-migration rates were highest among rural workers in both the 1860s and 1870s further supports this view.

Even more evident than patterns of out-migration, rates of in-migration tended to be highest in positions at the bottom of the occupational ladder. Within the agricultural labor force, migration into the rural workers category surpassed that for the farm operators category by at least 10 percent in all three decades. Perhaps more indicative of this pattern is the fact that in only one decade, the 1870s, did in-migration account for more than 10 percent of the wealthiest farm operator group. On the other hand, in only one decade did in-migration equal less than 50 percent of the farm laborer group. A similar pattern existed among non-agricultural occupations; in every decade, rates of in-migration into blue-collar occupations exceeded by at least 10 percent those into white-collar groups. Furthermore, higher rates of in-migration prevailed for white-collar workers than for farm operators and for blue-collar workers than for rural workers. Finally, in-migration rates for white-collar workers ranged within 3 percent of the rates for rural workers over the three decades.

Such findings concerning in-migration further support our suggested explanation for higher out-migration rates for agricultural workers. Though there was absolute growth throughout the period within all four broad occupational groups, farm operator positions were declining proportionately resulting in less potential security or advancement within the agricultural labor force. This, in turn, induced greater out-migration and less in-migration within that sector than within the non-agricultural sector. Such an explanation appears to contradict the work of both Morrison and Lowry who argue that in-migration rates correspond to local economic conditions while out-migration rates do not. Their studies, however, examine the overall in- and out-migration rates for a community and not groups within the community. Our data indicate, however, that the two rates vary widely between occupational categories and that the best possible explanation at this time appears to be that out-migration rates as well as in-migration rates reflect changes in the local economy and corresponding changes in the structure of the work force.[11]

Although few detailed community studies of in- and out-migration exist, there are a number of investigations of decennial rates of persistence denoting what proportion of male adults present at the beginning of a decade remain throughout the ten-year period. In order to facilitate comparisons with these studies (which did not distinguish between internal losses through death and external losses through migration), the persistence rates were computed for Holland by adding the estimated number of deaths and out-migrants together and then subtracting the result from the total labor force population at the beginning of the decade.

The persistence rates in Holland for the three decades between 1850 and 1880 of 61, 61 and 55 percent respectively are comparable to other findings and, if anything, tend toward the high side. More specifically, comparison with Stephan Thernstrom's compilation of persistence rates for selected urban areas between 1800 and 1958 indicates that the Holland community did not differ significantly from these communities. In more than three-quarters (24 of 31) of the cases he listed, persistence rates were between 40 and 60 percent. It should be further noted that Thernstrom found that persistence rates did not vary over time, among types of cities or among cities experiencing different growth rates.[12]

These patterns of persistence held not only for most cities in the last century and two-thirds but also for rural communities. In only 8 of the 26 communities included in the compilation did persistence rates fall outside of the 40 to 60 percent range; furthermore, communities in the early years of settlement accounted for 7 of the 8 deviant cases. In these settlements no more than a third of the adult males remained more than a decade. After this initial period of extreme fluidity, however, rural persistence rates approached the general level of those in cities.[13]

The magnitude of the difference between the persistence rates for the Holland community during its first two decades and these other new rural settlements suggests a more complex explanation than mere chance. One possible explanation is that rapidly growing areas would be more likely to keep their existing population. A comparison of population growth rates between Holland and three other settlements for which data are readily available from the U.S. Census does not indicate that this is a valid explanation. Both Wapello County, Iowa, and selected townships in eastern Kansas had growth rates about 15 percent below Holland's 84 percent. The population of Trempealeau County, however, increased over four-fold in its first decade. Thus, high persistence does not appear to be a correlate of rapid population growth in new settlements.[14]

A second possible explanation for the high persistence rates in the Holland community is that opportunity for advancement was greater there than in any of these other settlements. That is, it might be assumed that a community offering high levels of occupational mobility would be better able to retain its population than one that did not. Unfortunately data on occupational mobility exist only for Trempealeau County and Holland, making any conclusions regarding this relationship only suggestive. The existing data do indicate that greater opportunity for occupational mobility existed in Holland than in Trempealeau County—rates of total and upward occupational mobility during the first decade of their existence were 64 and 33 percent respectively in the former and 43 and 21 percent in the latter settlement. Such findings, although tentative at best, suggest that social scientists should look more fully at the relationship between vertical and geographic mobility in the nineteenth century.[15]

Another possible explanation is based on cultural and organizational factors. The founders of the Holland area sought to establish a homogeneous Christian community. As a result, it may be that the advance planning of the community along with its ethnic homogeneity and religious commitment offered an element of population stability in the early years that was not existent in these other settlements. That the persistence rate for the Dutch-born population in the 1870s was almost double that of the non-Dutch native born population (57 to 31 percent) further underscores the importance of these factors in explaining the settlement's high persistence rates during its early years. Similarly, those born in the United States of Dutch parentage had almost as high a persistence rate (56 percent) as the Dutch-born even though most were under 30—an age group generally found to be the most geographically mobile. It should be noted, however, that this type of stability did not exist in cities where ethnically homogeneous communities formed without prior planning or commitment.[16]

Although any explanation at this point must remain tentative, the data indicate that the population growth rate in new settlements is not a determinant of persistence. On the other hand, occupational mobility and ethnic homogeneity do seem to be related to persistence in new settlements. Based on the internal evidence from Holland on the differing persistence rates of the Dutch and the non-Dutch, an explanation based on cultural and organizational factors in new communities is indicated. But this explanation must remain only suggestive until further studies are undertaken which explicitly explore the degree of ethnic and religious homogeneity and the organizational nature of settlements at their foundings. While favoring this argument, we neither reject the possibility of a relationship between opportunity and persistence nor rule out an explanation based on a combination of both organizational factors and opportunity. In order to test the relationship between occupational mobility and persistence in new settlements, moreover, attention should focus on what skills are being favored in occupational mobility and the extent to which the existing population possesses those skills or can acquire them readily.

It is impossible, furthermore, to understand fully the relationship between occupational mobility and persistence and the effect of cultural and organizational factors on it unless out-migration is separated from deaths. That is, studies of persistence assume implicitly that the age structure and the death rate remain constant both within all ethnic segments of a community and between communities. This leads to a further assumption that the out-migration rate encompasses approximately the same proportion of the persistence rate's residual, i.e., out-migration equals persistence rate minus a constant. Thus, studies more sensitive to the death rate will facilitate more meaningful comparisons of differing rates of persistence.

More important for an understanding of the relationship between migration and labor force composition is the fact that the type of men who were most transient in Holland were also the most transient in other nineteenth-century American communities. In the Holland settlement, in- and out-migration rates were higher for blue- than white-collar workers and for rural workers than farm operators. Similarly, Thernstrom found that in the ten available tabulations for selected nineteenth- and early twentieth-century cities, blue-collar workers had lower rates of persistence than white-collar employees.[17] In addition, a recalculation of the available data pertaining to persistence in three rural communities indicates that similar patterns of turnover existed in these areas (see Table 6). In every case, persistence rates for farm operators surpassed those of rural workers and those for white-collar workers either exceeded or equaled the rates for blue-collar workers. Thus the selective pattern of out-migration found in Holland occurred in other nineteenth-century communities for which data are available.

Although some studies of persistence exist, no systematic examinations of in-migration are available for the nineteenth century. As a result, it is not possible to determine to what extent the pattern of higher in-migration rates for the less economically prestigious categories in Holland is typical. In the absence of studies to the contrary and given the fact that patterns of out-migration in Holland did not deviate from those of other nineteenth-century communities, there is no reason to suspect that the selective nature of migration into the settlement was unique.

Table 6—Rates of Persistence by Occupation for Selected Rural Communities.

Name of Settlement	Decade	Farm Operators	Rural Workers	White-Collar	Blue-Collar
Crawford Township	1850-60	24	4	n.a.	n.a.
Crawford Township	1860-70	40	3	n.a.	n.a.
Trempealeau County	1860-70	32	24	33	19
Trempealeau County	1870-80	39	22	25	25
Wapello County	1850-60	46	20	30	18

Source: William L. Bowers, "Crawford Township, 1850-70; A study of a Pioneer Community," *Iowa Journal of History*, LVIII (January, 1960), 8-10; Curti, 140-258; Throne, 305-30. (Percentages computed by the authors).

Migration and Occupational Mobility

The results of this case study have broader implications for both the nature and study of occupational mobility. If widespread in nineteenth-century America, the tendency of those at the bottom of the occupational ladder to be the most transient as well as the tendency for net-migration to supply disproportionate increases to less prosperous occupations while internal processes disproportionately increased the more prosperous groups implies that the geographically mobile tended to experience less upward vertical movement than those remaining in a settlement. That is, the nineteenth-century man on the move, unlike his twentieth-century counterpart, cannot be equated with the successful man on the make.[18]

These findings also suggest that studies of occupational mobility in any community are dealing with an unrepresentative sample skewed toward the most occupationally mobile. Thus, any analysis of nineteenth-century mobility based on data drawn from city directories or census manuscripts will inflate upward mobility rates. The degree of inflation, however, is open and will likely remain so for a long time since it is virtually impossible to examine directly the relationship between geographical and occupational mobility due to the difficulty in tracing large numbers of individuals from place to place through the manuscripts of the federal censuses. Only after migration and occupational mobility have been studied in a number of different types of communities can social scientists begin to make more precise inferences about the relationship between migration, persistence and vertical mobility.

Although the evidence for Holland indicates that migration may not have served as viable an avenue for upward mobility as persistence, it is possible that rates of net-migration and occupational mobility are still related. That is, it might be expected that net-migration would be greatest in those communities having the highest rates of vertical mobility. Data for Holland tend to support this generalization. Both rates of net-migration and upward occupational mobility steadily fell in the three decades between 1850 and 1880, the former dropping from 43 to 17 percent and the latter decreasing from 33 to 7 percent. Likewise, gross rates of occupational mobility fell from 64 to 21 percent.[19]

Because little systematic analysis of the relationship between occupational mobility and net-migration has been conducted, generalizations regarding the relationship of these two variables remain tentative. The only comparable study is Sidney Goldstein's examination of Norristown from 1910 to 1950 where he found (in contrast to Holland) that both gross and upward occupational mobility tended to increase as net-migration decreased. From these findings he argues that vertical mobility and migration complement each other in serving to meet the needs of an economy and in bringing about change in the occupational structure.[20]

The contradictory findings between the two studies suggest that the relationship between migration and occupational mobility is more complex than Goldstein suggests and involves other factors affecting both variables. For example, Goldstein's model ignores the impact of net natural processes on altering the size and composition of a labor force. A sudden increase from this process, assuming the occupational needs of a community remained constant, would certainly bring about a decrease in net-migration and potentially a decrease in occupational mobility. Also, the model assumes that occupational mobility is totally structurally induced; however, data indicate that only about half the rate of occupational mobility can be attributed to structural changes in the labor force.[21] Finally, implicit in the model is the idea that an increase in the labor force size will only affect the net-migration rate. However, where both the size of the labor force is increasing and especially where positions at the upper levels of the occupational hierarchy are expanding, it would be expected that both net-migration and occupational mobility would increase.

The findings from this study suggest that while certain relationships hold both in the nineteenth and twentieth centuries, others vary—implying that the relationships among structure and size of labor force, vertical mobility, migration, persistence and natural processes may depend on the historical period or period of economic development involved. They further suggest that some of the relationships generally posited between only two or three of these variables are but special cases of a process involving various factors interacting in a complex manner.

In addition, the findings regarding both the low economic status of migrants and the lack of a positive relationship between geographic mobility and upward vertical mobility in the nineteenth century and the contrary findings of Blau and Duncan emphasize the need to incorporate systematically these factors into historical studies of other social and political phenomena. In particular, future research should focus on the impact of the differing patterns of migration and their possible effects on family structure and behavior between classes over time. These migration patterns may also be important variables in understanding both the nature and the social control of dissent and discontent. Finally, the apparent differences in the mobility relationships over time indicate that an assessment of the influence of migration should be incorporated in both spatial and temporal studies of community power and political power in general.

Appendix I.
Components of change in the labor force of the Holland community by occupation and decade, 1850-80.

Table 1—Components of Change in the Labor Force
of the Holland Community, 1850-60
(based on 1860 labor force).

Occupation	Net-Migration		Net Occupational Mobility		Net Natural Processes	
	No.	%	No.	%	No.	%
White-Collar	31	52.2	13	19.4	0	0.0
Professionals	7	35.0	3	15.0	0	0.0
Big Businessmen*	3	42.9	3	42.9	0	0.0
Small Businessmen†	13	44.8	5	17.2	0	0.0
Clerical & Sales	8	72.7	2	18.2	0	0.0
Blue-Collar	82	35.0	-104	-44.4	-25	-10.7
Skilled Workers	57	45.6	-9	-7.2	-3	-2.4
Semiskilled Workers	28	77.8	5	13.9	2	5.6
Unskilled Workers	-3	-4.1	-100	-137.0	-24	-32.9
Farm Operators	117	36.4	150	46.7	4	1.2
Farmers (over $5000)	0	0.0	0	0.0	0	0.0
Farmers ($1001-$5000)	42	36.5	62	53.9	3	2.6
Farmers ($501-$1000)	45	33.8	75	54.9	5	3.8
Farmers ($500 & under)	30	41.1	13	17.8	-4	-5.5
Rural Workers	213	52.1	-59	-14.4	47	11.5
Gardeners	3	37.5	2	25.0	1	12.5
Tenants & Sharecroppers**	0	0.0	0	0.0	0	0.0
"Farmers without Farms"	138	49.8	-65	-23.5	9	3.2
Farm Laborers	72	58.1	4	3.2	37	29.8

*This category includes businessmen listed in the industrial census as being the owners or partners in a concern with a capitalization in excess of $1,000.

†This category includes all those listed in the general census as public officials, merchants, proprietors, and managers, and who are not listed in the industrial census as being the owner or partner in a concern with a capitalization of $1,000 or more.

**None listed in either the census of 1850 or 1860.

Appendix II.
Migration rates for the Holland community
by occupation and decade, 1850-80.

Table 1—Migration rates for the Holland Community, 1850-60.

Occupation	In-Migration No.	%	Out-Migration No.	%	Net-Migration No.	%
White-Collar	40	59.7	9	39.1	31	49.2
Professional	13	65.0	6	60.0	7	35.0
Big Businessmen	3	42.9	0	0.0	3	42.9
Small Businessmen	15	51.7	2	18.2	13	44.8
Clerical & Sales	9	81.8	1	100.0	8	72.7
Blue-Collar	166	70.9	84	29.1	82	35.0
Skilled Workers	82	65.6	25	31.3	57	45.6
Semiskilled Workers	28	77.8	0	0.0	28	77.8
Unskilled Workers	56	76.7	59	29.5	-3	-4.1
Farm Operators	128	39.9	11	22.0	117	36.4
Farmers (over $5000)	0	0.0	0	0.0	0	0.0
Farmers ($1001-$5000)	43	37.4	1	12.5	42	36.5
Farmers ($501-$1000)	47	35.3	2	25.0	45	33.8
Farmers ($500 & under)	38	52.1	8	23.5	30	41.1
Rural Workers	256	62.6	43	20.7	213	52.1
Gardeners	5	62.5	2	100.0	3	37.5
Tenants & Sharecroppers*	0	0.0	0	0.0	0	0.0
"Farmers without Farms"	175	63.2	37	18.0	138	49.8
Farm Laborers	76	61.3	4	27.5	72	58.1
Total	590	57.2	147	26.2	443	43.0

*None listed in either the census of 1850 or 1860.

Table 2—Migration Rates for the Holland community, 1860-70.

Occupation	In-Migration No.	%	Out-Migration No.	%	Net-Migration No.	%
White-Collar	109	53.4	18	26.9	91	44.6
Professionals	27	75.0	6	30.0	21	58.3
Big Businessmen	10	29.4	0	0.0	10	29.4
Small Businessmen	61	55.0	7	24.1	54	48.6
Clerical & Sales	11	47.8	5	45.5	6	26.1
Blue-Collar	381	74.6	81	34.6	300	58.7
Skilled Workers	147	70.7	38	30.4	109	52.4
Semiskilled Workers	63	63.6	13	36.1	50	50.5
Unskilled Workers	171	83.8	30	41.1	141	69.1
Farm Operators	241	37.1	39	12.1	202	31.1
Farmers (over $5000)	3	11.5	0	0.0	3	11.5
Farmers ($1001-$5000)	119	28.6	19	16.5	100	24.0
Farmers ($501-$1000)	88	56.4	9	6.8	79	50.6
Farmers (under $500)	31	60.8	11	15.1	20	39.2
Rural Workers	83	55.7	157	38.4	-74	-49.7
Gardeners	2	28.6	3	37.5	-1	-12.5
Tenants & Sharecroppers*	0	0.0	0	0.0	0	0.0
"Farmers without Farms"	42	47.2	96	34.7	-54	-60.7
Farm Laborers	39	73.6	58	46.8	-19	-37.7
TOTAL	814	53.8	295	28.7	519	34.3

*None listed in either the census of 1860 or 1870.

Table 2—Components of Change in the Labor Force
of the Holland Community, 1860-70
(based on 1870 labor force).

Occupation	Net-Migration No.	%	Net Occupational Mobility No.	%	Net Natural Processes No.	%
White-Collar	91	44.6	40	19.6	6	2.9
Professional	21	58.3	-4	-11.1	-1	-2.8
Big Businessmen	10	29.4	16	47.1	1	3.0
Small Businessmen	54	48.6	25	22.5	3	2.7
Clerical & Sales	6	26.1	3	13.0	3	13.0
Blue-Collar	300	58.7	-17	-3.3	-6	-1.2
Skilled Workers	109	52.4	-15	-7.2	-11	-5.3
Semiskilled Workers	50	50.5	6	11.5	7	7.1
Unskilled Workers	141	69.1	-8	-3.9	-2	-1.0
Farm Operators	202	31.1	141	21.7	-15	-2.3
Farmers (over $5000)	3	11.5	23	88.5	0	0.0
Farmers ($1001-$5000)	100	24.0	204	49.0	-3	-0.7
Farmers ($501-$1000)	79	50.6	-48	-30.8	-8	-5.1
Farmers ($500 and under)	20	39.2	-38	-74.4	-4	-7.8
Rural Workers	-74	-49.7	-164	-110.1	-22	-14.8
Gardeners	-1	-12.5	0	0.0	0	0.0
Tenants & Sharecroppers	0	0.0	0	0.0	0	0.0
"Farmers without Farms"	-54	-60.7	-119	-134.7	-15	-16.9
Farm Laborers	-19	-35.8	-45	-84.9	-7	-13.2

Table 3—Components of Change in the Labor Force
of the Holland Community, 1870-80
(based on 1880 labor force).

Occupation	Net-Migration No.	%	Net Occupational Mobility No.	%	Net Natural Processes No.	%
White-Collar	43	13.6	25	7.9	44	13.9
Professional	15	23.4	7	10.9	6	9.4
Big Businessmen	7	15.9	4	9.1	-1	-2.3
Small Businessmen	10	6.7	14	9.3	15	10.0
Clerical & Sales	11	19.0	0	0.0	24	41.4
Blue-Collar	138	20.4	-36	-5.3	65	9.6
Skilled Workers	52	18.9	1	0.4	14	5.1
Semiskilled Workers	118	41.0	4	1.4	67	23.3
Unskilled Workers	-32	-27.8	-41	-35.7	-16	-13.9
Farm Operators	91	13.2	16	2.3	-66	-9.6
Farmers (over $5000)	2	3.3	36	59.0	-3	-4.9
Farmers ($1001-$5000)	72	15.6	14	3.0	-40	-8.7
Farmers ($501-$1000)	16	12.4	-27	-20.9	-16	-12.4
Farmers ($500 & under)	1	2.6	-7	-18.4	-7	18.4
Rural Workers	85	19.7	-5	-1.2	203	47.0
Gardeners	-1	-20.0	0	0.0	-1	-20.0
Tenants & Sharecroppers	12	63.2	4	24.1	3	15.8
"Farmers without Farms"	13	7.6	-4	-2.3	74	43.0
Farm Laborers	61	25.8	-5	-2.1	127	53.8

Table 3—Migration Rates for the Holland Community, 1870-1880.

Occupation	In-Migration		Out-Migration		Net-Migration	
	No.	%	No.	%	No.	%
White-Collar	113	35.8	70	34.3	43	13.6
Professional	34	53.1	19	52.8	15	23.4
Big Businessmen	9	20.5	2	5.9	7	15.9
Small Businessmen	49	32.7	39	35.1	10	6.7
Clerical & Sales	21	36.2	10	43.5	11	19.0
Blue-Collar	366	54.0	228	446.	138	20.4
Skilled Workers	136	49.5	84	40.4	52	18.9
Semiskilled Workers	157	54.5	39	39.4	118	41.0
Unskilled Workers	73	63.5	105	51.5	-32	-27.8
Farm Operators	183	26.5	92	14.2	91	13.2
Farmers (over $5000)	3	4.9	1	3.8	2	3.3
Farmers ($1001-$5000)	108	23.4	36	8.7	72	15.6
Farmers ($501-$1000)	55	42.6	39	25.0	16	12.4
Farmers ($500 & under)	17	44.7	16	31.4	1	2.6
Rural Workers	161	37.3	76	51.0	85	19.7
Gardeners	2	40.0	3	42.9	-1	-20.0
Tenants & Sharecroppers*	12	63.2	0	0.0	12	63.2
"Farmers without Farms"	55	32.0	42	47.2	13	7.6
Farm Laborers	92	39.0	31	58.5	61	25.8
Total	823	38.9	466	30.8	357	16.9

*None listed in the census of 1870.

FOOTNOTES

1. Sidney Goldstein, "Migration and Occupational Mobility in Norristown, Pennsylvania," *American Sociological Review*, XX (1955), 402-8, has suggested that migration and occupational mobility tend to complement each other in meeting the community's occupational needs. That is, he found that occupational mobility tended to increase as net-migration declined.

2. Stephan Thernstrom, *Progress and Poverty: Social Mobility in a Nineteenth Century City* (Cambridge, Massachusetts, 1964), 86-89, has suggested that the unskilled workers who left Newburyport did not enjoy upward social mobility. Peter M. Blau and Otis Dudley Duncan, *The American Occupational Structure* (New York, 1967), 243-75, however, suggest that a strong positive relationship exists between geographic mobility and upward vertical mobility for the last two decades. Assuming that their observations are correct, this raises the question of whether or not there has been a decisive break in this relationship.

3. Page Smith, *As a City Upon a Hill: The Town in American History* (New York, 1966) 17-36.

4. For a further discussion of the background and early history of the Holland community, see Bertus Harry Wabeke, *Dutch Emigration to North America: 1624-1860* (New York, 1944), 84-95; Henry S. Lucas, *Netherlanders in America: Dutch Immigration to the United States and Canada, 1789-1950* (Ann Arbor, 1955), 42-106,

261-63; Gordon W. Kirk, Jr., "The Promise of American Life: Social Mobility in a Nineteenth Century Immigrant Community, Holland, Michigan, 1847-1894" (unpublished Ph.D. dissertation, Michigan State University, 1970), 22-60.

5. For a further discussion of the economic development of the Holland community based on data from both the federal and state censuses, see Kirk, 37-50.

6. For an insightful essay on the process and problems of linking by name individuals enumerated in different censuses, see Ian Winchester, "The Linkage of Historical Records by Man and Computer: Techniques and Problems," *Journal of Interdisciplinary History* I (Autumn, 1970), 107-25.

7. This would have the effect of raising equally the number of in- and out-migrants. In the case of sons, it would lower the number of new entrants into the labor force and raise the number of in-migrants, thus affecting the net-migration rate.

8. Net natural processes may appear to be a misnomer for the process we are describing. In this context, however, it refers specifically to "births" and "deaths" within the labor force and not to births and deaths within the larger Holland community.

9. No doubt if this measurement were calculated on an annual basis, the turnover rate would have been much higher.

10. Our data indicate that farm operators' sons comprised 11.2, 11.4 and 51.1 percent of the rural workers in 1860, 1870 and 1880 respectively. Such a trend may reflect the fact that as small farmers were declining (presumably for economic reasons) and the land-man ratio was decreasing that farmers were unable to pass on part of their farms to their sons until a later time. Phillip J. Greven, Jr., *Four Generations: Population, Land, and Family in Colonial Andover, Massachusetts* (Ithaca, 1970), has offered a similar explanation for the effects of a decreasing land-man ratio in that town.

11. Peter A. Morrison, "Urban Growth, New Cities, and 'The Population Problem,'" Rand Corporation Paper No. P-4515-1, 1970, 15; Ira S. Lowry, *Migration and Metropolitan Growth: Two Analytical Models* (San Francisco, 1966).

12. Stephan Thernstrom, "Migration and Social Mobility, 1800-1970: The Boston Case and the American Pattern" (paper presented to the Mathematical Social Science Conference on "International Comparisons of Social Mobility in Past Societies," Institute for Advanced Study, June 15-17, 1972), 2-17.

13. *Ibid.*, 8-10.

14. Data for Iowa are for employed males from Mildred Throne, "A Population Study of an Iowa County in 1850," *Iowa Journal of History*, LVII (1959), 305-30; data for Trempealeau County are for employed males from Merle Curti, *The Making of an American Community* (Stanford, 1959); eastern Kansas data are for farm operators in sample townships from James C. Malin, "The Turnover of Farm Population in Kansas," *Kansas Historical Quarterly*, IV (1935), 339-72. Population figures for the remaining four areas, (East-central Kansas, 1860-70; Roseburg, Oregon, 1870-80; Grant County, Wisconsin, 1885-95; and West Kansas, 1895-1905) were not available in the federal census of population.

15. Occupational mobility for purposes of this study was defined as movement from one of four broad occupational groups (urban white-collar, urban blue-collar, farm operator, rural worker) to another. Upward occupational mobility included only

movement from a blue-collar to a white-collar position and mobility from the rural workers to the farm operators category. For a further analysis of mobility in these communities, see Curti, 140-258; Kirk, 132-231.

16. Thernstrom, 16.

17. *Ibid.*, 12-17.

18. The most recent and thorough examination of mobility in contemporary America indicates a strong relationship between geographic and upward occupational mobility. Peter M. Blau and Otis Dudley Duncan, *The American Occupational Structure* (New York, 1967), 243-75.

19. Kirk, 132-92.

20. Goldstein, 402-8.

21. Blau and Duncan, p. 104, using contemporary survey research data have shown that changes in the occupational structure or more specifically changes in the distribution of occupations among members of their sample accounted for only about 50 percent of the total observed inter-generational occupational mobility.

IMMIGRANTS AND INDUSTRY:
THE PHILADELPHIA EXPERIENCE, 1850-1880[1]

Shortly after Stephan Thernstrom published *Poverty and Progress* (1964), the first study by an American historian of social mobility in an urban setting, interest in the mobility patterns of the past century mushroomed. "Nowhere, perhaps," was "there a more obvious fit between national ideology and scholarly preoccupation," Michael Katz reminds us, than with "this American concern with making it."[2] In our haste to "get on with it," however, historians turned to the sociological literature. And, in being "more attentive initially to the sociologists who developed this field than to economic and labor historians pursuing changes in the composition and experience of the work force in particular occupations or in the economy as a whole," we were guilty of a serious and time-consuming false start.[3]

Studies of occupational mobility, in particular studies which attempt to describe social mobility, *require* the construction of vertical stratification schema for the classification of occupations according to skill, income, status, and so forth. Mobility is frequently thought of as connoting improvement, but movement among strata can be in three directions: from lower to higher, from higher to lower, or horizontally between two positions on the same level. The role assumed by the stratification scheme in such studies is crucial. The empirical findings will be seriously flawed if the strata *at each point in time* do not reflect the accurate ranking of occupations.

Sociologists who study social mobility concentrate primarily on status. They are able to construct classification schema which are justifiable empirically. "Some individual titles apparently have shifted their relative position," surveys of public opinion have shown, "but the overall transformation of the hierarchy in the last fifty years has been glacial in nature."[4] Unfortunately, historians do not have comparably firm data about occupational status for the nineteenth century. Extrapolating the current trend backward in time to a period which was dissimilar in important respects (such as income, education, skill levels, and industrial structure) would be dubious at best and fundamentally ahistorical. The occupational stratification schema used by sociologists scrutinizing the twentieth century cannot simply be appropriated by historians who wish to understand the nineteenth.

In retrospect this should not be surprising. Industrialization in the nineteenth century had a significant impact on the occupational universe; it altered occupational patterns perhaps more fundamentally, and certainly differently, than it did in the twentieth century. Radical changes were brought about through the reorganization of work and the introduction of labor-saving technologies. The problem of constructing occupational stratification schema in such an environment should not be underestimated or ignored.

If, for example, both the shoemaker who worked with his hands to fashion a pair of shoes in 1850 and the shoemaker who worked with the aid of a pegging machine to complete only part of the work required to make a pair of shoes in 1880 were classified in the same stratum (vertical category), no change would be recorded by the historian. Yet significant change did occur. There was a clear dilution of skill, a possible drop in income, and probably a decline in status as well. Classification schema based on skill, income, and status, therefore, would consider the change in the work done by the shoemaker as downward mobility, regardless of the fact that the occupational designation "shoemaker" remained the same in both years. A useful occupational classification scheme must take all of these factors into account.

Where does one acquire such detailed knowledge about nineteenth-century occupations? Even for those occupations about which we know a great deal, such as shoemaking, the required information seems almost impossible to find. General studies are available which describe the industry in England and Massachusetts, but are of limited value. Like most industries, shoemaking varied greatly from place to place and knowledge of how the industry or occupation generally operated will not suffice when it is necessary to know the state of the industry or occupation for a *specific locale at a given time*. And if this is true for the few occupations and fewer industries about which we know relatively much, what about those of which we know little or nothing at all?

A considerable body of recent scholarship has produced important refinements in our understanding of the occupational structure by using the now familiar sources of the "new" social history — manuscript population censuses, city directories, and tax lists. Clyde Griffen argues, for example, that the line separating skilled craftsmen from proprietors is a blurred line, movement across which connotes as much downward as upward mobility.[5] Michael Katz suggests that the division between manual and nonmanual work was not as "firm or noticeable" as has been assumed.[6] Furthermore, it is now apparent that the category of "semiskilled" workers has rested on too little knowledge of work content to make it analytically useful. While these insights are valuable, the sources of the new social history suffer from several limitations: they cannot be employed systematically to devise strata sensitive to industrial changes in specific settings at specific dates; they can *describe,* but not *explain* the changing occupational patterns observed.

There is a source of information, however, which provides the requisite data. The manuscript schedules of the U.S. Census of Manufactures report wage rates, number and sex ratios of employees, mechanization, capital investment, and values of raw materials and finished products.[7] This detailed information for each firm makes possible the differentiation of industries and their ranking by *desirability* for the working man. When used in conjunction with the population manuscripts and impressionistic sources, they permit the description of the impact of industrialization on the occupational universe.

Systematic use of these data reveal how industrialization affected incomes, working conditions, and opportunities for career advancement. Specifically, the data point to further shortcomings in traditional occupational ranking schema. They reveal a considerable amount of variation in the objective conditions of skilled occupations which are usually assigned to a *single* category and indicate that the line separating skilled from unskilled workers blurs when one considers firm size and industry type. Above all, they demonstrate that industrialization shuffled the distribution of occupations within the occupational hierarchy. Traditional occupational ranking schema are static and, therefore, unable to capture the subtle changes in the occupational universe wrought by the process of industrialization.

What began for us as an attempt to improve the occupational stratification schema borrowed from sociologists has resulted in the determination that such schema are inappropriate to the tasks we have assigned them and that it makes sense to abandon the practice of using a priori occupational stratification schema as the *means* to the study of social mobility. For the time being we should concern ourselves with understanding the ways in which nineteenth-century occupations were actually stratified. Our new *means* might include socioeconomic and demographic profiles of individual occupations over time and sophisticated techniques of record linkage in order to reconstitute the actual careers of individuals. Our new *end* should be the accurate stratification of the nineteenth-century occupational universe.

To demonstrate both the opportunities and pitfalls inherent in such a reorientation of scholarly efforts, we focus in this paper on changes in the fourteen largest manufacturing industries in Philadelphia between 1850 and 1880. We seek to explain both how the industrial and occupational hierarchy changed and how this change affected the distribution of selected ethnic groups in the manual labor force.[8]

I. Patterns of Industrial Change

The fourteen industries under examination have been divided into manufacturers of consumer goods and manufacturers of producer goods.[9] The first group encompasses industries important in Philadelphia since the days of Dr. Franklin, namely shoemaking, clothing, baking, building construction, blacksmithing, printing, and traditional metal crafts. Included in the second group are textiles, hardware, machine tools, and iron and steel. With the exception of textiles, which appeared in colonial times but showed little growth before the Jackson period, these industries were new to the city. They emerged in the 1820s and 1830s when entrepreneur-inventors like Samuel Merrick, Matthias Baldwin, and Alfred Jenks opened foundries and machine shops and pioneered in the production of metal and metal products.

Though they were newer than the consumer industries, the producer industries developed more quickly and displayed greater industrial maturity in 1880. As Table 1 demonstrates, they were far more mechanized than the older industries both in 1850 and 1880. By 1880 nearly four-fifths of the firms in iron and steel and two-thirds of the firms in textiles and machine tools produced wares with the aid of steam or water power. Firms in the older industries were primitive by comparison. Printing and publishing houses showed the most advancement, but only 38.8 percent of them in 1880 boasted power-driven presses. Furniture makers rank a distant second: less than 12 percent of them were equipped with steam or water power, while less than 10 percent of the firms in each of the remaining industries used steam engines or water wheels.

The predominance of steam power in the newer industries helps account for the striking disparity in capitalization between them and the older industries (see Table 2). Median capitalization of these firms surpassed consumer industries in 1850 and 1880, and median capitalization in each producer-goods industry increased in the period. Capitalization also increased in printing and furniture-making, but they are exceptional. Capital costs of most consumer industries either remained constant between 1850 and 1880 or actually declined as in clothing, blacksmithing, harness making, shoemaking, and metal crafts.[10]

Table 1. Percentage Of Firms Using Steam Or Water Power*

Rank	1850		1880	
1.	Iron & Steel	76.3	Iron & Steel	79.1
2.	Textiles	50.6	Machines & Tools	67.4
3.	Machines & Tools	47.8	Textiles	66.3
4.	Hardware	17.6	Hardware	39.2
5.	Printing	15.1	Printing	38.8
6.	Metal	7.4	Furniture	12.3
7.	Building Construction	5.5	Metal	8.7
8.	Furniture	4.6	Clothing	6.2
9.	Clothing	2.2	Meat Processing	4.6
10.	Baking	1.2	Blacksmithing	4.0
11.	Shoes	0.2	Baking	3.2
12.	Harnesses	0	Building Construction	2.6
13.	Meat Processing	0	Harnesses	2.5
14.	Blacksmithing	0	Shoes	2.4

* SOURCE: United States Census Office, *Census of the United States, Manufacturing Schedule, County of Philadelphia, 1850* and *1880* (Microfilm MSS, National Archives).

Table 2. Median Capitalization (in $)*

	1850		1880	
1.	Iron & Steel	10,867	Iron & Steel	29,750
2.	Textiles	4,833	Textiles	9,194
3.	Hardware	4,500	Hardware	5,461
4.	Machines & Tools	3,250	Machines & Tools	5,250
5.	Printing	3,125	Printing	5,232
6.	Clothing	2,958	Clothing	2,487
7.	Furniture	1,538	Furniture	2,200
8.	Metal	1,375	Meat	1,479
9.	Meat	1,350	Metal	1,288
10.	Harness	1,030	Baking	1,036
11.	Building Construction	948	Building Construction	975
12.	Baking	839	Harness	780
13.	Shoes	690	Shoes	681
14.	Blacksmithing	582	Blacksmithing	492

* SOURCE: See Table 1.

Firms in the newer industries not only required more capital and used more power-driven machinery; they also employed more workers than firms turning out consumer goods. As Table 3 shows, the rank order did not change appreciably between 1850 and 1880. Table 4 analyzes shop size another way; it distinguishes firms with 1 to 5 employees, firms with 6 to 50 employees and firms with more than 50 employees. The aggregate picture conforms to our expectations in that categories 1 and 2 lost ground to category 3. Where in 1850 the largest firms employed 51 percent of the labor force, in 1880 they employed 61 percent. Exceptions to this pattern are apparent in textiles and hardware, where the largest firms gave way to middle-sized ones, but in these industries the largest firms still employed 58.0 and 60.2 percent of their labor force in 1880. In the consumer industries the trend toward larger firms is unmistakable, but even more striking is the persistence of small shops, especially in meat, baking, and blacksmithing. Even in shoes and clothing, where most of the labor force was located in large firms, there were still large numbers of small shops in 1880 (see Table 5).

Table 3. Median Number of Employees Per Firm*

	1850		1880	
1.	Textiles	19.50	Iron & Steel	31.88
2.	Iron & Steel	13.00	Printing	9.75
3.	Clothing	9.69	Textiles	9.50
4.	Printing	9.50	Hardware	6.92
5.	Machines & Tools	6.08	Machines & Tools	6.86
6.	Furniture	4.96	Clothing	6.06
7.	Building Construction	4.92	Furniture	3.98
8.	Hardware	4.71	Building Construction	3.39
9.	Shoes	4.55	Metal	2.52
10.	Harness	3.75	Shoes	2.14
11.	Metal	2.73	Blacksmithing	1.92
12.	Blacksmithing	2.65	Baking	1.61
13.	Baking	2.05	Harness	1.46
14.	Meat	1.41	Meat	1.39

* SOURCE: See Table 1.

Table 4. Percentages Of Workforce By Number Of Employees Per Firm*

| Industry | Number Of Employees Per Firm | | | | | |
| | 1850 | | | 1880 | | |
	1-5	6-50	50+	1-5	6-50	50+
Iron & Steel	1.7	34.1	64.2	0.7	16.9	82.4
Textiles	1.8	20.2	78.0	2.4	39.6	58.0
Hardware	11.8	23.9	64.3	3.9	35.9	60.2
Machines & Tools	6.2	38.2	55.6	4.8	38.2	57.0
Printing	5.0	51.2	43.8	3.6	37.7	58.7
Building Construction	22.6	54.0	23.4	24.0	45.7	30.2
Clothing	4.8	44.3	50.9	2.8	17.3	79.9
Furniture	17.9	62.1	20.0	11.7	45.5	42.8
Metal	48.6	33.0	18.3	22.2	41.3	36.5
Meat	67.2	32.8	-	59.7	27.3	12.9
Harness	15.8	41.0	43.2	15.3	30.5	54.2
Baking	71.1	28.9	-	45.2	34.8	19.9
Shoes	16.9	46.6	36.5	8.5	28.6	62.8
Blacksmithing	61.0	28.4	10.6	78.3	21.7	0
All 14 Industries	11.2	37.7	51.1	9.5	29.6	60.8

* SOURCE: See Table 1.

Table 5. Number Of Firms By Number Of Employees Per Firm*

| Industry | Number of Employees Per Firm | | | | | | | |
| | 1850 | | | | 1880 | | | |
	0-5	6-50	50+	Total	0-5	6-50	50+	Total
Iron & Steel	6	13	3	22	6	20	17	43
Textiles	46	87	53	186	25	59	8	92
Hardware	76	42	7	125	114	122	27	263
Machines & Tools	42	44	6	92	96	113	19	228
Printing	36	60	10	106	105	148	36	289
Building Construct.	83	59	3	145	588	227	18	833
Clothing	165	294	43	502	301	255	93	649
Furniture	84	66	3	153	185	105	20	310
Metal	83	11	1	95	166	47	5	218
Meat	81	3	0	84	458	23	2	483
Harness	32	15	3	50	96	21	2	119
Baking	384	29	0	413	910	73	8	991
Shoes	339	224	20	583	441	139	34	614
Blacksmithing	141	18	1	160	187	12	0	199

Note: Due to the fact that the census only recorded firms producing more than $500 per year, there may be serious undercounting of firms with one or no employees.

* SOURCE: See Table 1.

Data contained in the industrial census of 1880 confirm the suspicion that firms with less than five employees were not the proverbial handicraft shops of bygone days whose journeymen and masters produced custom goods on flexible work schedules and enjoyed relatively cordial relations. Instead, they were sweatshops characterized by frequent layoffs, the division of labor, and long hours under the rigid hand of severe taskmasters. Table 6 offers some insight into the abysmal working conditions in "sweated" industries — meat, baking, clothing, and shoemaking. The table shows that they were the most flagrant violators of the standard ten-hour day, operating in excess of ten hours as well as running on "short time" and capriciously shutting down in the middle of the day.

Table 6. Percentage Of Firms By Hours Worked Per Day May To November*

Industry	Under 10 Hours	10 Hours	Over 10 Hours
Iron & Steel	2.3	97.7	0
Textiles	14.1	81.5	4.4
Hardware	3.0	94.7	2.3
Machines & Tools	3.9	94.7	1.3
Printing	18.3	81.0	0.7
Building Construction	4.3	95.0	0.7
Clothing	14.8	81.4	4.0
Furniture	4.8	93.9	1.2
Metal	3.2	95.4	1.5
Meat	21.9	38.5	39.5
Harness	1.7	95.8	2.5
Baking	10.3	36.4	53.3
Shoes	8.4	85.4	6.4
Blacksmithing	1.5	93.5	5.0

* SOURCE: See Table 1.

We are also skeptical of the view put forth by some historians that large firms and heavy industry were the bane of the skilled worker. It is misleading to equate nineteenth-century foundries and iron and steel mills with modern factories and to envision those who labored in such settings as an undifferentiated mass of semiskilled workers. The production of iron, steel, and heavy machinery entailed a range of intricate processes. The various craftsmen, semiskilled workers, and unskilled workers who performed this labor were linked in an elaborate occupational hierarchy. The work environment could be disagreeable, the work itself was often dangerous, but skilled workers in large firms were well compensated for their endeavors. Cross tabulations of the wages of skilled workers by size of firm demonstrate that there was a direct relationship between firm size and average daily wage, so that *by 1880 the larger the firm, the higher the wage* (see Table 7). Some skilled workers, no doubt, objected to what one historian calls the "impersonal and mechanical" relations with employers.[11] Yet it is not entirely clear that factory work in heavy industry was as degrading in the eyes of the skilled worker as many historians believe. The perceptions of workers obviously deserve more treatment than is possible here, but it appears that some skilled workers found decided advantages in working for large employers, quite apart from the fact that they earned higher wages. One such worker, a machinist by trade though not a Philadelphian, tells us that

> Large firms can hire help to better advantage than small ones. The mass of workingmen like to feel that their situations are as permanent as possible, and this they cannot do when employed in a small shop. For one of limited means to secure the services of an expert and really valuable assistant, extra considerations must be offered, and even these will not retain such labor if the work seems likely to fail. The highly paid assistant hired in this small way, must be frequently employed upon a class of work which in a large shop would be done by the most unskilled, inexperienced, and, of course, poorly paid labor. ...[12]

Table 7. Average Daily Wages Paid By Number Of Employees
Per Firm in 1880*

Skilled Mechanic	1880 1-5	6-50	51+	Ordinary Mechanic	1880 1-5	6-50	51+
Iron & Steel	1.97	2.30	2.48	Iron & Steel	1.25	1.35	1.42
Textiles	1.84	1.99	2.00	Textiles	1.24	1.31	1.31
Hardware	2.04	2.25	2.44	Hardware	1.24	1.28	1.39
Machines& Tools	2.09	2.29	2.47	Machines & Tools	1.15	1.40	1.34
Printing	2.03	2.45	2.70	Printing	1.14	1.27	1.48
Building Construct.	2.07	2.18	2.29	Building Construct.	1.39	1.93	1.45
Clothing	1.90	2.14	2.55	Clothing	1.10	1.19	1.30
Furniture	2.08	2.18	2.27	Furniture	1.23	1.42	1.34
Metal	2.00	2.18	2.40	Metal	1.25	1.28	1.27
Meat	1.57	1.80	2.00	Meat	0.99	1.31	1.38
Harness	1.78	2.07	2.00	Harness	1.16	1.23	------
Baking	1.65	2.20	2.50	Baking	1.20	1.26	1.30
Shoes	1.65	2.06	2.54	Shoes	0.93	1.32	1.67
Blacksmithing	1.86	2.38	------	Blacksmithing	1.14	1.38	------

Note: Entries in this table have been weighted by the number of male employees in each firm.

* SOURCE: See Table 1.

When we translate daily wages into average yearly earnings, we begin to appreciate the plight of the small master craftsman and his journeymen under the stress of industrialization. Calculations of average yearly earnings of each industry are presented in Table 8. The table suggests that in 1850 handicraft producers enjoyed an enviable position in the marketplace since their journeymen earned the highest incomes. And while there was a considerable gap between industries, the range within industries was nominal. Thirty years later, however, industrialization undermined the small producer, who could not compete with larger, more efficient firms and whose workers held the least remunerative jobs. Workers employed by the largest and medium-sized employers, whether they were in the consumer or the producer group, secured the best incomes. In the consumer industries, for example, workingmen employed by the *largest* printers and publishers, boot and shoe manufacturers, and construction bosses, earned the highest incomes, as did workers in the remaining industries who found employment in the medium-sized firms. In the producer industries, workers employed in the largest firms (with the exception of textiles) garnered the best incomes.

Table 8. Average Yearly Wages Paid To Males By Number of Employees Per Firm*

1850	1-5	6-50	51+	Total	1880	1-5	6-50	51+	Total
Boots & Shoes	272	274	263	270	Boots & Shoes	378	462	492	469
Harness	322	339	378	353	Harness	440	484	n.a.	469
Textiles	268	226	197	206	Textiles	436	491	436	468
Clothing	319	333	236	287	Clothing	409	449	329	359
Baking	271	281	——	273	Baking	393	526	400	435
Meat	305	336	——	306	Meat	385	440	422	405
Furniture	373	335	374	351	Furniture	457	489	433	462
Blacksmithing	300	268	——	300	Blacksmithing	448	466	——	452
Printing	355	370	372	370	Printing	398	445	578	518
Building	375	340	159	307	Building	453	446	508	467
Hardware	391	329	320	330	Hardware	498	418	609	534
Metal	383	319	330	352	Metal	414	466	444	446
Machines & Tools	354	326	328	329	Machines & Tools	469	464	544	509
Iron & Steel	319	394	345	361	Iron & Steel	474	454	670	631

Estimation procedure for 1880:
(Average male wages) = (Total wages paid) /
([# males] + .4 [# females] + .3 [youths])

* SOURCE: See Table 1. Entries in this table have been weighted by the number of male employees in each firm.

In this thirty-year period, moreover, the disparity in earnings within industries increased considerably. To take a few examples, the range in incomes between wage earners in small and medium-sized shoemaking shops in 1850 was only $2, but widened to $84 in 1880. In the meat-packing and baking firms, the disparity between incomes was $31 and $10 respectively in 1850, $55 and $133 thirty years later. The same pattern holds for the new metal trades in which the margin between the smallest and largest iron and steel mills and machine shops was $26 in both in 1850 and $196 and $75 in 1880. This period also witnessed the development of major differentials between the incomes of workers in the producer and consumer groups. Table 9, which ranks each industry by average yearly income, shows that in 1850 neither group dominated; representatives of each were dispersed randomly in the rank order. But in 1880 the producer industries achieved superiority and occupied three of the top four positions in the ranking. The average yearly income of manual workers in these industries ranged between $468 and $631, while the range within the consumer groups, if we exclude printing for the moment, was between $359 and $469. Or, to put it another way, by 1880 the highest average earning in the consumer group was the lowest in the producer group.

Table 9. Average Yearly Wages Paid To Males*

1850		1880	
Printing	370	Iron & Steel	631
Iron & Steel	361	Hardware	534
Harness	353	Printing	518
Metal	352	Machine & Tools	509
Furniture	351	Boots & Shoes	469
Hardware	330	Harness	469
Machines & Tools	329	Textiles	468
Building Construction	307	Building Construction	467
Meat	306	All 14 Industries	464
Blacksmithing	300	Furniture	462
All 14 Industries	288	Blacksmithing	452
Clothing	287	Metal	446
Baking	273	Baking	435
Boots & Shoes	270	Meat	405
Textiles	206	Clothing	359

Note: Entries in this table have been weighted by the number of male employees in each firm.

* SOURCE: See Table 1.

These developments in industrial Philadelphia closely parallel the findings of Eric Hobsbawm in his brilliant study of the "Labour Aristocracy" in nineteenth-century Britain.[13] In both cases metal trades developed rapidly. Iron and steel mills, foundries, and machine shops proliferated and employed a highly diversified labor force comprised partly of iron puddlers, rollers, machinists, and other skilled workers who formed the aristocracy of labor, partly of semiskilled workers who toiled alongside the aristocrats, and partly of unskilled workers who performed menial tasks.[14]

Puddlers, rollers, machinists, and other skilled metal workers earned the highest incomes of all tradesmen, though superior earnings alone did not distinguish them from other workers. As Hobsbawm notes, a number of nonwage factors – conditions of work, relations with other workers and other social classes, styles of life – also figure in the equation. Historians are only beginning to treat these complex matters, but some evidence suggests that skilled metal workers occupied a more advantageous position in the workshop than most handicraft workers. Not the least of their advantages was considerable autonomy, despite the impressive advances in technology. They often combined managerial functions with manual skills, hiring their own crews and frequently determining the quantity and quality of outputs. It was precisely such autonomy that would inspire a determined effort by large employers and scientific managers to wrest control of the workplace from skilled workers in the 1890s and the early twentieth century. But in the third quarter of the nineteenth century, as David Montgomery demonstrates, skilled metal workers were the vanguard of tradesmen who exercised "control over the actual use of . . . . implements in the productive process. . . ."[15] Few if any of them could realistically aspire to become employers because of the enormous capital requirements, but they commanded considerable status and respect, both from employers who relied heavily on their skill and judgment and from wage earners below them in the occupational hierarchy.

Workers performing semiskilled tasks and ordinary labor in the new metal trades, moreover, were better off than their counterparts in the older industries. They earned slightly more per day than most ordinary workers in consumer industries and had more access to skilled jobs atop the occupational hierarchy because these industries had a greater ratio of skilled to unskilled jobs than did the old crafts. In the crafts, on the other hand, the division of labor diluted skills, and mobility held less promise for the ordinary workers who competed for a diminishing number of "skilled" jobs.

Within the consumer group certain industries expanded, namely printing and to a lesser extent, building construction. These industries contained their own occupational hierarchy with a sizable labor aristocracy, paid relatively high wages, and offered skilled workers considerable job satisfaction and prestige.[16] In fact, "aristocrats" could be found in most older industries, as in cabinet making, where a select few fashioned expensive furniture, or in clothing, where garment cutters whose ability to ruin employers with a fatal slip of the knife earned them prestige, respect, and high wages.[17]

In the main, however, working people found consumer industries less rewarding and less desirable between 1850 and 1880. These pursuits lacked the elaborate occupational hierarchy of the newer industries, which provided a career ladder for workers within a given firm. The alternative to rising within a firm was opening a small shop, which was still possible in many industries whose capital costs were not prohibitively high. Such was the case in meat processing, clothing, shoemaking, and baking, where shops capitalized at $500 were still common as late as 1880.

Yet it is improbable that journeymen bettered themselves by opening small shops. Small producers usually operated on the fringe of their industry as subcontractors producing specialized goods for large manufacturers.[18] The intense competition of subcontracting

Table 10. Average Gross Profits Of Firms
Reporting Capital Of $500 Or Less*

	1850 N	Average ($)	1880 N	Average ($)
Boots & Shoes	261	427	287	520
Harness	15	341	50	482
Textiles	14	428	5	818
Clothing	73	529	148	674
Baking	147	552	308	914
Meat	15	650	154	1665
Furniture	34	477	82	637
Blacksmithing	75	413	116	744
Printing	15	816	18	1058
Building Construction	50	780	333	877
Hardware	11	638	41	620
Metal	21	323	70	631
Machines & Tools	10	283	21	687
Iron & Steel	0	-----	0	--------
All 14 Industries	741	482	1633	907

* SOURCE: See Table 1.

forced small employers to "sweat" journeymen and even to work alongside them in the hope of cutting costs. This arrangement necessarily blurred the functional line between employer and employee in the shop, but the risk remained squarely on the shoulders of the employer who operated on a thin profit margin and was constantly haunted by the specter of ruin. Many, and perhaps most of them, did fail, and those who succeeded earned little more than the people they hired and less than many factory foremen (see Table 10).[19]

II. Patterns of Occupational Change

Changes in the ethnic composition and occupational distribution of the male labor force accompanied the transformation of Philadelphia's industrial activity.[20] Population doubled between 1850 and 1880, but the city's principal nativity groups — Irish and German immigrants and native-born whites — did not contribute equally to the population growth. Table 11 shows that Philadelphia's male work force grew from 100,404 in 1850 to 215,686 in 1880, an increase of over 100 percent. During this period the Irish maintained their standing as the city's largest immigrant group with 27,152 adult males in 1850 and 39,428 in 1880. But Irish immigration failed to keep pace with the city's expansion, and the Irish fell from 27 percent of the male work force in 1850 to 18 percent in 1880. German immigrants, on the other hand, increased at the rate of 137 percent, from 11,427 in 1850 to 27,099 in 1880. The number of native white males in Philadelphia increased from 56,754 to 139,716, an increase of 147 percent. Less than half of the native white entrants into the labor force in this period, however, were of native-born parentage. In 1880 there were 24,399 native-born sons of Irish immigrants and 13,860 native-born sons of German immigrants. (The columns headed "Irish 2," "German 2," and "Other 2" in Table 11 give the number of native-born sons with foreign-born parents.)

The proportion of each group which found employment in manufacturing declined between the two census years. The Germans showed the smallest decrease (64.1 to 61.1 percent), followed by the Irish (40.7 to 33.8 percent), and the native whites (53.7 to 44.0 percent). The sons of German immigrants were just about as heavily concentrated in manufacturing as their fathers in 1880 (59.7 percent). The sons of Irish immigrants, however, reversed the trend of their fathers and entered manufacturing, so that 47.3 percent of them worked in that sector of the economy in 1880.

Table 11. Male Workforce* By Ethnicity**

1850	Black	Irish	Irish 2	German	German 2	NWA	Other 2	Total
N =	5071	27152		11427		56754		100,404
% of total	5.1	27.0		11.4		56.5		100.0
1880								
N =	9443	39428	24399	27099	13860	87930	13527	215,686
% of total	4.4	18.3	11.3	12.6	6.4	40.8	6.3	100.0
% increase	86.2	45.2		137.1		54.9		114.8

* Males 18 years and older

** SOURCE: United States Census Office, *Census of the United States, Population Schedule, County of Philadelphia, 1850* microfilm MSS, National Archives).

What concerns us here are the skilled and unskilled workers employed in our 14 industries.[21] Occupations in these industries account for slightly less than half the skilled labor force in 1850, slightly more than half of it in 1880. Occupations in the consumer industries — shoemaker, tailor, butcher, and the like — represent a much larger segment of the "skilled" labor force in both census years than those in the producer industries. In the ensuing three decades, however, they declined from 25.3 percent of the labor force to 23.2 percent, while the occupations in the producer industries increased from 6.9 to 8.2 percent of the labor force. And there is every reason to believe that this trend continued, since the metal trades and other producer industries expanded dramatically in the following three decades.

Four consumer industries — meat, baking, printing, and the old metal crafts — increased their share of the labor force. All others lost ground, usually in the neighborhood of 0.5 percent of the total male work force. The most dramatic declines occurred in shoes, whose share of the laboring population fell from 6.2 to 3.4 percent, and in clothing, which declined from 3.4 to 2.7 percent in 1880 (see Table 12). Conversely, the producer industries grew, the only loss coming in textiles which dropped 1 percent of the labor force between 1850 and 1880 when the hand-loom weaving industry virtually disappeared.

Table 13 displays the occupational distribution of the Irish, German, and native-born groups, and it reveals few surprises. Even by a crude occupational rank order the Irish fare the worst of the three groups in 1850, for nearly half of them were located in day labor (30.3 percent), hand-loom weaving (11.6 percent), and carting (3.3 percent). Less than a third of them worked at "skilled" trades (excluding hand-loom weavers). The Germans also fulfill our expectations. We know that many of them arrived in America as skilled workers, and it is not surprising to find them less dependent upon unskilled labor and more heavily represented in the skilled trades than the Irish. In 1850 only 11.6 percent of them toiled as day laborers and nearly two-thirds worked at skilled trades. They were especially prevalent in shoemaking, tailoring, and baking, which together account for one-fifth of the German male labor force (see Table 13). The occupational superiority of the native-born whites requires little elaboration. Suffice it to note that they were much less involved in unskilled labor than the other groups and less evident than the Germans in clothing and shoemaking, but more concentrated in the prestigious building trades and printing and disproportionately represented in commerce and the professions.

Table 12. Percentage Of Ethnic Group By Industry*

Industry	Irish	Irish 2	German	German 2	NWA	Total
Iron & Steel						
'50	0.3		0.3		0.9	0.6
'80	1.4	2.2	0.6	1.3	1.6	1.4
Textiles						
'50	13.0		2.9		0.8	4.3
'80	4.0	6.4	3.2	2.6	1.9	3.3
Hardware						
'50	0.4		0.7		0.9	0.7
'80	1.1	1.6	0.8	1.8	1.2	1.2
Machines & Tools						
'50	0.6		1.4		1.8	1.3
'80	1.1	2.4	2.3	2.4	2.9	2.3
Printing						
'50	0.6		0.9		2.3	1.6
'80	0.7	3.2	1.3	3.1	3.3	2.4
Bldg. Construct.						
'50	4.2		2.6		10.2	7.4
'80	4.4	6.7	3.0	5.7	11.0	7.3
Clothing						
'50	2.9		8.6		2.9	3.4
'80	1.9	1.3	8.3	3.9	1.6	2.7
Furniture						
'50	0.5		4.7		1.7	1.7
'80	0.4	0.6	3.7	1.7	1.3	1.4
Metal						
'50	0.3		0.5		0.8	0.6
'80	0.4	1.4	0.9	1.3	0.9	0.9
Harness						
'50	0.3		0.5		0.7	0.5
'80	0.3	0.1	0.4	0.1	0.3	0.3
Baking						
'50	0.9		7.8		1.0	1.7
'80	0.6	0.3	7.7	5.1	0.7	1.8
Boots & Shoes						
'50	5.2		11.6		5.9	6.2
'80	4.2	2.1	8.1	3.1	2.4	3.4
Blacksmithing						
'50	1.4		1.7		2.0	1.7
'80	2.1	1.8	1.4	1.5	1.1	1.4
Medical/Legal						
'50	0.3		0.4		2.0	1.3
'80	0.3	1.4	0.5	1.3	2.9	1.7
Street Trades						
'50	4.3		1.0		1.2	2.1
'80	5.1	6.4	1.6	3.1	2.7	3.5

* SOURCE: See Table 11.

Table 13. Percentage Of Ethnic Group By Occupation*

Occupation	Irish	Irish 2	German	German 2	NWA	Total
Laborer						
'50	30.3		11.6		3.7	13.0
'80	30.0	14.7	6.4	6.1	5.8	12.6
Weaver						
'50	11.6		2.4		0.4	3.6
'80	1.6	1.7	1.1	0.9	0.2	0.9
Dyer						
'50	0.7		0.5		0.2	0.4
'80	0.4	1.1	0.6	0.3	0.3	0.5
Molder						
'50	.02		0.1		0.5	0.4
'80	0.4	1.2	0.1	0.6	0.6	0.5
Iron Molder						
'50	0.0		0.0		0.0	0.0
'80	0.2	0.4	0.1	0.3	0.3	0.3
Boiler Maker						
'50	0.1		0.1		0.1	0.1
'80	0.5	0.3	0.2	0.2	0.2	0.2
Machinist						
'50	1.5		3.3		2.7	2.3
'80	1.0	2.2	2.0	1.8	2.4	2.0
Printer						
'50	0.3		0.3		1.2	0.8
'80	0.3	1.5	0.4	1.3	1.5	1.1
Stone Mason						
'50	0.7		0.3		0.3	0.4
'80	0.8	0.2	0.6	0.2	0.2	0.4
Plumber						
'50	0.1		0.0		0.2	0.1
'80	0.3	1.1	0.1	0.3	0.8	0.6
Carpenter						
'50	2.7		1.6		6.5	4.6
'80	1.9	1.7	1.6	2.1	4.3	2.8
Painter						
'50	0.6		0.7		1.6	1.1
'80	0.6	1.2	0.6	1.3	2.0	1.3
Bricklayer						
'50	0.4		0.1		1.6	1.1
'80	0.4	1.2	0.2	0.3	0.9	0.7
Plasterer						
'50	0.3		0.0		0.9	0.6
'80	0.4	0.6	0.0	0.3	0.7	0.5

Table 13. (cont'd) Percentage Of Ethnic Group By Occupation

Occupation	Irish	Irish 2	German	German 2	NWA	Total
Tailor						
'50	2.4		7.4		1.9	2.6
'80	1.3	0.2	6.4	2.0	0.5	1.5
Turner						
'50	0.1		0.7		0.3	0.3
'80	0.0	-	0.1	0.2	0.1	0.1
Varnisher						
'50	0.1		0.1		0.1	0.1
'80	0.1	0.2	0.2	0.4	0.1	0.1
Cabinet Maker						
'50	0.4		4.0		1.1	1.2
'80	0.1	0.2	2.9	1.2	0.6	0.8
Locksmith						
'50	0.1		0.6		0.1	0.2
'80	0.0	-	0.4	0.2	0.1	0.1
Tinsmith						
'50	0.1		0.3		0.2	0.2
'80	0.3	1.0	0.6	0.5	0.6	0.6
Butcher						
'50	0.1		1.0		0.7	0.5
'80	0.3	0.7	3.5	3.5	1.5	1.5
Harness Maker						
'50	0.1		0.1		0.1	0.1
'80	0.2	0.1	0.3		0.2	0.2
Saddler						
'50	0.2		0.4		0.6	0.4
'80	0.1	-	0.1	0.1	0.1	0.1
Baker						
'50	0.8		6.3		0.5	1.2
'80	0.5	0.3	5.4	3.5	0.3	1.2
Shoemaker						
'50	3.5		7.4		4.2	4.2
'80	3.2	1.3	6.5	2.2	1.4	2.4
Blacksmith						
'50	1.4		1.8		2.0	1.7
'80	2.0	1.8	1.4	1.4	1.1	1.3
Lawyer						
'50	0.1		0.0		0.9	0.6
'80	0.1	0.6	0.0	0.3	1.0	0.5
Doctor						
'50	0.1		0.3		1.1	0.7
'80	0.1	0.3	0.4	0.6	1.5	0.8

Table 13. (cont'd) Percentage Of Ethnic Group By Occupation

Occupation	Irish	Irish 2	German	German 2	NWA	Total
Clerk						
'50	1.5		1.2		5.0	3.4
'80	0.3	2.3	0.4	2.4	3.8	2.2
Drayman						
'50	1.0		0.4		0.1	0.4
'80	0.3	0.1	0.0	-	0.0	0.1
Ostler						
'50	0.6		0.7		0.2	0.4
'80	0.6	0.0	1.0	0.2	0.2	0.4
Carter						
'50	3.3		1.4		0.9	1.6
'80	1.0	0.6	0.2	0.6	0.2	0.5
Teamster						
'50	0.0		0.0		0.1	0.0
'80	1.2	1.6	0.4	1.3	0.9	1.0

* SOURCE: See Table 13.

Thus at mid-century, native-white Americans and German immigrants dominated the most desirable skilled occupations. Heavily involved in printing, building, clothing, and shoemaking, they plied trades which promised fairly high wages and whose skills were just beginning to be diluted by segmentation of task or by machinery. Many of them were extremely articulate, a talent which they often parlayed into leadership positions in social organizations, trade unions, and local political parties. Local leaders of some prestige, they easily qualified as the labor aristocracy of their day.[22]

The occupational distribution of the immigrants in 1880 looks much as it did in 1850. Only two changes stand out. About 10 percent of the Irish ceased operating hand looms as weaving finally moved into the factory, and the proportion of German day laborers fell from 11.6 to 6.4 percent, an impressive change by any measure. Otherwise there were no striking changes. The Irish were still mired in unskilled labor, the Germans still employed chiefly in traditional crafts.

Upon closer examination, however, Table 13 indicates a trend barely perceptible among the immigrants, but apparent in the native whites and native-born sons of immigrants. These groups began to abandon traditional trades in the consumer industries (excluding printing and building trades), though they did so at slightly different rates. The desertion of sons of Germans is most impressive, for only 15.7 percent of them plied these trades compared to 30.1 percent of the 1850 immigrant cohort, a shift of 52.7 percent. The sons of Irish immigrants and native-born whites followed close behind and displayed shifts of 47.5 and 29.4 percent respectively. In 1880 only 5.7 percent of the sons of Irish immigrants and 6.6 percent of the native whites worked at these trades. It is perhaps ironic, but in the occupations of the consumer industries, the Irish sons and the native whites resemble one another more than the Germans. German immigrants were so concentrated in these crafts in 1850 and 1880 that their native-born sons constituted a sizable residual force despite the alacrity with which they abandoned the handicrafts.

An even broader parallel between the occupational distributions of the sons of immigrants and native whites emerges when we examine the ethnic composition of printing and the building trades. Unlike other older crafts, these trades still commanded relatively high wages in 1880. All of the groups entered the expanding printing industry in this period, but setting type was more of a magnet for the immigrant sons. The proportion of printers in the native-white population increased by only 0.3 percent (from 1.2 to 1.5 percent, Table 13), and the immigrant proportions hardly changed at all. The sons of immigrants, however, entered printing more rapidly than the native whites and more easily than their fathers and achieved parity with the native whites by 1880. In building construction the three native-born groups began to converge. The percentage of native whites declined from 11.1 in 1850 to 8.9 in 1880, while large numbers of immigrant sons became building tradesmen. Six percent of the Irish sons, for example, worked at skilled construction trades compared to 4.8 percent of the 1850 Irish cohort; the proportion of German sons in building was 4.6 percent, almost two percentage points higher than the Germans in 1850.

The sons of Irish immigrants also gained access to the prestigious jobs in the new metal industries. Slightly over 4 percent of them, compared to 1.8 percent of the 1850 cohort, plied skilled trades in machine shops, iron foundries, and rolling mills. Indeed, they had a higher proportion in these trades in 1880 than both the native whites (3.5 percent) and the sons of German immigrants (2.9 percent).

By 1880 German immigrants and their sons had as low a proportion of their numbers in casual labor as the native whites (roughly 6 percent). The percentage of native-white day laborers actually increased between 1850 and 1880 (from 3.7 to 5.8), probably as a result of in-migration from rural areas. A sizable share of Irish-born Philadelphians (30.0 percent) still worked as unskilled laborers in 1880, but casual labor was not as appealing to their sons. Only 14.7

percent of them were so employed in 1880. It appears, then, that the position of unskilled Irish sons paralleled that of skilled German sons in the traditional consumer crafts. Each group rapidly deserted the sphere of its fathers, but Irish immigrants were so dependent upon casual labor and German immigrants so concentrated in the older crafts that their sons could not help but remain heavily represented in those occupations.

III. Conclusion

The evidence presented here warrants two concluding observations and invites speculation about the relationship between immigrants, occupations, and industrial change. First, it is evident that the occupational distribution of Irish and German immigrants did not change significantly between 1850 and 1880. Aside from the Irish retreat from hand-loom weaving, which was not a matter of choice but a necessity since the industry disappeared, and the German shift out of day labor, each group clustered in the same occupations in 1850 and 1880.

The occupational distribution of these immigrants had less to do with the conditions in America than with prior experience in the old world. Rural, underdeveloped Ireland bequeathed her sons very little in the way of industrial experience or skill, which forced Irish immigrants in Philadelphia to assume positions at the bottom of the occupational hierarchy. They entered either day labor, occupations easily learned such as handloom weaving or shoebinding, or street trades which required no skill and small capital investment. Germans who left their country in the midst of the industrial revolution brought skills with them, and it is fitting that we find the majority of them in skilled trades in 1850 and 1880, especially in shoemaking, tailoring, and baking.

A combination of factors made it difficult for immigrants to take advantage of opportunities and shift into more rewarding occupations. Nativist feelings, which ran high in Philadelphia after the anti-Catholic riots of 1844 and which were directed chiefly against the Irish, probably inspired some employers to reserve the most remunerative jobs for native-born Americans. Germans could have been victimized by nativism to some extent as well, though one suspects that they had peculiar reasons not to seek new opportunities. Many of them came to America expressly to practice trades which were threatened by technology in the homeland. Wedded to the traditional crafts by habit and custom, they were not especially disposed to forsake the trades they valued so highly.[23] Shifting into new occupations also necessitated learning and acquiring skills, which took time and commitment, and German and Irish immigrants were much older than the native-born population in 1880. Well into their careers, they could not easily shift into more desirable jobs.

Second, our analysis of industrial change runs counter to the view held by many historians who see this period as an "Age of Industrialization," animated by the rapid and wholesale application of steam power and technological improvements.[24] This essential misunderstanding derives from equating industrialization with mechanization. The use of mechanized production techniques constitutes only a single *stage* (with greater import for the economics than the sociology of industrialization) which occurred relatively late in the process of industrialization. John R. Commons' classic study of the shoe industry made clear that significant changes in the organization of work, authority relationships, and production techniques transformed the role of the craftsman long before mechanization was introduced.[25]

Towns like Fall River, Massachusetts or Johnstown, Pennsylvania, which housed textile factories and iron and steel mills, shifted to mechanization early and rapidly. Perhaps the dramatic nature of the industrial change experienced by towns dominated by a single industry explains why some historians have mistakingly equated industrialization and mechanization. But in a large city with a diversified economy like Philadelphia, which produced everything from silk handkerchiefs to iron rails, the complexity and unevenness of industrial development precludes such a view.

In Philadelphia, mechanization did not reach much beyond heavy industry and textiles, which we referred to earlier as producer industries. Modern though they were, these pursuits employed a relatively small proportion of the manual labor force. Most of the city's male manual workers were located in the consumer industries, which were not as mechanized as we have been led to believe. Still, significant changes did occur. Between 1850 and 1880 these industries underwent considerable division of labor, used the latest hand tools, employed larger numbers of workers per firm, and produced their goods in factories even though they did not rely upon independent power supplies. It was not unusual in the 1870s, for example, for 150 shoemakers to be working under one roof without steam power.

Such transformations in the premechanized stages of work occurred at different times in different industries in different cities. A host of factors influenced these changes: the state and cost of local technology and the expertise of local craftsmen in fashioning new tools and machines; the strength of organized labor; the level of skills, availability, and ethnic composition of the labor force. In some industries innovations were so gradual that workers experienced no great or abrupt changes in procedures and work methods. Other industries changed more rapidly, which forced workingmen to make major adjustments to new methods. Whichever the case, it seems that the most important developments in authority relationships and work roles occurred prior to mechanization. The independent craftsman or skilled worker, in other words, was not reduced to the factory operative in one fell swoop. A major challenge facing historians will be to comprehend the socioeconomic consequences of such incremental changes for those who worked in this period of premechanized industrialization.

The nature of industrial change in Philadelphia, coupled with the occupational careers of its immigrants, sheds some light on our limited understanding of occupations and job mobility. All too often we treat skill as an absolute and assume that an occupation is either skilled or it is not, that a man who calls himself a tailor, carpenter, or butcher is a skilled worker. It should be clear, however, that skill is relative in that one skilled occupation may require more skill than another, though we hasten to add that measuring the differences is extremely difficult. It should also be evident that the skill level of an occupation changes over time, as do wage rates and the immediate environment of the workplace. We know, for example, that occupations such as butchering, tailoring, and shoemaking changed considerably relative to newer occupations in Philadelphia between 1850 and 1880. Division of labor diluted skills, sweatshops with rigorous work routines emerged, wages declined, and career opportunities for workingmen were limited because these operations lacked an articulate occupational hierarchy. The reverse occurred in the new metal trades, where both skilled and unskilled workers commanded relatively high wages, skill was at a premium, and career opportunities were probably good because of the developed occupational hierarchy.

All of which is to say that we must not assume that all skilled occupations were equally desirable or inherently *better* than unskilled occupations. Skilled jobs generally commanded higher wages in the period under discussion, but the wage differential between skilled and unskilled labor is not as great as we have been led to believe for the labor force overall. The line between these occupational groups blurs when we introduce the variable of shop size, for we find that wages of "skilled" workers in small shops in select consumer industries were hardly better than wages of "ordinary" workers in the largest shops in the new metal trades. Judging from wage rates presented in Table 7, moreover, it appears that there was as great a differential among rates paid to skilled workers as there was between the wages of the lowest paid skilled workers and unskilled laborers. Jobs in the consumer industries were even less desirable from the standpoint of career potential. Many of them were a cul de sac and no one realized this more than the sons of immigrants.

If we regard career potential as an important component of occupation then it behooves us to rethink our stereotype of unskilled labor. We might consider the possibility that German immigrants were not that much better off than their Irish counterparts simply because they were more likely to be "skilled" workers.[26] German immigrants were locked into declining crafts. Just as large numbers of Irish sons remained in day labor where their fathers were so heavily concentrated, the sons of German immigrants were still located principally in the crafts in 1880. But many of these first generation Americans perceived that better opportunities lay in the developing industries and assumed skilled jobs in printing, building construction, and heavy industry.

The means by which the sons of immigrants moved into these occupations is not known since we have not yet traced the careers of individuals. But we cannot resist the temptation to speculate that the Irish immigrants' lack of skills was not so great a disadvantage to their sons as has been thought.[27] It seems that the crucial occupational designation is *laborer*, which we normally associate with deprivation — low status, low wages, and limited dareer potential — and usually locate at the bottom of the occupational rank order. The problem with this assessment is that it fails to consider the career potential of some day laborers employed in building construction and the metal trades.[28] These laborers may have been engaged in on-the-job training, or what we should like to call "informal apprenticeship."[29] Toiling beside skilled workers on construction sites and in foundries and machine shops, they probably learned how to perform highly skilled jobs, which they later practiced as skilled workers. German sons followed a similar career pattern, but did so more slowly, partly because they did not have as much access as their Irish counterparts to the informal training ground of unskilled labor.[30]

By 1880 then, we find that the sons of Irish and German immigrants have begun to abandon occupations in the consumer industries and have gained a foothold in skilled occupations in printing, building construction, and the new metal industries. By entering these trades, they established themselves as labor aristocrats, an honor previously held by native-born Americans and some German immigrants. In abandoning the older crafts, they made room for the "new" immigrants who flocked to meat packing, the needle trades, and to unskilled positions in the iron and steel industry at the turn of the century.

University of Massachusetts   Bruce Laurie
University of Pennsylvania   Theodore Hershberg
University of Pennsylvania   George Alter

FOOTNOTES

1. This paper was prepared for a conference, "Immigrants in Industrial America, 1850-1920," sponsored by the Eleutherian Mills Historical Library and the Balch Institute (November 1-3, 1973). The essay was revised in 1974 and 1975. The data presented were collected by the Philadelphia Social History Project, directed by Dr. Theodore Hershberg, and are part of a larger study of the relationships between social mobility, family structure, neighborhood, industrialization, urbanization, and transportation. The paper was also presented to the *Sixth International Congress on Economic History*, Copenhagen, Denmark (August 19-23, 1974), and will appear in the volume of Eleutherian Mills conference proceedings edited by Richard Ehrlich and published by the University of Virginia Press (forthcoming, 1976).

The authors wish to express their appreciation to the Center for the Study of Metropolitan Problems of the National Institute of Mental Health whose financial support (MH 16621) has made this research possible. Bruce Laurie wishes to thank the National Endowment for the Humanities for supporting his research with a postdoctoral fellowship.

2. Michael B. Katz, *The People of Hamilton, Canada-West: Family and Class in a Mid-Nineteenth-Century City* (Cambridge, Mass., Harvard University Press, Forthcoming, 1976), chapter IV.

3. Clyde Griffen, "Occupational Mobility in Nineteenth-Century America: Problems and Possibilities," *Journal of Social History* 5 (1972): 310-30.

4. David L. Featherman and Robert M. Hauser, "On the Measurement of Occupation in Social Surveys," *Sociological Methods and Research* 2 (1973): 241.

5. Griffen, "Occupational Mobility," pp. 324-7.

6. Katz, *op. cit.*, chapter IV.

7. These documents report richly detailed information for each firm whose annual product was valued at $500 or more. The schedules for 1850 and 1860 are identical. Variables include: name of corporation, company, or individual; name of business, manufacture, or product; capital invested; raw materials used;

quantities, kinds, value; kind of motive power, machinery, structure, or resources; average monthly rate of male labor; average monthly rate of female labor; annual products: quantities, kinds, values.

The schedule for 1870 dropped some valuable detail, especially the separate reporting of average monthly wages paid to male and female employees, replacing them with a lump sum paid to all employees for the entire year, but added important information describing the kinds and numbers of machines used and the number of months the firm was in active operation. Variables include: name of corporation, company, or individual; name of business, manufacture, or product; capital invested; motive power: kind of power, if steam or water number of horse power; machines: name or description, number of; average number of hands employed: males above 16, females above 15, children and youth; total amount paid in wages during year; number of months in active operation reducing part time to full time; materials: kinds, quantities, value; production: kinds, quantities, value.

The schedule for 1880 changed more dramatically, dropping information on the specific kinds, quantities and values of raw materials and finished products, but adding a host of new detailed information including an invaluable distinction in wages paid to "skilled" and "ordinary" labor. Variables include: name of corporation, company, or individual; name of business, manufacture, or product; capital invested; greatest number of hands employed: males over 16, females over 15, children and youth; number of hours in ordinary day of labor: May to November, November to May; wages and hours of labor: average day's wages for a skilled mechanic, average day's wages for an ordinary laborer, total amount paid in wages during the year; months in operation: on full time, on 3/4 time only, on 2/3 time only, on 1/3 time only, idle; value of material; value of product; power used in manufacturing: if water used, on what river or stream, height of fall in feet, wheels: number, breadth in feet revolutions/minute, horsepower; if steam power used; number of boilers, number of engines, horsepower.

8. Our discussion focuses on three distinct groups of males above the age of 18: a) the "Irish and Germans," foreign-born immigrants identified by their place of birth; b) "second-generation Irish and Germans," American-born sons of Irish and German fathers; and c) "native-white Americans," American-born sons of native-whites only for the year 1880. The 1850 census identified the place-of-birth for the individual *only*, while the 1880 census reported the place-of-birth for the father and mother as well as for the individual. The 1850 figures for native-white Americans, then, include all native-born whites regardless of parental birth (see Table 3).

Although we have data available for all black males above the age of 18 as well, they have not been included in this analysis. Blacks were so excluded from the industrial sector of the economy that discussing their occupational patterns within the context of this paper would be counterproductive. Their occupational patterns are treated in Theodore Hershberg, "Free Blacks in Antebellum Philadelphia: A Study of Exslave, Freeborn and Socioeconomic Decline," *Journal of Social History* 5(1972): 191-2, 198-200. The occupational distribution of Philadelphia's Negro community is discussed in Theodore Hershberg, "Mulattoes and Blacks: Intra-Group Color Differences and Social Stratification," *Journal of American History* (forthcoming, 1976).

9. It should be added that these are crude categories constructed to facilitate our discussion. As will become evident, there are exceptions in each group, the most conspicuous of which are printing and building construction in the consumer group and textiles in the producer group.

10. Because of an undercounting of small firms in the 1850 manufacturing census, the figures for median capitalization presented in Table 2 may be somewhat inflated, masking a slight increase in capitalization by 1880. Any increase which might have occurred, however, remains small by comparison with the increases observed in the producer industries.

11. Edward C. Kirkland, *Industry Comes of Age: Business, Labor and Public Policy, 1860-1897* (Chicago, 1967), p. 351.

12. Massachusetts Bureau of the Statistics of Labor, *Report* (Boston: Wright and Potter, 1870), pp. 338-9.

13. E.J. Hobsbawm, *Labouring Men* (New York, 1964), pp. 272-315.

14. For an example of the range of wage rates and occupations in the metal industries, see *Annual Report of the Secretary of Internal Affairs of the Commonwealth of Pennsylvania, Part 3, Industrial Statistics*, Vol. 4, 1875-1876 (Harrisburg, 1877), pp. 546, 621, and ff. See also *Ibid.*, Vol. 6, 1877-1878, passim.

15. David Montgomery, "Trade Union Practice and the Origins of Syndicalist Theory in the United States" (Paper delivered at the Sorbonne, 1968), p. 3; United States Senate, *Report of the Committee of the Senate upon the Relations between Capital and Labor*, 5 vols (Washington, D.C., 1885) 2: 2-3; David Brody, *Steelworkers in America: The Non-Union Era* (Cambridge, Mass., 1960), p. 52.

16. Seymour M. Lipset, Martin Trow, and James S. Coleman, *Union Democracy* (Glencoe, Ill., 1956), pp. 1-76, and Robert Christie, *Empire in Wood* (Ithaca, N.Y., 1956), pp. 25-8.

17. See Montgomery, "Trade Union Practice," and Edwin T. Freedley, *Philadelphia and its Manufactures* (Philadelphia: Edward Young, 1858), p. 221.

18. Blanche E. Hazard, *The Organization of the Boot and Shoe Industry in Massachusetts Before 1875* (Cambridge, Mass., 1921), pp. 87-126. See also Charles Booth, *Labor and Life of the People* (New York, 1970), 1st ser., vol. 4, pp. 37-156 and 2nd ser., vol. 3, pp. 9-50.

19. A foreman blacksmith from Philadelphia reported to Pennsylvania's Secretary of Internal Affairs that his yearly income for 1880 was $900 *(Industrial Statistics*, vol. 8, 1879-1880, p. 247). This compares favorably with the average profit of small blacksmith firms, which was $744 in 1880 (see Table 10). The same source indicates that foremen in various industries earned daily wages ranging from $2.25 to $6.00 (annual incomes of $675 to $1800). See *Industrial Statistics*, vol. 4, 1875-1876, pp. 546-9; and vol. 9, 1880-1881, pp. 163-5.

20. Although we have collected data on the occupational patterns of women, they were not available for use in this essay. The discussion in this section, therefore, is based on the male work force above the age of 18.

21. "Unskilled" labor is of two types: *specified* occupations such as "watchman," and *unspecified* occupations such as "laborer," "day labor," "laboring man," etc. Our discussion here focuses on the *unspecified* category "laborer"; that is, occupations whose designation in the population manuscripts does not allow for categorization into an industry category.

22. See Bruce Laurie, "The Working People of Philadelphia, 1827-1853" (Ph.D. diss., University of Pittsburgh, 1971), chs. 7, 8, and Appendix C.

23. Mack Walker, *Germany and the Emigration, 1816-1885*, (Cambridge, Mass., 1964), p. 69.

24. See, for example, Thomas C. Cochran and William Miller, *The Age of Enterprise*, rev. ed. (New York, 1961), p. 223; Ray Ginger, *Age of Excess* (New York, 1965), pp. 35-6; and Carl N. Degler, *The Age of the Economic Revolution 1876-1900* (Glenview, Ill., 1967), p. 34.

25. John R. Commons, "American Shoemakers, 1648-1895," *Quarterly Journal of Economics* 24 (1910): 39-84.

26. If the ownership of real property is considered as a measure of "well-being," this possibility gains support. Although the proportion of Germans who were "skilled" workers was *twice* that of the Irish, the Germans were only 20 percent more likely to own real property. In 1870, 16.2 percent of the Germans and 13.6 percent of the Irish owned real property (these figures are age-standardized).

27. Stephan Thernstrom, *Poverty and Progress* (Cambridge, Mass., 1964), pp. 99-102, 109-11, and 155-7.

28. The problem, of course, is how operationally to differentiate among this large group of workers. The population census manuscripts do not provide any information beyond the designation "laborer" which can be used to resolve this problem. Although the manufacturing census manuscripts contain information which explicitly and implicitly describes the work environment, they do not list by name the individuals employed by each firm. Taken alone neither of these two sources of information is useful in overcoming the problem. But if they can be combined in some fashion, it may be possible to differentiate among laborers.
The Philadelphia Social History Project has worked out a method ("industrial geography") which links the residence of the individual worker to the location of the individual firm in which he may have worked (this method is not limited to laborers, but can be used in the linkage of any worker to any firm). Laborers who lived within roughly a two-block radius (empirically derived) of the firm are identified as likely to have worked in the firm and their careers are treated separately in analysis. A profile of their well-being, including ownership of real and personal property and whether wives worked and children attended school, can be constructed and compared to profiles of other groups of laborers. The profiles of laborers who are identified as employed by firms paying high wages, for example, should be better than those of laborers who were linked to firms paying low wages or to undifferentiated laborers who probably were employed on a very casual basis. This method of linking individuals to the firms in which

they may have worked will be most successful in the outlying areas of the city where heavy industry was located and where identification of potential employees will not be complicated by the dense concentration of people and firms at the city's center. "Industrial geography" is discussed in greater detail in Theodore Hershberg, "The Philadelphia Social History Project: A Methodological History" (Ph.D. diss., Stanford University, 1973).

29. See, for example, Robert Tressell, (psued., Robert Noonan), *The Ragged Trousered Philanthropists* (London, 1971), p. 15, and Sidney Pollard, *A History of Labour in Sheffield* (Liverpool, 1959), p. 84.

30. See the proportion of Irish and German sons with occupations in building construction, new metal trades, and printing (Tables 12 and 13).

"America is the woman's promised land": Swedish Immigrant Women and American Domestic Service

JOY K. LINTELMAN

DOMESTIC SERVICE WAS ONE of the most common forms of female wage-work in nineteenth- and early twentieth-century America. This occupation has captured the interest of several historians in recent years, perhaps most notably in David Katzman's *Seven Days a Week* and Daniel Sutherland's *Americans and Their Servants*.[1] These books represent important contributions to the historical literature on women and work in America, and have been well-received by scholars for analysis and detailed descriptions of household labor. In spite of this recent valuable work, our knowledge of domestic service remains incomplete. Both Katzman and Sutherland offer only limited information about one group of women who comprised a significant proportion of the domestic labor market—immigrant women. In 1890 foreign-born white women represented nearly 32 percent of the female servant population.[2] This essay will argue, based on material from Swedish immigrant domestics, that the experience of domestic service for immigrant women differed markedly from that of white native-born women.

While the literature on domestic service indicates that some women found domestic work a satisfying and enjoyable form of employment, the occupation is portrayed as a largely negative experience for the majority of domestic workers. Though certain attractions such as a steady income, room and board included with wages, and physical exercise are acknowledged, most domestics are described as generally unhappy with their work and eager to obtain other employment. This dissatisfaction, it is held, stems from several negative characteristics of domestic work, including physical over-exertion, lack of social prestige, lack of personal freedom, loneliness, and isolation.[3]

At the beginning of this research on single Swedish immigrant women, many of whom were employed as domestics, the expectation was to find the same unhappy souls described in the recent research: women forced into domestic work by lack of job skills, not by choice, and eager to leave household service as soon as possible. In fact, one might imagine that immigrant domestics would be even more frustrated with household service than native-born women. Immigrant domestics, often in their first months of employment, were also experiencing the adjustment of moving from one culture to another, with all of the pressures and anxieties such a transformation could entail. But the experiences described by many Swedish immigrant domestics are quite the contrary. Most came to America intending to find employment as domestics, were satisfied with their jobs, enjoyed cordial relationships with their employers, found their work tasks manageable, and led relatively active social lives.

To what should we attribute these sharply divergent pictures of domestic service? The confusion lies in the perspective researchers have taken toward household labor. Most of the current studies fail to distinguish between the experiences of native-born and immigrant domestics. For example, Katzman states that immigrant women represented a significant proportion of domestic workers, which, he explains, had to do with their cultural background of a service tradition, and in the case of Scandinavians, a tradition of farm to city migration to seek domestic work. He suggests that immigrant women saw domestic employment as an avenue for upward mobility through rapid acculturation. Young immigrant women with agrarian backgrounds were exposed to modern, industrialized America. But aside from these factors which attracted immigrant women to domestic service, Katzman argues that the experiences of immigrant and native-born household workers were very similar, and therefore largely negative.[4] This article indicates otherwise, suggesting that Swedish immigrants found greater satisfaction in domestic service than white native-born women.

Katzman's source materials may, in part, explain his lack of specific attention to the immigrant domestic. He utilizes many valuable and previously ignored resources on household labor, such as reports of investigations conducted by reformers and state labor bureaus. He also includes comments from several articles and a novel written by women who had worked as domestics. But most of these source materials reflect the experiences of native-born rather than immigrant domestics. And in his analysis of these materials, Katzman makes few attempts to distinguish between native-born and immigrant workers.[5] Sutherland's work also lacks detailed examination of domestic service from the immigrant woman's perspective.[6]

To document the ethnic domestic experience, it is necessary to know more about the specific situations of immigrant domestic workers. This essay describes the experiences of Swedish immigrant domestics, using

personal documents—"America letters," biographies, and autobiographies—
to develop an alternative picture of household labor and what it meant to
Swedish immigrant women. These personal sources shed a different light
on domestic service. Apparently the ethnic elements in these women's
lives shaped their experiences as domestics, making household labor a
positive and even attractive occupation, in contrast to the mostly negative
experiences of white native-born American domestics.

The sharp differences between the native-born domestics and the Swedish group have two central sources. The first is the cultural and social
background from which these women emigrated. Comparatively speaking, employment as a domestic in America was a marked improvement
from the same type of work in Sweden. The second source relates to the
attachments these women maintained with their family and friends, and
with the Swedish ethnic enclaves in the cities where they worked. These
ethnic and kinship ties countered the loneliness and isolation felt by
native-born domestics, and helped immigrant women adjust to a new
language, culture, and physical environment as well. For these women
who had this "connectedness" to an ethnic and/or familial support network, domestic service could be a positive and even rewarding
employment.[7]

The primary motivation for these women's migration to America was
economic. Few job opportunities existed for single females in Sweden at
the turn of the century other than domestic service or limited types of
factory work. Although some female high schools existed, higher education was generally too expensive for most young women from families
with limited means.[8] It was common for daughters of working class
families to obtain employment outside the home at a young age—after
confirmation at about age fourteen, and sometimes even younger. Family
size was large, and children were expected to contribute toward their own
economic support. Most of these young girls worked outside their homes
as domestic servants—called *pigor* in Swedish. In the primarily agrarian
society of nineteenth-century Sweden, many of these *pigor* worked on
farms and estates, where their duties included outdoor chores and field
work as well as household tasks. This type of employment offered only
low wages, or sometimes only payment in kind. While these women were
not able to make significant contributions to the family economy by
working as *pigor*, economic pressure on the family was relieved because
domestics received room and board from their employers.[9]

But such employment offered little hope for advancement. As the
Swedish immigrant stream to America expanded to its peak in the 1880s,

young Swedish women learned of the increased economic opportunities in the land to the west. Friends wrote home or visited, describing their success in America. Single women were interested in the possibilities of supporting themselves in America, and were logically interested in domestic service, an employment which was familiar to them at home in Sweden. Emigrants told of higher wages, easier job tasks, and increased social status for domestics in America. Young Swedish women responded to this information by immigrating in large numbers to America, particularly in the decades between 1880 and 1920 (see Table 1). Dina Peterson, who came to America in 1905, wrote about her decision to emigrate:

> After confirmation . . . I began work as a maid for a neighbor. I got thirty kronor for six months during the summer, and had to milk cows and look after the children and partake in all the work which occurred on the farm[.] [M]y oldest sister had immigrated in 1902, and came to a nice doctor's family in New York and liked it so well, and got twelve dollars a month. . . . I was also promised a job with them and I immediately became America-sick.[10]

This desire for and previous experience in domestic employment was a trait Swedish immigrant women also shared with their Finnish and Irish immigrant sisters.[11]

In many instances a sister or brother found the immigrant her first job. In 1909 Maja Johanson immigrated to America and was met by a sister who had immigrated five years earlier. Maja's sister made arrangements to have her own employer hire Maja.[12] In the case of Maria Sorensson,

TABLE 1

Single Female Emigration from Sweden to Non-European Nations, 1861-1915, expressed numerically and as a proportion of the total male and female non-European emigration from Sweden.

Years	Number of Single Women	Total Male & Female	Single Women as Percent of Total
1861-1870	14,465	93,119	15.5
1871-1880	22,672	102,501	22.1
1881-1890	85,343	327,505	26.1
1891-1900	68,661	204,513	33.6
1901-1910	66,232	224,043	29.6
1911-1915	19,868	63,361	31.4

Source: Statistiska Centralbyrån, *Historisk Statistik för Sverige. Del 1 Befolkningen.* (Stockholm, 1969), p. 129, table 49.

who immigrated to Sioux City, Iowa in the 1880s, a sister relinquished to Maria her position and found a new one for herself.[13] When one Swedish immigrant named Carl wrote to his sister Hulda in 1889, he sent her a ticket to America, gave her instructions for traveling safely and comfortably on the boat, and promised to have ready employment for her upon arrival.[14] Similarly, Anna J. Olson, after leaving Sweden in 1903, wrote home that her brother had found domestic work for her in Jersey City near his home.[15]

The initial assistance was, of course, especially important, because most of these women could not speak English upon arrival and would have had difficulty findings jobs alone. But this employment assistance did not end once the initial job was landed. Relatives along with friends made on the boat trip over kept in contact in America, comparing wages and working conditions, and helping with job leads. Katzman discusses the difficulty many domestics had in finding new domestic positions, stressing their lack of freedom of movement. He asserts that "few servants had adequate resources to remain out of work for long, since most were to some degree supporting their families." He emphasizes the tenuous living arrangements: "Often single women had no place to live other than an employer's household, and whatever savings they had put by would be eaten up by room and board while they were job-hunting."[16] Katzman notes how domestics maintained personal networks to find employment, but indicates that this job-seeking strategy declined markedly between the Civil War and World War I.[17]

Yet utilizing personal networks for obtaining employment was a common strategy among the Swedish domestics studied in this essay. Lina Eriksson wrote to her parents in 1882 from Moline, Illinois about a Swedish family who allowed her to stay with them until she had found a domestic job. In 1884 she left Moline to take a position with a friend in Paullina, Iowa. Neither of the young women liked working there and within two months they were back in Moline, employed together in a large household.[18] Another woman in Chicago, Illinois wrote to her niece in Sweden in 1902, "If you wish to come here you are very welcome . . . you can always stay with me when you want and I will do whatever I can to get you positions [as a domestic]."[19] Olga Johnsson stayed with a Swedish woman acquaintance for three days while waiting for a Swedish employment bureau in Chicago to locate a domestic position for her.[20]

These women who tapped ethnic and familial contacts both for their initial emigration and during their time spent in domestic service had considerable control over their lives and choices. Rather than feeling trapped in miserable positions, unable to find better jobs easily, and faced with a period of homelessness while in-between jobs—the situation depicted for many native-born domestics—these immigrant women relied on ethnic networks both to locate new employment and to find a place to stay while waiting for new jobs or taking time off. These networks allowed them to choose jobs carefully and lowered the risks involved in quickly leaving a position considered unsatisfactory.

Once in America and on the job, these women usually found their work as domestics easier than it had been in Sweden, offering better pay and improved working conditions. Hilda Pärsson wrote home in 1882 about her sister Tilda who had emigrated the year before. "It is a great difference now for Tilda than when she worked for farmers and slaved and got nothing except perhaps a little food and clothes when the year was over. But now she has fine clothes and paid off her ticket last spring." She continued by expressing pity for girls who had to work as domestics in Sweden because "they cannot protect themselves more than a slave and employers can have a maid instead of a farm-hand."[21] Describing her work tasks, Moli Nilsson wrote home from Omaha, Nebraska in 1890 that she "cooked and cleaned and baked and kept the house clean and avoided going outdoors even to get water because they have indoor plumbing." Nilsson continued, "I avoid going out and slaving like the poor girls in Sweden must do. I do not want to go back to Sweden because they work too hard."[22] Hanna Larsson wrote in 1888 that she "had quite a bit to do, so one still has to work here, though it is not like work in Sweden."[23] This kind of comparison appears frequently in Swedish immigrant women's letters. Even Swedish males in America recognized the benefits of working as a domestic in the United States. A young man named Carl wrote home to his sister Stina: "America is the woman's promised land. . . . A domestic is never asked to clean her employer's shoes, he does that himself." He described the typical work week for a domestic, with washing one day, ironing the next, and so on, including pre-determined times when the domestic was free to do as she wished. Carl added, "Swedish and Norwegian girls are always popular, especially if they can cook."[24]

No doubt one element in these comparisons of Swedish and American domestic service relates to differences between working in rural and urban households. Many of these Swedish immigrant women had been employed as *pigor* on farms in Sweden, and were pleased to discover that domestic employment in American urban areas was truly household, not farmyard, work. In terms of tasks performed, domestic labor in urban Sweden and urban America was probably quite similar. Yet other elements in these women's comparisons are unrelated to rural versus urban service. Domestics in America, Swedish women often pointed out, had determined work tasks and working hours. Maja Johanson's sister noted that "domestics had it much better [in America] than in Sweden [,] work was determined for every day and evenings were free." Maja herself later immigrated after working as a domestic in the city of Halmstad. "[T]here was no determined working-time so when I heard how much better domestics had it in America . . . I left."[25]

Despite the fact that domestics were viewed in American society as a "servant class," Swedish immigrant domestics viewed their move to America as an improvement in social status. This attitude originates from two sources. One, as indicated above, is that working conditions and wages were better in America than in Sweden. Whereas the domestic found it difficult to purchase her own clothing, let alone save any money, in Sweden on a servant's wages, Swedish women in America were able to support themselves, including clothing themselves, and often had money to spare to save or send home to the family. Maja Johanson wrote in 1909 about how much fun it was "to get one's wages and send money home and still have enough for oneself."[26]

The second source of improved social status relates to the treatment these women received from others—both from their employers and from their ethnic community. Women describing their improved situations in America pointed not only to job tasks, but to treatment by employers. Complaints about employers in the documents examined were rare, although there were some comments about deciding to change jobs because a particular position required too much work and the employer refused to raise the salary of the domestic.[27] But most Swedish household workers in the letters, biographies, and autobiographies had very positive relationships with their bosses. Olga Johnsson wrote in 1896, "I now have a place in a family. . . . They are as concerned for me as if I were their own daughter. If it rains when I am going out then the mistress lets me use their clothes so I won't ruin my own."[28] Maja Johanson wrote in 1909 about her new position where "all were friendly, one did not feel like a servant."[29] Anna Olson described the relationship with her employers as one like daughter and parents. She indicated that "they usually came down to the kitchen every evening and sat and read with me from a Swedish-English book."[30] Although not all women developed these nearly familial relationships with their employers, most were quite satisfied with their situations. In contrast to Sweden, a domestic in America was, as one woman put it, "treated like a human being."[31]

Some of these female letter-writers may have avoided telling their families about negative aspects of their work, though the number of these cases is probably limited. The fact that the stream of single women immigrating from Sweden to work in America remained of significant size for several decades suggests that the positives of immigration outweighed the negatives. Research by Swedish historian Ann-Sofie Kälvemark also suggests that rural domestics, like most of those described in this essay, who were immigrating to America were less dependent on their parents with regard to their decision to immigrate and the financing of immigration than *hemmadöttrar*—wealthier Swedish farmer's daughters who were not employed outside of the family household.[32] While the rural laboring women's families were probably concerned about the safety and happiness of their daughter/sibling, most of the women studied here had worked and lived away from their homes for several years prior to immigration. It is doubtful that these women felt any exaggerated need to assure their families of their well-being when they had already proven their capabilities as independent laborers.

Historians have depicted the domestic as desiring to leave household service at the first possible opportunity. The low social status connected to domestic work in America has been cited as a major reason for this attitude.[33] However, the Swedish women examined in this article were not so eager to obtain other forms of employment. Many worked as domestics for one to three years and some worked as long as ten to twenty years. Rather than bemoaning a low social status, they felt their status had improved compared to their past positions in Sweden. When examining ethnic domestics, the researcher must consider the values of the ethnic group as well as American social values. The Swedish women were able to support themselves, as well as to contribute to the support of their families in Sweden. Rather than feeling ashamed of employment in household labor, they felt proud of their economic independence, and were respected within their primary social network—the ethnic community. Although the research materials analyzed do not document the attitudes of the ethnic community per se, these women did not suggest in their writings that their countrymen and countrywomen viewed domestic service negatively. Research on community attitudes toward domestic service among Finnish immigrants has indicated that household employment was viewed with considerable respect.[34]

Social isolation and loneliness represent a final area in which the Swedish domestic experience differs markedly from that of native-born domestics. For example, Katzman comments that "long workdays seven

392

days a week and restricted free time left servants isolated from ordinary social interaction. More than anything else, servants felt this loss of freedom." Sutherland also states that "this lack of freedom, more than any other aspect of servants' lives, worsened the social stigma [attached to domestic service]."[35]

Judging from their letters and biographies, Swedish domestics led relatively active social lives, participating in functions sponsored by churches (usually Swedish) and the local ethnic community. They had friends among fellow domestics, as well as among other members of their ethnic group. Though their free time was certainly constrained by the demands of their employment, they made the most of their leisure time, and rarely expressed feeling isolated.

Most domestics were allowed some time during the day to tend to their own needs, as well as receiving an afternoon and an evening off when they were not expected to be in the employer's home. To the woman who had worked in Sweden, where time off was often undetermined, the American situation was a marked improvement. Moli Nilsson wrote in 1890: "[One has] . . . much more freedom here than at home. When one has finished work in the evenings then one can go and do as one wants. Usual quitting time is at 7:00 p.m."[36] She went on to describe the typical pattern of Thursday afternoons and Sunday evenings when domestics were free to go out in the town. Other women found positions which allowed extra personal time. Olga Johnsson wrote home in 1896 that "I don't work afternoons except for myself if I want, otherwise I go up and lie down."[37]

What did these women do with their free time? Were they too tired to enjoy leisure time, or too physically isolated from their friends and relatives to maintain and develop friendships? Most of the activities described by Swedish immigrant domestics center around the ethnic community, and much of it takes place via the ethnic church. Relating her free-time activities to her parents, Olga Johnsson wrote that on Thursday afternoons she usually went to visit a Swedish woman where "all the Swedish girls meet and have a good time." Every Sunday she attended church, where she participated in both a choir and a youth club. This woman also found other times during the week to socialize, because her good friend was employed in a home nearby so they could, as she wrote, "meet every day and talk about everything." Sometimes friends were able to be employed together in the same household. Lina Eriksson wrote home that she worked with two other Swedish girls and had lots of fun. But socializing was not limited to activities among fellow domestics, or just among females. The same woman wrote that she had "many good friends both girls and boys and so I am invited out two to three times a week."[38] Many of these Swedish domestics married Swedish immigrant men, supporting the assertion that these woman maintained close ties to the ethnic community despite the rather unique requirements of their employment: living in the employers' homes, often some distance from the Swedish ethnic community.

Whether or not women could leave their places of employment at other times varied from household to household. One Swedish woman working in New York around 1915 was allowed to go out to the theater two nights a week in addition to her regular time off. The only restrictions were that two persons needed to be present at her place of employment. The servants could decide among themselves who would go out and when.[39] Ellen Seagren, who worked in Minneapolis in the 1910s, told of asking for and receiving permission to attend certain church events on weeknights.[40]

Although holidays could be lonely times if the domestic had to stay and work in her employer's home, many of the women studied were able to take time off at Christmas to spend with friends or relatives. One woman took off a week at Christmas to spend with a friend, staying in the friend's sister's home during that time. She wrote that they "had parties every day and we had our friends there and we were out and visited and we slept until ten or eleven every day."[41] Because Swedish domestics usually worked in large cities such as Chicago, Minneapolis, and Boston, where good-sized Swedish ethnic communities existed, they could take advantage of the social events which took place within the ethnic group. Olga Johnsson wrote to her parents that "next Thursday the 12th of March I will go to a concert by the Swedish musical group Skandia. There will be a lot of music and singing and it will be lots of fun." Johnsson embellished that she had "much more fun here than at home. There were never any parties there like there are here."[42]

Proximity to the ethnic community seemed to be a key to avoiding isolation. Hasia Diner's research on Irish women suggests that isolation was not a major difficulty for domestics in that ethnic group. Irish servants worked most often in cities such as Boston, New York, and Philadelphia where there were significant numbers of male and female Irish immigrants, and a core Irish ethnic community or neighborhood around which social activities could resolve. However, the Finnish domestics studied by Carl Ross complained of isolation. Most of the male Finn immigrants were not living in urban ethnic communities—they were employed in smaller mining and lumbering towns.[43]

Swedish immigrant domestics certainly suffered some problems in their work, and some women probably felt America was not really a "promised land." What this essay documents, however, is that domestic employment for most Swedish immigrant women was a positive experience, in stark contrast to the largely negative experiences portrayed in studies on native-born white domestics. That Swedish domestics found their work attractive and rewarding is obvious from the letters, biographies, and autobiographies they have written containing comments about their work. Rather than feeling trapped in a job which lacked respect as well as opportunity for individual growth and personal recreation, these women capitalized on their ethnic networks to counter problems common to household workers. Most were not eager to leave domestic service. The positive attitude shared by Swedish-American domestic servants toward their work is suggested in the following statement of a woman who wrote: "you asked me if I had a fiancee. I can't say that I don't have one, but I haven't decided on one yet, because I believe that if I get married I won't have things as good as I have them now."[44]

Although these ethnic domestics spent more of their time in American households than in their ethnic communities, they did not automatically adopt the attitudes and values of native-born women. Swedish immigrant women functioned well as they moved between the two worlds of the American middle-class household and the Swedish-American ethnic community.[45] Their ethnic background and their continued contact with their ethnic group shaped their responses to domestic service, resulting in an experience quite different from that of their native-born sisters in service.

NOTES

A note on source materials: the primary research for this essay was conducted in Sweden under a Fulbright Grant in 1986–87. Collections at the *Utvandrarnas Hus* (Emigrant Institute) in Växjö and the *Folkminnessamling* (Folklore Archive) in Stockholm were examined. These collections included letters and short biographical and autobiographical essays concerning Swedes who had emigrated to America. The letters and essays by or about Swedish women emigrating from 1880 to 1920 were carefully analyzed, and represent the primary source material upon which the above work is based.

When an earlier form of this essay was presented as a conference paper in Sweden, the question of reliability of immigrant letters as source materials arose. Some scholars argued that immigrants rarely wrote home about their true feelings and circumstances, because to admit failure or dissatisfaction with life in their new homeland would bring great shame. I have considered this argument as I have analyzed several hundred immigrant letters by Swedish women, but I remain convinced of the value of letters as source materials. As with other historical sources, similarities in these documents in attitudes expressed and experiences related over time and across space suggest a common experience. That so many women had similar feelings about domestic work over a period of approximately forty years supports the validity of their statements.

The relationship between the writer and the addressee of the letters as well as the reason for writing are also important considerations. In many instances in the letters examined, the writer was responding to direct questions which had been posed to her in earlier letters. Young Swedish women often wrote to their friends and relatives who had immigrated, asking about working conditions and life in America because they were themselves contemplating emigration. Were the Swedish immigrant women in America to exaggerate or falsify the information in their responses to these inquiries, they might suffer the consequences by finding a newly immigrated sister or friend on their doorstep in a few months.

Not only do immigrant letters, at least those written by Swedish immigrant women which I have examined, represent an important source of information on immigrants and domestic service, they offer a wealth of other material as well. Women writing home to Sweden discussed many details of their new lives in America, from common work tasks and leisure activities to their opinions on American society and culture. Immigrant letters represent a nearly untapped resource for research on immigration and ethnicity, and especially for research on immigrant and ethnic women.

1. David M. Katzman, *Seven Days a Week: Women and Domestic Service in Industrializing America*, (New York, 1978); Daniel E. Sutherland, *Americans and Their Servants*, (Baton Rouge, La., 1981). Other studies of domestic service and household labor in America include Faye E. Dudden, *Serving Women: Household Service in Industrial America*, (Middletown, Conn., 1983); Blaine E. McKinley, "'Strangers in the Gates': Employer Reactions Toward Domestic Servants in America, 1825–1875" (Ph.D. diss., Michigan State University, 1969), and Susan Strasser, *Never Done: A History of American Housework* (New York, 1982).

2. United States Bureau of the Census, *Statistics of Women at Work* (Washington, D.C., 1907), pp. 159, 185; Joseph Hill, *Women in Gainful Occupations 1870 to 1920* Census Monographs 9 (Washington, D.C., 1929), p. 38. Though the number of immigrant domestics decreased over time, reflecting both the wide-scale entrance of Blacks into domestic work as well as a decline in immigration for those groups most likely to work as domestics, white foreign-born women still represented 21 percent of the servant population in 1920.

3. Katzman, *Seven Days*, pp. 7–43, passim; Sutherland, *Americans*, chapters 5 and 6, pp. 82–120.

4. Katzman, *Seven Days*, pp. 68–9, 171.

5. See Katzman's bibliographic essay "A Note on Sources", *Seven Days*, pp. 341–365. Katzman's discussion of immigrant domestics focuses upon propensities to work in household service, immigrants' proportion of the domestic population, ethnic preferences of employers, regional distribution, and tendencies of second-generation immigrants to avoid domestic work. While these are important considerations, they do not address the issue of individual experiences of immigrant versus native-born domestics.

6. Sutherland examined a few collections and volumes of immigrant letters, but these materials included only a limited number of servants' letters, and did not represent a significant source in his work. (see p. 292).

7. Several scholars of Swedish immigration have also found the Swedish single female immigrant experience to be a positive one for reasons similar to those detailed in my

research. Ann-Sofie Kälvemark has briefly documented the terrible conditions of Swedish domestics and their choice of immigration as a means to better their lives. See Ann-Sofie Kälvemark, "Utvandring och självständighet: Några synpunkter på den kvinnliga emigrationen från Sverige," *Historisk Tidskrift*, 2(1983): 140–174. H. Arnold Barton, who has also used immigrant letters as source materials, has pointed out the many attractions of American domestic work compared to work as a *piga* in Sweden, though he also asserts that the Swedish immigrant domestics quickly and eagerly adopted the "genteel" values of the American middle class—an assertion of which I am not convinced from my own research. See *Letters from the Promised Land: Swedes in America, 1840–1914*, ed. H. Arnold Barton, (Minneapolis, Minn., 1975), p. 112, and H. Arnold Barton, "Scandinavian Immigrant Women's Encounter with America," *Swedish Pioneer Historical Quarterly*, 25 (January, 1974): 37–42. Ingrid Semmingsen, a scholar of Norwegian immigration, has also questioned Barton's hypothesis regarding Swedish maids and Americanization, in "Women in Norwegian Emigration," in *Scandinavians in America: Literary Life*, ed. J.R. Christianson, (Decorah, Iowa, 1985), pp. 75–91. Byron Nordstrom's description of a female Swedish labor migrant's experiences provides a somewhat less rosy picture of life in America, though the woman described worked mostly as a live-out day-laborer rather than the traditional domestic work examined in this essay. See Byron J. Nordstrom, "Evelina Månsson and the Memoir of an Urban Labor Migrant," *Swedish Pioneer Historical Quarterly*, 31 (1980): 182–95.

8. The literature on nineteenth-century Swedish women is still quite sparse. One of the better pieces is a collection of essays by Swedish historian Gunnar Qvist, entitled *Konsten att blifva en god flicka: kvinnohistoriska uppsatser* (Stockholm, 1978), see also Kälvemark who describes interviews with a group of Swedish women immigrating to America, including comments about why they were leaving Sweden.

9. David Gaunt, *Familjeliv i Norden*, (Malmö, Sweden, 1983) and *Hembiträdet berättar om liv och arbete i borgerliga familjer i början av 1900-talet: uppteckningar ur kulturhistoriska undersökningens arkiv*, (Stockholm, Sweden, 1975).

10. Autobiography, Dina Peterson Collection, Folklore Archive, Nordic Museum, Stockholm, Sweden (immigrated 1905). (Note—the references below listing Folkminnessamling [Folklore Archive] are segments of two large manuscript collections. These collections are comprised of entries to two contests, one sponsored by a Stockholm newspaper and the other by a popular Swedish magazine, in the 1940s and 1960s which asked people to submit materials on immigration to compete for several prizes.)

11. Varpu Lindström-Best, "'I Won't Be a Slave!'—Finnish Domestics in Canada, 1911–30," in *Looking into My Sister's Eyes: An Exploration in Women's History*, ed. Jean Burnet (Toronto, Ontario, 1986), pp. 33, 36, 39; Hasia R. Diner, *Erin's Daughters in America: Irish Immigrant Women in the Nineteenth Century*, (Baltimore, Md., 1983), pp. 71–72, 86.

12. Biography, Maja Johanson Collection, Folklore Archive, (this woman immigrated to America in 1909).

13. Biography, Klara Jakobsson Collection, Folklore Archive (Jakobsson wrote about her mother and aunts who immigrated to America in the 1880s).

14. Letter, Adolph Larsson Collection, Folklore Archive, Carl Erik Karlgren to his mother and sisters, from Sioux City, Iowa, 5 May 1889.

15. Autobiography, Anna J. Olson (nee Nilsson) Collection, Folklore Archive (immigrated 1903).

16. Katzman, *Seven Days*, p. 140.

17. Ibid., pp. 96–99.

18. Letters, collection 10:3:19, Emigrant Institute, Växjö, Sweden, Karolina Eriksson to her parents and siblings in Mörtjuck, Sweden from Moline, Illinois, 17 May 1882;

Karolina Eriksson to her parents and siblings from Moline, 9 September 1884; Karolina Eriksson to her parents from Paullina, Iowa 3 December 1884; Karolina Eriksson to her parents and siblings from Moline, 5 February 1885.

19. Letter, collection 22:6:16:M:3:I, Emigrant Institute, Tillie Nelson to Hilma Ohlson from Chicago, Illinois, 12 February 1902.

20. Letter, collection 22:17:16:I:20, Emigrant Institute, Olga Henrietta Johnson to her father from Chicago, Illinois, 6 November 1896.

21. Letter, collection 22:1:14:A, Emigrant Institute, Hilda Pärsson to her brother Carl from Oneida (Illinois?), 30 August 1882.

22. Letter, Asta Fridström Collection, Folklore Archive, Moli Nilsson to her friend Maria Nilsson, from Omaha, Nebraska, 18 March 1890.

23. Letter, Sixten Nilsson Collection, Folklore Archive, Hanna Larsson to her aunt and uncle from Oskaloosa, Iowa, 22 January 1888.

24. Letter, Svea Jönsson Collection, Folklore Archive, Carl to his sister Stina from Sioux City, Iowa, 4 April 1910.

25. Autobiography, Maja Johanson Collection, Folklore Archive (immigrated 1909, returned to Sweden to live 1928).

26. Ibid.

27. Examples of descriptions of job changes in immigrant letters and biographies include the following: "Viola got a place as a cook with a doctor for 20 dollars. But she must move soon so that she can get better wages." (Biography, Kristina Vestberg Collection, Folklore Archive, biography of Vestberg's aunt who immigrated in 1903 at age 18)—and "I have now quit as a waitress. I was not there more than three weeks. I now have another place and it is much better. I have very little to do here. I have nearly every afternoon free, and my employer is very nice and friendly toward me." (letter, Elisabet Jönsson collection, Folklore Archive, Charlotte Bergstrom to her parents from Rockford, Illinois, circa 1890s).

28. Letter, collection 22:17:16:I:6, Emigrant Institute, Olga Johnsson to her father from Brighton, Massachusetts, 22 July 1896.

29. Biography, Maja Johanson Collection.

30. Autobiography, Anna J. Olson Collection.

31. Emigrationsutredningen, 21 parts in 9 vols. (Stockholm, 1908–13), 7: "Utvandrarnas egna uppgifter" (1908), p. 256.

32. Kälvemark, "Utvandring och självständighet," p. 166.

33. Katzman, Seven Days, pp. 8–9, 268, 278–9.

34. Lindström-Best, "'I Won't Be a Slave!'" p. 42.

35. Katzman, Seven Days, p. 115; Sutherland, Americans, p. 101.

36. Letter, Asta Fridström Collection, Folklore Archive, Moli Nilsson to friend Maria Nilsson from Omaha, Nebraska, 18 March 1890.

37. Letter, collection 22:17:16:I:6, Olga Johnsson to her father from Brighton, Massachusetts, 22 July 1896.

38. Letters, collection 10:3:19, Karolina Ericksson to her brother from Moline, Illinois, 10 December 1882; Karolina Ericksson to her parents and siblings from Moline, Illinois, 23 September 1885.

39. Inge Lund, En Piga i USA: Ett Pennskafts Äventyr, (Stockholm, 1917) p. 136.

40. Interview with Ellen Seagren, Minneapolis, Minnesota, 8 December, 1985.

41. Letter, collection 10:3:19, Karolina Ericksson to parents and siblings from Moline, Illinois, 16 January 1886.

42. Letter, collection 22:17:16:I:6, Olga Johnsson to her father from Cambridgeport, Massachusetts, 4 March 1896.

43. Diner, *Erin's Daughters*, p. 40. Another factor influencing the Irish immigrant woman's satisfaction with domestic service may have been the cultural tradition of gender segregation of adults, described by Diner in the first chapter of her book, especially pp. 20–22; Carl Ross, "Servant Girls: Community Leaders," in *Women Who Dared: The History of Finnish-American Women*, eds. Carl Ross and K. Marianne Wargelin Brown (St. Paul, Minn., 1986) p. 48.

44. Letter, Hulda Maria Hellberg Collection, Folklore Archive, Hädda Carlson to her brother(?) from Bradford, Pennsylvania, 10 September 1883.

45. Although a few of the domestics examined here were employed by wealthy immigrant families (usually Irish or Swedish), the majority were employed in the households of native-born and often old-stock Americans.

Tradition and Opportunity: The Japanese Immigrant in America

JOHN MODELL

The author is a member of the history department in the University of Minnesota

IN THE LATE NINETEENTH CENTURY Japan began experiencing far-reaching demographic changes which manifested themselves in a wide variety of ways. One of these was the Japanese attempt to gain political hegemony in Asia; another was the development of "a continuous and ascending movement of Japanese emigration."[1] The thrift and perseverance of those migrants whose ultimate destination was the United States are well known, as is the hostility shown them by white America. But the story of the internal differentiation of the Japanese-American community has been, in the main, untold.[2] This paper, based on retrospective evidence gathered by a structured interview schedule administered in the early 1960s to a representative sample of Issei (Japanese immigrants) living in the continental United States, will attempt to examine statistically the circumstances of the migration and some of the long-term consequences for those who undertook

---

[1] Imre Ferenczi, *International Migrations* (2 vols., New York, 1929), I, 160.

[2] The literature on Japanese-Americans is large and includes many excellent works. Aside from the well-known studies of discrimination, most of the research has dealt with the overall structure of the Japanese-American population, the organization of the Japanese-American community, or the split between the immigrant generation and its children. Among the better books treating such questions but dealing only tangentially with the question taken up in this paper are: Yamato Ichihashi, *Japanese in the United States* (Palo Alto, 1932); Mamoru Iga, "Acculturation of the Japanese Population in Davis County, Utah" (Ph.D. diss., University of Utah, 1955); Shotaro Frank Miyamoto, "Social Solidarity Among the Japanese in Seattle," *University of Washington Publications in the Social Sciences*, XI (1939), 57–130; John Modell, "The Japanese of Los Angeles: A Study in Growth and Accommodation, 1900–1946" (Ph.D. diss., Columbia University, 1969); William Carlson Smith, *Americans in Process* (Ann Arbor, 1937); Edward K. Strong, *The Second-Generation Japanese Problem* (Palo Alto, 1934); and Dorothy Swaine Thomas, *The Salvage* (Berkeley and Los Angeles, 1952).

it.[3] Specifically, we will seek to find out the extent to which the "success" of an immigrant was predetermined by his background and by the circumstances of his arrival in America.

Our data permit us to discuss important aspects of the current situation as results of a series of alterations in the original pattern of Japanese social relations brought over from the fatherland.[4] We will show that, on the whole, migration to America was a leveling experience, for much (but not all) of what had been known in Japan had to be abandoned or modified if success was to be achieved in America. Most Issei expected that their American stay would be only a temporary interruption in settled ways of doing things. But among those migrants who remained in America, the most tangibly rewarded were those best prepared or most inclined to accept change.

Migration from Japan to America attained sizable proportions shortly before the turn of the present century. At the time, Japanese factory employment was growing, with the number of laborers increasing from 500,000 to 1,500,000 during the first decade of the new century. Manufacturing would shortly surpass agriculture as the most valuable sector of the Japanese economy. Most rural areas were losing population to sparsely settled Hokkaido and to the industrializing cities.[5] Starvation

---

[3] The question of the representativeness of the sample is taken up in John Modell, "The Japanese-American Family: A Perspective for Future Investigations," *PHR*, XXXVII (1968), 67–81. The major deficiency of the generally adequate sample is that the survivors in the 1960s of such an elderly generation are necessarily unrepresentative of one important variable: date of arrival in America. Data gathered about male immigrants from their surviving spouses were adjudged too uncertain to include in the computations upon which the present paper is based; women's reports of their own histories were likewise excluded, for the women's history was a very different one. The total number of male respondents upon which this report is based is 695. The interviews were conducted under the auspices of the Japanese American Research Project, UCLA, with financial support from the Japanese American Citizens League and the Carnegie Corporation. Analysis is proceeding under a grant from the National Institute of Mental Health, Department of Health, Education, and Welfare. Computing assistance was obtained from the Health Sciences Computing Facility, UCLA, and sponsored by National Institutes of Health grant FR-3.

[4] Despite an abundance of "statistics," this paper pretends in no sense to be more "scientific" or even more credible than studies based on more conventional approaches. The sample is less than ideally representative, primarily because those Japanese who stayed for some period in the United States and then returned to their native land were never interviewed. The indicators employed are in some cases imperfectly matched to the purposes they are serving. And only the internal consistency of the responses leads us to place much trust in respondents' memories of such long-ago events. Nevertheless, the techniques employed permit the researcher to relate such diverse yet interrelated factors as family background, education, acculturation, occupational mobility, ethnic-group milieu, socioeconomic status, and assimilation.

[5] Irene B. Taeuber, *The Population of Japan* (Princeton, 1958), 39, 48, 125; Ryoichi Ishii, *Population Pressure and Economic Life in Japan* (London, 1937), 71; Ayanori Okasaki, *Histoire du Japon: L'Economie et la population* ("Travaux et documents," cahier no. 32, Institut national d'études demographiques; Paris, 1958), 87.

did not threaten Japan; rather, "subtle influences upon personal and family psychology, class relations, and national policy" followed from an excess of laboring hands, making emigration both attractive and feasible, especially to sons in large farm families.[6] The overseas migration from Japan was an extension of a much larger internal migration that swelled Japanese cities. A large proportion of the migrants to America, as our sample indicates, had themselves earlier moved from an agricultural to an urban setting within Japan. As was undoubtedly true for those who moved from farm to city in Japan, many if not most of the Japanese international migrants returned to the homes and family they had temporarily left. Although the return-migration rate is impossible to calculate with any accuracy, it is striking to note that, after a half-century of emigration, only a half-million Japanese were enumerated outside of their native land in 1930. Of these, one-fifth were in the United States.[7]

One exogenous factor did much to alter the multitude of minute decisions and unconscious changes that together created the characteristics of the Japanese migration to America: American immigration policy. Aside from the 1924 legislation that excluded Japanese immigrants from America, the most important element of this policy was the "Gentlemen's Agreement" of 1907. According to the terms of this understanding, the American government agreed to thwart attempts at discriminatory legislation on the part of the states in exchange for Japan's informal promise to give passports to America "only to such of its subjects as are non-laborers or are laborers who in coming to the continent, seek to resume a formerly acquired domicile, to join a parent, wife, or children residing there, or to assume active control of an already possessed interest in a farming enterprise in this country." Despite initial disagreement over definitions, Japan's enforcement of the understanding was sufficient to reduce the number of Japanese arrivals in the United States to less than the number of departures returning from there in 1908, the first year of operation following the agreement, and sharply to reduce the earlier male preponderance among the migrants.[8]

---

[6] William W. Lockwood, *The Economic Development of Japan* (Princeton, 1954), 154 and passim.

[7] Ishii, *Population Pressure*, 198; Okasaki, *Histoire*, 86.

[8] Henry Steele Commager, *Documents of American History* (6th ed.; 2 vols., New York, 1957), II, 225; U.S. Department of State, *Papers Relating to the Foreign Relations of the United States, 1924* (Washington, 1939), II, 361; Robert Esthus, *Theodore Roosevelt and Japan* (Seattle, 1966), 227–229.

The impact of the Gentlemen's Agreement is evident in our data. The new regulations seemed to crystallize a change already taking place in the attitude which Japanese families had toward migration to America. Our sample shows that pre-Agreement immigrants tended to be lone representatives of relatively large families. Later arrivals were more often from somewhat smaller families, which had sent or would send *several* members to America. Coincident with this new selectivity, Japanese contemplating an American adventure began to look toward group (and especially family) resources, rather than to individual effort, to develop the rich possibilities of America. A Japanese-American community, as distinct from a group of Japanese resident in America, was thus nurtured. After 1908, one-third of our sample Issei landed

TABLE I—CHARACTERISTICS OF ISSEI, BY ARRIVAL BEFORE OR AFTER GENTLEMEN'S AGREEMENT

	Arrived before Agreement (to 1907)	Arrived after Agreement (1909 or later)
Median age on arrival	19.0	17.5
Socioeconomic level of parents in Japan		
Low	6%	11%
Medium	53	57
High	41	32
Father's occupation in Japan		
Farm proprietor	49%	45%
Farm laborer	25	27
Nonagricultural	26	28
Student in Japan		
Yes	29%	60%
No	71	40
Relatives in U.S. at arrival		
Yes	41%	80%
No	59	20
Parents in U.S. at arrival		
Yes	5%	58%
No	95	42
Intended upon arrival to stay in U.S. permanently		
Yes	15%	36%
No	85	64
Number of cases:	336	348

after a sibling had already prepared the ground; before then, but one in five had.[9] Between 1920 and 1924, fully 45 percent of the Issei males arriving in America had siblings already in the country.

Table I summarizes differences in background and outlook of Issei arriving before and after the Gentlemen's Agreement. No doubt this table would be even clearer if "intentions to stay permanently" in the United States were more amenable to precise memory; even more revealing would be how long the successive waves of immigrants planned to remain in the country. Table I also shows that migrants were somewhat younger after the Gentlemen's Agreement than before.[10] In addition, it reveals that before the Agreement about thirty percent of our sample of male migrants had been students, while afterwards the proportion doubled, partly because of the provision in the Agreement permitting students to emigrate to the United States. However, fewer of these later students had a college education. Equally important are two characteristics that did *not* change: sons from farm families constituted about three-quarters of the migrant group at each date, and socioeconomic level of the parents of migrants (as measured by an index made up of measures of occupation, landholdings of farmers, and ascribed social status)[11] declined only slightly between the two dates.

---

[9] These and subsequent results are clarified by omitting from computations employing date of arrival those who reported that they arrived in 1908. These people in many instances apparently arrived before the Gentlemen's Agreement was being effectively enforced.

[10] The attrition through old age of Issei who arrived earlier would lead us to expect that larger distinctions in the same direction would have been the case.

[11] The use of indexes, here and elsewhere in this paper, requires some explanation. In general the convention followed is that of those working in quantitative social sciences who put into composite measures single items, which clearly relate to common dimensions and which are strongly correlated with one another. Several rationales explain this procedure. For one, it is seldom that single-item indicators can catch the complexity of a social dimension. In the case of socioeconomic level, neither occupation, nor landholdings, nor the noble–commoner distinction could tell us as much about a person's standing as could the three of them, with appropriate weighting. In addition, the use of indicators in combination permits finer distinctions to be made among patterns of responses. Finally, retrospective data, like those employed here, are indubitably imperfect in detail. If respondents do not *systematically* inflate or underestimate the several aspects of their parents' establishments, it seems reasonable to expect that composite measures will be more accurate than any single item. As here employed, the index of parental socioeconomic level is a three-step continuum divided into "low," "medium," and "high." A maximum of four factors were used to determine the socioeconomic level of the parents: (1) The most important of these was the principal occupation of the respondents' fathers; (2) those revealing farm backgrounds were then asked the size of their fathers' farms; and (3) whether in addition to farmland they owned mountain timberland; finally (4) all persons were also asked whether they were of noble descent. The 9 percent who claimed such lineage were (where appropriate) moved from the upper half of the "medium" level background into the "high" category, or from the upper half of the "low" background into "medium." Essentially (disregarding nobility), professionals, merchants with relatively large establishments, high-level sales persons, and higher clerical workers were considered to be

Table I also shows that the later male migrants were much more likely to enter the country with their parents or to join parents already there. The rise in such two-generation families (as well as in extended kinship groups) was one of the most distinct by-products of the Gentlemen's Agreement, and, as we shall see, one of the most consequential.[12] One in twenty of all pre-Agreement Issei in our sample accompanied or joined parents, as compared with six in ten after 1908. The corresponding rise for those who were seventeen years old or younger when they arrived was from about 33 to 86 percent! This tendency, moreover, was most common among Issei of relatively humble backgrounds. The growth in size of the Japanese-American family was of more than merely symbolic importance. The presence of the family created both pressure and means for the creation of an ethnic-group economy.

Initially, relatives served to aid the newcomer in finding a home, learning the ropes, gaining a job. Before the Gentlemen's Agreement, such aid was available to only one in five of the Issei who had attained their majority and for three in ten of those younger. Among those who arrived as minors after the Gentlemen's Agreement, no fewer than 84 percent were helped by relatives. At the same time, a decline was apparent in the frequency with which the newcomers found it necessary to call upon governmental or charitable agencies. In keeping with the well-known Japanese distaste for dependency, the number receiving such support never exceeded one in five; but the decline after the Gentlemen's Agreement was by almost half. As the family served to integrate the new immigrant into the ethnic economy and community, it also brought him into a world that was increasingly independent of the surrounding society. This is reflected in the fact that arrivals coming with or to meet parents were twice as likely as others to anticipate a

---

"high" in socioeconomic level, as were farm owners with large (12 or more acres) or middling (2.5 to 12 acres) farm establishments, owners of specialty farms, and renters of large farms. "Medium" socioeconomic level included the balance of farmers, except for renters of small farms, and merchants with small establishments, semi-professionals, highly skilled craftsmen, medium-level clerical workers, and all other salespersons. "Low" level backgrounds were ascribed to those whose fathers were renters of small farms, farm laborers, less-skilled craftsmen, lower clerical and sales personnel, operatives, public service workers, fishermen, and servants.

12 It is hard to escape the conclusion that some of this shift is an artifact of the sample—since we could obviously interview only living Issei and did so forty years after the last of them had arrived in America. But note the decline in the age-of-arrival of sample members! Could the sample be corrected for this flaw, fewer migrant sons and more migrant fathers would have been found. On the other hand, there is no valid objection to denoting the sons of migrants as themselves Issei, for the migration of the family as a social and economic institution is indeed part of the story this paper describes; moreover, since part of the significance of the term "Issei" is legal, Japanese immigrants of all ages were equally ineligible for American citizenship.

permanent stay in America, while those who were dependent upon help from the white community seldom did so.

Family aid was of particular importance in locating a first job. This kind of assistance depended upon the number and kind of relatives on hand when the young Issei arrived. Of the new arrivals who had neither siblings nor parents in America 84 percent found both their first and their second jobs without help from relatives. The proportions for those with either parents or siblings present was much lower—35 percent and 41 percent, respectively. And for Issei with both parents and siblings in America, only 19 percent were on their own in finding their first two jobs.

Many Japanese-American immigrants attribute the success of their group in America mainly to hard work and patience. However plausible this claim, other explanations are revealed in an examination of success or failure of individual migrants. Level of economic attainment and amount of friendly social contact with whites are two crucial dimensions of the careers of Japanese-Americans. These dimensions, moreover, can be adequately indicated by the somewhat impersonal data of a retrospective survey.[13] These two parameters of American "success" hardly exhaust the varieties of Japanese-American life, but it is fair to say that they were among the goals sought by most Issei, and success in them indicates a relatively comfortable accommodation to the new environment.[14]

---

[13] The economic attainment index combines a ranking of the occupation considered by the respondent to have been his main one in America, his highest single-year income (with no effort to adjust for changing real value), and certain kinds of investments. Since the interview did not reveal respondents' farm sizes or value, farm *owners* were as a first approximation counted as "medium-high" and farm *renters* or *managers* counted as "medium." Income and investments were then employed (as with nonfarm respondents) to distinguish among them. Nonfarm occupations were ranked in five categories, proceeding from professionals and managers at the top to servants and laborers at the bottom. In terms of weighting, occupational level was accorded a weight of four, income a weight of three (the highest income category was $15,000 or more, while the lowest was under $3000), and investments in real estate, stocks, or bonds a weight of one. Weighted scores were then summed, and cutting points established to create four nearly equal-sized categories.

The index of friendly contact with whites rests on three factors: visits to whites; visits from whites; and the number of friends and acquaintances who were whites. Those who visited and were visited by whites more than twice a year were accorded the maximum scores on those items. Those who said that half or more of their friends and acquaintances were white received the maximum score on that item. Minimum scores in all cases were for those with no contact with whites.

[14] The two dimensions are themselves interrelated but not identical. Those who achieved a "high" level of economic success in America were also far more likely than those with a "low" level to have achieved "much" contact with whites (27 percent as compared with 7 percent), and those with "much" white contact to have attained a "high" level of economic success (42 percent as compared with 18 percent for those with no contact). Which dimension caused which is a fruitless question; doubtless, contact with whites and prosperity were mutually facilitating.

Table II indicates the relationship between some of the background characteristics we have discussed, the level of economic attainment, and amount of friendly contact with whites. Although *a priori* one would have anticipated strong correlations in this table, the opposite is usually the case. Most striking in this regard is the weak relationship observed between the socioeconomic level of an Issei's father and his own ultimate levels of economic attainment and degree of friendly contact with whites. Even when immigrants are subdivided into those who were from primarily agricultural and from primarily nonagricultural backgrounds,

TABLE II—PREDICATORS OF LEVEL OF ECONOMIC ATTAINMENT IN AMERICA AND OF CONTACT WITH WHITES

	Level of Economic Attainment Index Score				Contact with Whites Index Score				Total Number of Cases
	Low %	Lo-Med. %	Hi-Med. %	High %	None %	Little %	Some %	Much %	
Parents' socioeconomic level									
Low	26	34	17	23	39	30	25	7	57
Medium	26	28	23	23	34	28	22	16	379
High	20	32	23	25	30	28	24	18	253
Father's occupation in Japan									
Farm proprietor	25	35	20	20	34	28	23	15	320
Farm laborer	23	26	25	27	31	30	22	17	180
Nonagricultural	23	26	25	26	32	27	25	16	189
Student in Japan									
Yes	23	21	20	27	27	31	24	18	310
No	25	30	25	21	38	26	22	14	374
Education in Japan									
≤5 yrs.	19	35	25	21	32	28	23	17	110
6–8 yrs.	27	30	24	19	36	26	25	13	311
9–11 yrs.	23·	28	19	30	31	30	20	19	146
≥12 yrs.	20	28	21	31	30	33	18	17	105
Interprefectural migration									
Moved to urban	17	19	25	39	22	39	17	22	60
Stayed in rural	26	32	20	21	37	25	23	15	456
Stayed in urban	19	28	28	25	27	33	25	16	167
Age at arrival in America									
≤12	16	41	30	13	25	16	34	25	37
13–14	24	24	24	28	36	25	21	18	28
15–17	25	31	21	23	29	27	25	19	199
18–20	26	27	20	27	32	30	24	14	224
21–23	22	27	27	23	31	32	21	16	101
≥24	19	37	22	21	45	29	17	9	96
Number of Cases:	159	204	151	159	215	186	151	103	

paternal socioeconomic level (as measured by our index) does not seem to have had a strong influence upon their sons' American attainment. Better-endowed sons simply did not seem to have had the kind of advantage that enabled them to achieve greater "success" than their fellows from less-favored backgrounds.

Only two background characteristics had even as much influence on subsequent success as parental socioeconomic status. The more important was earlier migration within Japan prior to coming to America: those who had moved from a rural to an urban prefecture frequently achieved success in America, both in terms of friendly contact and economic attainment. The other was age at arrival, which was related to friendly contact (younger arrivals found it easier to become friendly with whites) but not related to level of economic attainment. All told, Table II reveals that personal experiences, not family background, were translatable into advantages in America. For the most part, the proximate sources of differentiation within the Japanese-American community are to be sought in America.

At first, these findings seem to argue that the American setting was essentially an egalitarian one, since background rarely seemed to help or hinder the immigrant. Two somewhat more detailed lines of analysis will qualify and in some measure explain this inference. In the first, American education (which generally came early in the immigrant's stay) will be seen to have been a relatively certain route to facility with the English language, which in turn was a prime determinant of friendly contact with whites (although to some extent it was also a consequence of it). In the second line of analysis, the early occupational history of the new immigrants will be related to their background characteristics. This reveals the extent to which background and early career jointly prefigured the ultimate economic attainment of the Issei.

Orientation to America was dramatically connected with attendance at an American school. At the same time that educational opportunities were broadening in Japan, Japanese immigrants were availing themselves more frequently of American public schools; 19 percent of those who arrived before the Gentlemen's Agreement eventually obtained some formal American education. But 45 percent of those who arrived after 1908 received such education; even more of those arriving just before immigration was stopped obtained this schooling. At all times, the youngest arrivals were most likely to obtain American education; 29 percent of those seventeen years of age or younger who arrived before the Gentlemen's Agreement had such schooling; of those under eighteen arriving after the Agreement, 63 percent did. In part, this increase followed from the larger numbers of declared students who were admitted under the Gentlemen's Agreement. But even among such students the proportion who were educated in America grew. Six in ten of the post-Agreement student arrivals *continued* their education in America. Four in ten of pre-Agreement student arrivals did so. Students *constituted* 60 percent of all pre-Agreement arrivals who studied in America, and 82 percent of American-educated post-Agreement arrivals. Consequently, a closer correspondence developed between Japanese and Japanese-American life. In addition, a self-conscious realization of what constituted proper preparation for America may have also developed. In a sense, a new "sub-generation" of Issei arrived after 1908.

The increased availability of American education to immigrant Japanese did much to erase contrasts in socioeconomic background. The usual correlation between prosperity of parents and educational level of their children obtained among the Issei, but only for *Japanese* education, not for American. Forty-seven percent of those whose parents rated "high" on the socioeconomic index received at least secondary education in Japan, as compared with 28 percent of those whose parents' level was "low." But better-off Japanese usually came to America after having attained all the schooling they would ever attain, while children from lower-status homes, having received less education in Japan, more often resumed their education in America.

Of the Japanese students of lower- or middle-level backgrounds, 58 percent went to school in America; 44 percent of those from higher-level backgrounds did. This equalizing pattern was not intentional, but was rather the result of two simultaneous developments: the slight decline over time in the socioeconomic status of the migrant group, and the rapidly increasing availability of American education. When the sample is divided into pre- and post-Agreement arrivals, however, in neither group do Issei from lower-socioeconomic-level homes show an advantage in American education.

Education in America had for the Issei an open-ended value, one that in the long run could better adapt the poor boy to his new country than superior Japanese education could prepare the rich boy.[15] By virtue of

---

[15] As is usually the case in modern societies, higher education was strongly correlated among the Issei with a higher level of economic attainment, but this was the case only for American, not Japanese education. If we divide our sample into those who achieved their highest level of education in Japan (the more common) and those whose highest education was in America, we find two strikingly different patterns. Level of economic attainment did *not* vary by educa-

their sons' later arrival in America, lower-level parents were evidently more prepared by experience and by necessity to give their sons' fates wholeheartedly to the American environment. We find that the highest incidence of American education is among lower- and middle-level background Issei whose family had also helped them to get their first American job. Of these Issei, 43 percent received some American education, as compared with 30 percent of higher-level sons so aided, and only 27 percent of lower-level Issei who received no family aid in finding a job. Parents of relatively low socioeconomic level on the whole seem to have been readier to abandon the older bird-of-passage outlook.

A disadvantage in Japan, thus, became in a sense an advantage among those whose milieu was changed radically by migration. Those who were late arrivals, and particularly those whose parents were already in America, were most likely to have had opportunity to study in an American school. These same people also settled in a relatively complete family and ethnic context, and looked upon America as a place in which it was worthwhile to take formal steps to learn and to adapt to the culture. These persons, perhaps, even served as the American-born generation would later serve: as go-betweens who spanned the two cultures.

The most important aspect of American schooling was instruction in English. On an English language index, the components of which (weighted equally) are the interviewer's estimate of respondent's fluency in English and respondent's report of how often he used the language in a variety of informal settings, 37 percent were rated "good."[16] Of those rated "good," more than half had at least some American schooling (although fewer than a third of all respondents had been to school in this country). Of those who attended school in America 60 percent achieved "good" English; of those who did not attend American schools, only 26 percent were rated "good." Even elementary

---

tional level among those in the former group; about half at each level scored at one of the two higher levels of economic attainment. But for the latter group, economic attainment rose with level of education from 36 percent for those with only primary education, to 57 percent for those with intermediate education, to 70 percent for those with college education.

[16] Interviewers were invariably bilingual, and usually themselves second-generation Japanese-Americans. Each recorded at the conclusion of the interview whether the respondent knew no English, or whether he spoke it fluently, hesitantly, or brokenly. The largest category (45 percent) spoke "broken" English; only 17 percent were judged "fluent"; 14 percent had spoken no English, according to the interviewers. The other components of the English language index were respondents' reports on how often they spoke English with their relatives, friends, and other acquaintances. The reader should note that a "good" rating on the English language index does not necessarily imply that the Issei is *fluent* in the language, but only that he appears reasonably skillful and employs the language often.

education in America doubled the likelihood of an Issei's developing "good" English.

A rough indicator of the importance of English-language facility as an entree to the culture is the reading of American periodicals—something which three-quarters of all respondents at one time or another had done. Over 60 percent of those with "poor" English were so out of touch with their new land that they never read American periodicals. Over nine in ten whose English was "good" had been readers of periodicals. More intimate indicators of cultural involvement undoubtedly would vary in the same way, as did friendly contact with whites. Of the entire sample 35 percent were rated on this index as having "much" or "some" white contact; the comparable figure for those with "good" English was 56 percent.

But formal American education was certainly not the only way to gain such rudimentary sophistication about American matters. And, in fact, differing Issei backgrounds enhanced or altered the strong effect of American education. Interestingly, one such relevant characteristic was the level of *Japanese* education (which was itself positively related to education in America). Table III displays this joint relationship, showing the effects of Japanese education upon English skill and magazine reading for those who had and for those who had not had any American education. Likewise, Table III shows how American education modified the effects of characteristics of background and immigration upon skill in and employment of English.

Two general findings in Table III warrant emphasis: (1) in every instance American education had a crucial effect upon both linguistic skill and the use of such skills in reading American periodicals; and, (2) although other aspects of background combined with American education to promote these skills, parents' socioeconomic level did not. Family socioeconomic background was positively correlated with level of Japanese education (a "portable" characteristic), but this background itself was not "portable," in that it did not combine with American education to affect our measures of American cultural sophistication.

Let us examine the table in some detail. Looking first at the Japanese education column, we see that, among those lacking American education, the level of their training in Japan is a strong predictor of skill in English. The finding is not surprising, since schooling anywhere is usually a concomitant of an ability to master intellectual tasks, like learning a new language. Appropriately, these people display an equally strong relationship between level of Japanese education and the reading

TABLE III—CONTRIBUTION OF AMERICAN EDUCATION AND SEVERAL CHARACTERISTICS OF BACKGROUND AND MIGRATION TO ENGLISH FACILITY AND AMERICAN PERIODICAL READING (figures in parentheses are the total number of cases upon which the percentage is based).

	No American education		Some American education	
	With "good" English %	Has read American Periodicals %	With "good" English %	Has read American Periodicals %
Japanese education				
≤5 yrs.	15 (80)	41 (80)	67 (27)	89 (27)
6–8 yrs.	23 (221)	59 (215)	63 (87)	89 (87)
9–11 yrs.	38 (87)	75 (87)	59 (58)	91 (58)
≥12 yrs.	32 (63)	81 (63)	56 (41)	93 (41)
Parents' socioeconomic level				
Low	26 (35)	71 (35)	68 (22)	91 (22)
Medium	23 (253)	61 (246)	56 (123)	89 (124)
High	30 (177)	63 (176)	65 (74)	92 (74)
Father's occupation in Japan				
Farm proprietor	25 (233)	57 (232)	62 (87)	93 (87)
Farm laborer	20 (119)	61 (114)	47 (58)	90 (59)
Nonagricultural	32 (113)	73 (111)	69 (74)	86 (74)
Age at arrival in America				
≤12	35 (17)	82 (17)	75 (20)	95 (20)
13–14	60 (10)	60 (10)	61 (18)	89 (19)
15–17	27 (105)	72 (103)	62 (93)	89 (93)
18–20	25 (167)	62 (162)	53 (55)	89 (55)
21–23	27 (81)	61 (82)	65 (20)	90 (20)
≥24	19 (83)	46 (82)	45 (13)	92 (13)
Date of arrival in America				
Before Gentlemen's Agreement	19 (269)	54 (263)	60 (63)	87 (63)
After Agreement	34 (179)	73 (178)	61 (153)	91 (154)

of American periodicals—presumably a measure of interest as well as of mastery. But, regardless of their Japanese educational background, almost all Issei who attended school in America also read American periodicals. And for these people, additional education in Japan was *inversely* related to English language ability. For those with a strong educational background in Japan, immersion in the American world was seemingly less complete than for those whose American schooling was more nearly unique.

The table further shows that Issei whose fathers had not been farmers learned English better and used it more widely than those from agricultural backgrounds. Once again we see that, although socioeconomic ranking was scrambled by the move to America, the past was not buried, but rather expressed itself through complicated channels. As Table III also shows, the personal circumstances and timing of the migration also had effects upon English skill and reading of periodicals. The younger arrivals received more, and more effective, American education, and, in addition, apparently also benefited from informal education beyond that received by those who arrived at a more advanced age. For those with no American education, the younger the migrant, the better his English. English skill was predominant, of course, among those who gained American education and who had arrived before they were twelve years of age (over three in four being rated "good"); but fewer than half of those twenty-four years or older upon arrival developed "good" English, despite their American education. But, again, education was the more crucial of the variables under consideration: Issei with formal American education, even though they arrived relatively mature, were still more likely to develop "good" English, and read more American periodicals, than the youngest arrivals who never went to school in the United States.

Year of arrival in large part reflected the changes in migrant orientation and family setting brought about by the Gentlemen's Agreement. Post-Agreement immigrants were more likely than their predecessors to develop English skill, even in the absence of American schooling, and more likely to read American periodicals. Evidently, then, sharp cultural distinctions, based on American experiences mediated by background and circumstances of migration, developed *within* the Issei group. These distinctions modified the apparent competitive advantages some Issei had possessed before embarking for America.

Despite the constricted scope generally allowed members of the race, analogous but not identical mechanisms were at work in the occupational realm. Ignoring the long-range shifts in the occupational status of the Japanese-American group as a whole, let us here examine the first two jobs held by each male Issei in our sample, regardless of the duration of these jobs.[17] Table IV relates the broad occupational classification of the immigrants' first American jobs to background characteristics and

---

[17] Although one-tenth of the first jobs held by Issei were abandoned within one year, they were not different in type or distribution from those held by Japanese-American males in the 1910–1920 period.

TABLE IV—First American Job, by Selected Background
Characteristics and Occupational Category

	White Collar	Blue Collar	Servant	Agriculture	Total Number
Japanese education					
≤5 yrs.	10%	20%	19%	51%	70
6–8 yrs.	8	16	12	64	237
9–11 yrs.	10	25	22	42	116
≥12 yrs.	17	15	27	40	81
Parents' socioeconomic level					
Low	14	28	19	38	42
Medium	9	17	16	58	302
High	12	18	21	49	174
Father's occupation in Japan					
Farm proprietor	7	18	14	61	233
Farm laborer	9	16	15	61	144
Nonagricultural	16	24	27	33	141
Age at arrival in America					
≤12	12	14	15	59	34
13–14	19	14	24	43	21
15–17	9	22	17	53	152
18–20	10	17	17	56	154
21–23	8	20	19	53	87
≥24	13	19	19	79	69
Date of arrival in America					
Before Gentlemen's Agreement	8	21	22	29	221
After Agreement	11	17	15	57	282
Had American education					
Yes	12	12	27	48	336
No	9	22	13	56	180

American education. The first finding is an important one, suggesting some initial continuity of job type. Six out of ten Issei sons of Japanese farm proprietors or laborers entered farming as their first occupation in America; but only one in three of those whose fathers had not worked on farms did so. Forty-three percent of those whose first job was white-collar and 41 percent of those whose first occupation was as a servant came from nonagricultural backgrounds.

Despite this tendency to follow the occupation of one's father, only a tenuous relationship existed between the parents' socioeconomic level and the first American job of their migrant sons. Sons of low-status fathers often accepted blue-collar positions as their first job in their new country; those whose first job was in farming came very frequently from middle-level parents. But once again a clearer story emerges when Japanese education rather than parental socioeconomic level is examined: what *could* be carried over from Japan were learned qualities, like abilities, ambitions, and values; status, by contrast, could not be transplanted. Immigrants with more education, as a consequence, tended to shun farm employment, even in their first jobs, and to seek white-collar and servant occupations.

Those whose first jobs were as servants were by far the *most* likely to gain some American education, a reflection of the "schoolboy" tendency, whereby an aspiring young Issei would take a position as house-boy in exchange for a place to live and a small salary while he attended school. More than half of those who initially became servants gained some American education. Also high in this attainment were white-collar employees (who were mainly clerks). Those whose first American jobs were on farms, interestingly, gained more education in America than did the blue-collar workers (who were commonly day laborers). These patterns were in general constant throughout the migration period, and cannot be explained by the variations in ages of the immigrants. Farm employment as a first job did increase (from 49 percent before the Gentlemen's Agreement to 57 percent afterward) as Japanese-American farm enterprise grew. But at each period, education in Japan was the most important background characteristic in predicting what the first job would be.

The first jobs of post-Agreement arrivals, however, differed greatly from those of their predecessors in one surprising and significant way: the manner in which they were found. We have already seen that growing families in America cooperated with the expanding Japanese-American community to give several forms of aid to new arrivals. No form of aid was more important than that of finding a job. Of the Issei men who entered the United States before the Gentlemen's Agreement 15 percent were assisted by relatives in finding their first jobs; post-Agreement arrivals were so aided 52 percent of the time. Undoubtedly, this increased dependence reflects no decline in the "quality" or ambition of the migrants, but rather an accommodation to the limitations placed upon Japanese-Americans by white society, and the consequent elaboration of the distinctive ethnic-group economy.

Such assistance was not equally available to, or taken advantage of by, all Issei. Young arrivals were more likely to accept such aid, with the proportion availing themselves of family help dropping off rapidly after the age of about twenty. Approximately half of those who were below that age when they migrated gained their first jobs through family intercession, but only one-fourth who were older did so. Even steeper was the decline in those whose families helped them find their second jobs: from 30 percent of those under twenty to 10 percent of those older. Similarly, those who had been students in Japan were considerably more likely to be assisted by their families in gaining American jobs. Of the ex-students 15 percent gained *both* their first and second American jobs through family help, as compared with 5 percent of those who had held jobs in Japan before departure. The students were a relatively protected group, as were those with families (especially parents) in America.

Most significant, however, is the finding revealed in Table V. Here we see that it was the less well-off parents, not those of higher economic level, who arranged for the protection of their children in the unfamiliar American environment. Seven out of ten of those with high-level parents were on their own in the New World, insofar as finding first jobs was concerned, but only half of those of low status were. This pattern, moreover, is not merely a consequence of year of arrival. We have already seen that lower-level background seemed to predispose Issei to take up American education and generally to devote themselves wholeheartedly to their new setting. It now appears that lower-level parents were especially anxious to advance their migratory offspring in the American economic race and were more likely to place their sons in jobs. Of all Issei, the *most* likely to have family aid in finding one or both of his first two jobs was the immigrant of lower-status background who recalled that on arrival he had anticipated a permanent stay in America. By contrast, the *least* likely to have received such aid was the immigrant of higher-status background who expected to return to Japan. While

TABLE V—PARENTS' SOCIOECONOMIC STATUS BY FAMILY AID IN FIRST AMERICAN YEARS

	Low	Medium	High
Aid received in:			
Neither job	48%	57%	70%
First or second job	35	33	23
Both jobs	17	10	7
Number of cases:	52	336	220

six in ten of the former received family aid in securing a job, only one in four of the latter received such help.

About three in four of those whose families helped them find their first two American jobs were introduced in this way to farm work. Of those who were on their own in finding both their first two jobs, only about 43 percent went into agriculture. Those without aid, however, were twice as likely as the others to expend their effort in an ultimately less rewarding blue-collar position. Issei from lower-level backgrounds availed themselves often of family job assistance. But for these Issei the distribution of job types was no different than for Issei of higher-level background.

From arrival, then, many family members were led by their veteran kin into a channeling process through which they helped develop the characteristic Japanese-American economy. Here, in an ethnic-communal setting, the newcomer could begin the long and arduous haul that would bring relative prosperity to the immigrant generation and opportunity to its successors. Perhaps successful birds of passage were more common among the Issei children of higher socioeconomic background; and perhaps the American years of the successful returnees were intellectually more stimulating, because less dependent. But the "success" of the lower-background migrant was achieved by just this kind of steady, though perhaps unadventurous, application to immediate problems in the unsympathetic American social environment.

The road begun by family aid was no royal road to eventual success in America, however. Farming, the job most commonly provided by relatives, was for many a false step. Only 36 percent of those whose first two American jobs were in agriculture eventually achieved one of the two top positions on our index of economic attainment. By contrast, 58 percent of those whose first two jobs were off the farm achieved the top two rankings. And, appropriately, those with just one of their first two jobs in farming scored about midway on the scale of economic attainment. This tendency is even slightly heightened among those whose early farm jobs had been achieved through family intervention. Family aid could be a snare. This was true even when the aid was in locating a white-collar job, probably because such jobs were usually minor clerking positions in the petty retail businesses common to the Japanese-American ethnic economy. Although the degree of difference is perhaps exaggerated because few of our interviewees started out in white-collar jobs, the proportion who ultimately were scored "high" or "high-medium" on the index of economic attainment was 72 percent for those who found that job unaided by family, and only 27 percent for those whose family helped.

Table VI presents a somewhat paradoxical relationship between economic background and American economic attainment. In the table, it is apparent that where no family aid was involved, high-level-background Issei had a notable if not overwhelming advantage over their lower-status contemporaries. But—and here the paradox becomes the strongest—among those who were aided, the lower-level group came out distinctly ahead of those whose parents had been better off. Likewise, for low-status background Issei, family job assistance neither hindered nor aided eventual advancement, but for high-status Issei, such assistance was associated with a distinct hindrance to occupational achievement.[18] Perhaps only fashionable prejudice inclines one against interpretations that support the self-image of America as the land of individual opportunity, in which the best and most self-reliant man wins. But it seems more persuasive to infer that family job assistance among higher-status Issei led its no less capable recipients along a path of dependency that was a false one, *from the point of view of economic attainment in America.*

TABLE VI—LEVEL IN ECONOMIC ACHIEVEMENT IN AMERICA BY PARENTS' SOCIOECONOMIC LEVEL AND FAMILY AID IN FIRST TWO JOBS

	Low and Medium Level			High Level		
	No Aid	Aid in first or second job	Aid in both jobs	No Aid	Aid in first or second job	Aid in both jobs
Economic attainment index score						
Low	26%	27%	27%	17%	23%	24%
Low-medium	27	33	30	28	35	53
High-medium	22	22	16	25	22	18
High	25	18	25	30	20	6
Number of cases:	208	124	44	159	51	17

According to this interpretation, those of relatively favored background appear to have been the group best prepared to achieve success *in Japan.* They were, one supposes, more devoted to maintaining traditional ways, an outlook that could only be perpetuated by insulation

18 The same table showing contact with whites in place of level of economic attainment reveals parallel findings, though of lesser significance.

from the harsh facts of American discrimination. These people were also more set upon a return to the homeland, and likely to expend an important portion of their economic activity to this end. Many if not most of these people in fact did return to Japan—which might also explain why a greater proportion of the lower-background Issei stated that they had received job assistance from their families. But those who did not return were disadvantaged both in attitude and in training for America. A clear example comes in comparing the incidence of American education among low- and high-socioeconomic background Issei who were helped by their families in finding their first two jobs in America. Fifty-eight percent of the former but only 31 percent of the latter received American education, which, as we have seen, was crucial to some aspects of adaptation to America.

Although our sample is too small and the questionnaire too retrospective and limited to answer the question once and for all, this explanation provides a proposition that could be examined further with respect to Japanese or other migrant groups.[19] According to this hypothesis, those Issei whose adjustment in America was "best" in terms of American economic attainment and in terms of their acceptance into personal contact with whites were those relatively disadvantaged in Japan, and therefore least apt to cling to Japanese approaches to American problems. By necessity as well as by choice, these Issei took America on its own terms and, with intense devotion to hard work and economic success, won for themselves a relatively high position. Those who needed most to adapt, adapted and profited.

If this is the general outline of the story, a double irony results. America was the land of equal opportunity among the Issei in a peculiar sense: for a component of the "democratizing" agent may well have been the undemocratic discrimination suffered by Oriental immigrants, which hindered most those least willing and able to conform to the hostile demands placed upon them by prejudiced Americans. Those of humble origins could better submit to the halfway position permitted Japanese-Americans by white America. The success available to Japanese immigrants, though certainly low in comparison with that open to whites, and perhaps low in comparison with that available to those of higher status in Japan, offered yet a distinct opportunity for advancement to those furthest down on the socioeconomic level.

---

[19] The overall adaptive advantages (literacy, cohesion, relatively "modern" background, and a hard-work ethic) of the Japanese immigrant group must be kept in mind when extending this argument to other groups.

AN ETHNIC TRADE: THE CHINESE LAUNDRIES
IN EARLY CALIFORNIA

By Paul Ong

Introduction

Researchers have frequently cited the small Asian stores throughout much of urban America during the early part of the twentieth century as typical of ethnic entrepreneurship. An equally significant minority venture is the Chinese laundry trade in urban California during the latter part of the nineteenth century.[1]

The main characteristics of the ethnic laundry trade in California can be quickly outlined. The Chinese entered the laundry industry soon after they began immigrating to the United States in large numbers around 1848.[2] By 1853 the Chinese laundryman was a common sight in many parts of the state. By the end of that decade Chinese easily constituted a majority of the laundry workers, marking the beginnings of an occupational specialization.[3] In the following three decades the Chinese continued to dominate the occupation, comprising over three-quarters of the work force. During this period the Chinese also dominated the business end of the trade. Although some worked for White firms, most of the Chinese were either self-employed or worked for a fellow country-man in a prodigious number of small washhouses which on the average housed three to five workers. The earlier known Chinese washhouse was established in 1851.[4] By the 1880s Chinese owned and operated over three-fourths of all laundries in San Francisco, Napa, Sacramento, and other California cities.[5]

TABLE 1

LAUNDRY WORKERS IN CALIFORNIA

Year	Total	Chinese	% Chinese
1860	1,918	--	--[a]
1870	4,045	2,899	71.7%
1880	7,013	5,435[b]	77.5%
1890	9,302	6,400[c]	68.8%
1900	10,010	5,274[d]	52.7%
1910	15,647	--[e]	--

Data derived from census publication unless otherwise noted.

[a]From sample of the census manuscripts for San Francisco, the proportion appears to be substantially greater than half.

[b]Ping Chin, 1963: 65.

[c]Conservative estimate based on 6,585 male and 367 female "colored" workers.

[d]Includes, perhaps, about 1000 Japanese and Indians.

[e]Figure for Chinese and Japanese is 4,647 or 29.7%.

Like most ethnic enterprises in America, the Chinese laundry trade was highly urbanized. The trade was established in the hinterlands by Chinese who were driven out of the more profitable mining activities. However, with the

PAUL ONG lives in Berkeley, California.

The Journal of Ethnic Studies 8:4

emergence of industrialization in the state, the laundry trade eventually became more concentrated in the cities.[6] By 1880 about 40% of the Whites and Chinese in California resided in municipalities with 4,000 or more persons, located in such areas. The growth of the urban ethnic trade was due more to the opening of new firms than to the relocation of older ones from the outlying areas.

Within the cities, laundering was a major economic activity for the Chinese community. Over one-tenth of this minority population were laundrymen or laundry helpers,[7] and about one-third of all Chinese businesses were washhouses.[8] The trade served as a vital economic link between the ethnic and larger population. Since patrons were exclusively White, the washhouses exchanged Chinese labor for outside money.

The descriptive outline of the Chinese washhouses presents a socio-economic phenomenon which, if well understood, provides insights into the process of ethnic (and racial) divisions of the urban economy. Many of the scholarly works on small ethnic businesses in the twentieth century gave as explanation for the development of the early laundry trade the Chinese predilection for self-employment and their ability to raise capital through social institutions. Although ethnic culture did play an important role, it was not, as we shall see later, the only or determining factor in the developmental process. Further, a cultural thesis cannot explain the decline of the ethnic trade. Focusing solely on ethnic culture, then, would preclude an understanding of the far richer historical process. To better analyze this history, the role of ethnic culture must be located in the broader societal context and dynamics.

There appear to be three areas of consideration, of which one is related to ethnic culture. There is first the structural context, the emergence of a racially and hierarchically segmented labor market in an industrializing urban society with a surplus of workers. The second consideration is the capitalization on social ties to transform the laundry trade into an ethnic niche. Finally, although many factors contributed to the demise of the Chinese dominance of the trade, there is the rise of institutional racism which generated discriminatory practices beyond those normally found in a simple racial division of labor.

The Emergence of a Segmented Labor Market

The Chinese washhouses emerged as a part of a broader search for order in an industrializing urban society torn by racial strife. The Chinese had been in California since 1848, but racial conflict between Chinese and Whites in the cities was not significant until after the mid-1860s, with hostilities reaching a peak during the late 1870s and 1880s.[10] An immediate explanation for the timing of these events is that Chinese and Whites began to urbanize extensively only after the mid-1860s. Implicit is that racial hostilities were merely transplanted along with the population. However, this seems too simple and superficial an answer. Urbanization only brought the two groups together, but other circumstances precipitated animosity. The underlying cause of the urban violence (and urbanization) was a radical shift in the state's economy and employment opportunities. Gold mining had attracted a massive work force that was not readily absorbed by the subsequent economic expansion that was based in the cities.

Mining was California's economy during approximately the first dozen years after gold was discovered in 1848.[11] Placer mining increased within months of the discovery, and within five years produced over 81 million dollars worth of precious metal annually. Mining held its dominant economic role throughout the 1850s and even at the end of the decade the value of gold

96

extracted was nearly twice as great as the value of manufactured goods.[12] During this period, independent miners—the forty-niners—comprised the single largest occupational group. Despite the prodigious output, or perhaps because of it, mining was never more than a boom industry, for gold was exhaustible. As the surface gold became depleted, mining waned. Although mining still dominated the state's economy in 1860, its eclipse was evident. In that year the dollar value of gold output fell to about one-half of the 1853 output, and the proportion of the state's labor force working as miners also fell by about the same amount. By the mid-1860s, prospecting was but a shadow activity. At the end of the decade the dollar value of gold stood at only seventeen million, and because extracting the remaining gold required capital-intensive hydraulic equipment, corporate mining replaced independent and small group mining.

Manufacturing and agriculture rose to replace mining as the core of California economy. Although each is distinct, they shared common attributes. Both emerged from the needs and accumulations of the previous era: they expanded through outside and self-generated capital, and there was a need for a large pool of potential wage-workers comprised of ex-prospectors and a continual stream of newcomers. Both stimulated massive investments in infrastructure, which was necessary for an economic "take-off." The most obvious example of these investments was the railroad, the "octopus" that connected California with the national market and tied the state together. In short, manufacturing and agriculture economy was the core of an emerging capitalist economy. Although this economy suffered from short-term swings (boom-to-bust cycles) and contradictory developments, it set the state on an irrevocable course towards industrialization.

Small-scale manufacturing existed during the mining era to produce goods that were too expensive or impractical to import, but the Civil War was the impetus for manufacturing expansion in the state.[13] When the fighting curtailed importation of goods from the East, local production filled the void. Even after the war, production continued to expand, for manufacturing had reached a level of self-sustained growth. By 1879 California was the twelfth largest manufacturer in the nation, with annual sales of 116 million compared to 23.5 million two decades earlier.[14] This represents a long-term annual growth rate of more than 8%, and the rate was considerably higher during the latter part of this period. An increase in the number of firms accounted for part of this growth, but the most significant share occurred within firms. As manufacturing occupied an increasingly larger part of the economy, the firms were transformed into large capital ventures employing a sizable number of workers. During this period the average number of workers per establishment doubled and the average amount of capital invested almost quadrupled.

Capital and labor also transformed agriculture into a major economic sector.[15] Between 1869 and 1880, the value of farms increased four-fold, from 49 million to 202 million dollars. With this growth, agriculture took on the form of agribusiness—large corporate farming. The average size of all farms in the state was two to three times the average size of farms for the nation as a whole, and this large size made California dependent upon a large seasonal work force. Large amounts of capital were also needed. In fact, capital investments in some land reclamation projects far exceeded any investment in a single manufacturing plant of this period.[16] California farming, then, was more akin to industrial capitalism than to traditional family farming.

As in most other cases of economic development, industrialization in California was inextricably accompanied by rapid urbanization. Manufacturers

97

located in the city where capital, labor, and transportational facilities were concentrated. Agribusiness also added to urbanization. The valley towns became food processing centers, transport terminals, and the home bases for a large seasonal farm-labor force. So, between 1860 and 1890, a period encompassing the inception and maturation of the new economy, the population in urban areas with 2,500 or more persons grew more than six-fold, from 80,000 to over 500,000, representing an increase from 21% to 48% of the state's population.[17]

TABLE 2

URBANIZATION BY RACE IN CALIFORNIA

Year	Total	White Urban	% Urban	Total	Chinese Urban	% Urban
1860	323,177	73,720	22.8	34,933	3,950	11.3
1870	499,424	117,615	35.6	49,277	17,686	36.2
1880	767,181	310,940	40.5	75,132	29,495	39.3
1890	1,111,672	503,185	45.3	72,472	36,056	49.8

Urban areas are cities with 4,000 or more persons.

Figures derived from census reports.

The economic currents of the era drastically altered the fortunes of the Chinese. During the 1850s and early 1860s the flow of immigrants was to the mountains. After a brief layover in San Francisco, newcomers proceeded by steamer to towns along the Sacramento and San Joaquin Rivers, and then ventured to potential sites following the advice of more experienced miners.[18] By the early 1860s, 70-80% of the Chinese in the state were miners or in the mining regions. When mining waned, this migratory pattern reversed. By 1870 only 20% of the Chinese remained and those who left the placer fields joined a continuing influx of new immigrants in search of work outside the foothills and mountain areas. By 1880 three-fourths of the Chinese resided outside the mining region.

TABLE 3

PERCENTAGE OF POPULATION IN MINING REGIONS[a]

Year	Total Population	Chinese
1852	50.0% +	--
1860	35.0%	70.2%
1870	18.0%	34.9%
1880	15.4%	23.8%
1890	10.2%	1.8%

[a]Adapted from Warren S. Thompson, Growth and Changes in California's Population. (The Haynes Foundation, 1955)

An increasing number of the Chinese worked in the cities, but often with less than sanguine results. The urban ethnic community held out few job

98

opportunities. During the Gold Rush the Chinese enclaves had functioned as service, retailing, and entertainment centers for the much larger number of immigrants in the hinterlands.[19] This commercial base enabled the Chinese to be economically autonomous from the rest of the city which generated few jobs. Since the ethnic community could only absorb few, if any, of the large number of immigrants drifting into the city after the mid-1860s, employment had to be found within the larger urban economy.

TABLE 4

GEOGRAPHIC DISTRIBUTION OF CHINESE
(Calculated from census publications)

Year	Total	% of Mining Region	% in Cities 4,000 +	% in Towns and Rural
1860	34,933	70%	11%	19%
1870	49,277	35%	36%	29%
1880	75,132	24%	39%	37%
1890	72,472	2%	50%	48%

Generally in the enclave the most likely source of employment was wage work, which expanded with the economy. In the two decades following 1860 the number of agricultural workers, general laborers, and manufacturing employees-- the core of the emerging working class—generally tripled from 42,000 to 125,000. The Chinese were an ideal labor force. They were as productive as Whites since the early production processes required only crude rather than skilled labor; they were cheaper and more easily disciplined because of their marginal position in a society where employment was scarce.[20] This is not to say that the Chinese did not want or demand fair pay; rather, conditions weighed against such actions. Therefore, all others things being equal, employers as profit maximizers sought Chinese labor. In manufacturing alone, the sector that generated the largest number of new urban jobs, the number of Chinese workers increased from a few dozen in 1860 to over 1,200 in 1867 and to over 15,000 in 1876, a rate of growth noticeably higher than the rate for White workers.[21] Not all of the Chinese, however, were employed by White capitalists, as we shall see a little later.

TABLE 5

EMPLOYMENT TRENDS IN CALIFORNIA

	1869	1890	% Difference
Total	219,192	376,505	72%
Wage Work			
Farm Labor	10,421	23,856	129%
Laborers	25,394	57,510	126%
Manufacturing	6,610	43,693	561%
Miners	82,573	37,147	-55%
Merchants	5,087	14,920	193%
Domestic Servants	8,069	22,858	183%

99

White owners might have welcomed the Chinese, but other Whites were hostile.[22] Pre-existing racist attitudes laid the grounds for anti-Chinese sentiments, and economic stress activated it. Uneven and chaotic development in the economy placed grave burdens on the emerging White working class. A surplus of labor ensured intense competition and uncertainty in the labor market. Many of the existing jobs were often at the mercy of shifts of capital from one sector to another, the seasonal nature of agriculture employment, and business cycles. This tenuous situation led to anti-capitalist sentiments among the working class but these sentiments were not strong enough to motivate White workers to overcome their racial prejudices and unite with the Chinese workers. Instead, Whites saw the Chinese, who potentially constituted one-fifth of the wage workers, as undesirable and deleterious competitors who took jobs away from able-bodied Whites and who acquiesced to the capitalist's effort to drive down wages in favor of profits. Prompted by the leaders of the nascent unions and by political demagogues, White workers undertook a virulent and eventually successful campaign to drive "the coolies" out of manufacturing, construction, and other better paying sectors. The single biggest triumph of this campaign was the enactment of a series of federal statutes ending unrestricted immigration from China.[23] The Chinese, then, became the scapegoat for California's economic ills.[24]

What emerged from the racial agitation was a hierarchically segmented economy, a socio-economic structure now frequently called a dual labor market. White workers secured a group privilege to participate in the core of the economy where the better paid and more stable jobs were located. The Chinese were forcibly excluded from such participation. The determining factor behind the segmentation obviously was the radical shift in the economy, but it was not the shift per se but the characteristic of the ascending economy that generated the racial animosities and finally the segmentation.

The emergence of manufacturing and agribusiness also marked the emergence of capitalism as the dominant economic system in California. While class conflict may be endemic to this system, it also generated conflicts among workers through competition for jobs. In a society with a history of racism and a surplus of labor, racial hostility between workers of different color can readily displace class hostility as the primary societal conflict. This happened in California as White workers minimized their own losses and risks within a capitalistic economy by eliminating a competitor, the Chinese workers. And competition was eliminated through a segmented economy.

The Laundry Trade and Ethnic Mobilization

The ability of the Chinese to develop laundries into a major ethnic trade as a response to the increasing economic restrictions can be understood by examining the role of culture in a segmented economy. The formation of a racially divided economy entailed an incremental process of excluding the Chinese from participating in an ever increasing portion of the core of the economy. Exclusion from the mainstream rather than racially ascribed occupations is the key that differentiates a segmented economy in a capitalist society from a caste system. While a caste system would have locked the Chinese into specific occupational niches, exclusion allowed the Chinese some, yet very limited, room for action. During each stage in the development of the segmentation, the Chinese attempted to maximize their few opportunities. It is within this restricted arena for action that the cultural baggage of the excluded becomes an important factor. The strength of that group's social ties and institutions determines the degree and form of collective action. For example, these

100

ties and institutions enabled some Chinese to establish cigar, shoe, and clothing sweatshops that employed a number of their countrymen.

Since these firms were a response to racial hostilities, it is not surprising that their numbers increased more rapidly towards 1867 and 1876 when economic slumps heightened anti-Chinese violence.[25] These establishments, unfortunately, were far from being a total solution to the growing problems facing the Chinese, particularly in the smaller urban areas which had a small manufacturing base. Economic opportunities were still constricted, forcing many Chinese into the less desirable service sector.

Given the persistent economic woes, laundry work emerged as an important alternative for the Chinese. The laundry trade was one of the few areas where competition with Whites was minimal. Although Whites vehemently complained about Chinese competition in other occupations, complaints against Chinese laundrymen did not occur.[26] Whites shunned laundering for good reasons. Even among the Chinese who were at the bottom of the economic ladder, the wages and social status of laundry workers were among the lowest.[27] As small businesses, laundries were also risky investments with low returns to capital. Of 42 laundries existing in Sacramento in 1878, over 17 still operated in 1882. The Chinese, however, did not participate in this trade just to escape inter-racial economic confrontation. The washhouses provided opportunity for self-employment, which was highly prized among overseas Chinese.[28] For the owners, laundering was one of the better choices among the economic activities not coveted by Whites.

Although self-employment was an incentive, participation in the trade was hardly the result of individual action. Most Chinese could not readily overcome economic obstacles in establishing washhouses without capitalizing on social ties and institutions existing in the Chinese community. The major problems involved were raising capital, securing labor, and minimizing the risk of failure.

Although laundries were labor intensive businesses, capital was still needed. Initial investments were lowered by renting rather than buying the building that housed the business and by purchasing only the few items needed: soap, firewood, etc. Nevertheless, capital outlay was required for equipment and structural modifications to the rented building.[29] Investments ranged from $400 to $1,600, with the average being about $800.[30] Such sums were sizable, considering the annual income of a Chinese in one of the better occupations to be about $250 to $300.[31] With steady employment, which was unlikely, an immigrant could scarcely accumulate "a few hundred dollars in a few years." At that point, he would more likely return to China a relatively rich man than risk the savings in a washhouse. Consequently, most of the Chinese who wished to start laundries probably did not have the personal resources to do so.

Those who could not individually finance a washhouse turned to partnerships or to extensive borrowing. Partners were often from the same clan or native district.[33] This pattern occurred because partnerships depended upon a mutual trust between owners. During the first few months and other periods of slow business, there was little or no profit and no assurance of a better future. What prevented one co-owner from abandoning the business was only his personal commitment to the other. Without knowing in advance that this obligation existed in a potential partner, an immigrant was less likely to risk his hard earned, yet meager, savings on a laundry. Since such a sense of obligation existed among members of the same clan or same district association, partners were recruited along kinship and territorial lines.

101

Loans, whether taken out by individuals or partners, were used to meet outstanding capital or operating expenses. Although it is impossible to ascertain how these loans were acquired, money probably was borrowed from close relatives or through a rotating credit association of people from the same clan or native district. Both borrowing practices were commonly used by other overseas Chinese and by American Chinese laundrymen in the twentieth century.[34] These loans were made on the strength of familial and social ties; therefore, a Chinese was able to secure credit without any notable assets. Without such credit, it is doubtful that most laundries could meet all of their financial needs.

The major daily problem of a fully operating laundry was securing labor. The typical laundry consisted of five persons, of whom three or four were employees.[35] This size of work force was needed to meet fixed operating expenses. During the 1870s and 1880s, a washhouse in San Francisco paid an average of $750 a year for rent, taxes, and other charges.[36] Rent, the only variable cost in this list, was already at its lowest since most washhouses were located in small, cheaply constructed buildings. It is unlikely that one or two persons could take in the amount of work sufficient to generate the revenue to meet the fixed expenses, and also to retrieve loans and see a profit. Extra hands were needed if a washhouse was to operate profitably.

TABLE VI

LAUNDRYWORKER TO POPULATION RATIO

Year	California	Massachusetts	Illinois
1860	5.05	1.21	.59
1870	7.22	1.13	.61
1880	8.11	2.04	1.21

Male to Female Ratio

Male per 1 Female

	California		Massachusetts	Illinois
	Total	White		
1860	2.56	2.35	.94	1.12
1970	1.66	1.48	.95	1.08
1880	1.50	1.31	.93	1.06

Excess Male Population

Excess Males (Male-Female) — Laundryworkers Per 1,000 Excess Males

Year	California	Illinois	California	Illinois
1860	130,371	93,571	14.7	10.9
1870	95,872	93,183	42.2	16.7
1880	102,931	11,517	68.1	32.3

102

Help was often recruited along lineal or locality lines. When jobs were available, owners were obligated to give preference to a "cousin" or an immigrant from the same home district. It was not easy for operators to avoid this social responsibility, for the duties were based on the same social bonds that held partnerships together and supported the ethnic credit system. An owner who was remiss about his employment obligation undermined his own ability to capitalize and rely on the existing ethnic ties.

Social obligations also worked for the owners. The social bonds which were at the bases of the prevailing hiring practices lowered the potential for labor conflicts. More importantly though, the Chinese labor system allowed employers to expect more work from their help. Workers could not easily avoid this expectation, for later jobs would also be found through similar social ties. A worker could not afford to earn a reputation of not fulfilling his obligation, since any recalcitrance would be readily communicated to other employers through the social network. The Chinese laundry employees were a disciplined work force.

These reciprocal obligations enabled laundries to be a flexible economic unit. Laundry work was tedious and involved long hours. Whereas normal employees were hired for a fixed number of hours, Chinese workers were expected to devote whatever time was necessary to complete the work. On the other hand, when business was slack, workers were given at least room and board. Thus, variations in the work load were easily accommodated.

Although its social foundation enabled Chinese washhouses to survive longer than similar businesses based solely on economics, the laundries were not immune to bankruptcy. Business failure was a real threat because racial restrictions in the other sectors of the economy inflated the number of competitors beyond what the market would normally support. Even when prices lowered, the number of washhouses grew.[37] Compared to other industrialized or developing states, California had an exceedingly high laundry-to-population ratio, even after taking into account the large number of itinerant males in Califonia. In fact, the laundry trade grew even as the sex ratio among Whites became more balanced, indicating the extensive overcrowding in the supply of laundering services.

Without some form of business regulation, competition would escalate, resulting in ruinous price wars and a higher bankruptcy rate. Laundry guilds, modeled after trade guilds in China, emerged to control the allocation of business markets and prices. Violation of their rules was met with forceful economic retaliation or, if needed, violence.[38] At times the guilds demanded loyalty above the obligations to relatives and compatriots of the same home district. When a washhouse closed, those out of work were given first opportunity at jobs at other laundries and received temporary room and board from other members of the organization.[39] Those still in business provided this relief even at the expense of family. From the standpoint of a laundryman, this hierarchy of responsibility was acceptable because it was in his own interest. The rules lowered his own risk of bankruptcy and provided a rudimentary form of unemployment insurance. Over time, therefore, the guilds supplanted familial and other cultural bonds as the social foundation for the trade. While the familial and district bonds facilitated the establishment of individual laundries, the guilds emerged to sustain the trade by stabilizing it.

This social foundation of the trade, however, was not unflawed. Ownership of more than one firm by an individual was rare.[40] Laundry businesses were limited to a size where owners, partners, and employees could maintain face-to-face contact. Without constant surveillance, partners and workers would be tempted to lighten their own respective load, which would cause the washhouse

103

to operate at a loss. This limitation made laundries more a source of employment rather than a small investment for further capital accumulation. Even among those who provided monies to finance the needed starting capital, there was little or no interest attached to the loans. Investments in a laundry, as with many other small businesses peripheral to the economy, were not made for returns on capital but as a license to work.

The social bonds and guilds also fostered conservatism. So long as the trade provided some tangible benefits, it strengthened the social institutions upon which it was built. Those who were already established and had the most to lose used the institutions to protect their own interest. They prevented the introduction of new technology by prohibiting new firms from establishing in the better markets. Later, for example, many laundries eventually sent their wash to large commercial laundries, keeping only the ironing for themselves.

But size and technology did not significantly impede the Chinese after the turn of the century. Before then, the culturally based social factors were an asset to the Chinese in an increasingly racially segmented economy. Without these factors it is unlikely that they would have developed the trade as extensively as they did in California's urban areas.

Laundry Laws and the Control of Social Relations

The racially segmented economy was not sustained solely through economic forces but also depended upon an ideology that legitimized the inequities. The ideology was racism, a belief held by the dominant group that the subordinate group was culturally and genetically inferior and deserved their lower social status. While racism explained the segmentation, it also assumed a life beyond this function and created a set of social relationships not based on efforts to monopolize the better jobs. In other words, the stratified roles that had their bases in the economic structure permeated all other relationships between the races. So, despite the absence of direct economic competition with Whites, Chinese washhouses were not immune to the ambient racial turmoil.[41]

More than once, White mobs sacked and burned Chinese laundries. While this violence was an outgrowth of the larger anti-Chinese movement, a covert, yet more pernicious attack was directed specifically against the laundry trade. At the heart of the anti-laundry movement was a conflict between White residents and Chinese laundrymen over the use of urban space. This conflict did not materialize until the trade was in its latter stage of development. But once the conflict was underway, it led to an anti-laundry campaign that culminated into the unique set of laws enacted against the Chinese.

Inter-racial conflict over the use of urban land was minimal in the 1850s and 1860s. During this period the economic base of the Chinese urban community, which relied on the patronage of their countrymen in the hinterlands, encouraged ghettoization. By congregating together, Chinese purveyors and social organizations created an enclave that provided their clients with what they needed most, an illusion of being in their native country.[42] These clusters—Little Chinas or Chinatowns—formed soon after the Chinese began migrating to California. By the early 1850s these districts were a main commercial and residential neighborhood for the urban Chinese.[43] And by the beginning of the next decade, an overwhelming majority of the immigrants in the cities resided in these ghettos.[44] Within this segregated urban society, the few early washhouses, which were not yet highly dispersed, operated with little harassment.

The growth of the laundry trade after the 1860s ended this co-existence in

104

urban space. This was inevitable because of the territorial nature of the businesses. The viability of a laundry hinged on its location. The marginal profits of the business could not support an extensive delivery network, and clients were unwilling to travel great lengths to take in their clothes. Washhouses had to be located along the paths where potential clients travelled, or in close proximity to where they lived. Long term growth of the trade entailed opening new territorial markets.

The primary constraint on location was a desire to minimize the distance from the ethnic enclave for social and security reasons. Consequently, the earliest washhouses were located in Chinatowns.[45] But soon after, the enclave became saturated with laundries. Thereafter, the trade grew by dispersing away from the ghetto, a movement that was hastened by the guilds. The guilds protected the established firms by limiting the number of laundries in any one area.[46] This rule channelled newcomers even further away from the ghetto, and into untried markets where financial and physical risks were higher. By 1880 over nine-tenths of San Francisco's Chinese laundry workers were located outside Chinatown.[47]

The next market areas to become saturated were the central business districts (CBD), which were adjacent to the enclaves. The Chinese adapted well to the nuances of these districts. In areas within the CBD that were more heavily used by daily workers and shoppers, the immigrants opened more laundries.[48] On sites where rent was comparatively higher, they met the higher operating expense by using facilities intensively, e.g., two firms sharing the same washhouse but operating in shifts.[49] By using these adaptive mechanisms, the Chinese were able to establish large numbers of firms in the CBDs. Even so, these areas became saturated. By 1882 Stockton's ethnic laundry trade reached this point as businesses began to locate in the area bordering the residential districts.[50]

The final markets were the White residential neighborhoods which were taking form as the economy matured. By the 1870s and early 1880s large numbers of washhouses were moving into these areas in Sacramento, San Francisco, and even smaller towns such as Modesto.[51] Since laundry workers and owners lived in their shops, this movement made a sizable number of Chinese residents of the White neighborhoods. In San Francisco, the number probably grew to well over a thousand.[52] This dispersion away from the ghetto had grave implications. Many Whites looked on the Chinese and their washhouses with malice, and the intensity and prevalence of this view grew during the latter stage of the trade's development when laundries began encroaching on the residential districts. Some Whites might have tolerated the laundries at a distance, but few wanted one as a neighbor.[53]

Whites objected to the Chinese and their businesses on moral grounds.[54] The Chinese were accused of disrupting White families by taking away a task traditionally assigned to distaff members. The laundry men were characterized as being sexually perverted and predisposed towards violence. And the washhouses were depicted as gathering places for other, but equally corrupted, Chinese who resided outside Chinatown. It is questionable whether or not these hyperboles were taken seriously, but they exercised the intensity of White antipathy towards the immigrant laundries and laundry workers.

These sentiments became institutionalized into laws. With the exception of one aborted effort on the state level, all legislation directed at the laundries were enacted on the municipal level. The laundry issue remained the province of local politicians and public officials for two reasons. First, strong sentiments against the trade did not develop simultaneously because the Chinese entered the

PAUL ONG

residential areas in different cities at different times. Second, the laundry issue was a neighborhood concern, and such parochial problems were best handled by local jurisdictions. Local politicians, who had long learned to capitalize on racist attitudes by proposing and voting for discriminatory laws against the Chinese, were more than willing to take up the issue. Enacting laws against the Chinese washhouses was another means of maintaining or winning popularity.[55]

The first laundry laws were enacted in the 1870s, and they imposed a tax and prohibited workers from carrying poles in public. The purpose of the prohibition was purely to harass the Chinese since only they carried bundles suspended from the ends of poles. Tax schedules were heavily biased against the immigrants so the law makers could "rid themselves of a great plague (the Chinese."[56] In spite of the racist intent of these laws, they proved ineffective in stopping the growth and dispersion of the Chinese laundry trade.

The need for effective measures became pressing in the 1880s when laundries were appearing in large numbers in the residential areas. By then, a new state constitution had delegated more power to local jurisdictions, primarily the authority to enact ordinances to protect the general public's health, safety, and welfare.[57] Local politicians employed this new police power against the Chinese in three ways.[58] The first approach required laundries to meet health and safety standards and to restrict their hours of business. Because the regulations were applied almost exclusively to the small washhouses and those firms that had to operate long hours, the Chinese were the hardest hit. Moreover, local officials denied Chinese operating permits even after their washhouses satisfied the prescribed standards. The second strategy was to prohibit laundries from operating in neighborhoods unless a stated number of immediate residents gave their approval. This delegation of power enabled local anti-Chinese vigilante committees to prevent, through pressure and threats, White residents from giving their approval to Chinese operators.[59] The final approach, which became the norm, was to limit laundries to specific geographical areas, or in contemporary terms to designated zones. The township of Modesto introduced this restrictive land-use method in 1885, and it was subsequently adopted by other California cities.[60] When such laws were carefully constructed, they effectively halted further dispersion of the Chinese washhouses and expelled existing ones from White neighborhoods. There is little doubt that these laws were aimed at the Chinese laundries since no similar restrictions were evoked against any other businesses until decades later.

The Chinese laundry guilds challenged the constitutionality of these laws in court. The local officials responded that it was their duty to enact such restrictions to protect the public's welfare. According to the electorates, washhouses were a source of sewage that polluted water wells and were potential fire traps that endangered surrounding homes and buidings. The veracity of these allegations is marginal at best.[61] Serious fires among Chinese laundries were rare, and a good proportion of these resulted from arson. If the businesses did pollute water sources, the problem would have been eliminated by requiring proper drainage, an approach not used. The strongest evidence contradicting the accusations was the ability of the laundries to meet safety and sanitary standards established by fire and health departments. There was, then, no evidence that the Chinese washhouses were a nuisance or a hazard. As the guilds pointed out, politicians used the allegations to circumvent a legal proscription on blatant discrimination against the Chinese.[62]

In many cases the courts saw through the cities' arguments and recognized the discriminatory intent and effects. Beginning in 1880 various benches invalidated a series of laundry ordinances, declaring that the laws were either

106

432

discriminatory or based on spurious justifications.[63] In the mid-1880s Judge Sawyer alone struck down flagrantly discriminatory laws enacted by three different municipalities.[64] He would later become the justice who authored the U.S. Supreme Court's decision barring racial zoning. In 1886 the Chinese won their most notable victory. In Yick Wo vs. Hopkins, the highest court of the land ruled that discriminatory administration of the law violated the Fourteenth Amendment, a historical ruling that expanded the rights of all non-Whites.[65]

Unfortunately, the decisions favorable to the Chinese were only temporary setbacks for the cities. Local officials repeatedly revised their justifications and methods in order to overcome judicial objections. Furthermore, many justices were unwilling to examine the discriminatory intent and effects.[66] Instead, they questioned whether or not the local jurisdictions had the police powers to enact protective regulations, which the cities did. With limited resources, the guilds were unable to appeal many of these adverse rulings even when higher courts would likely have overturned the decisions. Inevitably, the cities won by default. Their most important victory came in 1885 when local jurisdictions won judicial approval to control the location of laundries.[67] This became the basis through which the dominant racial group could control the use of urban lands.

It is difficult to estimate the exact impact of the laws on the Chinese laundry trade. Without a doubt, the cities were earnest in their efforts to eliminate the washhouses. During the height of the anti-laundry activities. Scores of Chinese were arrested for violating at least one of the regulations. In situations where the restrictions withstood judicial scrutiny, the Chinese were forced out of business. Even when the laws were later invalidated, the initial threats of jail sentences and fines were probably sufficient to deter immigrants from opening new businesses and to drive some of those already in business into retirement. The laws certainly had some impact in slowing, if not altogether reversing, the rapid growth of the Chinese laundry trade.

Ironically, after the cities had developed the restrictive land-use method, the need for laundry laws dwindled. After the mid-1880s the larger anti-Chinese movement had slowed further migration from China to a trickle and forced a substantial proportion of the immigrants to leave the state in search of better opportunities. The diaspora not only relieved much of the economic stress that was the impetus for expanding the laundry trade, but the exodus also included many of the laundry workers.[68] Yet the mere fact that many Chinese laundrymnen left to establish their trade elsewhere testifies to the hostilities directed at them and to the unprofitable nature of their work in California.

As Chinese dominance of the laundry trade declined (the laundering industry itself, however, did not decline), the Chinese washhouses were no longer a major threat to White neighborhoods. Consequently, the fervor to implement more land-use restrictions against the washhouses waned in the 1890s. Nonetheless, the cities had established legal means to discriminate against a Chinese ethnic trade, a way of institutionalizing racism.

The purpose of this institutional racism was directed more at controlling social relationships across race lines than at excluding the Chinese from the core of the economy. Intense racism made either social distance or physical segregation between the two racial groups important mechanisms that lowered overt conflicts. Whites did not object to the presence of a subordinate role. For instance, although the number of Chinese domestic workers in White residential neighborhoods was at least as large as the number of Chinese laundry workers in such areas, the servants never became the target of exclusionary restrictions.[69] Their servile role made their presence acceptable to both White

107

employers and their White neighbors. On the other hand, the laundry workers entered White neighborhoods as independent entrepreneurs. Without being in a clearly recognized subordinate role, the Chinese laundry workers were eventually segregated from White areas.

While the discriminatory practices against the Chinese laundries were social controls, they were not without economic consequences. Competition in the labor market led White workers to drive the Chinese out to the mainstream of the economy, but this exclusionary process did not define the pariah activities that the Chinese could take up. The ideology of racism, which legitimized the segmented economy, did. Racism limited the range of social interaction between Whites and Chinese, and in doing so, limited the range of economic interactions. When racism is intense, as in the case of early California, it is unlikely that any ethnic enterprises would be viable—regardless of that group's ability to raise capital and labor through their social ties and institutions.

NOTES

[1] Perhaps the most recent and best known work is by Ivan Light, Ethnic Enterprise in America (University of California Press, 1972). Also see Nathan Glazer and Daniel Moynihan, Beyond the Melting Pot (MIT Press, 1970). An example of a study on economics is Thomas Sowell, Race and Economics (David McKay, 1975).

[2] The Manuscript Census of 1850 lists two Chinese laundry workers in Sacramento. See also Alexander McLeod's Pigtails and Gold Dust (Caxton Printers, 1947), p. 112-133; and Thomas Chinn's A History of the Chinese in California (Chinese Historical Society of America, 1969), p. 63.

[3] Based on a sampling of the Manuscript Census of 1860 for San Francisco and Chico.

[4] McLeod, pp. 112-113; and Chinn, p. 63.

[5] In Yick Wo v. Hopkins, 118 U.S. 356 (1886), 240 of 320 laundries in San Francisco were operated by Chinese; and in Sam Kee, 31 Fed. 681 (1887), six out of seven in Napa. See also California Bureau of Labor Statistics, Second Annual Report, 1884-1886 (State of California, 1886), pp. 630-746.

[6] San Francisco exemplified this pattern. In 1860 the city had about 8% of the state's Chinese and 10% of the state's Chinese laundry workers. Figures based on the Manuscript Census of 1860 and U.S. Census, Population of the United States, 1860 (GPO, 1866), pp. 24-27. In 1870 the respective figures were 24% and 47%; U.S. Census, Ninth Census, Volume 1, The Statitics of the Population of the United States (GPO, 1872), pp. 769 and 799. In 1880 the respective statistics are 29% and 46%. Estimates based on U.S. Census, Statistics of the Population of the United States at the Tenth Census (GPO, 1883), pp. 499 and 902. For a summary of the demographic trends of California's racial groups, see Warren S. Thompson, Growth and Changes in California's Population (The Haynes Foundation, 1955).

[7] In San Francisco 11% in 1870, and in Chico 8% in the same year. Percentage for San Francisco taken from the 1870 Census of the Population. Percentage for Chico tabulated from the Manuscript Census. In Sacramento, the percentage was nearly 20%, using estimates from Melford Weiss, Valley City: A Chinese Community in America (Schenkman Publishing, 1972), p.51.

108

[8]In Sacramento, 42 of the 103 Chinese businesses in 1878 were laundries, and 45 of 104 in 1882. Data from Wells, Fargo, and Co., Directory of Chinese Business Houses (Lith Britton and Rey, 1878 and 1882).

[9]U.S. Immigration Commission, Abstract of Reports of the Immigration Commission (Washington, D.C.: U.S. Government Printing Office, 1911), p. 659.

[10]Stanford Lyman, The Asians in the West (Western Studies Center, University of Nevada, 1970), pp. 19-24.

[11]Second Report of the State Minerologist of California, Dec. 1880-Oct. 1882 (Sacramento, 1882), pp. 171.

[12]U. S. Census, Manufactures of the U.S. in 1860 (GPO, 1865), pp. 35-36.

[13]See Julius Klein, "The Development of the Manufacturing Industry in California up to 1870," (M.A. Thesis, U.C. Berkeley, 1908).

[14]U.S. Census, 1865, op. cit., p. 36, and U.S. Census, Statistics of Manufactures (GPO, 1883), p. 91. For similar data on trends in value added, see Everet Lee, et al., Population Redistribution and Economic Growth, U.S., 1870-1950 (American Philosophical Society, 1957), pp. 692-694.

[15]For an insightful treatment of this topic, see Cary McWilliams, Factories in the Field (Peregrine Press, 1971).

[16]Ping, Chiu, Chinese Labor in California, 1850-1880 (The State Historical Society of Wisconsin, 1967), pp. 71-72.

[17]U. S. Census, Report on the Production of Agriculture, 1880 (GPO, 1883), p. 103; and Agriculture of the U.S. in 1860 (GPO, 1864), p. 10.

[18]Rev. William Speer, "An Humble Plea Addressed to the Legislature of California in Behalf of the Immigrants From the Empire of China to this State" (San Francisco, 1856).

[19]Gunther Barth, Bitter Strength: A History of the Chinese in the United States, 1850-1870 (Harvard Univ. Press, 1964), p. 110.

[20]This argument is at variance with Edna Bonacich's assertions as presented in "A Theory of Ethnic Antagonism: The Splite Labor Market," American Sociological Review 37:547-59 (Oct. 1972). Chinese wages were not necessarily lower because they expected less, as Bonacich would argue. There is little reason to believe that the Chinese would not have accepted higher wages, if available. Low wages are often the result of a surplus of labor relative to demand: i.e., overcrowding in the labor market creates downward pressure on prevailing wages. Since the Chinese were segmented into a smaller labor market—or conversely, Whites dominated a proportionately larger segment of the labor market—the workings of a competitive market would lead to lower wages for the Chinese. See Barbara Bergmann's "The Effect of White Incomes of Discrimination in Employment," Journal of Political Economy, 79 (1971), pp. 294-313, for discussion on the effects of labor segmentation and overcrowding on wages.

[21]Chiu, p. 64.

[22]This socio-economic development is within the framework proposed by Herbert Blumer in his article "Industrialisation and Race Relations," in Industrialisation and Race Relations edited by Hunter (Oxford University Press, 1965). According to Blumer, racism does not necessarily disappear with

industrialisation, even though racism is in conflict with the rationalism that underlies the new economic order. If the industrialists are not powerful enough to overturn traditional values—i.e., racism—then the industrialist accommodates and integrates the values.

[23]The two most notable were the Chinese Exclusion Act of May 8, 1882 and the Scott Act of October 1, 1888. The first suspended further immigration of Chinese laborers, and the second prohibited Chinese who had temporarily left the country from returning to the U.S.

[24]See Stuart C. Miller, The Unwelcome Immigrant: The American Image of the Chinese, 1785-1882 (University of California Press, 1969) for details on the anti-Chinese sentiments. There are numerous works on the economic roots of the anti-Chinese movement; e.g., Elmer C. Sandmeyer, The Anti-Chinese Movement in California (University of Illinois Press, 1973).

[25]In 1867 the number of Chinese cigar and manufacturing firms in San Francisco increased from 33 to 41 and 40 to 51, respectively, according to Daniel Cleveland's letter to J. Rose Brown (July 27, 1868—copy at Bancroft Library). Chiu, op. cit., reports large increases in 1876-77, p. 135.

[26]Complaints were relatively absent in the two most widely published governmental hearings on the "Chinese problem": U.S. Senate, Senate Report No. 689 Joint Special Committee on Chinese Immigration (GPO, 1877) and California Senate, Chinese Immigration (1877).

[27]California Bureau of Labor Statistics, First Biennial Report (1884), 166-167 on Chinese wages. John W. Stephens, "A Quantitative Study of San Francisco's Chinatown, 1870 and 1880," in The Life and Influence and the Role of the Chinese in the U.S., 1776-1960 (Chinese Historical Society, 1976), p. 82 for social status.

[28]In Re Wo Lee, 26 Fed. 471 (1886), briefs on file: "the Chinese laundry business, while not lucrative, has been remunerative and highly valuable." In regards to washhouses as a source of jobs, see Susan W. Book, The Chinese in Butte County, Ca., 1860-1920 (R. and E. Research, 1976), p. 32.

[29]Of the ten laundries recorded in the Manuscript Census of 1870 for Chico, only one appears to have been owned by a Chinese. Of the eight fires in Chinese washhouses that were reported by the San Francisco fire department for the period between July 1882 to June 1885, seven were in buildings owned by Whites. Modifications included constructing a drying platform on top of the shop and building counters and storage spaces. Since most owners and their workers lived in the laundry, the Chinese also constructed living quarters.

[30]Estimates from Yick Wo v. Hopkins, 118 U.S. 356 (1886), p. 359; Manuscript Census of 1870 for Chico; and fire reports published in San Francisco Municipal Reports, 1882 to 1885.

[31]Chiu, pp. 114 and 125.

[32]Walter Fong, "Chinese Labor Unions in America," Chautauquan 23 (1896), p. 402.

[33]McLeod, pp. 113-114; Paul Sui, "The Chinese Laundrymen," (Univ. of Chicago diss. 1954), p. 92; and the repeated occurrence of partners with the same surnames in the Manuscript Census of 1870 for Chico.

[34]Light, pp. 23-27; Sui, p. 112; Milton Barnett, "Kinship as a Factor

110

Affecting Cantonese Economic Adjustment in the U.S.," Human Organizatio 19 (1960), p. 41.

[35] California Senate, p. 151; and Manuscript Census of 1870 for Chico.

[36] McLeod, p. 115; Yick Wo, p. 359; and Hubert H. Bancroft, Essays and Miscellany (The History Company, 1898), p. 348.

[37] During the gold rush, the price was as high as eight dollars a dozen, but the price dropped to one dollar a dozen by the 1870s. A. A. Hayes, "A Symposium of the Chinese Question," Scribner 17(1878), p. 491.

[38] California Senate, p. 123.

[39] Fong, p. 402.

[40] California Senate, p. 32; Fong, pp. 400-401; and Light, p. 94.

[41] Hubert H. Bancroft, History of the Pacific States, Volume 18 (The History Company, 1898), p. 345; Connie Yu, "The Chinese in American Courts," Bulletin of Concerned Asian Scholars 3 (1972), p. 27; and Alexander Saxton, The Indispensable Enemy: Labor and the Anti-Chinese Movement in California (University of California Press, 1910), p. 150.

[42] Barth, p. 110.

[43] Frank Soule, et al., The Annals of San Francisco (New York: D. Appleton and Co., 1854), p. 381; and Daily Alta, Nov. 21, 1853.

[44] According to Stephens, 64% of the Chinese in 1860 in San Francisco resided in Chinatown.

[45] McLeod, pp. 112-113; Chinn, p. 63; and Sui, p. 52.

[46] Fong, p. 401.

[47] Using data from Stephens, about one-fifth of the Chinese laundrymen were in Chinatown, assuming that his sample is representative.

[48] For example, the Chinese washhouses in Napa were concentrated in the core of the CBD. Four of the six Chinese laundries were located in the more intensively used half of the downtown, while the other two were situated in the other half. This fact was presented in a brief filed in the case of In Re Sam Kee, 31 Fed. 681 (1887).

[49] Bancroft, 1890, p. 348; Chinn, p. 63; Jones, "Cathay on the Coast," American Mercury 8 (1926), p. 445.

[50] This pattern is based on a mapping of the locations of the laundries listed in Wells, Fargo, and Co.

[51] U.S. Senate, p. 63; Weiss, p. 51; Jeanette B. Maine, One Hundred Years, Modesto, California, 1870-1970 (Belt Printing, 1970), p. 19.

[52] In 1880 there were 2,450 Chinese laundry workers in San Francisco, with over 80% working outside of Chinatown. See Note 47.

[53] Soon Hing v. Crowley, 113 U.S. 703 (1895), p. 704; and Bancroft, 1890, p. 348.

[54] Miller, pp. 75 and 193; California Senate, pp. 123-124 and 132; and U.S. Senate, p. 718.

111

[55]For summary, see Charles Kneier, "Discrimination Against Aliens by Municipal Ordinances," Georgetown Law Journal 16 (1927-8); William J. Courtney, San Francisco Anti-Chinese Ordinances, 1850-1900 (R. and E. Research, 1976); and Yu, op. cit. For summary of anti-laundry laws, see Alfred Clarke, Report of Alfred Clarke, Special Counsel for the City and County of San Francisco in the Laundry Order Litigation (W. M. Hinton and Co., 1885).

[56]Clarke, briefs filed in the case of In Re Tie Loy, 26 Fed. 611 (1886); and San Francisco Orders No. 1569, 1679, and 1767.

[57]Noel Sargent, "California Constitutional Convention of 1878," California Law Review 6 (1917-18), pp. 21 and 129.

[58]U.S. Senate, p. 998; Clarke, p. 5; Soon Hong, p. 704; briefs filed in the case of In Re Hang Kie, 10 Pac. 327 (1886).

[59]For example, Won Pao Ling was able to obtain the required signatures, but the League of Deliverance intimidated signers to retract their approval. Event cited in briefs filed in the case of In Re Quong Woo, 13 Fed. 119 (1882).

[60]Robert A. Walker, The Planning Function in Urban Government (Univ. of Chicago Press, 1941), pp. 55-56.

[61]For fire rates, see Saxton, p. 150. Also, among San Francisco's Chinese washhouses, only eight fires were reported for the period from July 1882 to June 1885, half of which were minor. Moreover, many of the fires were likely the result of arson rather than carelessness. If this is so, the Chinese were victims of "blaming the victims." For pro-Chinese argument on economic grounds, see George F. Seward, Chinese Immigration in Its Social and Economic Aspects (Charles Scribner's Sons, 1881), p. 115. In regard to the fact that laundries were not a nuisance, see ruling in In Re Woo Yeck, 12 Pac. C.L.J. 383 (1880). In regard to the question of health hazards, see ruling in Tie Loy.

[62]Yick Wo v. Hopkins, 118 U.S. 356 (1886), p. 224.

[63]Woo Yeck, Quong Woo, Ex Parte Sing Lee, 21 Pac. 245 (1892); People v. Soon Kung, County Court of San Francisco (1874) was an earlier victory.

[64]Tie Loy; San Kee; and Yick Wo.

[65]Yick Wo, pp. 374-375: "Though the law itself be fair on its face, and impartial in applicance, yet, if it is applied and administered by public authority with an evil eye and unequal hand, so as practically to make unjust and illegal discrimination between persons in similar circumstance, material to their rights, the denial of equal Justice is still within the prohibition of the Constitution."

[66]Soon Hing, p. 711.

[67]In Re Hang Kie.

[68]The laundrymen were often the first to establish communities outside of California; David T. C. Cheng, Acculturation of the Chinese in the U.S.: A Philadelphia Study (Fukien University Press, 1948), pp. 68-69; Sui, p. 36. For a study of the Chinese laundry trade after 1910, see Peter Li, "Ethnic Business Among Chinese in the United States," Journal of Ethnic Studies 4:3 (1976), pp. 35-41. The high rate of dispersion among the Chinese laundrymen can be seen in the census statistics for 1930. In that year, 57% of the Chinese males over the age of 10 resided outside of the state; U.S. Census, Fifteenth Census of the United States: 1930 Population Volume V (GPO, 1933), pp. 95-97. This meant

112

only 6% of the Chinese males in California worked in laundries, while 24% of the Chinese males outside of California worked in laundries.

[69]According to the 1880 Census of the population, there were about 3,300 Chinese domestic workers and 2,450 Chinese laundry workers in San Francisco in 1880. According to Stephens, few of these workers resided in Chinatown (see footnote 6).

Journal of Interdisciplinary History, VII:4 (Spring 1977), 655–681.

Daniel T. Rodgers

Tradition, Modernity, and the American Industrial Worker:

Reflections and Critique

Much of the current writing on labor history begins in complaint. The field, it is said, suffers from fossilization; its techniques are old-fashioned, its guiding questions archaic, and its institutional preoccupations downright myopic. There is a measure of truth to these charges, but it is a rapidly diminishing measure. Evident signs of change abound: a wholesale embrace of statistical techniques with often iconoclastic results; an egalitarian effort to recover working-class history from the bottom up and, in consequence, a flight from the study of trade unions or, at least, of conservative ones; and a new interest in the complex web of social and cultural relations too often overlooked by earlier generations of economics-trained scholars.

Labor history has been driven before the winds of the present in less obvious ways as well. One change, unheralded but far-reaching, has been the impact of the internationalization of the industrial revolution. It is a commonplace, though a momentous one, that the non-Western world has experienced a massive upheaval in economic habits in the twentieth century. As the factory and the supermarket, the ethics of Samuel Smiles, and the precepts of Henry Ford burst the boundaries of the West, the study of industrialization shifted as well, from past to present and from history to sociology. The result has been the emergence of new models and new vocabularies which, in turn, have begun to recast the axioms of Western labor history.

The mediators between the non-Western present and the Western past were a corps of industrial sociologists and social theorists who turned to the study of international industrialization after 1945, and their contributions ran in separate but complementary directions. The first was to heighten interest in the strains experienced by the first generation of workers to encounter industrialization head on. As Luddites, as Chartists, or as Wobblies, these uprooted workers have always occupied a conspicuous place

Daniel T. Rodgers is Assistant Professor of History at the University of Wisconsin, Madison.

in Western social history. But the concerns of the industrial sociologists who took up the study of non-Western work forces were less political than managerial, and they were above all interested in the more pervasive, work-place tied issue that they called labor commitment—the process by which new industrial employees adjusted deeply set rural loyalties and work habits to the disrupting demands of factory labor. It was a difficult process, the first studies suggested. In the early stages of industrialization, the labor force remained mentally rooted in the ways of the past; stability and efficiency were rare, the lure of wage incentives weak, and turnover and absenteeism high. Beneath the exterior of the industrializing community, as Kerr and his associates summarized the existing studies in 1960, there "is always latent protest, seething and simmering."[1]

Over the long run, however, Kerr and others predicted a steady increase in the commitment of new workers. In their confidence in the "logic of industrialization" their conclusions meshed with those of a group of more theoretical students of international development who began to describe the fundamental process at work in the non-Western world as something that they called "modernization." The term has since acquired an ample train of imprecisions and confusions. Yet the roots of the idea belong to the long-standing sociological vision of comprehending change by dichotomizing the processes of history. From Henry Sumner Maine's effort to show how the age of status gives way to the age of contract, the bipolar habit of mind has had a firm hold on the sociological imagination, and the modernization hypothesis is its latest and most sophisticated recrudescence.[2]

Essentially the modernization hypothesis proposes to understand the larger processes of industrialization as the irreversible transition from one ideal social type, "traditional" society, to its mirror opposite, "modernity." Traditional society, on the one

---

1 Clark Kerr, et al., *Industrialism and Industrial Man: The Problems of Labor and Management in Economic Growth* (Cambridge, Mass., 1960), 202, 166–181, 202–210; Wilbert E. Moore, *Industrialization and Labor: Social Aspects of Economic Development* (Ithaca, 1951); Wilbert E. Moore and Arnold S. Feldman (eds.), *Labor Commitment and Social Change in Developing Areas* (New York, 1960); Charles A. Myers, *Labor Problems in the Industrialization of India* (Cambridge, Mass., 1958), 36–54; Walter Elkan, *Migrants and Proletarians: Urban Labor in the Economic Development of Uganda* (London, 1960), 97–110.

2 For a perceptive treatment of this theme, see Philip Abrams, "The Sense of the Past and the Origins of Sociology," *Past & Present*, 55 (1972), 18–32.

hand, is closed and static, organized around tightly woven patterns of kinship and village relations, tied to a subsistence economy, and committed to the worlds of the past and the unseen. Modern society, on the other hand, is socially and technologically innovative, open to a high degree of mobility, and highly rationalized; it is urban, industrial, and bureaucratic; and its capstone is said to be a new social nature. Definitions of "industrial" or "modern" man differ somewhat from writer to writer, but all are joined by the assumption that industrialized societies produce a character type which internalizes the needs of an expansive industrial economy. Mobile and ambitious, modern man has nonetheless made his peace with the new forms of labor. In the industrial sociologists' terms, the worker in modern society is fully committed, "dedicated to hard work, a high pace of work, and a keen sense of individual responsibility for performance of assigned norms and tasks." He is moved, Kerr and his associates write, not by grudging acquiescence, but by "an ideology and an ethic."[3]

Taken together, the work of the modernization theorists and the early students of new non-Western industrial employees formed a two-sided story. Industrialization begins with a short and turbulent period of uprooting; but, with time, resistance succumbs to the processes of acculturation and the result, ultimately, is something approaching harmony and stasis. The grandchild of the premodern peasant laborer adjusts to the time clock and the incentive wage; the primitive rebel is succeeded by the leader of a wage-conscious trade union.

Incompletely, but unmistakably, the new labor history has begun to echo this schema of generational shock and gradual acculturation. Led by Thompson, Gutman, Pollard, and Stearns, labor historians have consciously turned the industrial sociologists' questions of work habits and commitment to the first generations of workers to enter the factories in the West, and the results have been new and sensitive insights into what Gutman has called "the painful process by which an old way of life was discarded for a new one." Although Stearns would except the Ger-

3 Kerr, *Industrialism*, 43; Neil J. Smelser, "The Modernization of Social Relations," in Myron Weiner (ed.), *Modernization: The Dynamics of Growth* (New York, 1966); Daniel Lerner, *The Passing of Traditional Society: Modernizing the Middle East* (Glencoe, Ill., 1958); Alex Inkeles and David H. Smith, *Becoming Modern: Individual Change in Six Developing Countries* (Cambridge, Mass., 1974).

man peasant turned industrial laborer, the emphasis of these studies has been on the ways in which new industrial laborers stubbornly resisted the new work-forms, clinging to accustomed patterns of time, work, and social relations in the face of the factories' demands, refusing to respond to incentives in the ways the inventors of "economic man" predicted, and, on occasion, erupting in brief bursts of tradition-asserting protest. These were not necessarily the acts of conscious rebels, they stress, but of workers caught in the creases of time, whose habits and values, nurtured in pre-industrial cultures, could not but jar against the standards of work and discipline that industrialization demanded.[4]

Historians have not given comparable attention to the processes of acculturation. Yet there is a widespread assumption among these same writers that with time and generational change the initial tensions subsided, the worker was modernized, and the factory lessons were learned and accepted. Thompson, despite deep reservations about the literature of economic development, nonetheless agrees with its central premise, that the transition to "mature industrial society" entailed not only new disciplines and new incentives but "a new human nature upon which these incentives could bite effectively"—forged in England, he maintains, by the Methodist revivals. Stearns writes, to much the same end, that in Germany experienced industrial workers learned "the 'modern' idea of the wage" and made "the basic bargain industrialization requires" by accepting the new work forms in return for an increasing material standard of living. In yet another example, Dawley and Faler argue that the industrial revolution gave birth to a new, modern-minded person among the laboring classes of Europe and America, who gave up the traditionalist's casual work attitudes and raucous mores for a new ethic of self-control, self-denial, and self-improvement.[5] Frequently the acculturation as-

4 E. P. Thompson, "Time, Work-Discipline, and Industrial Capitalism," *Past & Present*, 38 (1967), 56–97; Herbert G. Gutman, "Work, Culture, and Society in Industrializing America, 1815–1919," *American Historical Review*, LXXVIII (1973), 531–587; Sidney Pollard, "Factory Discipline in the Industrial Revolution," *Economic History Review*, XVI (1963), 254–271; Peter N. Stearns, "Adaptation to Industrialization: German Workers as a Test Case," *Central European History*, III (1970), 303–331. The quotation is from Gutman, "The Worker's Search for Power: Labor in the Gilded Age," in H. Wayne Morgan (ed.), *The Gilded Age: A Reappraisal* (Syracuse, 1963), 40.
5 Thompson, "Time, Work-Discipline, and Industrial Capitalism," 57; Stearns, "Adaptation to Industrialization," 322, 323; Alan Dawley and Paul Faler, "Working-Class Cul-

sumption lurks more discreetly in the background, buried somewhere in the half-consciousness of historians, its presence marked by the currency of the terms "traditional," "premodern," and "modern" where "agrarian" and "industrial" once sufficed. The new terminology has created strange and not altogether compatible bedfellows. Above all, those who share the assumptions of initial shock and gradual accommodation are deeply divided as to the moral of the story—whether it should be read as tragedy or comedy, as the collapse of a viable working-class culture or the triumph of progress. But the tale itself has become an increasingly familiar part of contemporary scholarship.

Yet perhaps the story is wrong or, at best, oversimplified. In their quest for a coherent evolutionary order to labor history, it is possible that historians have exaggerated both the fractiousness of first-generation industrial workers and the docility of their descendants, just as it is possible that in accepting the concepts of "traditional" and "modern" man they have fallen too eagerly into formulations as mechanical as the "economic man" from which they were in pell-mell flight. Above all, it is possible that working-class cultures have been far too diverse and the ties between gross levels of economic development and working-class mores far too tenuous to fit the grand schemes half-consciously accepted. The confident grasp of the shape of the future which so strikingly marked studies in international development in the generation after the war has eroded sharply in recent years, and modernization theorists have become increasingly tentative about hypotheses that they boldly argued less than a decade ago. The uniform experience of newly industrializing work forces, the assumption of global convergence upon Western-style modernity, and the utility of the tradition-modernity polarity itself have all been seriously questioned by students of social change.[6]

---

ture and Politics in the Industrial Revolution: Sources of Loyalism and Rebellion," *Journal of Social History*, IX (1976), 466, 468. See also Bruce Laurie, "'Nothing on Compulsion': Life Styles of Philadelphia Artisans, 1820–1850," *Labor History*, XV (1974), 337–366; and, for a broader application, Richard D. Brown, "Modernization and the Modern Personality in Early America, 1600–1865: A Sketch of a Synthesis," *Journal of Interdisciplinary History*, II (1972), 201–228.

6 Morris D. Morris, *The Emergence of an Industrial Labor Force in India: A Study of the Bombay Cotton Mills, 1854–1947* (Berkeley, 1965); Manning Nash, *Machine Age Maya: The Industrialization of a Guatemalan Community* (Menasha, Wisc., 1958); Clark Kerr, *et al.*, "Postscript to *Industrialism and Industrial Man*," *International Labour Review*, CIII (1971), 519–540;

In their interdisciplinary zeal it would be a shame for historians to leap unwittingly onto an outmoded bandwagon. What follows is an attempt to pose the hypothesis of initial entrenchment and progressive acculturation against what can be gleaned about the behavior of factory workers in the United States, focusing primarily on the years from 1865 to 1919 and, more briefly, on the modern years since World War II. The results are cautious and skeptical reflections. But if the historian pays his way in doubts and a sense of alternatives, perhaps we should not insist that he be taxed entirely in the hard coin of certainty.

Two matters are open to relatively little question: that industrialization in America, as elsewhere, required a major assault on the existing norms of time and labor, and that during the years of that attack the factories were the site of frequent contest and widespread friction. Given the highly uneven development of the American economy, the assault on the old work norms was far from uniform. But as the nineteenth century wore on and as manufacturers learned to count the monetary value of time with increasing precision, they turned an arsenal of new weapons—precise work rules and personnel departments, the steam whistle and locked factory gates, the time clock and, eventually, the efficiency expert's stop watch—against the irregular work rhythms of pre-industrial America. Nor were their efforts without result. A French labor delegate who toured the industrial states in the 1890s marveled that, "work in the American shops is altogether different from what it is in France. Nobody talks, nobody sings, the most rigorous silence reigns."[7] But accommodation to work rules such as these (as often as not enforced by heavy fines) was far commoner than internalization of the new standards, and the new model workers that the factory masters tried to forge—punctual,

---

S. N. Eisenstadt, *Tradition, Change, and Modernity* (New York, 1973), 3–21, 98–115; Joseph R. Gusfield, "Tradition and Modernity: Misplaced Polarities in the Study of Social Change," *American Journal of Sociology*, LXXII (1967), 351–362; Robert A. Nisbet, *Social Change and History: Aspects of the Western Theory of Development* (New York, 1969), 240–304; Reinhard Bendix, "Tradition and Modernity Reconsidered," *Comparative Studies in Society and History*, IX (1967), 292–346; Dean C. Tipps, "Modernization Theory and the Comparative Study of Societies: A Critical Perspective," *ibid.*, XV (1973), 199–226.
7 E. Levasseur (trans. Thomas S. Adams), *The American Workman* (Baltimore, 1900), 173–174.

efficient, sober, disciplined to the clock and the incentive wage
—were not easily made.

A part of the evidence lies in the vigorous complaints of the
manufacturers themselves. Suspect and inextricably tangled in
ample doses of prejudice, employers' laments of drunkenness
among their hands, irregular attendance, and general inefficiency
are nonetheless too numerous to dismiss out of hand. Another
part of the evidence is to be found in the persistent dream of
shorter working hours, which captured the imagination of all of
the period's labor organizations and runs through the rank and file
testimony preserved in the records of the state bureaus of labor
statistics as a constant challenge to the factory masters' aim of constant, untiring labor. Still more direct were the repeated contests
between the new standards of toil and shop-maintained work patterns which undercut them. Like so many of the essential facts of
social history, the outlines of these shop cultures are often hidden
and difficult to recover, although something of them can be sur-
mised from the rules factory supervisors felt compelled to make
explicit—against leaving one's place during working hours, for
example—and something more from the controversy over scientific management which came to a head just before World War I.
As far as employers were concerned, worker-maintained production quotas were the nub of the issue. Only a few skilled factory
workers at the height of their power—glass blowers, potters, iron
molders, and puddlers and rollers in the iron and steel mills—
maintained openly acknowledged output limits. But the Bureau of
Labor report on the subject in 1904 concluded that clandestine
shop-level output agreements were far more common than this,
and, if often short-lived, the mood behind them was clearly serious. In 1901, in one of the most dramatic examples of the period,
sheep and cattle butchers slowed down the lines of the Chicago
packing plants by some 30 percent until the new regime fell apart
in a disastrous strike. And where workers could not actually control the factory pace, they could at least intimidate the exceptionally fast worker, branding him with shop names—hog, boss's pet,
bell-horse, rusher, swift—which amounted to a string of
epithets.[8]

8   U.S. Commissioner of Labor, *Eleventh Special Report: Regulation and Restriction of Output*
(Washington, 1904), 18, 715.

Quantitative evidence, on the whole, confirms the clash of work norms within the factories, although some of its dimensions are exceedingly difficult to determine. Absenteeism is a case in point. Throughout the period, employers complained of irregular attendance and tried to curb the habit by stiff fines, occasionally equivalent to a day's pay or more, for unexcused absences and tardiness. But typical absence rates are another matter. Payroll records from three late-nineteenth-century industrial firms show that a quarter of the employees stayed out at least one day a week, although some of the lost days may have been due to a shortage of work at hand, often a chronic problem. Another way to count absences is in the number of "spare hands" kept to fill the places of absentees. In isolated country mills, where the practice was widely used, the spares might amount to 10 to 25 percent of a mill's total labor force, although again the figure inflates the actual voluntary absence rate, for the system worked in a vicious circle, forcing regular employees to stay home in order to give enough work to the spare hands to keep them from drifting elsewhere.[9] By the turn of the century in the industrial Northeast, factory managers had clearly succeeded in reducing absences far below the levels typical of nonfactory trades—to less than 4 percent according to a Massachusetts survey of 1904 compared with rates of up to 17 percent in the state's shop and building trades.[10] Nonetheless, between factories absence rates varied widely. In 1916, when labor shortages may have begun to drive industrial absence rates upward, the handful of reported figures ranged from 2 percent at the reorganized Ford plant to 11 percent in a set of South Carolina textile mills. During the war years, observers forced to generalize set-

H. M. Gitelman, "The Labor Force at Waltham Watch during the Civil War Era," *Journal of Economic History*, XXV (1965), 229; Thomas R. Navin, *The Whitin Machine Works since 1831: A Textile Machinery Company in an Industrial Village* (Cambridge, Mass., 1950), 68; Robert S. Smith, *Mill on the Dan: A History of Dan River Mills, 1882–1950* (Durham, N.C., 1960), 48; U.S. Senate, Committee on Education and Labor, *Report upon the Relations between Labor and Capital* (Washington, 1885), III, 207–208; August Kohn, *The Cotton Mills of South Carolina* (Charleston, S.C., 1907), 61–63; U.S. Bureau of Labor, *Report on Condition of Woman and Child Wage-Earners in the United States*, 61st Cong., 2 sess. (1910–1912), XVI, 154–155.

10 *Massachusetts Labor Bulletin*, 32 (1904), 210–215. A replication of the survey in August of that year, however, produced such astonishingly low figures (0.1% in Fall River, for example) that these rates should be treated with some skepticism.

THE AMERICAN WORKER | 663

tled on 6 percent as the goal for a well-run industrial plant.[11] But how often and by how much that figure had been exceeded in the preceding half century is a matter of impressions and guesswork.

But if the rate at which workers stayed away from the factories is obscure, the rate at which industrial employees moved between jobs in the early twentieth century is not. The picture it shows is of an astonishingly restless and mobile labor force. The median job tenure for industrial workers seems to have been slightly less than three years, and a sizeable fraction moved much faster, deserting their jobs after a matter of days or weeks. The result was a constant shuffling of men. To keep a work force of about 8,000 employees, for example, Armour in Chicago hired 8,000 workers during the course of 1914, and the pattern was repeated over and again in the early-twentieth-century factories. Larger turnover surveys concluded that about one-third of the employees of a typical factory held on to their jobs a year or less, and, because they moved so often, annual factory turnover in normal times was at least as high as the 100 percent reported at Armour. Turnover in the wool industry between 1907 and 1910 varied between 113 and 163 percent; in 1913–1914 a Bureau of Labor Statistics survey of sixty-eight manufacturing plants found an average yearly turnover of 115 percent, despite the current economic slump. At casually managed plants or regions troubled by labor shortages, the turnover rate ran still higher. It reached 176 percent in the Southern textile industry in 1907, 252 percent in a sample of Detroit factories in 1916, and the bewildering rate of 370 percent at Ford in 1913. As turnover investigators were forced to rely on plants concerned enough about the transiency problem to have collected their own data, the Bureau of Labor Statistics figure of 115 percent seems a cautious estimate.[12]

11 John S. Keir, "The Reduction of Absences and Lateness in Industry," *Annals of the American Academy of Political and Social Science,* LXXI (1917), 140–155; Paul H. Douglas, "Absenteeism in Labor," *Political Science Quarterly,* XXXIV (1919), 591–608; Emil Frankel, "Labor Absenteeism," *Journal of Political Economy,* XXIX (1921), 487–499; Boris Emmet, "Labor Turnover and Employment Policies of a Large Motor Vehicle Manufacturing Establishment," U.S. Bureau of Labor Statistics (hereafter USBLS), *Monthly Labor Review,* VII (1918), 846; J. D. Hackett, "Absentism: A Quantitative Study," *Management Engineering,* II (1922), 85.
12 U.S. Commission on Industrial Relations, *Final Report and Testimony,* 64th Cong., 1 sess. (1916), IV, 3507, 3510; U.S. Tariff Board, *Wool and Manufactures of Wool,* 62nd Cong., 2 sess. (1912), IV, 963, 983; Sumner H. Slichter, *The Turnover of Factory Labor* (New York,

Systematic turnover data do not extend back before the turn of the century, but it is likely that the overall pattern then was much the same. A knowledgeable observer of the Lowell textile industry reported in 1873 that most of the operatives left within four years, and, even at the model Pullman plant in 1894, 21 percent of the workforce had less than a year's tenure. Certainly employers were aware of the "nomadic system of employing men" and made strenuous efforts to escape it by offering bonuses for steady work, requiring labor passes certifying that the worker had left his last job with the permission of his employer, or, most frequently, demanding that those who left without adequate notice forfeit one or two weeks' back wages. Called upon to defend the last practice in the 1870s, a Massachusetts textile mill agent insisted that if a mill did not withhold wages it would simply wake up to find all of its hands gone by morning.[13]

It is easier to count the transients than to know why so many workers changed jobs so often. Prior to 1919, few companies distinguished between those who quit and those who were laid off or fired, and, even then, such categories are far from clear cut. Quitting was undoubtedly more pleasant than being fired or waiting for the layoff one sensed was imminent. Nevertheless, the best students of early-twentieth-century turnover were convinced that in normal times layoffs and discharges directly accounted for well under half and perhaps as little as one quarter of all job separations. Fluctuations in the turnover rate bear out their emphasis on the high proportion of voluntary quitters. Turnover was far higher in years of prosperity than in depression years when all who had jobs worked hard and anxiously to keep them; and throughout the course of the year turnover rose in spring and fell in winter in a cycle which apparently had more to do with wanderlust than with industrial conditions.

1919), 16–27, 34–35, 44–45; Paul F. Brissenden and Emil Frankel, *Labor Turnover in Industry* (New York, 1922), 50–51, 118–119. I have recalculated Brissenden and Frankel's aggregate figures throughout to eliminate the nonfactory trades from their sample.
13   Massachusetts Bureau of Statistics of Labor (hereafter MBLS), *Fourth Annual Report* (Boston, 1873), 281; Stanley Buder, *Pullman: An Experiment in Industrial Order and Community Planning, 1880–1930* (New York, 1967), 248, n. 2; Wisconsin Bureau of Labor and Industrial Statistics, *Third Biennial Report* (Madison, 1888), 111–115; Melton A. McLaurin, *Paternalism and Protest: Southern Cotton Mill Workers and Organized Labor, 1875–1905* (Westport, Conn., 1971), 32; MBLS, *Third Annual Report* (Boston, 1872), 376. Withholding wages also served, of course, as a strike preventative.

Attempts to probe still further into the reasons behind the high quit rates were not particularly successful. Skilled workmen sometimes defended moving about as a way to learn more than one branch of their increasingly specialized trades. Yet very few of those who quit claimed that they had a better job in hand, and, in most of the plants investigated, less than a third cited better opportunities as their grounds for leaving. The quitters were "dissatisfied," looking for something else to turn up, leaving town—in all, taking a vacation from factory discipline. No statistics more clearly show the restlessness of the industrial work force than this army of voluntary migrants (perhaps one worker in seven in the year 1913–1914, according to one careful estimate) continually on the run from—and to—industrial labor. But their grievances may not have been essentially different from those who stayed behind. A machinist at the federal arsenal at Watertown, unnoticed by history save for his participation in a strike against the introduction of scientific management, told investigators that the new regime threatened to make a man stick to his work "every second of the eight hours, and if there is any man who can do that I don't believe I ever saw him." Industrialization in post–Civil War America pressed repeatedly and not always successfully against sentiments like these and against recalcitrant human materials.[14]

To grant the restlessness of the industrializing work force, however, only begins to answer the essential questions. How close was the match between factory rebels and neophyte industrial workers? To what extent was the persistent conflict in the factories due to what Gutman has called the central problem of American labor history, the repeated clash of "premodern" patterns of behavior with the industrial setting?[15] Certainly large numbers of first-generation industrial workers toiled in the factories of post–Civil War America. And it is often not hard to trace

14 Brissenden, *Labor Turnover*, 94–96; Slichter, *Turnover*, 163–185; Anne Bezanson, *et al.*, "Four Years of Labor Mobility: A Study of Labor Turnover in a Group of Selected Plants in Philadelphia, 1921–24," *Annals*, CXIX (1925), supplement, 70–72; U.S. House of Representatives, Special Committee to Investigate the Taylor and Other Systems of Shop Management, *Hearings* (Washington, 1912), I, 453. The estimate of the number of floaters is W. S. Woytinsky's, adjusted to eliminate nonfactory workers from his base data: *Three Aspects of Labor Dynamics* (Washington, 1942), 27.
15 Gutman, "Work, Culture, and Society," 541, 543.

direct connections between the turbulence which bedeviled employers and these new workers' attempts to cling to custom and memory in the face of the new and strange demands of the factories. The army of industrial transients included its regiments of the classically semi-committed: French-Canadian and Maine mill hands who deserted the factories for their farms or fishing villages each summer in a regular cycle, Southerners who drifted back to the land with rising cotton prices or who practiced "summer farming," and immigrant workingmen retreating homeward, their dreams fulfilled or their energies exhausted. Factory absence rates, too, were clearly inflated by the pull of the past—by workers not yet broken from the rural prerogative of taking a day off at will to go fishing and by immigrants who struggled hard to keep Old World holiday schedules intact against the factory demands of regular attendance. Cigar makers, potters, and other one-time hand workers caught in the vise of change figured prominently in the complaints of drunkenness and disorder as their artisan ways jostled painfully against new standards of industrial discipline.

None of this can be dismissed, yet the matter will not rest here. Some of the apparent rebellion against industrial discipline was not rebellion at all, but accommodation to the constant turbulence of the industrializing economy. Whether seasonal or afflicted by unpredictable changes in demand, few industries escaped repeated cycles of boom and famine which, for the workers, meant that short time and layoffs followed hard on the heels of bouts of overtime and rush work. The experience had a deep impact on the industrial work force. "At one time they drive us like slaves, and at other times we have to beg for work," a Brooklyn worker charged in the 1880s, and the complaint runs as a constant thread through the reports of the bureaus of labor statistics and through immigrant letters.[16]

Had the ethos of industrialization been all of one piece, employers might have cushioned the destabilizing effects of these cycles on their workers. But the economics of cheap labor took

16 Marion C. Cahill, *Shorter Hours: A Study of the Movement since the Civil War* (New York, 1932), 42. On the irregularity of employment: Constance M. Green, *Holyoke, Massachusetts: A Case History of the Industrial Revolution in America* (New Haven, 1939), 76–77; David Brody, *Steelworkers in America: The Nonunion Era* (Cambridge, Mass., 1960), 39–40; W. Jett Lauck and Edgar Sydenstricker, *Conditions of Labor in American Industries: A Summarization of the Results of Recent Investigations* (New York, 1917), 74–100, 137–164.

precedence over the ideal of steady, clockwork toil, although the result was to undermine the factory masters' disciplining efforts. Irregular employment helped fuel the shorter-hours drive by turning workers' dreams to shorter but steadier hours of labor. It fostered clandestine slowdown agreements as employees struggled to stretch out the work at hand and stave off the layoff they knew was coming. Finally, unstable employment contributed to the high industrial turnover, throwing initially steady workers out of their jobs so often that motion became an ingrained habit. Economic conditions were at the root of these matters, not memory or culture. In the case of the most transient laborers restlessness slides paradoxically into functional integration, for these highly mobile and uncommitted workers, complained of by employers, provided what the factories sorely needed—a reserve army of workers able to iron out the fluctuations of an expanding economy.

The picture is made still more complex by the fact that, far from resisting the new demands, some first-generation industrial workers labored considerably harder than the norm. Weber, noting the phenomenon among sojourning laborers in Germany, concluded that "the simple fact of a change in residence is among the most effective means of intensifying labour. . . . The same Polish girl who at home was not to be shaken from her traditional laziness by any chance of earning money, however tempting, seems to change her entire nature and become capable of unlimited accomplishment when she is a migratory worker in a foreign country." In considerably cruder language, many American employers of immigrant workers agreed. A Chicago clothing contractor in the early twentieth century warned his forelady that he had no use for experienced help: "I got to pay them good wages and they make me less work, but these greenhorns, Italian people, Jewish people, all nationalities, they cannot speak English and they don't know where to go and they just came from the old country and I let them work hard, like the devil, and these I get for less wages."[17] Obviously not all immigrants worked exception-

---

17   Max Weber (trans. Talcott Parsons), *The Protestant Ethic and the Spirit of Capitalism* (New York, 1958), 191; anon., "Bricks without Straw," *Survey*, XXV (1910), 425. The point, of course, can be carried past the brink into caricature, as in Gerald Rosenblum, *Immigrant Workers: Their Impact on American Labor Radicalism* (New York, 1973).

ally hard, and fewer still changed their entire nature in the crossing. But the "greenhorns" were a conspicuous feature of industrializing America. Their experience suggests something of the severe limits of the term traditional, certainly the danger of any easy equation of non-industrial cultures with premodernity. Moreover, it suggests that what shaped those who moved across the boundaries of industrial society was neither culture nor economic conditions but the highly specific interaction of the two—the ways in which expectation, memory, and habit met with the force of circumstance. The process contained not one, but a wide variety of potential outcomes.

The making of an exceptionally diligent workman out of a European immigrant began with the fact that, although relatively few immigrants in post-Civil War America brought industrial habits with them, they were not, as a necessary consequence, premodern—not the backward, fatalistic traditionalists described by students of social change. Immigration historians have repeatedly testified to the importance of economic ambition in the population movements which unsettled the continent in the late nineteenth and early twentieth centuries. Often the emigrant had been on the move before as a temporary laborer in Europe when tales of success manufactured from the letters of those who had left for America or from the example of the successful repatriate turned his thoughts toward the United States. Most immigrants, moreover, brought with them not only ambition but a faith in toil itself. Even in southern Italy, for example, where the working year might be half as long as in the United States, folk songs warned that "lazy" girls would not find a husband. The confidence and expectations ran deep. A young Polish Catholic, determined to make his fortune in two or three years in America, wrote an emigration assistance league that his priest had tried to dissuade him from the journey, "show[ing] me the dangers, the terrible work there which often costs one's life, and in general the reasons why it is not worth leaving here." "But," the emigrant concluded, "I was not persuaded."[18]

---

18 Phyllis H. Williams, *South Italian Folkways in Europe and America* (New Haven, 1938), 20; William I. Thomas and Florian Znaniecki, *The Polish Peasant in Europe and America* (Boston, 1919), III, 22.

Eagerness for success and willingness to work characterized large numbers of new immigrants. What happened next, it would appear, depended on highly particular circumstances. Some found "easy work" and wrote happily of the fact in letters home; others had their illusions stripped bare and reemigrated or became potential rebels; still others had the blow of adjustment cushioned by strong families or strong subcultures and effected a compromise with industrial expectations. But for the potential greenhorn the governing experience was the irregularity of work—the initial, painful shock of unemployment which led in turn to entrapment in a brutal round of temporary jobs.

Steiner, who emigrated from central Europe in the 1880s, may serve as an example for nameless others. Landing in New York City, he found his first job in the clothing industry, but the slack season soon dried up the work. He tried to eke out a living in other short-term jobs in a bakery, a feather-renovating shop, and a sausage factory, abandoned the city for harvest work, moved on to a Pittsburgh steel mill where his job ended in a layoff, worked in a coal mine until a strike halted production, tried a job in a South Bend plough factory until he became ill from the heat and the damp, moved on to a Chicago machine shop where he was fired for lecturing his fellow employees, and shuttled on through more harvest, mine, and factory work—all in the space of about two years.[19] Whether one went "on the tramp" like Steiner or scrambled for a foothold in the casual labor market of the city, the permanent job that the immigrant had so eagerly anticipated often eluded him. And the combination of extravagant hopes and the trauma of finding and keeping a job worked together to shatter village norms of toil, to undercut the props of tradition, and to confuse what was "proper" work and what was unacceptable drudgery.

The result was the ferocious energy observers repeatedly found in the American mills and sweatshops. Once a greenhorn was not always to remain a greenhorn. There is some evidence

19 Edward A. Steiner, *From Alien to Citizen: The Story of My Life in America* (New York, 1914), 53–208. For other examples of the immigrant's initial "tramping" period: Eli Ginzberg and Hyman Berman, *The American Worker in the Twentieth Century: A History through Autobiographies* (New York, 1963), 75–79; Charlotte Erickson, *Invisible Immigrants: The Adaptation of English and Scottish Immigrants in Nineteenth-Century America* (Coral Gables, Fla., 1972), 247–254.

that, with time, many such immigrants reassessed the bargain they had made with industrial society and grew as confident and stubborn as the more experienced workers around them.[20] If so, theirs was the mirror opposite of what is conventionally described as the modernizing experience; in any event, the greenhorns suggest how the combination of mobility, hope, and radically uncertain employment might produce far different results from those that formula implies.

The formula does not do much better with a second prominent group of first-generation industrial workers—the white farm and farm tenant families who took up work in the textile mills of the New South. Cultural and economic forces interacted here as well—not ambition and unstable employment but isolation together with changes in the ratio of labor supply and demand. Ultimately these combined to generate one of the most nomadic work forces in the country. But the process was not a straightforward one of challenge and resistance, for the restlessness of the southern mill hands took time to emerge and the habits which frustrated early-twentieth-century employers were not simply country ways carried into the factories.

The first part of that statement rests on inference from the thin and impressionistic evidence. Yet from an extensive series of manufacturers' comments on industrial conditions printed in the reports of the North Carolina Bureau of Labor Statistics from 1887 to 1908 it is possible to graph a curve of employers' complaints, and, even by the generous standards of the South, the level of criticism of the mill hands through the mid 1890s is strikingly low. Newly built mills seem generally to have found more applicants for work than they could employ, and the labor surplus gave manufacturers an enormous leeway to weed out the fractious from the tractable and orderly. This search for the most adaptable workers was a conscious policy, if the boasts of the southern mill men are to be believed, and it went on even within the mill families, drawing the women and children into the factories while many a potentially troublesome adult male was left to work only sporadically, at odd jobs outside the mills, or not at all. The mills

20 Rudolph J. Vecoli, "Chicago's Italians prior to World War I: A Study of Their Social and Economic Adjustment," unpub. Ph.D. diss. (University of Wisconsin, 1963), 435–440.

employed fifteen adult women for every ten adult men in 1870, seventeen women for every ten men in 1880, and, until the proportions finally equalized and reversed in the labor-short decade of the 1890s, the non-working father, or "cotton mill drone," was a common and functional feature of the southern mill villages. Even the most rigorous selectivity had its limits. Mill managers universally agreed that southern workers could not be induced to save their wages, and it is also clear that the general standards of efficiency were not always particularly high. Nevertheless, southern employers initially seem to have found more than enough workers capable of making the adjustment to industrial labor in ways that satisfied their expectations.[21] Even agricultural societies, it would appear, have their corps of the particularly flexible, not only the adventurous but the powerless, the dependent, and those with little reserves of resistance.

The mill building boom of the 1890s and the acute labor shortage which followed unsettled this early pattern. Complaints in North Carolina began to rise in the mid 1890s, grew increasingly shrill, and reached a peak in 1906–1907. Plants which once reported all hands stable and orderly began to deplore the growing restlessness "of late years," and by the early twentieth century wrote in despair that their hands were working only four days a week and left on the slightest pretext. The village drones were outlawed and forced into the mills throughout the southern states, and, if this proved a mixed blessing for the manufacturers, so did other tactics that they employed in their efforts to find sufficient workers to operate the new machinery. Wage increases seemed only to aggravate absenteeism, and raids on the labor forces of other mills simply encouraged transiency. By 1910, despite the easing of the most acute phase of the labor famine, the southern textile industry was no longer the same. Every mill claimed a core of steady, long term employees, but these rubbed shoulders with a turbulent army of floaters, variously estimated at 20 to 40 percent

---

21 Confirming evidence exists outside North Carolina: U.S. Senate, *Labor and Capital*, IV, 508–542, 582–597, 684–696, 721–756, 793–796; Broadus Mitchell, *The Rise of Cotton Mills in the South* (Baltimore, 1921), 176–209; McLaurin, *Paternalism and Protest*, 21, 55. On the sex ratio and sometimes very lax efficiency standards, see Elizabeth H. Davidson, *Child Labor Legislation in the Southern Textile States* (Chapel Hill, 1939), 8; North Carolina Bureau of Labor Statistics (hereafter NCBLS), *Tenth Annual Report* (Winston, 1897), 60–61; C. Vann Woodward, *Origins of the New South, 1877–1913* (Baton Rouge, 1951), 222–225.

of the work force—twice as mobile as northern textile workers, according to a study made in the early 1920s, and twice as prone to absenteeism.[22]

Undoubtedly the labor shortage had forced less adaptable rural folk into the industry, but the ways of the "floaters" were not simply more deeply set country work mores rattling against the confines of factory discipline. Only a fraction of the enormous turnover of the southern mill hands, for example, involved a return to farm work. Most of the job changing amounted to a restless movement from mill to mill; and it was greatest not in country mills but in the urban centers of the South and among workers who had drifted considerably farther from their pasts than a single step from the worn-out cotton fields. Southern landlords, moreover, fearful of mill habits, were not eager to take the textile workers back. Isolated and ostracized in the mill villages, the mill hands increasingly appeared to outsiders not as farm folk but as a separate people.[23]

These are threads of evidence, but what they seem to add up to is a process of cultural hybridization. Cut off from their pasts, southern workers built a half-new world of their own. That world could not escape the imprint of rural memory, particularly in its casual attitudes toward time and in its deep streak of fatalism. But the isolation of the southern workers and their ability to float on the tide of a labor-short economy transmuted the old into new forms—an apparently stable, quasi-industrial subculture, passed on to cotton mill children with the tricks of piecing threads and doffing spindles until the Great Depression shattered the economic conditions which had nurtured and supported it. Measured against

22 NCBLS, *Twelfth Annual Report* (Raleigh, 1899), 401; NCBLS, *Twentieth Annual Report* (Raleigh, 1906), 254, 261; NCBLS, *Twenty-second Annual Report* (Raleigh, 1908), 219–221; Kohn, *Cotton Mills of South Carolina*, 22, 60–66; U.S. Bureau of Labor, *Woman and Child Wage-Earners*, I, 126, 453; Smith, *Mill on the Dan*, 100–105; "Lost Time and Labor Turnover in Cotton Mills," U.S. Department of Labor, Women's Bureau, *Bulletin*, LII (1926), 39, 179. For indications of the extent of the "floating" population: Lois MacDonald, *Southern Mill Hands: A Study of Social and Economic Forces in Certain Textile Mill Villages* (New York, 1928), 49, 89, 124; Jennings J. Rhyne, *Some Southern Cotton Mill Workers and Their Villages* (Chapel Hill, 1930), 107; U.S. Bureau of Labor, *Woman and Child Wage-Earners*, I, 127.

23 *Ibid.*, XVII, 22; II, 585–587; U.S. Women's Bureau, "Lost Time and Labor Turnover," 191, 46; Kohn, *Cotton Mills of South Carolina*, 29; Liston Pope, *Millhands and Preachers: A Study of Gastonia* (New Haven, 1942), 67–69; John K. Morland, *Millways of Kent* (Chapel Hill, 1958).

the conventional story of shock, entrenchment, and gradual accommodation, the southern experience was an extensive detour.

Examples such as these should not minimize our sense of the toll industrialization exacted of those caught in the upheaval of work processes. All such workers faced a sharp break in habits and values and an enforced recasting of their sense of self and place in society. But since they came from widely different pasts into a far from uniform economy, the encounter with industrialization could not but be complex and multiform. The groups sketched here—uprooted and mobile Southerners, success-striving immigrants, workers who struggled to be rational in an irrational economy, and tradition-asserting rebels—do not exhaust the possibilities. Other groups of industrial newcomers spring quickly to mind, each worth careful and imaginative study: women workers of many backgrounds and cultures, black workers (including those who entered industrial work through the uncomfortable role of strikebreaker), Jewish workers carrying a culture no more peasant than it was industrial, artisans forced into factory labor, downwardly mobile children of white-collar families, or farm boys seeking their fortunes in the cities. In each case culture, expectation, and the particular economic circumstances of the encounter met in different ways, with different compromises, and with different outcomes. The mills had many doorways.

Can more be said for the premise of acculturation? Did industrial experience extended over several generations produce increasingly convergent accommodations and ultimately make a "modern man" of the American factory worker?

For the years before 1919, second- and third-generation industrial workers are far less easy to identify in the factories than are newcomers. One reasonable place to look for acculturated workers, however, is among immigrants from the Lancashire towns where the Western industrial revolution began. Many such workers could be found in the late-nineteenth-century American factories, particularly in the New England textile mills where they filled the more skilled places, most conspicuously those of tending the complex and temperamental spinning mules used in the manufacture of fine grade yarn. But if the mill agents are to be believed, the Lancashire-raised mule spinners were as "rowdy, drinking, [and] unprincipled" a set of workingmen as existed in

459

America. The largest concentration of British textile workers collected in Fall River. By 1878 the city had already acquired a justified reputation as a second Manchester, and, through repeated contrast to Lowell, which was said to run placidly on the labor of its native-born, Irish, and French-Canadian workers, an equally wide reputation for industrial disorder. Part of the "rowdiness" with which the Fall River spinners were charged had more to do with their stubborn propensity to strike than with work habits. But the mule spinners not only challenged the economic power of the Fall River manufacturers but also flaunted industrial discipline, taking their holidays when they thought they needed them and rarely working full time even when the mills ran at full production.[24] Refractory as these habits were, they were neither preindustrial nor artisanal customs, for mule spinning by the 1870s had been a factory occupation in England for well over a generation, reached by a long apprenticeship from childhood at simpler mill tasks.[25] The Lancashire spinners were, to be sure, not typical second-generation workers but highly skilled factory aristocrats who built their quasi-industrial subculture on the rock of their indispensability. But their factory-nurtured, disorderly habits make it clear that industrial experience did not invariably result in acquiescence to the ideals of the new economic order.

It is perhaps unfair, however, to expect to find modern workers in the imperfectly rationalized economy of the late nineteenth and early twentieth centuries. If one turns instead to the years since 1945 the hypothesis appears more promising, for in the interim the behavior of factory workers has changed in important ways. Turnover in manufacturing began to decline in the 1920s, rose once more in the labor-short years of World War II, but has remained at levels half or less than the pre-World War I estimate in all but four years since 1950. And although the overall absence rate

24 Rowland T. Berthoff, *British Immigrants in Industrial America, 1790–1950* (Cambridge, Mass., 1953), 30–36; MBLS, *Report* (Boston, 1871), 469; MBLS, *Thirteenth Annual Report* (Boston, 1882), 194–415; Mosely Industrial Commission to the United States of America, *Reports of the Delegates* (London, 1903), 127; U.S. Industrial Commission, *Reports* (Washington, 1900–1902), XIV, 571.
25 Sydney J. Chapman, *The Lancashire Cotton Industry: A Study in Economic Development* (Manchester, 1904), 69–70, 216; Neil J. Smelser, *Social Change in the Industrial Revolution: An Application of Theory to the Lancashire Cotton Industry, 1770–1840* (London, 1959), 193–204. Robert Howard, for example, the Fall River spinners' most prominent spokesman, began his career at age eight as a piecer in a Cheshire silk mill.

in the factories still remains a matter of considerable guesswork, the 5 to 6 percent levels personnel managers in the early twentieth century thought normal are now sufficient to trigger considerable alarm. The closing of unrestricted immigration, the introduction of systematic personnel policies and industrial welfare programs in the 1920s, the searing experience of the Great Depression, and the incentives to stability built into the factories since the 1930s by union seniority rules, non-transferable pensions, and the requirements of unemployment compensation have all left their mark. Highly mobile and overtly restless workers still exist, but they are now most common outside the factories where statisticians rarely tread.[26]

But modernity is a matter of values as well as behavior, and, if some of the overt restlessness of industrial workers has been tamed, it remains far from clear that they have internalized the rules by which modern man is said to live. These rules are not merely matters of speculation, according to many social scientists, but can be proved to cohere in complex and empirically tested syndromes. Modern man is said to be a rationalist who believes in science, technology, and the inherent logic of things—convictions inculcated in part through exposure to the orderly and routine processes of the modern factory, according to Inkeles' findings. He is an inveterate optimist—an "activist"—who is convinced that societies and individuals shape their destinies, and who responds to the survey question, "Can an able, smart, industrious boy succeed against fate?" with the answer, "Yes." Modern man is an individualist—ambitious, hardworking, and possessed of a high esteem for efficiency and punctuality. He is flexible, open to change, and eager for new experiences—"empathetic," to use Lerner's term.[27]

26 Ewan Clague, "Long-Term Trends in Quit Rates," USBLS, *Employment and Earnings*, III (Dec. 1956), iii–ix; "Handbook of Labor Statistics, 1973," USBLS, *Bulletin* no. 1790 (1973), 124; USBLS, *Monthly Labor Review*, IC (April 1976), 76; Janice N. Hedges, "Absence from Work—A Look at Some National Data," *ibid.*, XCVI (July 1973), 24–30; "Absent Workers—A Spreading Worry," *U.S. News & World Report* (Nov. 27, 1972), 48–49.
27 Joseph A. Kahl, *The Measurement of Modernism: A Study of Values in Brazil and Mexico* (Austin, 1968), 3–44, 133–134; Inkeles and Smith, *Becoming Modern*, 15–35, 154–191; *idem*, "The OM Scale: A Comparative Socio-Psychological Measure of Individual Modernity," *Sociometry*, XXIX (1966), 364–365; Lerner, *Passing of Traditional Society*, 47–52. A comprehensive list of "modern" traits would be considerably longer and would include at the minimum an active interest in the mass media, a preference for urban life, and participation in organizations.

Not all of these characteristics have been tested against present-day American industrial workers, but some of those most directly related to work values have, and some of them fit. The bureaucratic labor union structure, which has everywhere pushed aside older, fraternal forms of workers' organizations, and the responsiveness of contemporary workers to incentive wage formulas both attest to the ascendancy of rationalistic attitudes in the working class. Not that union behavior is a perfect exercise in rationality or shop behavior in income maximization. Workers still test their wits against the time-study man and still set output limits on their work in a battle governed as much by custom and frustration as by careful estimation of the effects of output on the prevailing piece rates.[28] Nevertheless, fining is a far less common practice in contemporary factories than it once was, and few employers find it necessary, as Robert Owen did, to reward each day's performance with a visible, non-pecuniary badge of merit.

But other, central aspects of modernity simply do not apply to modern American industrial workers. The majority do not believe in the efficacy of striving up the occupational ladder against the pull of fate. Several studies of factory employees made in the decade after World War II failed to turn up more than one worker in three who admitted he would like to move out of the blue-collar ranks into a supervisory position, a foreman's job in most cases; at least as many workers told the interviewers they would not take a foreman's job if it were offered to them. Industrial workers do dream of success in other ways. In surprising numbers they harbor entrepreneurial hopes of a business of their own, or at least did so in recent years. Bendix and Lipset's study of Oakland, California, in 1949–50 found that two thirds of the blue-collar heads of families had at one time thought of going into business for themselves, a rate exceeded only by salesmen. Studies of the automobile industry in the late 1940s and early 1950s seemed to confirm their findings. Auto workers told interviewers of their hopes for a farm of their own, an auto repair shop, a gas station, or a "little" stationery store—where you can "give your own orders and not have to take them from anybody else." These are not newfangled dreams of rising to the top, however, but old ones of

28 Donald Roy, "Quota Restriction and Goldbricking in a Machine Shop," *American Journal of Sociology*, LVII (1952), 427–442.

getting out of the factory and the employee relationship, akin to the Knights of Labor's hope to evade the wage system through the cooperative workshop. And for the majority of factory workers the optimism of modern man is undercut by the conviction that neither the corporate ladder nor entrepreneurship holds much chance at all.[29]

Finally, what of work itself? How committed are present-day workers to the tasks industrial society provides them? A "work ethic"—an abstract belief in the value of toil—is still strong among industrial workers. From 1953 to 1973, a half dozen samples of male factory employees and blue-collar men in general have been asked whether, suddenly given a comfortable income, they would continue to work. At least one half, and generally closer to two thirds, said that they would keep working. The answer has the force of tradition behind it. Struggling for status and respect in a society which has at once honored work and demeaned the industrial laborer, American workers have repeatedly insisted on the necessity and worth of manual toil. They once proudly called themselves the "producing classes," the "horny-handed sons of toil," the "knights of labor," the bedrock of the nation, and the feelings behind such phrases have not yet been extinguished. This same pride carries over into the unwillingness of laboring men to demean the jobs they do. A majority of industrial workers— skilled or unskilled, assembly-line workers or craftsmen—tell interviewers they are "satisfied" with their jobs and find them "interesting." But the response tells much more about working-class culture than of the satisfaction it is frequently presumed to measure. When the question is rephrased and respondents are given an open choice, a majority of male industrial workers would exchange their jobs for something else, in numbers larger than most of the rest of the population. In two surveys designed to probe further the bonds blue-collar men have with their work, only a tenth of those questioned talked about the intrinsic rewards of

29 *Fortune*, XXXV (May 1947), 10; Ely Chinoy, *Automobile Workers and the American Dream* (Garden City, N.Y., 1955), 47–61, 82–95; Robert H. Guest, "Work Careers and Aspirations of Automobile Workers," *American Sociological Review*, XIX (1954), 157–158, 162; Bennett M. Berger, *Working-Class Suburb: A Study of Auto Workers in Suburbia* (Berkeley, 1960), 17; Seymour M. Lipset and Reinhard Bendix, "Social Mobility and Occupational Career Patterns," *American Journal of Sociology*, LVII (1952), 502. For more recent confirmation: Curt Tausky, "Occupational Mobility Interests," *Canadian Review of Sociology and Anthropology*, IV (1967), 246.

what they did; for the largest number of respondents—71 to 76 percent in the groups surveyed—what came first to mind about their jobs when they thought about quitting them was that they kept them busy and preserved them from the boredom of having nothing to do.[30]

Specific comparison of these responses with the moods of earlier generations of industrial workers remains an open and vexing question. Within it lie shifts in the styles and grounds of discontent at least as important as the persistent conflict itself. But experience with factory labor has not yet won over the inner minds of most of those who do it. In the midst of a society which, in structural terms, is fully modern, the ancient contest over norms and styles of work persists, not only where the latest arrivals—southern migrants and black and Spanish-speaking Americans—are most numerous but also throughout the contemporary factories.[31]

Nor has American society as a whole gone modern in quite the way that theorists of economic development predicted. Modernity is not only a highly class-bound phenomenon but it is time-bound, and in the West its peak may well be over. Certainly to historians familiar with the literature of Anglo-American Victorianism, modern man's faith in science, success, individualism, work, and progress is bound to have a suspiciously archaic ring. The sober-sided ambitions Kahl ascribes to modern man are barely distinguishable from those that Smiles preached to multitudes of nineteenth-century readers. As for Inkeles' conviction that machine civilization forms an effective school for orderly

30 Nancy C. Morse and Robert S. Weiss, "The Function and Meaning of Work and the Job," *American Sociological Review*, XX (1955), 196, 197; Tausky, "Occupational Mobility Interests," 246; William H. Form, "Auto Workers and Their Machines: A Study of Work, Factory, and Job Satisfaction in Four Countries," *Social Forces*, LII (1973), 5, 8–9; Harold L. Sheppard and Neal Q. Herrick, *Where Have All the Robots Gone? Worker Dissatisfaction in the '70s* (New York, 1972), 52, 74n; 1969–70 Survey of Working Conditions and 1972–73 Quality of Employment Survey, unpub. data made available by the Survey Research Center, Institute for Social Research, University of Michigan; Robert P. Quinn, *et al.*, *Job Satisfaction: Is There a Trend?* U.S. Department of Labor, Manpower Research Monograph no. 30 (Washington, 1974); Robert Blauner, "Work Satisfaction and Industrial Trends in Modern Society," in Walter Galenson and Seymour M. Lipset (eds.), *Labor and Trade Unionism* (New York, 1960); idem, *Alienation and Freedom: The Factory Worker and His Industry* (Chicago, 1964), 202; Harold L. Wilensky, "Varieties of Work Experience," in Henry Borow (ed.), *Man in a World at Work* (Boston, 1964), 136–137.

31 Cf. S. M. Miller and Frank Riessman, "Are Workers Middle Class?" *Dissent*, VIII (1961), 507–513; John H. Goldthorpe, *et al.*, "The Affluent Worker and the Thesis of Embourgeoisement: Some Preliminary Research Findings," *Sociology*, I (1967), 11–31.

habits and rational thought processes, this too was a nineteenth-century article of faith, reiterated most firmly when revolt from below seemed most imminent, and ultimately put in classical form by Veblen—although Veblen wisely thought that the virus of rationalism would infect the engineers and technocrats long before it reached the semiskilled machine operators.[32] One may not press the parallel between the moderns and the Victorians too far. The nineteenth-century middle class was not particularly empathetic, in Lerner's use of the term. Prophets of success and technological rationalism, moreover, are still abroad and prominent in the West. But the Norman Vincent Peales and the Buckminster Fullers have been forced to alter the nineteenth-century tune in telling ways not as yet comprehended by the fabricators of modernity scales. Perhaps America, unique in so many ways, is an exception to the pressures of modernity. But it is more likely that technology is not the potent determinant of culture that it is sometimes said to be and that, as a shaper of the men it needs, the industrial revolution has been overrated.

If the hypothesis of initial shock and gradual acculturation to the political economy of the factory is not the highway to the promised land and if the modernization hypothesis is suspect, what are the alternatives? Of first importance is a de-escalation of the levels of generalization. Tradition and modernity are too homogenizing of the intractable variety of both past and present to serve historians well. They may be of real help in distinguishing a hunting and gathering tribesman from a twentieth-century engineer, but for most historical questions the terms barely suffice at all. They carry their sway in part on the basis of their appeal to the obvious. No one would deny that in the millennium or so after the Middle Ages the West has changed from something like a collection of traditional societies to a society far more modern. Nor would anyone deny that the reflex of these changes has had an enormous impact on the non-Western world, transforming its traditions in ways past reversing. But the modernization hypothesis does not merely restate the evident—that medieval society broke down with momentous consequences. Behind the

---

32 Thorstein Veblen, *The Instinct of Workmanship and the State of the Industrial Arts* (New York, 1914), 299–355; *idem, The Theory of Business Enterprise* (New York, 1904), 312–313.

terms tradition and modernity lies a law of societal evolution, which carries with it implicit assumptions of historical linearity and of a determinate relationship between culture, personality, and gross levels of economic development. As long as workers use machines and the technology of work processes remains essentially additive, there will always be a degree of linearity to labor history. But workers are more than appendages to economic and work relationships, and it is possible to embrace the insights, the sensitivity, and the humanity of the newest labor history without also embracing its evolutionary framework.[33] Historians would do well to subject the current revival of evolutionism in the social sciences to critical scrutiny.

One can state the whole question differently: all men in all cultures are born premodern, with concepts of time and activity profoundly unsuited to the modern factory. Throughout much of childhood and through many adolescent subcultures, time still runs as irregularly as it ever did before the coming of the factory system. And the passage from childhood to industrial work remains as potentially long and difficult. How a working-class child makes that passage has much to do with the institutions and values which push and shape him until he finally stands at the factory gate. His play and rearing; the precepts taught him by elders, peers, and schools; the heroes (real and mythological) offered him for emulation; and the shape adolescence takes in his society—all of these factors hold important clues for labor historians. What did the nineteenth-century emergence of full-blown adventure stories for the young mean for the values that working-class boys would carry with them into adulthood? What was the experience of a child laborer besides abuse and exploitation? What have schools taught working-class children?

To think of labor history in these ways is to recognize that working-class cultures are not made once and set in motion but must be refashioned with each generation. Not only early life experiences matter but later stages of life as well—the shape of marriage, adulthood, old age, and work in specific times and cultures.

33 For example, Gareth S. Jones, "Working-Class Culture and Working-Class Politics in London, 1870–1900: Notes on the Remaking of a Working Class," *Journal of Social History*, VII (1974), 460–508; William H. Sewell, Jr., "Social Change and the Rise of Working-Class Politics in Nineteenth-Century Marseille," *Past & Present*, 65 (1974), 75–109.

The source materials for labor history of this kind are not easy to locate and to interpret, as the few tentative probes in this direction have found.[34] But within this material there are rich and original working-class histories waiting to be written.

The collateral advantages are many. Recasting labor history as collective working-class biography would greatly help to recover the varieties of subcultures within the working class, the continuities, reversions, and departures between working-class generations, and the strikingly different ways new workers have met the encounter with industrial labor. And if it helped to recover the variety of the past, it might also curb the long-standing habit among labor economists to see the present as in stasis. It might make it understandable why, in what are called fully industrialized societies—where the gulf between the child and the adult has been stretched wide and the winds of pleasure blow strongly—adjustment to the factory can still be an intensely difficult experience. It might remind us that, even in the West, industrialization remains a fact of the present.

34 John Demos, *A Little Commonwealth: Family Life in Plymouth Colony* (New York, 1970), 128–178; Joseph F. Kett, "Growing Up in Rural New England, 1800–1840," in Tamara K. Hareven (ed.), *Anonymous Americans: Explorations in Nineteenth-Century Social History* (Englewood Cliffs, N.J., 1971), 1–16.

Race, Ethnicity, and Gender in the Railroad Work Force: The Case of the Far Northwest, 1883-1918

W. THOMAS WHITE

"A new destiny is upon us," the *Portland Oregonian* pronounced on September 9, 1883, celebrating the completion of the Northern Pacific's line to the Northwest Coast.[1] The fundamental importance of transcontinental railroads for western settlement is well known. In the Far Northwest (Washington, Oregon, Idaho, and Montana), as elsewhere, the railroads' arrival heralded a new era of settlement and communication, at the same time profoundly influencing the economic and cultural development that derived from the fast-growing American-built environment in the region. With the burgeoning mines, the railroads were the harbingers of large-scale corporate enterprise and all that that implied in the Far Northwest.[2]

Less appreciated is the significance of the roads' impact on labor relations in the Far West. With the railroads came a new, industrial work force, possessed of a heritage of earlier conflicts with managers in the East. Their experience, too, served as a model for other industries on the wageworkers' frontier.[3] This case study will focus upon one segment of the new work force—the unskilled laborers who performed the roads' maintenance-of-

W. Thomas White is curator of the James Jerome Hill Reference Library in Saint Paul, Minnesota.

[1] *Portland Oregonian*, September 9, 1883. See also Murray Morgan, *Puget's Sound: A Narrative of Early Tacoma and the Southern Sound* (Seattle, 1979), 192-93; Michael P. Malone and Richard B. Roeder, *Montana: A History of Two Centuries* (Seattle, 1976), 132-33.

[2] Alfred D. Chandler, Jr., *The Visible Hand: The Managerial Revolution in American Business* (Cambridge, MA, 1977), 120; Alfred D. Chandler, Jr., comp. and ed., *The Railroads: The Nation's First Big Business, Sources and Readings* (New York, 1965). For a general assessment of the impact of the railroad on American culture, consult John R. Stilgoe, *Metropolitan Corridor: Railroads and the American Scene* (New Haven, 1983).

[3] For the laboring milieu of the Far Northwest, consult Carlos A. Schwantes, "Coxey's Montana Navy: A Protest against Unemployment on the Wageworkers' Frontier," *Pacific Northwest Quarterly*, 73 (July 1982), 98-107; and Carlos A. Schwantes, *Radical Heritage: Labor, Socialism, and Reform in Washington and British Columbia, 1885-1917* (Seattle, 1979), 3-21. For earlier generations of railway workers in the East and Midwest, consult Walter Licht, *Working for the Railroad: The Organization of Work in the Nineteenth Century* (Princeton, 1983).

way and construction work. Their experience contrasted sharply with that of skilled workers in the industry but was typical of that of many in the vast trans-Mississippi migrant labor pool that formed an indispensable part of the West's developing economy before the First World War.[4]

The thousands of migrant laborers who built and maintained the roads received the least pay and endured the worst conditions in the industry. As late as 1914, Washington Commissioner of Labor Edward W. Olson declared unequivocally that "the worst conditions in the state are to be found on highway and construction work." Usually recruited by large labor contractors, workers often had to travel long distances to receive an average $1.75-$2.25 per day (Japanese and southern and eastern Europeans received less), out of which they paid $5.50-$7.00 per week for board, hospital fees, transportation, and a miscellany of other charges. Sanitary and housing conditions were "detestable" and the general treatment of workers "reprehensible," Olson fumed, and "would not be permitted if generally known and realized."[5] The labor commissioner touched on a key aspect of the problem confronting the masses of unskilled railway workers—their invisibility. That fact, accentuated in the sprawling, sparsely populated West, coupled with the seasonal nature of section and construction work, obscured the plight of many unskilled workers from the general populace. For the laborers confronted by the grim realities of low pay, isolation, poor housing, and the other unfortunate aspects of unskilled, casual railroad work, those conditions formed an unhappy milieu that alternately spawned militant protests and later demoralized workers and hindered their success in those protest movements.

Like unskilled laborers everywhere, railway workers were divided sharply by race, ethnicity, and gender. Consequently, they were nearly powerless to overcome the many obstacles confronting them and realize any form of meaningful redress for their substantial problems. Only in the anti-Chinese

---

[4] For details on this regional study, see W. Thomas White, "A History of Railroad Workers in the Pacific Northwest, 1883-1934" (doctoral dissertation, University of Washington, 1981). For a national perspective, consult Andrew Dawson, "The Paradox of Dynamic Technological Change and the Labor Aristocracy in the United States, 1880-1914," *Labor History*, 20 (Summer 1979), 325-51; Christopher L. Tomlins, "AFL Unions in the 1930s: Their Performance in Historical Perspective," *Journal of American History*, LXV (March 1979), 1021-42; K. Austin Kerr, *American Railroad Politics, 1914-1920: Rates, Wages, and Efficiency* (Pittsburgh, 1968); Graham Adams, Jr., *Age of Industrial Violence, 1910-1915: The Activities and Findings of the United States Commission on Industrial Relations* (New York, 1966), 128-45; Reed C. Richardson, *The Locomotive Engineer, 1863-1963: A Century of Railway Labor Relations and Work Rules* (Ann Arbor, 1963); Albert Theodore Helbing, *The Departments of the American Federation of Labor* (Baltimore, 1931), 72-74. For the International Association of Machinists in particular, see David Montgomery, *Workers' Control in America: Studies in the History of Work, Technology, and Labor Struggles* (New York, 1979); Mark Perlman, *The Machinists: A New Study in American Trade Unionism* (Cambridge, MA, 1961).

[5] Washington State, *Ninth Biennial Report of the Bureau of Labor Statistics and Factory Inspection, 1913-1914* (Olympia, WA, 1914), 27-28.

campaigns of the mid-1880s and in the turbulence of 1894, when most employed on the roads were native white or north European men, did rank and file, skilled and unskilled workers alike, join together to launch serious, industry-wide challenges to management prerogatives. More typically, the Chinese, Japanese, Greeks, Bulgarians, blacks, women in a singular way, and others, many of whom also served as scapegoats for the accumulated grievances of others, proved unable to forge their own form of effective protest. For them the reality of the region's "new destiny" occasioned little cause for celebration.

The origins of the railroad labor movement can be traced to the completion of the Northern Pacific in 1883 and the Oregon Short Line the following year. The skilled operating brotherhoods earlier had established locals at Portland and other points, but they represented only a small minority of railway employees. It was the industrially organized Knights of Labor, which probably included many operating and shopcraft workers, that quickly became the most important force in the railway labor relations of the 1880s. Founded at Philadelphia in 1869, the Order was a national, comprehensive organization that welcomed wage earners, farmers, small businessmen, and professionals alike—only bankers, stockbrokers, gamblers, and those involved in the manufacture or sale of liquor were excluded. Despite its national jurisdiction, the Order's leadership was preoccupied with organizational problems and paid little attention to the activities of Knights in the Far Northwest. Consequently, the Order there was almost an indigenous labor organization. As such, it became an important vehicle for the expression of regional attitudes on race and labor organization.[6]

The onset of a severe depression, which triggered general labor unrest and the order's success in the Gould Southwestern Strikes of 1884-1885, helped boost memberships in the new assemblies of the region. Within four years at least 204 local assemblies, which included many railroad workers, were functioning in Washington, Oregon, Idaho, and Montana.[7]

[6] Harry W. Stone, "Beginning of Labor Movement in the Pacific Northwest," *Oregon Historical Quarterly*, 47 (June 1946), 155-64; and Jack E. Triplett, "History of Oregon Labor Movement Prior to the New Deal" (master's thesis, University of California, Berkeley, 1961), 6. See also Carlos A. Schwantes, "Protest in a Promised Land: Unemployment, Disinheritance, and the Origin of Labor Militancy in the Pacific Northwest, 1885-1886," *Western Historical Quarterly*, XIII (October 1982), 373-90.

[7] Standard accounts of the Knights of Labor include Norman J. Ware, *The Labor Movement in the United States, 1860-1895* (New York, 1929); Gerald N. Grob, *Workers and Utopia: A Study of Ideological Conflict in the American Labor Movement* (Evanston, IL, 1961); Terence V. Powderly, *The Path I Trod: The Autobiography of Terence V. Powderly*, eds. Harry J. Carman, Henry David, and Paul N. Guthrie (New York, 1940), but they should be read in conjunction with more recent scholarship, including Leon Fink, *Workingmen's Democracy: The Knights of Labor and American Politics* (Urbana, 1983); and Michael J. Cassity, "Modernization and Social Crisis: The Knights of Labor and a Midwest Community, 1885-1886," *Journal of American History*, 66 (June 1979), 41-61. For specific information on the locals in the Far Northwest, see Jonathan Garlock, comp., *Guide to the Local Assemblies of the Knights of Labor* (Westport, 1982).

The sudden rise of the Knights of Labor in the Far Northwest cannot be attributed solely to the hard times occasioned by economic depression or the Order's early success in other areas. Much more important was the heavy reliance organizers placed on the widespread anti-Chinese prejudice in the region. Racial tensions had existed for some time as Chinese workers migrated to the region to labor in the mines and other developing industries. In their final construction phase, however, the railroads became their principal employers. As the Northern Pacific completed its line through the Pacific Northwest, it employed fifteen thousand Chinese construction workers in Washington Territory alone, and an estimated six thousand were at work in Montana and Idaho territories in 1882.[8] With the completion of that line, thousands of Chinese workers reentered the Northwest's already overburdened labor market. White laborers' job fears then combined with smoldering racial and cultural resentments to lay the groundwork for a racial confrontation.

The Knights immediately capitalized on popular fears of being deluged with Chinese immigrants. They and, to a lesser extent, the International Workingmen's Association, a radical organization founded at San Francisco in 1881, led the movement to purge the Chinese from the region's burgeoning frontier communities. Their adopted mission was to establish a high degree of cultural and racial homogeneity within the Northwest and, by doing so, to preserve jobs for the large number of unemployed whites. Railway workers participated in the general exclusionist campaign and in the racial incidents that became commonplace throughout the region, finding their most spectacular expression in the Seattle and Tacoma confrontations of 1885-1886.[9]

For all that, the Knights' strength was short-lived, and with the exception of the Spokane area, they had declined precipitously by the early 1890s. Discredited nationally by their poor leadership in the second round of strikes on the Gould system in 1886 and by the popular fears of labor organizations that intensified after the Haymarket Square bombing, the Order was in full retreat by the end of the 1880s. In the Far Northwest, those factors, combined with rising employment and the cooling of anti-Chinese passions as the new immigration restrictions took hold, left the order a bankrupt and, in most cases, a collapsing organization.[10]

---

[8] Robert Edward Wynne, *Reaction to the Chinese in the Pacific Northwest and British Columbia, 1850-1910* (New York, 1978), 85. For more on the reactions of Pacific Coast wage earners to Chinese immigration, consult Alexander Saxton, *The Indispensable Enemy: Labor and the Anti-Chinese Movement in California* (Berkeley and Los Angeles, 1971).

[9] *Union Pacific Employees Magazine* (Denver), September 1889; Wynne, *Reaction to the Chinese*, 173-283; Morgan, *Puget's Sound*, 212-52; Schwantes, *Radical Heritage*, 22-34; Jules A. Karlin, "The Anti-Chinese Outbreaks in Seattle," *Pacific Northwest Quarterly*, 39 (August 1948), 103-30; and Triplett, "Oregon Labor Movement," 8-19.

[10] Schwantes, *Radical Heritage*, 27-29; and Wynne, *Reaction to the Chinese*, 288.

Nonetheless, the Knights left a fundamentally important legacy. Long after the Order's decline, exclusionist sentiment and the drive for industrial unionism remained constant themes in the experience of white railway workers. The potential danger to employers of an aroused, ethnically homogeneous, and united work force first became manifest in 1894 when the Panic reached its nadir. Coxeyism, the Great Northern Strike, and the Pullman Boycott demonstrated the Gilded Age pattern of labor militance at high tide in the Far Northwest. Freed from the internal divisiveness of great racial and ethnic diversity, native-born whites joined northern and western Europeans in industry-wide protests against the Grover Cleveland administration and the railroads. In the case of the Great Northern and Pullman strikes, that protest took the form of a resounding endorsement of Eugene V. Debs's infant American Railway Union, heir to the Knights' legacy of industrial unionism.[11]

The emergence of Coxey's armies in the spring of 1894, the worst year of the 1893-1897 depression, dramatized the plight of the nation's unemployed. Several thousand men and women, including many recently laid off by the railroads, quickly imitated Jacob Coxey's Ohio example and formed their own "armies" in Butte, Spokane, Seattle, Tacoma, Portland, and smaller locales. Determined to carry their protest to the nation's capital and willing to hijack trains when all else failed, they were among the most militant of the country's "commonwealers." As such, they thoroughly alarmed local authorities as well as the Cleveland administration, which employed federal marshals and regular troops to check their progress in what became a dress rehearsal for intervention in the Pullman Strike.[12]

While they focused attention on the unemployed, northwestern Coxeyites also served as a vehicle for the populist and general antirailroad attitudes then sweeping the region. They attracted popular sympathy nearly everywhere. Yet the "commonwealers" enjoyed their greatest support in the smaller, more isolated communities that were highly dependent on the railroads, resentful of Cleveland's monetary policies, and smarting under what many considered excessive freight rates.[13]

[11] Schwantes, *Radical Heritage*, 25-36. See also White, "Railroad Workers," 13-123, which finds a pattern of community-based protest similar to that discovered in Pennsylvania by Herbert G. Gutman, "Trouble on the Railroads in 1873-1874: Prelude to the 1877 Crisis?" *Labor History*, 2 (Spring 1961), 215-35. For more recent assessments of the role of community in railway labor relations, see Fink, *Workingman's Democracy*; James H. Ducker, *Men of the Steel Rails: Workers on the Atchison, Topeka & Santa Fe Railroad, 1869-1900* (Lincoln, 1983); Nick Salvatore, "Railroad Workers and the Great Strike of 1877: The View from a Small Midwest City," *Labor History*, 21 (Fall 1980), 522-45; and Cassity, "Modernization and Social Crisis."

[12] Donald L. McMurry, *Coxey's Army: A Study of the Industrial Army Movement of 1894* (1929; reprint, Seattle, 1968), 199-226. See also Jerry M. Cooper, *The Army and Civil Disorder: Federal Military Intervention in Labor Disputes, 1877-1900* (Westport, CT, 1980), 106-14; and Gerald G. Eggert, *Richard Olney: Evolution of a Statesman* (University Park, PA, 1974), 67, 115-27.

Popular support was perhaps the most pronounced in Montana, where the Northern Pacific's attempt to claim a substantial part of the state's mineral lands as part of its land grant outraged nearly everyone. Consequently, anti-NP, pro-Coxeyite sentiments did not evaporate when William Hogan and five hundred followers, impatient with the road's refusal to carry them to Washington, D.C., broke into the Northern Pacific's Butte roundhouse on April 21. Defying a federal injunction, the Hoganites, who included a number of experienced railroad men and a reporter from the *Anaconda Standard*, commandeered the train and immediately began their race to the East. En route, onlookers, particularly in railroad towns such as Livingston, cheered the "commonwealers" and offered them supplies, while fresh recruits flocked to their banner. When the local citizenry in Billings joined the Hoganites to repel an attack by the trailing federal marshals, Governor John E. Rickards added his voice to the conservative clamor for U.S. troops, insisting it was "impossible for [the] State militia to overtake them." The Cleveland administration agreed, and federal troops apprehended the bulk of the force outside Forsyth. Nonetheless, pro-Hoganite passions were so intense in Butte and other Northern Pacific towns that the prisoners had to be taken to Helena for trial.[14]

Throughout the Northwest, community support for the Coxeyite cause remained strong after the Hoganites' adventure and after other "armies" had begun to move. Consequently, when Frank "Jumbo" Cantwell, formerly a saloon bouncer, prizefighter, and a member of the Knights of Labor, led his four-hundred-man contingent out of Tacoma, he saw no reason to allay the fears of jittery officials. Asked about the Hoganite precedent, he confidently retorted: "We ain't too proud to steal a train. Them fellers in Congress has broke the law. Why can't we?"[15]

---

[13] In addition to local newspapers, see the Coxeyite publications, *Industrial Army News* (Seattle), April 1894, Northwest Collection, University of Washington, Seattle; and Anaconda (MT) *Keep Off the Grass*, June 1, 1894, University of Montana Archives, Missoula. See also the prolabor *Tacoma Morning Union*, March-June 1894. Useful manuscript collections include Records of the Department of Justice, RG 60, Year File 4017-1894, National Archives; Letters sent by the Headquarters of the Army (Main Series), RG 108, U.S. Navy and Old Army Branch, Military Archives Division, National Archives; Robert W. Baxter to E. Dickinson, May 7, 1894, Union Pacific Collection, Nebraska Historical Society, Lincoln; Minutes of the Tacoma Trades Council, April 26, 1894; Pierce County Central Council Records, University of Washington Library (UWL), Seattle; and *Report of the Secretary of War*, 53d Cong., 3d sess., 1894, H.E.D. 1, pt. 2, vol. 1. See also Carlos A. Schwantes, "Law and Disorder: The Suppression of Coxey's Army in Idaho," *Idaho Yesterdays*, 25 (Summer 1981), 10-15, 18-26; and Herman C. Voeltz, "Coxey's Army in Oregon, 1894," *Oregon Historical Quarterly*, LXV (September 1964), 263-95.

[14] Thomas A. Clinch, "Coxey's Army in Montana," *Montana the Magazine of Western History*, 15 (Autumn 1965), 2-11; and "The Northern Pacific Railroad and Montana's Mineral Lands," *Pacific Historical Review*, XXXIV (August 1965), 323-35. See also *Anaconda Standard*, April 26, 1894 [quotation].

[15] Morgan, *Puget's Sound*, 283-85.

Despite Cantwell's blunt reply, Coxeyites in all the major (and many of the smaller) population centers worked hard to enlist community support by holding parades and benefits. In the case of the Seattle group, they established a women's auxiliary "to assist all poor working girls and unemployed women to earn an honest livelihood for themselves and aid those in distressed circumstances."[16]

Further, they constructed an inclusive, Populist platform designed to appeal to a wide variety of potential supporters. Calls for the free coinage of silver and general currency reform held an obvious appeal for the region's mining communities as well as for those interested in currency inflation. Calls for immigration restriction and for restrictions on alien land ownership easily appealed to wage earners and farmers, whereas demands for government ownership of the railroads and telegraphs, public works, direct election of senators, and the initiative and referendum appealed to insurgent white communities throughout the region. Reflecting the views of their railroad members, as well as their support for strikers on the Great Northern, the Coxeyites reiterated their enthusiasm for the American Railway Union and urged "organized and unorganized labor to pull together for the good of all."[17]

Called to protest repeated wage cuts and layoffs, the Great Northern Strike of April 1894 occurred simultaneously with the Coxeyite turbulence. Together they illustrated the unrest among unemployed and working railway men. In the GN Strike, unorganized white workers and members of the established brotherhoods alike flocked to the new American Railway Union, hopeful that at last they would have an effective organization. Later the myth that a great victory had been won further swelled the ARU's membership rolls.

The insurgent workers of the Far Northwest played a central role in that strike that so benefited the young industrial union. Ignoring President Eugene V. Debs's instructions, militants led by the youthful James Hogan (one of the ARU's national organizers) called the strike in western Montana when one of their number intercepted a coded message from the road calling for the dismissal of all ARU members in the Butte, Helena, and Great Falls yards. Until Debs arrived at Saint Paul for the negotiations and arbitration proceedings that ended the dispute, strike headquarters were in Butte, where Hogan dispatched organizers east and west of the Rocky Mountains to direct the fight. Meanwhile, GN employees in the Cascade

[16] *Anaconda Standard*, April 4-26, 1894; Clinch, "Coxey's Army," 6; *Seattle Post-Intelligencer*, April 17 [quotation], April 18-19, 1894; *Industrial Army News* (Seattle), April, 1894; *Tacoma Morning Union*, April 14-29, 1894; and Morgan, *Puget's Sound*, 282; *Portland Oregonian*, April 18-20, 1894; and Voeltz, "Coxey's Army in Oregon," 274-75.

[17] *Industrial Army News* (Seattle), April 1894; and *Keep Off the Grass* (Anaconda), June 1, 1894.

and coastal areas also ignored the initial calls for caution by Debs.In the case of the engineers, firemen, trainmen, and conductors, many defied their national leaders' explicit orders and joined the strikers.[18]

After an arbitration board chaired by Charles Pillsbury awarded the ARU what essentially was wage parity with workers on the Northern Pacific, the new union claimed a great victory. The claim had little substance, but the widespread belief that a smashing victory had been won led directly to the ARU's tragic involvement in the Pullman Strike two months later.[19]

At their first convention, held in June at Chicago, the ARU delegates ignored Debs's pleas for restraint and declared a sympathy boycott against the Pullman Palace Car Company.[20] As the dispute escalated, it paralyzed all roads west of Chicago, with the exception of the Great Northern. Throughout the region, but again most strikingly in the northern Rockies, various elements of society threw their support to the ARU strikers. Farmers donated their crops. A host of elected officials, merchants, clergymen, professionals, labor organizers, and others vigorously protested the road's labor policies. Populist sympathizer Governor Sylvester Pennoyer of Oregon castigated the Southern Pacific "for stopping other cars than Pullmans to seriously discommode the travelling and business public for the sole purpose . . . of settling a dispute between an exacting monopolist and his employes." Further, he strenuously objected to the SP's enlistment of federal power when the dispute "should rightfully be settled by arbitration." In Washington state, the Spokane and Sprague contingents of the National Guard refused to move against the strikers. Similarly, members of the railroad brotherhoods ignored direct orders from their national leaders to honor the boycott.[21]

[18]Department of Justice Year File 4017-1894; Minutes of the Western Central Labor Union, April 11-May 2, 1894, Archives and Manuscripts Division, UWL; President's subject files 107 and 2572, Great Northern Eastern Railway, Great Northern Railway Company Records, Minnesota Historical Society (MHS), Saint Paul; *Railway Times* (Chicago), *Tacoma Morning Union, Seattle Post-Intelligencer, Spokane Review, Anaconda Standard, Great Falls Tribune,* January-June 1894. See also Nick Salvatore, *Eugene V. Debs: Citizen and Socialist* (Urbana, 1982), 119-25; Almont Lindsey, *The Pullman Strike: The Story of a Unique Experiment and of a Great Labor Upheaval* (Chicago, 1942), 113-14; Eggert, *Richard Olney,* 127-30; and Albro Martin, *James J. Hill and the Opening of the Northwest* (New York, 1976), 415-16.

[19]For the assertion that there was more myth than substance in the American Railway Union (ARU) victory over the Great Northern, see Martin, *James J. Hill,* 416; White, "Railroad Workers," 71-75. See also Hill's suggestive response as quoted in Joseph Gilpin Pyle, *The Life of James J. Hill,* vol. 2 (Garden City, NY, 1916-17), 81.

[20]For accounts largely concerned with the Pullman Strike in Chicago, see Senate, *United States Strike Commission Report,* 53d Cong., 3d sess., 1894; Lindsey, *Pullman Strike;* Stanley Buder, *Pullman: An Experiment in Industrial Order and Community Planning, 1880-1930* (New York, 1967); Cooper, *Army and Civil Disorder;* and Salvatore, *Eugene Debs.* See also the ARU's *Railway Times* and the ARU *Proceedings of the General Managers Association of Chicago, 1893 and 1894* (Chicago, 1893-94).

[21]In addition to local newspapers see W. Thomas White, "Boycott: The Pullman Strike in Montana," *Montana the Magazine of Western History,* 29 (Autumn 1979), 2-13; *Appendix to*

The fact that the ARU represented white, largely native-born, and northern and western European workers, many of whom were solid members of their respective communities, was an important element in the high degree of support accorded strikers in much of the region. Indeed, cultural affinity, combined with shared economic hardships occasioned by the Panic and with the rising Populist tide, worked to form a crucible of discontent in the Far Northwest.[22]

The solidarity demonstrated by community and region in the Pullman Strike proved insufficient, however. In concert with the Cleveland administration and the General Managers Association (an organization of all railroads with terminals in Chicago), the Northern Pacific, Union Pacific, and Southern Pacific railroads easily destroyed the American Railway Union.[23] While it thoroughly frightened the railroads and their allies, the Pullman Strike also demonstrated the inadequacy of local and regional protests when confronted by a combination of large-scale corporate enterprise and an unsympathetic national government.

More to the point here, the turbulence of the 1890s, which the Pullman Strike demonstrated so spectacularly, triggered an abrupt change in the road's hiring policies. By the end of 1894, employers saw clearly that the racial and cultural homogeneity of the work force was a fundamental factor in the comparative unity exhibited by railway workers in all sectors of the industry and in the widespread community support they enjoyed. Since the anti-Chinese agitation of the 1880s, the roads had employed, for the most part, native whites and immigrants drawn from northern and western Europe. After 1894 the roads radically altered their employment practices, recruiting Japanese and southern and eastern European workers to fulfill the tasks in their unskilled sectors. Following the Pullman Strike, labor organizers in the industry were forced to deal, again, with the inescapable problem of ethnic and racial diversity.

the Annual Report of the Attorney General of the United States for the Year 1896 (Washington, DC, 1896); Adjutant General's Office Records Pertaining to the Chicago Pullman Strike of 1894, RG 94, National Archives; Letters sent by the Headquarters of the Army. See also *Portland Oregonian*, July 3, 1894 [quotation]; and Patrick McLatchy, "The Development of the National Guard of Washington as an Instrument of Social Control, 1854-1916" (doctoral dissertation, University of Washington, 1973), 284-91.

[22] The ARU specifically restricted membership to whites (Lindsey, *Pullman Strike*, 110), and the large-scale importation of southern and eastern Europeans did not begin until after the Pullman Strike. For general assessments of the economic and social milieu of the Far Northwest and the West during this period, consult Schwantes, *Radical Heritage*, 3-79; and Melvyn Dubofsky, *We Shall Be All: A History of the Industrial Workers of the World* (Chicago, 1969), 5-56.

[23] For details on the defeat of the ARU by federal intervention, consult the Adjutant General's Records; Letters sent by the Headquarters of the Army; *Report of the Secretary of War*, 1894; Cooper, *Army and Civil Disorder*, 114-43; and Lindsey, *Pullman Strike*, 147-78, 256-307.

The experience of Japanese workers, recruited largely into the unskilled maintenance-of-way and construction trades paralleled that of Mexican laborers in the Southwest and was decidedly different from that of the "labor aristocracy" of the operating brotherhoods. At the very bottom of the railroad labor hierarchy, they received less pay than "foreigners" (European immigrants) and "white men." They also bore the burden of anti-Asian prejudice, while they shared the harsh working conditions, routine exploitation by labor contractors, and general uncertainty connected with migrant work that beset all employed in that sector of the railroads' work force.[24]

Japanese began arriving in the Far Northwest in significant numbers in the 1890s. By 1906 their number had risen to thirteen thousand, mostly construction and section hands employed on western railroads. Of those, the Northern Pacific, Great Northern, Southern Pacific, Union Pacific, and Milwaukee lines were the principal employers. Indeed, at its peak, the Great Northern alone employed five thousand of the newcomers, although their number declined rapidly in the wake of the Gentlemen's Agreement of 1907-1908.[25]

To anxious managers desperate for large numbers of cheap tractable workers, Japanese immigrants, by the racial stereotypes of the day, seemed an ideal solution. "Jap section laborers . . . are certainly more reliable than either Greeks, Italians or white labor generally," GN Assistant Superintendent H. A. Kennedy wired from Spokane, adding that they "seem to be peculiarly adapted to section work." Kennedy's superior, F. E. Ward, seemed overjoyed that "the Japs are turning out so well" in Montana, and he entertained the notion of placing "our main reliance on them and having nothing to do with Italians or other outside labor."[26]

[24]White, "Railroad Workers," 170-79. For more on the working conditions facing all workers in this sector and on the pay differentials, see Yuji Ichioka, "Japanese Immigrant Labor Contractors and the Northern Pacific and Great Northern Railroad Companies, 1898-1907," *Labor History*, 21 (Summer 1980), 325-50; Senate, *Industrial Relations: Final Report and Testimony Submitted to Congress by the Commission on Industrial Relations Created by the Act of August 23, 1912*, 64th Cong., 1st sess., 1916, S.D. 415, I:29, 77-78, and V:4381-86, 4553-54, 4673, 4721-23, 4745-63; Senate, *Immigrants in Industries*, 61st Cong., 2d sess., 1911, S.D. 633, XXV:23; Washington State, *Third Biennial Report of the Bureau of Labor, 1901-1902* (Seattle, 1903), 11-12; Washington State, *Ninth Biennial Report of the Bureau of Labor*, 27-28; and H. W. Osborn to J. R. W. Davis, May 24, 1909, Great Northern Railway Vice President-Operating, General Manager subject file 34-09, Great Northern Railway Company Records, MHS. See also Shank and Smith to F. E. Ward, January 11, 1902, Great Northern and Northern Pacific Railway Company Records, Subject Files Relating to Japanese Labor, 1897-1942, MHS.

[25]Ichioka, "Japanese Labor Contractors," 325-29; *Immigrants in Industries*, XXV:37; and Roger Daniels, *The Politics of Prejudice: The Anti-Japanese Movement in California and the Struggle for Japanese Exclusion* (Berkeley, 1962), 31-45.

[26]*Immigrants in Industries*, XXII:38-39, XXV:20-22; H. A. Kennedy to G. T. Slade, June 24, 1903 [first quotation], and General Superintendent to P. T. Downs, June 7, 1900 [second quotation], Great Northern Vice President-Operating Subject File 34-01; Great Northern Assistant General Superintendent to Oriental Trading Company, February 27, 1903,

The growing Japanese presence on the railroads and in other industries quickly ignited an intense opposition, spearheaded by organized labor. As the new century began, *Seattle Union Record* editor Gordon A. Rice commenced a long-term anti-Japanese campaign, warning: "The Northwest is on the verge of a gigantic struggle with Oriental labor" similar to that waged against Chinese workers in the 1880s. "Jim Hill [president of the Great Northern] will have Japs as yardmen, engineers and conductors if a check is not put upon his career of greed," Rice fumed, and the *Spokane Freemen's Journal* and other prolabor publications broadcast a similar message throughout the region. In Oregon the Portland Central Labor Council registered its decided opposition to the "Mongolization of western states." To the east the *Butte Reveille* charged: "J. J. Hill is very fond of the Japs; they work cheaper than the Irishman, or Englishman, or Dutchman, and then besides they will stand all kinds of abuse from their employers."[27]

Many factors played into the anti-Japanese stance adopted by labor in the Progressive Era. Fears of job displacement meshed with general apprehensions felt in the white community over the introduction of alien races and cultures. Anti-Japanese sentiment also held obvious institutional advantages for organized labor, as instanced in the fall of 1900 when the Great Northern replaced a number of white workers with Japanese immigrants at Everett, Washington. Local merchants joined with their white customers in the labor force to protest the road's decision, a development suggestive of the continuing force of community loyalties that had supported much of the nineteenth-century industrial protest. Spying the main chance for AFL organizers, the *Union Record* rejoiced: "Everett is fast coming to the front as a union town. . . . [T]he anti-Jap agitation is the chief incentive and it is a powerful one." Other labor papers immediately carried the story and its moral to the interior, and discussions of the "Asiatic labor question" became an important rationale for the formation of the Washington state federation.[28]

Alienated from the labor movement and from the region's communities, Japanese workers had scant opportunity to remedy the conditions under which they toiled. In at least one instance, however, they did try to organize,

and J. M. Gruber to G. H. Emerson, June 28, 1909, Great Northern and Northern Pacific Records, MHS.

[27] *Union Record* (Seattle), May 4 and October 27, 1900, and August 10, 1901; *Freeman's Labor Journal* (Spokane), April 11, 18, and 24, 1902, and January 25, 1901; and *Portland Labor Press*, March 16, 1911. For more on the Asian exclusion movement, see Daniels, *Politics of Prejudice*, 16-19; Saxton, *Indispensable Enemy*, 249-57; John Higham, *Strangers in the Land: Patterns of American Nativism, 1860-1925* (New Brunswick, NJ, 1955), 166-75; and Joseph Cellini, ed., *Proceedings of the Asian Exclusion League, 1907-1913* (New York, 1977). See also Aileen S. Kraditor, *The Radical Persuasion, 1890-1917: Aspects of the Intellectual History and the Historiography of Three American Radical Organizations* (Baton Rouge, 1981).

[28] *Union Record* (Seattle), November 3-24, 1900; and *Freeman's Labor Journal* (Spokane), October 19, 1900.

forming their own union at Seattle in 1906. Angered by the exploitive practices of the Oriental Trading Company—the largest Japanese labor contractor in the region—the new union, led by K. Saskai and Jikei Hashiguchi,
editor of *The Japan Current*, tried to strike up an alliance with the AFL
organizations of western Washington. Predictably, their efforts proved
unavailing, and no other effective agency emerged to challenge the roads'
contractors.[29]

In this hostile atmosphere, Japanese workers tended to signal their disaffection by voting with their feet. Some found work on other roads, such
as the Milwaukee, which completed its line to the coast during those years.
Ultimately, however, most left railway work to find other jobs on farms,
in the coastal cities, or, particularly after the outbreak of the Russo-Japanese
War, they returned to Japan. When the Gentlemen's Agreement curtailed
further Japanese immigration to the United States, the roads were compelled, once more, to discover new sources of unskilled laborers.[30]

Suddenly, the new immigrants from eastern and southern Europe
assumed a vastly greater importance. Although they had been arriving since
the mid-1890s, the new Europeans now became the principal means of
meeting the unskilled labor shortfall left by the 1907-1908 understanding.
Generally, they were paid somewhat better than Asian workers—roughly
twenty-five cents more per day—although they received less than native white
workers until after 1911. Of course, all shared the same poor working conditions.[31]

Like Japanese workers, most of the new Europeans were recruited by
labor contractors. In its 1911 investigation, the Immigrant Labor Commission observed that each road employed one such agent to handle all non-
English-speaking, European immigrant laborers. Like the Oriental Trading
Company, the European contractors routinely exploited their charges through
commissions, overpriced supplies, and a variety of other devices.[32]

[29] *Union Record* (Seattle), September 21-28, 1907; *Spokane Daily Chronicle*, October 2, 1907;
and D. W. Hertel, *History of the Brotherhood of Maintenance of Way Employees:
Its Birth and Growth, 1887-1955* (Washington, DC, 1955), 38.

[30] Ichioka, "Japanese Labor Contractors," 344-47. See also General Manager to J. D.
Farrell, September 26, 1904; Howard Elliott to D. W. Willard, April 7, 1906; C. T. Takahashi
to J. M. Gruber, September 9, 1908; E. D. Sewall to J. M. Gruber, January 7, 1909; C.
T. Takahashi to George T. Slade, November 9, 1909; and [?] to E. L. Brown, December
10, 1909, all in Great Northern and Northern Pacific Records, MHS. For the Japanese reaction
to the exclusion movement and to other aspects of their sojourn in the United States, consult Kazuo Ito, *Issei: A History of Japanese Immigrants in North America*, trans. by Shinichiro
Nakamura and Jean S. Gerard (Seattle, 1973).

[31] White, "Railroad Workers," 179-92; *Industrial Relations*, I:29, 77-78; Washington State,
Ninth Biennial Report of the Bureau of Labor, 27-28; *Immigrants in Industries*, XXV:15-16; and
Yuzo Murayama, "The Economic History of Japanese Immigration to the Pacific Northwest,
1890-1920" (doctoral dissertation, University of Washington, 1982), 151-237.

[32] *Immigrants in Industries*, XXV:28; Ichioka, "Japanese Labor Contractors," 348-50. See
also Theodore Saloutos, "Cultural Persistence and Change: Greeks in the Great Plains and

H. W. Osborn's ⏎ Company supplied immigrant laborers to the Grea⏎ on typical of other agencies throughout the country. ⏎ Paul, Duluth, Bemidji, Sioux City, Grand Forks, Fargo, ⏎ e northwestern cities of Seattle, Portland, and Spokane, Osb⏎ possessed an extensive network for the recruitment and distr⏎ kers. Until the road dispensed with his services in 1910 becau⏎ arges against the company and exploitation of workers that resu⏎ owdowns, Osborn was the principal supplier of Greek, Bulgarian, ⏎ ian, and other European laborers. Clearly operating on a grand scale, in 1908 the Western Employment Company supplied over four thousand such workers (and 5,745 "white men") at Spokane alone.[33]

Like Japanese workers, southern and eastern European railway laborers bore the additional burden of hostility and nativism levied by labor and the local populace. Though such sentiments were not as intense as those expressed toward Asians, nativist pronouncements by organized labor still served as a strong bar to any substantive improvement in the new immigrants' condition. Outside the region's communities, the new Europeans could not rely on the same social structure that had cut across class lines and supported earlier efforts at organization and militant action.

Ed Teasdale of Portland exemplified the contrast between the support commonly tendered native white and northwestern Europeans and the reception accorded new immigrants. A fiery Knights of Labor leader, Teasdale had been an important activist and ally of the Coxeyites and the ARU in 1894. By 1912 he was concerned principally with "the evils impending from a flood of unskilled labor from Southern Europe." Similarly, Washington Labor Commissioner William Blackman, formerly an ARU stalwart in Seattle, successfully urged the State Federation of Labor, as one of its first official pronouncements, to declare "the immigration of labor from the South and East of Europe is a menace to the American standard of living."[34]

At the 1913 Immigration Conference in Portland, in newspapers, and in other forums throughout Washington, Oregon, Idaho, and Montana, AFL spokesmen pounded home the constant refrain that the region was a "white man's country" and that the new European immigration benefited only "the great combinations of Capital that sponsored it." Equally significant, the weak Brotherhood of Maintenance of Way Workers, which had

Rocky Mountain West, 1890-1970," *Pacific Historical Review*, XLIX (February 1980), 77-103.

[33]H. W. Osborn's activities can be traced in the Great Northern Vice President-Operating, General Manager subject file 34-09, 1905-9; and H. A. Kennedy to J. M. Gruber, February 3, 1910, Great Northern President subject file 4000, MHS.

[34]*Portland Labor Press*, May 16, 1912 [first quotation]; and Washington State, *Third Biennial Report of the Bureau of Labor*, 21-22 [second quotation]. See also Jonathan Dembo, "A History of the Washington State Labor Movement, 1885-1935" (doctoral dissertation, University of Washington, 1978), 99-100; and Higham, *Strangers in the Land*, 114-16, 123-30.

jurisdiction over that sector of the industry, seemed almost determined to obstruct its own growth by retaining its color bar and by reiterating its implacable opposition to "Italian and Greek labor that takes from honest American laborers the money and work that are rightfully theirs."[35]

As in the case of Japanese workers, some of the new Europeans did attempt to organize and better their lot, principally through the United Brotherhood of Railway Employees and the Industrial Workers of the World. Although both groups were largely indigenous to the region, neither had any lasting impact in the railroad industry. They lacked both the popular, community base that the Knights of Labor and the American Railway Union had enjoyed and the strategic job skills and effective, nationally centralized organization and leadership that the operating brotherhoods were learning to use with such telling effect in the Progressive Era.

The short-lived UBRE was organized by George Estes at Roseburg, Oregon, in 1901. An industrial union in the KL/ARU mold, Estes's group absorbed a Winnipeg-based organization of the same name and affiliated with the American Labor Union, which aspired to become an important rival of the AFL. Despite that rivalry, Estes quietly sought to lead the UBRE into Samuel Gompers's fold. When the AFL soundly rebuffed him and after a disastrous strike on the Canadian Pacific Railway in 1903, the UBRE disbanded. Many of its members probably followed their leader into the IWW in 1905. Estes himself soon fell into oblivion until after World War I, when he resurfaced as an important spokesman for the Oregon Ku Klux Klan.[36]

The IWW was somewhat more active in the region, launching job actions at Odessa, Washington, and in Montana, at Whitefish, Troy, and Columbia Falls. However, south of the Canadian border, the Wobblies focused their principal organizing efforts on the Northwest's logging camps, mills, mines, and fields. It was not until 1920, according to one of the Northern Pacific's Pinkerton infiltrators, that a much weakened IWW decided to launch

---

[35] *Portland Labor Press*, April 21, 1913 [first quotation], and June 9, 1913; *Union Record* (Seattle), February 9, 1907 [second quotation], and April 4, 1908; and *Industrial Relations*, V:4392-93.

[36] Schwantes, *Radical Heritage*, 142-50; Dubofsky, *We Shall Be All*, 71-76; J. Hugh Tuck, "The United Brotherhood of Railway Employees in Western Canada, 1898-1905," *Labour/Le Travailleur*, 11 (Spring 1983), 63-88; Canada, *Report of the Royal Commission on Industrial Disputes in the Province of British Columbia*, Sessional Paper No. 36a, 9th Parl., 3d sess. (Ottawa, 1903), 2-29; American Federation of Labor (AFL) Records: The Samuel Gompers Era, 1877-1937 (microfilm, Sanford, NC, 1979), rolls 142-43; San Francisco *Railway Employees Journal*, June-July 1903. For an example of Estes's bombast, see his bizarre account of his fight on behalf of the Order of Railroad Telegraphers against the Southern Pacific in which he claimed to have affected "the welfare of every English speaking railroad man in the world," George Estes, *Railway Employees United: A Story of the Railroad Brotherhoods* (Portland, 1931), 70. After World War I, Estes became well known in Oregon as author and publisher of *The Old Cedar School* (Troutdale, OR, 1922), a Ku Klux Klan tract written in support of compulsory *public* education of all children between eight and sixteen.

a serious organizational effort on the region's roads. The campaign bore partial fruit two years later in the Shopmen's Strike, but even that belated show of strength proved insufficient to wrest concessions from the roads.[37]

Spurned by organized labor and excluded from even the marginal relief benefits conferred by agencies such as the Itinerant Workers Union (Hoboes Union), the new Europeans reacted much like their Asian counterparts, thereby aggravating the roads' chronic labor shortage. They sought other jobs or, particularly after the outbreak of World War I, returned to their home countries. To meet the new shortage, the railroads called for a reintroduction of Japanese workers. When that effort failed, they again were compelled to seek out new sources.[38]

To meet the wartime challenge, the northwestern roads turned their recruitment efforts to enlist petty criminals, blacks, and women. Expressed resentments toward the newcomers, however, were more muted and decidedly different than those levied against their predecessors. In large measure, this comparative quiescence was due to the intervention of the federal government in the railroad industry. Anxious to prevent strikes or any further slowdowns on the roads, Woodrow Wilson created the Railroad Administration, which improved wages and working conditions throughout the nation. The RA also encouraged organization among the AFL unions, including the Maintenance of Way Brotherhood, which grew from only thirty thousand in 1917 to over three hundred thousand members by the end of 1920.[39] While such policies defused worker unrest on the roads, they also deflected potential attacks on the new workers.

Desperate to employ more unskilled laborers, the carriers first attempted to obtain the services of men convicted of misdemeanors. Great Northern

[37]Dembo, "Washington Labor Movement," vii-viii, 68; Hannon to Gompers, May 9, 1912, AFL Records, roll 39; *One Big Union Monthly* (Chicago), November 1919; *Union Record* (Seattle), January 22, 1916; M. J. Lins, "Report of Chief Special Agent, Fiscal Year Ending June 30, 1917," Great Northern Vice President-Operating file 1114; A. H. Hogeland to J. M. Gruber, June 12, Gruber to R. H. Aishton, June 25, L. W. Hill to William Sproule, June 26, 1917, Great Northern President subject file 6860; J. M. Hannaford to Howard Elliott, October 25, 1917, Northern Pacific President subject file 591-G; and Charles Donnelly to W. T. Tyler, November 12, 1920, Northern Pacific President subject file 591-G-7, all in MHS.

[38]*Industrial Relations*, V:4242-48, 4721-23, 4745-63; *Immigrants in Industries*, XXV:3-36; J. B. Powles to Austin E. Griffiths, November 20, 1914, Austin E. Griffiths Papers, Archives and Manuscripts Division, UWL; *Portland Oregonian*, December 16, 1914; Roger A. Bruns, *Knights of the Road: A Hobo History* (New York, 1980), 115-19; C. T. Takahashi to J. M. Gruber, February 28, R. Budd to Col. J. H. Carroll, April 10, 1918, Great Northern President subject file 6860, MHS; and David M. Kennedy, *Over Here: The First World War and American Society* (New York, 1980), 252-53. See also Kerr, *American Railroad Politics*, 39-71; Robert D. Cuff, "The Politics of Labor Administration during World War I," *Labor History*, 21 (Fall 1980), 546-69; and Frank L. Grubbs, Jr., *The Struggle for Labor Loyalty: Gompers, the A. F. of L. and the Pacifists, 1917-1920* (Durham, NC, 1968).

[39]Kerr, *American Railroad Politics*, 40-44, 72, 91-92 [quotation]; Kennedy, *Over Here*, 252-53; William Gibbs McAdoo, *Crowded Years: The Reminiscences of William G. McAdoo* (Cambridge, MA, 1931), 446-47; Walker D. Hines, *War History of American Railroads* (New Haven, 1928), 152-53; and H. D. Wolf, *The Railroad Labor Board* (Chicago, 1927), 10-13, 58-59.

President Ralph Budd instructed his subordinates to utilize "laborers who have been jailed for petty offences at such points as Havre, Great Falls, etc., where help is hard to get." Refusing to be caught up in the anti-German hysteria, Budd also directed that no German-born applicant would be barred from the road unless there was firm evidence to "suspect him of being an enemy of the Government."[40]

The roads also expanded their campaign to recruit black workers. Typical of that effort, the Great Northern obtained black workers through labor agencies such as the Minneapolis-based Fogg Brothers, which had connections to the Pinkerton's National Detective Agency and the Koenig Labor Agencies of Saint Louis and Kansas City, Missouri. In May 1917 the Fogg Brothers instructed their Missouri contacts "to get every possible negro you can get into Great Falls . . . the next bunch of nigers [sic] to Glasgow . . . and the next bunch . . . to Havre for pipe culvert work, [at] 20 cents per hour."[41]

Black workers proved no more satisfied with low pay, poor conditions, and long hours than whites or Asians. "Negroes don't seem [to] be [a] paying investment," C. O. Jenks wired from Sand Point, Idaho, since "they don't stay long enough."[42] As the surging wartime economy provided more and better paying jobs, there seemed little reason to settle for low wages and harsh working conditions in remote areas. With the possible exception of Pullman porters, blacks never became a numerically significant part of the Northwest's railway work force.

At the same time, the roads considered recruiting Puerto Rican and, like their counterparts in the Southwest, Mexican laborers. They quickly discarded such notions, however, largely because of the high cost necessary to transport such workers in large numbers over great distances. Further, Mexican railway workers could remain legally in the United States only for the duration of the war. Although the Southern Pacific employed some Mexican workers in Oregon, their large-scale importation into the Northwest made little economic sense to the officials of other roads in the region.[43]

Women, however, did provide an important new source of labor for the roads. By the end of 1918, they numbered 2,384 on the Northern Pacific alone, including over 900 in Washington, Idaho, and Montana. Most held

---

[40] R. Budd to J. M. Gruber, August 25 [quotation] and July-August, 1917, Great Northern President subject file 8324, MHS.

[41] Fogg Brothers to G. A. Weston and D. E. Dwyer, May 7; and [?] to G. A. Weston, May 22, 1917, Great Northern Vice President-Operating, General Manager subject file 34-13, MHS.

[42] C. O. Jenks to H. W. Lillegren, June 27, 1917, ibid.

[43] George Hodges-Louis W. Hill Correspondence, July 1917, Great Northern President subject file 6860; and Northern Pacific President subject file 591-G-8, MHS. For a synthesis of Mexican laborers in the Southwest, consult Mark Reisler, *By the Sweat of Their Brow: Mexican Immigrant Labor in the United States, 1900-1940* (Westport, CT, 1976).

clerical jobs, but many women also worked in machine shops, on the tracks, and in roundhouses.[44] They constituted only a fraction of the work force, but women employees attracted considerable attention from federal and state officials concerned with the type and conditions of their work.

RA Director William Gibbs McAdoo worried particularly about the employment of women in freight houses and on section gangs. Most "expressed themselves as thoroughly satisfied with the conditions of work," NP General Manager J. M. Rapelje reassured him, adding that "they are not asked to exert themselves beyond their strength." While he also tried to deflect McAdoo's anxieties, Federal Manager Jule M. Hannaford (formerly of the Northern Pacific) instructed his subordinates that although "the labor situation is [not] yet in such shape, especially on the West End, that we can dispose entirely with female labor in these classes . . . as rapidly as consistent, our officers will see that his [McAdoo's] wishes are complied with."[45]

At the state level, Washington Commissioner of Labor C. W. Younger also worried about women's welfare on the roads, as well as their impact on society. While he seemed generally satisfied with women's working conditions in Washington and he applauded McAdoo's policy of nondiscrimination in wages, Younger cautioned: "Only under the sternest necessity should [women] be taken out from under the ancient shelter of the home." His bureau's investigation of the Tacoma, Parkwater, and Spokane railway shops revealed a generally beneficent new "shelter," but he could not "forbear . . . a few words of warning." "Woman is not always a good judge of her own strength," the labor commissioner fretted, while he worried over the "real danger that she will in an excess of zeal undertake tasks too heavy for her."[46]

Younger failed to specify his principal concern about women in the industrial workplace. Certainly, the perceived dangers of women working outside the home included a potential threat to the traditional family structure, as Younger and others viewed it. Also, there were "moral risks" attendent upon "night work," which he felt "should be discouraged." Not least among Younger's and other progressives' apprehensions was the fear that if women worked night shifts they would "not get the requisite amount of rest, going home in the morning, preparing breakfast and then tackling the house work." Such pronouncements were hardly exceptional, and con-

[44]J. M. Hannaford to R. H. Aishton, December 17, 1918, Northern Pacific Federal Manager subject file 2223, MHS.

[45]Federal Manager to George T. Reid and J. M. Rapelje, October 3, J. M. Rapelje to J. M. Hannaford, October 5, R. H. Aishton to J. M. Hannaford, November 13, 1918, ibid.; and Aishton to A. L. Dickson, December 2, C. R. Gray to A. L. Dickson, October 3, 1918, Pierce County Central Labor Council Records, Archives and Manuscripts Division, UWL.

[46]Washington State, *Eleventh Biennial Report of the Bureau of Labor, 1917-1918* (Olympia, 1918), 42-44.

sequently, they illustrated the additional burdens women confronted in the industrial workplace, including those in comparatively well-regulated industries.[47]

The wartime workers were last in the succession of varied groups that had entered the railroads' unskilled labor pool since the arrival of the first transcontinental in the Far Northwest. After the Great War, the roads' demand for such workers declined, while postwar legislation restricted immigration. In the lean years of the 1920s, the remaining unskilled wage earners fought hard, though unsuccessfully, to retain the benefits conferred upon them by the Railroad Administration.[48] Not until the early days of the New Deal, however, did they obtain the legal tools to organize and bargain collectively to better their condition.[49]

Between the years 1883 and 1917, unskilled workers in the Far Northwest, as elsewhere, proved unable to better their situation. Many factors militated against their success. The very nature of the railroad industry, which dictated that many workers be widely dispersed to maintain the road, was a constant underlying obstacle, one that proved particularly troublesome in the sparsely populated West. The intransigence of the region's railroad managers to wide-scale collective bargaining and union recognition, like that of their counterparts in other industries, remained an important hurdle for those interested in organization of the entire industry. Yet the same managers could and did make exceptions for smaller organizations representing skilled workers. On occasion, they utilized those relationships to their advantage by alliances with the national leaders of the Big Four—Brotherhood of Locomotive Engineers, Brotherhood of Locomotive Firemen and Enginemen, Brotherhood of Railroad Trainmen, and Order of Railway Conductors—and of the AFL to oppose industrial unionism, which threat-

[47] Ibid., 43 [quotation]; Maurine Weiner Greenwald, "Women Workers and World War I: The American Railroad Industry, A Case Study," *Journal of Social History*, 9 (Winter 1975), 173; and Maurine Weiner Greenwald, *Women, War and Work: The Impact of World War I on Women Workers in the United States* (Westport, CT, 1980). See also Alice Kessler-Harris, *Out to Work: A History of Wage-Earning Women in the United States* (New York, 1982), 117, 219-24.

[48] White, "Railroad Workers," 212-304; and Hertel, *Brotherhood of Maintenance of Way Employees*, 97-100. For more on railway labor and politics in the 1920s, consult David P. Thelen, *Robert M. La Follette and the Insurgent Spirit* (Boston, 1976); Robert H. Zieger, *Republicans and Labor, 1919-1929* (Lexington, KY, 1969); Hamilton Cravens, "A History of the Washington Farmer-Labor Party, 1918-1924" (master's thesis, University of Washington, 1962); Irving Bernstein, *The Lean Years: A History of the American Worker, 1920-1933* (Cambridge, MA, 1960); Leonard A. Lecht, *Experience under Railway Labor Legislation* (New York, 1955); Edward Keating, *The Story of "Labor": Thirty-Three Years on Rail Workers' Fighting Front* (Washington, DC, 1953); Kenneth Campbell MacKay, *The Progressive Movement of 1924* (New York, 1947); and Edward Berman, *Labor Disputes and the President of the United States* (New York, 1924).

[49] Irving Bernstein, *Turbulent Years: A History of the American Worker, 1933-1941* (Boston, 1970), 214-15; and Irving Bernstein, *The New Deal Collective Bargaining Policy* (Berkeley and Los Angeles, 1950), 41-56. See also White, "Railroad Workers," 304-19.

ened the established unions' jurisdictions and prerogatives no less than those
of management.

The presence of such powerful forces did not automatically preclude
effective attempts at mass organization. Both the Knights of Labor and the
American Railway Union did present comparatively united, industry-wide
challenges to management. In both cases, they were able to rely upon insurgent community support peculiar to the developing region, which, like
so much of the Far West, was almost entirely dependent on the railroads,
subject to the vagaries of a largely extractive economy, remote from much
of the national marketplace, and imbued with the fires of frustrated expectations. Yet their protests were, in one sense, an aberration, since they were
launched when there was comparative ethnic and racial homogeneity in
the railway work force.

After the great turbulence of the 1890s, the roads changed all that.
In their perennial quest for cheap labor, the railroads, frightened by the
Coxeyites and the ARU strikes of 1894, were no less aware than their counterparts in other industries and in other regions of the benefits to be gained
by employing workers of diverse origins to do their unskilled, often seasonal, work. As the roads sought out new sources of labor, the resulting
demographic challenge emerged as a decisive factor militating against unifica-
tion of the work force, which was divided increasingly along the lines decreed
by race, ethnicity, and gender. Subsequent attempts at mass organization,
including the Japanese workers' organization in Seattle, the UBRE, and
the IWW, proved to be short-lived, and finally only futile, experiments.

Consequently, nearly all involved in unskilled railroad work remained
divided, unorganized, poorly paid, subject to the vicissitudes of casual labor, and victims of the generally harsh conditions imposed by employers
and labor contractors. Not until the federal government intervened to resolve the transportation crisis of the First World War on a national level
did the unskilled sector realize significant, albeit temporary, gains in pay,
working conditions, and union organization. Aside from that brief moment,
most workers in the industry experienced only lean years between the settlement of the far northwestern frontier and the onset of the New Deal.

REVIEW ESSAY

INDUSTRIALIZING AMERICA AND THE IRISH: TOWARDS THE NEW DEPARTURE

By ROBERT SEAN WILENTZ

The publication of a forty-two volume series* on so undeveloped a field as Irish-American history is cause for celebration—and some bemusement. Until the last few years, both the "old" and the "new" social and labor historians largely ignored the Irish. The few monographs that appeared before 1976 tended to retain some version of the "breakdown-assimilation" thesis first sketched out by Oscar Handlin more than three decades ago. The suggestions of a few historians, notably David Montgomery, that the Irish—and Irish workers in particular—deserved a complete re-evaluation were not followed up. Thanks to the very recent work of Michael Gordon, Eric Foner, Carol Groneman, and others, Irish-American history has at last begun its own New Departure with a focus on Irish-American labor and radicalism. Herein, however, rest the major problems with this Arno Press collection. The editors, with so little to work with, could hardly have delivered the conventional wisdom on their subject; such a

---

* Lawrence J. McCaffrey, Margaret E. Conners, David N. Doyle, and James P. Walsh, eds., "The Irish-Americans," New York: Arno Press, 1976, 42 volumes. (Robert G. Athearn, *Thomas Francis Meagher: An Irish Revolutionary in America;* Bruce Francis Biever, *Religion, Culture, And Values: A Cross-Cultural Analysis of Motivational Factors in Native Irish and American Irish Catholicism;* Stephen Garrett, *The Irish Character In American Fiction, 1830-1860;* Henry J. Browne, *The Catholic Church And The Knights Of Labor;* John Patrick Buckley, *The New York Irish: Their View of American Foreign Policy, 1914-1921;* Alice Lida Cochran, *The Saga Of An Irish Immigrant Family: The Descendants of John Mullanphy;* James J. Corbett, *The Roar Of The Crowd;* Harry C. Cronin, *Eugene O'Neill: Irish and American; A Study in Cultural Context;* Joseph Edward Cuddy, *Irish-American and National Isolationism, 1914-1920;* James Michael Curley, *I'd Do It Again: A Record of All My Uproarious Years;* Mary Deasy, *The Hour*

"series" would have run to perhaps a quarter of the size of the one at hand. Nor, in this age of diminished expectations, could they have commissioned a comprehensive overview of a field distinguished chiefly by its lacunae. The New Departure itself, meanwhile, is of too recent a vintage to have produced a satisfying yield. Within these limits, the editors have compromised with a collection of over a score of unrevised dissertations fleshed out with some valuable reprints and anthologies. The result, not surprisingly, is of uneven quality. Rather than to define the field, the series invites an assessment of where Irish-American studies have been and offers some tantalyzing suggestions about where they might be headed.[1]

The most influential study of Irish-American history is, with-

Of Spring; Joseph Dineen, *Ward Eight;* David Noel Doyle, *Irish-Americans, Native Rights, And National Empires: The Structure, Divisions, and Attitudes of the Catholic Minority in the Decade of Expansion;* Jack Dunphy, *John Fury;* Charles Fanning, ed., *Mr. Dooley And The Chicago Irish: An Anthology;* James T. Farrell, *Father And Son;* Thomas J. Fleming, *All Good Men;* Michael F. Funchion, *Chicago's Irish Nationalists, 1881-1890;* William A. Gudelunas, Jr., and William G. Shade, *Before the Molly Maguires: The Emergence of the Ethno-Religious Factor in the Politics of the Lower Anthracite Region, 1844-1872;* Thomas McLean Henderson, *Tammany Hall And The New Immigrants: The Progressive Years;* Robert Francis Heuston, *The Catholic Press And Nativism, 1840-1860;* William Leonard Joyce, *Editors And Ethnicity: A History of the Irish-American Press, 1848-1883;* Audrey Lockhart, *Some Aspects Of Emigration From Ireland To The North American Colonies Between 1660-1775;* Edward J. Maguire, ed., *Reverend John O'Hanlon's The Irish Emigrant's Guide For The United States: A Critical Edition with Introduction and Commentary;* Lawrence J. McCaffrey, ed., *Irish Nationalism And The American Contribution;* Grace McDonald, *History Of The Irish In Wisconsin In The Nineteenth Century;* Francis G. McManamin, *The American Years of John Boyle O'Reilly, 1870-1890;* Edward McSorley, *Our Own Kind;* James H. Moynihan, *The Life Of Archbishop John Ireland;* Earl F. Niehaus, *The Irish In New Orleans, 1800-1860;* Joseph Patrick O'Grady, *Irish-Americans And Anglo-American Relations, 1880-1888;* James Paul Rodechko, *Patrick Ford And His Search For America: A Case Study of Irish-American Journalism;* Frank Roney, *Irish Rebel And California Labor Leader: An Autobiography,* ed., by Ira B. Cross; James Edmund Roohan, *American Catholics And The Social Question, 1865-1900;* James Shannon, *Catholic Colonization On The Western Frontier;* Douglas V. Shaw, *The Making Of An Immigrant City: Ethnic and Cultural Conflict in Jersey City, New Jersey, 1850-1877;* Harry Sylvester, *Moon Gaffney;* Marie Veronica Tarpey, *The Role Of Joseph McGarrity In The Struggle For Irish Independence;* JoEllen McNergney Vinyard, *The Irish On The Urban Frontier: Nineteenth Century Detroit;* James P. Walsh, ed., *The Irish: America's Po'itical Class;* Howard Ralph Weisz, *Irish-American And Italian-American Educational Views And Activities, 1870-1900: A Comparison*).

[1] David Montgomery, *Beyond Equality: Labor And The Radical Republicans, 1862-1872* (NY, 1967); Michael A. Gordon, "The Labor Boycott In New York City, 1880-1886," *Labor History,* 16 (1975), 184-229; Eric Foner, "Class, Ethnicity, And Radicalism In The Gilded Age: The Land League And Irish-America," *Marxist Perspectives,* 2 (1978), 6-55; Carol Groneman Pernicone, " 'Bloody Ould Sixth': A Mid-Nineteenth Century Working-Class Community," (unpublished PhD diss., Univ. of Rochester, 1976). See also Lynn Lees and John Modell, "The

out question, Oscar Handlin's *Boston's Immigrants* (1941, rev. ed. 1957). Compared with *The Uprooted*—the author's subsequent tone poem, *Boston's Immigrants* is a tightly structured *etude*—the model of a hard-nosed, firmly-grounded local social history. Handlin, while still a graduate student, pioneered in the use of such tools as census records and immigrant newspapers and set the standard for later studies of urban communities. By treating the Irish immigrants as products of unbearably harsh conditions, he rescued them from genetic stereotypes of the intemperate, gentle-hearted, improvident Paddies. In his search for a Durkheimian "environmental" history, however, Handlin struck upon the dubious "breakdown-assimilation" framework that was to dominate all work on American immigration, including his own, for decades to come. *Boston's Immigrants,* with all of its virtues, is a case study of the perils of interpreting people from their surroundings and equating material deprivation with cultural poverty.

Handlin begins with a dark—and superficial—account of social and cultural life in pre-Famine Ireland. The peasantry appear as oppressed by "relentless historical forces," "hopeless," "reconciled," and plagued by habits of "shiftlessness," "laziness," and "drunkeness." To the Irish outlook, Handlin ascribes an "immense sadness, a deep-rooted pessimism," tempered by "a deep respect for class divisions." Some misgivings about this description arise on consulting the footnotes only to learn that too often, the "bereft" are not allowed to speak for themselves. Handlin draws his depressing panorama from the impressions of English travellers and officials. To help prove Irish "subservience," he quotes from an Irish charity school text prepared by the English Sunday school reformer Sarah Trimmer. The chasm separating these writers from the Irish makes their remarks suspect; one

Irish Countryman Urbanized," *Journal of Urban History,* 3 (1977), 391-408. More conventional accounts appear in Thomas N. Brown, *Irish-American Nationalism, 1870-1890* (Philadelphia, 1966), and Dennis Clark, *The Irish In Philadelphia: Ten Generations of Urban Experience* (Philadelphia, 1973). A major exception to the rule is Robert Ernst, *Immigrant Life in New York City, 1825-1863* (NY, 1949), which avoids the pitfalls of the "uprooted" thesis and includes valuable material on immigrant labor and the Irish; it well deserves republication. Lawrence J. McCaffrey's recent *The Irish Diaspora in America* (Bloomington, IN, 1976), corrects some of the false impressions about the Irish background and the "breakdown" in America discussed below, but concentrates almost exclusively on the Irish-American middle-class and on inter-class "ethnicity."

wonders whether the proselytizing words of a crusading English
Protestant, no matter how influential they might have been in
shaping Irish school children, could ever be extrapolated to account for Irish character and culture. Handlin both relies on these
sources and disregards abundant evidence of plebeian awareness
and unrest. The pre-Famine secret societies, organized by the
peasantry and often successful in holding down rents, are dismissed as "reckless." Their urban counterparts in the Catholic
Ribbon societies that mixed Paineite republicanism with industrial terrorism, are not mentioned. Handlin barely considers the
popular movements led by Daniel O'Connell for Catholic Emancipation and Repeal and their possible effects on Irish "pessimism" and "deference." Such rich material as the "blue book"
testimony before the numerous Parliamentary committees on the
state of Ireland is untapped.[2]

Boston's Immigrants fails to delve beyond the surface of Irish
rural society. Nowhere does Handlin describe harvest routines or
the regular fairs and festivities which enlivened peasant life and
distressed Dublin Castle as possible breeding grounds of violence
and sedition. Other community bonds, such as wakes and proces-
sions, are neglected. If the Irish enjoyed any semblance of family
affection, Handlin does not examine it. More obvious cultural
riches, including music, dance, and crafts, are absent, as is the
Gaelic Erin of the west of Ireland. Aside from a summation of
Catholic conservative dogma, there is little information on the
social position of the Church and the local priest, or on Catholic
support for reform and radical movements. Handlin instead

---

[2] Oscar Handlin, *Boston's Immigrants: A Study In Acculturation* (Cambridge, MA,
1941; rev. ed., 1957), 38-47, 131-132. The first edition of the book breaks at
1865, while the second (to which all citations here refer) extends the study to
1880. While Handlin treats all immigrant groups in Boston, the Irish justifiably
command the most attention. George C. Lewis, *On Local Disturbances In Ireland*
(London, 1836), remains the most revealing source on rural movements, but see
also Kevin B. Knowlan, "Agrarian Unrest In Ireland, 1800-1845," *University
Review*, 2 (1958), 8-16; Wayne G. Broehl, *The Molly Maguires* (Cambridge, MA,
1968), 1-10; Gale E. Christianson. "Secret Societies And Agrarian Violence in
Ireland, 1790-1840," *Agricultural History*, 46 (1972), 369-384; and T. Desmond
Williams, ed., *Secret Societies In Ireland* (Dublin, 1973), especially 13-35, 58-78.
Joseph Lee's fine article on the Ribbonmen in the Williams volume covers the
rural side of the movement, but ignores the cities and towns, for which there is
evidence in Public Record Office, Dublin, Official Papers, Combinations, 1790-
1831; Informer Reports, Sirr Papers, Trinity College, Dublin; Halliday Pam-
phlets, Royal Irish Academy, Dublin, #1237. See also Bernard Reaney, "Industrial Terrorism in Pre-Famine Ireland," *History Workshop Journal*, forthcoming.
The "blue books" are used to good effect in the early chapters of Pernicone.

leaves a hollow people, clutching to their pratties and milk. His Irish were on the verge of social chaos even before they arrived in Boston.

Handlin also underestimates the importance of popular culture and Irish protest on the American side of the Atlantic. His description of the wretchedness of the Boston Irish community after the Famine, itself a masterful account of urban squalor, leads irrevocably to his contention that Boston realities "perverted" and "warped" Irish sensibilities. He points to Irish drunkenness, crime, and prostitution as signs of their fall, sometimes stretching the evidence in the process. As drunkenness was, according to Handlin, already a problem in pre-Famine Ireland, it is unclear whether Boston Irish insobriety actually stemmed from desperation with Boston. Handlin considers drinking, meanwhile, only as a sign of self-destruction; he never explores the inner life of the Irish neighborhood saloon, or the links between Irish bars and such local institutions as political clubs. He admits that the Irish were rarely guilty of worse than misdemeanors associated with drink, but cites Irish lawbreaking as another index of Irish maladjustment. On Irish prostitution, Handlin notes relatively high illegitimate birth rates among Irish girls in 1860; these alone do not prove that "new exigencies" drove "many" Irish girls to become street-walkers.[3]

These shortcomings in Handlin's work should not be the cue for a lyrical romance on the lot of the Irish or of the Irish-Americans. Life in English-dominated Ireland could be brutal; along with the hardships of famine, eviction, and resettlement, the legacy of colonial subordination certainly impoverished every feature of Irish life. No one who has learned of the social impact of "modernization" in Ireland itself, or felt the shock of recognition that goes with reading Studs Lonigan can fantasize that a hearty Irish culture survived the collision with industrial capitalism intact. But neither were the Irish ciphers, the victims of a world that they did not make. As much recent work has shown, contrary to Handlin's formulations, important social ties and institutions endured—families, customary forms of protest such as the boycott, and political networks—the Atlantic crossing.

---

[3] Handlin, 120-123. For a refutation of the "breakdown" thesis for Irish newcomers to England see Lynn Hollen Lees, Exiles of Erin: Irish Immigrants in Victorian London (Ithaca, NY, 1979).

A far richer culture than the one Handlin imagines provided the immigrants with the basis for their adjustments to the New World. The "breakdown," the total disruption of Irish life and the attendant pathology of Irish-American existence, did not occur— and probably could not have occurred—as Handlin describes it, even in Yankee Boston.[4]

Nor did the Irish assimilate in the manner that Handlin claims they did. For Handlin, assimilation means the achievement of middle-class respectability and accommodation to Boston society. By concentrating on the efforts of well-known Irish clergymen, journalists, and politicians, he notes how, after the horrors of the post-Famine period, the Irish congealed into a community with at least the appearance of stability. This is no starry-eyed success story: Handlin discloses that by the 1880s, most of Boston's Irish remained, in his term, "proletarian." But Handlin subordinates social distinctions among the Irish to his idealized notions of their community "group consciousness," and interethnic conflict. The measure of Irish Boston's success was in its ability to substitute a new ethnic identity for the "sundered fabric of familiar social patterns," by establishing Irish-American institutions and following such lace-curtain representatives as John Boyle O'Reilly, the editor of the prestigious Boston *Pilot*. Handlin blames any failure on "fearful and insecure" natives and on Irish politicos and die-hards who could not be "soothed by the calm assurance that their interests were identical with those of the rest of the community." By the 1880s, Handlin writes, Boston, although still "divided within itself," "had learned it could survive through tolerance." He concludes on the hopeful note that, even with the resurgence of ethnic strife, there were always "some men in every group"— one senses these are Handlin's heroes—"who recognized the community of interest which transcended the particular divisions in Boston's population."[5]

This pluralist historical model, while suffused with an admirable desire for ethnic harmony, virtually ignores the question of class. The Irish were hardly as dependent upon reputable leaders as Handlin suggests. For some, assimilation entailed entering trade unions, subscribing to such radical periodicals as *The Irish*

---

[4] On Irish "modernization," see Nancy Scheper-Hughes, "Inheritance Of The Meek: Land, Labor, & Love In Western Ireland," *Marxist Perspectives*, 5 (1979), 46-77.
[5] Handlin, 178-206, 278-279.

World and American Industrial Liberator, and opposing both British policies in Ireland and American imperialist initiatives elsewhere. Handlin, by slighting this side of Irish life, tends to homogenize Irish views; too often, for example, the editorial policy of the *Pilot* is taken to represent Boston Irish opinion. By stressing the unquestionably important bonds of ethnic solidarity, he skirts the equally important tensions within the Irish community and misses the alliances that Irish workers might have made with other ethnic groups on matters ranging from currency reform to the eight-hour day. The point, again, is not to romanticize the Irish into fraternal working class heroes, nor to discount how ethnic identity and the political machine blurred class divisions and muffled discontent. Ethnicity must not, however, be interpreted either as the only source of Irish "community" or as the undertaker of class consciousness. Indeed, following Herbert Gutman's lead, it would be more fruitful to explore how Irish ethnicity shaped an identifiably Irish-American working class outlook, and then see how these developments were challenged, engulfed, and muted by the kind of inter-class "group consciousness" that Handlin outlines.[6]

Boston's Immigrants, with all of its flaws, nevertheless continues to command the Irish-American field because no other book in print matches its research or challenges its broad interpretations. The articles of the New Departure chip at the foundations of the "breakdown-assimilation" thesis, but revisionary syntheses are badly needed. Major efforts are required from labor historians. Not only will a history of Irish-American workers rectify the Handlinesque biases, but such a history is crucial to any understanding of the formation and ideology of the American working class. By the 1850s and 1860s, Irish men and women comprised the bulk of the workforce in unskilled and some skilled trades, not only in the Northeastern seaboard cities, but in the mining counties of Pennsylvania, the entrepots of the Middle West, and even in the urban South. By the 1870s, Irish immigrants and their sons were a most conspicuous power among local and national trade union leaders. Radical labor parties from the Greenback-Laborites to the Georgite single taxers drew signifi-

---

[6] *Ibid.,* 217-219; Herbert Gutman, *Work, Culture, And Society In Industrializing America* (NY, 1976).

cant support from Irish workers. The continuing battles of the radical Irish nationalists, both at home and abroad, had an as yet untold impact upon the organization of working-class sentiment among Irish and non-Irish alike. An American labor history minus a thorough account of the Irish cannot even pretend to the name.[7]

Any such account must begin with a firm grasp of the Irish background. Little is known, except in the most general way, about where, precisely, the Irish immigrants to America came from at different points in time. The overall nineteenth-century trend, which saw the main sources of migration shift from the more developed areas of the north and east towards the central and southern districts and finally to the west, is in itself significant, considering the vast differences between these areas. That the pattern of immigration seems to have conformed chronologically both to the spread of capitalist agriculture and petty manufacturing, and to shifts in the American trade cycle, must have had a tremendous impact on the shape of the Irish communities in the United States. Apart from pinning this pattern down, historians must try to be more precise about the ecology of overseas migration from within different parts of Ireland at different times before and after the Famine. How many were actually the "pre-industrial" peasants discussed by Handlin (and, in a very different way, by Gutman) and how many were agricultural laborers or small townsmen? How many of even the peasantry were familiar with the emerging industrial capitalist regime from their initial settlement in Liverpool or Manchester or from their seasonal migrations across the Irish Sea? Even if a thorough quantitative evaluation of these questions is unattainable, they must be posed at the outset, and taken into account lest the image of the Irish remain ensnared in either depressing or romantic stereotypes.[8]

---

[7] See, from the Arno collection, the works by Gudelunas and Shade, Vinyard, and Niehaus. The range of Irish labor radicalism is briefly surveyed in Foner.

[8] Useful on the Irish migration are William Forbes Adams, *Ireland And Irish Emigration To The New World From 1815 To The Famine* (New Haven, 1932); K. H. Connell, *The Population Of Ireland, 1750-1845* (Oxford, 1950); S. H. Cousens, "The Regional Variations in Emigration from Ireland between 1821 and 1841," *Transactions and Papers of the Institute of British Geographers* 37 (1965), 22-29; the volume by Audrey Lockhart in this series; George Rex Crowley Keep, "The Irish Migration To North America In The Second Half Of The Nineteenth Century" (unpublished thesis, Trinity College, Dublin, 1951); and Robert E. Kennedy, *The Irish: Emigration, Marriage, And Fertility* (Berkeley, 1973). See

Next, Americanists must understand plebeian outlooks and popular movements in Ireland and how these might have shaped similar activities in the United States. Michael Gordon's work on the boycott and Wayne Broehl's on the Molly Maguires are exemplary of this, but more is necessary, particularly with regard to the links between republican ideals, religious sectarianism, and urban and rural unrest after 1798. Two world of the Irish artisans, both in large cities and in the countryside, needs to be studied. The Irish journeymen were, as the Webbs pointed out long ago, the best organized in the British Empire as early as 1760. The impact of this experience upon Irish-American labor, upon both the immigrant artisans and the unskilled who knew of these organizations, has never been fully worked out. The possible circulation on Paineite principles throughout the country, and the relations between them and the demand for Catholic citizenship and early labor organizing, warrants our attention, as does the entire range of "primitive" rebellion, from rent wars to assassinations.[9]

On the American side, there must be a complete evaluation of the breadth of Irish dispersal throughout the country in the nineteenth century, and a mapping of where, at different times, the Irish fit into the many tiers of the working class. Special attention should be paid to the sizable sector of Irish skilled workers that emerged between 1875 and 1890 and that formed the backbone of such movements as the left-wing unions and the George campaign of 1886. In addition, study is badly needed on Irish women workers, especially in the needle trades prior to 1880. This, in turn, must lead to some idea of the ideological and organizational contributions made by the Irish to the gamut of local institutions —not just political machines and more respectable groups, but trade unions, working class fraternal clubs, reform efforts, even sports. Most important, work must focus on how the "philosophy" of Irish labor—a "philosophy" denied them by labor historians since David Saposs—blended and/or conflicted with

also Barbara M. Kerr, "Irish Seasonal Migration To Great Britain, 1800-1830," *Irish Historical Studies*, 3 (1942-43), 365-380; and John M. Werly, "The Irish In Manchester, 1832-1849," *Irish Historical Studies*, 18 (1972-73), 345-358; Lees, 22-41.

[9] On Irish labor, J. Dunsmore Clarkson, *Labour And Nationalism In Ireland* (New York, 1925), is a thorough expansion of the Webbs, but see also Fergus d'Arcy, "The Artisans Of Dublin And Daniel O'Connell, 1830-47: An Unquiet Liaison," *Irish Historical Studies*, 17 (1970-71), 221-243.

those of natives and other ethnic groups. Alan Dawley, in his study of Lynn, describes how the Anglo-American tradition of "Equal Rights" was a foundation of workers' opposition. Yet far from Lynn, in towns and cities from New York to San Francisco where the Irish were numerous, remarkably similar appeals emerged throughout the late nineteenth century, occasionally uniting the Irish with natives, Germans, and Eastern Europeans. How, and why, did this happen? And how, and why, did Irish political participation and the many alliances between Irish workers and the Irish middle class blunt—and, alternatively, encourage—different styles of Irish labor militancy? The crucial period for this work should be the 1880s, when the radical artisan republicanism forged during the Jacksonian period began to shade off into all varieties of socialism and radical trade-unionism. The Irish, like the Germans, had a major hand in this transformation, bringing their own experience and contacts with their countrymen to bear in the creation of a distinctly American working class socialism that would culminate with the Debsites in the 1890s.[10]

Moving into the twentieth century, all of the strands of Irish-American working class life—strands personified by such clashing personalities as Elizabeth Gurley Flynn, Michael Quill, and Cardinal Spellman—must be traced against the shifting fortunes of Irish-America. The image of the Irish-American as the quintessence of the right-wing worker needs to be placed in the context of earlier events and challenged in its own right. If Paul Cowan's impressive investigations on other ethnic workers (a case of journalism instructing the academy) are heeded, the Irish-Americans' "conservatism" may turn out to be of far more recent origins than imagined, and may not seem as total or as consistent as others have suggested.[11]

It is a huge task, one deserving of a large collective effort and a long series of books. The Arno Collection "The Irish-Americans" is not that series, but it provides some important materials

[10] David Saposs, "The Role of the Immigrant in the Labor Movement," *Amalgamated Illustrated Almanac* (NY, 1924), 150; Alan Dawley, *Class and Community: The Industrial Revolution in Lynn* (Cambridge, MA, 1976). On Irish women workers, David Katzman, *Seven Days A Week* (NY, 1978) includes suggestive material on domestic service.
[11] Paul Cowan, "Whose America Is This?" *Village Voice*, April 2, 1979. See also Cowan's *The Tribes of America* (NY, 1979). On Irish "conservatism," see Andrew M. Greeley, *That Most Distressful Nation* (NY, 1973).

with which to begin, as well as some lessons of false starts. Among the series' fifteen reprints is a gem, Frank Roney's *Irish Rebel and California Labor Leader*, edited by Ira Cross. Roney, a Belfast-born iron moulder, was in turn an Ulster trade unionist, a "soldier" in the Irish republican and Fenian conspiracies of the 1860s, a political exile, an immigrant to America, a leader of the San Francisco Workingman's Party, a socialist, an organizer for the Knights of Labor, and a participant in almost every West Coast labor struggle until 1903. Readers of Alexander Saxton's *The Indispensable Enemy* will recognize Roney as the man whose career demonstrated the tortuous relationship between left-wing unionism and anti-Chinese bias and whose politics indicated the strength of socialism in the American labor movement.[12] Roney's huge autobiography, which Saxton used extensively, elaborates the connections between Irish republicanism, American trade unions, and political radicalism while providing a wealth of description of the personalities and social conditions Roney encountered at every step. It surely ranks with the memoirs of Gompers, Powderly, Flynn, and the handful of other classic American labor memoirs; indeed, because of the breadth of Roney's experience and because of his particular immigrant-republican slant, it may be the most helpful text of all in continuing the New Departure. It must be read, and re-read.

Several other of the reprints are worthy of note. Henry J. Browne's *The Catholic Church and the Knights of Labor* (1943) is the only extensive treatment of this crucial topic, and its republication should be welcomed amidst the current resurgence of interest in the Knights. Jim Curley's memoirs, *I'd Do It Again* (1957), are cluttered with the types of anecdotes that too often pass for Irish-American history. They are also a valuable insight into the mentality of urban Irish electoral politics and the social life of the machine, and cannot be ignored. Republication of a Farrell novel is to be commended (especially now that his pen is stilled) and *Father and Son* (1940), from the Danny O'Neill series is no exception. Edward McSorely's novel, *Our Own Kind* (1946) evokes working-class family life in Providence, R.I. James Shannon's *Catholic Colonization On the Western Frontier*

---

[12] Alexander Saxton, *The Indispensable Enemy: Labor And The Anti-Chinese Movement In California* (Berkeley, 1971), 39-40, 120-126, 155-199, 213-227, 264-268.

(1957), Grace McDonald's *History of the Irish in Wisconsin in the Nineteenth Century* (1954), and Earl F. Niehaus' *The Irish in New Orleans, 1800-1860* (1965), help pull attention away from the Eastern cities, although the Shannon and Niehaus volumes are by far the superior. *The Life of Archbishop John Ireland* (1953), by James H. Moynihan, should be read with an eye for the enormous discrepancies between the prelate and socialists like Roney, and for a starting place on understanding Irish liberal opinion, the complexities of Irish religious life, and the Midwest Irish-Americans. Jim Corbett's memoirs, *The Roar of the Crowd* (1925), should interest those who wish to learn more about Irish working-class leisure and sport.

Each of the four anthologies brings together useful articles of high merit. James Walsh's collection on the Irish-Americans in party politics and Lawrence McCaffrey's on Irish nationalism in America, would be useful to students and teachers of American politics as synopses of the fields, although they should be supplemented with the on-going work of the New Departure. Emmet Larkin has stirred considerable controversy in Ireland with his articles on the rise of Irish devotionalism after the Famine and on church wealth and politics. In anthologized form, these articles should now win the attention of American historians as well. Perhaps the most charming collection (though a bit in the antiquarian vein) is Charles Fanning's *Mr. Dooley and the Chicago Irish*, in which the editor presents the "original" transcripts of pub conversations that F. P. Dunne would eventually turn into his celebrated Dooley dialogues.

The dissertations are, however, the heart of the series, and they are a mixed lot indeed. As a group, they have the merit of covering a great deal of the country: Irishmen in New York City, Missouri, Pennsylvania, New Jersey, and Michigan all find their historians here. The concentration on work covering the period 1870-1923 is a mixed blessing; while the gaps on the pre-Famine arrivals and twentieth-century Irish for the most part remain; yet the series adds much to our understanding of the years just after Handlin leaves off. But in some cases, perhaps because of the editors' desire for comprehensive, regional studies, publication only brings embarrassment. Alice Lida Cochran's thesis, for example, promises *The Saga of An Irish Immigrant Family*, but delivers little more than the geneaology of the Mullanphys of St. Louis. Francis G. McManamin's treatment of John Boyle O'Reilly's American years presents at length as much of importance as Handlin and Arthur Mann present concisely.[13] Others suffer from being unrevised dissertations that might have been much better if rewritten or boiled down to lengthy articles. Bruce Biever's "cross cultural analysis," for example, proves that Irish American Catholics are more "secularized" than Irish Catholics, but takes such plodding measures to do so that the effort does not seem worth the candle.

A few of the dissertations are top-flight but limited by their conventional framework. Jo Ellen Vinyard's *The Irish On The Urban Frontier: Nineteenth Century Detroit,* is an impeccable local study in the Handlin mode that blends intensive research, methodological sophistication, and a useful survey of the Irish economic background. She proves that in Detroit, where the earliest European settlers were not Yankee Protestants but French Catholics, the Irish had a far easier time adjusting to American life. In making this useful corrective, however, Vinyard implicitly accepts Handlin's environmental logic: the "breakdown" did not occur in Detroit because the urban frontier was so different from Boston. While she occasionally departs from this context to discuss Irish working class life, she never confronts the Handlin analysis head-on, thus diminishing the power of her work. James Rodechko's biography of the radical editor Patrick Ford is a gold mine of information about Irish labor, journalism, and discontent in late nineteenth-century New York City. Ford, who ran the *Irish World,* was at the forefront of local radical opinion in activities ranging from the Land League to the George campaign. His career, which began with his working as a printer's devil for William Lloyd Garrison on *The Liberator,* embodied the confluence of the native reform impulse and Irish labor radicalism. Rodechko, confined to the biographical form and limiting his study to the years after 1870, never quite captures the broad significance of this mixture. His description of Ford's "search for America" needs to be taken further to include the search of Irish-American labor as a whole; as it stands, it is an important build-

---

[13] Arthur Mann, *Yankee Reformers In the Urban Age: Social Reform In Boston, 1880-1900* (Cambridge, MA, 1954), 24-44.

ing block, to be used along with such works as the Roney autobiography. Michael Funchion's study of Chicago Irish nationalism is of similar calibre and usefulness.

A few of the dissertations stand out because they offer both fresh material and interpretive outlines (not all of them successfully) different from Handlin's. David Doyle, one of the editors of the series, has discovered a large and divided Irish middle class in late nineteenth-century America, and demonstrated the dangers of assuming that the Irish were monolithically "conservative." His *Irish-Americans, Native Rights, and National Empires* explains how the long-established Irish concerns with the welfare of the Church and the rights of colonies clashed during the 1890s. While some Irish Catholics were determined that American foreign policy should support the beleaguered Spanish in the Philippines and Cuba, others were active anti-imperialists. Doyle stresses that the split had wide political ramifications, since the Irish, as leaders of the American Catholic community, helped forge Catholic political opinion. Without elaborating the point, the study fits nicely with recent work on late nineteenth-century politics that suggest that urban ethnics gave crucial backing to the various Progressive reform drives.

Doyle, looking for the social basis of this division, scrutinizes the 1900 Federal Census and finds that in the United States as a whole, the Irish were far more socially diverse and economically successful than had been previously thought. He convincingly shows that Irish-America cannot be assumed to have been composed of a "proletarianized" mass led by a few worthies. The complexity of class structure and opinion shown to have existed so soon after the terminus of *Boston's Immigrants* opens the field to complete reinvestigation.

Unfortunately, Doyle's study also has its drawbacks. By using national statistics, he no doubt glosses over regional variations in social structure that would seriously qualify his argument. The discussions of demography and opinion never quite merge, as Doyle never attempts to clearly state how social or class position might have encouraged either pro- or anti-imperialist politics. Finally, there is Doyle's paradoxically Handlinesque focus on the Irish middle-class. By describing the differentiation of the Irish, Doyle proves that Irish men and women could be found at almost every level of skill and income within the working class. But he then jumps quickly to discuss only prominent middle-class opinion, leaving few clues about how Irish workers might have thought or felt. He implies that it was the middle-classes, after all, who were the decisive "opinion-makers," for the Irish and for American Catholics at large, bringing us full-circle back to Handlin. Doyle's sensitive treatment of Irish diversity, valuable as it is, is only part of the story he sets out to tell.

Before the Molly Maguires, by William Gudelunas, Jr., and William Shade, examines Schuykill County, Pennsylvania, during the thirty years before the outburst of industrial strife in the region's mines in the 1870s. An example of the "new" political history, the study analyzes voting data to argue that ethnic conflict was the basis of political alignments. The conclusion, like others of this genre, is a useful cultural antidote to any lingering temptations to economic determinism. It also implies that, at least in Pennsylvania, the Irish community was tightly-knit by the early 1840s, before the Famine, suggesting that ethnic cohesion could be achieved without a preliminary "breakdown." But Gudelunas and Shade fail to advance beyond this point. In interpreting ethnic differences, they consign the Irish Catholic world view, along with that of the German Lutherans, to the static category of "devotionalist." Such reduction, an easy operation for "scientific" historians to perform, eviscerates Irish culture even more than *Boston's Immigrants* does. Taken alone, voting is not the only nor even the best indication of social consciousness. Moreover, Gudelunas and Shade do not provide any way of understanding the intense class conflict which united miners across ethnic lines in the 1870s. Surely the rebellion of 1877, the emergence of the Knights of Labor, and the strong vote in the Schuykill area for the Greenback-Labor Party do not fit the pattern of ethnic upheaval. To describe the convergence of class and ethnicity would have been more rewarding than the authors' artificial-segmentation of the two, but this would have required greater awareness of the subtleties of Irish working class life than they muster in this book. Their road, which ends with a lifeless parody of the suggestive work on voting begun by Lee Benson in 1961, is one that is best not taken.

Far more satisfactory is Douglas V. Shaw's history of the Irish in *The Making of an Immigrant City: Class and Ethnicity in Jersey City, 1850-1877*. Jersey City was a particular kind of city that is too often ignored in studies of American industrialization —a transportation center, without heavy industry, that fed the increasing railroad traffic between the hinterland and the burgeoning metropolis, New York. Shaw is sensitive to this difference, and his study, like Vinyard's and Doyle's, demonstrates that Irish-American workers did not fit a single proletarian "type." In tracing the sources of labor unrest in Jersey City, Shaw confirms that a wide breach separated the Protestant elite from the Irish Catholic workingmen. Shaw's Irishmen, however, are not broken. They challenged their betters, on fronts ranging from politics to the workshop. Ethnic hatreds managed to mold and complicate these class struggles; in examining the interplay between class and ethnicity, Shaw makes the valuable observation that nativism persisted long after most historians believed that it had died out.

Although conflict was articulated in ethnic terms, however, Shaw is not blind to class distinctions among the Irish. In a discussion of a middle-class Irish attempt to form a breakaway Democratic organization, he reveals how Irish workers refused to follow their socially prominent countrymen. He pinpoints those movements that made some progress across class lines—Irish nationalism and temperance—but shows that while the Irish could agree, they also divided on labor and political issues. As Shaw makes clear, the ethnic workers were neither wholly "Irish" nor "workers" but both, a reality that cannot be fractured by simple subdivision. While the study examines the traditional fare of the labor historian—strikes, lockouts, unions—it is enriched by discussions of how community activities shaped the Irish. His analysis suggests the importance of looking at the possible splits between work and community as well as their links, and at the ambiguous position of the party machines in the working class neighborhoods. Shaw might have made more of the Irish background and of the relations between the Jersey City Irish and the emerging Irish labor movement across the river in New York; at times, his "community" seems closed off from the rest of the world, a problem that seems to plague studies of this type. But Shaw's book might be a model for monographs on other "immigrant cities" in industrializing America, provided that future historians broadened their vision.

The remainder of the dissertations, alas, are either of such passing importance or so narrowly focused that they can be recommended only to dedicated specialists. In all, *The Irish-Americans* should be greeted with a quiet and brief celebration, not a *feis*. Much work remains to be done, and we need clear heads and energetic souls. The series' greatest contribution may be to point out some of the pitfalls to avoid and some of the riches to be sought if the New Departure is to succeed. Labor historians cannot afford for it to fail.

ACKNOWLEDGMENTS

James R. Barrett, "Unity and Fragmentation: Class, Race, and Ethnicity on Chicago's South Side, 1900–1922," *Journal of Social History*, 18 (Fall 1984), 37–55. Reprinted with the permission of the *Journal of Social History*. Courtesy of George E. Pozzetta.

Ira Berlin and Herbert G. Gutman, "Natives and Immigrants, Free Men and Slaves: Urban Workingmen in the Antebellum American South," *American Historical Review*, 88:5 (December 1983), 1175–1200. Courtesy of Yale University Library.

John E. Bodnar, "The Impact of the 'New Immigration' On the Black Worker: Steelton, Pennsylvania, 1880–1920," *Labor History*, 17:2 (Spring 1976), 214–229. Reprinted with the permission of *Labor History*. Courtesy of Yale University Library.

John E. Bodnar, "Immigration and Modernization: The Case of Slavic Peasants in Industrial America," *Journal of Social History*, 10 (Fall 1976), 45–71. Reprinted with the permission of the *Journal of Social History*. Courtesy of George E. Pozzetta.

John E. Bodnar, Michael Weber, and Roger Simon, "Migration, Kinship, and Urban Adjustment: Blacks and Poles in Pittsburgh, 1900–1930," *Journal of American History*, 66:3 (December 1979), 548–565. Reprinted with the permission of the *Journal of American History*. Courtesy of Yale University Library.

Edna Bonacich, "Small Business and Japanese American Ethnic Solidarity," *Amerasia Journal*, 3 (Summer 1975), 96–112. Reprinted with the permission of *Amerasia Journal*. Courtesy of *Amerasia Journal*.

John J. Bukowczyk, "'Polish Rural Culture and Immigrant Working Class Formation, 1880–1914'," *Polish American Studies*, 41:2 (Autumn 1984), 23–44. Reprinted with the permission of *Polish American Studies*. Courtesy of Yale University Library.

David Emmons, "An Aristocracy of Labor: The Irish Miners of Butte, 1880–1914," *Labor History*, 28 (Summer 1987), 275–306. Reprinted with the permission of *Labor History*. Courtesy of Yale University Library.

Clyde Griffen, "Occupational Mobility in Nineteenth-Century America: Problems and Possibilities," *Journal of Social History*, (Spring 1972), 310–330. Reprinted with the permission of *Journal of Social History*. Courtesy of Yale University Library.

Herbert G. Gutman, "Work, Culture, and Society in Industrializing America, 1815–1919," *American Historical Review*, 78 (June 1973), 531–588. Courtesy of Yale University Library.

Robert F. Harney, "The Padrone and the Immigrant," *Canadian Review of American Studies*, 5:2 (Fall 1974), 101–118. Reprinted with the permission of *Canadian Review of American Studies*. Courtesy of *Canadian Review of American Studies*.

Theodore Hershberg, Michael Katz, Stuart Blumin, *et al.*, "Occupation and Ethnicity in Five Nineteenth-Century Cities: A Collaborative Inquiry," *Historical Methods Newsletter*, 7:3 (June 1974), 174–216. Reprinted with the permission of *Historical Methods Newsletter*. Courtesy of Yale University Library.

John R. Jenswold, "In Search of a Norwegian-American Working Class," *Minnesota History*, 50, no. 2 (Summer 1986), 63–70. Reprinted with the permission of *Minnesota History*. Courtesy of George E. Pozzetta.

Gordon W. Kirk, Jr. and Carolyn Tyirin Kirk, "Migration, Mobility and the Transformation of the Occupational Structure in an Immigrant Community: Holland, Michigan, 1850–80," *Journal of Social History*, 7, no. 2 (Winter 1974), 142–164. Reprinted with the permission of *Journal of Social History*. Courtesy of George E. Pozzetta.

Bruce Laurie, Theodore Hershberg, and George Alter, "Immigrants and Industry: The Philadelphia Experience, 1850–1880," *Journal of Social History*, 9:2 (Winter 1975), 219–248. Reprinted with the permission of *Journal of Social History*. Courtesy of Yale University Library.

Joy K. Lintelman, "'America is the woman's promised land': Swedish Immigrant Women and American Domestic Service," *Journal of American Ethnic History* 8:2 (Spring, 1989), 9–23. Reprinted with the permission of *Journal of American Ethnic History*. Courtesy of the Library of Congress.

John Modell, "Tradition and Opportunity: The Japanese Immigrant in America," *Pacific Historical Review*, 40:2 (May 1971), 163–182. Reprinted with the permission of the *Pacific Historical Review*. Courtesy of Yale University Library.

Paul Ong, "An Ethnic Trade: The Chinese Laundries in Early California," *Journal of Ethnic Studies*, 8:4 (Winter 1981), 95–113. Reprinted with the permission of the *Journal of Ethnic Studies*. Courtesy of the *Journal of Ethnic Studies*.

Daniel T. Rodgers, "Tradition, Modernity and the American Industrial Worker: Reflections and Critique," *Journal of Interdisciplinary History*, 7:4 (Spring 1977), 655–681. Reprinted with the permission of the *Journal of Interdisciplinary History*. Courtesy of Yale University Library.

W. Thomas White, "Race, Ethnicity, and Gender in the Railroad Work Force: The Case of the Far Northwest, 1883–1918" *Western Historical Quarterly*, 16:3 (July 1985), 265–283. Reprinted with the permission of *Western Historical Quarterly*. Courtesy of Yale University Library.

Robert Sean Wilentz, "Industrializing America and the Irish: Towards the New Departure," *Labor History*, 20:4 (Fall 1979), 579–595. Reprinted with the permission of *Labor History*. Courtesy of George E. Pozzetta.